INSTITUTIONAL INVESTORS, OTHER TOPICS IN PORTFOLIO MANAGEMENT, AND CASES

CFA® Program Curriculum
2023 • LEVEL III • VOLUME 5

WILEY

© 2022, 2021, 2020, 2019, 2018, 2017, 2016, 2015, 2014, 2013, 2012, 2011, 2010, 2009, 2008, 2007, 2006 by CFA Institute. All rights reserved.

This copyright covers material written expressly for this volume by the editor/s as well as the compilation itself. It does not cover the individual selections herein that first appeared elsewhere. Permission to reprint these has been obtained by CFA Institute for this edition only. Further reproductions by any means, electronic or mechanical, including photocopying and recording, or by any information storage or retrieval systems, must be arranged with the individual copyright holders noted.

CFA®, Chartered Financial Analyst®, AIMR-PPS®, and GIPS® are just a few of the trademarks owned by CFA Institute. To view a list of CFA Institute trademarks and the Guide for Use of CFA Institute Marks, please visit our website at www.cfainstitute.org.

This publication is designed to provide accurate and authoritative information in regard to the subject matter covered. It is sold with the understanding that the publisher is not engaged in rendering legal, accounting, or other professional service. If legal advice or other expert assistance is required, the services of a competent professional should be sought.

All trademarks, service marks, registered trademarks, and registered service marks are the property of their respective owners and are used herein for identification purposes only.

ISBN 978-1-953337-15-3 (paper)
ISBN 978-1-953337-39-9 (ebk)

10 9 8 7 6 5 4 3 2 1

Please visit our website at www.WileyGlobalFinance.com.

CONTENTS

How to Use the CFA Program Curriculum ix
    Background on the CBOK ix
    Organization of the Curriculum x
    Features of the Curriculum x
    Designing Your Personal Study Program xi
    CFA Institute Learning Ecosystem (LES) xii
    Prep Providers xiii
    Feedback xiv

Portfolio Management

Study Session 12   **Portfolio Management for Institutional Investors** 3

Reading 24   **Portfolio Management for Institutional Investors** 5
    Institutional Investors: Types and Common Characteristics 6
        Institutional Investors: Common Characteristics 7
    Overview of Investment Policy 11
    Pension Funds: Types and Stakeholders 14
        Stakeholders 16
    Pension Funds: Liabilities, Investment Horizon, and Liquidity Needs 18
        Liabilities and Investment Horizon 18
        Liquidity Needs 22
    Pension Funds: External Constraints 23
        Legal and Regulatory Constraints 24
        Tax and Accounting Constraints 25
    Pension Funds: Risk Considerations 26
    Pension Funds: Investment Objectives and Asset Allocation 29
        Investment Objectives 30
        Asset Allocation by Pension Plans 31
    Sovereign Wealth Funds: Types and Stakeholders 35
        Stakeholders 37
    Sovereign Wealth Funds: Liabilities, Investment Horizon, Liquidity Needs, and External Constraints 37
        Liabilities and Investment Horizons 38
        Liquidity Needs 40
        External Constraints Affecting Investment 40
    Sovereign Wealth Funds: Investment Objectives and Asset Allocation 41
        Investment Objectives 41
        Asset Allocation by Sovereign Wealth Funds 43
    University Endowments and Private Foundations: Introduction and External Constraints 45
        External Constraints Affecting Investment 47
    University Endowments: Stakeholders, Liabilities, Investment Horizon, and Liquidity Needs 48
        University Endowments—Liabilities and Investment Horizon 49

◯ indicates an optional segment

	University Endowments—Liquidity Needs	50
	Private Foundations: Types, Stakeholders, Liabilities, Investment Horizon, and Liquidity Needs	51
	Private Foundations—Liabilities and Investment Horizon	51
	Private Foundations—Liquidity Needs	53
	University Endowments: Investment Objectives and Asset Allocation	54
	University Endowments	54
	Asset Allocation	58
	Private Foundations: Investment Objectives and Asset Allocation	62
	Private Foundations	64
	Banks and Insurers: Introduction and External Constraints	66
	External Constraints Affecting Investment	68
	Banks: Stakeholders, Liabilities, Investment Horizon, and Liquidity Needs	71
	Banks—Liabilities and Investment Horizon	71
	Banks—Liquidity Needs	72
	Insurers: Stakeholders, Liabilities, Investment Horizon, and Liquidity Needs	73
	Insurers—Liabilities and Investment Horizon	74
	Insurers—Liquidity Needs	75
	Banks and Insurers: Investment Objectives	76
	Banks	76
	Insurers	77
	Banks and Insurers: Balance Sheet Management and Investment Considerations	79
	Banks and Insurers: Investment Strategies and Effects on Asset and Liability Volatility	86
	Banks and Insurers: Implementation of Portfolio Decisions	91
	Summary	97
	Practice Problems	101
	Solutions	108
Study Session 13	**Trading, Performance Evaluation, and Manager Selection**	**115**
Reading 25	**Trade Strategy and Execution**	**117**
	Introduction	117
	Motivations to Trade	118
	Profit Seeking	118
	Risk Management/Hedging Needs	120
	Cash Flow Needs	121
	Corporate Actions/Index Reconstitutions/Margin Calls	122
	Trading Strategies and Strategy Selection	124
	Trade Strategy Inputs	124
	Reference Prices	128
	Pre-Trade Benchmarks	129
	Intraday Benchmarks	130
	Post-Trade Benchmarks	130
	Price Target Benchmarks	131
	Trading Strategies	131
	Short-Term Alpha Trade	132
	Long-Term Alpha Trade	133

◉ indicates an optional segment

Contents

Risk Rebalance Trade	134
Client Redemption Trade	134
New Mandate Trade	135
Trade Execution	**137**
Trade Implementation Choices	137
Algorithmic Trading	140
Comparison of Markets	**145**
Equities	145
Fixed Income	146
Exchange-Traded Derivatives	147
Over-the-Counter Derivatives	147
Spot Foreign Exchange (Currency)	148
Trade Cost Measurement	**149**
Implementation Shortfall	149
Expanded Implementation Shortfall	151
Evaluating Trade Execution	**157**
Arrival Price	158
VWAP	158
TWAP	159
Market on Close	159
Market-Adjusted Cost	160
Added Value	162
Trade Governance	**163**
Meaning of Best Order Execution within the Relevant Regulatory Framework	164
Factors Used to Determine the Optimal Order Execution Approach	165
List of Eligible Brokers and Execution Venues	166
Process Used to Monitor Execution Arrangements	167
Summary	*169*
Practice Problems	*172*
Solutions	*181*

Reading 26   **Portfolio Performance Evaluation**   **189**

Introduction	190
Introduction to Performance Evaluation and Attribution	190
Performance Attribution	192
Equity Return Attribution	195
A Simple Return Attribution Example	196
Equity Return Attribution—The Brinson–Hood–Beebower Model	197
Brinson–Fachler Model	201
Fixed- Income Return Attribution	203
Fixed-Income Return Attribution	206
Risk Attribution	212
Return Attribution Analysis at Multiple Levels	214
Macro Attribution—An Example	215
Micro Attribution—An Example	217
Asset-Based and Liability-Based Benchmarks	221
Asset-Based Benchmarks	224

◘ indicates an optional segment

	Benchmark Properties, Evaluating Benchmark Quality, and Choosing the Correct Benchmark	226
	Evaluating Benchmark Quality: Analysis Based on a Decomposition of Portfolio Holdings and Returns	228
	Importance of Choosing the Correct Benchmark	230
	Benchmarking Alternative Investments	232
	Benchmarking Hedge Fund Investments	232
	Benchmarking Real Estate Investments	233
	Benchmarking Private Equity	234
	Benchmarking Commodity Investments	234
	Benchmarking Managed Derivatives	235
	Benchmarking Distressed Securities	235
	Performance Appraisal: Risk-Based Measures	235
	Distinguishing Investment Skill from Luck	236
	Appraisal Measures	236
	Performance Appraisal: Capture Ratios and Drawdowns	242
	Capture Ratios	242
	Drawdown	244
	Evaluation of Investment Manager Skill	251
	Performance Attribution Analysis	251
	Appraisal Measures	252
	Sample Evaluation of Skill	253
	Summary	255
	Practice Problems	257
	Solutions	261
Reading 27	**Investment Manager Selection**	**265**
	Introduction	265
	A Framework for Investment Manager Search and Selection	266
	Defining the Manager Universe	268
	Type I and Type II Errors in Manager Selection	269
	Qualitative considerations in Type I and Type II errors	270
	Performance implications of Type I and Type II errors	271
	Quantitative Elements of Manager Search and Selection	272
	Style Analysis	272
	Capture Ratios and Drawdowns in Manager Evaluation	275
	The Manager's Investment Philosophy	279
	Investment Philosophy	279
	Investment Personnel	283
	The Manager's Investment Decision-making Process	283
	Signal Creation (Idea Generation)	283
	Signal Capture (Idea Implementation)	284
	Portfolio Construction	284
	Monitoring the Portfolio	285
	Operational Due Diligence	286
	Firm	287
	Investment Vehicle	289
	Evaluation of the Investment's Terms	290

◉ indicates an optional segment

	Management Fees	292
	Assets under Management Fees	293
	Performance-Based Fees	293
	Summary	298
	Practice Problems	301
	Solutions	316
Study Session 14	**Cases in Portfolio Management and Risk Management**	**329**
Reading 28	**Case Study in Portfolio Management: Institutional**	**331**
	Introduction	331
	Background: Liquidity Management	332
	Liquidity Profiling and Time-to-Cash	333
	Rebalancing, Commitments	335
	Stress Testing	336
	Derivatives	337
	Earning an Illiquidity Premium	337
	QUINCO Case: Background	338
	Quadrivium University Investment Company (QUINCO)	340
	Investment Strategy: Background and Evolution	340
	QUINCO Case: Strategic Asset Allocation	342
	QUINCO Case: Liquidity Management	347
	QUINCO Case: Asset Manager Selection	352
	QUINCO Case: Tactical Asset Allocation	355
	QUINCO Case: Asset Allocation Rebalancing	359
	QUINCO Case: ESG Integration	363
	Summary	366
	Practice Problems	367
	Solutions	373
Reading 29	**Case Study in Risk Management: Private Wealth**	**379**
	Introduction and Case Background	379
	Background of Eurolandia	380
	The Schmitt Family in Their Early Career Stage	382
	Identification and Analysis of Risk Exposures: Early Career Stage	383
	Specify the Schmitts' financial objectives	383
	Identification of risk exposures	384
	Analysis of identified risk	386
	Risk Management Recommendations: Early Career Stage	388
	Recommendations for managing risks	388
	Monitoring outcomes and risk exposures	392
	Risk Management Considerations associated with Home Purchase	392
	Review of risk Management Arrangements Following the House Purchase	392
	Identification and Analysis of Risk Exposures: Career Development Stage	394
	Case Facts: The Schmitts Are 45	394
	Financial Objectives in the Career Development Stage	395
	Identification and Evaluation of Risks in the Career Development Stage	397

indicates an optional segment

	Risk Management Recommendations: Career Development Stage	399
	Disability insurance	399
	Life insurance	400
	Investment risk recommendations	402
	Retirement planning recommendation	403
	Additional suggestions	404
	Identification and Analysis of Risk Exposures: Peak Accumulation Stage	404
	Review of Objectives, Risks, and Methods of Addressing Them	406
	Assessment of and Recommendations concerning Risk to Retirement Lifestyle and Bequest Goals: Peak Accumulation Stage	412
	Analysis of Investment Portfolio	414
	Analysis of Asset Allocation	416
	Recommendations for Risk Management at Peak Accumulation Stage	417
	Identification and Analysis of Retirement Objectives, Assets and Drawdown Plan: Retirement Stage	418
	Key Issues and Objectives	419
	Analysis of Retirement Assets and Drawdown Plan	420
	Income and Investment Portfolio Recommendations: Retirement Stage	422
	Investment Portfolio Analysis and Recommendations	423
	The Advisor's Recommendations for Investment Portfolio in Retirement	424
	Summary	425
	Practice Problems	426
	Solutions	429
Reading 30	**Integrated Cases in Risk Management: Institutional**	**433**
	Introduction	433
	Financial Risks Faced by Institutional Investors	434
	Long-Term Perspective	434
	Dimensions of Financial Risk Management	435
	Risk Considerations for Long-Term Investors	437
	Risks Associated with Illiquid Asset Classes	440
	Managing Liquidity Risk	443
	Enterprise Risk Management for Institutional Investors	445
	Environmental and Social Risks Faced by Institutional Investors	447
	Universal Ownership, Externalities, and Responsible Investing	447
	Material Environmental Issues for an Institutional Investor	448
	Material Social Issues for an Institutional Investor	454
	Case Study	455
	Case Study: Introduction	456
	Case Study: Background	456
	R-SWF'S Investments: 1.0	456
	Investment Committee Meeting 1.0	462
	R-SWF'S Investments: 2.0	472
	Investment Committee Meeting 2.0	476
	R-SWF'S Investments: 3.0	484
	Glossary	**G-1**

◎ indicates an optional segment

How to Use the CFA Program Curriculum

Congratulations on your decision to enter the Chartered Financial Analyst (CFA®) Program. This exciting and rewarding program of study reflects your desire to become a serious investment professional. You are embarking on a program noted for its high ethical standards and the breadth of knowledge, skills, and abilities (competencies) it develops. Your commitment should be educationally and professionally rewarding.

The credential you seek is respected around the world as a mark of accomplishment and dedication. Each level of the program represents a distinct achievement in professional development. Successful completion of the program is rewarded with membership in a prestigious global community of investment professionals. CFA charterholders are dedicated to life-long learning and maintaining currency with the ever-changing dynamics of a challenging profession. CFA Program enrollment represents the first step toward a career-long commitment to professional education.

The CFA exam measures your mastery of the core knowledge, skills, and abilities required to succeed as an investment professional. These core competencies are the basis for the Candidate Body of Knowledge (CBOK™). The CBOK consists of four components:

- A broad outline that lists the major CFA Program topic areas (www.cfainstitute.org/programs/cfa/curriculum/cbok);
- Topic area weights that indicate the relative exam weightings of the top-level topic areas (www.cfainstitute.org/programs/cfa/curriculum);
- Learning outcome statements (LOS) that advise candidates about the specific knowledge, skills, and abilities they should acquire from readings covering a topic area (LOS are provided in candidate study sessions and at the beginning of each reading); and
- CFA Program curriculum that candidates receive upon exam registration.

Therefore, the key to your success on the CFA exams is studying and understanding the CBOK. The following sections provide background on the CBOK, the organization of the curriculum, features of the curriculum, and tips for designing an effective personal study program.

BACKGROUND ON THE CBOK

CFA Program is grounded in the practice of the investment profession. CFA Institute performs a continuous practice analysis with investment professionals around the world to determine the competencies that are relevant to the profession, beginning with the Global Body of Investment Knowledge (GBIK®). Regional expert panels and targeted surveys are conducted annually to verify and reinforce the continuous feedback about the GBIK. The practice analysis process ultimately defines the CBOK. The CBOK reflects the competencies that are generally accepted and applied by investment professionals. These competencies are used in practice in a generalist context and are expected to be demonstrated by a recently qualified CFA charterholder.

© 2021 CFA Institute. All rights reserved.

The CFA Institute staff—in conjunction with the Education Advisory Committee and Curriculum Level Advisors, who consist of practicing CFA charterholders—designs the CFA Program curriculum in order to deliver the CBOK to candidates. The exams, also written by CFA charterholders, are designed to allow you to demonstrate your mastery of the CBOK as set forth in the CFA Program curriculum. As you structure your personal study program, you should emphasize mastery of the CBOK and the practical application of that knowledge. For more information on the practice analysis, CBOK, and development of the CFA Program curriculum, please visit www.cfainstitute.org.

ORGANIZATION OF THE CURRICULUM

The Level III CFA Program curriculum is organized into six topic areas. Each topic area begins with a brief statement of the material and the depth of knowledge expected. It is then divided into one or more study sessions. These study sessions should form the basic structure of your reading and preparation. Each study session includes a statement of its structure and objective and is further divided into assigned readings. An outline illustrating the organization of these study sessions can be found at the front of each volume of the curriculum.

The readings are commissioned by CFA Institute and written by content experts, including investment professionals and university professors. Each reading includes LOS and the core material to be studied, often a combination of text, exhibits, and in-text examples and questions. End of Reading Questions (EORQs) followed by solutions help you understand and master the material. The LOS indicate what you should be able to accomplish after studying the material. The LOS, the core material, and the EORQs are dependent on each other, with the core material and EORQs providing context for understanding the scope of the LOS and enabling you to apply a principle or concept in a variety of scenarios.

The entire readings, including the EORQs, are the basis for all exam questions and are selected or developed specifically to teach the knowledge, skills, and abilities reflected in the CBOK.

You should use the LOS to guide and focus your study because each exam question is based on one or more LOS and the core material and practice problems associated with the LOS. As a candidate, you are responsible for the entirety of the required material in a study session.

We encourage you to review the information about the LOS on our website (www.cfainstitute.org/programs/cfa/curriculum/study-sessions), including the descriptions of LOS "command words" on the candidate resources page at www.cfainstitute.org.

FEATURES OF THE CURRICULUM

End of Reading Questions/Solutions   All End of Reading Questions (EORQs) as well as their solutions are part of the curriculum and are required material for the exam. In addition to the in-text examples and questions, these EORQs help demonstrate practical applications and reinforce your understanding of the concepts presented. Some of these EORQs are adapted from past CFA exams and/or may serve as a basis for exam questions.

Glossary   For your convenience, each volume includes a comprehensive Glossary. Throughout the curriculum, a **bolded** word in a reading denotes a term defined in the Glossary.

Note that the digital curriculum that is included in your exam registration fee is searchable for key words, including Glossary terms.

LOS Self-Check   We have inserted checkboxes next to each LOS that you can use to track your progress in mastering the concepts in each reading.

Source Material   The CFA Institute curriculum cites textbooks, journal articles, and other publications that provide additional context or information about topics covered in the readings. As a candidate, you are not responsible for familiarity with the original source materials cited in the curriculum.

Note that some readings may contain a web address or URL. The referenced sites were live at the time the reading was written or updated but may have been deactivated since then.

Some readings in the curriculum cite articles published in the *Financial Analysts Journal®*, which is the flagship publication of CFA Institute. Since its launch in 1945, the *Financial Analysts Journal* has established itself as the leading practitioner-oriented journal in the investment management community. Over the years, it has advanced the knowledge and understanding of the practice of investment management through the publication of peer-reviewed practitioner-relevant research from leading academics and practitioners. It has also featured thought-provoking opinion pieces that advance the common level of discourse within the investment management profession. Some of the most influential research in the area of investment management has appeared in the pages of the *Financial Analysts Journal*, and several Nobel laureates have contributed articles.

Candidates are not responsible for familiarity with *Financial Analysts Journal* articles that are cited in the curriculum. But, as your time and studies allow, we strongly encourage you to begin supplementing your understanding of key investment management issues by reading this, and other, CFA Institute practice-oriented publications through the Research & Analysis webpage (www.cfainstitute.org/en/research).

Errata   The curriculum development process is rigorous and includes multiple rounds of reviews by content experts. Despite our efforts to produce a curriculum that is free of errors, there are times when we must make corrections. Curriculum errata are periodically updated and posted by exam level and test date online (www.cfainstitute.org/en/programs/submit-errata). If you believe you have found an error in the curriculum, you can submit your concerns through our curriculum errata reporting process found at the bottom of the Curriculum Errata webpage.

DESIGNING YOUR PERSONAL STUDY PROGRAM

Create a Schedule   An orderly, systematic approach to exam preparation is critical. You should dedicate a consistent block of time every week to reading and studying. Complete all assigned readings and the associated problems and solutions in each study session. Review the LOS both before and after you study each reading to ensure that you have mastered the applicable content and can demonstrate the knowledge, skills, and abilities described by the LOS and the assigned reading. Use the LOS self-check to track your progress and highlight areas of weakness for later review.

Successful candidates report an average of more than 300 hours preparing for each exam. Your preparation time will vary based on your prior education and experience, and you will probably spend more time on some study sessions than on others.

You should allow ample time for both in-depth study of all topic areas and additional concentration on those topic areas for which you feel the least prepared.

CFA INSTITUTE LEARNING ECOSYSTEM (LES)

As you prepare for your exam, we will email you important exam updates, testing policies, and study tips. Be sure to read these carefully.

Your exam registration fee includes access to the CFA Program Learning Ecosystem (LES). This digital learning platform provides access, even offline, to all of the readings and End of Reading Questions found in the print curriculum organized as a series of shorter online lessons with associated EORQs. This tool is your one-stop location for all study materials, including practice questions and mock exams.

The LES provides the following supplemental study tools:

Structured and Adaptive Study Plans The LES offers two ways to plan your study through the curriculum. The first is a structured plan that allows you to move through the material in the way that you feel best suits your learning. The second is an adaptive study plan based on the results of an assessment test that uses actual practice questions.

Regardless of your chosen study path, the LES tracks your level of proficiency in each topic area and presents you with a dashboard of where you stand in terms of proficiency so that you can allocate your study time efficiently.

Flashcards and Game Center The LES offers all the Glossary terms as Flashcards and tracks correct and incorrect answers. Flashcards can be filtered both by curriculum topic area and by action taken—for example, answered correctly, unanswered, and so on. These Flashcards provide a flexible way to study Glossary item definitions.

The Game Center provides several engaging ways to interact with the Flashcards in a game context. Each game tests your knowledge of the Glossary terms a in different way. Your results are scored and presented, along with a summary of candidates with high scores on the game, on your Dashboard.

Discussion Board The Discussion Board within the LES provides a way for you to interact with other candidates as you pursue your study plan. Discussions can happen at the level of individual lessons to raise questions about material in those lessons that you or other candidates can clarify or comment on. Discussions can also be posted at the level of topics or in the initial Welcome section to connect with other candidates in your area.

Practice Question Bank The LES offers access to a question bank of hundreds of practice questions that are in addition to the End of Reading Questions. These practice questions, only available on the LES, are intended to help you assess your mastery of individual topic areas as you progress through your studies. After each practice question, you will receive immediate feedback noting the correct response and indicating the relevant assigned reading so you can identify areas of weakness for further study.

Mock Exams The LES also includes access to three-hour Mock Exams that simulate the morning and afternoon sessions of the actual CFA exam. These Mock Exams are intended to be taken after you complete your study of the full curriculum and take practice questions so you can test your understanding of the curriculum and your readiness for the exam. If you take these Mock Exams within the LES, you will receive feedback afterward that notes the correct responses and indicates the relevant assigned readings so you can assess areas of weakness for further study. We recommend that you take Mock Exams during the final stages of your preparation for the actual CFA exam. For more information on the Mock Exams, please visit www.cfainstitute.org.

PREP PROVIDERS

You may choose to seek study support outside CFA Institute in the form of exam prep providers. After your CFA Program enrollment, you may receive numerous solicitations for exam prep courses and review materials. When considering a prep course, make sure the provider is committed to following the CFA Institute guidelines and high standards in its offerings.

Remember, however, that there are no shortcuts to success on the CFA exams; reading and studying the CFA Program curriculum *is* the key to success on the exam. The CFA Program exams reference only the CFA Institute assigned curriculum; no prep course or review course materials are consulted or referenced.

SUMMARY

Every question on the CFA exam is based on the content contained in the required readings and on one or more LOS. Frequently, an exam question is based on a specific example highlighted within a reading or on a specific practice problem and its solution. To make effective use of the CFA Program curriculum, please remember these key points:

1. All pages of the curriculum are required reading for the exam.
2. All questions, problems, and their solutions are part of the curriculum and are required study material for the exam. These questions are found at the end of the readings in the print versions of the curriculum. In the LES, these questions appear directly after the lesson with which they are associated. The LES provides immediate feedback on your answers and tracks your performance on these questions throughout your study.
3. We strongly encourage you to use the CFA Program Learning Ecosystem. In addition to providing access to all the curriculum material, including EORQs, in the form of shorter, focused lessons, the LES offers structured and adaptive study planning, a Discussion Board to communicate with other candidates, Flashcards, a Game Center for study activities, a test bank of practice questions, and online Mock Exams. Other supplemental study tools, such as eBook and PDF versions of the print curriculum, and additional candidate resources are available at www.cfainstitute.org.
4. Using the study planner, create a schedule and commit sufficient study time to cover the study sessions. You should also plan to review the materials, answer practice questions, and take Mock Exams.
5. Some of the concepts in the study sessions may be superseded by updated rulings and/or pronouncements issued after a reading was published. Candidates are expected to be familiar with the overall analytical framework contained in the assigned readings. Candidates are not responsible for changes that occur after the material was written.

FEEDBACK

At CFA Institute, we are committed to delivering a comprehensive and rigorous curriculum for the development of competent, ethically grounded investment professionals. We rely on candidate and investment professional comments and feedback as we work to improve the curriculum, supplemental study tools, and candidate resources.

Please send any comments or feedback to info@cfainstitute.org. You can be assured that we will review your suggestions carefully. Ongoing improvements in the curriculum will help you prepare for success on the upcoming exams and for a lifetime of learning as a serious investment professional.

Portfolio Management

STUDY SESSIONS

Study Session 1	Behavioral Finance
Study Session 2	Capital Market Expectations
Study Session 3	Asset Allocation and Related Decisions in Portfolio Management
Study Session 4	Derivatives and Currency Management
Study Session 5	Fixed-Income Portfolio Management (1)
Study Session 6	Fixed-Income Portfolio Management (2)
Study Session 7	Equity Portfolio Management (1)
Study Session 8	Equity Portfolio Management (2)
Study Session 9	Alternative Investments Portfolio Management
Study Session 10	Private Wealth Management (1)
Study Session 11	Private Wealth Management (2)
Study Session 12	Portfolio Management for Institutional Investors
Study Session 13	Trading, Performance Evaluation, and Manager Selection
Study Session 14	Cases in Portfolio Management and Risk Management

This volume includes Study Sessions 12–14.

© 2021 CFA Institute. All rights reserved.

TOPIC LEVEL LEARNING OUTCOME

The candidate should be able to prepare an appropriate investment policy statement and asset allocation; formulate strategies for managing, monitoring, and rebalancing investment portfolios; and evaluate portfolio performance.

PORTFOLIO MANAGEMENT
STUDY SESSION

12

Portfolio Management for Institutional Investors

Broadly defined, institutional investors include retirement plans such as defined-benefit or defined-contribution plans, grant making organizations, endowments, insurance companies, banks, sovereign wealth funds, and investment intermediaries. These institutions typically have a well-defined purpose or business model in which their investment portfolio plays a pivotal role. Each group faces a unique set of investment objectives and constraints.

This study session provides a conceptual, yet practical, framework for understanding institutional portfolio management. Concepts and practices important in determining the investment policy statement (IPS) are presented for different types of institutional investors.

READING ASSIGNMENT

Reading 24   Portfolio Management for Institutional Investors
by Arjan Berkelaar, PhD, CFA, Kate Misic, CFA, and Peter Stimes, CFA

READING
24

Portfolio Management for Institutional Investors

by Arjan Berkelaar, PhD, CFA, Kate Misic, CFA, and Peter C. Stimes, CFA

Arjan Berkelaar, PhD, CFA, is at KAUST Investment Management Company (USA). Kate Misic, CFA, is at Telstra Super Pty Ltd (Australia). Peter C. Stimes, CFA, is a private investor in Fallbrook, California (USA).

LEARNING OUTCOMES

Mastery	The candidate should be able to:
☐	a. discuss common characteristics of institutional investors as a group;
☐	b. discuss investment policy of institutional investors;
☐	c. discuss the stakeholders in the portfolio, the liabilities, the investment time horizons, and the liquidity needs of different types of institutional investors;
☐	d. describe the focus of legal, regulatory, and tax constraints affecting different types of institutional investors;
☐	e. evaluate risk considerations of private defined benefit (DB) pension plans in relation to 1) plan funded status, 2) sponsor financial strength, 3) interactions between the sponsor's business and the fund's investments, 4) plan design, and 5) workforce characteristics;
☐	f. prepare the investment objectives section of an institutional investor's investment policy statement;
☐	g. evaluate the investment policy statement of an institutional investor;
☐	h. evaluate the investment portfolio of a private DB plan, sovereign wealth fund, university endowment, and private foundation;
☐	i. describe considerations affecting the balance sheet management of banks and insurers.

CFA Institute would like to thank Karl Mergenthaler, CFA, for his contributions to earlier drafts of this reading.

© 2019 CFA Institute. All rights reserved.

1 INSTITUTIONAL INVESTORS: TYPES AND COMMON CHARACTERISTICS

a discuss common characteristics of institutional investors as a group

Institutional investors are corporations, trusts, or other legal entities that invest in financial markets on behalf of groups or individuals, including both current and future generations. On a global basis, institutional investors represent more than US$70 trillion in investable assets, and, as such, wield significant influence over capital markets.

The universe of institutional investors includes, but is not limited to, defined benefit and defined contribution pension plans, sovereign wealth funds, endowments, foundations, banks, and insurance companies. Pension plans, which account for approximately US$35 trillion in investable assets or roughly half of global institutional assets under management, include both defined benefit plans, in which the sponsor (employer) assumes investment risk, and defined contribution plans, in which the individual makes investment decisions and assumes the investment risk. Sovereign wealth funds, which account for about US$7 trillion in assets as of the end of 2016, are government-owned investment funds that invest in financial and/or real assets. Endowments and foundations, which account for approximately US$1.6 trillion in assets, manage assets on behalf of educational institutions, hospitals, churches, museums, and other charitable organizations. Banks and insurance companies, comprising net financial assets on the order of US$9 trillion, are financial intermediaries that balance portfolios of securities, loans, and derivatives for the purposes of (i) meeting the claims of depositors, counterparties, policyholders, and creditors and (ii) providing adequate returns to their contractual capital holders. The universe of institutional investors is comprised of large, complex, and sophisticated investors that must contend with a multitude of investment challenges and constraints.

There has been an important shift in the asset allocation of institutional investors over the last half century. In the 1970s, most pensions and endowments invested almost exclusively in domestic, fixed-income instruments. In the 1980s, many institutional investors began to invest in equity markets and often pursued a long-term strategic allocation of 60% equities/40% fixed income. In the 1990s, investors recognized the benefits of diversification and many made their first forays into international equity markets. At the turn of the 21st century, many of the world's largest pension funds and endowments further diversified their portfolios and increased investments in alternative asset classes, including private equity, hedge funds, real estate, and other alternative or illiquid assets.

Meanwhile, institutional investors have seen broad shifts in their strategic investment behavior. The trend toward Liability Driven Investing (LDI), long a mainstay of banks and insurance companies, has taken hold among many defined benefit pension plans, particularly US corporate and public pension funds. Sovereign wealth funds have amassed significant assets over the past several decades, and many have implemented innovative investment approaches characterized by active management. Many endowments have adopted the "Endowment Model" of investing that involves significant exposure to alternative investments. Meanwhile, banks and insurers must navigate a complex and ever-changing economic and regulatory environment.

In this reading, we endeavor to put the numerous factors that affect investment by institutional investors into context. Section 1 discusses common characteristics of institutional investors as a group. Section 2 provides an overview of investment policies for institutional investors. Detailed coverage by institutional investor type begins with Sections 3–7, pension funds, where we discuss various factors that influence investments, including: stakeholders, liability streams, investment horizons, and liquidity needs; major legal, regulatory, accounting, and tax constraints; investment objectives and key components of Investment Policy Statements; and, finally, asset allocation and investment portfolios that emanate from the foregoing factors and constraints. Sections 8–10 follow the same approach for sovereign wealth funds, and Sections 11–15 do the same for university endowments and private foundations. Sections 16–19 covers banks and insurers and includes balance sheet management considerations. A summary of key points concludes the reading.

1.1 Institutional Investors: Common Characteristics

For the purposes of this reading, institutional investors include pension plans, sovereign wealth funds, endowments, foundations, banks, and insurance companies. As we will see in upcoming sections where we cover each of these six institutional types in detail, their objectives and constraints can vary widely. First, in this section we discuss important defining characteristics of institutional investors as a group, characteristics that set them apart from individual (retail and high-net-worth) investors. The common defining characteristics of institutional investors include the following:

1. **Scale (i.e., asset size):** The issue of scale is relevant for institutional investors because it may impact investment capabilities, access to investment strategies, liquidity, trading costs, and other key aspects of the investment process.
2. **Long-term investment horizon:** Institutional investors generally have a long-term investment horizon that is often determined by a specific liability stream, such as the benefit obligation of a pension plan, the spending policy of an endowment, or other obligations.
3. **Regulatory frameworks:** Institutional investors must contend with multiple regulatory frameworks that frequently vary by jurisdiction and complexity and are often evolving.
4. **Governance framework:** Institutional investors typically implement their investment programs through an investment office that often has a clearly defined governance model.
5. **Principal–Agent issues:** As institutional investors manage assets on behalf of others, principal–agent issues must be recognized and managed appropriately.

We discuss these five common characteristics in more detail next.

1.1.1 Scale

Institutional investors' assets under management can range from relatively small (e.g., less than US$25 million) to relatively large (e.g., more than US$10 billion). Smaller institutions may face challenges in building a diversified portfolio spanning public and private asset classes because they may be unable to access certain investments that have a high minimum investment size. For example, smaller institutions are less likely to be able to invest in private equity or real estate assets (i.e., property). Small institutional investors may also face challenges in hiring skilled investment professionals. As a result, they are more likely to outsource investments to external asset managers and rely on investment consultants. Larger institutional investors experience scale benefits that allow them access to a wider investment universe, and they can readily hire investment professionals. They may potentially manage part of their portfolios in-house if benefits outweigh costs. The largest institutional investors, however, may experience dis-economies of scale. For example, they might be unable to invest in certain niche investments like venture capital ("VC"). Given the huge asset size of investments under management, a small allocation to VC may not generate sufficient returns to justify the position (including due diligence costs). The largest institutional investors may also be unable to deploy as much capital as desired with some external managers as certain investment strategies are capacity constrained. External managers who want to avoid jeopardizing their ability to generate superior returns will close the strategy to new investors. To overcome these constraints, some of the largest institutions buy private companies, property, and infrastructure assets directly and manage their traditional asset-class portfolios in-house. Large institutional investors also face the costs of market impact given their sizable trading orders.

Rapidly growing institutional investors may experience high cash inflow relative to the size of their portfolios, which requires them to continuously invest inflows and to maintain the appropriate asset mix (strategic asset allocation). Ensuring access to investments capable of absorbing their growth in assets under management may be challenging when investing in capacity-constrained strategies, such as small-cap equity or venture capital.

1.1.2 Long-Term Investment Horizon

Pension funds, sovereign wealth funds, endowments, and foundations all typically have long investment horizons and relatively low liquidity needs. Cash outlays are relatively modest as a percent of assets under management, with net payouts typically around 5% or less. However, there are exceptions: For example, frozen defined benefit plans might be in a de-risking mode that increases their liquidity needs. Relatively low liquidity needs allow these institutions to invest in a broad range of alternative asset classes, including private equity, private real estate, natural resources, infrastructure, and hedge funds. Banks and insurance companies, however, tend to be much more asset/liability focused while operating within tight regulations designed to ensure adequacy of capital.

1.1.3 Regulatory Frameworks

Institutional Investors are typically subject to different legal, regulatory, tax, and accounting frameworks than individual investors. These frameworks define the set of rules an institutional investor must follow to qualify for reduced tax rates or tax-exempt status. Importantly, these frameworks and rules typically differ by national jurisdiction in which the institutional investor operates. Some examples of important relevant legal, regulatory, taxation, and accounting frameworks and organizations include the following:

- United States:
  - Employee Retirement Income Security Act (ERISA)
  - Pension Protection Act (PPA)
  - Uniform Prudent Management of Institutional Funds Act (UPMIFA)
  - Uniform Prudent Investor Act (UPIA)
  - Freedom of Information Act (FOIA)
  - Governmental Accounting Standards Board (GASB)
  - Generally Accepted Accounting Principles (GAAP) set by the Financial Accounting Standards Board (FASB)
  - Statutory Accounting Principles (SAP) set by the National Association of Insurance Commissioners (NAIC)
- United Kingdom:
  - Pensions Act
  - Finance Acts (various)
- European Union:
  - Institutions for Occupational Retirement Provision (IORP) II
- South Korea:

Institutional Investors: Types and Common Characteristics

- Employee Retirement Benefit Security Act
■ Australia:
- Superannuation Industry (Supervision) Act (SIS Act)
■ International:
- International Financial Reporting Standards (IFRS) set by the International Accounting Standards Board (IASB)
- International Organization of Securities Commissions (IOSCO)

Many relevant regulatory bodies govern and supervise institutional investors and their portfolios globally. The International Organization of Securities Commissions (IOSCO) is the international body that brings together the world's securities regulators, and it has 217 members. Ordinary members (127) include the national securities commissions or similar governmental bodies. Associate members (24) are supranational governmental regulators, subnational governmental regulators, intergovernmental international organizations, and other international standard-setting bodies. Affiliate members (66) include self-regulatory organizations, securities exchanges, and other financial market infrastructure and international regulatory bodies.

The key drivers of the legal and regulatory frameworks faced by institutional investors are investor protection, safety and soundness of financial institutions, and integrity of financial markets. Changes to these frameworks following the 2007–2009 global financial crisis focused on leverage limits, enhanced collateral requirements, increased liquidity requirements, central clearing, proprietary trading limits, private equity limits, trading tax implementation, brokerage fee limits, compensation limits, and requirements for more transparent reporting. Examples of regulations focusing on such reforms include the following:

■ United States:
- Dodd-Frank Wall Street Reform and Consumer Protection Act (Dodd-Frank)
- Section 619 (12 U.S.C. Section 1851) of the Dodd-Frank Act (Volcker Rule)
- Foreign Account Tax Compliance Act (FATCA), which has international implications
■ United Kingdom:
- Retail Distribution Review (RDR)
■ European Union (with most adopted by the United Kingdom):
- Undertakings for the Collective Investment of Transferable Securities V (UCITS V)
- Alternative Investment Fund Managers Directive (AIFMD)
- Solvency II Directive (Solvency II)
- Markets in Financial Instruments Directive II (MIFID II)
- European Market Infrastructure Regulation (EMIR)
- Financial Transaction Tax (FTT)
- Packaged Retail Investment and Insurance Products (PRIIPs)
■ International:
- Third Basel Accord / Capital Requirements Directive (Basel III / CRD IV)
- Santiago Principles (Generally Accepted Principles and Practices for Sovereign Wealth Funds)
- Principles of the Linaburg-Maduell Transparency Index (Sovereign Wealth Funds)

1.1.4 Governance Framework

Institutional investors typically operate under a formal governance structure. The governance structure generally includes a board of directors and an investment committee. The board may comprise company representative directors, employee representative directors, and independent directors. Independent directors are usually selected to increase the board's overall investment expertise. Investment committees can be sub-committees of the board with delegated authority to oversee investment policy. Alternatively, investment committees can be internal and consist of investment staff tasked with implementing the investment policy set by the board. The board and/or investment committee provide a key role in establishing the organization's investment policy, defining the risk appetite, setting the investment strategy, and monitoring the investment performance.

The board often sets the long-term strategic asset allocation and can delegate the setting of medium-term tactical asset allocation to its investment staff. It may also delegate manager selection to investment staff. Notably though, many institutional investor boards will seek to retain control through overseeing hiring and firing of managers. Best practice suggests, however, that it is better to delegate the hiring and firing of external managers to investment staff to ensure that the board focuses on such broader issues as governance, investment policy, and strategic asset allocation.

Institutional investors typically implement their investment strategy through an investment office. The investment office can be structured in different ways, but the most common model involves a Chief Investment Officer, who is supported by a team of asset-class specialists or a team of generalists working across asset classes. Institutional investors may manage investments in-house (e.g., some large Canadian pension plans and Australian superannuation funds) or outsource investment management partially or entirely to external assets managers. The factors affecting the decision to manage assets internally include the size of assets under management, capability of internal resources, or a desire to pursue custom strategies not readily offered by external managers. It can be costly to build the capability to manage assets internally, so in most cases asset owners need to achieve a certain threshold of assets under management before the benefits outweigh the costs of internalization.

For pension funds, sovereign wealth funds, endowments, and foundations, outsourcing elements of the investment function to external asset managers—or even outsourcing the entire investment operation to an outsourced chief investment officer (CIO) firm—is much more common than managing investments in-house. Such asset owners typically rely on specialized consultants to assist with asset allocation decisions and investment manager selection. These consultants often provide macroeconomic forecasts and capital market assumptions for asset classes that are integral to determining the investor's optimal asset allocation. In addition, the consultant assists in monitoring the large universe of external asset managers. Finally, the consultant may provide independent performance attribution and reporting and may monitor any internally managed investments and benchmark them against the external asset manager universe.

In contrast, banks and insurance companies undertake most of their investing, risk budgeting, compliance, and balance sheet management activities internally.

1.1.5 Principal–Agent Issues

Institutional investors frequently experience conflicts of interest that stem from principal–agent issues. The principal–agent issue arises if one person, the agent, makes decisions on behalf of another person or institution, the principal, and their interests are not aligned. A dilemma exists for the agent when he/she may be motivated to act in his/her own best interests and not in the best interests of the principal. Because of operational and investment complexity, institutional investors generally rely on various parties (i.e., agents) to act on their behalf. Agents may be internal or external. Internal agents include investment committee members and investment staff. External agents include third-party asset managers, broker/dealers, consultants, and board members. A typical example of the principal–agent problem is where performance fee structures are designed by external fund managers to provide attractive compensation to them via a high base fee, which is due regardless of fund performance. This fee structure gives little incentive for the fund manager to produce superior performance. Such fee arrangements are common among hedge funds and have led to greater demand for fee transparency and alignment of interest between hedge fund managers and their clients. To manage principal–agent issues, institutional investors will typically have highly developed governance models and high levels of accountability with a board and/or investment committee typically overseeing the investment office. Such models should be designed to explicitly acknowledge and manage conflicts of interest and align the interests of all agents with those of the principals.

OVERVIEW OF INVESTMENT POLICY

b discuss investment policy of institutional investors

Institutional investors codify their mission, investment objectives, and guidelines in an Investment Policy Statement (IPS). The IPS establishes policies and procedures for the effective administration and management of the institutional assets. A well-crafted IPS can help minimize principal–agent challenges by providing clear guidance on day-to-day management of the assets. Besides mission and investment objectives (i.e., return and risk tolerance), the IPS should cover any constraints that affect the asset allocation, asset allocation policy with ranges and asset class benchmarks, rebalancing policy, guidelines affecting the implementation of the asset allocation policy, and reporting requirements. The IPS should be reviewed annually; however, revisions should be infrequent, such as when material changes occur in investor circumstances and/or the market environment, as the IPS serves as the foundation for the investment program. The asset allocation policy and investment guidelines are typically included in an appendix that can be modified more easily.

Investment objectives flow from the organization's overall mission. For banks and insurance companies, the investment objective is to maximize net present value by balancing (i) the expected returns on assets, (ii) the expected cost of liabilities, (iii) the overall risks of assets and liabilities, and (iv) the economic relationships between and among assets and liabilities.

The investment objectives are more straightforward for the other types of institutions covered in this reading. For example, the overall objective of a DB pension fund might be to maintain a funded ratio in excess of 100%; for an endowment, it may be to maintain long-term purchasing power while providing needed financial support to its university. Investment objectives are typically expressed as a desired return target over the medium-to-long term (which should be clearly specified) with an acceptable level of risk. This return target should be evaluated in the context of the organization's overall mission and should be tied to the evaluation of liabilities (e.g., discount rate used to value DB pension plan liabilities or spending rate for an endowment). When expressing the return target in real terms, the relevant inflation metric must be defined. For example, GIC—Singapore's sovereign wealth fund—uses global inflation defined as G3 (the US, Japan, and Eurozone) inflation, while some US endowments use the Higher Education Price Index (HEPI) published by Commonfund (an independent asset management firm serving non-profit organizations and promoting best practices among institutional investors).

Investment objectives and return targets must be consistent with an organization's risk tolerance and other constraints. Risk tolerance can be expressed in different ways, such as for:

- DB pension funds: surplus volatility (standard deviation of asset returns in excess of liability returns);
- Sovereign wealth funds (SWFs): probability of investment losses (or probability of not maintaining purchasing power) over a certain time period;
- Endowments and foundations: volatility of total returns (standard deviation of total returns); and
- Banks and insurance companies: value at risk (VaR) or conditional VaR (CVaR) and comprehensive, scenario-based stress tests.

Finally, constraints (legal, regulatory, tax, and accounting) have a bearing on investment objectives and should be incorporated into the design of an investment policy. For example, constraints might limit the scope of acceptable risk and available asset classes.

Once the investment objectives—the desired risk and return characteristics—have been established, a strategic asset allocation or policy portfolio is designed. The investment portfolio of an institutional investor is designed to meet its objectives and should reflect the appropriate risk and liquidity considerations addressed in the IPS. For example, a large allocation to private equity is probably not appropriate for institutions with a relatively short investment horizon and high liquidity requirements. Similarly, a large fixed-income allocation might not be appropriate for an institution with a long investment horizon and low liquidity requirements. While institutional investors each have unique liability characteristics, several investment approaches have emerged over the past couple of years. Broadly speaking, these can be grouped into four different approaches:

1 **Norway Model** popularized by Norway's global pension fund, Government Pension Fund Global (GPFG). The Norway model is characterized by an almost exclusive reliance on public equities and fixed income (the traditional 60/40 equity/bond model falls under the Norway model), with largely passively managed assets and with very little to no allocation to alternative investments. Investments are usually managed with tight tracking error limits. The advantages of this approach are that investment costs/fees are low, investments are transparent, the risk of poor manager selection is low, and there is little complexity for a governing board. The disadvantage is that there is limited potential for value-added (i.e., alpha from security selection skills) above market returns. However, Norway's GPFG has begun to seek additional value over market-capitalization benchmarks by attempting to capture systematic risk factors.

2 **Endowment Model** popularized by the Yale Endowment. The endowment model is characterized by a high allocation to alternative investments (private investments and hedge funds), significant active management, and externally managed assets. This investment approach stands in almost direct contrast to the Norway model. Although labeled 'endowment model,' this investment approach is not only followed by many university endowments and foundations but also by several sovereign wealth funds and defined benefit pension funds. The endowment model is appropriate for institutional investors that have a long-term investment horizon, high risk tolerance, relatively small liquidity needs, and skill in sourcing alternative investments (the nature of alternative investments is such that there is large variation between the worst and best performing asset managers, and selecting the right manager is therefore critically important). The endowment model is difficult to implement for small institutional investors as they might not be able to access high quality managers.

Overview of Investment Policy

It might also be difficult to implement for very large institutional investors because of their very large footprint. The endowment model is more expensive in terms of costs/fees compared to the Norway model.

3 **Canada Model** popularized by the Canada Pension Plan Investment Board (CPPIB). The Canada model, just like the endowment model, is characterized by a high allocation to alternatives. Unlike the endowment model, however, the Canada model relies more on internally managed assets. The innovative features of the Canada model are the: a) reference portfolio, b) total portfolio approach, and c) active management. The reference portfolio is a passive mix of public equities, fixed income, and cash that represents a cheap and easily implementable portfolio that is expected to achieve the long-term expected return consistent with the institution's investment objectives and risk appetite. The reference portfolio effectively defines a transparent, risk-equivalent benchmark for the investment portfolio, and serves as a low-cost alternative to the fund's actual portfolio. The reference portfolio might be different from the institution's strategic asset allocation or policy portfolio. Importantly, the reference portfolio is typically made up of only publicly traded securities (in the form of common public market indices in equities and fixed income) that can be more easily understood by the governing board, while the strategic asset allocation may include target allocations to private markets and hedge funds. The total portfolio approach is the method of constructing the portfolio to ensure that planned risk exposures at the total portfolio level are maintained as individual investments enter, leave or change in value. It is an approach that is aimed at minimizing the unintended exposures and uncompensated risks that may arise as added value is sought by extending investments beyond the reference portfolio. For example, if private equity is added, management considers that it is leveraged equity and as a result the exposure to public equities needs to be reduced by more than the proposed allocation to private equity and the allocation to fixed-income needs to be increased to offset the leverage. Although the Canada model starts with a passive reference portfolio, it is important to note that the Canada model employs active management from tilting asset allocation through to stock selection. A good example of a sovereign wealth fund that has embraced the concept of the reference portfolio is the New Zealand Superannuation Fund.

4 **Liability Driven Investing (LDI) Model** has gained significant importance, particularly among corporate defined benefit pension plans in the United States, although some of the European pension funds—particularly in Denmark and in the Netherlands—adopted the LDI concept even prior to the 2007–2009 global financial crisis. In the LDI model, the primary investment objective is to generate returns sufficient to cover liabilities. As such, the investor's focus shifts away from operating in an asset-only context, to a focus on maximizing expected surplus return (excess return of assets over liabilities) and managing surplus volatility. Although the implementation and resultant asset allocation may vary significantly, LDI portfolios—other than for banks and insurance institutions—typically have a significant exposure to long duration fixed-income securities. In some LDI implementations, institutional investors separate their portfolios into a hedging portfolio (this portfolio usually hedges the main risk factor in the liabilities, which is interest rate risk) and a return-generating portfolio (this portfolio needs to generate sufficient returns to offset the growth rate of liabilities, other than changes in the discount rate). The hedging portfolio for defined benefit pension funds, sovereign wealth funds, and endowments/foundations usually consists of long duration fixed-income securities and may entail

the use of derivatives, such as interest rate swaps, to extend the duration of the portfolio. The return-generating portfolio usually includes public equities and alternative investments.

Exhibit 1 summarizes these four investment approaches.

Exhibit 1   Common Investment Approaches Used by Institutional Investors

Investment Approach	Description
Norway Model	Traditional style characterized by 60%/40% equity/fixed-income allocation, few alternatives, largely passive investments, tight tracking error limits, and benchmark as a starting position. *Pros*: Low cost, transparent, suitable for large scale, easy for board to understand. *Cons*: Limited value-added potential.
Endowment Model	Characterized by high alternatives exposure, active management and outsourcing. *Pros*: High value-added potential. *Cons*: Expensive and difficult to implement for most sovereign wealth funds because of their large asset sizes.
Canada Model	Characterized by high alternatives exposure, active management, and insourcing. *Pros*: High value-added potential and development of internal capabilities. *Cons*: Potentially expensive and difficult to manage.
LDI Model	Characterized by focus on hedging liabilities and interest rate risk including via duration-matched, fixed-income exposure. A growth component in the return-generating portfolio is also typical (exceptions being bank and insurance company portfolios). *Pros*: Explicit recognition of liabilities as part of the investment process. *Cons*: Certain risks (e.g., longevity risk, inflation risk) may not be hedged.

3   PENSION FUNDS: TYPES AND STAKEHOLDERS

c   discuss the stakeholders in the portfolio, the liabilities, the investment time horizons, and the liquidity needs of different types of institutional investors

Pension funds are long-term saving and investment plans designed to accumulate sufficient assets to provide for the financial needs of retirees. There are two main types of pension plans: **defined benefit**, in which a plan sponsor commits to paying a specified retirement benefit, and **defined contribution**, in which contributions are defined but the ultimate retirement benefit is not specified or guaranteed by the plan sponsor. Globally, there are many variations and nuances of these two broad categories of pension plans. Exhibit 2 compares the key features of defined benefit and defined contribution pension plans.

Exhibit 2 Comparison of Defined Benefit and Defined Contribution Pension Plan Features

Characteristics/Features	Defined Benefit Pension Plan	Defined Contribution Pension Plan
Benefit payments	Benefit payouts are defined by a contract between the employee and the pension plan (payouts are often calculated as a percentage of salary).	Benefit payouts are determined by the performance of investments selected by the participant.
Contributions	The employer is the primary contributor, though the employee may contribute as well. The size of contributions is driven by several key factors, including performance of investments selected by the pension fund.	The employee is typically the primary contributor—although the employer may contribute as well or may have a legal obligation to contribute a percentage of the employee's salary.
Investment decision making	The pension fund determines how much to save and what to invest in to meet the plan objectives.	The employee determines how much to save and what to invest in to meet his/her objectives (from the available menu of investment vehicles selected by the plan sponsor).
Investment risk	The employer bears the risk that the liabilities are not met and may be required to make additional contributions to meet any shortfall.	The employee bears the risk of not meeting his/her objectives for this account in terms of funding retirement.
Mortality/Longevity risk	Mortality risk is pooled. If a beneficiary passes away early, he/she typically leaves a portion of unpaid benefits in the pool offsetting additional benefit payments required by beneficiaries that live longer than expected. As a result, the individual does not bear any of the risk of outliving his/her retirement benefits.	The employee bears the risk of not meeting his/her objectives for this account in terms of funding retirement. The employee bears longevity risk.

Source: World Economic Forum, "Alternative Investments 2020: The Future of Alternative Investments" (2015).

Pension funds are significant players in the global investment landscape. Over the past 20 years, there has been a move away from defined benefit (DB) plans (especially non-government DB plans) to defined contribution (DC) plans. Among drivers of this shift are DC plans' lower financial risk for plan sponsors, absence of risk of becoming underfunded, and ease of portability (simplifies job mobility). Willis Towers Watson reports in its "Global Pension Assets Study 2018" covering the seven largest pension markets, the "P7" (Australia, Canada, Japan, the Netherlands, Switzerland, the United Kingdom, and the United States) that during the past 20 years DC pension plans have risen from 33% to 49% of total plan assets.

The split between DB and DC plans can vary significantly from country to country. One of the challenges of classifying countries by this split is that many countries offer hybrid pension plans, such as that in Switzerland where defined contribution connotes a cash balance plan in which all assets are pooled and the plan sponsor shares the investment risk. There are basically no pure DC plans in Switzerland. Exhibit 3 presents the split between DB and DC plans for the P7 countries. Together these countries comprise more than 80% of worldwide pension assets. In these data, DB plans and hybrid plans are combined (as for Switzerland). Note that a substantial difference exists between countries. Some countries rely almost exclusively on DC plans (like Australia), while others predominantly use DB plans (like Canada).

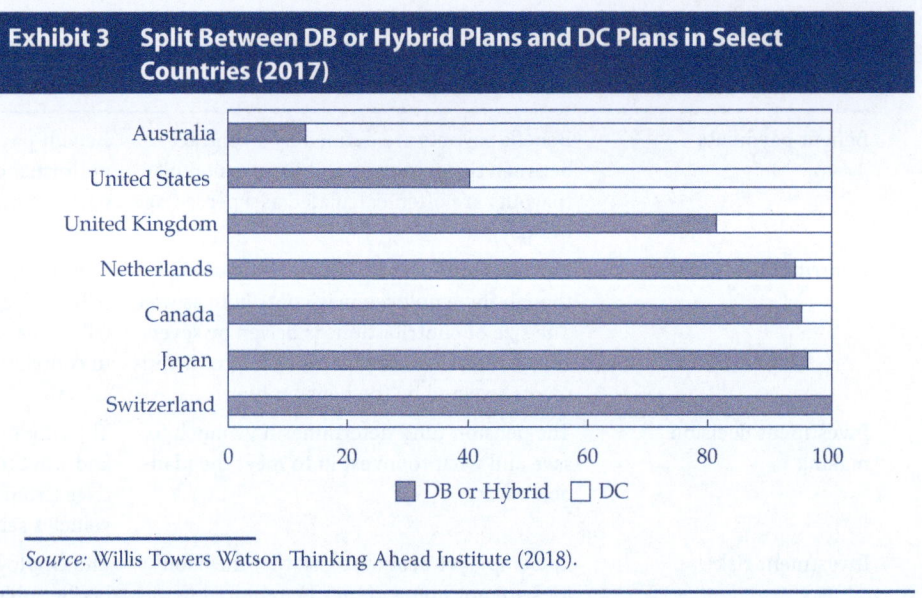

Exhibit 3   Split Between DB or Hybrid Plans and DC Plans in Select Countries (2017)

Source: Willis Towers Watson Thinking Ahead Institute (2018).

3.1 Stakeholders

Many entities are involved with institutional retirement plans. These include the employer, employees, retirees, unions, management, the investment committee and/or board, and shareholders. Governments have generally encouraged pension plans as a tool to assist individuals to build sufficient financial resources to fund their retirement needs. Government support typically comes in the form of favorable tax treatment for both companies and individuals who contribute to or manage pension plans, provided they operate according to local pension plan regulations. The government and taxpayers will bear some of the shortfall risks (in terms of added welfare or social security payments) in instances of employers failing to pay agreed on defined benefit payments and where individuals fail to accumulate sufficient wealth for retirement.

3.1.1 Defined Benefit Pension Plans

The stakeholders of a defined benefit pension plan are the employer [typically referred to as the plan sponsor and usually represented by management and the Chief Financial Officer (CFO)]; plan beneficiaries (employees and retirees); the Chief Investment Officer (CIO) and investment staff; the investment committee and/or board; and the government, unions, and shareholders in the case of corporate DB plans. Defined benefits promised to beneficiaries create liabilities for the plan sponsor. In operating the pension plan, the sponsor and investment staff must make investment decisions in the interest of the ultimate beneficiaries (employees and retirees). Defined benefit pension liabilities are typically funded from two sources: 1) employer and employee contributions and 2) investment returns on funded assets. Employee contributions can be fixed or variable, but employer contributions usually vary depending on the plan's funded status. Although each of the stakeholders has a strong interest in plan assets being invested appropriately, opinions might differ over the acceptable level of investment risk and the magnitude of employer contributions to the plan.

The plan sponsor may have an interest in 1) minimizing employer contributions due to budget constraints and/or 2) managing the volatility of employer contributions (by aiming for less volatility in investment returns). This allows management to plan future contributions with less uncertainty. Management and the CFO may also want to manage the impact of pension assets and liabilities on the sponsor's balance sheet. Employees and retirees, however, want to maximize the probability that plan liabilities are met and thus want the sponsor to make timely and sufficient plan contributions. Finally, the CIO and investment staff should be interested in meeting the investment objectives and constraints of the investment policy statement.

In a defined benefit pension plan, the sponsor bears the ultimate risk of the portfolio falling short of meeting liabilities. This risk manifests itself in the form of higher contributions from the plan sponsor when the plan becomes underfunded. In the extreme case of default, however—when the plan sponsor can no longer meet its legal obligations and cannot contribute further to the plan—the employee bears the ultimate risk and may need to find alternative means to meet financial needs in retirement. Some of this risk may be shared by taxpayers via additional social security or welfare payments, making the government a stakeholder in a defined benefit pension plan.[1]

The investment office of the DB pension plan is tasked with investing assets appropriately and may have variable compensation (bonuses) tied to investment performance. The investment committee or board will consider recommendations from investment staff, such as setting strategy and investment manager selection. In setting and executing strategy, all stakeholders' positions must be considered, including the sponsor's ability to make plan contributions. Ultimately, however, the board has a fiduciary duty to employees and retirees.

Finally, for corporate DB plans the company's shareholders are stakeholders. They are interested in the sustainability of the pension plan because if it is underfunded, any shortfall becomes a liability on the balance sheet, reducing the value of the company. Contributions to an underfunded plan also reduce net income. Underfunded status also increases financial risk, which may cause higher volatility in the stock price.

3.1.2 Defined Contribution Pension Plans

The main stakeholders of a defined contribution pension plan are the plan beneficiaries, the employer, the board, and the government.

A key stakeholder in a DC plan is the participant. Each participant has an individual account into which contributions are made on a regular basis—either by the employee, the employer, or both. Plan participants must ensure that 1) adequate contributions are made and 2) appropriate investment options are selected to generate sufficient investment returns. For a DC pension plan, the individual participant bears the investment risk of the portfolio failing to meet future liabilities (i.e., retirement needs). If plan participants outlive their savings, they will need to find other ways to meet their financial needs in retirement. In that case, the government (via taxpayers) may need to provide additional social welfare benefits, making the government another stakeholder in a DC plan.

Although DC plan participants control the investment decisions for their individual accounts, perhaps acting upon the advice of their financial adviser, the plan sponsor still has important fiduciary responsibilities, including overseeing the appropriate investment of plan assets (either by internal staff or by third-party asset managers or a combination thereof), offering suitable investment options, and selecting administrative providers. The plan sponsor, therefore, is an important stakeholder in a DC plan. The plan sponsor typically has an obligation to contribute to the DC plan on behalf of the employee as specified by the employment contract or through a government-mandated system. In some countries, a plan sponsor may also have an obligation to provide employees with a choice of different investment options within the employer-sponsored DC plan or even the choice of different DC plans. The sponsor typically must ensure that the investment options provide appropriate

---

[1] Some risk is also shared by other plan sponsors through agencies like the Pension Benefit Guaranty Corporation (PBGC) in the US. It is not funded by the government; rather, PBGC's funding comes primarily from insurance premiums paid by DB plan sponsors, assets of failed pension plans it takes over, and investment income.

levels of diversification. It may also need to provide investment education and communications so that employees can make well informed investment choices. Running DC plans can be more expensive than DB plans given their increased complexity of administration and meeting regulatory compliance, all of which may result in higher fees for DC plan participants.

The board of a DC plan sponsor must consider the differing levels of sophistication among participants and provide adequate disclosure in communications to ensure participants are well informed. The board may be required to select a default investment option when participants do not explicitly make an investment choice. In such cases, the board has a higher obligation because by entering the default option, the participant is indicating that he/she either does not have sufficient understanding to make an informed choice or that he/she trusts the board of the pension plan to make the best choice.

4. PENSION FUNDS: LIABILITIES, INVESTMENT HORIZON, AND LIQUIDITY NEEDS

c discuss the stakeholders in the portfolio, the liabilities, the investment time horizons, and the liquidity needs of different types of institutional investors

4.1 Liabilities and Investment Horizon

4.1.1 Defined Benefit Pension Plans

The liabilities of a DB pension plan are the present value of the future payments it will make to beneficiaries upon retirement, disability, or death. Calculating DB liabilities is complex and typically undertaken by actuaries employed by the plan sponsor or by external actuaries. Here we will highlight some key elements and focus on the discount rate used in calculating the present value of future benefit payments.

The first step in determining DB liabilities is to calculate the expected future cash flows (i.e., retirement benefits). These depend on the design and specifics of the pension plan. Some of the key elements common among DB plans in the calculation of expected cash flows are:

1 **Service/tenure:** The number of years the employee has been with the company or organization (or service years) determines the defined benefit the employee is expected to receive upon retirement. The higher the service years, the higher the retirement benefit. Sometimes a minimum number of service years is required before retirement benefits become vested (i.e., the employee becomes eligible to receive a pension).

2 **Salary/earnings:** The salary or earnings level of the employee affects the calculation of the defined benefit the employee is expected to receive upon retirement. The defined benefit may be a function of the average earnings over the entire career or the average earnings over the last several years prior to retirement (e.g., last three years).

3 **Mortality/longevity:** The length of time that retirement benefits are expected to be paid to plan participants is important in calculating expected cash flows. This requires assumptions about employees' and retirees' life expectancies. Importantly, ever-increasing life expectancies is a key factor in making DB

pension plans less affordable from the sponsor's perspective. Longevity risk is the risk to the plan sponsor that participants will live longer than assumed in the pension liabilities calculations.

In estimating future benefits, the plan sponsor must make several key assumptions, such as the growth rate of salaries, expected vesting, and mortality and disability assumptions. **Vesting** means that employees only become eligible to receive a pension after meeting certain criteria, typically a minimum number of years of service. In measuring defined benefit obligations, the plan sponsor must consider the likelihood that some employees may not satisfy the vesting requirements. Under both International Financial Reporting Standards (IFRS) and US generally accepted accounting principles (GAAP), pension obligations are determined as the present value of future benefits earned by employees for service provided to date. Assumptions about future salary increases, expected vesting, and life expectancy change over time and will change the estimated pension obligation. Given the importance of these factors, pension plans require periodic actuarial reviews to determine the value of the liabilities and the sponsor's annual required contribution rate.

Once expected future benefits are calculated, they must be discounted to determine their present value. Practices of marking-to-market liabilities using market discount rates can vary considerably based on country, or even within a country, between private and public pension plans. Typical discount rates include government bond yields or swap rates, corporate bond yields, and constant actuarial discount rates (long-term expected rate of return). Plan sponsors might be inclined to use a higher discount rate that will, all else equal, result in lower pension liabilities, a better funded status, and potentially lower contributions. Beneficiaries prefer to see a lower discount rate being used that will, all else equal, result in higher pension liabilities, a worse funded status, and potentially higher contributions. There is a delicate balance, however, because if contributions become unsustainable, the plan sponsor might decide to shut down its DB plan and substitute it with a less risky DC plan.

Over the past 15 years, a shift has occurred in many countries toward tying the discount rate to market rates. As a result, many pension plans have adopted a more liability-driven investment approach to partially or fully hedge the interest rate risk in their liabilities. Given the low interest rate environment since the 2007–2009 financial crisis, this has posed tremendous challenges for pension funds globally.

Discount Rates for Defined Benefit Plans in the US

In the United States, private and corporate DB pension plans may discount liabilities at rates based on high-grade bond yields averaged over 25 years. This was allowed under the 2012 update to the Pension Protection Act (PPA), part of broader legislation known as MAP-21. The change effectively raised the applicable discount rates (and reduced DB pension liabilities), providing some relief to defined benefit plans given what were perceived to be 'artificially' low interest rates. Prior to the PPA, corporate DB plans had to discount liabilities using current investment-grade corporate bond yields, not a historical average.

US public DB pension plans use actuarial discount rates which, as required by the US Governmental Accounting Standards Board (GASB), are based on the expected return of the pension plan asset portfolio. These are typically far higher than bond rates. The higher discount rates lower their liabilities and raise their funded status. However, this may cause such pension plans to potentially make inadequate plan contributions and take on excessive risk by investing heavily in equities and alternatives in hope of generating an expected rate of return that supports the high discount rate.

Exhibit 4 summarizes the key elements in the calculation of defined benefit pension plan liabilities.

Exhibit 4 Factors Affecting Calculation of Defined Benefit Liabilities

Factor	Impact on Liabilities
Service/tenure	Depending on plan design, often the longer the period of service or tenure, the larger the benefit payments.
Salary/earnings	The faster salaries or earnings grow, the larger the benefit payments.
Additional or matching contributions	Additional or matching contributions are often rewarded by a step change increase in benefit payments.
Mortality/Longevity assumptions	If life expectancy increases, the obligations or liabilities will increase.
Expected Vesting	If employee turnover decreases, expected vesting will increase.
Expected Investment Returns	In some cases, increases in expected returns will result in a higher discount rate being used—hence, lower obligations or liabilities.
Discount Rate	A higher (lower) discount rate results in lower (higher) liabilities.

The main objective of a DB plan is to have sufficient assets to cover future benefit payments. A common pension industry metric used to gauge asset sufficiency is the funded ratio, also known as the vested benefit index (VBI) in some countries. The funded ratio is defined as:

Funded ratio = Fair value of plan assets/PV of Defined benefit obligations

In some countries, if the funded ratio is less than 100%, the sponsor must increase contributions until it exceeds 100%. Improving the plan's funded ratio can transform the pension obligation from a liability to an asset on the plan sponsor's balance sheet. It is important to note that in some cases, underfunded pension plans may take more investment risk in the hope of achieving higher returns and growing assets sufficiently to return to fully funded status. In other cases, underfunded pension plans reduce investment risk and rely on other actions to improve their funded status, such as increasing contributions or reducing benefits.

Additional considerations in DB pension design are:

1 the size of the pension plan relative to the size of the sponsor's balance sheet; and

2 the cyclicality of the plan sponsor's core business.

If plan assets and liabilities are small relative to the sponsor's balance sheet, then there may be more flexibility in taking investment risk and more tolerance for volatility in employer contributions. If, on the other hand, plan asset and liabilities are large in relation to the sponsor's balance sheet, then there may be less appetite for volatility of employer contributions and hence a reduced desire for taking investment risk.

Another important factor is the core business of the plan sponsor. If the plan sponsor's revenues are highly cyclical, it will not want plan funded status to deteriorate when the core business suffers from a cyclical downturn. In such cases, the DB plan's asset allocation would be modified to ensure adequate diversification so as not to have significant exposure to assets highly correlated with the sponsor's core business or industry. In sum, it is desirable for plan assets to have low (high) correlations with the sponsor's operating assets (liabilities).

The plans sponsor's ability to tolerate volatility of contribution rates may impact the investment horizon, and hence the pension plan's appetite for such illiquid investments as private equity and venture capital. Another important factor determining the investment horizon is the mix of active plan participants (i.e., current employees) versus retirees. The higher the proportion of retirees (so the higher the liability associated with retirees only) relative to the proportion of active participants (or the liability associated with active participants), the more mature the plan—hence, the lower its risk tolerance. Some mature DB pension plans have been frozen (closed to new participants) as they typically experience negative cash flow where benefit payments exceed contributions. Generally, the more mature a pension fund, the shorter its investment horizon, which directly affects risk tolerance and the allocation between fixed-income assets and riskier assets.

4.1.2 Defined Contribution Pension Plans

In a DC plan, participants' pension benefits are based on amounts credited to their individual accounts in the form of contributions (from the employee and possibly the employer) and investment returns. Consequently, the liabilities of a DC pension plan sponsor are equal only to its required contributions. DC plan assets are typically pooled, and the sponsor invests according to the investment choices selected by plan participants. Often the DC plan may invest in a broadly diversified portfolio that may include investments not generally offered to retail investors, such as private equity and hedge funds. This is possible since pooling of assets gives rise to scale and the long-term horizon of the aggregate beneficiaries. In such case, the plan sponsor takes on the residual investment risk of its asset allocation. Once invested in such alternative asset types, the DC plan sponsor bears liquidity risk if any event occurs that causes a significant proportion of its participants to exit the plan. The asset allocation may be impacted to such an extent that the plan sponsor is unable to provide the asset allocation promised to its participants. Such a circumstance will have regulatory and reputational consequences for the DC plan sponsor.

Individuals in a DC plan are at different stages of their careers, so each has a different investment time horizon (the time period from his/her current age until expected death or expected death of a spouse, whichever is longer) as well as different risk tolerances. Therefore, key considerations for most DC plans are participants' ages and invested balances. If the plan has a larger proportion of older (younger) participants with large (small) invested balances, the investment options might reflect a shorter (longer) investment horizon. Many DC plans offer investment options that allow participants to select the investment horizon that best aligns with their own investment horizon. Examples are life-cycle options or target date options, which feature a glide path that manages the asset mix based on a desired retirement date. In the United States, most DC plans offer target-date options as default options; in Hong Kong SAR it is mandated that every default option plan have a life-cycle option.

There are two main types of life-cycle options. **Participant-switching life-cycle options** automatically switch members into a more conservative asset mix as their age increases. There may be several automatic de-risking switches at different age targets. A **participant/cohort option** pools the participant with a cohort that has a similar target retirement date. For example, if a participant is 40 years old in 2020 and plans to retire at the age of 65, he/she could invest in an option with a target date of 2045 and the fund would manage the appropriate asset mix over the next 25 years. In 2020, the assets might be 90% invested in equities and 10% in bonds. As time passes, however, the fund would gradually change the asset mix (less equities and more bonds) to reflect an appropriate allocation given the time to retirement.

4.2 Liquidity Needs

Although pension plans typically have long investment time horizons, they still must maintain sufficient liquidity relative to their projected liabilities. Liquidity needs are driven by:

- Proportion of active employees relative to retirees—The former contribute to the plan, while the latter receive benefit payments. More mature pension funds have higher liquidity needs. Frozen DB pension plans, often facing negative cash flow, must hold even more cash and other liquid investments compared to open mature plans.

- Age of workforce—Liquidity needs rise as the age of the workforce increases, since the closer participants are, on average, to retirement, the sooner they will switch from the contribution phase to benefit payment stage. This is true for both DB and DC plans.

- DB plan funded status—If the plan is well funded, the plan sponsor may reduce contributions, generating a need to hold higher balances of liquid assets to pay benefits.

- Ability of participants to switch/withdraw from plan—If pension plan participants can switch to another plan or withdraw on short notice, then higher balances of liquid assets must be held to facilitate these actions. This applies to DB and some DC plans.

A pension plan with lower liquidity needs can hold larger balances in private investments—such as real estate, infrastructure, private equity, and hedge funds—and can invest a higher proportion in equities and credit. A pension plan with higher liquidity needs, however, must invest a higher proportion of its assets in cash, government bonds, and highly liquid, investment-grade corporate bonds.

It is important for pension plans to regularly perform liquidity stress tests, which may include stressing the value of their assets and modelling reduced liquidity of certain asset classes in a market downturn. Such stress-testing may also help DC plans anticipate whether participants might switch out of more volatile investment options during market downturns.

EXAMPLE 1

Comparing Defined Benefit (DB) and Defined Contribution (DC) Pension Plans

Geoff Albright is 35 years old and has been working at Henley Consulting in Melbourne, Australia, for 10 years. Henley Consulting offers a defined benefit (DB) pension plan for its employees. The defined benefit plan is fully funded. Geoff Albright's benefit formula for monthly payments upon retirement is: final monthly salary × benefit percentage (=1.5%) × number of years of service, where final monthly salary equals his average monthly earnings for the last three financial years immediately prior to retirement date. Having been at Henley Consulting for 10 years, his benefits have vested and can be transferred to another pension plan.

Geoff has been offered a job at rival Australian firm, Horizon Ventures Consulting, which is offering a similar salary; however, Horizon Ventures Consulting offers a defined contribution (DC) pension plan for its employees. Horizon Ventures Consulting will pay 15% of annual salary into the plan each year. Employees can choose to invest in one of three diversified portfolios offered by the plan sponsor—Horizon Growth, Horizon Balanced, and Horizon

Conservative—based upon their risk appetite, and employees can elect to make additional contributions to the plan. The monthly pension payments will depend on what has accumulated in Geoff's account when he retires.

Discuss the features that Geoff should consider in evaluating the two plans. Please address benefit payments, contributions, shortfall risk, and mortality/longevity risks.

Solution:

- Geoff notes his benefits at Henley Consulting have vested and can be transferred to Horizon Ventures Consulting's DC plan.
- Henley Consulting's plan provides a defined benefit payment linked to years of service and final salary, whereas Horizon Ventures Consulting's plan provides an uncertain benefit payment linked to the company's and Geoff's contribution rates and investment performance of plan assets. The benefits he can achieve in Henley Consulting's DB plan increase both by time employed as well as by growth in his wages. Geoff considers his capacity to achieve wage growth and compares this to the return objectives of his chosen option in Horizon Ventures Consulting's DC plan. Geoff notes his risk appetite and time horizon are suited to the Horizon Growth option.
- Although Henley Consulting's contribution rate is not known, Geoff is aware that the plan is currently fully funded and that it is Henley Consulting's obligation to maintain a fully funded status. Horizon Ventures Consulting's contribution rate is known (15% of annual salary), and Geoff can also make additional contributions himself.
- Geoff notes that the shortfall risk of plan assets being insufficient to meet his retirement benefit payments falls to his employer in the case of Henley Consulting's DB plan. But, for Horizon Ventures Consulting's DC plan, the shortfall risk falls to Geoff and depends on the contribution rate (15% from the company plus any additional contributions he chooses to make) and the performance of his chosen investments.
- Henley's DB plan pools mortality risk such that those in the pool who die prematurely leave assets that help fund benefit payments for those who live longer than expected. Horizon Venture Consulting's DC plan pays out the amount accumulated in Geoff's account, and he bears the risk of outliving his savings.

PENSION FUNDS: EXTERNAL CONSTRAINTS | 5

d describe the focus of legal, regulatory, and tax constraints affecting different types of institutional investors

In this section, we take a high-level view of some of the legal and regulatory constraints faced by pension funds. In the next section, we consider tax and accounting constraints that may affect investing by pension funds.

5.1 Legal and Regulatory Constraints

Regulatory bodies supervising pension funds typically cover financial services licensing and regulation, prudential supervision, capital adequacy, market integrity, and consumer protection. Breeching key regulations may result in loss of operating licenses and/or loss of tax benefits, where applicable, which provides a strong incentive to comply. Regulations do vary from country to country; for example, some countries specify minimum and maximum percentage allocations to certain asset classes, while other countries require a minimum contribution rate by employers, particularly if the plan's funded ratio falls below 100%. However, despite national differences, there are similar themes in regulation globally.

Reporting and transparency are heavily influenced by regulatory requirements, as some regulators now require extensive reporting, not only on direct investment fees and costs incurred by pension plans but also on indirect fees and costs of external commingled vehicles. Drivers of more detailed reporting and transparency are avoidance of corruption by government officials involved with public pension plans and increased consumer protection for private pension plans so participants and stakeholders make appropriate investment choices. Many countries have increased personal liability for pension trustees to ensure they act in the best interests of ultimate beneficiaries. For example, DC plan participants must choose their contribution rates and the investment risk they are willing to bear. However, regulators are aware that many DC plan participants have little understanding of how to invest for retirement. Although regulators may require the plan sponsor to provide investor education to their employees, DC plan trustees, as fiduciaries, are still required to operate with prudence and as if they were the asset owners.

In Australia, for example, most employees are covered by the DC Superannuation Guarantee, under which employers must contribute 9.5% of an employee's salary. Since many participants do not actively make investment decisions, the government applies strict licensing and other obligations for trustees when offering the default option (MySuper), including: providing a single diversified investment strategy as a default option suitable for the majority of participants; avoiding unnecessary or excessive fees; and delivering value for money (measured by long-term net returns). A similar default DC plan account exists in the United States (known as the Qualified Default Investment Alternative), which must also be diversified.

In Europe the updated Institutions for Occupational Retirement Provision (IORP II) will lead to regulatory changes for pension plans. Although each country will interpret the provisions slightly differently, the changes relate to governance, risk management, and disclosure. A number of key functions are defined, such as an internal audit, and standards are applied to those executing these key functions, including a requirement that such a person does not carry out a similar function for the plan sponsor. Many pension plans will need to document their risk management policies and procedures. For example, each fund must document its "own risk assessment" covering items such as the risk of not meeting benefit obligations and operational risk, including administrative error or fraud. For disclosure, there will also be greater harmonization of pension benefit statements with certain items required to be included.

US corporate pension plans are subject to significant regulatory oversight. The Employee Retirement Income Security Act of 1974 (ERISA) regulates vesting, funding requirements, and payouts. ERISA includes a fiduciary code of conduct and required disclosures. ERISA established the Pension Benefit Guaranty Corporation, a US government agency that collects premiums from pension plan sponsors and pays benefits to participants (approximately 630,000) in terminated plans. Although ERISA protects benefits that workers have earned, an employer may still terminate a plan, essentially freezing a worker's ability to earn additional benefits. Moreover, the US Pension Protection Act of 2006 established minimum funding standards for DB plans, while later revisions raised the rates corporations could use to discount their liabilities (high-grade bond yields averaged over 25 years). Importantly, a potential consequence of using higher discount rates is these DB plans must generate higher returns for their funding status to remain sustainable, which typically requires taking on greater investment risk.

5.2 Tax and Accounting Constraints

Governments around the world encourage citizens to save for retirement by typically providing favorable tax treatment to retirement savings. Favorable tax treatment may come in different forms: reduced taxes on retirement plan contributions, favorable tax rates on investment income and/or capital gains, and lower tax rates on benefit payments drawn throughout retirement (versus higher taxes on lump sum payments). Foregone tax revenues from such favorable tax treatment are costly, so to ensure pension plans actually reduce tax burdens for retirement savers, governments typically place restrictions on plan design, governance, and investment activities in order for plans to qualify for the favorable tax treatment.

In the United States, 401(k) plans are tax deferred as participants make pre-tax contributions and do not pay tax on investment earnings; benefit payments, however, are taxed as ordinary income. To encourage savings retention within the pension plan, early withdrawals before age 59½ are taxed an additional 10%. In the United Kingdom, private pension plans are also tax deferred, with no tax on contributions or on investment earnings. The first 25% of benefit payments are tax free, and the remaining 75% is taxed as ordinary income after a tax-free personal allowance. In China, companies providing occupational pensions (known as Enterprise Annuities) are given tax relief amounting to 4% of wages; however, there are taxation differences between regions.

Pension plans taxed on investment earnings must be aware of tax implications of their investment activities. For example, there may be favorable capital gains tax treatment for investments held over 1 year, which should incentivize investing in lower turnover strategies. Also, pension plans must consider tax implications when returns from investing via futures and other derivatives are treated as income and taxed at higher rates than returns from investing in the underlying securities, which are typically taxed at lower capital gains and dividend rates. When investing internationally, double taxation may occur when the same income or capital gain is taxed both by the jurisdiction in which it is earned *and* in the jurisdiction where the pension fund resides. To achieve tax efficiency, pension plans should invest via legal structures that provide access to double taxation treaties, whereby taxes paid in the country of residence are exempt in the country where they arise (alternatively, the plan receives a foreign tax credit in its country of residence to reflect taxes withheld in the country where the income/gain arose).

Accounting treatment is another important external factor that drives investment decision making by pension funds. These treatments may differ across countries, so it is important to be fully aware of them. Here we focus on the United States to illustrate how accounting treatment may influence investment choices. Corporate DB pension plans must follow generally accepted accounting principles—notably, Accounting Standards Codification (ASC) 715, Compensation—Retirement Benefits, which requires that an overfunded (underfunded) plan must appear as an asset (liability) on the balance sheet of the corporate sponsor. Such plan sponsor must also report gains, losses, and service costs as part of net income. This accounting treatment significantly increased the transparency of US plans' funded status, and it prompted many corporate plans to implement liability-driven investing techniques to reduce the effect of funded ratio volatility on their financial statements.

Public pension plans in the US must follow Governmental Accounting Standards Board (GASB) rules. Under GASB rules, public plan sponsors must report fair market values of plan assets and can use a blended approach to valuing plan liabilities. The latter involves discounting the funded portion of pension liabilities using the (higher) expected return on plan assets as well as discounting the unfunded portion of liabilities based on the (lower) yield on tax-exempt municipal bonds. Using a higher discount rate for the funded portion of liabilities skews the risk tolerance of public pension plans and incentivizes them to allocate relatively large proportions of assets to equities and alternative investments.

6. PENSION FUNDS: RISK CONSIDERATIONS

e evaluate risk considerations of private defined benefit (DB) pension plans in relation to 1) plan funded status, 2) sponsor financial strength, 3) interactions between the sponsor's business and the fund's investments, 4) plan design, and 5) workforce characteristics

Despite the long-term trend in the shift away from DB plans toward DC plans, as previously demonstrated, DB plans (and their hybrids) are still a key part of the pension landscape in several P7 countries, such as Canada, Japan, the Netherlands, and Switzerland. As such, it is important to review risk management considerations of private defined benefit pension plans—a topic that has intensified following the global financial crisis of 2007-2009. Key risk considerations of such plans must be measured and managed.

1 Plan funded status

   When a defined benefit pension plan is fully funded, the value of assets is greater than or equal to the present value of the liabilities. If the value of the assets falls below the present value of the liabilities, the pension plan is considered to be underfunded and the plan sponsor is left with a financial liability. The plan sponsor can take several approaches in order to minimize the risk of generating a financial liability:

   a Seek to match assets to liabilities in terms of quantity, timing, and risk using a Liability Driven Investing (LDI) approach. Duration gap management or cash flow–matching suits plans that are close to fully funded and seek to maintain that status.

   b Seek to grow assets at a higher rate of return than the expected growth in liabilities—which typically involves taking on more investment risk. This form of investment suits plans that are underfunded and wishing to return to a fully funded status. It may also suit fully funded plans that are seeking to lower their contribution rate over time and are willing to endure the increased volatility in funded status that this approach entails.

   c Seek to invest in more defensive assets expected to deliver less volatile returns. This may suit defined benefit pension plans where the plan sponsor is willing to make higher contributions over time in exchange for less variability in the plan funded status.

   In cases where a plan is adequately funded, the sponsoring corporation may seek to remove pension-driven balance sheet volatility by engaging pension risk transfer through such mechanisms as:

   - offering lump sum payments to beneficiaries in exchange for voluntarily leaving the plan; or

- negotiating a transfer of the risk to an insurance provider.

2 Sponsor financial strength

When a defined benefit pension plan sponsor is not financially strong, there is a considerable risk that it may fail to make the necessary contributions to the plan. The plan sponsor may not be able to meet its defined benefit pension plan liabilities if there is a funding shortfall. If the plan sponsor files for bankruptcy protection, an underfunded pension plan is in the same difficult position as other creditors, having to join the queue claiming the firm's remaining assets.

The relative size of the plan also influences the sponsor's ability to assume risk. If the pension plan is small (large) relative to the size of the sponsor, then volatility in pension assets, liabilities, and/or contributions will have a smaller (larger) effect on the sponsoring company's balance sheet.

3 Interactions between the sponsor's business and the fund's investments

In the past, many private defined benefit pension plans have held significant stakes in the equity of the sponsor company. However, due to the risk involved, many regulators have restricted how much a plan may invest in the stock of the sponsor company. This risk materializes in circumstances in which the company performs poorly and its share price falls, thereby increasing the risk that pension plan assets fall below liabilities. This may coincide with a point in time when the sponsor's financial strength is poor, constraining its ability to make additional contributions necessary to address the developing funding shortfall. For this reason, it is advisable for the plan to diversify out of the sponsor company's stock. It is also prudent to diversify away from companies operating in the same industry, because their risk and return are expected to be highly correlated with those of the sponsor company's stock.

4 Plan design

Poor plan design can contribute many risks for the private defined benefit pension plan sponsor. When setting out the formula for calculation of defined benefit payments, the plan sponsor must balance adequacy (will the benefit payment be sufficient to meet income needs in retirement) and sustainability (what contribution rate is sustainable, and what investment return can realistically be achieved) within the context of its risk tolerance. There is a significant risk that a company will be overly optimistic in predicting its ability to make contributions to its pension plan decades into the future.

The plan design is informed by its purpose as an employee retention tool to mitigate the risk of losing employees to a competitor. The company/sponsor may also wish to increase future defined benefit payments to address worker unrest, which may otherwise lead to strike action or lengthy negotiations with unions. If a company does not have immediate excess cash flow, it may prefer to increase future defined benefit payments instead of granting immediate pay raises.

5 Workforce characteristics

The nature of the workforce is an important risk consideration for companies because it impacts what the duration of the assets should be. The younger the workforce, the longer the duration of assets and the greater risk tolerance the plan will have. If a company's workforce has high turnover, it may have few employees whose entitlements to defined benefit payments will vest. On the other hand, if the average tenure of the workforce increases, then more liabilities will vest, thereby reducing the plan's funded status. If the workforce is older and nearer to retirement age, an important risk consideration is keeping sufficient liquidity so the plan can meet liabilities when they become due. Conversely, in a plan where the workforce is younger, on average, the sponsor may take on more liquidity risk. A workforce with a high level of vested benefits may constrain the company in terms of flexibility in managing its workforce. For example, a company may prefer to downsize its workforce, but doing so might require it to pay out excessive vested benefits.

Retired workers also influence the longevity risk of DB plans. Longevity risk is the risk that an individual will live longer than expected and draw more in benefit payments than the amount determined in the calculation of plan liabilities. In private DB pension plans, longevity risk is pooled such that if a participant dies earlier than expected, he/she leaves more assets in the pool that can then cover additional payments for those who live longer than expected. However, this pooling of longevity risk does not mitigate the effect of rising life expectancies, which implies, all else equal, an increase in total DB plan liabilities.

In setting a risk objective, plan sponsors must consider plan status, sponsor financial status and profitability, sponsor and pension fund common risk exposures, plan features, and workforce characteristics, as shown in Exhibit 5.

Exhibit 5 Factors Affecting Risk Tolerance and Risk Objectives of Defined Benefit Plans

Category	Variable	Explanation
Plan status	▫ Plan funded status (surplus or deficit)	▫ Higher pension surplus or higher funded status implies potentially greater risk tolerance.
Sponsor financial status and profitability	▫ Debt to total assets ▫ Current and expected profitability ▫ Size of plan compared to market capitalization of sponsor company	▫ Lower debt ratios and higher current and expected profitability imply greater risk tolerance. ▫ Large sponsor company size relative to pension plan size implies greater risk tolerance.
Sponsor and pension fund common risk exposures	▫ Correlation of sponsor operating results with pension asset returns	▫ The lower the correlation, the greater the risk tolerance, all else equal.
Plan features	▫ Provision for early retirement ▫ Provision for lump-sum distributions	▫ Such options tend to reduce the duration of plan liabilities, implying lower risk tolerance, all else equal.
Workforce characteristics	▫ Age of workforce ▫ Active lives relative to retired lives	▫ The younger the workforce and the greater the proportion of active lives, the greater the duration of plan liabilities and the greater the risk tolerance.

EXAMPLE 2

Andes Sports Equipment Corporation—Defined Benefit Plan

1 Frank Smit, CFA, is chief financial officer of Andes Sports Equipment Company (ADSE), a leading Dutch producer of winter and water sports gear. ADSE is a small company based in Amsterdam, and all of its revenues come from Europe. Product demand has been strong in the past few years, although it is highly cyclical. The company has rising earnings and a strong (low debt) balance sheet. ADSE is a relatively young company, and as such, its defined benefit pension plan has no retired employees. This

essentially active-lives plan has €100 million in assets and an €8 million surplus in relation to the projected benefit obligation (PBO). Several facts concerning the plan follow:

- The duration of the plan's liabilities (which are all Europe-based) is 20 years.
- The discount rate applied to these liabilities is 6 percent.
- The average age of ADSE's workforce is 39 years.

Based on the information provided, discuss ADSE's risk tolerance.

2   Smit must set risk objectives for the ADSE pension plan. Because of excellent recent investment results, ADSE has not needed to make a contribution to the pension fund in the two most recent years. Smit considers it very important to maintain a plan surplus in relation to PBO. Because an €8 million surplus will be an increasingly small buffer as plan liabilities increase, Smit decides that maintaining plan funded status, stated as a ratio of plan assets to PBO at 100 percent or greater, is his top priority.

Based on the information provided, state an appropriate risk objective for ADSE.

Solution to 1:

ADSE appears to have above average risk tolerance for the following reasons:

a   The plan has a small surplus (8 percent of plan assets); that is, the plan is overfunded by €8 million.

b   The company's balance sheet is strong (low use of debt).

c   The company is profitable despite operating in a cyclical industry.

d   The average age of its workforce is low.

Solution to 2:

Given Smit considered it very important to maintain a plan surplus in relation to PBO, an appropriate risk objective for ADSE relates to shortfall risk with respect to the plan's funded status falling below 100 percent. For example, ADSE may want to minimize the probability that funded status falls below 100 percent, or it may want the probability that funded status falls below 100 percent to be less than or equal to 10 percent. If a plan surplus is maintained, ADSE may experience more years in which it does not need to make a contribution. Indeed, a major motivation for maintaining a plan surplus is to reduce the contributions ADSE needs to make in the future. As such, another relevant type of risk objective would be to minimize the present value of expected cash contributions.

PENSION FUNDS: INVESTMENT OBJECTIVES AND ASSET ALLOCATION

7

f   prepare the investment objectives section of an institutional investor's investment policy statement

g   evaluate the investment policy statement of an institutional investor

h   evaluate the investment portfolio of a private DB plan, sovereign wealth fund, university endowment, and private foundation

7.1 Investment Objectives

7.1.1 Defined Benefit Pension Plans

Defined benefit pension plans ultimately need to meet pension liabilities through a combination of investment returns and contributions. In practice, the investment objective of a DB pension plan is often to achieve a long-term rate of return on plan assets that exceeds the assumed rate of return used by the pension plan actuaries, typically the discount rate used in valuing pension liabilities. Importantly, targeting a long-term return based on the discount rate may be inappropriate in some cases. For example, when the discount rate is set using yields on government bonds, the target return is likely too low. In such a case, it may be preferable to fully hedge interest rate risk by adopting a liability-driven investing approach.

In determining an appropriate target return, it is worth noting that, ideally, the asset base should grow—through investment returns and contributions—in line with the growth of liabilities. If a plan is underfunded, the asset base must grow faster than liabilities. Because the growth of liabilities is met through investment returns and contributions (from the plan sponsor and/or employees), the DB plan's board and investment committee must consider the appropriate level of portfolio risk relative to the plan sponsor's willingness and ability to raise contribution rates should investment returns fall short of expectations.

In summary, the primary objective for DB pension plans is to achieve a long-term target return (usually defined in nominal terms) over a specified investment horizon (3–5 years or even as long as 10 or 25 years) with an appropriate level of risk that allows the plan to meet its contractual liabilities. The secondary objective could be to minimize the present value of expected cash contributions.

In setting overall investment strategy, many DB pension plans engage in detailed Asset Liability Management studies every 3–5 years. These studies include Monte Carlo simulations of thousands of scenarios for asset returns and factors driving pension liabilities (importantly, the discount rate) aimed at producing probability distributions for funded ratios and contribution rates at different horizons. These distributions are useful for determining key metrics, such as the expected funded ratio in 10 or 15 years, surplus volatility, surplus-at-risk, and volatility of contribution rates. Additionally, many pension funds engage in detailed liquidity modeling and stress testing that involve modeling contributions, benefit payments, capital calls for funding private equity investments, stressed asset values, and reduced liquidity of certain asset classes in market downturns. Besides providing an assessment of the appropriateness of the pension fund's liquidity profile, such stress testing provides insights into meeting liquidity needs during a financial crisis.

7.1.2 Defined Contribution Pension Plans

The main objective of defined contribution pension plans is to prudently grow assets that will support spending needs in retirement. Defined contribution plans usually offer a variety of investment options with differing investment objectives to suit participants of different ages, asset balances, and risk appetites. The investment options offered by the DC plan sponsor can be managed either in-house or externally as well as passively or actively. Most DC pension plans also provide a default option for disengaged participants. Plan trustees/boards must set an appropriate investment objective of the default option after reviewing the characteristics of existing default participants. Unsurprisingly, many DC plans end up with a balanced asset allocation mix as the default option—frequently in the form of a life-cycle fund. In cases where a DC plan provides participants a balanced asset allocation option with active management, a secondary objective may be to outperform the long-term policy benchmark consisting of the weighted average of individual asset class benchmarks and the policy weights defined by the strategic asset allocation. Finally, for some DC plans it is important their investment options outperform those of other DC pension plans, which is particularly relevant in countries where participants can voluntarily switch between DC plan providers.

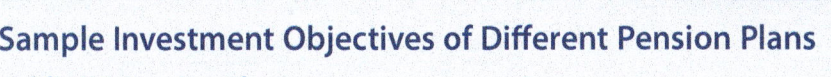

Sample Investment Objectives of Different Pension Plans

Public DB Pension Plan:

1. The assets of Public Plan will be invested with the objective of achieving a long-term rate of return that meets or exceeds the Public Plan actuarial expected rate of return.
2. Public Plan will seek to maximize returns for the level of risk taken.
3. Public Plan will also seek to achieve a return that exceeds the Policy Index.
4. Public Plan will seek to achieve its objectives on an after fees basis.

Corporate DB Pension Plan:

The Trustee wishes to ensure that the Corporate Plan can meet its obligations to the beneficiaries while recognizing the cost implications to the Company of pursuing excessively conservative investment strategies. The objectives of the Plan are defined as: wishing to maximize the long-term return on investments subject to, in its opinion, an acceptably low likelihood of failing to achieve an ongoing 105% funding level.

Corporate DC Pension Plan:

The Fund currently offers a range of investment options to its participants and has adopted an age-based default strategy for participants who do not choose an investment option.

The investment strategy of the Fund is to put in place portfolios to achieve the objectives of its stakeholders over a reasonable period of time with a reasonable probability of success.

In establishing each option's investment objectives, the Trustee takes into account the average participant's age, account balance, and risk appetite. The participant's choice of investment option indicates his/her risk appetite.

For example, a participants selecting the growth option indicates a higher risk tolerance over a longer investment time horizon. The investment objective for the growth option is to build an investment portfolio to outperform inflation + 4% per annum over 7-year periods while accepting a high level of risk that is expected to generate 4–6 negative annual returns over any 20-year period.

7.2 Asset Allocation by Pension Plans

An examination of pension fund asset allocations shows very large differences in average asset allocations by country. Moreover, examining pension fund asset allocations within a country also typically shows large differences despite these plans seeking to achieve similar goals. Such inter- and intra-national differences are driven by many factors discussed earlier in this reading, including the differences in legal, regulatory, accounting, and tax constraints; the investment objectives, risk appetites, and investment beliefs of the stakeholders; the liabilities to and demographics of the ultimate beneficiaries; the availability of investment opportunities; and the expected cost of living in retirement.

Exhibit 6 presents the average asset allocation of pension funds in the world's largest pension fund markets. The data are an aggregation of both DB and DC plans as presented (the split between DB and DC plans for each of the P7 countries is shown in Exhibit 3).

Note the category 'Other' includes hedge funds, private equity funds, loans, structured products, other mutual funds (i.e., not invested in equities, bonds, or cash), land, buildings, and other miscellaneous investments.

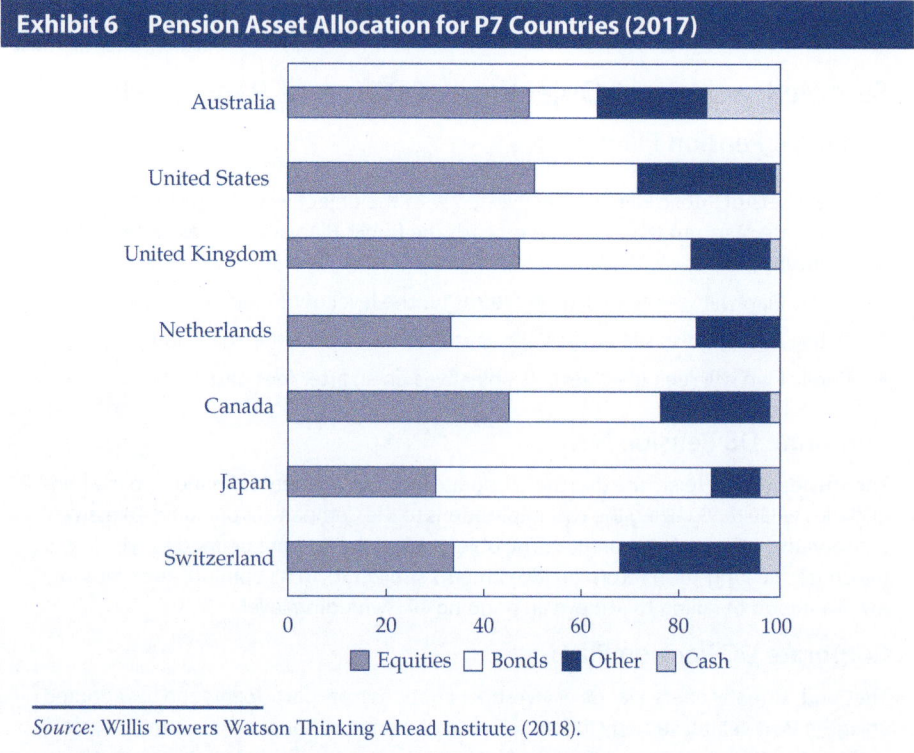

Exhibit 6   Pension Asset Allocation for P7 Countries (2017)

Source: Willis Towers Watson Thinking Ahead Institute (2018).

The key observations regarding the data presented in Exhibit 6 are as follows:

- *Equities*: Equities provide a long-term risk premium over bonds and cash and are typically viewed as the asset class of choice for long-term investors, like pension plans because of the higher expected returns they offer. Traditionally, equities are also viewed as an inflation hedge, as opposed to bonds that do not perform well in an inflationary environment. However, over the past decade, there has been a decrease in the equity allocation in several countries, particularly in Japan, the United Kingdom, and the United States. In aggregate, the resulting reallocation has been to the category 'Other,' which includes such alternatives as private equity and debt, real assets, and hedge funds, as well as to bonds (and fixed income, generally) as DB pension funds have reduced their risk appetite to lower the volatility of their funded ratios. Australia and the US have the largest proportions of DC pension assets and also the largest allocations to equities. Although not shown in Exhibit 6, it is worth noting that the United States, Australia, and the Netherlands have the highest proportions of their equities allocations invested in their local markets. Given the size of the domestic equities markets in Australia and the Netherlands, this implies significant home bias.

- *Fixed Income*: Fixed income plays a defensive role in pension fund portfolios, because during times of financial market stress, equity markets and interest rates tend to fall. Fixed-income investments also help DB pension plans hedge the interest rate risk relative to their pension liabilities. Many regulators, in fact, require DB pension plans to hold a minimum allocation in fixed-income investments. Over the last decade, US corporate pension plans have increased their allocations to fixed-income investments, despite low expected returns, driven by the desire to reduce their funded ratio volatility. Conversely, US public pension plans have reduced their fixed-income allocations overall while increasing their allocations in the fixed-income space to high yield (riskier) bonds. The reallocation and repositioning are driven by the large gap that has opened between their expected rate of return and the yield available on long-term government securities.

- *Alternatives (Other)*: This category includes private equity and debt markets, real estate, hedge funds, and real assets. As a group, these alternative assets tend to have low, or negative, correlations with traditional investments as well as lower drawdowns. In the case of hedge funds, this may be explained by the lower volatility of these strategies versus equity markets. Private asset classes have historically also exhibited lower drawdowns compared to equities. This may be partially explained by a lack of fully marking-to-market because of limited market transactions as well as appraisal-based valuations that lag changes in market pricing. Overall, the perception of institutional investors is that alternatives can produce equity-like returns over the long run with relatively low drawdowns, which has been the motivation for the shift from equities to alternatives over the past decade and a half. However, given the complexity and skill required to manage alternative investments, these investments come with high fees; thus, fee-sensitive institutions with significant liquidity needs may be unable to make sizable allocations to alternatives. Furthermore, attractive investment opportunities in private markets and in hedge fund strategies may be scarce. Increased competition and the huge amounts of capital deployed on a global scale by institutional investors may put downward pressure on future returns. Although still a smaller part of most institutional portfolios, allocations to real assets have increased significantly because they are considered an attractive way to hedge inflation. Japan has been slowest among the select countries to increase allocations to alternatives; however, the transition is underway with the country's largest pension plan, Government Pension Investment Fund (GPIF), which is reducing its allocation to domestic bonds in favor of alternatives.

EXAMPLE 3

Asset Allocation by a Public Defined Benefit Plan

Susan Liew, CFA, is the chief investment officer of the Lorenza State Pension Plan (LSPP), a public DB plan. The plan maintains an asset allocation of 30% US equities, 30% international equities, 30% US fixed income, and 10% international fixed income. Liew's investment team developed the following long-term expected real returns for the asset classes in which the LSPP has traditionally invested. The outlook for US and international equities is slightly below long-term averages, while the outlook for US and international fixed income is well below long-term averages.

Asset Class	Expected Long-Term (10-Year) Annual Return
US equities	4.0%
International equities	5.0%
US fixed income	1.0%
International fixed income	−0.5%

Given the poor prospects for fixed income and the mediocre expectations for equities, Liew is exploring making allocations to various alternatives and has asked LSPP's asset consultant to provide comments on considerations for each alternative asset class, as shown here:

Asset Class	Comments
Alternative debt	Represents a diverse range of high yielding and floating-rate debt expected to return 300 bps annually over traditional fixed income (default-adjusted basis). The additional returns are compensation for increased liquidity risk in private debt, added credit risk in high yield and EM debt, and non-performing loans.
Infrastructure funds	Strong income-like characteristics given contracted cash flows for most underlying infrastructure projects. This asset class entails increased liquidity risk but offers some inflation protection (many contracted cash flows are linked to inflation).
Hedge funds	Provide access to various diversifying strategies, including those with potential to generate gains in both rising and falling markets. Expected to return 250 bps annually over traditional long-only equities. Careful manager selection and underlying strategy selection (especially exposure to equity market beta) are important factors.

Liew recommends to LSPP's Board of Trustees the following change in asset allocation:

Asset Class	Current Asset Allocation	Recommended Asset Allocation
US equities	30%	25%
International equities	30%	25%
US fixed income	30%	15%
International fixed income	10%	5%
Alternative debt	—	10%
Infrastructure funds	—	10%
Hedge funds	—	10%

How would the recommended change in asset allocation be expected to affect LSPP's funded status?

Solution:

The recommended changes in asset allocation would likely affect LSPP's funded status as follows:

- The changes would increase expected returns, implying higher expected asset values for LSPP over time.
- Given that both alternative debt and hedge funds have higher projected long-term returns than traditional debt and equities, respectively, the discount rate applied to LSPP's liabilities can be increased, thereby reducing their present value.
- On balance, LSPP's funded status would be expected to improve because of the recommended changes in asset allocation. In addition to generating higher asset values and lower present value of liabilities, the volatility of assets (and therefore the risk to funded status) should be reduced because of the lower correlation among asset returns.

> Note that although these alternative investments entail reduced liquidity, this does not impact funded status; in fact, funded status improves because of the factors mentioned previously. However, the reduced liquidity must be considered to ensure sufficient coverage of prospective liabilities. Alternative investments entail greater manager selection risk and larger dispersion of returns around the policy benchmark relative to a passive allocation to public markets. Careful manager selection would likely require resources that would increase internal costs, and also require paying higher fees to access skilled alternative asset managers.

Exhibit 7 shows the evolution of pension fund asset allocation trends from 1997–2017 for the P7 countries. It is apparent that the allocation to equities has decreased from about 57% in 1997 to about 46% in 2017, while allocations to the 'Other' category of alternatives has increased from about 4% to 25% over the same time period. This is consistent with the general trend among institutional investors of diversifying out of equities and into alternative investments, including private equity, natural resources, real estate, and hedge funds.

Exhibit 7 Evolution of Pension Asset Allocation from 1997 to 2017

Source: Willis Towers Watson Thinking Ahead Institute (2018).

SOVEREIGN WEALTH FUNDS: TYPES AND STAKEHOLDERS

8

c discuss the stakeholders in the portfolio, the liabilities, the investment time horizons, and the liquidity needs of different types of institutional investors

Sovereign wealth funds (SWFs) are state-owned investment funds or entities that invest in financial or real assets. Sovereign wealth funds have increased significantly in number and size over the past two decades. Governments have established SWFs from budget surpluses to meet different objectives. The International Monetary Fund

(IMF) has defined five broad types of sovereign wealth funds, and each pursues different investment objectives. Exhibit 8 summarizes these five types with their main objective and some notable examples.

Exhibit 8   Major Types of Sovereign Wealth Funds

Type	Objective	Examples
Budget stabilization funds	Set up to insulate the budget and economy from commodity price volatility and external shocks.	Economic and Social Stabilization Fund of Chile; Timor-Leste Petroleum Fund; Russia's Oil Stabilization Fund
Development funds	Established to allocate resources to priority socio-economic projects, usually infrastructure.	Mubadala (UAE); Iran's National Development Fund; Ireland Strategic Investment Fund
Savings funds	Intended to share wealth across generations by transforming non-renewable assets into diversified financial assets.	Abu Dhabi Investment Authority; Kuwait Investment Authority; Qatar Investment Authority; Russia's National Wealth Fund
Reserve funds	Intended to reduce the negative carry costs of holding reserves or to earn higher return on ample reserves.	China Investment Corporation; Korea Investment Corporation; GIC Private Ltd. (Singapore)
Pension reserve funds	Set up to meet identified future outflows with respect to pension-related contingent-type liabilities on governments' balance sheets.	National Social Security Fund (China); New Zealand Superannuation Fund; Future Fund of Australia

Source: International Monetary Fund, "Sovereign Wealth Funds—A Work Agenda" (29 February 2008).

Exhibit 9 shows some of the largest sovereign wealth funds, which manage a total of about US$3.6 trillion in assets—close to 50% of all SWF assets (more than US$7.3 trillion).

Exhibit 9   Select Large Sovereign Wealth Funds

Fund	Inception Date	Country	Type
Saudi Arabian Monetary Authority (SAMA) foreign holdings	1952	Saudi Arabia	Reserve Fund
Kuwait Investment Authority	1953	Kuwait	Savings Fund
Abu Dhabi Investment Authority	1976	Abu Dhabi, United Arab Emirates	Savings Fund

Exhibit 9   (Continued)

Fund	Inception Date	Country	Type
Norway's Government Pension Fund—Global	1990	Norway	Budget Stabilization/ Savings/Pension Reserve
China Investment Corporation	2007	China	Reserve Fund

Source: SWF Institute (www.swfinstitute.org).

8.1 Stakeholders

SWF stakeholders include the citizens, the government, and external asset managers as well as the SWF management, investment committees, and boards.

The ultimate SWF stakeholders are the current and future citizens (or residents) of the country. Depending on the objectives of the SWF, these stakeholders either benefit directly in the form of payments (e.g., for pension reserve funds) or indirectly through stabilization of government budgets, lower taxes, or investments by the SWF in the domestic economy. If the SWF fails to meet its objectives, citizens/residents might be impacted through higher future taxes. Several SWFs are explicitly set up to benefit not only the current generation but also future generations. When such intergenerational wealth transfer is part of the objective, significant transparency and communication are required by the SWF and government to gain support from all stakeholders. This also requires long-term thinking by the government, which can be challenging when some governments have tenures of only a few years and when fiscal budgets vary significantly over the economic cycle.

The management or investment office of an SWF is tasked with investing its assets according to the investment policy and objectives of the fund. They monitor assets, make recommendations on investment strategy, and either select external asset managers or manage assets in-house. Appointment to an SWF's board, which oversees the management or investment office, is typically executed through a formal process that may include appointment by the current ruling government. In any case, the board has a fiduciary duty to the ultimate beneficiaries, the nation's current and future generations.

SOVEREIGN WEALTH FUNDS: LIABILITIES, INVESTMENT HORIZON, LIQUIDITY NEEDS, AND EXTERNAL CONSTRAINTS

9

c   discuss the stakeholders in the portfolio, the liabilities, the investment time horizons, and the liquidity needs of different types of institutional investors

d   describe the focus of legal, regulatory, and tax constraints affecting different types of institutional investors

9.1 Liabilities and Investment Horizons

There is a wide variety in investment objectives, liabilities, investment horizons, and liquidity needs among the five types of SWFs, so we will discuss each type separately. As a group, however, SWFs are different from the other institutional investors covered in this reading when it comes to liabilities. The liabilities of DB pension funds, endowments and foundations, insurance companies, and banks are clearly defined, which facilitates asset/liability management (ALM) processes. SWFs, however, do not generally have clearly defined liabilities given their mission of intergenerational wealth transfer. It is also worth noting that SWFs do not necessarily fit neatly into one of the five different types discussed in this section. For example, Norway's Government Pension Fund Global (formerly known as Norway's Petroleum Fund) undertakes elements of stabilization and sterilization, accumulating pension reserves, and saving for future generations.

9.1.1 Budget Stabilization Funds

Budget stabilization funds are established to insulate the fiscal budget from commodity price volatility and other external shocks, particularly if a nation's revenue is tied to natural resource production or other cyclical industries. These funds have uncertain liabilities and relatively short investment horizons. Their main purpose is risk management because such funds may be needed on a short-term basis to help support the government budget. The investment objective is usually to deliver returns in excess of inflation with a low probability of a negative return in any year. Budget stabilization funds typically avoid assets that are highly correlated with the main sources of government revenue, and they may engage in hedging against declines in prices of commodities that are important revenue generators for the local economy. These funds mainly invest in government bonds and other debt securities. Examples of budget stabilization funds include the Economic and Social Stabilization Fund of Chile and Russia's Oil Stabilization Fund.

9.1.2 Development Funds

Development funds are established to support a nation's economic development through investing in essential infrastructure, innovation, or by supporting key industries. Liabilities are not clearly defined and typically uncertain for development funds, but their overall objective is to raise a country's economic growth or to diversify the economy. As such, these funds have an implicit real return target: to increase real domestic GDP growth and productivity. Some initiatives, such as infrastructure/industrial development, may be ongoing and long-term, while others may have a fixed, medium-term horizon, such as a medical research fund. Examples of development funds include Mubadala Development Corp. (UAE) and the National Development Fund of Iran.

9.1.3 Savings Funds

Savings funds are typically established to transform proceeds from the sale of non-renewable natural resources into long-term wealth and a diversified portfolio of financial assets. The mission of a savings fund is wealth transfer to future generations after the sources of natural wealth have been depleted. As such, their liabilities are long-term. Some savings funds have a real return objective or an explicit spending policy (like endowments). Norway's Government Pension Fund Global (GPFG) uses a fiscal spending rule whereby it intends to withdraw 3% of the fund's value annually with the goal of gradually phasing oil revenue into the Norwegian economy. This spending rate is linked to the expected real return earned by the GPFG. A special case of savings funds involves government investment holding companies, which are funded from the privatization proceeds of national companies (e.g., Singapore's

Temasek Holdings). Because of their long-term horizons, savings funds invest in risky and illiquid assets, including equities and a wide range of alternative investments. Of course, savings funds should avoid investing in assets highly correlated with the non-renewable resources from which the government is trying to diversify.

9.1.4 Reserve Funds

Reserve investment funds are established from central bank excess foreign currency reserves. The objective is to achieve a return higher than that on FX reserves (usually invested in low-duration, high-grade debt instruments) and to reduce the negative cost-of-carry of holding FX reserves. Reserve funds are common in export-intensive economies that have built up large FX reserves. Central banks accumulate such reserves as they print local currency to buy FX (like US dollars or euros) from local firms selling export goods. The central banks then issue monetary stabilization bonds to absorb the excess local currency. So, the central banks typically end up with FX reserves invested in low-yielding US Treasury or other high-quality sovereign debt instruments, while their liabilities (monetary stabilization bonds) pay much higher yields that create the negative cost-of-carry. Countries mitigate this cost by creating sovereign wealth reserve funds, placing excess FX reserves in these funds, and investing them globally in higher yielding, risky assets. Although their true liabilities are the central bank's monetary stabilization bonds, in practice, reserve funds operate somewhat similarly to endowments and foundations by having either a nominal or real return target. Also, their investment horizons are very long, with typically no immediate or interim payout expectation. Consequently, reserve funds generally invest in diversified portfolios with significant exposure to equities and other high-yielding alternative investments. Examples of reserve funds include China Investment Corporation (CIC), Korea Investment Corporation (KIC), and GIC Private Limited (GIC), formerly known as Government of Singapore Investment Corporation.

9.1.5 Pension Reserve Funds

Pension reserve funds are established to help prefund contingent pension-related liabilities on the government's balance sheet. Pension reserve funds are usually funded from fiscal surpluses during economic booms. The goal is to help reduce the burden on future taxpayers by prefunding social security and health care costs arising from aging populations, so these funds generally have long-term investment horizons. There is usually an **accumulation phase** (**decumulation phase**) where the government predominantly contributes to (withdraws from) the fund. However, additional uncertainty also exists around expected cash flows, particularly in the case of funding health care because those costs are quite volatile. The investment objective of pension reserve funds is to earn returns sufficient to maximize the likelihood of meeting future pension, social security, and/or health care costs as they arise. Therefore, such funds will typically invest in a diversified portfolio with the majority in such equities and alternative investments as property, infrastructure, hedge funds, and private markets. An example of a pension reserve fund is Future Fund of Australia (FFA). Its goal is to meet unfunded pension liabilities (retirement payments or superannuation payments in Australia) that will be owed to former public employees starting in 2020. FFA was funded from budget surpluses and privatization proceeds of Telstra, an Australian telecommunications company that was formerly a state-owned enterprise. The investment mandate for FFA is to achieve an average annual return of at least the Consumer Price Index (CPI) + 4% to 5% per year over the long term with an acceptable level of risk.

9.2 Liquidity Needs

9.2.1 *Budget Stabilization Funds*

Stabilization funds must maintain a high level of liquidity and invest in assets that have a low risk of significant losses over short time periods. For example, in the event of a negative commodity price shock, the government might experience a significant budget deficit caused by lower commodity-based revenues. To stabilize the budget and meet spending needs, the stabilization fund's assets must be readily accessible. As a result, budget stabilization funds invest a significant portion of their portfolios in cash and high-grade, fixed-income instruments that are very liquid and carry little risk of significant drawdown.

9.2.2 *Development Funds*

A development fund supports national economic development. Liquidity needs depend on the particular strategic economic development initiatives the fund was created to support. For example, infrastructure investments are very long-term, so funds established to develop infrastructure would have low liquidity needs. Development funds designed to promote research and innovation may also require long time periods to see the fruits of investments in innovation and research and are likely to have low liquidity needs as well.

9.2.3 *Savings Funds*

Savings funds have a very long-term investment horizon and low liquidity needs. Their main objective is to grow wealth for future generations, so their liquidity needs, being long-term in nature, are comparable to those of endowments and foundations. In instances where the savings fund was established to transform the proceeds from the sale of non-renewable commodities into long-term wealth, the fund's liquidity needs may change once the nation's natural resources have been depleted because the government is more likely to begin withdrawing money from the fund to support its budgetary needs.

9.2.4 *Reserve Funds*

Reserve funds operate to offset negative carry effects of holding FX reserves, and consequently, excess reserves are invested in higher growth investments. The liquidity needs of reserve funds are lower than those of stabilization funds but higher than those of savings funds. Reserve funds typically hold 50%–70% in equity or equity-equivalent investments to achieve their return targets. The remainder, however, is likely to be invested in liquid fixed-income securities that could be readily sold should a dramatic change in the balance of trade require additional central bank reserves.

9.2.5 *Pension Reserve Funds*

Pension reserve funds need to meet future pension or health care liabilities when they come due. Depending on when significant fund withdrawals are expected, liquidity needs change over time. During the accumulation phase, reserve funds can hold a significant part of their portfolios in equities and relatively illiquid investments. Once the decumulation phase begins, the asset allocation will gradually shift toward more liquid, high-quality, fixed-income investments.

9.3 External Constraints Affecting Investment

In this section and the next, we briefly highlight some legal/regulatory and tax constraints, respectively, that sovereign wealth funds must consider when investing.

9.3.1 Legal and Regulatory Constraints

Sovereign wealth funds are typically established by national legislation that contains details on: the fund's mission; contributions to the fund; circumstances allowing withdrawals from the fund; and governance structure, including selection of board members, their roles, and the level of board independence. Some SWFs are set up with clear rules on asset allocation. For example, a technology development fund may be required to be 100% invested in offshore technology assets to provide diversification (versus local economic drivers) and eventual technology transfer. Alternatively, an industrial development fund may be required to invest 100% locally to support the development of key industries in the domestic economy. In any case, SWFs should operate in a transparent and accountable manner as they are ultimately established for the benefit of a nation's people and future generations. Sound governance, independence, transparency, and accountability are all essential to ensure that SWFs are protected from political influence.

The International Forum of SWFs (IFSWF) is a self-governing body established to promote best practices among SWFs. All IFSWF members have endorsed a set of generally accepted principles and practices (GAPP). Known as the "Santiago Principles" for the city where they were drafted, the GAPP provide a best practices framework by which SWFs should operate that addresses such key elements as sound legal framework, well-defined mission, independence, accountability, transparency, disclosure, ethics and professionalism, effective risk management, and regular review for compliance with the Santiago Principles.

9.3.2 Tax and Accounting Constraints

Typically, sovereign wealth funds are given tax-free status by the legislation that governs them. However, SWFs may be ineligible to claim withholding taxes or tax credits that are ordinarily available to taxable investors. As SWFs invest in offshore markets, they also need to consider any tax treaties that may exist between the countries in which they are investing and their own country. Some regulators allow SWFs to be exempt from domestic tax rules that have been put in place to deter tax avoidance by corporations and individuals. To prevent any international diplomatic issues, SWFs should be sensitive to ensuring they are not perceived as trying to avoid paying taxes in any offshore jurisdictions where they operate or invest.

SOVEREIGN WEALTH FUNDS: INVESTMENT OBJECTIVES AND ASSET ALLOCATION

10

f prepare the investment objectives section of an institutional investor's investment policy statement

g evaluate the investment policy statement of an institutional investor

h evaluate the investment portfolio of a private DB plan, sovereign wealth fund, university endowment, and private foundation

10.1 Investment Objectives

10.1.1 Budget Stabilization Funds

The investment objective of budget stabilization funds is capital preservation. This is achieved by endeavoring to deliver returns in excess of inflation with a low probability of a negative return in any given year. In addition, budget stabilization funds should avoid cyclical assets whose returns are highly correlated to the main sources of government revenue (such as natural resources industries). According to the stated investment objectives of Chile's Economic and Social Stabilization Fund, *"the main aim of its investment policy is to maximize the fund's accumulated value in order to partially cover cyclical reductions in fiscal revenues while maintaining a low level of risk. Its risk aversion is reflected by the choice of an investment portfolio with a high level of liquidity and low credit risk and volatility, thereby ensuring the availability of the resources to cover fiscal deficits and preventing significant losses in the fund's value."*

10.1.2 Development Funds

Development funds are established to support a nation's economic development with the ultimate goal of raising a country's long-term economic growth. The implicit investment objective of development funds is therefore to achieve a real rate of return in excess of real domestic GDP or productivity growth. Accordingly, Khazanah Nasional Berhad, the strategic investment fund of the government of Malaysia, *"strives to create sustainable value and cultivate a high-performance culture that helps contribute to Malaysia's economic competitiveness. Utilizing a proactive investment approach, we aim to build true value through management of our core investments, leveraging on our global footprint for new growth, as well as undertaking catalytic investments that strategically boost the country's economy. We also actively develop human, social and knowledge capital for the country."*

10.1.3 Savings Funds

The mission of savings funds is to ensure wealth transfer to future generations. Therefore, their primary objective is to maintain purchasing power of the assets in perpetuity while achieving investment returns sufficient to sustain the spending necessary to support ongoing governmental activities. According to Alaska Statutes 37.13.020, the Alaska Permanent Fund, *"should provide a means of conserving a portion of the state's revenue from mineral resources to benefit all generations of Alaskans; the fund's goal should be to maintain safety of principal while maximizing total return; the fund should be used as a savings device managed to allow the maximum use of disposable income from the fund for purposes designated by law."*

10.1.4 Reserve Funds

The investment objective of reserve funds is usually to achieve a rate of return above the return the government must pay on its monetary stabilization bonds, thereby eliminating the negative cost-of-carry of holding excess FX reserves (that are typically invested in low duration, high-grade, fixed-income instruments). For example, Singapore's Government Investment Corporation (GIC) has a clearly defined purpose: *"We aim to achieve good long-term returns for the Government—a reasonable risk-adjusted rate above global inflation over a 20-year investment horizon. By achieving these returns, we meet our responsibility to preserve and enhance the international purchasing power of Singapore's foreign reserves. The reserves provide a stream of income that can be spent or invested for the benefit of present and future generations."*

10.1.5 Pension Reserve Funds

The investment objective of pension reserve funds is to earn sufficient returns to maximize the likelihood of being able to meet future unfunded pension, social security, and/or health care liabilities of plan participants as they arise. Accordingly, among its mandates, the Australian government states that its Future Fund should *"maximise the return earned on the Fund over the long term; ... adopt an average return of at least the Consumer Price Index (CPI) +4 to +5 per cent per annum over the long term as the benchmark return on the Fund; [and] in targeting the benchmark return, the Board must determine an acceptable but not excessive level of risk for the Fund...."*

> **EXAMPLE 4**
>
> ### The People's Fund of Wigitania—A Pension Reserve Fund
>
> The People's Fund is a pension reserve fund established by the government of Wigitania by setting aside current government surpluses. Its objective is to meet future unfunded social security payments caused by an aging population. The following is an extract from the People's Fund IPS.
>
>> Effective from 2030, the government will have the ability to withdraw assets to meet pension and social security liabilities falling due each year. Actuarial projections estimate annual payouts to be about 5% of the total fund value at that time. Given this level of cash flow, the Fund is expected to maintain most of its asset base for the foreseeable future. As such, 2030 does not represent an 'end date' for measurement purposes. A long-term investment horizon remains appropriate at present. However, the appropriate timeframe, risk tolerance, portfolio construction and liquidity profile may change.
>
> 1 What are the liquidity needs of the People's Fund?
> 2 What factors does the Board need to consider when reviewing the Fund's investment horizon?
>
> **Solution to 1:**
>
> From the extract, we see that the unfunded pension and social security liabilities that the Fund is meant to cover are expected to be about 5% of total fund value per year, starting in 2030. Management of the fund will need to ensure that they have sufficient liquidity at that time to meet those ongoing liabilities. Until that time, liquidity needs are very low, which should allow the People's Fund to invest a significant part of its portfolio in less-liquid alternative asset classes.
>
> **Solution to 2:**
>
> The Board should consider two separate phases when reviewing the Fund's investment horizon and investment policy: an accumulation phase and a decumulation phase. The accumulation phase lasts until 2030 and allows the Fund to invest with little to no liquidity needs and little concern for interim volatility. The decumulation phase starts after 2030, when the government expects to withdraw about 5% of the assets on an annual basis. The investment horizon, liquidity needs, and risk tolerance will need to be modified during the decumulation phase, which will affect the investment policy.

10.2 Asset Allocation by Sovereign Wealth Funds

Each of the five types of sovereign wealth funds have very different objectives and purposes. Not surprisingly then, these funds have very different asset allocations. Development funds usually have little flexibility with their asset allocations as they operate within a limited investment universe as part of their mandate (e.g., they are required to invest in local infrastructure development projects). Given that national development projects can be different in nature and purpose between countries, it would be difficult to envision a 'typical' asset allocation for a development fund. The other four types of sovereign wealth funds are more homogeneous within their respective groups, for which Exhibit 10 provides illustrative asset allocations.

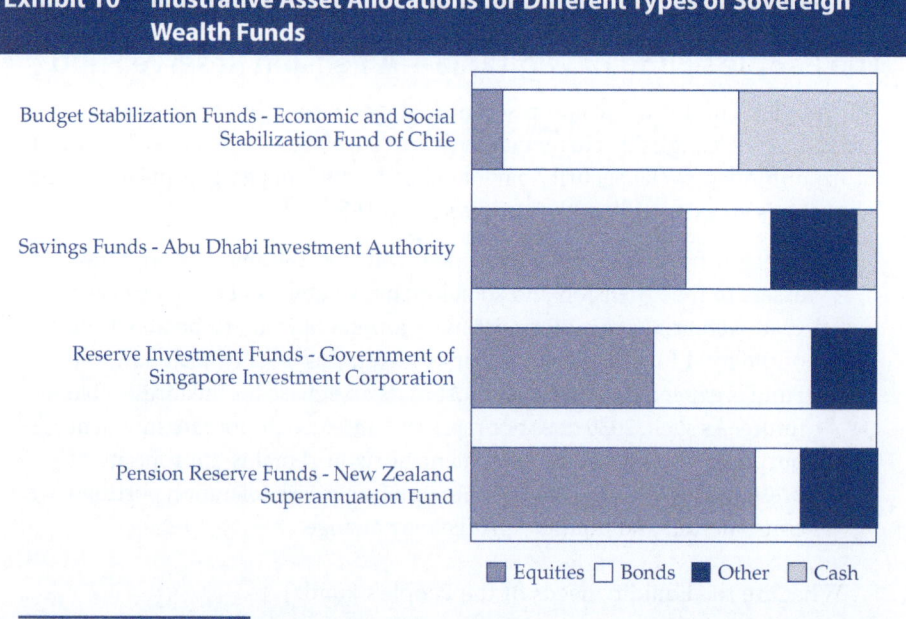

Exhibit 10 Illustrative Asset Allocations for Different Types of Sovereign Wealth Funds

Sources: 1. Economic and Social Stabilization Fund of Chile website; 2. Abu Dhabi Investment Authority (ADIA), *2015 Review*; 3. Government Investment Corporation (GIC), *Report on the Management of the Government's Portfolio for the Year 2016/17*; 4. NZSUPERFUND, *New Zealand Superannuation Fund Annual Report 2017*.

Several key points stand out from the data in Exhibit 10:

- The portfolios of budget stabilization funds are dominated by fixed-income investments because of their defensive nature, relatively stable investment returns, and diversification against cyclically-sensitive factors (such as commodity prices) that drive government budget revenues in some countries. The conservative asset allocation may be partly explained by the fact that several major stabilization funds are managed by their countries' central bank or Ministry of Finance; these entities tend to be relatively risk averse.

- The portfolios of savings funds are shown to be tilted toward growth assets, equities, and alternatives (the "Other" category). Due to their very long investment horizons, these funds can take on more equity-related risks, and they consequently hold relatively high allocations to such alternative investments as real assets, private equity and debt (loans), and hedge funds.

- Reserve investment funds have a similar allocation to savings funds but they tend to allocate less to alternatives. This may be partially explained by reserve funds having potentially higher liquidity needs compared to savings funds because of central bank activities. Public equities are typically the most liquid growth asset available and help counter the negative carry generated by foreign exchange reserves, while bonds and other fixed-income investments help to reduce reserve funds' portfolio volatility.

- The portfolios of pension reserve funds are relatively heavily tilted toward equities with a significant allocation to alternative assets, such as real assets and infrastructure, private equity and debt markets, and hedge funds. Pension reserve funds generally have long-term investment horizons (but not necessarily inter-generational as with savings funds) and low liquidity needs during their accumulation phases, which can explain their high allocation to alternatives compared with other SWFs.

Sovereign wealth funds with savings or pension reserve objectives typically follow the endowment investment model. Some also adopt the Canada reference portfolio model. An example of the latter is the New Zealand Superannuation Fund (NZSF). As noted previously, this model makes use of a reference portfolio comprising passive investment in stocks and bonds that are expected to meet the fund's investment objectives. The total portfolio is then invested to replicate the risk factors of the reference portfolio, while individual investments are benchmarked against a combined stock and bond benchmark representing the risk factors driving the individual investments. Both models result in higher allocations to alternative investments, as observed in Exhibit 10.

In the Asia Pacific region, sovereign wealth funds are the largest institutional investors. Some examples include China Investment Corporation (CIC), State Administration of Foreign Exchange (SAFE) Investment Company (China), Hong Kong Monetary Authority Investment Portfolio (HKMAIP) and Government Investment Corporation of Singapore (GIC). Given the huge size of their assets, these SWFs tend to dominate the regional investment landscape. They typically have fewer investment constraints than other Asia Pacific institutional investors. These SWFs also have broader investment mandates, minimal investment management fee constraints, and longer time horizons as compared to (for example) pension funds. Such flexibility allows these SWFs to implement higher allocations to alternative assets.

UNIVERSITY ENDOWMENTS AND PRIVATE FOUNDATIONS: INTRODUCTION AND EXTERNAL CONSTRAINTS

11

d   describe the focus of legal, regulatory, and tax constraints affecting different types of institutional investors

This section introduces university endowments and private foundations. As will be seen shortly, these two types of institutional investors have some similarities but also important differences that affect their investing activities.

University Endowments

Many institutions have endowments, including universities, churches, museums, and hospitals. These endowments are typically funded through gifts and donations and are intended to help the institutions provide for some of their main services. Endowment funds invest in capital markets to provide a savings and growth mechanism that allows the institution to meet its mission in perpetuity. The main objective is to provide intergenerational equity. As James Tobin wrote in 1974: "The trustees of an endowed institution are the guardians of the future against the claims of the present. Their task is to preserve equity among generations."

Throughout this reading, for simplicity we will focus on university endowments. The investment objectives and philosophies of the endowments of other institutions are typically not very different from those of university endowments. Exhibit 11 shows some large (by assets) university endowments.

Exhibit 11	Select US University Endowments
University	Assets (US$ bn)
Harvard University	34.5
Yale University	25.4
University of Texas System	24.2
Stanford University	22.4
Princeton University	22.2

Source: Commonfund and the National Association of College and University Business Officers (NACUBO), *2016 NACUBO–Commonfund Study of Endowments (NCSE).*

Private Foundations

Foundations are nonprofit organizations that typically make grants to outside organizations and persons who carry out social, educational and other charitable activities. Many foundations are located in the United States, but some large foundations are outside the United States, such as the Wellcome Trust in the United Kingdom. Foundations are more common in the United States because of favorable tax treatment. Outside the United States, charitable giving is typically undertaken by family offices.

There are four different types of foundations:

1 *Community foundations*: These are charitable organizations that make social or educational grants for the benefit of a local community (e.g., the New York Community Trust). These foundations are usually funded by public donations.

2 *Operating foundations*: Organizations that exist to operate a not-for-profit business for charitable purposes. They are typically funded by individual donors or donor families.

3 *Corporate foundations*: These are established by businesses and funded from profits.

4 *Private grant-making foundations*: These are established by individual donors or donor families to support specific types of charities. Most of the largest foundations in the US fall into this category.

Community foundations are a type of public charity associated with such community organizations as hospitals, schools, and churches. They are funded by many relatively small donors, and they typically provide charitable support in the region or community where they are located. Private operating foundations are established to provide funding and support for related programs and activities (e.g., operating a museum) rather than giving grants to outside organizations or activities.

Private grant-making foundations (also called private non-operating foundations) are by far the largest group (in number of foundations and in total assets), so they are our primary focus. Private grant-making foundations support different types of charities and usually run a large grant-making operation in addition to an investment office. The main objective of most private grant-making foundations is to maintain purchasing power into perpetuity, so that the organization can continue making grants. In recent years, however, there has been a trend toward limited-life foundations as original donors seek to maintain control over foundation spending during their lives.

The focus of grants varies widely and includes issues such as health, education, environment, arts, and culture. Some foundations make large and targeted grants to very specific causes while others make many smaller grants to a wide variety of causes. Exhibit 12 shows some large US foundations and their missions.

Exhibit 12	Select US Foundations
Foundation	**Mission**
Bill & Melinda Gates Foundation	Focus on global health and poverty. In US focus on education.
Ford Foundation	Focus on inequality.
Robert Wood Johnson Foundation	Improve health and health care of all Americans.
Lilly Endowment Inc.	Support religion, education, community development.
William and Flora Hewlett Foundation	Help people build measurably better lives by focusing on education, the environment, global development, performing arts, philanthropy, and population. Also supports disadvantaged communities in San Francisco.

Source: Foundation Center (www.foundationcenter.org).

11.1 External Constraints Affecting Investment

In this section and the next we briefly touch on some legal/regulatory and tax constraints, respectively, that affect investing by university endowments and private foundations.

11.1.1 *Legal and Regulatory Constraints*

Charitable organizations, including endowments and foundations, are typically subject to rules and regulations in their country of domicile that: 1) require investment committees/officers/boards to invest on a total return basis and consider portfolio diversification when managing assets (i.e., follow the principles of modern portfolio theory, MPT); and 2) require investment committees/officers/boards to exercise a duty of care and prudence in overseeing the assets and making investment decisions (i.e., fiduciary duty).

In the United States, endowments and foundations are governed by the Uniform Prudent Management of Institutional Funds Act of 2006 (UPMIFA). Two important features of UPMIFA include:

1 Allowing charitable organizations flexibility in spending decisions, which could be adjusted for fluctuations in the market value of assets. Endowments, particularly, could meet the fiduciary standard of prudence by maintaining purchasing power of the fund.

2 Modernizing the standard of prudence for the management of charitable funds by adopting the principles of MPT established by the Uniform Prudent Investor Act (1994).

UK endowments and foundations are typically organized as trusts. Until 2000, UK trusts were limited to spending only income earned from investments (not capital gains). The Trustee Act (2000) changed that and, like UPMIFA in the United States, required trustees to manage trust assets based on MPT principles. The act also imposed a duty of care upon trustees. The shift toward managing portfolios using MPT principles has enabled endowments and foundations to embrace a broader range of asset classes compared to the traditional 60/40 equity/bond mix. It has also allowed them to focus on total return rather than solely on income return (high coupon bond and/or high-dividend-yield stocks).

11.1.2 Tax and Accounting Constraints

Endowments and foundations typically enjoy tax-exempt status. Tax-exempt status has three elements:

1 *Taxation of gifts and donations to endowments and foundations*: Gifts and donations to endowments and foundations are usually tax-deductible (up to a certain percentage of adjusted gross income) for the person or entity making the gift or donation.

2 *Taxation of income and capital gains on assets*: Income and capital gains on assets are usually tax-exempt in countries that have endowments and charitable organizations, which are tied to such non-profit, tax-exempt organizations as universities, religious organizations, or museums.

3 *Taxation on payouts from endowments and foundations*: Payouts are tax exempt if the receiving institution is exempt from income tax. If payouts are made to support the operating budget of a for-profit business, then that business is required to treat the payout as taxable income.

In the United States, private grant-making foundations enjoy the same tax-exempt status as endowments. But unlike endowments, such private foundations are subject to minimum payout (spending) requirements, whereby they must distribute a minimum of 5% of their asset value on an annual basis in grants that support their mission. Failing to meet this spending requirement subjects such foundations to 30% tax on undistributed income. Most tax-exempt private foundations also have an excise tax of 2% on their net investment income. In the United Kingdom, charitable organizations do not pay taxes on most of their income and gains if these are used for charitable purposes; however, taxes must be paid on funds that are not used for charitable purposes.

12 UNIVERSITY ENDOWMENTS: STAKEHOLDERS, LIABILITIES, INVESTMENT HORIZON, AND LIQUIDITY NEEDS

c discuss the stakeholders in the portfolio, the liabilities, the investment time horizons, and the liquidity needs of different types of institutional investors

Stakeholders of a university endowment include current and future students, alumni, current and future university faculty and administrators, and the larger university community. Each of these stakeholders has a strong interest in seeing the endowment invested prudently. There is potential, however, for tension between increasing spending to meet current needs versus preserving sufficient funds to serve future generations. Endowment boards or investment committees, therefore, need to determine an appropriate balance.

University endowments are generally funded by gifts and donations from alumni. It is common that donors specify the handling and use of their gifts—for example, that only the income portion be spent or that only specific scholarships, programs, or departments benefit. Other gifts may be unrestricted and can be spent for general purposes. Alumni are concerned about current students and faculty and also future generations, so they expect endowment assets to be invested for the long-run. Endowment payouts support the university's operating budget and provide an important source of income. Endowments provide stability and continuity when other revenues sources, such as tuition and government funding, fluctuate. Endowments also allow universities to more readily undertake long-term capital projects, knowing required resources are available to meet those future commitments.

Stakeholders of a university endowment often have representation on the endowment's board or investment committee, including alumni who are investment professionals running or working for financial services organizations.

12.1 University Endowments—Liabilities and Investment Horizon

Although most endowments operate on an asset-only basis, their main purpose is to support the university's operating budget based on the principle of intergenerational equity. The investment horizon for endowments is thus perpetuity, and their main objective is to maintain long-term purchasing power. An endowment's liabilities are the future stream of payouts to the university, which are typically codified in an official spending policy. The spending policy serves two important purposes: 1) to ensure intergenerational equity; and 2) to smooth endowment payouts to partially insulate contributions to the university from capital market volatility.

Although the spending policy defines how much of the endowment's assets are paid out annually, several other liability characteristics should be considered when designing an appropriate investment policy, including:

a   What is the university's capacity for fund-raising: How much in gifts and donations are contributed (on average) each year?

b   What percentage of the university's operating budget is supported by the endowment?

c   Balance sheet health: Does the endowment or university have the ability to issue debt?

We first discuss different types of spending policies and then discuss other important liability-related characteristics. Broadly speaking, there are three different types of endowment spending policies:

1   *Constant Growth Rule*: The endowment provides a fixed amount annually to the university, typically adjusted for inflation (the growth rate). The inflation rate is usually based on the Higher Education Price Index (HEPI)[2] in the United States or a more general consumer price index elsewhere, possibly with an additional spread. A shortcoming of constant growth spending rules is that spending does not adjust based on the endowment's value. If the endowment experiences weak (strong) average returns, the spending amount expressed as a percentage of assets may become very high (low). This spending rule is therefore commonly complemented with caps and floors, typically between 4% and 6% of average assets under management (AUM) over one or three years.

---

[2] The Higher Education Price Index is calculated annually by Commonfund and tracks the most important components in the cost of higher education. More information can be found at https://www.commonfund.org/commonfund-institute/higher-education-price-index-hepi.

2. *Market Value Rule*: The endowment pays a pre-specified percentage (the spending rate) of the moving average of asset values, typically between 4% and 6%. Asset values are usually smoothed using a 3- to 5-year moving average. A disadvantage of this spending rule is that it tends to be pro-cyclical; when markets have performed well (poorly), the overall payout increases (decreases).

3. *Hybrid Rule*: Spending is calculated as a weighted average of the constant growth and market value rules. Commonly referred to as the Yale spending rule, weights can range from 30% to 70%. This spending rule was designed to strike a balance between the shortcomings of the respective spending rules.

All three spending rules can be summarized by the following formula:

Spending Amount in Year $t + 1$ = $w \times$ [Spending Amount in Year $t \times (1 +$ Inflation Rate)] $+ (1 - w) \times$ Spending Rate $\times$ Average AUM,

where w denotes the weight put on the prior year's spending amount. When $w = 1$, the formula simplifies to a constant growth rule; when $w = 0$, it simplifies to a market value rule. For any other choice of w ($0 < w < 1$), the formula represents a hybrid spending rule. Most US endowments use a market value spending rule, but some of the larger ones use a hybrid rule. As noted, a market value spending rule is pro-cyclical: This may not be an issue for universities that receive only a small percentage of their operating budgets from their endowment, but this may be more problematic otherwise. The goal of providing intergenerational equity means university endowments aim to maintain their purchasing power. Therefore, endowments target a real rate of return (after inflation) equal to or greater than their spending rates. Given that endowments pay out (on average) between 4% and 6% of assets annually, they typically target a 5% to 5.5% real, long-term rate of return.

Other liability-related factors must be considered when managing an endowment. Universities regularly raise money from donors. Depending on the wealth of their alumni base, such fund-raising activity may be more or less successful. Because of gifts and donations, endowments' net spending rate tends to be lower than the headline spending of 4% to 6% of assets previously discussed. On average, net spending is closer to 2% to 4% of assets. Another important distinction between endowments is how much the university relies on its endowment to support the operating budget. Such support may be less than 5% for some universities, while in other cases, 40% to 50% of the university's operating budget is provided by its endowment. All else equal, endowments that support a smaller percentage of the overall budget should be able to tolerate more market, credit, and liquidity risk. In practice, however, this important distinguishing factor is typically insufficiently incorporated in the design of investment policies. It is common for university endowments to be benchmarked against each other, which creates herding behavior even though the organizations might have very different liability characteristics. A final consideration is the debt issuance capability of the endowment (or university). Some endowments access the public and private debt markets on a regular basis. The capability to access debt markets, especially during periods of market stress, affects the levels of risk and illiquidity endowments can accept in their investments.

12.2 University Endowments—Liquidity Needs

The liquidity needs of university endowments are relatively low (compared to foundations). On average, endowments' annual net spending is 2% to 4% of assets, after factoring in gifts and donations. Low liquidity needs combined with long investment horizons allow endowments to accept relatively high short-term volatility in pursuit of superior long-term returns. Consequently, many university endowments have relatively high allocations to equity markets and illiquid private asset classes and small allocations to fixed income. Having significant allocations to illiquid asset classes, such as private equity and private real estate, creates additional liquidity needs to meet annual net capital calls from general partners managing these assets. Finally, to the extent that endowments use derivatives for rebalancing or portable alpha strategies, there may be further liquidity needs—particularly during times of financial market stress—to meet margin calls or to cover higher collateral demands.

13. PRIVATE FOUNDATIONS: TYPES, STAKEHOLDERS, LIABILITIES, INVESTMENT HORIZON, AND LIQUIDITY NEEDS

c discuss the stakeholders in the portfolio, the liabilities, the investment time horizons, and the liquidity needs of different types of institutional investors

Stakeholders of a foundation include the founding family, donors, grant recipients, and the broader community that may benefit indirectly from the foundation's activities. Each has a strong interest in seeing the foundation's assets invested appropriately. As with university endowments, a tension may exist between increasing current grant spending versus preserving sufficient funds to serve future generations of grant recipients. The founding family and donors typically want their donations to support grant recipients in perpetuity. There is a trend, however, toward limited-life foundations as donors seek to maintain control over foundation spending during their lives. Finally, the government (Internal Revenue Service in the United States) may also be a stakeholder because of the favorable tax treatment that foundations enjoy. The government's main concern is that foundations remain engaged strictly in charitable work.

The boards of foundations tend to be different in terms of skill sets than the boards of endowments. University endowments typically have alumni sitting on their boards—people with a special relationship to the university and who may have significant financial market skills (for example, in private equity or hedge funds). Board members for foundations, however, are typically individuals involved with grant making and not necessarily investment professionals. This difference in skill sets may affect the quality of board oversight, the level of delegation of decision making to investment staff, and the quality of investment decisions.

Mission-related investing (also known as "**impact investing**"), which aims to direct a significant portion of assets in excess of annual grants into projects promoting the foundation's mission, is becoming increasingly important. For example, the Ford Foundation has allocated up to US$1.0 billion (more than 8% of assets) over 10 years to investments related to its mission of addressing global inequality. The challenge for foundations is to ensure that mission-related investments generate financial returns commensurate with risks assumed. As typically lower yielding mission-related investments are undertaken at the expense of higher return investment opportunities, portfolio returns (expected and realized) may decline, which could result in foundation assets being spent down sooner and annual grant-making activities being reduced.

13.1 Private Foundations—Liabilities and Investment Horizon

In practice, the investment philosophy of private foundations is typically similar to that of university endowments, despite important differences between them in terms of liabilities and liquidity needs. Foundations and endowments both typically have perpetual investment horizons (although, as noted shortly, some foundations may have finite lives) and both invest to maintain purchasing power; however, foundations generally have higher liquidity needs. In the United States, private grant-making foundations are legally required to pay out 5% of assets (on a trailing 12-month basis) plus investment expenses, while university endowments have more-flexible spending rules. In addition, foundations must spend any donations in the year received, known as flow-through (but this is not necessarily the case outside the United States). Foundations typically use a smoothing formula similar to that of university endowments to ensure payouts do not fluctuate with the market volatility of assets. The constant growth spending rule and the hybrid spending rule, discussed previously for university endowments, are rarely used by foundations.

Foundations sometimes issue bonds. The capability to access debt markets, especially during periods of market stress, is positively associated with the levels of investment risk and liquidity risk that foundations can accept in their investments. The Wellcome Foundation (United Kingdom), with a credit rating of AAA, has occasionally issued bonds. For example, in early 2018, it issued £750 million of century bonds (i.e., 100-year maturity) with a coupon of 2.517%.[3] Proceeds from such bonds have been used to support charitable work, and bondholders are repaid by the returns generated on the investment portfolio.

Spending Rate and Investment Expenses of Foundations

Costs of running a foundation are included in the 5% required payout, excluding investment expenses, which means the investment office is considered a cost center. Consequently, the investment office of a foundation will typically be much smaller compared to that of a similar-sized (by AUM) endowment, leading to potentially different investment behavior. For example, many small foundations have limited investment staff and therefore rely on an outsourced CIO model, whereby assets are managed by an external organization that assumes fiduciary duty and takes responsibility for the strategic asset allocation and investments across various asset classes. Although many outsourced CIOs do offer allocations to alternative asset classes, the result of such outsourcing may typically be a heavier allocation to public markets, more-intensive use of passive strategies, and a heavier reliance on beta as a driver of returns.

Many foundations typically receive a one-time gift from the founding family. Some foundations are allowed to raise money on an ongoing basis, but in the US, any such donations must be spent on a flow-through basis. Unlike universities that derive revenues from other sources besides their endowments, such as tuition and research grants, foundations rely almost exclusively on their investment portfolios to support operating budgets. This high dependency has important implications for risk tolerance, and as a result, foundations (on average) have more conservative, more-liquid investment portfolios compared to endowments.

Typically, the original gift must be maintained in perpetuity (principal protection). There is, however, a trend toward **limited-life foundations**, as some founders seek to maintain control of spending while they (or their immediate heirs) are still alive. For example, the Bill and Melinda Gates Foundation is mandated to spend down assets to zero within 30 years of the Gates' death. There is risk—and concern by some founding donors—that as the foundation's leadership changes over time, the mission may move away from the founder's vision. Thus, to minimize this risk, more limited-life foundations are being established. Importantly, a limited-life foundation

---

[3] In late 2017, Oxford University issued a century bond with the same size and similar coupon.

faces a different investment problem than a perpetual foundation: As the investment horizon of a limited-life foundation shortens, its liquidity needs increase and risk tolerance decreases.

Real-Life Example of a Limited-Life Foundation

The Atlantic Philanthropies, set up by Chuck Feeney in 1982, is among the largest limited-life foundations to complete its grant-making activities. After giving a total of US$8 billion over 35 years to human rights, health care, and education causes, the last grant was made in 2016 and the Atlantic Philanthropies expects to close in 2020. All stakeholders have been informed of the spend-down process and critical challenges are being addressed, including: 1) choosing who will oversee the portfolio wind-down process with staff departing for other employment opportunities; and 2) deciding how best to liquidate private investments. As a limited-life foundation gives away its assets, liquidity needs increase and risk tolerance decreases, resulting in lower financial returns and thus limiting the size of the grants that can be made. The de-risking process requires a very "hands-on" investment approach and includes liquidating private portfolios by reducing/stopping commitments, selling private portfolios in the secondary markets, and reinvesting distributions. This becomes increasingly challenging as talented investment staff depart the organization. Actions taken and lessons learned by The Atlantic Philanthropies provide a great case study for other limited-life foundations.

13.2 Private Foundations—Liquidity Needs

The liquidity needs of foundations are relatively low but still higher than those of university endowments. US foundations are legally required to spend 5% of assets or face a tax penalty. They must set aside monies to pay one-year grants and to meet annual installments for longer-term (typically two- to five-year) grants. Having a significant allocation to such relatively illiquid asset classes as private equity and private real estate creates additional liquidity needs to meet general partners' annual net capital calls. Also, derivatives use for such activities as portfolio rebalancing or implementing portable alpha strategies may result in added liquidity demands to meet increased margin calls or to cover higher collateral demands (especially during times of financial market stress).

Exhibit 13 presents a summary comparison of foundations and endowments.

Exhibit 13	Comparison Between Private US Foundations and US University Endowments	
	US Foundation	**US University Endowment**
Purpose	Grant-making for social, educational, and charitable purposes; principal preservation focus.	General support of institution or restricted support; principal preservation focus.
Stakeholders	Founding family, donors, grant recipients, and broader community that may benefit from foundation's activities.	Current/future students, alumni, university faculty and administration, and the larger university community.
Liabilities/Spending	Legally mandated to spend 5% of assets + investment expenses + 100% of donations (flow-through).	Flexible spending rules (headline spending rate between 4% and 6% of assets) with smoothing.
Other liability considerations	Future gifts and donations, or just one-time gift?	Gifts and donations, percentage of operating budget supported by endowment, and ability to issue debt.

(continued)

Exhibit 13 (Continued)

	US Foundation	US University Endowment
Investment time horizon	Very long-term/perpetual (except limited-life foundations).	Perpetual
Risk	High risk tolerance with some short-term liquidity needs.	High risk tolerance with low liquidity needs.
Liquidity needs	Annual net spending is at least 5% of assets.	Annual net spending is typically 2% to 4% of assets, after alumni gifts and donations.

14 UNIVERSITY ENDOWMENTS: INVESTMENT OBJECTIVES AND ASSET ALLOCATION

   f   prepare the investment objectives section of an institutional investor's investment policy statement

   g   evaluate the investment policy statement of an institutional investor

   h   evaluate the investment portfolio of a private DB plan, sovereign wealth fund, university endowment, and private foundation

We now consider the investment objectives and investment policy statement for university endowments and the investment objectives of private foundations.

14.1 University Endowments

A university endowment's mission is to maintain the purchasing power of the assets into perpetuity while achieving investment returns sufficient to sustain the level of spending necessary to support the university budget. For a university endowment, investment policy and spending policy are intertwined, so the IPS should cover spending policy. As discussed previously, endowments use different spending rules. In general, endowments target a spending rate of about 5% of (average) assets. The effective spending rate will, however, be reduced after accounting for gifts and donations. An endowment's primary investment objective is typically to achieve a total real rate of return (after inflation) of $X\%$ with an expected volatility of $Y\%$ over the long term (K years). A common target for $X\%$ is 5%, with inflation being measured using the Higher Education Price Index (HEPI), to be achieved over 3 to 5 years (i.e., $K = 3$ or 5). The expected volatility of returns, $Y\%$, is typically in the range of 10% to 15% annually. Note that the target rate of return may also be expressed as a nominal (as opposed to real) return.

Endowments sometimes have secondary and tertiary investment objectives. A secondary objective might be to outperform the long-term policy benchmark. A third objective might be to outperform a set of pre-defined peers (e.g., outperform the average of the 20 largest university endowments). Peer comparison can lead to herding behavior and be detrimental to long-term success if the focus moves away from managing investments based on each organization's unique liability characteristics to exploit their own comparative advantages. To achieve their objectives, endowments invest in a broad range of asset classes, including fixed income, public equities, hedge fund strategies, private equity, private real estate, and natural resources (e.g. energy and timber). Given that endowments aim to maintain the purchasing power of their assets, they tend to have significant allocations to real assets that are expected to generate returns commensurate with inflation.

The following box provides two examples of investment objectives found in IPSs for real-life endowments.

Investment Objectives of University Endowments

Oxford University Endowment: *"The Oxford Endowment Fund aims to preserve and grow the value of perpetuity capital across the collegiate University of Oxford, while providing a sustainable income stream. ... The Oxford Endowment Fund's investment objective is to produce an average (often referred to as annualised) real return of 5% in excess of the Consumer Price Index (CPI) over the long term."*

Source: http://www.ouem.co.uk/wp-ontent/uploads/2017/10/OUem_Fund_Report_17.pdf.

Note: Oxford Endowment Fund defines its investors as the University of Oxford, including 23 of its colleges and five associated foundations and trusts.

Massachusetts Institute of Technology Endowment: *"Our primary long-term goal is to generate sufficient investment returns to maintain the purchasing power of the endowment after inflation and after MIT's annual spending. Assuming inflation will average around 3% over the long-term and MIT's spending rate will average around 5%, we need to earn approximately 8% to meet this goal. As a secondary check on the quality of our performance, we compare our returns to other endowments and to passive benchmark alternatives."*

Source: http://www.mitimco.org/wp-content/uploads/2017/03/MITIMCo-Alumni-Letter.pdf.

One of the lessons from the 2007–2009 global financial crisis is that liquidity risk must be managed carefully, particularly for institutions that invest heavily in illiquid assets. Most endowments now engage in detailed cash flow modeling for the illiquid portions of their portfolios, and some use a liquidity risk band as part of their overall risk profile. The liquidity risk band is defined as total NAV allocated to illiquid investments plus uncalled commitments to total fund AUM. If the liquidity band is violated (i.e., when the total allocation to illiquid investments exceeds a pre-specified upper bound), this may trigger a reduction (or even a stoppage) of commitments or possibly a sale of some illiquid investments in secondary markets to bring the overall illiquid allocation back to within the liquidity risk band.

EXAMPLE 5

Investment Objectives of the Ivy University Endowment

The hypothetical Ivy University Endowment was established in 1901 by Ivy University and supports up to 40% of the university's operating budget. Historically, the endowment has invested in a traditional 20% public US equities and 80% US Treasury portfolio, entirely implemented through passive investment vehicles. The investment staff at the endowment is relatively small. With the appointment of a new chief investment officer, the investment policy is being reviewed. Endowment assets are US$250 million, and the endowment has an annual spending policy of paying out 5% of the 3-year rolling asset value to the university.

An investment consultant hired by the new CIO to assist with the investment policy review has provided the following 10-year (nominal) expected return assumptions for various asset classes: US equities: 7%, Non-US equities: 8%, US Treasuries: 2%, hedge funds: 5%, and private equity: 10%. Additionally, the investment consultant believes the endowment could generate an extra 50 bps per year in alpha from active management in equities. Expected inflation for the next ten years is 2% annually.

1 Draft the investment objectives section of the IPS of the Ivy University Endowment.
2 Discuss whether the current investment policy is appropriate given the investment objectives of Ivy University Endowment.
3 What decisions could the CIO and board of the Ivy University Endowment take to align the investment policy and the spending policy?

Solution to 1:

The mission of the Ivy University Endowment is to maintain purchasing power of its assets while financing up to 40% of Ivy University's operating budgeting in perpetuity. The investment objective, consistent with this mission, is to achieve a total real rate of return over the Higher Education Price Index (HEPI) of at least 5% with a reasonable level of risk; the volatility of returns should not to exceed 15% annually.

Solution to 2:

Given the expected returns provided by the consultant, a portfolio of 80% fixed income and 20% public equities, invested passively, is expected to provide a nominal expected return of 3% per year (= 0.8 × 2% + 0.2 × 7%). Given, expected inflation of 2%, this implies a 1% real rate of return, which falls well short of the 5% spending rate and the stated objective of a 5% real rate of return. The endowment will see its purchasing power deteriorate over time if it continues with its current asset mix and spending rate.

Solution to 3:

The CIO and board could either change the investment policy by adopting an asset mix that has a more reasonable probability of achieving a 5% real rate of return (an asset allocation including non-US equities and private equity); they could change the spending rate to more accurately reflect the expected real rate of return of the current investment policy; or the new CIO may want to recommend a combination of both.

Below is an example of a university endowment Investment Policy Statement. In this case the university endowment has clearly articulated primary and secondary investment objectives.

University Endowment Investment Policy Statement

A Introduction

The hypothetical Ivy University Endowment Fund (the "Endowment") has been established to fund scholarships, fellowships, faculty salaries, programs, activities, and facilities designed to promote and advance the mission of Ivy University (the "University"). This investment policy statement (IPS) is established by the

Investment Committee of the Board of Trustees (the "IC") for the guidance of the IC, the Investment Office, the Endowment's investment managers, and other fiduciaries in the course of investing the monies of the Endowment. This IPS establishes policies and procedures for the administration and investment of the Endowment's assets. This document formally defines the goals, objectives, and guidelines of the Endowment's investment program.

B Mission and Investment Objectives

The Endowment provides financial support for the operations of the University. Investment and spending policies are designed to balance the current goals of the University with its future needs, in order to achieve parity in supporting both current and future generations of Ivy students. The goal for the Endowment is to provide a real total return that preserves the purchasing power of the Endowment's assets while generating an income stream to support the academic activities of the University.

The primary investment objective of the Endowment is to earn an average annual real total return (net of portfolio management fees) of at least 5% per year over the long term (rolling five-year periods), within prudent levels of risk. Attainment of this objective will be sufficient to maintain, in real terms, the purchasing power of the Endowment's assets and support the defined spending policy.

A secondary investment objective is to outperform, over the long term, a blended custom benchmark based on a current asset allocation policy of: 30% MSCI World Index, 20% Cambridge Associates LLC US Private Equity Index, 10% NCREIF Property Index, 10% Consumer Price Index for All Urban Consumers (annualized CPI-U) + 5%, 20% HFRI Fund of Funds Index, and 10% Citigroup US Treasury Index.

C Spending Policy

The Endowment's spending policy was developed to meet several objectives, namely to: (a) provide a sustainable level of income to support current operations, (b) provide year-to-year budget stability, and (c) meet intergenerational needs by protecting the future purchasing power of the Endowment against the impact of inflation. Under this policy, spending for a given year equals 80% of spending in the previous year, adjusted for inflation (CPI within a range of 0% and 6%), plus 20% of the long-term spending rate (5.0%) applied to the 12-quarter rolling average of market values. This spending policy has two implications. First, by incorporating the previous year's spending, the policy eliminates large fluctuations and so enables the University to plan for operating budget needs. Second, by adjusting spending toward a long-term rate of 5.0%, the policy ensures that spending levels will be sensitive to fluctuating market value levels, thereby providing stability in long-term purchasing power.

D Asset Allocation Policy, Allowable Ranges, and Benchmarks

The single most important investment decision is the allocation of the Endowment to various asset classes. The primary objective of the Endowment's asset allocation policy is to provide a strategic mix of asset classes that produces the highest expected investment return within a prudent risk framework. To achieve this, the Endowment will allocate among several asset classes with a bias toward equity and equity-like investments caused by their higher long-term return expectations. Other asset classes may be added to the Endowment to enhance returns, reduce volatility through diversification, and/or offer a broader investment opportunity set.

To ensure broad diversification among the major categories of investments, the Endowment has adopted the following capital allocation policy ranges for each asset class within the overall portfolio set forth in the Annex. This asset allocation framework is reviewed annually by the IC, but because of the long-term nature of the Endowment, changes to the framework are expected to be infrequent:

Asset Class	Policy Range	Benchmark
Global equity	20%–40%	MSCI World Index
Private equity & venture capital	15%–25%	Cambridge Associates LLC US Private Equity Index
Private real estate	5%–15%	NCREIF Property Index
Real assets	5%–15%	Consumer Price Index for All Urban Consumers (annualized CPI-U) + 5%
Absolute return strategies	15%–25%	HFRI Fund of Funds Index
Fixed income & cash	5%–15%	Citigroup US Treasury Index

The following core investment principles provide the foundation for the asset allocation policy:

- Equity dominance: Equities are expected to be the highest-performing asset class over the long term and thus will dominate the portfolio.
- Illiquid assets: In general, private illiquid investments are expected to outperform more-liquid public investments by exploiting market inefficiencies.
- Global orientation: The Endowment will consider the broadest possible set of investment opportunities in its search for attractive risk/return profiles.
- Diversification: Thoughtful diversification within and between asset classes by region, sector, and economic source of return can lower volatility and raise compound returns over the long term.

E Rebalancing

The IPS establishes the long-term asset allocation targets for the endowment and policy ranges for the various asset classes approved by the IC. The role of the capital allocation ranges is to allow for short-term fluctuations caused by market volatility or near-term cash flows, to recognize the flexibility required in managing private investments, and to provide limits for tactical investing. The IC will rely on investment staff to determine allocations within the stated ranges and to regularly manage actual asset class allocations to be within the ranges where possible. In addition, the IC will review actual asset allocations relative to this asset allocation framework at each quarterly meeting.

F Reporting

The Investment Team, with the oversight of management, must provide adequate reporting to the Board of Trustees, the IC, and other stakeholders. The reporting structure should include the following:

- Performance measurement and attribution for the quarter and trailing periods for the portfolio both in absolute terms and relative to the established benchmarks
- Asset allocation of the total portfolio
- Market value of the total portfolio

14.2 Asset Allocation

We now consider asset allocation, investment portfolios, and investment performance of university endowments. We follow with a similar discussion focusing on private foundations.

14.2.1 *University Endowments*

Most large endowments follow the endowment investment model and rely heavily on alternative investments to achieve their long-term investment objectives. This approach is not without risks. During the global financial crisis, several large endowments faced significant liquidity challenges and were forced to either sell portions of their private investment portfolios in the secondary markets, reduce payouts to their universities, or issue bonds to bridge their liquidity needs. The rapid post-crisis recovery arguably bailed out many endowments, but had the crisis lasted longer, the pain would have been substantially worse. David Swensen, the longtime CIO of the Yale Endowment, and his colleagues have regularly warned against a blanket application of the endowment model. Yale and some of the other large endowments have enjoyed a first-mover advantage in their private investments, and their alumni networks have provided access to investment opportunities that may not be as easily accessible to other institutions.

Exhibit 14 shows the average asset allocation for US endowments by size at the end of June 2017 using data from a study in which more than 800 colleges and universities participated. Here alternatives include private equity and venture capital, hedge funds and other marketable alternative strategies, private real estate, energy and natural resources (e.g., oil, gas, timber, commodities, and managed futures), and distressed debt.

These data reveal several important points. First, the larger endowments have a significantly higher allocation to alternatives. Larger endowments have achieved better returns over the past 10 years, and their larger allocation to alternatives has played an important role. Second, the larger endowments do not face the "home bias" issue that smaller endowments seem to suffer. The allocation of smaller endowments to US equities is significantly larger than their allocation to non-US equities. Finally, the larger endowments hold a significantly smaller amount of their assets in fixed-income securities. This might pose a challenge during liquidity crises—such as in the 2007–2009 global financial crisis when some larger endowments struggling to meet their liquidity needs pressured managers of private investment funds to delay any calls (i.e., demands) for additional capital. Some universities also issued bonds during the crisis to help relieve the liquidity pressures faced by their endowments.

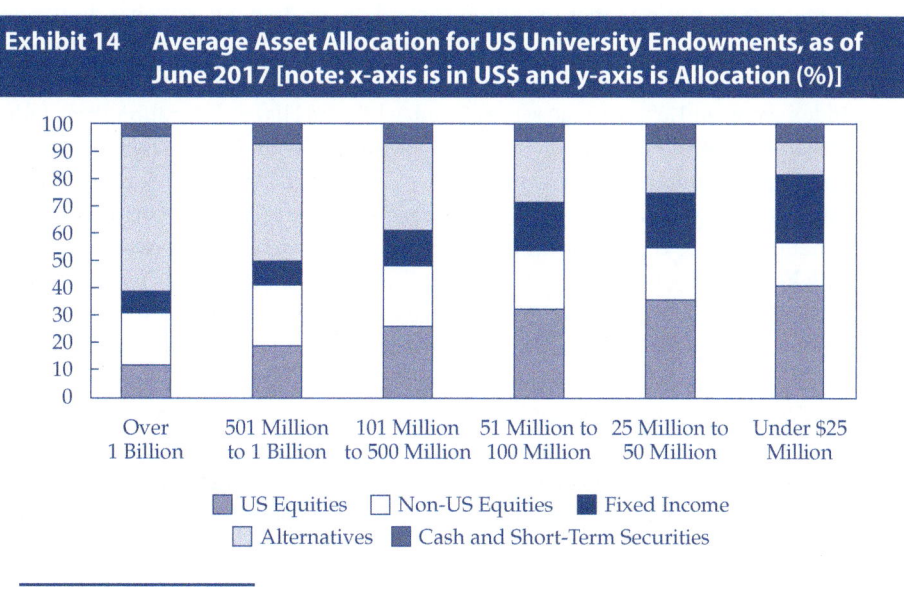

Exhibit 14 Average Asset Allocation for US University Endowments, as of June 2017 [note: x-axis is in US$ and y-axis is Allocation (%)]

Source: Commonfund and the National Association of College and University Business Officers (NACUBO), *2017 NACUBO–Commonfund Study of Endowments*.

Exhibit 15 shows the average asset allocation at the end of FY 2002 and at the end of FY 2017 for university endowments of more than US$1 billion in size. During this period, the largest endowments significantly increased their allocation to alternatives from 32% to 57%. Although not shown here, most of the increase has been in the allocations to private equity, venture capital, and private real estate—with the allocation to hedge funds remaining roughly the same. This increased allocation to alternatives has come at the expense of public equities (reduced from 45% to 32%) and fixed income (reduced from 21% to 7%).

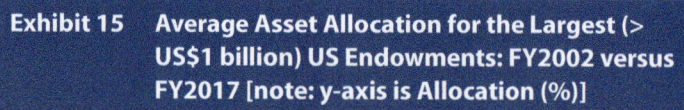

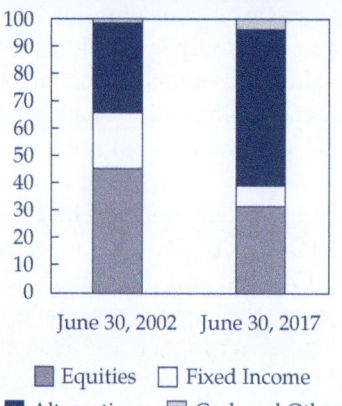

Sources: Commonfund and the National Association of College and University Business Officers (NACUBO), *2002 NACUBO–Commonfund Study of Endowments* and *2017 NACUBO–Commonfund Study of Endowments*.

Given asset allocations that are tilted toward alternative investments, how have endowments fared over the past 10 years? Exhibit 16 shows the average annual 10-year return (net of fees) for US endowments by size as of end-June 2017. The US Consumer Price Index averaged 1.6% over the same period, while the Higher Education Price Index (HEPI) averaged 2.4%. It is apparent, overall, that US endowments have fallen well short of generating an annualized real return of 5% over the past 10 years. Moreover, larger endowments have generally been able to generate higher returns during this period. Endowments of more than US$1 billion have generated anywhere between 50 bps to 60 bps higher returns (annually) compared to the smaller endowments (with less than US$500 million). This difference compounds to a significant gap over a 10-year period. These higher returns have allowed the larger endowments to payout a larger part of their assets to support their universities. Interestingly, the smallest endowments (less than US$25 million) have produced a 10-year return identical to those of the largest endowments. This can be attributed to their large allocation to US equities which outperformed other international markets by a significant margin over the last 10 years.[4] It is worth noting that the 10-year period ending 30 June 2017 is time-period

---

[4] The S&P 500 Index experienced a 100% cumulative total return over the 10-year period to 1 July 2017, while the MSCI World ex-US Index (developed markets) and the MSCI Emerging Market Index increased by 10% and 20%, respectively, over the same period.

specific. A different 10-year period might lead to a different conclusion. However, this 10-year period is reasonably representative of long-term asset class returns because capital markets have generally rewarded growth assets over the period.

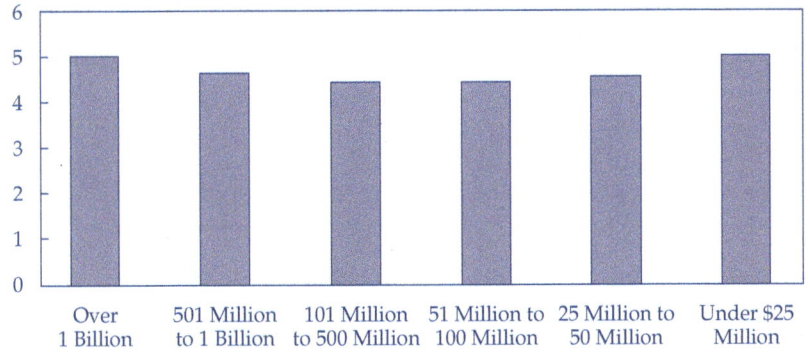

Exhibit 16 Average Annual 10-Year Nominal Returns for US University Endowments as of June 2017 [note: x-axis is in US$ and y-axis is Nominal Return (%)]

Source: Commonfund and the National Association of College and University Business Officers (NACUBO), *2017 NACUBO–Commonfund Study of Endowments*.

EXAMPLE 6

Investment Portfolio of the Ivy University Endowment

The hypothetical Ivy University Endowment was established in 1901 and supports Ivy University. The endowment supports about 40% of the university's operating budget. Historically, the endowment has invested in a traditional 20% public US equities, 80% US Treasury portfolio, and it is entirely implemented through passive investment vehicles. The investment staff at the endowment is relatively small. With the appointment of a new chief investment officer, the investment policy is being reviewed. Endowment assets are US$250 million, and the endowment has a spending policy of paying out 5% of the 3-year rolling asset value to the university.

The new CIO has engaged an investment consultant to assist her with the investment policy review. The investment consultant has provided the following 10-year (nominal) expected return assumptions for various asset classes: US equities: 7%, Non-US equities: 8%, US Treasuries: 2%, hedge funds: 5%, private equity: 10%. In addition, the investment consultant believes that the endowment could generate an additional 50 bps in alpha from active management in equities. Expected inflation for the next 10 years is 2%.

The new CIO was at a previous endowment that invested heavily in private investments and hedge funds and recommends a change in the investment policy to the board of Ivy University Endowment. She recommends investing 30% in private equity, 30% in hedge funds, 30% in public equities (15% US and

15% non-US with *active* management), and 10% in fixed income. This mix would have an expected real return of 5.1% based on the expected return assumptions provided by the investment consultant.

1. Given the expected return assumptions from the investment consultant, provide an asset mix that would be more appropriate for Ivy University Endowment?
2. Should the board approve the new CIO's recommendation? Provide your reasoning.

Solution to 1:

To achieve a 5% real rate of return, the endowment will need to accept significantly more equity risk, diversify its assets internationally, allocate some of its assets to hedge funds and private equity, and engage in active management. There are several possible combinations that could result in a portfolio with a 5% expected real rate of return. Here are two possible asset mixes:

I: 40% in US equities with active management (7.5% expected return), 40% in non-US equities with active management (8.5% expected return), 10% in US Treasuries (2% expected return), 10% in hedge funds (5% expected return). This asset mix would result in an expected nominal return of 7.1% or an expected real return of 5.1%.

II: 50% in US equities with passive management (7% expected return), 30% in non-US equities with active management (8.5% expected return), 10% in US Treasuries (2% expected return), 10% in private equity (10% expected return). This asset mix would result in an expected nominal return of 7.25% or an expected real return of 5.25%.

Solution to 2:

The board should reject the CIO's recommendation. This is a very significant departure from the current practice. The size of the investment team is small, and they have no prior experience in managing hedge fund and private equity portfolios (except for the new CIO). Additionally, given the size of the endowment, it is unlikely to have access to top quartile managers in the hedge fund and private equity spaces. The CIO should explain why the recommended asset mix with 60% in alternatives is preferable over asset mixes that deliver the same or higher expected real return (such as I and II in Solution 1).

15. PRIVATE FOUNDATIONS: INVESTMENT OBJECTIVES AND ASSET ALLOCATION

f prepare the investment objectives section of an institutional investor's investment policy statement
g evaluate the investment policy statement of an institutional investor
h evaluate the investment portfolio of a private DB plan, sovereign wealth fund, university endowment, and private foundation

As discussed previously, private foundations in the United States are legally required to pay out a minimum of 5% of assets annually to be eligible for tax-exempt status. Foundations strive to be capable of making grants that support their overall missions in perpetuity while meeting the minimum 5% payout requirement. The primary investment objective for foundations is typically to generate a total real return over consumer price inflation of 5%, plus investment expenses, with a reasonable expected volatility (approximately 10%–15% annual standard deviation) over a 3- to 5-year period. A secondary investment objective may include outperforming the policy benchmark with a specified tracking error budget. Monte Carlo-based modeling for generating expected returns and risk distributions as well as liquidity modeling and asset stress testing mentioned earlier for DB pension plans are also used by management and consultants to develop cogent investment objectives and policies for foundations and endowments. Foundations, like endowments, invest in a broad range of asset classes, including fixed income, public equities, hedge fund strategies, and private equity.

The following box provides two real-life examples of investment objectives for foundations.

Investment Objectives for Private Foundations

Wellcome Trust (UK):

"Our overall investment objective is to generate 4.5% real return over the long term. This is to provide for real increases in annual expenditure while preserving the Trust's capital base to balance the needs of current and future beneficiaries. We use this absolute return strategy because it aligns asset allocation with funding requirements and provides a competitive framework in which to judge individual investments."

Note: Wellcome Trust's IPS mentions that the real return is based on an average of US and UK consumer price inflation.

Source: https://wellcome.ac.uk/about-us/investments.

Robert Wood Johnson Foundation:

"The Robert Wood Johnson Foundation's mission is to help Americans lead healthier lives and get the care they need. Reflecting that mission and our Guiding Principles, we recognize that as a private foundation, 'We are stewards of private resources that must be used in the public's interest.' ... Achieving comprehensive and meaningful change in health and health care will require sustained attention over many years to come. The Foundation therefore seeks to earn an investment return that, over time, equals or exceeds the sum of its annual spending, as a percentage of the Foundation's assets plus the rate of inflation. This balance of investment return and spending is designed to spread risk and promote a steady, stable flow of support for our grantees."

Source: http://www.rwjf.org/en/about-rwjf/financials.html.

The IPS of a private foundation is not very different from that of a university endowment and follows a similar format as outlined in the previous section. The mission statement would be framed slightly differently, but the IPS would cover the same elements.

15.1 Private Foundations

Foundations tend to follow a similar investment approach compared to endowments, despite important differences in their liability structures. Two of the most notable differences between foundations and endowments that should have a bearing on their asset allocation are that:

1 foundations support the entire budget of their organization, while universities have significant other sources of financing available besides the endowment; and

2 foundations (in the United States) are mandated to pay out at least 5% of their assets to maintain tax-exempt status and typically receive no additional inflows in the form of gifts and donations (or, if there are gifts/donations, these need to be spent in the same year that they are received and do not count against the 5% mandated payout), whereas university endowments typically have a net payout of less than 5%.

Exhibit 17 shows the average asset allocations for US foundations by size and type at year-end 2016. The underlying data cover 203 institutions (123 private foundations and 80 community foundations). Here, alternative investments include private equity and venture capital, hedge funds and other marketable alternative strategies, private real estate, energy and natural resources, and distressed debt.

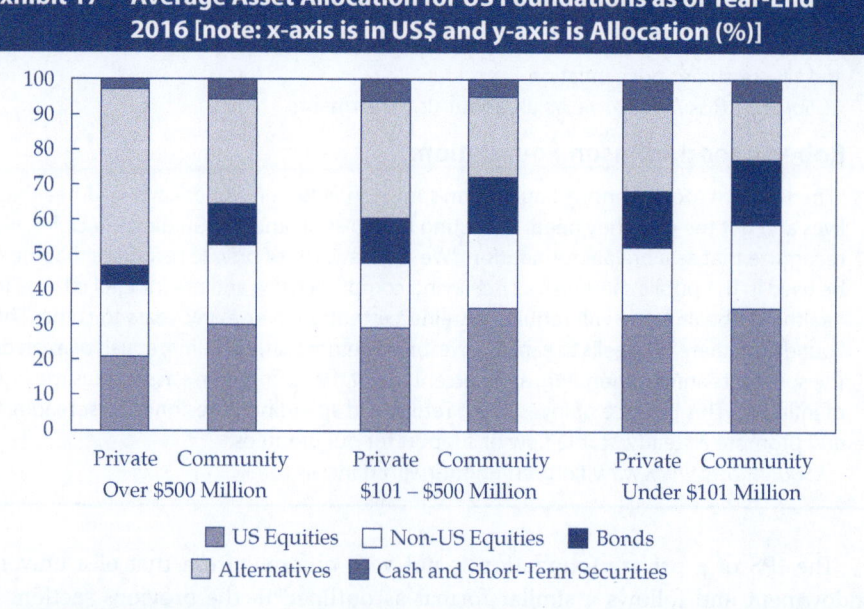

Exhibit 17 Average Asset Allocation for US Foundations as of Year-End 2016 [note: x-axis is in US$ and y-axis is Allocation (%)]

Source: Council on Foundations–Commonfund, *2016 Council on Foundations–Commonfund Study of Investment of Endowments for Private and Community Foundations (CCSF)*: https://www.cof.org/content/2016-council-foundations-commonfund-study-investment-endowments-private-and-community.

These data highlight several key points. The larger foundations have a significantly higher allocation to alternatives, and private foundations have higher allocations to alternatives compared to community foundations. The largest private foundations (more than US$500 million) have about half of their assets invested in alternatives. Although not shown, the largest private and community foundations have similar allocations to marketable alternatives (hedge funds), but the private foundations have significantly higher allocations to the higher-return-generating, illiquid alternatives—such

Private Foundations: Investment Objectives and Asset Allocation

as private equity, venture capital, private real estate, and distressed debt. Smaller foundations seem generally to have a higher allocation to US equities compared to the larger foundations. Finally, the larger private foundations hold a smaller amount of their assets in fixed-income securities.

Foundations must generate real (net of fee) returns above 5% to maintain their purchasing power. Exhibit 18 shows that over the 10-year period to year-end 2016 (when US CPI averaged 1.8%), US foundations have fallen well short of this minimum target. As a result, their purchasing power has deteriorated. However, during this period larger private foundations (more than US$500 million) have been able to generate higher returns—anywhere between 10 bps to 60 bps higher returns (annually)—compared to medium/small private foundations. Their larger allocation to alternatives likely played a key role in this outperformance. Note that the effective spending rate in 2016 was 5.8% for private foundations.

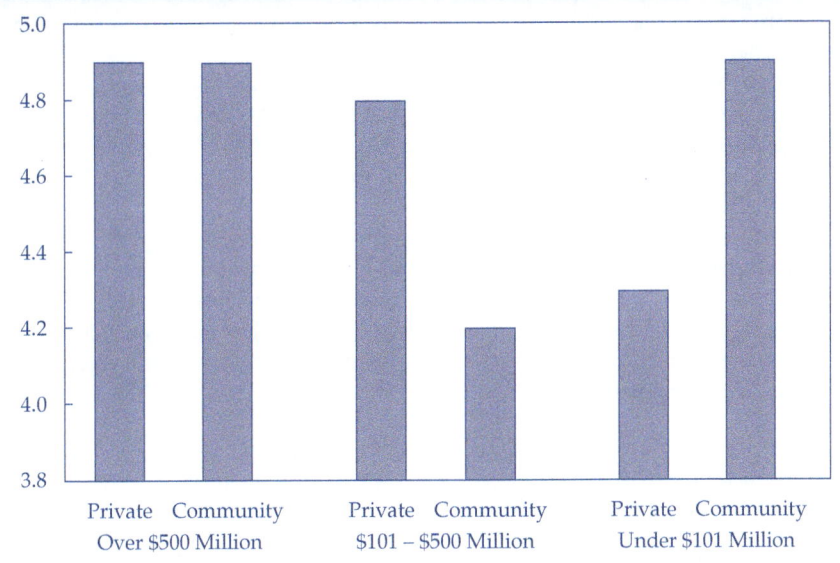

Exhibit 18 Average Annual 10-Year Nominal Return for US Foundations as of Year-End 2016 [note: x-axis is in US$ and y-axis is Nominal Return (%)]

Source: Council on Foundations–Commonfund, *2016 Council on Foundations–Commonfund Study of Investment of Endowments for Private and Community Foundations (CCSF)*: https://www.cof.org/content/2016-council-foundations-commonfund-study-investment-endowments-private-and-community.

Real-Life Case Study: Wellcome Trust (UK)

Wellcome Trust ("the Trust") provides an interesting study of how a foundation transformed its investment approach and asset allocation and, in the process, significantly improved its investment performance. The Wellcome Trust was founded in 1936 and manages about £23 billion in its investment portfolio (as of end-September 2017). The investment portfolio supports all of the charitable work of the Trust, which provides funding for scientific and medical research to improve health worldwide. During FY2016–17, charitable grants were more than £1 billion.

Between 1936 and 1986, the Trust was the sole owner of Burroughs Wellcome, the pharmaceutical company founded by Henry Wellcome. In 1986, the Trust began selling shares in the company and used the proceeds to diversify its assets. Over the past two decades, the portfolio has generated an average annual (nominal) return of 14%. The overall investment objective is to generate a 4.5% real return over the long term. The Trust used to target a payout rate of 4.7% of the weighted average value of the portfolio over the previous three years. Historically, this resulted in an average annual payout of 4.3%.

Daniel Truell joined the Trust as CIO in 2005 and initiated radical changes to its investment approach and asset mix, shifting from short-term, liquid, and low-risk assets to longer-term, less-liquid, and higher risk assets. The most notable changes were an increase in the allocation to private equity (including buyout and venture capital funds) and hedge funds as well as reduced allocations to public equities and cash. In addition to radically changing its allocations, the decision was made to concentrate assets with fewer managers and in fewer, higher quality investments, such that by 2017 less than 100 investments represented nearly 85% of the portfolio's value. The Trust also shifted to more direct investments, and active management in public equities was brought predominantly in-house and conducted by an investment team of more than 30 professionals.

At end-September 2017, the Trust's investment portfolio consisted of 53% in public equities, 9% in hedge funds, 24% in private equity, 9% in property and infrastructure, 1% in commodity futures and options, and 4% in cash. The Trust has issued bonds totaling £2 billion—representing about 8% of total assets. Proceeds from the bond issuance are used for investments.

In 2017, the Trust adopted a new approach to determine how much to fund its charitable activities. According to the latest IPS (October 2017), the Trust now "*targets an annual real cash spend in the Primary Fund (based on UK CPI) of £900 million in 2017 prices. This level of spending will be reviewed in 2022, or earlier in the event of declines in the investment portfolio below £20 billion in 2017 prices.*"

The Trust manages risk by ongoing monitoring of the following key risk factors: 1) 95% value-at-risk at a one-year horizon (if more than 20%, then this is highlighted to the Investment Committee), 2) foreign currency exposure (if more than 85%, then this is highlighted to the Investment Committee), 3) forecast of cash levels (unencumbered cash should exceed 2% of gross assets within a 5-year forecast period), and 4) estimated equity beta for the portfolio should be in the range of 0.4 to 0.8.

Sources: 1. Wellcome Trust, "Investment Policy" (October 2017): https://wellcome.ac.uk/sites/default/files/investment-policy-october-2017.pdf. 2. Wellcome Trust, *Annual Report and Financial Statements 2016* (https://wellcome.ac.uk/sites/default/files/WellcomeTrustAnnualReportFinancialStatements_160930.pdf). 3. Wellcome Trust, Annual Report and Financial Statements 2017 (https://wellcome.ac.uk/sites/default/files/wellcome-trust-annual-report-and-financial-statements-2017.pdf). 4. World Economic Forum, "Alternative Investments 2020: The Future of Alternative Investments" (2015). 5. Steve Johnson, "Uncovering Little Investment Gems among the Shrunken Heads," *Financial Times* (12 April 2014): https://www.ft.com/content/c49bb40c-be63-11e3-b44a-00144feabdc0.

16 BANKS AND INSURERS: INTRODUCTION AND EXTERNAL CONSTRAINTS

i. describe considerations affecting the balance sheet management of banks and insurers

This section focuses on institutional investors that are also financial intermediaries, namely banks and insurance companies.

Banks

Banks are financial intermediaries that take deposits, lend money, safeguard assets, execute transactions in securities and cash, act as counterparties in derivatives transactions, provide advisory services, and invest in securities. The universe of banks is quite large and diverse, ranging from small community banks to global diversified financial services institutions. A precise estimate of total worldwide banking assets is difficult to obtain; nevertheless, using publicly available data from such sources as the Bank for International Settlements (BIS), Reuters, and individual balance sheets for the largest public banks, an estimate of more than US$100 trillion seems reasonable.[5] An order-of-magnitude estimate for bank equity capitalization works out to US$7 trillion. Our focus here is on the largest, most globally important banks—the two to three dozen banks that account for the great majority of international commercial bank assets and liabilities. Exhibit 19 shows some of these banks, all of which are designated as global systemically important banks by the Financial Stability Board, an international body that monitors the global financial system.

Exhibit 19 Select Large Global Banks

Bank	Country/Region
Industrial & Commercial Bank of China	China
China Construction Bank Corp.	China
Agricultural Bank of China	China
Bank of China	China
HSBC Holdings Plc	Hong Kong SAR/United Kingdom
JPMorgan Chase & Co.	United States
BNP Paribas	France
Mitsubishi UFJ Financial Group	Japan
Bank of America	United States
Credit Agricole Group	France

Source: Kevin P. Johnston, "The World's Top 10 Banks." Investopedia (25 April 2017).

Insurers

The universe of insurance companies can be divided into two broad categories:

- Life insurers
- Property and Casualty (P&C) insurers

According to the OECD (Organization for Economic Co-Operation and Development) data on 35 large countries (ex-China and India), aggregate direct-insurance assets for both types of insurers had combined totals of more than US$22 trillion, with equity capitalization of more than US$2.2 trillion.[6]

The life insurance product set includes traditional whole and term insurance, variable life insurance and annuity products, as well as health insurance. The P&C product suite encompasses insurance against a wide range of perils—covering commercial

---

[5] Inter-company and cross-border transactions, non-contemporaneous reporting dates, differing accounting treatment (IFRS vs. GAAP, for example), and currency exchange rate conversions are inescapable complications.
[6] OECD (2016).

property and liability, homeowner's property and liability, and automotive as well as such multiple specialty coverage lines as marine, surety, and workers' compensation. Exhibit 20 lists some of the largest global insurance companies.

Exhibit 20 Select Large Global Insurance Companies	
Entity	**Country/Region**
AXA	France
Zurich Insurance Group	Switzerland
China Life Insurance	China
Berkshire Hathaway	United States
Prudential plc	United Kingdom
United Health Group	United States
Munich Re Group	Germany
Assicurazioni Generali S.p.A.	Italy
Japan Post Holding Co., Ltd.	Japan
Allianz SE	Germany

Source: Prableen Bajpai, "World's Top 10 Insurance Companies," Investopedia (23 March 2016).

16.1 External Constraints Affecting Investment

The legal and regulatory environments, as well as tax and accounting constraints, faced by banks and insurers are complex and may vary according to the national and local jurisdictions in which these institutional investors do business. In this section, we take a high-level view of some of the major legal and regulatory constraints within which banks and insurers must operate. In the following section, we consider tax and accounting constraints that affect investing by banks and insurers.

16.1.1 Legal and Regulatory Constraints

For banks and insurance companies, the liabilities to depositors, the claims of policyholders, and the amounts due to creditors are clearly and contractually defined. This is different from the other types of institutions discussed previously where there typically can be a great deal of discretion in the timing and amounts due and paid to stakeholders. Furthermore, banks and insurance companies carry out important functions with respect to the underlying economies in which they operate. These include facilitation of individual and commercial payments, extensions of credit, safeguarding of assets, and transfers of risk—to name the more important. The activities of companies in the financial industry not only are deeply intertwined with the non-financial, or *real*, economy, but their activities also are deeply intertwined with each other. Thus, a disturbance in the operation of individual banks and insurance companies can spread through the entire financial industry with great speed and with compounding damage; significant adverse effects can easily overflow into the real economy. Such negatives can include depositor runs on a banking system, credit crunches whereby companies or governments cannot obtain funding for maintaining operations, or the failure of insurance companies that undermine the viability of large sectors of the economy, such as residential housing or the health care markets. Consequently, banking and insurance regulators in most jurisdictions are intensely focused on capital adequacy, liquidity, and leverage to mitigate systemic or contagion risk.

Banks and insurance companies are primarily regulated at national and state levels and are increasingly overseen by supranational regulatory and advisory bodies. The need to regulate banks and insurance companies at high, rather than local, levels stems from the fact that financial institutions are mainly large and spread across many local and national jurisdictions. At its most essential, the regulation of financial institutions centers on making sure banks and insurance companies have adequate capitalization to absorb losses rather than allowing losses to be borne by the rest of the financial system or the real economy—including depositors, insurance policyholders, creditors, or taxpayers.

Lowering the risk of assets through regulation is the first way to lower the potential strains on bank and insurance company capitalization. This can be through requirements for diversification, asset quality (including adequate reserve provisioning for credit, market, and operational risk losses) and liquidity maintenance. Likewise, setting requirements on liabilities can lower potential stress on bank and insurance capital resources. Such regulation of liabilities may include requirements for funding sources to be diversified over time and among different groups of depositors and debtholders. In the case of insurance companies, potential losses from liabilities can be regulated through rules limiting the size and concentration of potential policy claims. In addition to limiting potential losses from assets and liabilities—or from other operational risks—regulators may mandate certain minimum required capitalization.

Turning to insurers, the US insurance industry is regulated by individual states, each having its own administrative agency; the federal government does not play a major role in oversight. The National Association of Insurance Commissioners (NAIC), of which every state is a member, provides a forum for industry issues and sets accounting policies and financial reporting standards for the industry. In Europe, regulators have developed the Solvency II framework to standardize insurance regulation across member states.

The size and diversity of financial institutions result from powerful economies of scale. These economies of scale arise because most activities of banks and insurance companies (such as extension of credit, underwriting health or property risks, or taking of deposits) are made in large numbers, where the successes and failures of individual transactions are not normally highly correlated among each other. By the law of large numbers, the volatility of the weighted sum of independent risks decreases as a function of the square root of the number of independent risks assumed. This diversification effect would be a benefit to a financial firm that grows larger than its competitors. In fact, it would represent increasing returns to scale because the largest institution could hold a portfolio of assets with less capital than its competitors, because asset and liability volatility would be much less and would result in a higher and less volatile return on capital for the largest institution. Of course, offsetting factors keep this effect from dominating. Other marginal costs of operation, communications, and management keep the industry from eventually evolving into one giant financial firm. Nevertheless, the powerful impacts of diversification in terms of credit defaults, deposit funding, casualty insurance claims, and life-and-health mortality/morbidity claims are very strong factors in contributing to the existence of a small number of large national and international financial firms that comprise most of the financial industry's assets and earnings.

These few large firms are regarded as systemically important financial institutions (SIFIs). Since the worldwide financial system meltdown of 2008–2009, legislators and regulators worldwide have moved in the direction of bolstering the financial system by raising capital requirements—directly, by requiring higher absolute amounts of primary capital, and indirectly, by (1) effectively increasing the amount of capital needed to support the holding of certain investments, (2) limiting the payout of dividends and repurchases of common equity, and (3) making subordinated debt and preferred shareholders less able to assert their claims in the event of bankruptcy or regulator-mandated restructuring. Furthermore, regulators' actions have resulted in tightening regulations on the use of derivatives, proprietary trading, and off-balance-sheet liabilities/guarantees. These actions require institutions through stress testing to show how they can survive severe economic and financial market turbulence, and they impose more stringent accounting/disclosure rules and reserving requirements. The consequences of a relatively small number of SIFIs dominating the financial industry and the existence of regulatory cycles mean that the management of a financial institution must take into account the actions of its SIFI competitors and must integrate its asset and liability portfolio decisions with a view to where the rules are today *and* where they are likely heading.

16.1.2 Accounting and Tax Considerations

Three different types of accounting systems apply for every financial institution. For the enterprise and its subsidiaries, the first is standard financial accounting, whether in the form of GAAP or IFRS, and which is used for communicating results to shareholders (or members), deposit or policyholders, and suppliers of debt capital. Regulators of banks and insurance companies, in addition, impose a second type of accounting in various forms and known as *statutory* accounting. Statutory accounting rules can be very different across different national and local regulatory jurisdictions. Although statutory results are normally available to the public, they mostly are utilized by regulators. Finally, the third type, true economic accounting, marks all assets and liabilities (net of imputed income taxes) to current market values.

Each accounting system is designed with a particular objective in mind, and it is incumbent upon financial institution managers and investment analysts to understand the purposes of all three. Economic or mark-to-market (MTM) accounting provides the best picture of an entity's assets, liabilities, and changes in economic well-being. MTM earnings are the most volatile of all because they reflect all value changes contemporaneously rather than being smoothed over time. The results of MTM reporting are likely to differ from those from financial reporting, where the reporting rules are consistently and conservatively applied over time (but where asset and liability values may depart from reported balance sheet amounts). Financial reporting has moved increasingly in the direction of MTM accounting over the past several decades, although changes in asset and liability values often are reported by way of balance sheet comprehensive income accounts rather than directly through an income statement. On balance, financial reporting will provide the smoothest reporting of income and asset/liability valuations.

Statutory accounting represents essentially a system of adjustments to standard financial accounting. For both bank and insurance regulators, this means most significantly the subtracting of intangible assets from asset and common equity accounts and/or the acceleration of certain expenses, such as policy underwriting and sales costs. In other cases, it is the recognition and assignment of additional reserves against losses on assets or unexpectedly large losses on guarantees or insurance claims. Statutory accounting usually results in lower earnings and lower common equity capital than in financial accounting. Capital requirements for both banks and insurance companies are predicated on one or another version of statutory reporting.

In terms of taxation, banks and insurance companies typically are taxable entities, and the industry-specific tax rules can be quite complicated. As taxable entities, banks and insurance companies must manage their investment programs with consideration of after-tax returns.

BANKS: STAKEHOLDERS, LIABILITIES, INVESTMENT HORIZON, AND LIQUIDITY NEEDS

i. describe considerations affecting the balance sheet management of banks and insurers

Bank stakeholders include external parties (such as shareholders, creditors, customers, credit rating agencies, regulators, and even the communities where they operate) as well as internal parties (such as employees, management, and boards of directors). A bank's investment program must meet the needs and expectations of multiple parties. Most large, international banks are typically companies with publicly issued securities, which are expected to maximize the net present value of shareholders' capital. As will be seen shortly in greater detail, this hinges importantly on the ability of banks to manage the volatility of the value of shareholders' capital.

On the liability side, bank customers are comprised of a variety of depositors, including individuals, corporations, and municipalities. Individuals deposit cash and depend on banks to safeguard their assets over time. Legal entities, ranging from small privately held companies to large publicly listed corporations, often have multiple banking relationships and depend on banks to provide financing throughout economic cycles. Similarly, municipalities and other public entities deposit funds and rely on banks' safekeeping and transaction services. In addition, both for their own account and for the benefit of customers, banks are important counterparties to both publicly traded and over-the-counter derivatives transactions. Finally, most global banking institutions are significant issuers of fixed-income securities, either directly or via such other means as asset-backed trusts.

On the asset side, bank customers include both retail and commercial borrowers. Individuals borrow money from banks to finance large purchases, such as houses that are often financed with mortgages. On the corporate side, real estate developers often require bank financing through commercial real estate loans. Additionally, large companies require commercial and industrial loans from banks in order to finance working capital, ongoing operations, or capital improvements.

Internal stakeholders include a bank's employees, management, and board of directors. Notably, the largest banks may each have more than 200,000 employees around the globe. At banks with a national or global presence, management teams are often highly visible in regulatory and economic affairs. At the regional and local level, bank management teams are often integrated within the local business community.

17.1 Banks—Liabilities and Investment Horizon

Banks are unique in that they originate assets (loans), liabilities (deposits, derivatives, fixed-income securities), and capital (preferred and common stock) in the normal course of business. The ability to originate and manage both assets and liabilities has implications for the management of a bank's interest rate risk exposure (i.e., asset/liability gap management) and the volatility of equity capitalization.

The largest component of bank assets is loans, typically comprising up to 50% or more of the assets of the large, international banks that dominate the sector. The next largest component of assets is debt securities, typically accounting for 25% or more of total assets. The largest remaining portion of assets consists of currency, deposits with central banks (e.g., Bank of Japan or Bank of England), receivables, and bullion.

Banks' liabilities are comprised of deposits and also include short-term funding, such as commercial paper, as well as longer term debt. Deposits are the largest component of liabilities, usually more than half of total liabilities. Bank deposits include the following:

- **Time deposits** or **term deposits** – These interest-bearing accounts have a specified maturity date. This category includes savings accounts and certificates of deposit (CDs). Banks have visibility on the duration of these deposits because they require advance notice prior to withdrawal.

- **Demand deposits** – These accounts can be drawn upon regularly and without notice. This category includes checking accounts and certain savings accounts that are often accessible through online banks or automated teller machines (ATMs). Consequently, banks have limited visibility on the expected lives of these accounts and tend to assume they are short-term in duration.

In addition to deposits, banks can access wholesale funding, sources of which include Federal Funds, public funds, and other government-supported, short-term vehicles. Banks must actively monitor the expected cash outlays and timing of their liabilities. For time deposits, the amount and timing of the cash outlay are known, while for demand deposits, the amount is known but the timing is uncertain. Other liabilities comprise (1) long-term debt, 10%–15% of total balance sheet; and (2) such items as trading/securities payables and repurchase finance payables, also on the order of 10%–20% of balance sheet liabilities.

The tactical investment horizon for a bank's investment portfolio is directly impacted by the nature and maturities of its asset base and liability structure.[7] Although commercial banks, as corporations, have a perpetual time horizon (possibly longer than the other institutions in this reading), the instruments held in a bank portfolio tend to have far shorter maturities than those held by other financial institutions.

The difference between the long time horizon of the institution and the much shorter maturity of most of its assets and liabilities may seem counterintuitive. Suppose that in the current market, the credit spreads on loans are narrow and the economy is nearing recession. The long-term horizon of the bank is evidenced by it: (1) cutting back new lending, (2) selling part of its existing loan portfolio, (3) increasing allocations to short-maturity, liquid securities, and (4) decreasing leverage through fewer large wholesale time deposits. The bank is sacrificing current earnings while looking forward to an uncertain time horizon when it can aggressively expand in the more favorable future environment. The long-term time horizon means that it expects to apply similar tactics—with medium to short-term maturity assets and liabilities—many more times over the indefinite future.

17.2 Banks—Liquidity Needs

Liquidity management is a core consideration in the management of bank portfolios. Given the short duration of deposits, as well as the potential need for increased liquidity in adverse market conditions, management and regulators have developed a robust framework around liquidity management for bank portfolios. Apart from asset or cash flow securitization, banks must have the ability to liquidate their investment portfolios within a certain period to generate adequate cash in the event of a crisis.

Bank liquidity needs have evolved since the global financial crisis of 2007–2009. Prior to that period, deficiencies in liquidity from deposits were made up with wholesale funding; banks would use their portfolios as a source of return so were invested

---

[7] Its strategic horizon is perpetuity because of its corporate structure, which makes it as long, or longer, than many defined benefit plans, endowments, foundations, and sovereign wealth funds.

in lower quality, less liquid securities. In the post-crisis environment, however, bank portfolios are increasingly comprised of higher quality, more liquid securities. This trend to more conservative management of investment portfolios has largely been driven by increased regulatory scrutiny on a global basis, most noticeably through the introduction of mandated liquidity coverage ratios (LCRs) and net stable funding ratios (NSFRs).[8]

In general, contrasting commercial banks and retail-oriented banks, commercial banks have a higher cost of funds and lower liquidity because of wholesale funding of loan commitments and other contingent commitments. Conversely, retail banks have a lower cost of funds and better liquidity because their retail deposits are relatively low cost and tend to be more stable.

INSURERS: STAKEHOLDERS, LIABILITIES, INVESTMENT HORIZON, AND LIQUIDITY NEEDS

18

i. describe considerations affecting the balance sheet management of banks and insurers

The stakeholders of insurers include such external parties as shareholders, derivatives counterparties, policyholders, creditors, regulators, and rating agencies as well as such internal parties as employees, management, and boards of directors. Insurance companies are organized as either companies with publicly listed securities or mutual companies.

In North America and Europe, most large insurers are companies with publicly issued securities, with the inherent shareholder concerns and pressures. As such, there is significant interest and scrutiny on quarterly investment performance, corporate earnings, and balance sheet strength. Within this context, as with banks, optimal management must focus on the long-term maximization of net present value of shareholders' capital. Concretely, this requires balancing expected returns on investments and policy writing in such a way that all insurance liabilities will be met. This requires a very strong focus by management and regulators on maintaining tight control over the volatility of the value of shareholder capital. Capital must be maintained at all investment horizons and under all scenarios so that the company will be able to honor its obligations, especially to policyholders.

Mutual companies are owned by policyholders. Mutual companies either retain profits as surplus or rebate excess cash to policyholders in the form of dividends or premium reductions.[9] Although mutual companies are free from the shareholder pressure for earnings performance, they have less access to capital markets than peers with publicly issued securities. Mutual companies remain quite prevalent in the United States, Canada, Japan, and many European countries. To provide certainty that policyholders are paid under all economic conditions, the need to control and maintain capital surplus is fundamentally the same as in the case of for-profit insurers.

Customers are primarily policyholders who have a need to protect themselves against specific risks. The main objective of any insurance company investment program is to fund policyholder benefits and claims.

---

[8] LCRs require that highly liquid assets must constitute more than 100% of highly probable near-term expected cash outflows. NSFRs set minimum requirements for stable funding sources relative to assets; such stable sources include capital, long-term debt, and non-volatile deposits.
[9] Mutual companies can also increase the amount of "paid up insurance" for whole-life policies.

Given the nature and requirements of their product suite, life insurers maintain both a **general account** and **separate accounts**. For traditional life insurance products and fixed annuities, insurers bear all the risks—particularly mortality risk and longevity risk, respectively—so they maintain a general account of assets to fund future liabilities from these products. However, in the case of variable life and variable annuity products, customers make investment decisions from a menu of options and themselves bear investment risk. Consequently, insurers invest the assets arising from these products within separate accounts. Exhibit 21 summarizes the main bearers of investment risk and the account structure for the major categories of insurance and annuity products.

Exhibit 21	Main Investment Risk Bearers for Different Insurance Products	
Products	Bearer of Investment Risk	Account
Whole and term life insurance	Company	General
Universal life insurance	Company	General
Fixed annuities	Company	General
Variable life insurance	Policyholder	Separate
Variable annuities	Policyholder	Separate

The insurance industry is tightly regulated in most countries, usually by state or national authorities. The regulatory environment, including constraints impacting insurance asset management, will be discussed shortly. The rating agencies—including A.M. Best, Standard & Poor's, Moody's, and Fitch—are stakeholders in the management of insurance investment portfolios because they monitor the financial stability of insurance companies and provide credit ratings and data on the industry to the investment community globally.

An insurance company's management team and employees are also direct stakeholders. The large global insurance companies may have thousands of employees spread over many countries. Their management teams are often highly visible in terms of regulatory and economic affairs. Clearly, the employees are impacted by the amount of risks taken on an insurance company's balance sheet.

18.1 Insurers—Liabilities and Investment Horizon

Insurance companies manage their investment portfolios with an intense focus on asset/liability management (ALM). Within the insurance industry, the business line is critical because it determines the nature and structure of the liabilities. Further, effective management of liabilities is crucial to the long-term viability of any insurance company.

18.1.1 *Life Insurers*

Broadly speaking, life insurers face a liability stream and time horizon with a long duration. Life insurance involves a range of products, including Individual Life, Group Life and Disability, Individual Annuity, and Retirement Plan products. Life insurance portfolios are comprised of asset accumulation products, with some nuances in the associated liability stream. The liability stream is driven by the predictability of claims, which can vary based on the specific product line. For example, Term Life products have a one-time payout and the predictability is relatively high using statistical and actuarial analyses on large portfolios with many policies. Meanwhile, annuity products involve an ongoing payout with shorter duration that is subject to longevity risk. The nature of the liability stream has important implications for the amount of investment risk that can be tolerated.

Within life insurance, product features and resulting liabilities as well as policyholder behavior are key determinants of the associated portfolios' investment horizons. Historically, life insurance companies set portfolio return objectives with long time horizons of 20 to 40 years.

18.1.2 Property & Casualty Insurers

In general, P&C insurers face a shorter duration liability stream and investment horizon than life insurers. Further, P&C insurance involves events with lower probability of occurrence and potentially higher cost (especially in the case of natural disasters), leading to highly volatile business claims. This results in a liability stream with short duration and high uncertainty.

For example, a P&C insurance company may initiate policies against catastrophic events, such as hurricanes or other natural disasters. By definition, this insurance involves unpredictable and infrequent events that are difficult to hedge against. Insurance companies utilize statistical and actuarial analyses to forecast liability cash flows on a probabilistic (scenario) basis. P&C insurers may benefit from developing global, diversified portfolios that are more applicable to statistical analysis because of the law of large numbers. In any case, P&C insurers face a liability stream with a shorter duration and more potential volatility than life insurers.

With both life and P&C insurers, as with banks, the nature and timing of expected policy claims strongly influence the time horizon and nature of investments held. Even so, the ultimate management time horizon is perpetuity. A natural and frequently occurring example for both types of insurers is the case of underwriting cycles. Such cycles relate to the pricing of newly issued policies relative both to then-existing expected security returns and to the actuarial outlook for life and casualty loss claims. Long-term strategic investment and balance-sheet management policies result in modifications to portfolios and overall company leverage at different points in time to adjust to the varying relative attractiveness of bearing investment risk versus bearing underwriting risk and/or financial (leverage) risk.

18.2 Insurers—Liquidity Needs

Insurance companies must actively manage and monitor the liquidity of their portfolios. The level of liquidity required has important implications across the portfolio management process, including the insurer's ability to utilize leverage. Further, liquidity needs can vary greatly based on the business line.

Both life and P&C insurers need a sound, two-part liquidity plan that includes internal and external components. An insurer's internal liquidity includes cash and cash equivalents maintained on the balance sheet. Insurers must actively manage cash from operations (including investment income) that involves steady inflows and outflows. Further, insurers manage and project the cash flows from investment portfolio income and principal repayments. An insurer's external liquidity includes the ability to issue bonds in the capital markets and to access credit lines through syndicated commercial bank credit lines or other lines of credit. Finally, insurers manage short-term liquidity by actively buying and selling repurchase agreements. In this way, insurers consistently manage both internal and external sources of liquidity.

The liquidity needs of life insurance companies must also be considered in the context of the interest rate environment. In periods of rising/high interest rates, insurance companies may face the risk of significant net cash outflow as policies are surrendered by customers searching for higher yields in other investments. P&C insurers face uncertainty regarding both the value and timing of the payment of benefits.

This significant cash flow uncertainty necessitates maintaining ample liquidity and results in P&C portfolios comprised of high proportions of cash and cash substitutes as well as short-term fixed-income instruments.

Insurers segment general account investment portfolios into two major components: **reserve portfolio** and **surplus portfolio**. Insurance companies are typically subject to specific regulatory requirements to maintain a reserve portfolio that is intended to ensure the company's ability to meet its policy liabilities. The surplus portfolio is intended to realize higher expected returns. Insurance companies manage reserve assets relatively conservatively. The size of the reserve portfolio is typically dictated by statute, and assets must be highly liquid and low risk. Meanwhile, insurance companies have more of an ability to assume liquidity risk in the surplus portfolio. Insurance companies are often willing to manage these assets aggressively with exposure to alternative assets, including private equity, hedge funds, and non-security assets.

19 BANKS AND INSURERS: INVESTMENT OBJECTIVES

i. describe considerations affecting the balance sheet management of banks and insurers

We now consider the investment objectives of banks followed by a discussion of investment objectives and an investment policy statement for insurers.

19.1 Banks

The investment securities portfolio of a bank is an integral component of the overall banking enterprise. The primary objective of a bank's securities investment portfolio is to manage the bank's liquidity and risk position relative to its non-securities assets, derivatives positions, liabilities, and shareholders' capitalization. Given the highly regulated nature of the industry, banks typically have formally documented investment policies as well as multiple levels of oversight in the form of internal committees and external regulators.

What follows provides a real-life example of how investment objectives are framed at banks.

Bank Investment Objective
JPMorgan Chase & Co., Treasury and Chief Investment Officer Overview

"Treasury and CIO are predominantly responsible for measuring, monitoring, reporting and managing the Firm's liquidity, funding and structural interest rate and foreign exchange risks, as well as executing the Firm's capital plan. ... The risks managed by Treasury and CIO arise from the activities undertaken by the Firm's four major reportable business segments to serve their respective client bases, which generate both on- and off-balance sheet assets and liabilities.

> Treasury and CIO achieve the Firm's asset-liability management objectives generally by investing in high-quality securities that are managed for the longer-term as part of the Firm's investment securities portfolio. Treasury and CIO also use derivatives to meet the Firm's asset- liability management objectives."
>
> *Source:* JPMorgan Chase & Co., *Annual Report 2016*, https://www.jpmorganchase.com/corporate/investor-relations/document/2016-annualreport.pdf.

Banks establish an asset/liability management committee ("ALMCo") that provides direction and oversight of the investment portfolio. The ALMCo has significant visibility with the bank's management and board of directors, as well as with external regulators. This ALMCo sets the investment policy statement (IPS), monitors performance on an ongoing basis, and has the ability to mandate adjustments on the asset and liability sides of the balance sheet. The ALMCo also ensures that market (interest rate and FX), credit, liquidity, and solvency (capital adequacy) risk positions are within the limits of the bank's specified risk tolerances. Once the overall investment objectives and risk levels are set, the investment team establishes policy benchmarks. The investment team monitors performance and such portfolio characteristics as duration and convexity relative to the benchmark for each asset class. Further, the investment team may monitor performance relative to a set of peers with comparable business models and investment objectives. Finally, the investment team makes periodic presentations to senior management and the board of directors regarding performance and characteristics of the investment portfolio.

19.2 Insurers

Given the highly regulated nature of the insurance industry, a detailed and well-documented Investment Policy Statement is of paramount importance. It is a best practice for an IPS to take a holistic approach and include the parent company's strategic enterprise risk management framework. Similar to banks, insurers manage their investment portfolios with a focus on liquidity as well as interest rate, foreign exchange, credit, and other risk factors.

The investment oversight function is a critical part of an insurer's overall governance. Insurers typically have a committee on the board of directors that maintains oversight of all investment policies, procedures, strategies, and performance evaluation. Insurers provide significant transparency to their underlying portfolios—including showing the inherent duration, credit, and other risks to regulators and other external stakeholders.

The IPS should encompass the insurer's appetite for market risk, credit risk, and interest rate risk. An insurer's risk tolerance may vary relative to the competitive environment for various product lines, regulatory and tax changes, market conditions, and other factors. Moreover, the IPS should be a "living document" that evolves as market, regulatory, and business conditions change.

Hypothetical Life Insurance Company—Investment Policy Statement

I. Introduction

XYZ Life Insurance Company ("the Company") underwrites and markets life insurance and annuity products. The Company is licensed to provide insurance products in all 50 US states, as well as several foreign countries. This investment policy statement ("IPS") documents the policies and procedures that govern the Company's general account securities portfolio. There are detailed policy statements for each asset segment within the portfolio that provide a more granular breakdown of investment guidelines.

II. Governance and Stakeholders

The Company's investment policies, including investment objectives and constraints, are the responsibility of the Investment and Finance Committee ("IFC") of the board of directors ("BoD"). The insurer's senior management team ("Mgmt") is responsible for implementation of the investment program consistent with this policy. In turn, the investment team ("InvTeam") manages the investment portfolio on a day-to-day basis.

The IFC will review the investment policy on an annual basis. The IFC must consider changes to the Company's strategic direction, regulatory changes, tax changes, financial market conditions, and any other relevant factors that may arise. The IFC proposes adjustments to the IPS to the BoD, and all material changes must be approved by the BoD in their entirety.

The IFC has responsibility to employ appropriate resources for the management of the investment portfolio. The IFC may retain or dismiss InvTeam personnel at its discretion. Further, the IFC may retain investment consultants or other advisers to manage specific asset classes or other sub-components of the portfolio. All consultant, external investment managers, and other advisers are required to comply with this IPS.

III. Mission and Investment Objective

The core mission of the general account is twofold:

1 Provide liquidity for the payment of policyholder claims in the normal course of insurance operations.

2 Grow the Company's surplus over the long-term.

The investment objective must follow prudent investing practices and achieve an appropriate balance between maintaining short-term liquidity and contributing to long-term asset growth.

IV. Risk Tolerance and Constraints

The Company is subject to significant scrutiny from internal and external stakeholders, including shareholders, regulators, and others. The general account investment program must take into account the following key factors:

- **Liquidity.** The investment portfolio must maintain sufficient liquidity to meet all policyholder claims that may arise on a short-term and long-term basis. The InvTeam monitors investment cash flow to ensure the Company's ability to meet all obligations in a timely manner. Further, the InvTeam may liquidate publicly traded securities as a secondary source of liquidity.
- **Interest Rate Risk.** The InvTeam monitors the portfolio's exposure to changes in interest rates, including the relative exposure of both assets and liabilities.
- **Credit Risk.** The InvTeam monitors the credit (default) risk inherent in the portfolio and must continually monitor the financial health of key counterparties.
- **Foreign Exchange Risk.** The Company is subject to foreign exchange risk in the normal course of business. The InvTeam monitors the aggregate foreign exchange risk of the portfolio.
- **Regulatory Requirements.** All investments must adhere to the insurance code of the Company's state of domicile as well as all other applicable domestic and foreign guidelines. Further, the investment program must comply with risk-based capital considerations and rating agency requirements.

- **Tax Considerations.** Further, the securities portfolio must account for tax considerations, and all investment decisions should be evaluated on an after-tax basis. The income tax planning of the Company may impact the timing of realization of capital gains and losses.

V. Asset Allocation Policy, Allowable Ranges, and Benchmarks

The primary investment vehicles within the Company's investment portfolio will consist of highly liquid instruments, including US and foreign government obligations, corporate debt, and other fixed-income instruments. Further, the Company may invest in private placement bonds, commercial mortgage loans, and other less liquid instruments within the parameters specified. Further, the Company may invest in real estate and private equity in order to enhance long-term returns and contribute to the surplus growth of the company. However, strict guidelines apply for less liquid asset classes.

The IFC establishes the strategic asset allocation that is consistent with the long-term constraints of the Company. The IFC will review the strategic asset allocation annually and may make adjustments as appropriate. Further, the IFC sets out allowable ranges of allocation for each asset class. Further, the IFC approves appropriate benchmarks for each asset class upon consultation with the InvTeam.

VI. Investment Guidelines

The InvTeam should seek to diversify holdings in terms of economic exposure, counterparty, and other applicable attributes to the extent possible. Securities that are guaranteed by the US government or its agencies must constitute at least 25% of the portfolio.

VII. Reporting

The InvTeam, with the oversight of Mgmt, must provide adequate reporting to the BoD and other stakeholders. The reporting structure should include the following:

- Daily Flash Report: Summary of market values, yield, and interest rate position of entire portfolio
- Monthly Investment Performance Detail: Detailed investment performance by asset class, including market values, yields, and interest rate position
- Quarterly Investment Summary: Detailed analysis of market values, yield, and interest rate exposure, including long-term performance metrics and attribution

BANKS AND INSURERS: BALANCE SHEET MANAGEMENT AND INVESTMENT CONSIDERATIONS | 20

i. describe considerations affecting the balance sheet management of banks and insurers

We turn now to the portfolio investment strategy for banks and insurance companies. The objectives and constraints are very different from what we have seen with respect to pensions, sovereign wealth funds, endowments, and foundations. In the case of banks and insurance companies, the need is to fund deposits, policy claims, derivatives payoffs, and debtholders. A financial institution's fundamental purpose is to assure such contractual parties the full and timely payment of claims when they come due. A firm can only hope to earn a profit if it can provide counterparties assurance it will be able to meet all claims with extremely high probability.

The financial claims against banks and insurers may not always be known with certainty, but they are, at any point in time, measurable. Such measurement may require the use of probabilistic methods to account for such outcomes as: (1) the liquidation of bank deposits; (2) insurance policy claims and surrenders; (3) losses on derivatives, guarantees, or forward purchase commitments; and (4) returns on variable annuities, among other outcomes. Thus, in the case of banks and insurers, the well-defined, contractual nature of the financial claims, along with their measurability, imply that—unlike with defined benefit and defined contribution pension plans, sovereign wealth funds, endowments, and foundations—the underlying investment strategy is mainly liability driven investing (LDI as earlier defined).

We can obtain insight about both investment strategy and regulation of financial institutions by applying a fairly simple but intuitive economic model. The model's first two equations define the relationship between an institution's assets A, liabilities (claims) L, and residual equity of the institution's shareholders or members E:

$$A = L + E \tag{1}$$

$$\Delta A = \Delta L + \Delta E \tag{2}$$

Assets are equal to the sum of contractual claims and residual ownership. Likewise, all changes in assets must equal the sum of changes in the value of contractual claims and ownership interest (equity capitalization). These equations are set forth in terms of current market—or economic—values, which will not necessarily coincide with GAAP, IFRS, or regulatory/statutory values. However, using current market values will facilitate the subsequent application of these other accounting valuations.

These equations can be used to understand not just market value changes but also the impact of earnings, the consequences of adding or selling off assets in total, and changes in an institution's capital structure. All of these are relevant to investment strategy and are additional layers of complexity as compared with the other portfolio strategies in this reading.

By multiplying the various terms by 1 (i.e., $A \div A$ or $L \div L$), dividing both sides by E, and doing a little regrouping, we obtain a useful expression, namely:

$$\frac{\Delta A}{A}\left(\frac{A}{E}\right) = \frac{\Delta L}{L}\left(\frac{L}{E}\right) + \frac{\Delta E}{E} \tag{3}$$

Using Equation 1 and moving liabilities and assets to the same side of the equation, we rewrite this as:

$$\frac{\Delta E}{E} = \frac{\Delta A}{A}\left(\frac{A}{E}\right) - \frac{\Delta L}{L}\left(\frac{A-E}{E}\right) = \frac{\Delta A}{A}\left(\frac{A}{E}\right) - \frac{\Delta L}{L}\left(\frac{A}{E}-1\right) \tag{4}$$

Equation 4 provides an easy way to see how percentage changes in market value of both assets and liabilities are magnified by the leverage factors.

To demonstrate this point, Exhibit 22 presents the effects on the market value of the institution's equity capital as a function of (i) declines in underlying asset value,[10] and (ii) beginning degree of leverage. Asset values can decline for several reasons, such as deterioration in credit quality and/or liquidity of loans or securities held. The value of assets can also be hurt by rising interest rates in the case of fixed-rate loans or securities.

---

[10] Which, for our analysis, focuses on the investment portfolio assets. The net equity described here is net financial equity. The portion of an institution's equity associated with financing other assets, such as buildings and equipment, are not a focus of this reading.

Exhibit 22   Effects on Market Value of Equity Due to Change in Market Value of Assets (Given Beginning Degree of Leverage)

Beg. Equity to Assets Ratio (E÷A)	Leverage (x) (A÷E)	Percentage Change in Institution's Equity Value Due to Change in Asset Value of:			
		−0.5%	−1.0%	−1.5%	−2.0%
20%	5.0	−2.5%	−5.0%	−7.5%	−10.0%
15%	6.7	−3.3%	−6.7%	−10.0%	−13.3%
10%	10.0	−5.0%	−10.0%	−15.0%	−20.0%
5%	20.0	−10.0%	−20.0%	−30.0%	−40.0%

This analysis reveals that even small losses in the market value of assets can have a pronounced negative effect on the institution's equity capital account because of the leverage factor. Naturally, it works in reverse; Small gains in assets can have a very positive impact for equity capital holders. These relationships give rise to a conflict of interest: Because equity capital holders can only lose the value of their investment but also can make extremely large gains if assets perform well, liability holders require some form of protection against the potential inclination of the institution to take excessive risks. Contractual, regulatory, and reputational methods all come into play to provide such protection. In one form or another, they relate to limiting the volatility of assets and providing for a capital cushion so that equity capital holders, rather than liability holders, are expected to absorb unforeseen losses on assets.

Similarly, financial institutions face the possibility of loss from adverse changes in the market value of liabilities. In the case of insurance companies, unexpectedly high policy loss claims are the most notable cause of expanding liabilities. For banks, it could be having to make a forward-funding commitment to a struggling company, the exercise of a guarantee, or a loss on forward currency purchase contracts. Exhibit 23 uses Equation 4 to illustrate the effect on the market value of the institution's equity capital as a function of (i) increases in its liabilities and (ii) beginning degree of leverage.

Exhibit 23   Effects on Market Value of Equity Due to Change in Market Value of Liabilities (Given Beginning Degree of Leverage)

Beg. Equity to Assets Ratio (E÷A)	Leverage (x) [(A÷E) − 1]	Percentage Change in Institution's Equity Value Due to Change in Liability Value of:			
		+0.5%	+1.0%	+1.5%	+2.0%
20%	4.0	−2.0%	−4.0%	−6.0%	−8.0%
15%	5.7	−2.8%	−5.7%	−8.5%	−11.3%
10%	9.0	−4.5%	−9.0%	−13.5%	−18.0%
5%	19.0	−9.5%	−19.0%	−28.5%	−38.0%

Exhibit 23 bolsters the conclusions reached in Exhibit 22. Mainly, liability holders, regulators, and owners (equity shareholders) of a financial institution all are motivated to limit the volatility and magnitude, relative to the base capital level, of market value changes in the institution's liabilities.

Now we must integrate the analysis of both sides of the balance sheet with the capital management strategy of the financial institution. To do this, we would like to have a framework for understanding various interactions in a more rigorous manner.

A customary starting point is with an analysis of interest rate risk. Our framework comfortably accommodates the standard duration-based model of value changes with respect to interest rate changes. In order to find the percentage change in the value of the institution's equity capital associated with a change in the reference yield, y, on the asset holdings, we divide Equation 4 by the change in such yield, thereby obtaining:

$$\frac{\Delta E}{E \Delta y} = \frac{\Delta A}{A \Delta y}\left(\frac{A}{E}\right) - \frac{\Delta L}{L \Delta y}\left(\frac{A}{E} - 1\right) \qquad (5)$$

Likewise, we want to understand how this relates to the change in the effective yield on the liabilities, i. Multiplying by $1 = \Delta i \div \Delta i$ in the appropriate location, we restate Equation 5 as:

$$\frac{\Delta E}{E \Delta y} = \frac{\Delta A}{A \Delta y}\left(\frac{A}{E}\right) - \frac{\Delta L}{L \Delta i}\left(\frac{\Delta i}{\Delta y}\right)\left(\frac{A}{E} - 1\right) \qquad (6)$$

Recall that the modified duration of asset W with respect to its yield-to-maturity, r, (D_W^*) is defined as:

$$D_W^* = -\frac{\Delta W}{W \Delta r} \qquad (7)$$

This allows us to revise Equation 6 to a practical and intuitive analytical tool, namely,

$$D_E^* = \left(\frac{A}{E}\right)D_A^* - \left(\frac{A}{E} - 1\right)D_L^*\left(\frac{\Delta i}{\Delta y}\right) \qquad (8)$$

Over reasonably modest yield changes, Equation 8 provides a useful way to break down the volatility of a financial institution's equity capital as a function of degree of leverage, comparative (modified) duration of assets and liabilities, and correlation (or sensitivity) of changes in yields of assets and liabilities.

Exhibits 24 and 25 show how sensitive the valuation of equity is to changes in the security portfolio yield for differing degrees of mismatching of asset and liability durations. In both these exhibits, the x-axis shows the duration of the financial institution's liabilities, the y-axis shows the duration of its security portfolio assets, and the z-axis (vertical axis) shows the resulting duration of the institution's shareholders' equity. The yields on liabilities are assumed to move only 90% as much as the yields on portfolio assets. That is,

$$\frac{di}{dy} = \frac{\Delta i}{\Delta y} = 0.90$$

Exhibits 24 and 25 show results for differing initial degrees of leverage, as measured by the equity-to-assets ratio, which is 20% and 10%, respectively.

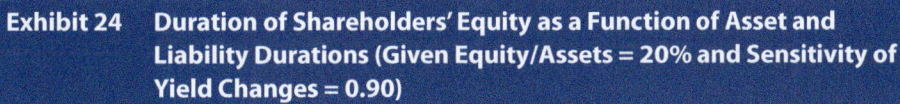

Exhibit 24 Duration of Shareholders' Equity as a Function of Asset and Liability Durations (Given Equity/Assets = 20% and Sensitivity of Yield Changes = 0.90)

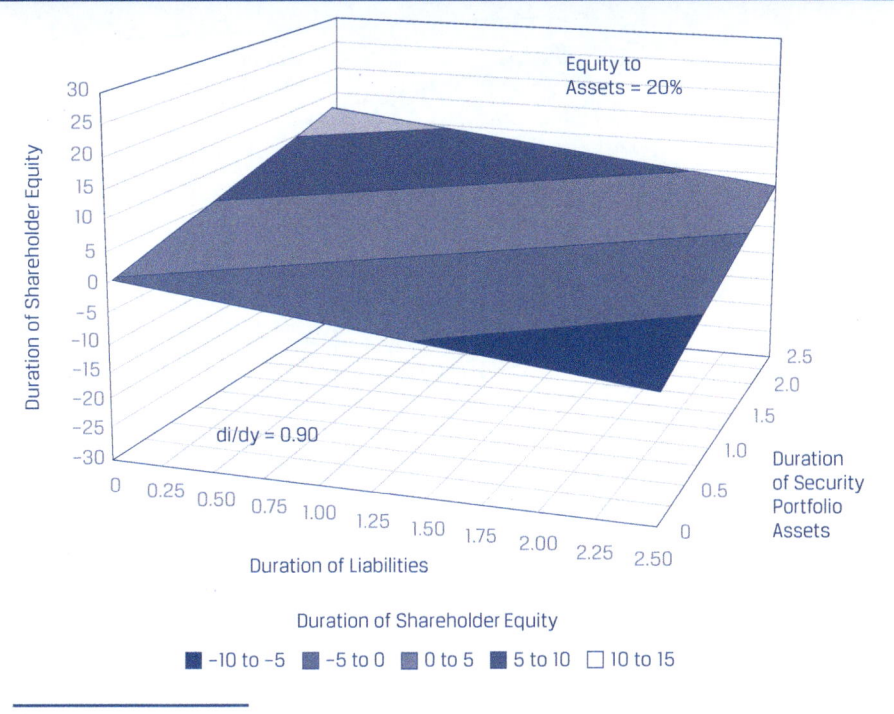

Source: Authors

Exhibit 24 indicates that, even at relatively high capital ratios of 20%, moderate differences between asset and liability durations can imply durations for equity that can be sizable in either a positive or negative direction. Remember that, by definition, the modified duration of a zero-coupon bond is its final maturity divided by one plus its yield. Thus, by comparison, a 10-year zero coupon bond would have a modified duration around 9.75. Utilizing Equation 7, a +/− 100 basis point change in interest rates when multiplied by a modified duration of 9.75 implies an approximate +/− 10% change in value. It is highly unlikely that regulators would like to see large asset/liability duration mismatches, since regulators want equity capital to remain stable in periods of large adverse interest rate changes.

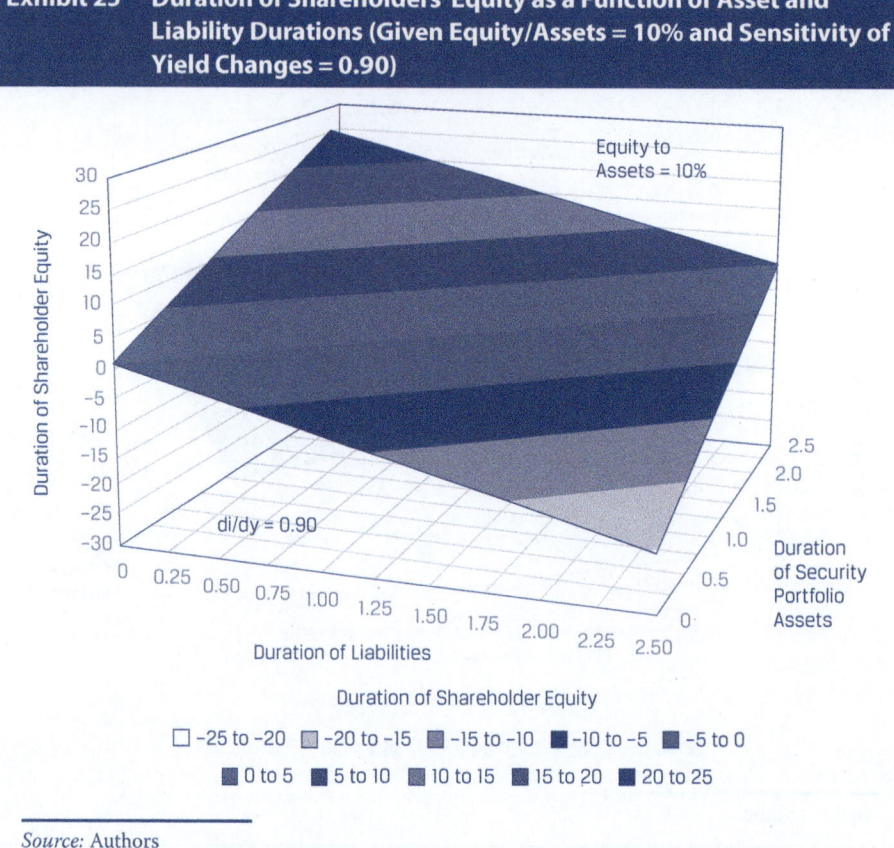

Exhibit 25 Duration of Shareholders' Equity as a Function of Asset and Liability Durations (Given Equity/Assets = 10% and Sensitivity of Yield Changes = 0.90)

Source: Authors

In Exhibit 25, we see that lowering the equity capital ratio to 10% means that in order to avoid very high durations for equity capitalization, it is all the more necessary to keep assets and liabilities from having large differences in duration. It is often mistakenly thought that banks (and to a lesser degree, insurance companies) climb the yield curve by raising capital through the issuance of short maturity deposits that they then invest in longer duration loans and securities. The foregoing exhibits indicate the potential dangers of such an asset/liability mismatch. In Exhibit 25, assuming a liability duration of close to zero (very short-term deposits and overnight borrowing), even if the security portfolio duration is only 2.5 years, the duration of shareholder's equity reaches 25 years (about the equivalent of a 26-year zero coupon bond). In such a case, a +/– 100 basis point change in asset yields would produce a +/– 25% change in shareholder equity value. The loss potential is a danger that neither deposit holders, creditors, stockholders, nor regulators would be keen to embrace.

In actuality, in order to lower asset duration, financial institutions hold cash, deposits at central banks, foreign currency reserves, and other highly liquid (zero duration) assets. Also, as a means of lowering effective asset durations, banks typically make business loans that float according to market reference rates, which are expected to move in line with the variable cost of deposits. Likewise, credit card and many real estate loans are tied to variable rate indexes in order to minimize the sensitivity of values to interest rates. Moreover, many fixed-rate mortgage loans are securitized and sold off to private investors. All these foregoing techniques are ways of limiting the duration of asset portfolios.

On the liability side, there are many ways in which the duration of liabilities can be extended far beyond the implicit zero duration of demand deposits. These include issuance of intermediate and longer-term debt instruments, deeply subordinated capital securities, and perpetual preferred stock. Finally, banks can and do utilize financial futures and interest rate swaps to alleviate asset/liability mismatches.

In the light of persistent low interest rates since the global financial crisis of 2007–2009, many large international banks have an asset/liability structure where earnings are poised to benefit from a rise in interest rates. In such cases, the duration of assets is actually shorter than the duration of liabilities. This is clearly not the naïve "borrow short and lend long" strategy.

EXAMPLE 7

MegaWorld Bancorp has an equity capital ratio for financial assets of 9%. The modified duration of its assets is 2.0 and of its liabilities is 1.5. Over small changes, the yield on liabilities is expected to move by 85 bps for every 100 bps of yield change in its asset portfolio.

1. Compute the modified duration of the bank's equity capital.
2. What would be the impact on the value of shareholder capital of a 50 basis point rise in the level of yields on its asset portfolio?
3. Management is considering issuing common stock, selling investment portfolio assets, and paying off some liabilities in order to achieve an equity capitalization ratio of 10%. Assuming no change in the durations of assets and liabilities and assuming no change in the sensitivity of liability yields to asset yields, what is the resulting modified duration of the bank's equity capital?
4. Using the facts in question 3 but assuming the bank rebalances its investment portfolio to achieve a modified duration of assets of 1.75, what happens to the duration of the bank's equity capital?

Solution 1:

Using Equation 8, $A \div E = 1/0.09 = 11.11$; $(A \div E) - 1 = 10.11$; $D_A^* = 2.0$; $D_L^* = 1.5$; and $\Delta i \div \Delta y = 0.85$.

Therefore, the modified duration of shareholders' capital is:

$$D_E^* = (11.11 \times 2) - (10.11 \times 1.50) \times 0.85 = 9.33$$

Solution 2:

Using the implications of Equation 7, the change in equity capitalization value is computed as:

0.5% × −9.33 = −4.67%.

Solution 3:

With this less leveraged balance sheet, $A \div E = 1/0.1 = 10$; $(A \div E) - 1 = 9$; and the duration of shareholders' equity is:

$$D_E^* = (10 \times 2) - (9 \times 1.50) \times 0.85 = 8.53$$

Solution 4:

The duration of shareholders' capital now declines to:

$$D_E^* = (10 \times 1.75) - (9 \times 1.50) \times 0.85 = 6.03$$

21. BANKS AND INSURERS: INVESTMENT STRATEGIES AND EFFECTS ON ASSET AND LIABILITY VOLATILITY

i. describe considerations affecting the balance sheet management of banks and insurers

Our previous discussion has given us some insight into the effects of leverage and the volatility of underlying assets and liabilities on the value of a financial institution's equity. The degree of leverage was given; the sensitivity of changes in liability to asset yields (di/dy) was constant; and the durations of assets and liabilities varied. Although quite useful in many circumstances, such duration analysis captures the effects of only small changes in overall levels of interest rates and only over short time intervals.[11] Although of great significance, changes in the overall levels of interest rates are only one source of volatility. An expansion of Equation 4 is therefore necessary. A natural step is to extend it in a probabilistic way. We can thereby capture the volatility of the market value change in the financial institution's equity capital as shown in Equation 9. Volatility is defined here as standard deviation, where $\sigma_{\frac{\Delta E}{E}}$, $\sigma_{\frac{\Delta A}{A}}$, and $\sigma_{\frac{\Delta L}{L}}$ represent the standard deviations of the percentage changes in market value of equity capital, asset holdings, and liability claims, respectively.[12] Furthermore, $-1 \leq \rho \leq 1$ denotes the correlation between percentage value changes of assets and liability claims.[13]

$$\sigma^2_{\frac{\Delta E}{E}} = \left(\frac{A}{E}\right)^2 \sigma^2_{\frac{\Delta A}{A}} + \left(\frac{A}{E} - 1\right)^2 \sigma^2_{\frac{\Delta L}{L}} - 2\left(\frac{A}{E}\right)\left(\frac{A}{E} - 1\right) \rho \sigma_{\frac{\Delta A}{A}} \sigma_{\frac{\Delta L}{L}} \quad (9)$$

Equation 9 states the relationship in precise mathematical terms. It also incorporates the concept of correlation, which is an essential element of liability-driven investing. Exhibit 26 is a graphical representation of Equation 9 and illustrates the magnitude of the asset/liability correlation effect (ρ is measured on the x-axis) on the volatility of the financial institution's equity capital ($\sigma_{\frac{\Delta E}{E}}$ is measured on the y-axis) for various levels of leverage (the downward-sloping dotted lines). For purposes of this exhibit, the volatilities of asset and liability percentage value changes ($\sigma_{\frac{\Delta A}{A}}$, $\sigma_{\frac{\Delta L}{L}}$) are both assumed to be constant at 1.5%.

Exhibit 26 demonstrates that over the range of leverage shown (equity/assets ratios from 5% to 20%), the volatility of the financial institution's equity capital decreases as the correlation between asset and liability *value changes* (ρ) increases toward +1.0. This beneficial effect is most pronounced when the financial institution is highly leveraged.

---

[11] Most notably, the duration model does not reflect well on non-linear factors, such as convexity and embedded options in many fixed-income securities and derivatives.

[12] The variance of any random variable is equal to the square of the standard deviation of the variable.

[13] Transforming Equation 4 into Equation 9 follows the basic statistical property that, for any random variable Z, which is a linear sum of two other random variables X and Y (specifically, $Z = AX + BY$), the variance of Z is $\sigma^2_Z = A^2\sigma^2_X + B^2\sigma^2_Y + 2AB\rho\sigma_X\sigma_Y$. This expression does not depend on the nature and shape of the underlying probability distributions of either X or Y.

For example, assuming leverage of 20% (assets/equity = 5x) and correlations (ρ) of 0.5 and then 0.9, the volatility of equity declines from 6.9% to 3.5%. However, if higher leverage is assumed, at 5% equity/assets, and ρ takes the same two values, then the decrease in volatility of equity from 29.3% to 13.2% is more dramatic.

If the correlation between assets and liabilities is 1.0, the volatility of shareholders' equity capital shrinks to minimal amounts, even for high leverage (equity to assets = 5.0%). However, the flip side is that any divergence in correlations—such as can often occur in turbulent markets—causes equity volatility to increase and especially dramatically when leverage is high.

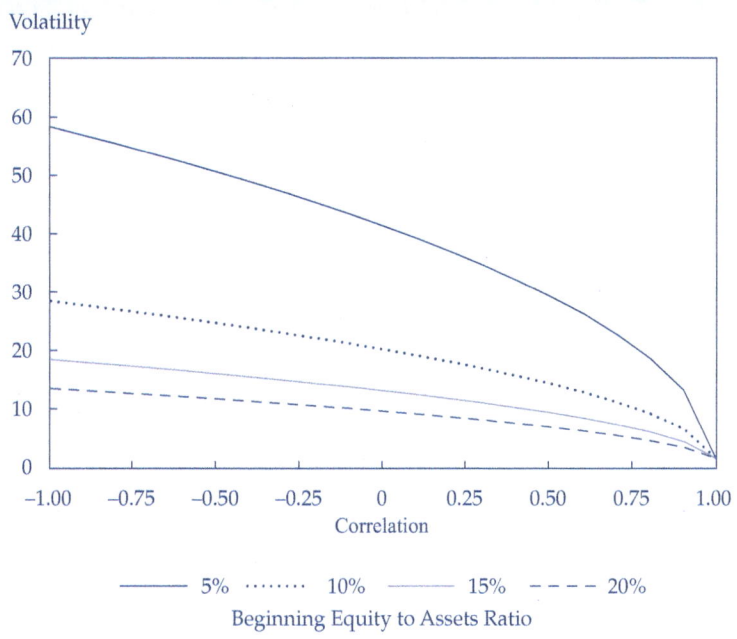

Exhibit 26 Volatility of Value of Shareholders' Equity as a Function of Correlation of Asset and Liability Value Changes and Beginning Leverage

Source: Authors

With the comprehensive framework provided by Equation 9, we next turn to a brief catalogue, shown in Exhibit 27, of how differing portfolio strategies and actions affect the inputs and thus the results of the volatility paradigm in Equation 9. Before doing so, however, it is important to note that hedging with derivatives, duration-based portfolio management and funding, and other techniques for raising the correlation between asset and liability values are not a cure-all. High correlations between assets and liabilities are not easy to achieve in practice, and often breakdown during periods of financial industry stress or stress in an individual institution. In the final analysis, techniques for raising correlations are not a pure substitute for maintaining adequate capitalization buffers.

Exhibit 27 Investment Strategies and Effects on Bank/Insurer Asset & Liability Volatility

Portfolio Strategy Considerations	Main Factors Affected	Explanation/Rationale	Additional Regulatory Concerns
Diversified fixed-income investments	Decreases $\sigma_{\Delta A}/A$	Debt securities are less volatile than common equities, real estate, and other securities.	Effective diversification involves a multiplicity of issuers and industries, both domestic and foreign.
High-Quality bond/debt investments	Decreases $\sigma_{\Delta A}/A$	Overall, higher quality securities are less likely to be downgraded or default, thereby lessening the probability of significant loss of value through either losses or widening of credit spreads.	Regulatory structures and central banks favor sovereign issuers most for this reason.
Maintain reasonable balance between asset and liability durations, key rates durations, and sensitivity to embedded borrower and claimant options	Increases ρ	Requires more in-depth analysis than simple duration-matching strategy, because must account for convexity and asymmetric payoffs due to (i) defaults, (ii) principal payoffs prior to maturity, and (iii) annuity, life-insurance policy, and bank CD surrenders in high interest rate scenarios.	Regulatory structures penalize institutions with unjustifiable asset/liability mismatches.
Common Stock Investments	Increases $\sigma_{\Delta A}/A$, typically decreases ρ	Equity and other high-volatility assets provide only slight diversification benefits while adding to volatility. Also, common stock returns do not correlate well with financial institution returns, which pushes correlation, ρ, away from 1.0 toward 0.0.	Most regulatory structures require 100% or more risk weighting for common stock investments, thus such investments are ineligible for backing financial liability issuance.
Derivatives transparency, collateralization	Decreases both $\sigma_{\Delta A}/A$ and $\sigma_{\Delta L}/L$, and increases ρ	Whether derivatives are used to hedge or synthesize (i) assets or (ii) liabilities, the more "plain vanilla" (and protected against counterparty default) they are, the less likely they will revalue in unexpected directions.	Transparency fosters regulatory "financial stress test" confidence. It also allows regulators and claimants to ascertain whether derivatives are being used in a justifiable manner.
Liquidity of portfolio investments	Decreases $\sigma_{\Delta A}/A$	Includes short-maturity debt securities of highly rated issuers, currency reserves, access to credit lines, and access for banks to emergency central bank borrowing.	Problems occur for regulators when financial contagion extends beyond just a few institutions.
Surrender penalties	Decreases $\sigma_{\Delta L}/L$	For typical life insurance, annuities, and bank deposits, such penalties cushion losses to financial institutions for having to pay back liabilities "at par" when rising interest rates would otherwise have reduced the discounted present value of the obligations.	Properly computed surrender penalties must account for interest rate volatility and slope of the yield curve. Typically, regulators/customers do not tolerate economically justified surrender penalties (they are usually priced too low to offset the institution's risk).

Exhibit 27 (Continued)

Portfolio Strategy Considerations	Main Factors Affected	Explanation/Rationale	Additional Regulatory Concerns
Prepayment penalties on debt investments	Increases ρ	When interest rates are declining, borrowers must incur a penalty to repay loans at par to refinance. Also, prepayment penalties help institutions offset rising values of their fixed-rate liabilities in falling rate environments.	None.
Catastrophic insurance risks	Increases $\frac{\sigma_{\Delta L}}{L}$	By definition, these losses faced by insurance companies are less predictable and possibly very large.	Regulators and insurance customers usually expect (i) higher capital ratios, (ii) higher quality and liquid investment portfolios, and (iii) strong reinsurance agreements compared with typical home, health, auto, and fire insurance.
Predictability of underwriting losses	Decreases $\frac{\sigma_{\Delta L}}{L}$	High frequency, low cost loss events caused by law of large numbers make total insurance liabilities less uncertain.	Adverse changes in legal or regulatory systems cannot be offset by actions on the asset side of the financial institution. These are risks borne by owners of the institution's equity capital.
Diversifying insurance business	Decreases $\frac{\sigma_{\Delta L}}{L}$	Diversifying across several business lines increases aggregate risk-reduction potential (due to law of large numbers).	None.
Variable annuities	Increases ρ, and $\frac{\sigma_{\Delta A}}{A}$, $\frac{\sigma_{\Delta L}}{L}$ diminish in relevance	Where equity/bond market risks are fully borne by policyholders, the correlation between asset and liability returns approaches 1.0, independent of investment performance of the underlying, segregated account assets.	Assuming adequate risk disclosure to policyholders, and sufficient asset custody protections, regulators permit greater investment flexibility than in insurer's standard business lines.

The last key implication of the aggregate risk framework in Equation 9 relates to the importance of raising equity capitalization externally. The ability to raise capital is not just the key to expanding operations; more importantly, it is a way of buffering financial uncertainty. It diminishes both the probability of default to liability holders and the total volatility of equity capitalization values.[14] Over the past several decades, the financial industry has moved increasingly to publicly traded, for-profit, corporations, rather than mutual or membership co-ops. This is primarily because publicly traded companies can issue new common stock capital in cases of either opportunity or emergency. Mutual and membership co-ops (for example, credit unions) are restricted by the growth of their membership, which usually cannot change much over short periods of time.

---

[14] Although raising equity ratios negatively impacts return on common equity (ROCE) and earnings per share of financial companies, the diminished volatility of earnings and economic value acts toward raising price-earnings and market-to-book ratios. Perhaps somewhat counterintuitively, the issuing of common stock by financial companies can be neutral or even a net benefit to pre-existing shareholders.

EXAMPLE 8

Foresight International Assurance is an international multiline insurance conglomerate. Under its overall strategic financial plan, it computes the annualized standard deviation of returns on investment assets as 5.0% and on liabilities as 2.5%. The bulk of its liabilities are constituted by the net present value of expected claims payouts. The correlation between asset and liability returns is therefore a very low 0.25. Foresight's common equity to financial assets ratio is 20.0%.

1. What is the standard deviation of changes in the value of Foresight's shareholder capitalization?

2. Management believes the overall risk profile of the company is too high and desires to increase the common equity ratio by issuing additional shares of common equity and listing such shares on several international stock market exchanges. The new target equity ratio will be 25.0%. All other things being equal, how does this impact the volatility of value changes in shareholder capitalization?

3. Management believes it also needs to lower the volatility of its assets. It shifts out of low-quality bonds into higher quality, more liquid government securities and, by doing so, expects to lower the standard deviation of asset returns to 4.0% per year without having any impact on the correlation ratio between assets and liabilities. Along with the stronger capital ratios premised in question 2, what does this do to the volatility of shareholder equity value?

4. What is the impact of the various portfolio and capitalization changes on the value of Foresight's common shares outstanding? Explain your answer.

Solution to 1:

We use Equation 9 recognizing that $A \div E = 1/0.20 = 5$; $(A \div E) - 1 = 4$; the standard deviation of asset returns ($\sigma_{\frac{\Delta A}{A}}$) = 0.05; the standard deviation of changes in liability values ($\sigma_{\frac{\Delta L}{L}}$) = 0.025; and the correlation between asset and liability value changes (ρ) = 0.25.

First, we compute the variance of shareholders' capital value changes:

$$\sigma^2_{\frac{\Delta E}{E}} = 5^2 \times 0.05^2 + 4^2 \times 0.025^2 - 2 \times 5 \times 4 \times 0.25 \times 0.05 \times 0.025 = 0.06.$$

The standard deviation of shareholder capital valuation change is the square root of the variance. Thus,

$$\sigma_{\frac{\Delta E}{E}} = \sqrt{\sigma^2_{\frac{\Delta E}{E}}} = \sqrt{0.06} = 0.245 = 24.5\% \text{ per year.}$$

Solution to 2:

The new asset to equity ratio is $A \div E = 1/0.25 = 4$, and so $(A \div E) - 1 = 3$. Using the existing values of the other variables in Equation 9, we obtain

$$\sigma^2_{\frac{\Delta E}{E}} = 4^2 \times 0.05^2 + 3^2 \times 0.025^2 - 2 \times 4 \times 3 \times 0.25 \times 0.05 \times 0.025 = 0.038125$$

from which we see $\sigma_{\frac{\Delta E}{E}} = \sqrt{\sigma^2_{\frac{\Delta E}{E}}} = \sqrt{0.038125} \approx 0.195 = 19.5\%$ per year.

Solution to 3:

Equation 9 now produces the following results:

$$\sigma^2_{\frac{\Delta E}{E}} = 4^2 \times 0.04^2 + 3^2 \times 0.025^2 - 2 \times 4 \times 3 \times 0.25 \times 0.04 \times 0.025 = 0.025225$$

from which we obtain $\sigma_{\frac{\Delta E}{E}} = \sqrt{\sigma^2_{\frac{\Delta E}{E}}} = \sqrt{0.025225} \approx 0.159 = 15.9\%$.

Solution to 4:

We note that the proposed changes are likely to reduce earnings per share, first by having a greater number of shares outstanding and second by lowering the expected returns on assets (because there will now be a greater percentage of safer, lower yielding assets). All other things being equal, this would pressure the common stock price. However, Foresight is also lowering its overall equity risk exposure while strengthening its reputation as a more soundly operated and capitalized insurance company. The lower risk profile might well result in a higher credit rating and a lower discount rate at which the lower earnings per share trajectory is valued. Also, the improved long-term survivability and underwriting strength could result in a higher *long-term* growth outlook. In sum, the impact on common equity prices cannot be predicted merely by a change in capital structure and near-term reduction in earnings and portfolio expected returns.

BANKS AND INSURERS: IMPLEMENTATION OF PORTFOLIO DECISIONS   22

i. describe considerations affecting the balance sheet management of banks and insurers

With sovereign wealth funds, endowments, foundations, and employee benefit plans (DB and DC), the investment adviser must primarily focus on the investment of assets. In the case of financial institutions, optimal management must simultaneously focus on liabilities, particularly the volatility and convexity of asset and liability payouts. Consequently, the investment strategy of financial institutions must also consider the appropriate degree of leverage and total amount of common equity capital. Returning to the basic framework of Equations 2 and 4, the proper way to maximize long-term economic earnings thus might be to raise (lower) leverage through: (a) the acquisition (disposal) of portfolio assets; (b) the underwriting (retirement) of liabilities; or (c) the repurchase (issuance) of capital stock.

The financial management of a bank or insurer has not only to deal with the level and direction of interest rates, credit spreads, derivatives markets, economic cycles, and stock markets as they impact the investment portfolio, but we also now see it needs to have a keen understanding of the valuation of its own common equity and debt capital securities. Financial management also requires a view on the actions of competitors. For example, will they create a housing bubble through excessive lending to low-quality borrowers? Will they drive down insurance policy premiums through overly aggressive underwriting? Finally, financial management must satisfy all existing regulations as well as the ones that may evolve with changes in global economic circumstances and other political pressures.

In sum, financial and portfolio management of banks and insurance companies is an attempt to create positive net present value for capital holders by solving simultaneously several different conditions with several different variables. Consequently, key decisions are typically made at the highest levels of the institution's management. Specific analysts and investment managers are typically assigned only to specialized subsets of the institution's varied assets and liabilities.

In such dynamically changing economic and regulatory environments, it is difficult to specify particular portfolio investment rules and policies. Therefore, the following mini-case studies are offered to provide illustrations of the types of high-level portfolio decisions that are required.

EXAMPLE 9

Mini-Case A:

A bank considers reducing its ownership of commercial loans in smaller businesses. These loans pay interest quarterly at various contractually pre-specified spreads above the floating market reference rate (MRR). The runoff of the loan portfolio through repayments, together with proceeds of outright sales and securitizations of other loans, are to be reinvested in a portfolio of fixed-rate government securities of comparable maturities. The securities will be hedged fully against general interest rate risk through the use of publicly traded options and futures on government securities. Additionally, hedging interest rate risk completely would create a synthetic variable rate asset. If interest rates rise, gains on hedges can be reinvested to raise overall portfolio income; if interest rates fall, losses on hedges will require some assets to pay counterparties, thereby lowering overall portfolio income.

1. How would this portfolio restructuring affect the asset/liability profile of the bank?
2. What is the expected impact on the volatility of bank shareholder equity valuation?
3. What is the likely impact on bank earnings?
4. What are reasons that argue in favor of this portfolio redeployment?

Solution to 1:

Switching from variable rate to fixed-rate assets of similar maturities increases the duration of the bank's overall portfolio. However, entering into hedging positions with futures and options on fixed-rate assets has the effect of shortening overall duration. As described, the net effect of the portfolio alteration likely should have little effect on the bank's existing asset/liability duration profile, because floating-rate corporate loans also have little price exposure in the event of rising or falling interest rates.

Solution to 2:

The overall volatility of assets and bank capitalization should decrease, because a hedged portfolio of government securities is more liquid than a portfolio of individual small business loans and also less subject to volatility arising from changes in credit default spreads on corporate loans.

Solution to 3:

Bank earnings would be expected to decline, independent of subsequent changes in the overall level of interest rates. This is because the yields on business loans, adjusting for expected default rates, are higher than on government securities, adjusting for the costs of hedging the government securities. Furthermore, if overall interest rates subsequently rise, the business loan portfolio would generate higher income to the bank. However, hedges on the government securities generate gains when interest rates rise—offsetting losses on the underlying securities and thus permitting more money to be reinvested in now higher yielding government securities. Similarly, a decline in interest rates would lead to a loss on the hedges and a sale of appreciated underlying government securities to cover these hedge losses. The portfolio value is approximately unchanged, but the (reduced) ability to generate income has tracked interest rates downward. In sum, *changes* in overall interest rates impact income-generating ability similarly for both the loan portfolio and the hedged securities portfolio. This is the flip side of the coin; in other words, the two portfolios have similar modified durations. In any environment, the net yields on the hedged government securities are lower than on the business loans. Thus, bank net income is unambiguously lower because of the portfolio rebalancing.

Solution to 4:

Although the proposed redeployment is expected to lower bank earnings, there are at least three good reasons for this action, any of which would justify the decision: (a) the bank believes it needs to have a more liquid investment portfolio because of the risk of unexpected claims against assets; (b) the bank needs to raise its regulatory "equity to risky assets" ratio (by substituting low credit-risk for high credit-risk assets); and (c), the bank believes it will be able to reverse the trade in the future after a recession has driven up the effective default-adjusted spreads (i.e., driven down the prices) on small business loans. In all three rationales, overall volatility is expected to decline and the reduction in volatility is expected to provide a benefit that more than offsets the anticipated reduction in earnings. That is, the risk-adjusted return is projected to rise.

Mini-Case B:

A medium size insurance company plans to sell a large portion of its diversified, fixed-rate, investment-grade-rated securities in order to redeploy proceeds into a special purpose trust holding a diversified portfolio of automobile loans with original loan lives of 5 years. The loans are collateralized by direct liens on the vehicles, and the underlying borrowers meet minimum consumer credit scores set by a national credit rating agency. The underlying loans were randomly selected for the trust, and the collateral constitutes a nationwide sample of automobiles of different foreign and domestic manufacturers.

1. What does this transaction reveal about the regulatory capital of this insurer?
2. What key information must the insurer know about the automobile loans held by the trust in order to manage its asset/liability duration profile?
3. What external factors might the insurer need to consider with respect to the duration of trust assets?
4. What is the expected impact from the proposed investment transaction on (a) the insurer's earnings, and (b), the overall volatility of the insurer's common equity capitalization?

Solution to 1:

The portfolio redeployment reduces the insurer's liquidity. Given that the insurer is able to undertake this action, the company has excess regulatory capital, because the underlying illiquid loans require more regulatory capital than high-quality/investment-grade, marketable, fixed-income securities.

Solution to 2:

The insurer must make actuarial projections of contractual cash flows from the auto loans, which must take into account full and partial pre-payments because of accidents, auto trade-ins, and loan defaults. The acceptable credit quality of the borrowers and the geographical and brand diversity contribute to the accuracy of such predictions. The overall asset/liability profile for the insurer might well change depending on how the projected modified duration of the auto loan receivables compares with the investment-grade marketable securities to be sold. A material difference might require management to undertake (a) changes in the modified duration of the insurance company's liabilities, such as by altering the maturities of future debt issuances; or (b), implementation of interest rate-hedging transactions.

Solution to 3:

The insurer must be concerned about an adverse change in the economic cycle, changes in technology, and/or energy prices—all of which could adversely impact the value of the auto loan receivables (as compared with the marketable securities portfolio to be sold) and which could undermine the cash flow assumptions made with respect to setting the company's overall asset/liability profile.

Solution to 4:

The portfolio redeployment is likely to raise the insurer's earnings, because the expected yield on the auto loans, net of credit losses, is higher than for investment-grade, liquid securities. However, the company is taking on more credit risk, which should translate into higher volatility of the value of assets and, thus, higher volatility of equity capitalization.

Mini-Case C:

Floating-rate securities, paying a fixed spread over the floating MRR, are trading at historically narrow yield spreads over MRR. In addition, issuers of these securities tend to be concentrated disproportionately in a small number of industries—notably in banks, insurers, and other financial services companies. A bank's investment manager considers selling the bank's portfolio holdings of these floating-rate securities, which have a 5-year maturity and trade at 0.1% over MRR. The proceeds will be used to buy more-diversified (by issuer type), investment-grade, fixed-rate securities that are selling at more normal spreads versus government bond yields of comparable duration (which trade at 1.0% over 5-year US Treasury bond yields). The fixed-rate securities portfolio is to be combined with pay-fixed/receive-floating interest rate swaps under standard mark-to-market collateralization terms. The 5-year interest rate swap terms permit one to receive MRR while paying 0.4% over Treasury yields.

1. What does the portfolio alteration do to required regulatory risk-based capital?
2. What might indicate that the bank's senior managers are more concerned about risks to equity capitalization than are regulators?
3. What is the expected effect on the bank's asset/liability profile?
4. What is the expected effect on expected earnings?
5. Summarize the rationale for the portfolio alteration.

Solution to 1:

To a first approximation, substituting one kind of marketable security for another should have little effect on regulatory risk-based capital requirements, because there is little apparent change in average credit quality. The new portfolio will have more issuer and industry diversification than the securities being sold. Thus, under robust scenario simulation testing, the new portfolio should be somewhat more resistant to loss than the more-concentrated portfolio assets being sold.

Solution to 2:

The bank's senior managers appear to be concerned about systemic risk in the financial sector, especially since the securities the bank plans to sell are concentrated in the financial sector and are trading at unusually high prices (narrow spreads to MRR). Apart from interest rate risk, the probability of underperformance for financial company securities is higher than for a diversified portfolio of fixed-rate securities. In the bank's view, the prospective volatility of floating-rate bank assets—and thus, the company's own equity capital—is higher than what is reflected in the regulatory risk-weight framework, because the latter does not take into account relative price risk. Thus, from the bank's perspective, the proposed trade lowers asset and equity volatility.

Solution to 3:

Substituting fixed-rate securities in place of variable-rate securities tends to increase the modified duration of the bank's assets. However, entering into a pay-fixed/receive-floating swap is equivalent to creating a synthetic liability, which becomes (i) smaller as interest rates rise and (ii) greater as interest rates fall. The interest rate swap can be tailored to offset the tendency of the newly acquired fixed-rate securities to lose value as interest rates rise and gain value as interest rates fall. Said differently, the synthetic liability increases the duration of the bank's liabilities to counterbalance the rise in asset duration from replacing variable-rate with fixed-rate debt securities.

Solution to 4:

Earnings are expected to rise. The securities sold pay a low spread over MRR. The new package (fixed-rate securities plus pay-fixed/receive-floating interest rate swap) pays a higher expected spread over MRR. The high yield received on the fixed-rate securities, net of the fixed-rate leg of the interest rate swap paid, represents the new built-in spread that is then added to the MRR received in the floating-leg of the interest rate swap. Specifically, the new portfolio will (i) receive 5-year Treasury yield plus 1.0% on the fixed-rate securities, (ii) pay 5-year Treasury yield plus 0.4% on the fixed leg of the interest rate swap, and (iii) receive MRR on the floating side of the interest rate swap. The net result is that the hedged, fixed-rate holdings will pay the bank the 5-year Treasury yield (T) + 1.0% − (T + 0.4%) + MRR = MRR + 0.6%. This synthetic floating-rate portfolio compares with the original floating-rate portfolio that paid just MRR + 0.1%.

Solution to 5:

A pay-fixed/receive-floating interest rate swap is "plain vanilla"; it is easy to value and unwind. The trade would thus not have any major adverse impact on the institution's liquidity. The bank, by selling securities in the banking and financial services industry, can lower its own exposure to systemic financial risk. In essence, the trade achieves better diversification while creating cheap (i.e., higher yielding) synthetic MRR floaters in place of true MRR floaters. The regulatory system in which the bank operates likely has a statistical system that penalizes excessive use of derivatives by deeming worst-case liabilities in a stress test. This should not be an issue assuming the proposed trade is small enough, relative to the institution's size, to have no significant impact on stress test results. Overall, the trade would be a duration-neutral trade, achieving higher net earnings and lower asset and equity risk without significantly impacting the bank's regulatory capital ratios.

Mini-Case D:

In the aftermath of prolonged financial turmoil and a recession, a large pan-European life insurance company believes that corporate debt securities and asset-based securities are now very attractive relative to more-liquid government securities. The yield spreads more than compensate for default and credit downgrade risk. Interest rates for government securities are near cyclical lows. The insurance company is concerned that rates may rise and that, as a result, many outstanding annuities might be surrendered. The insurer believes the probability of a large, adverse move in interest rates is much higher than is currently reflected by the implied volatility of traded options on government securities in the eurozone. The insurer's regulatory capital and reserves are deemed to be healthy.

1 What are the consequences of lowering allocations to government securities and raising allocations to corporate and asset-backed securities?

2 Are there steps that the insurer should take on the liability side?

Solution to 1:

These proposed asset reallocations have several implications. First, corporate debt securities have higher yields and thus shorter durations than government securities of similar maturity. Asset-backed securities tend to have lower effective durations than corporate and government bonds. Thus, the proposed rebalancing would likely lower the overall duration of the investment portfolio, which is consistent with the insurer's concerns about rising interest rates and the expected consequences. Second, the change in portfolio allocation would likely lower the company's overall liquidity and lower regulatory risk-based capital measures, because the new securities are treated less favorably for regulatory purposes (less liquid, higher credit risk corporate debt and asset-backed securities require a higher equity charge than liquid, low credit risk government securities, so regulatory "equity to risky assets" is reduced). Thus, the proposed portfolio moves make sense only if the regulatory capital position of the insurer is already ample and if the existing liquidity elsewhere in the portfolio is enough to fund an uptick of annuity surrenders in the case of rising interest rates. Finally, the reallocation would increase expected earnings (from higher interest income) and set the stage for price gains if credit spreads versus government securities contract to more normal levels.

Solution to 2:

Because overall interest rates are low, the company must also deal with an asymmetric risk separate and apart from the reallocation of its investment portfolio. In other words, the insurer must alter its liability profile in order to minimize potential adverse changes in its common equity capitalization. A spike up in interest rates could result in a rise in surrenders of annuities during a time when asset values are coming under pressure. Because the company is more concerned about higher interest rate volatility than is reflected in current option prices, the insurer might consider purchasing out-of-the-money puts on government securities and/or purchasing swaptions with the right to be a fixed-payer/floating-receiver. Sharp rises in rates would make both positions

> profitable[15] and offset some of the burden of premature annuity surrenders. If time passes without any substantial rise in interest rates, the cost of purchasing option protection would detract from the incremental benefits from the proposed switch into higher yielding securities.

SUMMARY

This reading has introduced the subject of managing institutional investor portfolios. The key points made in this reading are as follows:

- The main institutional investor types are pension plans, sovereign wealth funds, endowments, foundations, banks, and insurance companies. Common characteristics among these investors include a large scale (i.e., asset size), a long-term investment horizon, regulatory constraints, a clearly defined governance framework, and principal–agent issues.
- Institutional investors typically codify their mission, investment objectives, and guidelines in an Investment Policy Statement (IPS).
- Four common investment approaches to managing portfolios used by institutional investors are the Norway model, the Endowment model, the Canada model, and the Liability Driven Investing (LDI) model.
- There are two main types of pension plans: defined benefit (DB), in which a plan sponsor commits to paying a specified retirement benefit; and defined contribution (DC), in which contributions are defined but the ultimate retirement benefit is not specified or guaranteed by the plan sponsor.
- Pension plan stakeholders include the employer, employees, retirees, unions, management, the investment committee and/or board of directors, and shareholders.
- The key elements in the calculation of DB plan liabilities are as follows:
  - Service/tenure: The higher the service years, the higher the retirement benefit.
  - Salary/earnings: The higher the salary over the measurement period, the higher the retirement benefit.
  - Mortality/longevity: The longer the participant's expected life span, the higher the plan sponsor's liability.
  - Vesting: Lower turnover results in higher vesting, increasing the plan sponsor's liabilities.
  - Discount rate: A higher discount rate reduces the present value of the plan sponsor's liabilities.
- DB plan liquidity needs are driven by the following:
  - Proportion of active employees relative to retirees: More mature pension funds have higher liquidity needs.

---

15 A put option becomes valuable to the holder if prices of the underlying asset fall. A swaption with the right to enter a swap paying fixed and receiving floating is economically analogous to a put option on a bond. If rates rise, the swaption owner has the right to receive a rising stream of floating payments in exchange for what will have then become a stream of reasonably low fixed payments. The swaption contract will have gained in value.

- Age of workforce: Liquidity needs rise as the age of the workforce increases.
- Plan funded status: If the plan is well funded, the sponsor may reduce contributions, generating a need to hold higher balances of liquid assets to pay benefits.
- Flexibility: Ability of participants to switch among the sponsor's plans or to withdraw from the plan.

■ Pension plans are subject to significant and evolving regulatory constraints designed to ensure the integrity, adequacy, and sustainability of the pension system. Some incentives, such as tax exemption, are only granted to plans that meet these regulatory requirements. Notable differences in legal, regulatory, and tax considerations can lead to differences in plan design from one country to another or from one group to another (e.g., public plans vs. corporate plans).

■ The following risk considerations affect the way DB plans are managed:
- Plan funded status
- Sponsor financial strength
- Interactions between the sponsor's business and the fund's investments
- Plan design
- Workforce characteristics

■ An examination of pension fund asset allocations shows very large differences in average asset allocations by country and within a country despite these plans seeking to achieve similar goals. Such inter- and intra-national differences are driven by many factors, including the differences in legal, regulatory, accounting, and tax constraints; the investment objectives, risk appetites, and investment views of the stakeholders; the liabilities to and demographics of the ultimate beneficiaries; the availability of suitable investment opportunities; and the expected cost of living in retirement.

■ The major types of sovereign wealth funds (SWFs) follow:
- Budget Stabilization funds: Set up to insulate the budget and economy from commodity price volatility and external shocks.
- Development funds: Established to allocate resources to priority socioeconomic projects, usually infrastructure.
- Savings funds: Intended to share wealth across generations by transforming non-renewable assets into diversified financial assets.
- Reserve funds: Intended to reduce the negative carry costs of holding foreign currency reserves or to earn higher return on ample reserves.
- Pension Reserve funds: Set up to meet identified future outflows with respect to pension-related, contingent-type liabilities on governments' balance sheets.

■ Stakeholders of SWFs include the country's citizens, the government, external asset managers, and the SWF's management, investment committee and board of directors.

■ Given their mission of intergenerational wealth transfer, SWFs do not generally have clearly defined liabilities, so do not typically pursue asset/liability matching strategies used by other institutional investor types.

■ Sovereign wealth funds have differing liquidity needs. Budget stabilization funds require the most liquidity, followed by reserve funds. At the other end of the spectrum are savings funds with low liquidity needs, followed by pension reserve funds.

Summary

- The investment objectives of SWFs are often clearly articulated in the legislative instruments that create them. They are often tax free in their home country, though must take foreign taxation into consideration. Given their significant asset sizes and the nature of their stakeholders, SWFs have aimed to increase transparency regarding their investment activities. In this regard, the Santiago Principles are a form of self-regulation.

- The typical asset allocation by SWF type shows budget stabilization funds are invested mainly in bonds and cash given their liquidity needs. Reserve Funds invest in equities and alternatives but maintain a significant allocation of bonds for liquidity. Savings funds and pension reserve funds hold relatively higher allocations of equities and alternatives because of their longer-term liabilities.

- Endowments and foundations typically invest to maintain purchasing power while financing their supporting university (endowments) or making grants (foundations) in perpetuity—based on the notion of intergenerational equity. Endowments and foundations usually have a formal spending policy that determines how much is paid out annually to support their mission. This future stream of payouts represents their liabilities. For endowments, other liability-related factors to be considered when setting investment policy are: 1) the ability to raise additional funds from donors/alumni, 2) the percentage of the university's operating budget provided by the endowment, and 3) the ability to issue debt.

- Foundations and endowments typically enjoy tax-exempt status and face relatively little regulation compared to other types of institutional investors.

- Foundations face less flexible spending rules compared to endowments; foundations in the US are legally mandated to pay out 5% of their assets annually to maintain tax-exempt status. Endowments and foundations have relatively low liquidity needs. However, foundations have somewhat higher liquidity needs (vs. endowments), because they 1) typically pay out slightly more as a percentage of assets, and 2) finance the entire operating budget of the organization they support.

- Endowments and foundations typically have a long-term real return objective of about 5% consistent with their spending policies. This real return objective, and a desire to maintain purchasing power, results in endowments and foundations making significant allocations to real assets. In general, endowments and foundations invest heavily in private asset classes and hedge funds and have relatively small allocations to fixed income.

- Banking and insurance companies manage both portfolio assets and institutional liabilities to achieve an extremely high probability that obligations on deposits, guarantees, derivatives, policyholder claims, and other liabilities will be paid in full and on time.

- Banking and insurance companies have perpetual time horizons. Strategically, their goal is to maximize net present value to capital holders; tactically, this may be achieved by liability driven investing (LDI) over intermediate and shorter horizons.

- Financial institutions are highly regulated because of their importance to the non-financial, or real, sectors of the economy. Such institutions are also regulated in order to minimize contagion risk rippling throughout the financial and real sectors.

- The underlying premise of regulation is that an institution's capital must be adequate to absorb shocks to both asset and liability values. This implies limiting the volatility of value of the institution's shareholder capital.

- The volatility of shareholder capital can be managed by (a) reducing the price volatility of portfolio investments, loans, and derivatives; (b) lowering the volatility from unexpected shocks to claims, deposits, guarantees, and other liabilities; (c) limiting leverage; and (d) attempting to achieve positive correlation between changes in the value of assets and liabilities.
- Ample liquidity, diversification of portfolio and other assets, high investment quality, transparency, stable funding, duration management, diversification of insurance underwriting risks, and monetary limits on guarantees, funding commitments, and insurance claims are some of the ways management and regulators attempt to achieve low volatility of shareholder capital value.

REFERENCES

OECD. 2016. *OECD Insurance Statistics 2008–2016*. https://read.oecd-ilibrary.org/finance-and-investment/oecd-insurance-statistics-2016_ins_stats-2016-en#page1.

Tobin, James. 1974. "What Is Permanent Endowment Income?" *American Economic Review* 64 (2), Papers and Proceedings of the Eighty-Sixth Annual Meeting of the American Economic Association (May): 427–432.

Willis Towers Watson Thinking Ahead Institute. 2018. "*Global Pension Assets Study 2018*" (February). https://www.willistowerswatson.com/-/media/WTW/Images/Press/2018/01/Global-Pension-Asset-Study-2018-Japan.pdf.

PRACTICE PROBLEMS

The following information relates to Questions 1–7

William Azarov is a portfolio manager for Westcome Investments, an asset management firm. Azarov is preparing for meetings with two of Westcome's clients and obtains the help of Jason Boulder, a junior analyst. The first meeting is with Maglav Inc., a rapidly growing US-based technology firm with a young workforce and high employee turnover. Azarov directs Boulder to review the details of Maglav's defined benefit (DB) pension plan. The plan is overfunded and has assets under management of $25 million. Boulder makes the following two observations:

Observation 1   Maglav's shareholders benefit from the plan's overfunded status.

Observation 2   The funded ratio of Maglav's plan will decrease if employee turnover decreases.

Maglav outsources the management of the pension plan entirely to Westcome Investments. The fee structure requires Maglav to compensate Westcome with a high base fee regardless of performance. Boulder tells Azarov that outsourcing offers small institutional investors, such as Maglav's pension plan, the following three benefits:

Benefit 1: Regulatory requirements are reduced.

Benefit 2: Conflicts of interest are eliminated from principal–agent issues.

Benefit 3: Investors have access to a wider range of investment strategies through scale benefits.

In the meeting with Maglav, Azarov describes the investment approach used by Westcome in managing the pension plan. The approach is characterized by a high allocation to alternative investments, significant active management, and a reliance on outsourcing assets to other external asset managers. Azarov also explains that Maglav's operating results have a low correlation with pension asset returns and that the investment strategy is affected by the fact that the pension fund assets are a small portion of Maglav's market capitalization. Azarov states that the plan is subject to the Employee Retirement Income Security Act of 1974 (ERISA) and follows generally accepted accounting principles, including Accounting Standards Codification (ASC) 715, *Compensation—Retirement Benefits*.

Azarov's second meeting is with John Spintop, chief investment officer of the Wolf University Endowment Fund (the Fund). Spintop hired Westcome to assist in developing a new investment policy to present to the Fund's board of directors. The Fund, which has assets under management of $200 million, has an overall objective of maintaining long-term purchasing power while providing needed financial support to Wolf University. During the meeting, Spintop states that the Fund has an annual spending policy of paying out 4% of the Fund's three-year rolling asset value to Wolf University, and the Fund's risk tolerance should consider the following three liability characteristics:

Characteristic 1   The Fund has easy access to debt markets.

Characteristic 2   The Fund supports 10% of Wolf University's annual budget.

Characteristic 3 The Fund receives significant annual inflows from gifts and donations.

The Fund has a small investment staff with limited experience in managing alternative assets and currently uses the Norway model for its investment approach. Azarov suggests a change in investment approach by making an allocation to externally managed alternative assets—namely, hedge funds and private equity. Ten-year nominal expected return assumptions for various asset classes, as well as three proposed allocations that include some allocation to alternative assets, are presented in Exhibit 1.

Exhibit 1 10-Year Nominal Expected Return Assumptions and Proposed Allocations

Asset Class	Expected Return	Allocation 1	Allocation 2	Allocation 3
US Treasuries	4.1%	45%	10%	13%
US Equities	6.3%	40%	15%	32%
Non-US Equities	7.5%	10%	15%	40%
Hedge Funds	5.0%	0%	30%	5%
Private Equity	9.1%	5%	30%	10%

Expected inflation for the next 10 years is 2.5% annually.

1. Which of Boulder's observations regarding Maglav's pension plan is correct?
   A Only Observation 1
   B Only Observation 2
   C Both Observation 1 and Observation 2

2. Which of the benefits of outsourcing the management of the pension plan suggested by Boulder is correct?
   A Benefit 1
   B Benefit 2
   C Benefit 3

3. Westcome's investment approach for Maglav's pension plan can be *best* characterized as the:
   A Norway model.
   B Canadian model.
   C endowment model.

4. The risk tolerance of Maglav's pension plan can be *best* characterized as being:
   A below average.
   B average.
   C above average.

5. Based on Azarov's statement concerning ERISA and ASC 715, which of the following statements is correct?
   A Maglav is not allowed to terminate the plan.
   B Maglav can exclude the plan's service costs from net income.
   C Maglav's plan must appear as an asset on Maglav's balance sheet.

6. The risk tolerance of the Wolf University Endowment Fund can be *best* characterized as:

Practice Problems

- **A** below average.
- **B** average.
- **C** above average.

7 Which proposed allocation in Exhibit 1 would be *most appropriate* for the Fund given its characteristics?
- **A** Allocation 1
- **B** Allocation 2
- **C** Allocation 3

The following information relates to Questions 8–12

Bern Zang is the recently hired chief investment officer of the Janson University Endowment Investment Office. The Janson University Endowment Fund (the Fund) is based in the United States and has current assets under management of $12 billion. It has a long-term investment horizon and relatively low liquidity needs. The Fund is overseen by an Investment Committee consisting of board members for the Fund. The Investment Office is responsible for implementing the investment policy set by the Fund's Investment Committee.

The Fund's current investment approach includes an internally managed fund that holds mostly equities and fixed-income securities. It is largely passively managed with tight tracking error limits. The target asset allocation is 55% equities, 40% fixed income, and 5% alternatives. The Fund currently holds private real estate investments to meet its alternative investment allocation.

8 **Identify** the investment approach currently being used by the Investment Committee for managing the Fund. **Justify** your response.

Identify the investment approach currently being used by the Investment Committee for managing the Fund. (circle one)			
Norway Model	Endowment Model	Canadian Model	LDI Model

Justify your response.

9 **Discuss** the advantages and the disadvantages of the investment approach currently being used by the Investment Committee.

Discuss the advantages and the disadvantages of the investment approach currently being used by the Investment Committee.

Advantages

Disadvantages

10 **Describe** how *each* of the following common characteristics of institutional investors supports the Fund's allocation to private real estate:

  i. Scale
  ii. Investment horizon
  iii. Governance framework

Describe how *each* of the following common characteristics of institutional investors supports the Fund's allocation to private real estate.
Scale
Investment Horizon
Governance Framework

After a thorough internal review, Zang concludes that the current investment approach will result in a deterioration of the purchasing power of the Fund over time. He proposes a new, active management approach that will substantially decrease the allocation to publicly traded equities and fixed income in order to pursue a higher allocation to private investments. The management of the new investments will be outsourced.

11 **Identify** the new investment approach proposed by Zang for managing the Fund. **Justify** your response.

Identify the new investment approach proposed by Zang for managing the Fund. (circle one)
Norway Model   Endowment Model   Canadian Model   LDI Model
Justify your response.

12 **Discuss** the advantages and the disadvantages of the new investment approach proposed by Zang.

Discuss the advantages and the disadvantages of the new investment approach proposed by Zang.
Advantages
Disadvantages

13 Fiona Heselwith is a 40-year-old US citizen who has accepted a job with Lyricul, LLC, a UK-based company. Her benefits package includes a retirement savings plan. The company offers both a defined benefit (DB) plan and a defined contribution (DC) plan but stipulates that employees must choose one plan and remain with that plan throughout their term of employment.

The DB plan is fully funded and provides full vesting after five years. The benefit formula for monthly payments upon retirement is calculated as follows:

- Final monthly salary × Benefit percentage of 2% × Number of years of service

- The final monthly salary is equal to average monthly earnings for the last five financial years immediately prior to the retirement date.

The DC plan contributes 12% of annual salary into the plan each year and is also fully vested after five years. Lyricul offers its DC plan participants a series of life-cycle funds as investment choices. Heselwith could choose a fund with a target date matching her planned retirement date. She would be able to make additional contributions from her salary if she chooses.

Discuss the features that Heselwith should consider in evaluating the two plans with respect to the following:

   i. Benefit payments

   ii. Contributions

   iii. Shortfall risk

   iv. Mortality/longevity risks

	Discuss the features that Heselwith should consider in evaluating the two plans with respect to the following:
Benefit Payments	
Contributions	
Shortfall Risk	
Mortality/ Longevity Risks	

14 Dianna Mark is the chief financial officer of Antiliaro, a relatively mature textile production company headquartered in Italy. All of its revenues come from Europe, but the company is losing sales to its Asian competitors. Earnings have been steady but not growing, and the balance sheet has taken on more debt in the past few years in order to maintain liquidity. Mark reviews the following facts concerning the company's defined benefit (DB) pension plan:

- The DB plan currently has €1 billion in assets and is underfunded by €100 million in relation to the projected benefit obligation (PBO) because of investment losses.
- The company to date has made regular contributions.
- The average employee age is 50 years, and the company has many retirees owing to its longevity.
- The duration of the plan's liabilities (which are all Europe based) is 10 years.
- The discount rate applied to these liabilities is 6%.
- There is a high correlation between the operating results of Antiliaro and pension asset returns.

Determine whether the risk tolerance of the DB plan is below average or above average. **Justify** your response with *two* reasons.

Determine whether the risk tolerance of the DB plan is below average or above average. (circle one)	Justify your response with *two* reasons.
Below Average	1.
Above Average	2.

The following information relates to Questions 15–17

The Prometheo University Scholarship Endowment (the Endowment) was established in 1950 and supports scholarships for students attending Prometheo University. The Endowment's assets under management are relatively small, and it has an annual spending policy of 6% of the five-year rolling asset value.

15 **Formulate** the investment objectives section of the investment policy statement for the Endowment.

Prometheo University recently hired a new chief investment officer (CIO). The CIO directs her small staff of four people to implement an investment policy review. Historically, the endowment has invested 60% of the portfolio in US equities and 40% in US Treasuries. The CIO's expectation of annual inflation for the next 10 years is 2.5%.

The CIO develops nominal 10-year return assumptions for US Treasuries and US equities, which are presented in Exhibit 1.

Exhibit 1 Asset Class Return Assumptions

Asset Class	10-Year Return Assumptions (Nominal)
US Treasuries	4.0%
US Equities	7.4%

16 **Discuss** whether the current investment policy is appropriate given the Endowment's annual spending policy.

Upon completion of the investment policy review by her four-person staff, the CIO makes some recommendations to the Endowment's board regarding the investment objectives and asset allocation. One of her recommendations is to adopt the endowment model as an investment approach. She recommends investing 20% in private equity, 40% in hedge funds, 25% in public equities, and 15% in fixed income.

17 **Determine** whether the board should accept the CIO's recommendation. **Justify** your response.

Determine whether the board should accept the CIO's recommendation. (circle one)	Justify your response.
Accept	
Reject	

18 Meura Bancorp, a US bank, has an equity capital ratio for financial assets of 12%. Meura's strategic plans include the incorporation of additional debt in order to leverage earnings since the current capital structure is relatively conservative. The bank plans to restructure the balance sheet so that the equity capitalization ratio drops to 10% and the modified duration of liabilities is 1.90. The bank also plans to rebalance its investment portfolio to achieve a modified duration of assets of 2.10. Given small changes in interest rates, the yield on liabilities is expected to move by 65 bps for every 100 bps of yield change in the asset portfolio.

Calculate the modified duration of the bank's equity capital after restructuring. **Show** your calculations.

SOLUTIONS

1. C is correct. Both observations are correct. For a corporate defined benefit plan, Maglav's shareholders are stakeholders. These stakeholders are interested in the sustainability of the pension plan, and the overfunded status is an asset on the balance sheet, potentially increasing the value of Maglav's stock. The overfunded status also allows management to potentially lower employer contributions to the plan and increase net income. It also lowers financial risk, which may reduce volatility in the stock price. In addition, decreasing employee turnover will increase plan liabilities and worsen the funded ratio. With high turnover, fewer workers will be vested and entitled to defined benefit payments. Conversely, if employee turnover decreases, expected vesting will increase, leading to higher plan liabilities and a lower funded ratio.

2. C is correct. Scale (asset size) is a defining characteristic for institutional investors since it affects key aspects of the investment process. Maglav's pension plan is small, with $25 million in assets under management. Smaller institutions may be unable to access certain investments that have a high minimum investment, such as private equity and real estate assets. These smaller institutions may also have difficulty in hiring skilled investment professionals. As a result, small institutional investors, such as Maglav's pension plan, are more likely to outsource all or most of the investment operations to external asset managers or investment consultants.

3. C is correct. The endowment model operates in an asset-only context and is characterized by a high allocation to alternative investments, including private investments and hedge funds; significant active management; and outsourcing to external managers. These characteristics describe the investment approach used by Westcome. The skill in sourcing alternative investments is critically important given the large variation in performance among asset managers, especially for alternative investments.

4. C is correct. The risk tolerance for Maglav's defined benefit plan is high and thus above average. Several factors influence the plan sponsor's ability to assume risk. For Maglav, the overfunded status of the pension fund allows the plan to withstand more volatility, and its small size relative to the company size implies greater risk tolerance. The low correlation of Maglav's operating results with pension asset returns also results in greater risk tolerance. Finally, the workforce characteristics imply greater risk tolerance. The younger workforce increases the duration of the plan liabilities and enables the sponsor to take on more liquidity risk. The high turnover of the workforce means fewer employees may be vested, reducing the number of employees entitled to receive defined benefit payments. All these factors contribute to an above average risk tolerance for Maglav's defined benefit plan.

5. C is correct. ASC 715, *Compensation—Retirement Benefits* requires that an overfunded (underfunded) plan appear as an asset (liability) on the balance sheet of the corporate sponsor. Maglav's plan is overfunded, so it appears as an asset on Maglav's balance sheet.

6. C is correct. The risk tolerance of the Wolf University Endowment Fund is above average since endowments that support a small percentage of the university's operating budget (10% in this case) should be able to tolerate more market, credit, and liquidity risk. In addition, the Fund's ability to access debt markets, especially during periods of market stress, increases the level of risk the endowment can accept in its investments. Finally, because of the significant

inflows from gifts and donations, the effective spending rate will be lower than the annual spending policy of paying out 4% of the Fund's three-year rolling asset value. Thus, the Fund can rely less on investment returns to generate the income stream needed to support the university and can accept higher-risk investments.

7 C is correct. Allocation 3 is the most appropriate allocation for the Fund. The annual expected returns for the three allocations are as follows:

$$\text{Allocation 1 exp. return} = (0.45 \times 4.1\%) + (0.40 \times 6.3\%) + (0.10 \times 7.5\%) + (0.05 \times 9.1\%)$$
$$= 5.57\%.$$

$$\text{Allocation 2 exp. return} = (0.10 \times 4.1\%) + (0.15 \times 6.3\%) + (0.15 \times 7.5\%) + (0.30 \times 5.0\%) + (0.30 \times 9.1\%)$$
$$= 6.71\%.$$

$$\text{Allocation 3 exp. return} = (0.13 \times 4.1\%) + (0.32 \times 6.3\%) + (0.40 \times 7.5\%) + (0.05 \times 5.0\%) + (0.10 \times 9.1\%)$$
$$= 6.71\%.$$

The real return for Allocation 1 is 3.07% (= 5.57% − 2.50%), and the real return for Allocation 2 and Allocation 3 is 4.21% (= 6.71% − 2.50%).

Therefore, Allocation 1 is not appropriate because the expected real rate of return is less than the annual spending rate of 4%. With expected spending at 4%, the purchasing power of the Fund would be expected to decline over time with Allocation 1.

Allocations 2 and 3 both offer an expected real rate of return greater than the annual spending rate of 4%. Thus, the purchasing power of the Fund would be expected to grow over time with either allocation. However, Allocation 3 is more appropriate than Allocation 2 because of its lower allocation to alternative assets (hedge funds and private equity). The total 60% allocation to alternative assets in Allocation 2 is well above the 15% allocation in Allocation 3 and is likely too high considering the Fund's small investment staff and its limited experience with managing alternative investments. Also, given the Fund's relatively small size of assets under management ($200 million), access to top hedge funds and private equity managers is likely to be limited.

8

Identify the investment approach currently being used by the Investment Committee for managing the Fund.
(circle one)

Norway Model	Endowment Model	Canadian Model	LDI Model

Justify your response.

The investment approach currently used to manage the Fund's assets is the Norway model. This approach is characterized by a heavy allocation to public equities and fixed-income securities with little allocation to alternatives and largely passively managed assets with tight tracking error limits.

9		
		Discuss the advantages and the disadvantages of the investment approach currently being used by the Investment Committee.
	Advantages	Advantages of using the Norway model are that investment costs/fees are low, investments are transparent, manager risk is low, and there is little complexity for a governing board (the model is easy to understand).
	Disadvantages	The disadvantage of using the Norway model is that there is limited potential for value-added (i.e., alpha from security selection skills), above-market returns.

10		
		Describe how *each* of the following common characteristics of institutional investors supports the Fund's allocation to private real estate.
	Scale	The Fund has $12 billion of assets under management. Its relatively large size allows it access to a broad investment universe and to investments that have a high minimum investment size, such as private real estate.
	Investment Horizon	Alternative investments, such as private real estate, require a long-term investment horizon. Janson, like most university endowments, has a long-term investment horizon and relatively low liquidity needs. This makes private real estate an appropriate investment and also helps the endowment maintain long-term purchasing power.
	Governance Framework	Institutional investors usually operate under a formal governance framework. Janson has a well-structured governance framework that includes an Investment Committee that is part of the board overseeing the endowment's investment portfolio. This framework also includes an Investment Office that implements the investment policy approved by the Investment Committee. The decision to invest in private real estate had to go through an approval process that is set and maintained by the governance structure in place.

11

Identify the new investment approach proposed by Zang for managing the Fund.
(circle one)

Norway Model	**Endowment Model**	Canadian Model	LDI Model

Justify your response.

The new investment approach proposed by Zang is the endowment model. This model is characterized by significant active management, a high allocation to alternative investments, and externally managed assets (which distinguishes it from the Canadian model, an approach that relies more on internally managed assets).

12

	Discuss the advantages and the disadvantages of the new investment approach proposed by Zang.
Advantages	The primary advantage of using the endowment model is a higher potential for value-added, above-market returns.
Disadvantages	The endowment model can be difficult to implement for small institutional investors because they might not be able to access high-quality managers. The endowment model may also be difficult to implement for a very large institutional investor because of the institutional investor's very large footprint. Furthermore, relative to the Norway model, the endowment model is more expensive in terms of costs/fees.

13

	Discuss the features that Heselwith should consider in evaluating the two plans with respect to the following:
Benefit Payments	Heselwith notes that the vesting schedule with regard to the company's contributions is the same in both plans, although her contributions in the DC plan are vested immediately. The DB plan provides a defined payment linked to final salary and years of service, whereas the DC plan provides an uncertain benefit based on Lyricul's and Heselwith's contributions as well as the investment performance of the plan assets.
Contributions	Lyricul's contribution rate to the DB plan is not known, but the plan is fully funded. However, there is no guarantee that it will remain fully funded or that Lyricul is committed to maintaining the DB plan's fully funded status. The rate for the DC plan is stated to be 12% of annual salary.
Shortfall Risk	Heselwith notes that the shortfall risk of plan assets being insufficient to meet her retirement benefit payments falls to her employer, Lyricul, with the DB plan. However, for the DC plan, the shortfall risk falls to her and depends on the 12% contribution rate from the company, plus any additional contributions she chooses to make, as well as the performance of the chosen investments.
Mortality/ Longevity Risks	The DB plan pools mortality risk such that those in the pool who die prematurely leave assets that help fund benefit payments for those who live longer than expected. Heselwith bears the risk of outliving her savings with the DC plan.

14.

Determine whether the risk tolerance of the DB Plan is below average or above average. (circle one)	Justify your response with *two* reasons.
Below Average	• The plan is underfunded, and the discount rate being used is fairly aggressive. 1. The DB plan already has a deficit, despite regular contributions, and is suffering from investment losses. The discount rate is already aggressive and should not be increased to lower the contribution. • The uncertain financial condition of the company. 2. The uncertain condition of Antiliaro may constrain its ability to make contributions to the DB plan. Lack of earnings growth and increasing debt on the balance sheet over the last few years imply below-average risk tolerance.
Above Average	• The plan suffers from investment losses. 3. Often, investment losses can lead a DB plan to take on more investment risk to achieve higher returns, but the other constraints, such as the plan's underfunded status and the company's financial condition, prevent this approach. • The older age of employees necessitates liquidity. 4. The average employee age is 50 years, and the company has many retirees because of its longevity. These characteristics generate a need for liquidity, which lowers the amount of risk the plan can assume. • The high correlation between the operating results of Antiliaro and pension asset returns lowers the risk tolerance of the pension plan. 5. The high correlation between the operating results of Antiliaro and the pension asset returns suggests a low risk tolerance. If Antiliaro is performing poorly as a company, this will constrain its ability to make additional contributions that may be necessary to address the shortfall in the pension's funding.

15. The mission of the Prometheo University Scholarship Endowment is to provide scholarships for students attending the university. In order to achieve this mission, the Endowment must maintain the purchasing power of the assets in perpetuity while achieving investment returns sufficient to sustain the level of spending necessary to support the scholarship budget. Therefore, the investment objective of the endowment should be to achieve a total real rate of return (after inflation) of at least 6% with a reasonable level of risk.

16. GUIDELINE ANSWER:

- The policy is not appropriate.
- The expected real return of 3.54% is less than the spending policy rate of 6%.
- Therefore, the current allocation and investment objectives are not sustainable.

The nominal expected return on the current portfolio, according to the nominal return assumptions in Exhibit 1, is 6.04% per year (0.6 × 7.4% + 0.4 × 4.0% = 6.04%). The expected real return is approximately 3.54% (6.04% − 2.5% = 3.54%), which is below the 6% spending rate and the stated objective of a 6% real return. Therefore, this real return is not sufficient to meeting the spending policy, which makes the Endowment's goals unsustainable. The Endowment will need to change its asset allocation to earn higher returns and/or lower its spending policy rate.

17.

Determine whether the board should accept the CIO's recommendation. (circle one)	Justify your response.
Accept **Reject**	The board should reject the CIO's recommendation. This recommendation is a significant departure from current practice and entails a much higher level of risk. The size of the investment team is small, with only four people, and it may not have adequate access to or experience in alternative investments. Given the relatively small size of the Endowment, it is unlikely that it has access to top managers in the hedge fund and private equity spaces.

18. The modified duration of the bank's equity capital after restructuring is 9.89 years:

$$D_E^* = \left(\frac{A}{E}\right)D_A^* - \left(\frac{A}{E} - 1\right)D_L^*\left(\frac{\Delta i}{\Delta y}\right)$$

$$= \left(\frac{1}{0.10}\right) \times 2.10 - \left(\frac{1}{0.10} - 1\right) \times 1.90 \times 0.65$$

$$= 9.89 \text{ years}$$

PORTFOLIO MANAGEMENT
STUDY SESSION

13

Trading, Performance Evaluation, and Manager Selection

The investment process is not complete until securities are bought or sold, and so the quality of trade execution is an important determinant of investment results. The first reading examines how portfolio managers need to work closely with traders to determine the most appropriate trading strategy given their motivation for trading, risk aversion, trade urgency, and other factors such as order characteristics and market conditions. Portfolio manager motivations to trade, inputs to trade strategy selection, and the range of trade implementation choices, trading algorithms, and a comparison of various markets are discussed. Guidance is provided on evaluating a firm's trading procedures for good governance practices, measuring trade costs, and evaluating success in trade execution.

Performance evaluation is one of the most critical areas of investment analysis. Performance results can be used to assess the quality of the investment approach and suggest changes that might improve it. They are also used to communicate the results of the investment process to other stakeholders and may even be used to compensate the investment managers.

The second reading on performance evaluation includes three primary components, each corresponding to a specific question needed to answer to evaluate a portfolio's performance:

- performance measurement—what was the portfolio's performance?;
- performance attribution—how was the performance achieved?; and
- performance appraisal—was the performance achieved through manager skill or luck?

The last reading of this study session addresses the complex and detailed process involved in in evaluating an investment manager. The focus is on understanding how the investment results were achieved and on assessing the likelihood that the investment process that generated these returns will produce superior or at least satisfactory

© 2021 CFA Institute. All rights reserved.

investment results going forward. It also entails an evaluation of a firm's integrity, operations, and personnel. This reading provides a framework that introduces and describes the important elements of the manager selection process.

READING ASSIGNMENTS

Reading 25	Trade Strategy and Execution by Bernd Hanke, PhD, CFA, Robert Kissell, PhD, Connie Li, and Roberto Malamut
Reading 26	Portfolio Performance Evaluation edited by Marc A. Wright, CFA
Reading 27	Investment Manager Selection by Jeffrey C. Heisler, PhD, CFA, and Donald W. Lindsey, CFA

READING 25

Trade Strategy and Execution

by Bernd Hanke, PhD, CFA, Robert Kissell, PhD, Connie Li, and Roberto Malamut

Bernd Hanke, PhD, CFA, is at Global Systematic Investors LLP (United Kingdom). Robert Kissell, PhD, is at Molloy College and Kissell Research Group (USA). Connie Li (USA). Roberto Malamut (USA).

LEARNING OUTCOMES

Mastery	The candidate should be able to:
☐	a. discuss motivations to trade and how they relate to trading strategy;
☐	b. discuss inputs to the selection of a trading strategy;
☐	c. compare benchmarks for trade execution;
☐	d. recommend and justify a trading strategy (given relevant facts);
☐	e. describe factors that typically determine the selection of a trading algorithm class;
☐	f. contrast key characteristics of the following markets in relation to trade implementation: equity, fixed income, options and futures, OTC derivatives, and spot currency;
☐	g. explain how trade costs are measured and determine the cost of a trade;
☐	h. evaluate the execution of a trade;
☐	i. evaluate a firm's trading procedures, including processes, disclosures, and record keeping with respect to good governance.

1. INTRODUCTION

This reading discusses trading and execution from a portfolio manager's perspective. The reading covers a broad range of topics related to trade strategy selection and implementation and trade cost measurement and evaluation. Growth in electronic trading has led to increased automation in trading, including the use of algorithmic trading and machine learning to optimize trade strategy and execution. Various markets,

© 2019 CFA Institute. All rights reserved.

including equities, fixed income, derivatives, and foreign exchange, are examined. Adequate trading processes and procedures are also discussed from a regulatory and governance perspective.

Portfolio managers need to work closely with traders to determine the most appropriate trading strategy given their motivation for trading, risk aversion, trade urgency, and other factors, such as order characteristics and market conditions. Trade execution should be well integrated with the portfolio management process, and although trading strategies will vary on the basis of market and security type, all trade activity should be evaluated for execution quality and to assess broker and trade venue performance consistent with the fund's objectives. Additionally, firms should have proper documentation of trade procedures in place to meet regulatory and governance standards.

This reading is organized as follows: Section 2 discusses portfolio manager motivations to trade. Sections 3–5 discuss inputs to trade strategy selection and the trade strategy selection process. Sections 6 and 7 cover the range of trade implementation choices and trading algorithms and provide a comparison of various markets. Sections 8 and 9 explain how trade costs are measured and how to evaluate trade execution. Section 10 provides guidance on evaluating a firm's trading procedures for good governance practices. The final section concludes and summarizes the reading.

2 MOTIVATIONS TO TRADE

a discuss motivations to trade and how they relate to trading strategy

Portfolio managers need to trade their portfolio holdings to ensure alignment with the fund's underlying investment strategy and objectives. The reasons for trading, or motivations to trade, and the extent of trading vary by investment strategy and circumstance. Even a passive buy-and-hold index portfolio requires some trading because of corporate actions, fund flows, or changes in the benchmark index. Portfolio managers for actively managed funds have additional reasons for trading based on their changing views for individual assets and market conditions. A portfolio manager's motivation to trade in addition to the fund's investment objectives play an important role in determining an overall trading approach.

Broadly speaking, a portfolio manager's motivation to trade falls into one of the following categories:

- Profit seeking
- Risk management/hedging needs
- Cash flow needs
- Corporate actions/index reconstitutions/margin calls

2.1 Profit Seeking

The primary added value that most active managers seek to provide is risk-adjusted outperformance relative to their benchmark. Superior returns originate from a manager having a unique insight that can be capitalized on ahead of the market. Trading in these cases is based on information portfolio managers have uncovered that they believe is not fully recognized by the market and, therefore, offers the potential to earn an excess return from the trade. Active managers will seek to transact in securities believed to be mispriced (under- or overvalued) at more favorable prices before the rest of the market recognizes the mispricing.

To prevent information leakage, or the disclosure of information about their trades, which might alert the market to the mispricing, active managers take steps to hide their trades from other market participants by executing in multiple or less transparent trade venues. *"Lit" markets* (a term referring to illumination), such as exchanges and other displayed venues, provide pre- and post-trade transparency regarding prices, volumes, market spreads, and depth. In contrast, alternative trading systems, such as dark pool trading venues, are available only to select clients and provide far less transparency, reporting only post-trade transactions and quantities. Because of these characteristics, orders in dark pool venues have a higher likelihood of going unfilled since clients receive executions only if an offsetting order arrives while their order is pending. For example, to prevent information about their trading activity from leaking to the market, a manager executing a large, directional trade may choose to execute the order in a less transparent venue.

As their investment views change with changing market and macroeconomic environments, portfolio managers will trade their holdings to align the portfolio with their views. Portfolio managers seeking longer-term profits may have relatively stable views from one period to the next whereas, in contrast, managers seeking shorter-term profits may have more rapidly changing views based on short-term movements in the market or individual securities that require higher turnover and trading.

To capitalize on investment views ahead of the market, trading the order faster, at an accelerated pace, may be needed. Portfolio managers may execute their orders at prices nearer to the market if they believe the information they have uncovered is likely to be realized by the rest of the market in the near term. **Trade urgency** refers to how quickly (aggressively) or slowly (patiently) the order is executed over the trading time horizon. Greater trade urgency is associated with executing over shorter execution horizons, whereas lower trade urgency is associated with executing over longer execution horizons.

A portfolio manager with a short-term event-driven strategy will trade with greater urgency if the expected alpha, or return payoff associated with the investment view over the trading horizon, is likely to be rapidly acted on by other market participants. In this case, the rate or level of expected alpha decay is high. In a trading context, **alpha decay** refers to the erosion or deterioration in short-term alpha once an investment decision is made. Portfolio managers following a longer-term strategy based on company fundamentals will trade more patiently, with less urgency, if the rate or level of expected alpha decay is lower.

Following are examples of short-term and long-term profit-motivated trading with differing levels of trade urgency.

2.1.1 *Michigan Index of Consumer Sentiment (short-term profit seeking)*

The University of Michigan Index of Consumer Sentiment (ICS) is one of the primary indicators of US consumer confidence. It is based on a nationwide survey of households. The ICS is closely watched by market participants, and changes in the index can prompt significant moves in the US equity market. Since 2007, Thomson Reuters, a financial data vendor, has held the exclusive right to disseminate the ICS. Until mid-2013, the firm had a two-tiered process for disseminating the ICS. A small number of trading clients received the ICS at 9:54:58, or two seconds earlier than the broader market release at 9:55:00. The two-tiered process was abolished in July 2013 after receiving negative public attention. Hu, Pan, and Wang (2017) examined how quickly the information contained in the ICS was incorporated into S&P 500 Index prices during the period of the two-tiered process.[1] They found that most of the

---

[1] Hu, G., J. Pan and J. Wang, 2017. "Early peek advantage? Efficient price discovery with tiered information disclosure". *Journal of Financial Economics* 126(2), 399–421.

price adjustment happened within the first 200 milliseconds. This is an example of profit-driven trading with high associated trade urgency and an extremely short-term execution horizon.

2.1.2 Value manager (long-term profit seeking)

An investment manager following a value strategy might attempt to identify undervalued companies on the basis of such metrics as earnings yields and price-to-book ratios. The manager might favor companies that score well according to these metrics. To capitalize on their views, individual positions may be held for months or years by value managers. Minimal trading is required, and any necessary trading can often be carried out in a more patient manner. Trading in this case has no trade urgency, given the managers' much longer trade execution horizons.

As more news and market information become available on a close-to-real-time basis, combined with the increase in electronic trading, markets have become more competitive. Information is being incorporated into security prices at even faster rates. Surprises in companies' earnings announcements, interest rate changes by central banks, and other macroeconomic announcements are being incorporated into security prices on a nearly instantaneous basis. Portfolio managers trying to act on this information must trade quickly and ahead of others to capitalize on the perceived opportunity. If more immediate execution cannot be achieved at a reasonable trading cost and risk, the trade may not be worthwhile given high rates of alpha decay. Therefore, these trades may be possible only in more liquid markets, such as equities, exchange-traded derivatives, foreign exchange, and fixed-income Treasury. In less liquid markets, such as non-Treasury fixed income or over-the-counter (OTC) markets where more immediate executions cannot be achieved, trades may not be worthwhile. For active managers seeking to maximize net returns to the portfolio, the expected rate of alpha decay of the security being traded is an important trading consideration.

2.2 Risk Management/Hedging Needs

As the market and the risk environment change, portfolios need to be traded or rebalanced to remain at targeted risk levels or risk exposures. Risk horizons and risk forecasts used by portfolio managers vary by investment strategy type and by investment time horizon. Fixed-income portfolio managers, for example, may have investment objectives to adhere to target portfolio durations. For these managers, portfolio rebalancing is usually required to match a benchmark duration target over time. Trading may be required because of a changing interest rate environment, a change in the benchmark index, or the passage of time. Equity portfolio managers may wish to manage their portfolio's beta or remain market neutral by hedging market risk and targeting a beta of zero relative to the equity market. To do this, the manager could trade to adjust holdings in the underlying portfolio or trade futures or exchange-traded funds (ETFs) to adjust the fund's equity beta to zero. Similarly, hedge fund managers may wish to maintain exposure to higher market volatility without having a view on directional price movement.

In general, the risks being managed, or hedged, in addition to such factors as security liquidity considerations and the fund's investment mandate, determine whether derivatives can be used or whether trades in the underlying portfolio (cash) securities are necessary. For example, an equity portfolio's beta to a broad equity market may be managed to the portfolio's target beta by trading equity index futures (e.g., S&P 500 futures, FTSE 100 Index futures, or Nikkei 225 futures). Using futures for hedging is often a simpler, more cost-effective approach because many futures contracts are liquid and can be traded at minimal cost. In addition, the standardization of futures contracts makes them attractive to investors. They can also be traded on margin, requiring relatively small amounts of capital. Similarly, for fixed-income strategies in the United States, interest rate risk can often be (at least partially) hedged using futures on Treasury securities, such as T-bond futures. Using liquid derivatives for risk management can provide an inexpensive and straightforward means of hedging versus trading in the underlying cash securities. In addition, the ability to trade derivatives or underlying securities may depend on the fund's investment mandate. In some cases, the fund's investment mandate may not allow the use of derivatives, and the portfolio manager must instead trade ETFs or the underlying to achieve the desired exposures.

For quantitative funds, targeted volatility is usually explicitly stated in the fund's offering documents whereas for fundamental funds, it may be an implicit assumption within the investment process. Regardless of fund type, portfolio managers should understand target risk levels and when changes in the market environment might require trading to adjust portfolio risk back to targeted volatility.

Portfolio managers may also trade to hedge risks when they do not have a view on the specific risk in question. For example, a global fixed-income long/short manager without strong currency views may choose to minimize currency exposure through a currency hedging trade. A fixed-income manager who wants to trade expected changes in the shape of the yield curve may not have a view on the level of the yield curve. In this case, the manager's yield curve trade would incorporate a hedge for duration risk. A manager of a high-yield bond portfolio may need to manage portfolio sector risk as well as geographical risk. Although credit default swaps (CDSs) might be used to manage this type of risk, finding a counterparty for a more specialized CDS can be difficult and costly. Because few derivatives to manage these risks exist, the underlying cash securities are generally traded. Using more illiquid securities for these risk trades generally increases the difficulty and cost of implementation.

A portfolio manager using option strategies may want to hedge the portfolio against certain risk factors: for example, the buyer of a long straddle position (a long position in a call and a put option on the same underlying security, both with the same strike price) who is implementing a view on higher expected volatility, irrespective of whether higher volatility will lead to higher or lower security prices. This is inherently an investment view on volatility that requires hedging directional price movement in the security.

The amount and nature of trading required for risk management generally depend on the risk profile of the portfolio as well as the amount of leverage used in the fund. Although various types of funds permit the use of leverage, leverage is typically used more by hedge funds that hold both long and short positions. For highly levered funds, risk must be monitored closely because the portfolios can quickly accumulate large losses with sudden increases in market risk. This strong risk sensitivity makes trading for risk management crucial.

2.3 Cash Flow Needs

A considerable amount of trading for portfolios is neither return seeking nor for risk management purposes but instead is driven by cash flow needs. Cash flow needs may involve high or low trade urgency depending on their nature. For example, collateral/margin calls could require close-to-immediate liquidation, whereas a fund redemption due to longer-term client asset allocation changes might not require immediate liquidation.

This type of trading is often client driven, arising from fund inflows (orders, mandates) and outflows (redemptions, liquidations). Fund inflows and outflows require capital to be invested or positions to be liquidated. To minimize cash drag on a portfolio, or fund underperformance from holding uninvested cash in a rising market, fund inflows may be equitized using futures or ETFs until the next portfolio rebalance or positions in the underlying can be traded. Equitization in this case refers to a strategy of temporarily investing cash using futures or ETFs to gain the desired equity exposure before investing in the underlying securities longer term. Equitization may be required if large inflows into a portfolio are hindered by lack of liquidity in the underlying securities. For example, a large inflow into a small-capitalization equity portfolio often cannot be invested immediately in the underlying stocks owing to limited market liquidity. Instead, the manager may equitize the cash using equity futures or ETFs and then gradually trade into the underlying positions and trade out of the futures/ETF position. For client redemptions, fund holdings may need to be liquidated if redemptions are larger than expected and cannot be funded by portfolio cash or offsetting fund inflows. Currency trades in which one currency needs to be exchanged (traded) into another may be required if fund inflows or outflows are not in the desired currency for receipt or payment. Many funds offer daily liquidity, which means investors can invest or redeem on a daily basis, often without limitation. Cash positions for these funds must be carefully managed in order to satisfy all fund flows and, at the same time, minimize the fund's cash drag. Trading is often required to manage the fund's cash position appropriately.

Hedge funds often have lockup periods in which fund redemptions are made according to a regular schedule, such as calendar quarter-ends. The stated objective is to protect remaining investors from incurring transaction charges resulting from other investors' redemption activity. These types of fund liquidations generally must be requested in advance to allow fund managers time to trade out of potentially illiquid positions and thereby minimize trading costs.

In most cases, client redemptions are based on the fund's net asset value (NAV), where NAV is calculated using the closing price of the listing market for listed securities. Clients receive proceeds based on the fund's NAV calculation. In these cases, trading at the closing price eliminates the risk (to the fund and the trader) associated with executing at prices different from those used to calculate the fund's NAV and resulting redemption proceeds.

Trading to raise or invest cash proceeds may not require specific securities to be traded to meet cash flow needs. Instead, these trades may involve strategically choosing from those securities considered optimal to trade from a risk–return or cost perspective. Trade size and security liquidity considerations play a determining role, and understanding trade-offs between costs, liquidity, and other factors is key. For example, selling a liquid security that generates a substantial tax liability is preferred over selling an illiquid security that has a smaller associated tax liability with substantially higher trading costs that overwhelm any savings in tax liability. Similar considerations apply to risk–return and liquidity trade-offs.

2.4 Corporate Actions/Index Reconstitutions/Margin Calls

Trading may also be necessitated by such activity as corporate actions and operational needs (e.g., dividend/coupon reinvestment, distributions, margin calls, and expiration of derivative contracts). The companies held in a manager's portfolio might be undergoing corporate actions, such as mergers, acquisitions, or spinoffs, that require trading. Cash equity dividends or bond coupons may need to be reinvested. For funds that make regular distributions, the timing of distributions may not align with the timing of dividends or coupons received on the individual securities. Therefore, raising proceeds for fund distributions may require individual holdings to be sold to meet distribution needs.

Cash needs can also arise from margin calls on leveraged positions as portfolio managers are asked to increase cash collateral on trades that have moved against them. Margin or collateral calls may drive high levels of trade urgency, given a need

Motivations to Trade

for the immediate sale of portfolio holdings. For example, the use of derivatives within a portfolio often requires collateral posting, which can necessitate a move to more liquid government bonds or cash in order to meet or fund collateral requirements.

Long-only managers may manage funds using a market-weighted index as a benchmark (e.g., the S&P 500, the MSCI World Index). If the benchmark constituents change, it could affect the manager's desired portfolio composition. If the manager runs an active portfolio, in the case of a change in index constituents, the manager might choose to sell holdings in a security that has been removed from the benchmark index.

For index tracking portfolios, such index changes as additions, deletions, and constituent weight changes are generally traded in the manager's portfolio to reflect benchmark exposure. Since the fund's NAV is calculated using the official market close for each security, trading index changes at the closing price ensures that the same price is used for fund and benchmark valuation (which also uses the closing price in its calculation) and thus minimizes the fund's tracking error to the benchmark index.

IN-TEXT QUESTION

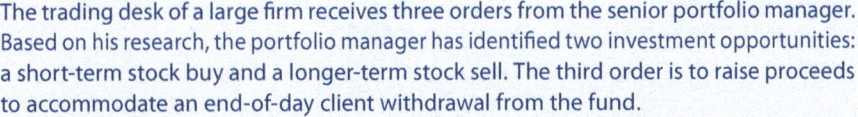

The trading desk of a large firm receives three orders from the senior portfolio manager. Based on his research, the portfolio manager has identified two investment opportunities: a short-term stock buy and a longer-term stock sell. The third order is to raise proceeds to accommodate an end-of-day client withdrawal from the fund.

Discuss the motivation to trade and the associated trade urgency for each order:

a Short-term buy
b Longer-term sell
c Client withdrawal

Solution:

a This is a profit-seeking trade because the portfolio manager has identified the short-term buy as an investment opportunity. Short-term profit-seeking trades typically involve higher levels of trade urgency as managers attempt to realize short-term alpha before it dissipates (decays). These managers seek to transact before the rest of the market recognizes the mispricing and as a result are less price sensitive and more aggressive (seek to transact at accelerated rates) in their trading.

b This is a profit-seeking trade because the portfolio manager has identified the longer-term sell as an investment opportunity. Managers seeking long-term profits are typically more patient in trading and willing to wait for favorable prices by spreading executions over a longer time horizon, which may be days or weeks. Managers trading for long-term profits generally have much lower trade urgency for these orders.

c This is a cash flow–driven trade arising from the need to raise proceeds for the client withdrawal. For funds that offer daily liquidity, clients can invest and redeem at the end of each trading day. In this case, managers raising proceeds for client withdrawals will generally target end-of-day closing prices to match trade prices to those used to calculate the fund's valuation and redemption proceeds to the client. Hedge funds that hold less liquid positions may allow redemptions only at quarter-end and with a relatively long notice period (e.g., one month), allowing them more time to sell illiquid positions. Client-driven redemptions usually involve much lower levels of trade urgency.

3 TRADING STRATEGIES AND STRATEGY SELECTION

b   discuss inputs to the selection of a trading strategy

Once a portfolio manager has made an investment decision, the portfolio manager and the trader must work together to identify the most appropriate trading strategy to meet the portfolio manager's trade objective given cost, risk, and other considerations. Selecting the appropriate trading strategy involves a number of important trade input considerations to ensure the strategy is transacted in the most efficient manner possible.

3.1 Trade Strategy Inputs

In addition to a portfolio manager's motivation to trade, other factors play a role in the selection of a trading strategy by affecting trade urgency, expected costs, and risks for the desired trade. Portfolio managers can manage the trading costs and execution risks they incur through their selection of an appropriate trading strategy.

Key inputs for trade strategy selection include

- order characteristics,
- security characteristics,
- market conditions, and
- individual risk aversion.

3.1.1 Order Characteristics

Order-related considerations include the following:

- **Side:** the side or trade direction of the order—for example, buy, sell, cover, or short
- **Size:** the total amount or quantity of the security being transacted
- **Relative size (% of ADV):** order size as a percentage of the security's average daily volume (ADV)

The side of the order, such as buy or sell, may be important when there is expected price momentum associated with trading the security or when trading a basket of securities where managing the risk of the entire trade list is required. If prices are rising, executing a buy order may take longer than executing a sell order, given the presence of more buyers (liquidity demanders) than sellers (liquidity suppliers) in the market. Trading a list that consists of only buys or only sells will have greater market risk exposure than a list of buys and sells in which the securities have offsetting market risk exposures.

Order size is the amount or quantity of the security being traded. Larger order sizes create greater market impact in trading. Market impact is the adverse price movement in a security caused by trading an order and is one of the most significant costs in trading. Larger orders usually take longer to trade than smaller orders do, and portfolio managers will often trade larger orders in a more patient manner (lower trade urgency) to reduce market impact. All else equal, trading larger order sizes more quickly will increase market impact cost whereas trading smaller order sizes more slowly will decrease market impact cost.

To have a consistent order size measure across securities, portfolio managers often divide the order size by the security's ADV. For example, a 1 million share order in Stock ABC may be much different than a 1 million share order in Stock XYZ. If Stock ABC has an average daily volume of 50 million shares, the 1 million share order represents 2% (1 million/50 million) of ADV. If Stock XYZ has an average daily volume of 4 million shares, its order represents 25% (1 million/4 million) of ADV. The larger the size of the trade expressed as a percentage of ADV, the larger the expected market impact cost.

3.1.2 Security Characteristics

Security-related considerations include the following:

- **Security type:** the type of security being traded (underlying, ETF, American depositary receipt, global depositary receipt)
- **Short-term alpha:** the expected price movement in the security over the trading horizon
- **Price volatility:** the annualized price volatility of the security
- **Security liquidity:** the liquidity profile of the security (e.g., ADV, bid–ask spread, average trade size)

The security type distinguishes the instrument being traded and can include underlying securities, ETFs, American depositary receipts (ADRs), global depositary receipts (GDRs), derivative contracts, and foreign exchange currencies. Identifying the best means of exposure—for example, whether to trade a foreign security in its local market or trade its associated ADR (if US listed) or GDR (if non-US listed)—requires an evaluation of the trade-offs. Trading costs and liquidity will vary by local exchange. Gaining emerging market exposure, in particular, may be less expensive and operationally easier when trading available ADRs and GDRs than when trading the security in the local market. In addition, compliance, regulatory, and custody costs can be lower with ADRs and GDRs.

Short-term alpha in a trading context is the expected movement in security price over the trading horizon (independent of the trade's impact). Short-term alpha (also called *trading alpha* or *trade alpha*) may arise from an appreciation, a depreciation, or a reversion (i.e., reversal) in security price.

Alpha decay is the erosion in short-term alpha that takes place after the investment decision has been made. Alpha decay results from price movement in the direction of the investment forecast and occurs regardless of whether the trade takes place. Alpha decay is a function of the time required for a relevant piece of information (used by a portfolio manager to form her investment view) to be incorporated into a security's price. If this information is rapidly incorporated into the security's price, then its alpha is considered to decay quickly. High rates of alpha decay, or alpha loss, require faster, or more accelerated, trading to realize alpha before it is traded on by other market participants.

Depending on the expected rate of alpha decay, portfolio managers may be better off trading the order faster (higher trade urgency) or slower (lower trade urgency). In an adversely trending market—for example, buying in a rising market or selling in a falling market—portfolio managers may trade at an accelerated rate if less favorable prices are expected later in the trading horizon. In a favorably trending market—for example, buying in a falling market or selling in a rising market—portfolio managers are better off trading more slowly to execute at more favorable prices expected later in the trading horizon. Adverse price movements increase trading costs, whereas favorable price movements decrease trading costs.

The price volatility of a security primarily affects the execution risk of the trade. *Execution risk* is the risk of an adverse price movement occurring over the trading horizon owing to a change in the fundamental value of the security or because of trading-induced volatility. Execution risk is often proxied by price volatility. Securities with higher levels of price volatility have greater exposure to execution risk than securities with lower price volatility.

A security's liquidity profile affects how quickly the trade can be executed, in addition to expected trading cost, and is a significant consideration in determining trade strategy. All else being equal, greater liquidity reduces execution risk and trading costs, such as market impact. Bid–ask spreads indicate round-trip trading costs for trades of a given maximum size (as they are associated with a maximum quantity). As a result, bid–ask spreads indicate both trading costs and the amount of a security that can be traded at a given point in time (market depth), which affects how larger trades might need to be broken down into smaller orders for trading. Average trade sizes observed in past data provide additional information on quantities that can be traded at reasonable trading costs for a given security.

3.1.3 Market Conditions

Inputs relating to market conditions include the following:

- **Liquidity crises:** deviations from expected liquidity patterns due to periods of crisis

Market liquidity refers to the liquidity conditions in the market at the time the order is traded. At the time of trading, current or realized market conditions, such as traded volumes, price volatility, and bid–ask spreads, are additional factors that affect trade strategy selection, given that real-time market conditions are likely to be different from those anticipated and the conditions at the time the investment decision was made.

During market events or crises, the volatility and liquidity of the market and the security will be critical to consider as conditions result in sudden and significant deviations from normal trade patterns. Such seasonal considerations as local market holidays and quarter-end or year-end dates may have more predictability in their liquidity variations and are also important to consider.

Security liquidity will also change over time, often because of changes in market-wide liquidity. For example, in August 2007, stocks with high exposure to widely used quantitative factors became very hard to liquidate as many quantitative asset managers tried to reduce their exposures to certain factors around the same time. In the fall of 2008, during the credit crisis, short selling in certain stocks, mostly financials, was banned. During this time, many structured credit securities became "toxic assets" and became extremely difficult to liquidate.

Even during "normal" market environments, liquidity will vary. For example, over time certain companies reach market values that may result in them being added to or removed from widely used equity indexes. When this happens, their stocks' liquidity often improves or deteriorates as their shares become more widely or more narrowly held. Government bonds are generally liquid as long as they are the most recently issued (so-called on the run) among a particular bond type. However, once they become off-the-run bonds, their liquidity generally decreases.

Moreover, market volatility and liquidity are dynamic. They are also generally negatively related, which becomes apparent especially during periods of crisis, when volatility increases and liquidity decreases. For example, during the 1987 stock market crash, the Long-Term Capital Management crisis in 1998, and the global financial crisis in 2008, market volatility increased sharply and market liquidity collapsed. Portfolio managers can be hurt in such environments: Lower liquidity might suggest a longer trading horizon for order completion, but higher volatility might lead people to speed up their trades and incur higher costs. However, as trading horizon lengthens, market risk increases, particularly during periods of high volatility.

3.1.4 User-Based Considerations: Trading Cost Risk Aversion

In addition to order, security, and market considerations, the risk aversion of the individual(s) trading affects trade strategy selection.

Risk aversion is specific to each individual, and in a trading context, it refers to how much risk the portfolio manager or trader is willing to accept during trading. A portfolio manager or trader with a high level of risk aversion is likely to be more concerned about market risk and will tend to trade with greater trade urgency to avoid the greater market exposure associated with trading more patiently. A portfolio manager with a low level of risk aversion might be less concerned about market risk and may tend to trade more patiently (more passively), with lower levels of trade urgency.

3.1.5 Market Impact and Execution Risk

The temporary market impact cost of trading an order is the often short-lived impact on security price from trading to meet the need to buy or sell. For example, in situations where a portfolio manager is looking to buy shares but there are not enough sellers in the market to complete the order, the portfolio manager will need to increase his buying price to attract sellers to complete the order. In situations where a portfolio manager is looking to sell shares but there are not enough buyers in the market to complete the order, the portfolio manager will need to decrease his selling price to attract buyers to complete the order. In these situations, there is usually price reversion after the trade has been completed since the price change was driven by short-term buying or selling pressure rather than a fundamental change in security value. Therefore, post-trade prices should revert, with prices decreasing after buy order completion and increasing after sell order completion.

The permanent component of price change associated with trading an order is the market price impact caused by the information content of the trade. Trading in the market often conveys information to other market participants that the asset may be under- or overvalued. If market participants discover there are more buyers demanding liquidity than sellers supplying liquidity, the market interprets this situation as the pricing being relatively too low and prices will move in the direction of the trade imbalance on average. In this case, market participants will increase their selling price.

If market participants find out that there are more sellers than buyers, the market interprets this situation as the pricing being relatively too high and market participants will decrease their buying price. In other words, market participants may believe there is some information component of the trade that is causing the counterparty to buy or sell shares in the market that they have not yet discovered or incorporated into their own asset valuations. Therefore, market participants will adjust the price at which they are willing to buy or sell to reflect this potential new information.

To minimize information leakage, which may result in market participants adjusting the prices at which they are willing to buy or sell, portfolio managers may attempt to hide their trading activity by executing orders across different venues and using a mix of order types, such as market and limit orders. Market (marketable) orders instruct execution at the best available price at the time of trading, whereas limit orders instruct execution at the best available price as long as the price is equal to or better than the specified limit price—that is, a price equal to or lower than the limit price in the case of buys and equal to or higher in the case of sells. To hide their activity, portfolio managers will also trade less on displayed venues (e.g., exchanges with greater trade transparency regarding the intentions of market participants) and make greater use of dark pool venues.

Execution risk—the risk of adverse price movement during the trading horizon due to a change in the fundamental value of the security—arises as time passes and occurs even if the order is not traded. Trading faster (greater trade urgency) results in lower execution risk because the order is executed over a shorter period of time, which decreases the time the trade is exposed to price volatility and changing market conditions. Trading slower (lower trade urgency) results in higher execution risk because the order is executed over a longer period of time, which increases the time the trade is exposed to price volatility and changing market conditions.

Trader's dilemma. To alleviate the market impact effect of entering a large order into the market, traders will "slice" the order into smaller pieces to trade over time. This results in a lower market price impact on the value of the asset, but in trading in smaller pieces over time, the fund is exposed to market risk, which could result in an even higher trading cost than if the order was entered into the market in its entirety. This phenomenon is known as the trader's dilemma and is stated as follows:

Trading too fast results in too much market impact, but trading too slow results in too much market risk.

The goal in selecting a trading strategy is to choose the best price–time trade-off given current market conditions and the unique characteristics of the order.

> **IN-TEXT QUESTION**
>
> Discuss how order size and security liquidity considerations affect market impact and execution risk for an order.
>
> **Solution:**
>
> Trading a large order creates greater market impact than trading a smaller order, all else being equal. To minimize market impact, large orders are often traded over longer trade time horizons, which increases the corresponding execution risk of the order. Smaller orders have less market impact and can be traded more quickly over shorter time horizons, with lower associated execution risk. The liquidity profile of a security has important implications for trading strategy. More liquid securities (higher traded volumes, tighter bid–ask spreads, etc.) have lower levels of market impact and execution risk given that they can be transacted over shorter time horizons with greater certainty of execution. Finally, higher rates of alpha decay would speed up order execution time horizons and increase market impact costs given greater trade order urgency, whereas lower rates of alpha decay would increase trade time horizons and associated execution risk.

4 REFERENCE PRICES

c compare benchmarks for trade execution

Reference prices, also referred to as *price benchmarks*, are specified prices, price-based calculations, or price targets used to select and execute a trade strategy. Reference prices are used in determining trade prices for execution strategy and in calculating actual trade costs for post-trade evaluation purposes. Following is a discussion of reference prices used in the selection and execution of a trade strategy.

Reference prices are categorized as follows:

- pre-trade benchmarks, where the reference price for the benchmark is known before trading begins;
- intraday benchmarks, where the reference price for the benchmark is computed on the basis of market prices that occur during the trading period;
- post-trade benchmarks, where the reference price for the benchmark is established after trading is completed; and
- price target benchmarks, where the reference price for the benchmark is specified as a price to meet or beat (transact more favorably).

4.1 Pre-Trade Benchmarks

A pre-trade benchmark is a reference price that is known before the start of trading. For example, pre-trade benchmarks include decision price, previous close, opening price, and arrival price. A pre-trade benchmark is often specified by portfolio managers who are buying or selling securities on the basis of decision prices (the price at the time the investment decision was made) or seeking short-term alpha by buying undervalued or selling overvalued securities in the market. Portfolio managers making trading decisions based on quantitative models or portfolio optimizers that use historical trading prices, such as the previous close, as model inputs may also specify a pre-trade benchmark.

4.1.1 Decision price

The **decision price** benchmark represents the security price at the time the portfolio manager made the decision to buy or sell the security. In many situations, portfolio managers have exact records of the price when they decided to buy or sell the security. Quantitative portfolio managers will often have records of their decision price because these prices may be inputs into their quantitative models.

There are times, however, when portfolio managers do not have a record of their decision price. In these situations, portfolio managers may decide to buy or sell securities on the basis of long-term growth prospects or higher-than-expected return potential and will specify the previous close or opening price as their reference price benchmark.

4.1.2 Previous close

The previous close benchmark refers to the security's closing price on the previous trading day. A previous close benchmark is often specified by quantitative portfolio managers who incorporate the previous close in a quantitative model, portfolio optimizer, or screening model. The previous close is often used as a proxy for the decision price by quantitative portfolio managers.

4.1.3 Opening price

An opening price benchmark references the security's opening price for the day. This benchmark price is most often specified by portfolio managers who begin trading at the market open and wish to minimize trading costs. The opening price is often used as a proxy for the decision price by fundamental portfolio managers who are investing in a security for long-term alpha or growth potential. Portfolio managers may choose an opening price instead of the decision price or previous close because, unlike a reference price from the prior day or earlier, the opening price does not have associated overnight risk, or the risk that prices will adjust at market open to incorporate information released after the close of the previous business day.

If the trade is to be executed in the opening auction, then using the opening price as a reference benchmark is not appropriate because the trade itself can influence the reference benchmark. An auction in this case is a market where buyers compete for order execution and orders are aggregated for execution at a single price and point in time. An auction taking place at market open is referred to as an opening auction, and one taking place at market close is a closing auction. The impact of trading any amount of the order in the opening (or closing) auction would be incorporated in the opening (or closing) price auction calculation, thus inappropriately influencing the reference benchmark level.

4.1.4 Arrival price

The **arrival price** is the price of the security at the time the order is entered into the market for execution. Portfolio managers who are buying or selling on the basis of alpha expectations or a current market mispricing will often specify an arrival price benchmark. In these cases, the portfolio manager's goal is to transact at or close to current market prices in order to complete trade execution and realize as much potential alpha as possible. Portfolio managers looking to minimize trading cost will also in many cases specify the arrival price as their benchmark.

4.2 Intraday Benchmarks

An intraday price benchmark is based on a price that occurs during the trading period. The most common intraday benchmarks used in trading are volume-weighted average price (VWAP) and time-weighted average price (TWAP).

Portfolio managers often specify an intraday benchmark for funds that are trading passively over the day, seeking liquidity, and for funds that may be rebalancing, executing a buy/sell trade list, and minimizing risk. Portfolio managers who do not expect the security to exhibit any short-term price momentum commonly select an intraday benchmark.

4.2.1 VWAP

The VWAP benchmark price is the volume-weighted average price of all trades executed over the day or the trading horizon. Portfolio managers may specify the VWAP benchmark when they wish to participate with volume patterns over the day.

Portfolio managers who are rebalancing their portfolios over the day and have both buy and sell orders may select the VWAP as a price benchmark. In these situations, the preference is to participate with market volume. Exposure to market risk is reduced in this case by having a two-sided trade list of buys and sells, as opposed to a trade list containing all buys or all sells. Portfolio managers who are rebalancing and using cash from sell orders to purchase buy orders will also often select an intraday benchmark, such as VWAP. Doing so allows the portfolio managers to structure their executions over time to ensure cash received from sell orders is sufficient to fund remaining buy orders. If trades are not executed properly, portfolio managers could be short cash for buy orders and need to raise additional money for order completion.

4.2.2 TWAP

The TWAP benchmark price is defined as an equal-weighted average price of all trades executed over the day or trading horizon. Unlike VWAP, TWAP price does not consider volume traded and is simply the average price of trades executed over the specified time horizon. Portfolio managers may choose TWAP when they wish to exclude potential trade outliers. Trade outliers may be caused by trading a large buy order at the day's low or a large sell order at the day's high. If market participants are not able to fully participate in these trades, then TWAP may be a more appropriate choice. The TWAP benchmark is used by portfolio managers and traders to evaluate fair and reasonable trading prices in market environments with high volume uncertainty and for securities that are subject to spikes in trading volume throughout the day.

4.3 Post-Trade Benchmarks

A post-trade benchmark is a reference price that is determined at the end of trading or sometime after trading has completed. The most common post-trade benchmark is closing price. Portfolio managers for funds valued at the closing price on the day or who wish to minimize tracking error to an underlying benchmark price, such as index funds, often select a post-trade reference price, such as the official closing price. In this case, the objective is to target consistency between the trade execution price and the price used in fund valuation and benchmark calculation.

4.3.1 *Closing price*

The closing price is typically used by index managers and mutual funds that wish to execute transactions at the closing price for the day. For managers with index mandates, where the fund's securities are typically valued using the official market close for each security, it is important to know how close their executions are to the benchmark price, which also uses the official market close in its calculation. A portfolio manager who is managing tracking error to a benchmark will generally select a closing price benchmark since the closing price is the price used to compute the fund's valuation and resulting tracking error to the benchmark.

An advantage of the closing price benchmark is that it provides portfolio managers with the price used for fund valuation and thus minimizes potential tracking error. A disadvantage is that the benchmark price is not known until after trading is completed. Thus, portfolio managers have no way of knowing whether they are performing more or less favorably relative to the benchmark until after trading is completed.

4.4 Price Target Benchmarks

Portfolio managers seeking short-term alpha may select an alternative benchmark known as a price target benchmark. In this case, a portfolio manager would like to transact in a security—believed to be undervalued or overvalued—at a more favorable price. For example, if a stock currently trading in the market at $20.00 is believed to be undervalued by $0.50, the portfolio manager will seek to purchase shares by specifying a price target of $20.50 or better (better being lower than $20.50 in the case of a buy). In this example, the benchmark price is specified as the perceived fair value price of $20.50. In this setting, the portfolio manager wishes to purchase as many order shares as possible at a price equal to or better (lower) than the specified price target.

TRADING STRATEGIES

5

d recommend and justify a trading strategy (given relevant facts)

The primary goal of any trading strategy is to balance the expected costs and risks associated with trading the order in the market consistent with the portfolio manager's trading objectives, risk aversion, and other known constraints. A portfolio manager's motivation to trade, risk aversion, trade urgency for the order, and other factors, such as order size and market conditions at the time of trading, are thus key in determining an appropriate trade strategy.

Will the value in completing the trade dissipate if the trade is not completed in a timely enough manner? Trade urgency, the importance of execution certainty, is critical in determining trade strategy. For alpha-driven trades, trading with greater urgency to maximize short-term alpha capture must be weighed against the costs of trading faster and expected alpha decay. For trades with low or no trade urgency, trading over a longer trade horizon or at the market close may be optimal.

Portfolio managers also have expectations or insights regarding short-term market conditions, such as price trends and market liquidity, particularly if these factors are used in the security selection process. For example, does the stock exhibit momentum, where any observed trend will continue through the end of the day, or does the stock exhibit reversion, where the observed trend is more likely to reverse during the day? Portfolio managers may also have insights into expected trading volumes for assets and whether trading volumes may be expected to continue or may reverse in direction. Traders will also have insights regarding volume patterns and potential information leakage during execution. These expectations combined with actual market conditions at the time of trading help inform an appropriate trade strategy.

The selection of a trade strategy is best illustrated through a discussion of common trade types. Trading strategies for the following types of trades involving equities, fixed income, currency, and derivatives are explained in this section:

- **Short-term alpha:** short-term alpha-driven equity trade (high trade urgency)
- **Long-term alpha:** long-term alpha-driven fixed-income trade (low trade urgency)
- **Risk rebalance:** buy/sell basket trade to rebalance a fund's risk exposure
- **Cash flow driven:** client redemption trade to raise proceeds
- **Cash flow driven:** cash equitization (derivatives) trade to invest a new client mandate

5.1 Short-Term Alpha Trade

A portfolio manager has determined that the market has overreacted to weak earnings announced in the pre-market trading session for Stock XYZ. The stock price is trading at a significant discount in the pre-market relative to the portfolio manager's valuation and now represents a significant buying opportunity based on the portfolio manager's analysis. The portfolio manager would like to buy 50,000 shares, which represents 10% of the stock's average daily volume. Based on the heavy pre-market trading, however, the trader believes that this order will only constitute 2% of the day's volume.

The pre-market price is currently $50, down $15 relative to the previous night's close. The portfolio manager believes that the stock's fair value is in the low $60 range and sets her limit price at $60.

In this situation, the portfolio manager believes that the market has overreacted to the weak earnings announced by the company. If she is correct and the market eventually adopts her view going forward, Stock XYZ's price should increase closer to her estimated fair value in the low $60 range. In setting her limit price of $60, the portfolio manager is also specifying the reference price for the trade, which, in this case, represents a price target benchmark.

Given the possibility of short-term price increases in XYZ, this order has associated trade urgency and the trader does not have the benefit of trading the order passively (such as using a VWAP or TWAP participation strategy) during the day, since XYZ's price could increase to fair value at any time. To trade this order, the trader would not likely attempt to use dark pool venues, given their greater risk of unfilled executions if offsetting orders do not arrive. The trader will likely want to trade a portion of the order in the opening auction and then continue trading any residual in the open market. Doing so provides greater execution certainty, which is important in this situation given the trade urgency of the order.

Since the order represents approximately 2% of expected volume, the trader would not likely place the full order into the opening auction. Research shows the US opening auction typically makes up between 1% and 4% of a day's volume,[2] so sending the entire order into the opening auction would result in the ordering being

---

[2] See J. Bacidore, K. Berkow, and J. Wong, "Inside the Opening Auction," *Journal of Trading* 7 (Winter 2012): 7–14.

roughly 50%–200% of the expected opening auction volume, on average. Because this is an unusual trading day, the trader could use volume information from pre-market trading and any auction-related data made available by the exchanges to determine the optimal amount to place into the opening auction.

Given the trade urgency of the order, the very liquid market for XYZ, and the order size not being large relative to XYZ's expected volume, the trader could trade any remaining shares using an arrival price trade strategy that would attempt to execute the remaining shares close to market prices at the time the order was received. This strategy could be executed using a programmed strategy to electronically execute, also known as an algorithm, such as an arrival price algorithm. Most importantly, the trader will want to make sure that the orders sent to the auction and traded in the open market use limit prices consistent with the portfolio manager's price view, reflected in her limit price of $60.

5.2 Long-Term Alpha Trade

A portfolio manager believes that a company whose bonds he holds is likely to experience a deteriorating credit position over the next year. The deterioration in credit is expected to be gradual as information becomes available over the next several quarters, confirming the company's deteriorating financial position. The portfolio manager's position is not large in aggregate, but the market for these bonds is not very active, with infrequent transactions and low volumes. The portfolio manager approaches the trader to determine how best to liquidate his holdings in the bond so that he can exploit his view while still getting a favorable execution.

Because the market for these bonds is not very liquid, it is likely the trader will need to approach various dealers to get quotes for these bonds. Given the portfolio manager's view that the deterioration in credit will occur gradually over the coming year, there is no order urgency from a trading perspective. Because the position is not large, the trader believes he could execute it over the next day or two if needed.

The trader, however, may not want to execute this quickly for two reasons. First, the sudden trading in an illiquid security may inadvertently leak information, leading the dealer involved to think the order is an information-based trade and consequently to price the trade less favorably for the trader. Second, requiring dealers to take on substantial illiquid inventory exposes them to risk, for which they will demand compensation in the form of inferior (unfavorable) pricing.

Therefore, a reasonable trade approach would be to sell these bonds off gradually over the course of a few days or even weeks, depending on the relative size of the bond holdings and their liquidity. By selling off smaller portions, varying the amounts sold, and trading over a longer execution horizon, the trader can reduce information leakage regarding the order and avoid placing pressure on dealer inventories, which would result in inferior pricing. Using this approach, the dealers will likely provide better (more favorable) initial quotes, and subsequent quotes may also be more favorable if the dealers have enough time between trades to reduce their inventory.

The use of reference prices for fixed-income trades executed over multiple days is not widespread and can be difficult in practice. A decision price, for example, would not only capture market impact and alpha loss but would also reflect unrelated market moves, which can be much larger than the former when a trade is spread out over days or weeks. Impact costs, for example, would decrease as the trade horizon lengthens, whereas price volatility impact would increase with time.

5.3 Risk Rebalance Trade

A macro fund manager is concerned that potential trade tariffs and a deteriorating financial situation in a number of key emerging markets may lead to a significant increase in currency volatility. The manager is holding long and short developed market currency positions and has, so far, not seen a significant impact on his fund's valuation because the fund's long and short positions have been constructed to offset one another, immunizing the fund from sudden price moves. The fund's mandate, however, specifies a target risk level of 10%. With the increase in volatility, the fund's risk level is currently closer to 14%. Although the increase has not caused the portfolio to breach any guidelines, the portfolio manager believes that volatility will remain at current levels for the next several months and wishes to reduce risk in a controlled and gradual manner by liquidating positions to bring the fund's volatility back to its target risk level. The portfolio manager approaches a trader to discuss an appropriate strategy.

In this situation, the macro fund manager is holding long and short positions and has no view as to whether the fund's value will rise or fall in the near term owing to the sudden increase in volatility. Consequently, the hedge fund manager simply wishes to reduce current positions (as opposed to rebalancing the fund's relative positions). The holdings in developed market currencies are actively traded, and it is unlikely the positions are large enough that they would dislocate (substantially move) the currency markets, as long as trading is done in an appropriate manner.

Although volatility has significantly increased, the risk exposure of the trade is more limited if the list of buys and sells is balanced in market risk exposure, such as a buy/sell trade list with a net beta of approximately zero (i.e., the trade-weighted average beta of the securities traded is zero). Therefore, the trader does not have the same trade urgency as a trade with a positive or negative net beta, such as one containing all buys or all sells, which might involve significantly more risk arising from exposure to potential market movement. Risk-averse market participants will typically have greater trade urgency for trades that have directional market exposure than for trades that are balanced, or hedged, in market exposure.

Since the portfolio is not in breach of its guidelines and the portfolio manager wishes to reduce risk on a controlled and gradual basis, the trader can trade this order in a passive manner to lower the fund's risk level. In this situation, using a TWAP reference price for the trade and a TWAP algorithm to execute over the next day or two (or longer, depending on the size of the position) would be an appropriate trading strategy. By trading all the orders over the same trading horizon using a TWAP strategy, the trader is maintaining the hedge that exists between the buys and sells, which helps reduce execution risk. And because currency markets in developed economies are very liquid and deep, trading algorithmically will not likely dislocate prices.

5.4 Client Redemption Trade

A client has decided to redeem its position in a small-cap/mid-cap value fund managed by ABC Investment Advisers. The fund holdings are US small- and mid-cap stocks, with the only constraints being that the stocks satisfy the criteria of the fund (e.g., stocks meet the definition of a small- or mid-cap stock, stocks are listed on a major exchange). Client redemptions from the fund are done at the fund's net asset value at the close of trading, where the NAV is calculated using the closing price of the stock's listing market. To raise the necessary cash to meet the client redemption request, the portfolio manager asks the trader to sell 0.1% of every position held in the fund.

In this scenario, the client will receive the NAV of the fund *regardless of how well or poorly the trader executes the trade.* Therefore, the trader bears risk (for executing at any price other than the closing price) unless she can guarantee that each position is executed at the closing price. A closing price reference price is, therefore, most appropriate for this trade. Because these stocks are traded on either the NASDAQ or the NYSE, the trader can send the order to the closing auction for these exchanges and receive the auction-guaranteed closing price on all orders submitted to the auction. Such a strategy eliminates all potential risk of executing at prices that are different from those used to calculate the fund's NAV.

However, the trader should make sure that the size of the orders does not have an undue impact on the closing price. Executing a relatively large sell order in the closing auction (e.g., 50% of the closing volume) may lead to a significant price decline at the close, lowering calculated NAV and resulting in less cash being returned to the client.

Following a strategy to receive a guaranteed closing price on all orders submitted eliminates risk to the fund (and trader) since the client is receiving proceeds at NAV. From a fiduciary standpoint, however, trading in a manner that will lead to a poorer (less favorable) execution for a client is inappropriate. An alternative approach that portfolio managers follow when their trades are large relative to expected liquidity in the closing auction is to execute in the market and in the closing auction. For example, they would identify a reasonable amount to send to the closing auction (e.g., 90% of the order to be sent to the closing auction), trade the order remainder in the market prior to the close of trading (e.g., 10% of the order to be traded VWAP in the market up to the close of trading),[3] and then send the identified amount (90% of the order) to the closing auction.

5.5 New Mandate Trade

An investment manager has just been awarded a $150 million mandate to track the Russell 2000 Index benchmark with a 3% tracking error. The investment manager and the client have agreed that performance measurement of the mandate will begin at the current day's close. The appropriate reference price for the trade is, therefore, also the closing price. Given the large size of the investment mandate, the trader is concerned that trading into the positions at the close of trading will cause significant price impact. The trader would instead prefer to trade into the positions over multiple days. The client, however, requests that the mandate be fully invested as quickly as possible. The portfolio manager for the fund also prefers not to have the fund holding cash, given that the performance evaluation for the mandate begins as of the close of trading. Holding a cash position in the fund exposes the portfolio manager to significant performance risk relative to the fund's Russell 2000 benchmark. For example, if the Russell 2000 increases while the fund is holding cash, the fund's uninvested cash amounts would result in underperformance (arising from cash drag) relative to the Russell 2000.

The trader can get more immediate exposure to the Russell 2000 by buying $150 million worth of futures near the end of the trading day. After establishing this initial exposure, the trader can begin building the underlying stock positions over time and unwinding (selling) the equivalent futures exposure. This approach allows the client mandate to achieve full $150 million exposure to the Russell 2000, eliminating the opportunity cost of holding cash balances in the fund. This approach also gives the trader additional time to establish the underlying positions, thereby receiving (hopefully) better execution prices. For smaller mandates in more liquid securities, the trader could possibly skip the equitization-via-futures step and instead invest

---

[3] Some brokers provide special "close algorithms" that will size the closing auction trade appropriately, route the order into the closing auction, and trade any residual in the open market, effectively automating the strategy discussed in this example.

directly in the underlying securities. For larger mandates, however, investing in the index via liquid futures contracts initially is often an effective means to equitize cash and reduce tracking error for the client mandate and fund.

Two considerations should be noted in this situation. First, futures markets may not have closing auctions, as is the case with the Russell 2000 futures contract. If no closing auction exists, the trader will likely want to time the trade as close to the benchmark close as possible; for example, in the United States, this equates to a 4:00 p.m. cash close. For a small trade that is less than the quoted size, the trader could send a market order at 4:00 p.m. For larger trades or less liquid futures, the trader may trade using a VWAP or TWAP algorithm into the market close. Second, this futures-based strategy assumes the fund's investment mandate allows the use of derivatives. If the fund's mandate does not allow the use of derivatives, such as futures, but does permit ETF usage, the trader could equitize cash using a liquid Russell 2000 ETF.

IN-TEXT QUESTION

A portfolio manager for a global fixed-income index fund is required to trade for quarterly index changes taking place at the end of the trading day. To keep the fund in line with the anticipated index constituent changes, the portfolio manager generates a fund rebalance list consisting of buys and sells. He approaches the senior trader to discuss the best trade strategy for the list.

1. Identify the most appropriate reference price benchmark for his trade.
2. Select and justify the most appropriate trading strategy to execute his trade.

Solution:

1. A closing price is the most appropriate reference price benchmark for an index fund. The portfolio manager needs to trade to maintain the same security holdings and weights as the benchmark index. Since the index fund will be valued using official closing prices, he should select the closing price as the reference price benchmark for trading the rebalance names. By executing the buys and sells at the close, he will be minimizing the fund's potential tracking error to the benchmark index.

   The previous close would not be an appropriate reference price benchmark since it would be the security's closing price on the previous trading day. A previous close benchmark is often used by quantitative portfolio managers whose models or optimizers incorporate the previous close as an input or who wish to use this price as a proxy for the decision price. The opening price benchmark would not be an appropriate benchmark because it references the security's opening price on the day and is often selected by portfolio managers and traders who wish to begin trading at the market open. The opening price may also be used as a proxy for the decision price.

2. A market-on-close (MOC) trade strategy would be the most appropriate strategy for his rebalance list. Trading the rebalance list at the market's closing prices best aligns the trade execution prices with the same closing prices used for the fund's NAV and benchmark calculation, thus minimizing tracking error of the fund to the benchmark index.

TRADE EXECUTION

e describe factors that typically determine the selection of a trading algorithm class

Once the appropriate trade strategy is determined by the portfolio manager and the trader, the trade must be executed in a market and in a manner consistent with the trade strategy chosen. A variety of implementation choices are available based on the specific order, market, and trade strategy involved. Trade implementation choices range from higher-touch approaches, which involve greater degrees of human interaction for order completion, to fully automated trade execution through electronic trading venues with varying levels of trade transparency. Higher-touch orders include principal and agency trades, the main difference being who assumes the risk of trading the order. In **principal trades**, the executing broker assumes all or part of the risk related to trading the order, pricing it into her quoted spread. In **agency trades**, the broker is engaged to find the other side of the trade but acts as an agent only, and risk for trading the order remains with the buy-side portfolio manager or trader. Electronic trading includes alternative or multilateral trading venues (ATS or MTF), direct market access (DMA), and dark pools.

6.1 Trade Implementation Choices

In general, trading in large blocks of securities requires a higher-touch approach involving greater human engagement and the need for a dealer or market maker to act as counterparty and principal to trade transactions.[4] For these transactions, also called *principal trades* or *broker risk trades,* market makers and dealers become a disclosed counterparty to their clients' orders and buy securities into or sell securities from their own inventory or book, assuming risk for the trade and absorbing temporary supply–demand imbalances. In the case of a less active security, the expected time to offset the trade for the dealer is longer. For taking on this additional risk, the dealer will demand greater compensation, generally by quoting a wider bid–ask spread.

Markets characterized by dealer-provided quotes may be referred to as *quote-driven*, *over-the-counter*, or *off-exchange markets*. In such bilateral dealer markets, customers trade at prices quoted by dealers. Depending on the instrument traded, dealers may work for commercial banks, investment banks, broker/dealers, or proprietary trading firms. Worldwide, most trading besides that in stocks, ETFs, and exchange-traded derivatives takes place in quote-driven markets, where the matching of buyers and sellers takes longer because of less frequent trading and greater market illiquidity.

In some cases, dealers may be unable or unwilling to hold the securities in their inventories and take on position (principal) risk. In agency trades, dealers try to arrange trades by acting as agents, or brokers, on behalf of the client. Brokers are often used for transactions in securities or markets in which finding a buyer or a seller is difficult.

High-touch approaches involve human sell-side traders as intermediaries. These traders, employed by sell-side brokerage firms, may first attempt to fill a customer order by matching it with offsetting orders from other customers before trying to fill it from their own position book. Crossing an order with a broker's own book is known as a broker risk trade or principal trade. If this does not occur, the broker would then route the order to the open market and "slice," or divide, the order into smaller pieces

---

[4] Large trades that exceed the normal trade size in a given security are often referred to as "block trades." Brokers offer dedicated services for block trades where human facilitation is higher than for regular trades, particularly for less liquid securities.

to trade in the market. This approach involves human judgment unique to each trade and is suited to trading illiquid securities in which the execution process is difficult to automate.

A variation of quote-driven markets often used to trade less liquid securities is a **request for quote** (RFQ). In RFQ markets, dealers or market makers do not provide quotes continuously but do so only upon request by a potential buyer or seller. These quotes are nonbinding and are valid only at the time they are provided.

For relatively liquid, standardized securities where continuous two-way trading may exist, buyers and sellers display prices and quantities at which they are willing to transact (limit orders) on an exchange or other multilateral trading venue. In order-driven markets, order-matching systems run by exchanges, brokers, and other alternative trading systems use rules to arrange trades. Trading is done electronically with multiple venues, often through a consolidated limit order book that presents a view of the limit buy (bid)/sell (ask) prices and order sizes for all venues with orders for a security. Centralized clearing for trades exists on those venues. Equities, futures, and exchange-traded options are generally traded using this approach.

Exhibit 1 shows the proportion of trading that was conducted electronically in 2012 and 2015. In most asset classes, electronic trading increased over the period to more than 50% of total trading volume. Markets with higher trading activity have seen strong growth in electronic trading. For example, cash equities and futures are now predominantly traded electronically, whereas some other (generally less liquid) markets, such as high-yield bonds, still feature trading with a high-touch, manual approach.

Trade Execution

Exhibit 1   Electronic Trading in Various Asset Classes (in %)

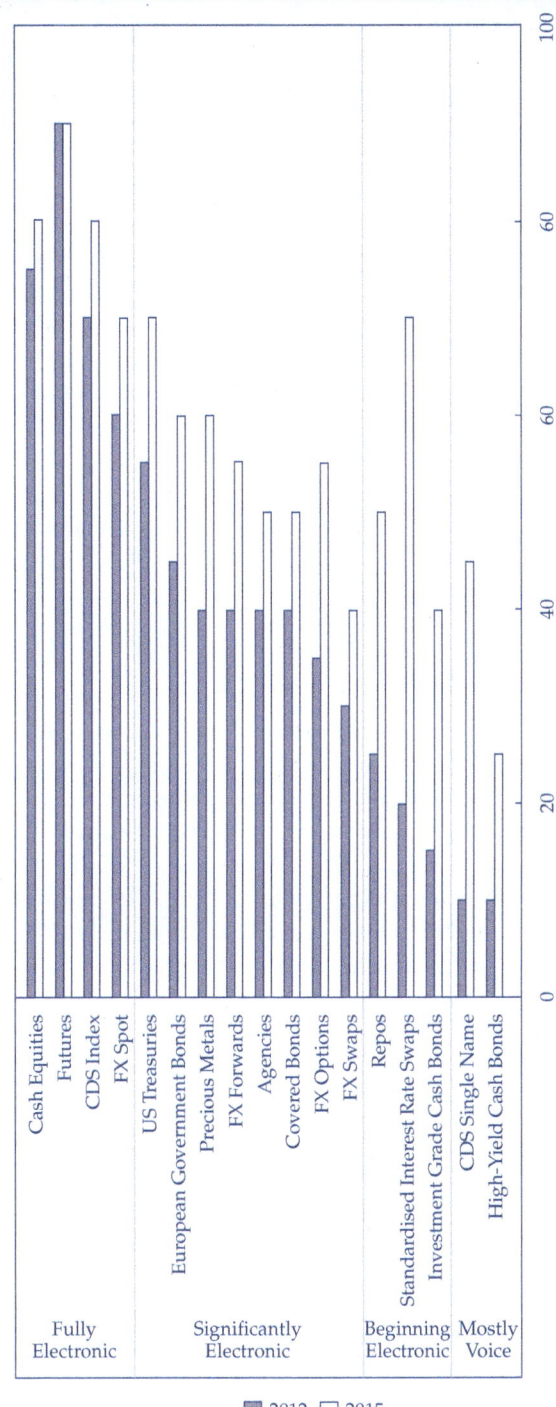

Source: Bank for International Settlements, "Electronic Trading in Fixed-Income Markets," Markets Committee Study Group (2016).

Automated execution approaches work well for liquid securities and most trade sizes other than extremely large orders (relative to the total volume traded of a particular security), which might require a more customized, high-touch approach. *Algorithmic trading*, or the use of programmed strategies to electronically trade orders, is well established in most equity, foreign exchange, and exchange-traded derivative markets. In fixed income, algorithmic execution is mostly limited to trading highly liquid government securities, such as US Treasury securities.

For liquid securities that trade in high volumes, high-touch execution approaches are generally inefficient, opaque, slow, and susceptible to front running. Front running occurs when speculative traders try to profit by buying ahead of other traders' anticipated activity. Front running is illegal in many jurisdictions if the information acted on is improperly obtained. Moreover, given that they require human involvement for each execution, they tend to be costly. Hence, for straightforward trades in liquid securities' low-touch automated execution strategies are often preferred whenever available. These generally involve direct market access (DMA) and/or execution algorithms.

Direct market access (DMA) gives all market participants a way to interact directly with the order book of an exchange, usually through a broker's exchange connectivity. This activity is normally restricted to broker/dealers and market-making firms. With DMA, buy-side firms use a broker's technology infrastructure and market access to execute orders themselves rather than handing orders over to the broker. DMA often involves the use of algorithms.

Alternatively, a broker can be instructed to execute client orders using certain execution algorithms. The desired urgency of an order is a key input for the choice and nature of the execution algorithm.

6.2 Algorithmic Trading

Algorithmic trading is the computerized execution of the investment decision following a specified set of trading instructions. An algorithm's programmed strategies used to electronically execute orders will slice larger orders into smaller pieces and trade over the day and across venues to reduce the price impact of the order. The primary goal of algorithmic trading is to ensure that the implementation of the investment decision is consistent with the investment objective of the fund. In this section, we describe factors that help determine the selection of a trading algorithm class.

Trading algorithms are primarily used for two purposes—trade execution and profit generation.

6.2.1 Execution algorithms

An execution algorithm is tasked with transacting an investment decision made by the portfolio manager. The manager determines what to buy or sell on the basis of his investment style and investment objective and then enters the order into the algorithm. The algorithm will then execute the order by following a set of rules specified by the portfolio manager.

6.2.2 Profit-seeking algorithms

A profit-seeking algorithm will determine what to buy and sell and then implement those decisions in the market as efficiently as possible. For example, these algorithms will use real-time price information and market data, such as volume and volatility, to determine what to buy or sell and will then implement the decision consistent with the investment objective. Profit-seeking algorithms are used by electronic market makers, quantitative funds, and high-frequency traders.

This section describes the common classification of execution algorithms and their use.

6.2.3 Execution Algorithm Classifications

Although there are many different types of execution algorithms, they can generally be classified into the following categories.

6.2.3.1 Scheduled (POV, VWAP, TWAP) Scheduled algorithms send orders to the market following a schedule that is determined by historical volumes or specified time periods. Scheduled algorithms include *percentage of volume (POV)* algorithms, *volume-weighted average price* algorithms, and *time-weighted average price* algorithms.

POV algorithms (also known as participation algorithms) send orders following a volume participation schedule. As trading volume increases in the market, these algorithms will trade more shares, and as volume decreases, these algorithms will trade fewer shares. Investors specify the POV algorithm through the participation rate, which determines the volume participation strategy. For example, a participation rate of 10% indicates that the algorithm will participate with 10% of the market volume until the order is completed. In this case, for every 10,000 shares that trade in the market, the algorithm will execute 1,000 shares. An advantage of volume participation algorithms is that they will automatically take advantage of increased liquidity conditions by trading more shares when there is ample market liquidity and will not trade in times of illiquidity. While POV algorithms incorporate real-time volume, by following (or chasing) volumes, they may incur higher trading costs by continuing to buy as prices move higher and to sell as prices move lower. An additional disadvantage of these algorithms is that they may not complete the order within the time period specified.

VWAP and TWAP algorithms release orders to the market following a time-specified schedule, trading a predetermined number of shares within the specified time interval; for example, trade 5,000 shares between 10:00 a.m. and 1:00 p.m. An advantage of a time slicing strategy is that it ensures the specified number of shares are executed within the specified time period. A disadvantage of a time slicing strategy is that it will force the trades even in times of insufficient liquidity and will not take advantage of increased liquidity conditions when available.

VWAP algorithms slice the order into smaller amounts to send to the market following a time slicing schedule based on historical intraday volume profiles. These algorithms typically trade a higher percentage of the order at the open and close and a smaller percentage of the order during midday. Because of this, the VWAP curve is said to resemble a U-shaped curve. Following a fixed schedule as VWAP algorithms do may not be optimal for illiquid stocks because such algorithms may not complete the order in cases where volumes are low.

TWAP algorithms slice the order into smaller amounts to send to the market following an equal- weighted time schedule. TWAP algorithms will send the same number of shares and the same percentage of the order to be traded in each time period.

Scheduled algorithms are appropriate for orders in which portfolio managers or traders do not have expectations of adverse price movement during the trade horizon. These algorithms are also used by portfolio managers and traders who have greater risk tolerance for longer execution time periods and are more concerned with minimizing market impact. Scheduled algorithms are often appropriate when the order size is relatively small (e.g., no more than 5%–10% of expected volume), the security is relatively liquid, or the orders are part of a risk-balanced basket and trading all orders at a similar pace will maintain the risk balance.

6.2.3.2 Liquidity seeking Liquidity-seeking algorithms, also referred to as *opportunistic algorithms*, take advantage of market liquidity across multiple venues by trading faster when liquidity exists at a favorable price. These algorithms may trade aggressively with offsetting orders when sufficient liquidity is posted on exchanges and alternative trading systems at prices the algorithms deem favorable (a practice called "liquidity sweeping" or "sweeping the book"). These algorithms may also use dark pools and trade large quantities of shares in dark venues when sufficient liquidity is present. If liquidity is not present in the market at favorable prices, these algorithms may trade only a small number of shares. These algorithms will often make greater use of market order types than limit order types.

Liquidity-seeking algorithms are appropriate for large orders that the portfolio manager or trader would like to execute quickly without having a substantial impact on the security price. Liquidity-seeking algorithms are also used when displaying sizable liquidity via limit orders could lead to unwanted information leakage and adverse security price movement. In these cases, the priority is to minimize information leakage associated with order execution and avoid signaling to the market the trading intentions of the portfolio manager or trader. These algorithms are also appropriate for trading securities that are relatively less liquid and thinly traded or when liquidity is episodic (e.g., the order book is typically thin with wide spreads but occasionally experiences tight spreads or thick books).

6.2.3.3 Arrival price Arrival price algorithms seek to trade close to current market prices at the time the order is received for execution. Arrival price algorithms will trade more aggressively at the beginning of trading to execute more shares nearer to the arrival price, known as a front-loaded strategy. Arrival price algorithms tend to be time schedule based but can also be volume participation based.

Arrival price algorithms are used for orders in which the portfolio manager or trader believes prices are likely to move unfavorably during the trade horizon. In these cases, the portfolio manager wishes to trade more aggressively to capture alpha ahead of the unfavorable prices expected later in the trade horizon. These algorithms are also used by portfolio managers and traders who are risk averse and wish to trade more quickly to reduce the execution risk associated with trading more passively over longer time horizons. These algorithms are used when the security is relatively liquid or the order is not outsized (e.g., the order is less than 15% of expected volume) such that a participatory strategy is not expected to result in significant market impact from order execution.

6.2.3.4 Dark strategies/liquidity aggregators Dark aggregator algorithms execute shares away from "lit" markets, such as exchanges and other displayed venues that provide pre- and post-trade transparency regarding prices, volumes, market spreads, and depth. Instead, these algorithms execute in opaque, or less transparent, trade venues, such as dark pools.

Dark aggregator algorithms are used in trading when portfolio managers and traders are concerned with information leakage that may occur from posting limit orders in lit venues with pre- and post-trade transparency. These algorithms are used when order size is large relative to the market (i.e., a large percentage of expected volume) and when trading in the open market using arrival price or VWAP strategies would lead to significant market impact. These algorithms are appropriate for trading securities that are relatively illiquid or have relatively wide bid–ask spreads. Since trading in dark pools offers less certainty of execution (offsetting orders may never arrive), these algorithms are appropriate for trades in which the trader or portfolio manager does not need to execute the order in its entirety.

6.2.3.5 Smart order routers Smart order routers (SORs) determine how best to route an order given prevailing market conditions. The SOR will determine the destination with the highest probability of executing the limit order and the venue with the best market price—known in the United States as the National Best Bid and Offer (NBBO)—for market orders. The SOR continuously monitors real-time data from exchanges and venues and also assesses ongoing activity in dark pools.

SORs are used when a portfolio manager or trader wishes to execute a small order by routing the order into the market as either a market(able) or non-marketable (limit) order.

Trade Execution

Market orders. SORs are used for orders that are sufficiently small that they will not have a large market impact if sent as marketable orders—for example, when the order size is less than the quantity posted at the best bid or offer. SORs are also best used for orders that require immediate execution because of imminent price movement, high portfolio manager or trader risk aversion, or abnormally high risk levels. Using SORs for marketable orders is also appropriate in cases where the market moves quickly, such that having the trader choose the venue(s) could lead to inferior executions (e.g., the trader chooses the venue but the venue with the best price changes before she can send the order).

Limit orders. SORs are also used for orders that are small enough that posting the order as a limit order will not leak information to the market and move prices (e.g., orders that are similar to those currently posted in the market). In addition, SORs are appropriate for stocks that have multiple markets actively trading the stock and for which it is not obvious to which venues the order should be routed (e.g., there are multiple venues currently posting orders at the trader's limit price).

IN-TEXT QUESTION

A portfolio manager has identified a stock with attractive long-term growth potential and would like to place an order of moderate size, relative to the stock's average traded volume. The stock is very liquid and has attractive short-term alpha potential. The portfolio manager expects short-term buying pressure by other market participants into the market close, ahead of the company's earnings call scheduled later in the day.

1. Explain when the following algorithms are used: (a) arrival price, (b) dark aggregator, and (c) SOR.
2. Discuss which of the three algorithms is most suited to trading this order.

Solution:

1.
   a. Arrival price algorithms are used for relatively liquid securities and when the order is not expected to have a significant market impact. Arrival price algorithms are also used when portfolio managers and traders have higher levels of risk aversion and wish to trade more aggressively at an accelerated pace to reduce the execution risk associated with trading over longer time horizons.
   b. Dark aggregator algorithms are appropriate for trading securities that are relatively illiquid or that have relatively wide bid–ask spreads or for relatively large order sizes in which trading in the open market is expected to have a significant price impact. Additionally, they are used by portfolio managers and traders who are concerned with information leakage that may occur when posting limit orders in lit venues. Given their higher risk of unfilled executions, these algorithms are also used when the order does not need to be filled in its entirety.
   c. Smart order routing systems are used to electronically send small orders into the market. Based on prevailing market conditions, SORs will determine which trade destinations have the highest probability of executing for limit orders and which trading venues have the best market prices for market orders and will route orders accordingly. SORs continuously monitor market conditions in real time in both lit and dark markets.
2. An arrival price algorithm would be most appropriate for trading this order because the portfolio manager has adverse price expectations. In this case, the portfolio manager wants to trade more aggressively to capture alpha ahead of less favorable prices expected later in the day. By trading the order more quickly,

> the portfolio manager can execute at more favorable prices ahead of the adverse price movement and the less favorable prices expected from other participants' buying pressure into the close, in line with his trade urgency.

Algorithmic Selection

Choosing the best algorithm to execute a given trade can be a difficult and complex decision. There has been a proliferation of choices for the buy-side trader, with multiple broker offerings and multiple algorithm types per broker, such as VWAP, POV, and implementation shortfall. For a given stock, what is the best algorithm to choose? Intuitively, it seems that selecting an algorithm by considering specific characteristics about the stock and its liquidity profile should be superior to selecting an algorithm without regard for these attributes. Additionally, it seems intuitive that stocks with similar characteristics might best be executed in a similar manner. This rationale has motivated firms that provide execution services to apply a machine learning technique called "clustering" to the problem of algorithmic strategy selection.

Clustering, generally used in unsupervised machine learning, groups data objects solely on the basis of information found in the data. The use of clustering for algorithmic strategy selection for stocks will generally include microstructure factors, such as bid–ask spread, trade size, price volatility, tick size, depth of the order book queue, and trading volume. Stocks are characterized from the results of the data analysis (i.e., placed into groups, or clusters, based on similarities informed by the data). For each cluster, the historical executions for each stock are examined for comparative performance. From this analysis, the optimal algorithmic strategy can be selected.

To illustrate a simple intuitive example, stocks with wider bid–ask spreads may be more effectively traded using an algorithm that executes more in off-exchange venues (such as dark pools) since on those venues trading can occur at mid-market if an offsetting order arrives and the cost of crossing the bid–ask spread (buying at the offer or selling at the bid) is high. In contrast, for a cluster of stocks with tight bid–ask spreads, the benefit of trading at mid-market is smaller and the optimal algorithm is likely to trade less on off-exchange/dark venues.

In some cases, the optimal decision may be clear from the data because the performance of one algorithm dominates all other choices. In other cases, even if the optimal choice is unclear, the historical execution data of the given cluster help narrow the research space and form the basis for further optimization using either traditional regression-based or machine learning techniques. Although our example is quite simple and the rationale intuitive, one might ask, if the answer is that obvious, why bother with machine learning at all? In practice, the answers are usually much less obvious and the conditions far more complicated.

High-Frequency Market Forecasting

One of the primary challenges in trading (and investing) is forecasting asset prices. Even for a long-term investor, the ability to forecast short-term market direction can help make execution more efficient.

Building a model to forecast short-term market movements involves two steps: The first is to identify key factors, or predictors (independent variables in a regression context), and the second is to estimate the model. One might identify many (hundreds, if not more) potential predictors; for example, for a period of time, one stock—perhaps for which there has been a significant news release—may "lead" the rest of the market and be a good predictor of short-term movement in other stocks.

LASSO (least absolute shrinkage and selection operator) is a machine learning technique used to help with this identification problem. LASSO is a penalized regression technique that relies on the underlying assumption of sparsity, meaning that at any point in time, even in the presence of many potential predictors, only a handful of variables are significant. LASSO minimizes the residual sum of squares, which has the effect of reducing many of the coefficients to zero, leaving only the most significant variables.

For example, consider a trader building a forecast model to predict the near-term value of the S&P 500 ETF (SPY). There are a multitude of variables that she might want to consider, including the order book imbalance (excess of buys or sells for a given price) on each exchange, SPY trade executions, SPY returns over a number of recent time horizons, and similar attributes for correlated instruments, such as other ETFs, equity index futures contracts, and stocks making up the underlying portfolio of the ETF. It is clear that there are hundreds of potential variables. Working with a regression model to identify the most important variables would likely be unwieldy and challenging, given potential collinearity. Using LASSO, the trader can reduce the problem to a more manageable number of variables.

COMPARISON OF MARKETS 7

f contrast key characteristics of the following markets in relation to trade implementation: equity, fixed income, options and futures, OTC derivatives, and spot currency

Although algorithmic trading is common in highly liquid, technologically developed markets, such as equities, trades in other markets require different implementation treatment, with greater human involvement. In this section, we compare and contrast key characteristics relating to trade implementation for the following markets:

- Equities
- Fixed income
- Exchange-traded derivatives (options and futures)
- Off-exchange (OTC) derivatives
- Spot currencies

7.1 Equities

Equities are generally traded on exchanges and dark pools. Exchanges are known as lit markets (as opposed to dark markets) because they provide pre-trade transparency—namely, limit orders that reflect trader intentions for trade side (buy or sell), price, and size. Dark pools provide anonymity because no pre-trade transparency exists. However, regardless of the trading venue, transactions and quantities are always reported. On exchanges, trade price, size, quote, and depth of book data are publicly available. However, detailed book data can be costly and may be available only to some market participants.

Most countries with open economies have at least one stock exchange. The United States has a total of 13 stock exchanges. There are more than 40 **alternative trading systems** (ATS)/dark pools globally. In Europe, these alternative trading venues are called **multilateral trading facilities** (MTF) and *systematic internalisers (SI)*. MTFs are operated by investment firms or market operators that bring together multiple third-party buying and selling interests in financial instruments. SIs are single-dealer liquidity pools. In the United States and Canada, these venues are called alternative trading systems (ATS). They are non-exchange trading venues that match buyers and sellers to find counterparties for transactions. They are typically regulated as broker/

dealers rather than as exchanges (although an ATS can apply to be regulated as a securities exchange). In the United States, ATS must be approved by the Securities and Exchange Commission (SEC).

In Asia, although trading volume on alternative trading venues has grown rapidly over the last few years, such activity remains less common than in North America and Europe. Even in markets with the highest share of dark pool trading, most equity trading still takes place on traditional exchanges. In emerging markets, dark pool trading volume is minimal compared with trading volume on traditional exchanges.

Equities are the most technologically advanced market. Algorithmic trading is common, and most trades are electronic. Equity exchanges may use different trading systems for stocks depending on their level of liquidity. Large, urgent trades, particularly in less liquid small-cap stocks, are generally executed as high-touch broker risk trades, where the broker acts as dealer and counterparty. Large, non-urgent trades may be executed using trading algorithms (particularly for more liquid large-cap stocks) or, for less liquid securities, a high-touch agency approach. For small trades in liquid securities, most buy-side traders use electronic trading.

In recent years, average trade sizes have generally decreased for most asset classes; market participants break down their trades into smaller pieces that they trade either sequentially on the same trading venue or simultaneously across different venues. In equities, growth in the number of trading venues has resulted in fragmentation of trading and increased competition among trading venues.

7.2 Fixed Income

Fixed-income markets are quite different from equity markets. Market transparency and price discovery for fixed-income markets are generally much lower; information available and how quickly it is made available vary by market. Individual bond issuers can have a large number of bonds outstanding with very different features—for example, different maturities, coupons, and optionality. As a result, fixed income is a very heterogeneous asset class that encompasses a large number of individual securities. Institutional investors will often hold bonds until maturity or may trade large quantities infrequently. Trade imbalances often occur in corporate bonds owing to illiquidity. As a result, sourcing market liquidity relies heavily on dealers acting as counterparties (i.e., principal trades), and matching buyers and sellers is generally difficult in the corporate bond market.

Fixed-income securities are generally traded in a bilateral, dealer-centric market structure.[5] Investors will generally get quotes from dealers, often banks, which make markets in the securities. Historically, these quotes were accessed via phone, but they increasingly are disseminated using electronic chat (e.g., Symphony, Bloomberg) or electronic RFQ platforms. Just as it was before the onset of these electronic platforms, dealers do not provide quotes continuously; they provide them only on request by a potential buyer or seller.

There is limited algorithmic trading in bond markets, except for on-the-run (most recently issued) US Treasuries in benchmark maturities and bond and interest rate futures contracts. Although algorithmic/electronic trading in corporate bonds is growing, it remains a relatively low proportion of overall corporate bond trading.[6] The combination of market illiquidity and the large size and low frequency of potential trades creates challenges for algorithmic trading and electronic trading generally. For other fixed-income instruments, high-touch trading persists, particularly for larger

---

[5] Some fixed-income securities trade on exchanges (e.g., the NYSE, the London Stock Exchange, and some Italian exchanges list corporate bonds). However, the volume traded on centralized exchanges is small.
[6] As of 2018, Greenwich Associates has estimated that as of 2018, a fifth of all investment-grade US corporate bond trades are now traded electronically—almost double the volume of a decade ago.

trades and less liquid securities. Small trades and large, urgent trades are usually implemented through broker risk trades (via RFQs), where the broker acts as the counterparty, because securities are hard to source otherwise. Large, non-urgent trades are generally implemented using a high-touch approach, with brokers acting as agents to source liquidity (agency trades instead of principal trades).

7.3 Exchange-Traded Derivatives

As of 2018, there were fewer than 1,000 liquid and highly standardized exchange-traded derivatives outstanding. The market is very large, and trading volume exceeds several trillion dollars per day. Most of the trading volume is concentrated in futures, although the number of futures is considerably smaller than the number of options outstanding. Similar to exchange-traded equities, market transparency is high and trade price, size, quote, and depth of book data are publicly available.

Electronic trading is widespread for exchange-traded derivatives; however, algorithmic trading is not as evolved as in equity markets and is currently used more for trading in futures than in options. Large, urgent trades "sweep the book" where market depth is relatively good. In these cases, trades are executed against the most aggressive limit orders on the other trade side first and then against decreasingly aggressive limit orders until the entire order has been filled. Large, non-urgent trades are generally implemented electronically through trading algorithms. Buy-side traders generally use direct market access, particularly for small trades.

7.4 Over-the-Counter Derivatives

In recent years, regulators have been placing pressure on OTC markets to introduce central clearing facilities and to display trades publicly. Although liquidity has increased for more standardized OTC trades that are centrally cleared, liquidity has decreased for OTC instruments not suited to central clearing or trade reporting.

OTC derivative markets have historically been opaque, with little public data about prices, trade sizes, and structure details. Regulatory efforts have focused on increasing transparency and reducing counterparty risk in these markets. In the United States, the Dodd–Frank Wall Street Reform and Consumer Protection Act, enacted in 2010, significantly increased post-trade transparency in the OTC derivative markets with the establishment of swap data repositories (SDRs) to which trade details must be submitted. Under the Dodd–Frank regulation, swaps entered into by parties exempt from mandatory clearing and exchange trading (and where at least one counterparty to the swap is a US person) are still subject to data reporting rules. Dodd–Frank forms part of a broader 2009 agreement by the G–20 countries whose primary long-term focus includes the trading of all OTC derivatives on exchanges or other electronic platforms with centralized clearing for all more standardized derivatives.

Trading OTC derivatives takes place through dealers. Because this type of security is typically traded by institutions, trade sizes are relatively large. Large, urgent trades are generally implemented as broker risk trades, where risk is transferred to a broker who takes the contract into his inventory. Large, non-urgent trades are generally implemented using a high-touch agency trade, where the broker attempts to match buyers and sellers directly. Doing so can be difficult, however, since OTC derivatives are often highly customized. Hence, at times, a strong price concession is required to find a buyer or seller.

7.5 Spot Foreign Exchange (Currency)

There is no exchange or centralized clearing place for the majority of spot foreign exchange (currency) trades. Spot currency markets consist of a number of electronic venues and broker markets. The currency market is an entirely OTC market. Despite being a global market, there is almost no cross-border regulation.

The spot currency market consists of multiple levels. The top level is called the interbank market, where participants are mostly large international banks and other financial firms that act as dealers. Trades between these foreign exchange dealers can be extremely large. The next market level is generally made up of small and medium-sized banks and other financial institutions that turn to the dealers in the interbank market for their currency trading needs and that, therefore, pay slightly higher bid–ask spreads. The level below that one consists of commercial companies and retail traders that turn to the second-level institutions for their currency trading. Once again, a higher bid–ask spread applies to these market participants.

The spot currency market is sizable in terms of daily trading volume, with often more than $1 trillion traded per day. Although large, the spot currency market is relatively opaque; there are usually only quotes available and only from some venues.

Electronic trading in currencies has grown substantially over the years in parallel with algorithmic trading strategies of equities. For large, urgent trades, RFQs are generally submitted to multiple dealers competing for a trade. Large, non-urgent trades are mostly executed using algorithms (such as TWAP) or a high-touch agency approach. Small trades are usually implemented using DMA.

IN-TEXT QUESTION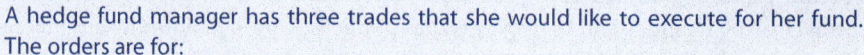

A hedge fund manager has three trades that she would like to execute for her fund. The orders are for:

1. a large, non-urgent sell of OTC options,
2. a large, urgent sell of corporate bonds, and
3. a small, non-urgent buy of six liquid emerging market currencies.

Describe factors affecting trade implementation for each trade.

Solution:

1. A large, non-urgent sell of OTC options would generally involve a broker agency trade in which the broker would act on behalf of the manager to find a matching buyer for the options. Depending on the level of contract customization, however, a significant price concession may be required by the manager to complete order execution.

2. A large, urgent sell of corporate bonds would usually involve a broker risk trade via the RFQ process. Because of corporate bond illiquidity, the likelihood of finding a matching buyer is low. For more immediate (urgent) order execution, a broker would be needed to act as counterparty to the trade, taking the bonds and their associated risk into his inventory.

3. Small, non-urgent trades in foreign exchange are generally executed using direct market access. DMA allows the buy-side trader to electronically route orders using the broker's technology infrastructure and market access and typically involves algorithmic trading.

TRADE COST MEASUREMENT

g explain how trade costs are measured and determine the cost of a trade

After trade implementation is complete, it is important for portfolio managers and traders to assess the trading that has taken place. Was the trade implemented in a manner consistent with the trade strategy chosen? What costs were incurred from trading the order, where did costs arise, and were these reasonable given market conditions? How well did the trader, broker, or algorithm selected for trade execution perform?

Unfortunately for the portfolio manager, trade implementation is not a frictionless transaction. In economic terms, trade costs are value paid by buyers but not received by sellers and value paid by sellers but not received by buyers. In finance, trade costs represent the amount paid above the investment decision price for buy orders and the discount below the decision price for sell orders. An important aspect of trade cost measurement is to identify where costs arise during implementation of the investment decision. Understanding where these costs arise will help portfolio managers carry out proper trade cost management, more efficient implementation, and better portfolio construction. This ultimately leads to lower trading costs and higher portfolio returns.

Proper trade cost management begins with an understanding of the implementation shortfall formulation.

8.1 Implementation Shortfall

The **implementation shortfall** (IS) metric[7] is the most important *ex post* trade cost measurement used in finance. The IS metric provides portfolio managers with the total cost associated with implementing the investment decision. This spans the time the investment decision is made by the portfolio manager up to the completion of the trade by the trader. IS also allows portfolio managers to identify where costs arise during the implementation of the trade.

IS is calculated as the difference between the return for a notional or paper portfolio, where all transactions are assumed to take place at the manager's decision price, and the portfolio's actual return, which reflects realized transactions, including all fees and costs.

Mathematically, IS is calculated as follows:

IS = Paper return − Actual return

The paper return shows the hypothetical return that the fund would have received if the manager were able to transact all shares at the desired decision price and without any associated costs or fees (i.e., with no friction):

Paper return = $(P_n - P_d)(S) = (S)(P_n) - (S)(P_d)$

Here, S represents the total order shares, $S > 0$ indicates a buy order, $S < 0$ indicates a sell order, P_d represents the price at the time of the investment decision, and P_n represents the current price.

The actual portfolio return is calculated as the difference between the current market price and actual transaction prices minus all fees (e.g., commissions):

Actual return = $\left(\sum s_j\right)(P_n) - \sum s_j p_j$ − Fees

---

[7] A.F. Perold, "The Implementation Shortfall: Paper versus Reality," *Journal of Portfolio Management* 14 (Spring 1988): 4–9.

Here, s_j and p_j represent the number of shares executed and the transaction price of the jth trade, respectively, $\left(\sum s_j\right)$ represents the total number of shares of the order that were executed in the market, and "Fees" includes all costs paid by the fund to complete the order.

This IS formulation decomposes the total cost of the trade into three categories: execution cost, opportunity cost, and fixed fees. **Execution cost** corresponds to the shares that were transacted in the market. Execution cost occurs from the buying and/or selling pressure of the order, which often causes buy orders to become more expensive and sell orders to decrease in value, thus causing the fund to incur higher costs and lower realized returns. Execution cost will also occur owing to price drift over the trading period. For example, buying stocks that are increasing in value over the trading period and selling stocks that are decreasing in value over the trading period.

It is important to note that since there is no guarantee that the portfolio manager will be able to execute the entire order, the number of shares transacted in the market may be less than the original order size—that is, $\sum s_j \leq S$ for a buy order and $\sum s_j \geq S$ for a sell order. **Opportunity cost** corresponds to the unexecuted shares of the order. It is the cost associated with not being able to transact the entire order at the manager's decision price and is due to adverse price movement over the trading period. Opportunity cost may also arise in times of insufficient market liquidity, when the fund is not able to find counterparties to complete the trade. The opportunity cost component provides managers with insight into missed profit opportunity for their investment idea.

The *fixed fees* component includes all explicit fees, such as commissions, exchange fees, and taxes.

The IS formulation decomposing costs into these categories is calculated as follows:

$$\text{IS} = \underbrace{\sum s_j p_j - \sum s_j p_d}_{\text{Execution cost}} + \underbrace{\left(S - \sum s_j\right)\left(P_n - P_d\right)}_{\text{Opportunity cost}} + \text{Fees}$$

Consider the following facts:

On Monday, the shares of Impulse Robotics close at £10.00 per share.

On Tuesday, before trading begins, a portfolio manager decides to buy Impulse Robotics. An order goes to the trading desk to buy 1,000 shares of Impulse Robotics at £9.98 per share or better, good for one day. The benchmark price is Monday's close at £10.00 per share. No part of the limit order is filled on Tuesday, and the order expires. The closing price on Tuesday rises to £10.05.

On Wednesday, the trading desk again tries to buy Impulse Robotics by entering a new limit order to buy 1,000 shares at £10.07 per share or better, good for one day. During the day, 700 shares are bought at £10.07 per share. Commissions and fees for this trade are £14. Shares for Impulse Robotics close at £10.08 per share on Wednesday.

No further attempt to buy Impulse Robotics is made, and the remaining 300 shares of the 1,000 shares the portfolio manager initially specified are canceled.

The paper portfolio traded 1,000 shares on Tuesday at £10.00 per share. The return on this portfolio when the order is canceled after the close on Wednesday is the value of the 1,000 shares, now worth £10,080, less the cost of £10,000, for a net gain of £80.

The real portfolio contains 700 shares (now worth 700 × £10.08 = £7,056), and the cost of this portfolio is 700 × £10.07 = £7,049, plus £14 in commissions and fees, for a total cost of £7,063. Thus, the total net gain on this portfolio is –£7. The implementation shortfall is the return on the paper portfolio minus the return on the actual portfolio, or £80 – (–£7) = £87.

We can break this IS down further, as follows:

- Execution cost, which is calculated as the difference between the cost of the real portfolio and of the paper portfolio and reflects the execution price paid for the amount of shares in the order actually filled: (700 × £10.07) − (700 × £10.00) = £7,049 − £7,000 = £49.
- Opportunity cost, which is based on the amount of shares left unexecuted and reflects the cost associated with not being able to execute all shares at the decision price: (1,000 shares − 700 shares) × (£10.08 − £10.00) = £24.
- Fixed fees, which are equal to total explicit fees paid: £14.

IS (£) is equal to the sum of execution cost, opportunity cost, and fixed fees: £49 + £24 + £14 = £87. More commonly, the shortfall is expressed as a fraction of the total cost of the paper portfolio trade: £87/£10,000 = 87 bps.

8.2 Expanded Implementation Shortfall

Wagner (1991) further expanded the IS measure to decompose the execution cost component into a delay-related cost component and a trading-related cost component.[8] These two decomposed execution components allow portfolio managers to more precisely isolate where their execution costs arise during the implementation cycle and help traders better manage overall execution quality and reduce trading costs.

The expanded implementation shortfall can be broken down as follows:

Expanded IS =

$$\underbrace{\underbrace{\left(\sum s_j\right)p_0 - \left(\sum s_j\right)p_d}_{\text{Delay cost}} + \underbrace{\sum s_j p_j - \left(\sum s_j\right)p_0}_{\text{Trading cost}}}_{\text{Execution cost}} + \underbrace{\left(S - \sum s_j\right)(P_n - P_d)}_{\text{Opportunity cost}} + \text{Fees}$$

In this representation, the additional notation p_0 represents the arrival price, and it is defined as the asset price at the time the order was released to the market for execution.

This expanded IS formulation decomposes execution cost further into two categories: delay cost and trading cost. **Delay cost** arises when the order is not submitted to the market in a timely manner and the asset experiences adverse price movement, making it more expensive to transact. Delay cost is often caused by a delay in selecting the most appropriate broker or trading algorithm to execute the order and by adverse price movement (also known as price drift) over the trading period.

Delay cost, however, can be minimized by having proper trading practices in place to provide traders with all the information they need to make an immediate decision, such as pre-trade analysis and post-trade analysis.

For example, consider the same Impulse Robotics example from before but with the following additional fact: *The buy-side trading desk releases the order to the market 30 minutes after receiving it, when the price is £10.03.* We now have additional information that helps identify where costs arise during the implementation of the trade.

---

[8] Wagner, W. (Ed.), 1991. *The Complete Guide to Security Transactions.* John Wiley.

The execution cost component in the expanded implementation shortfall can be decomposed into the following:

- Delay cost, which reflects the adverse price movement associated with not submitting the order to the market in a timely manner and is based on the amount of shares executed in the order: (700 × £10.03) − (700 × £10.00) = £7,021 − £7,000 = £21.

- Trading cost, which reflects the execution price paid on shares executed: (700 × £10.07) − (700 × £10.03) = £7,049 − £7,021 = £28.

While,

- Opportunity cost (£24) and fixed fees (£14) remain unchanged.

Therefore, expanded implementation shortfall (£) = £21 + £28 + £24 + £14 = £87.

The expanded IS provides further insight into the causes of trade costs. The delay cost is £21, which accounts for 24.1% (£21/£87) of the total IS cost, whereas the opportunity cost of £24 accounts for 27.6% (£24/£87) of the total IS cost. Quite often, delay cost and opportunity cost account for the greatest quantity of cost during implementation. These costs can often be eliminated with proper transaction cost management techniques.

Improving Execution Performance

In many situations, delay cost arises from a lag in time between when the buy-side trader receives the order from the portfolio manager and when the trader determines which broker or algorithm is most appropriate for the specific order. Delay costs can be reduced by having a process in place that provides traders with broker performance metrics. Traders can then immediately release the order to the broker without any delay or corresponding adverse price movement. In theory, the delay cost component should have an expected value of zero. In practice, however, the delay cost component is often due to the simultaneous buying and selling pressure from multiple funds buying and selling the same stocks on the same side and over similar trading horizons, resulting in adverse price movement over the trading period. Stock alpha may also contribute to the delay cost component.

Portfolio managers can use IS to help determine appropriate order size for the market within the portfolio manager's price range and to minimize the opportunity cost of the order. For example, IS analysis will help portfolio managers determine the number of shares that can be transacted within the manager's price range or better, and if the manager has incremental cash on hand from specifying a smaller order size, she can invest this amount into her next most attractive investment opportunity at presumably better market prices. If the portfolio manager does not perform IS analysis, she may try to transact a position size that is too large to execute in the market within the desired price range and may not realize this until it is too late to change the investment decision. If the manager knew beforehand that her position size was too large to execute within her price range, she could have reduced the order size for the stock and invested the remaining capital into the next most attractive investment opportunity.

Similar to the delay cost, opportunity cost is not mean zero and often represents a cost to the fund. This is due to two reasons: adverse price movement and illiquidity. First, portfolio managers will often buy shares at a specified price or better. If prices decrease over the trading period, the order will likely be filled. If prices increase by too much, the manager may feel that the asset is no longer an attractive investment opportunity, will cancel the order, and invest in a different asset, thus realizing an opportunity cost. Second, traders may not be able to complete the order if there is insufficient market liquidity. In times of favorable prices, fund managers may be willing to incur additional market impact to attract additional counterparties into the market. But during times of adverse market prices, fund managers may not be as willing to increase their purchase price to attract additional sellers into the market because doing so might increase the stock price to a level where it is no longer deemed an attractive investment opportunity. Thus, the order is less likely to be completed in times of adverse price movement and insufficient market liquidity. Both of these situations result in an opportunity cost to the fund.

Delay Cost

A portfolio manager decides to buy 100,000 shares of RLK at 9:30 a.m., when its price is $30.00. The manager gives the order to his buy-side trader and requests the order be executed in the market at a price no higher than $30.50. The trader is then tasked with determining the best broker and/or the best algorithm to execute the trade. We next discuss two different scenarios to illustrate how a trader's actions can affect the delay cost component.

Scenario 1: The trader receives the order for 100,000 shares at 9:30 a.m., when its price is $30. The trader is not familiar with RLK and needs to review the stock's liquidity, volatility, and intraday trading patterns and current market conditions. The trader next needs to review the historical performance of brokers trading similar order sizes and trading characteristics. After a thorough review, the trader determines the best broker to execute the order is Broker KRG. The trader then submits the order to Broker KRG at 10:30 a.m. but the market price increases to $30.10. The buy-side trader's delay in submitting the order to the broker is caused by the trader's need to evaluate and determine the best broker to execute the order given the order characteristics and market conditions. This delay costs the fund $0.10 per share. Note that if the price had decreased to $29.90, the delay would have benefited the fund by $0.10 per share.

Scenario 2: The trader receives the order for 100,000 shares at 9:30 a.m., when the price is $30.00. Because the buy-side trader exercises proper transaction cost management practices, the trader has analyses on hand indicating who is the best broker and what is the best algorithm to execute the order. The trader is able to immediately submit the order to Broker KRG for execution when the market price is $30.00 per share.

Opportunity Cost

The research department of an asset management firm identifies two stocks currently undervalued in the market. Stock ABC is currently trading at $30.00 and is undervalued by $0.50/share. Stock XYZ is also currently trading at $30.00 and is undervalued by $0.40/share.

The portfolio manager has $3 million and is looking to invest in the stock(s) that will provide the highest return for the fund. What stock(s) should she buy?

On the surface, it may appear most appropriate to invest the entire $3 million in Stock ABC because it is the most undervalued ($0.50/share) and represents the highest short-term alpha. However, if the portfolio manager does not incorporate opportunity cost into her analysis, she is unlikely to achieve the highest return for the fund.

The effect of opportunity cost on fund performance is explained in the following two scenarios.

Scenario 1: The portfolio manager decides to purchase 100,000 shares of ABC because it represents the highest short-term alpha potential. The portfolio manager does not want to purchase shares at a price higher than $30.50, which the research department has determined to be fair value for ABC. The trader tries to execute 100,000 shares of ABC but finds that only 80,000 shares can be executed at an average price of $30.25

before the price increases above $30.50. After ABC reaches a price of $30.50, it remains at this price through the end of the day. Additionally, Stock XYZ closes at its fair value of $30.40.

In this situation, the portfolio manager incurred an opportunity cost of $10,000 (20,000 shares multiplied by $0.50 = $10,000) and realized a profit of $20,000 (80,000 shares multiplied by $0.25 = $20,000).

Since Stock XYZ (which was the second most attractive investment opportunity at the beginning of the day) also increased to its fair value over the day, the portfolio manager is no longer able to invest the residual dollar value in XYZ and capture alpha. Thus, the portfolio manager has missed out on an opportunity to achieve maximum returns.

Scenario 2: The portfolio manager of the fund exercises proper transaction cost management practices. Based on pre-trade analysis, the manager determines that she can purchase only 80,000 shares of ABC before its price will recover to its fair value of $30.50. Because the manager will not be able to invest all funds into Stock ABC, she decides to invest the residual dollar value into Stock XYZ (the second most attractive asset) and buy 20,000 shares.

In this scenario, the portfolio manager transacts all shares from both orders at prices below the fair value. The manager purchases 80,000 shares of ABC at an average price of $30.25 and purchases 20,000 shares of XYZ at an average price of $30.20. Stock ABC closes at its fair value of $30.50, and Stock XYZ closes at its fair value of $30.40. Since the manager executed all shares, she does not incur any opportunity cost.

The manager realizes an overall profit of $24,000. Stock ABC realized a profit of $20,000 (80,000 shares multiplied by $0.25/share). Stock XYZ realized a profit of $4,000 (20,000 shares multiplied by $0.20/share).

In this scenario, where the portfolio manager practiced proper trading cost management and evaluated opportunity cost prior to submitting the order, she was able to increase portfolio returns by $4,000.

Knowledge of where costs arise during execution allows portfolio managers and traders to take necessary steps to reduce and manage these costs appropriately. For example, the delay cost component can be reduced by knowing beforehand which broker is best suited to execute the trade and/or which algorithm is the most appropriate given the order, price benchmark, and investment objectives. Opportunity cost can be reduced by knowing the order size and share quantity that is most likely to be executed in the market within a specified price range. The trading cost component can also be effectively managed so that it is consistent with the underlying investment objectives of the fund by selecting the proper price benchmarks and trading urgency.

IN-TEXT QUESTION

Implementation Shortfall

A portfolio manager decides to buy 100,000 shares of RLK at 9:00 a.m., when the price is $30.00. He sets a limit price of $30.50 for the order. The buy-side trader does not release the order to the market for execution until 10:30 a.m., when the price is $30.10. The fund is charged a commission of $0.02/share and no other fees. At the end of the day, 80,000 shares are executed and RLK closes at $30.65. Order and execution details are summarized as follows:

Trade Cost Measurement

Order	
Stock Ticker	RLK
Side	Buy
Shares	100,000
Limit Price	$30.50

Trades	Execution Price	Shares Executed
Trade 1	$30.20	30,000
Trade 2	$30.30	20,000
Trade 3	$30.40	20,000
Trade 4	$30.50	10,000
Total		80,000

a Calculate execution cost.
b Calculate opportunity cost.
c Calculate fixed fees.
d Calculate implementation shortfall in basis points.
e Discuss how opportunity cost could be minimized for the trade.
f Calculate delay cost.
g Calculate trading cost.
h Show expanded implementation shortfall in basis points.
i Discuss how delay cost could be minimized for the trade.

Solution:

a **Execution cost** is calculated as the difference between the costs of the real portfolio and the paper portfolio. It reflects the execution price(s) paid for the amount of shares in the order that were actually filled, or executed. Execution cost can be calculated as follows:

$$\text{Execution cost} = \sum s_j p_j - \sum s_j p_d$$

$$= (30{,}000 \text{ shares} \times \$30.20 + 20{,}000 \text{ shares} \times \$30.30 +$$
$$20{,}000 \text{ shares} \times \$30.40 + 10{,}000 \text{ shares} \times \$30.50) -$$
$$80{,}000 \times \$30.00$$
$$= \$2{,}425{,}000 - \$2{,}400{,}000$$
$$= \$25{,}000$$

b **Opportunity cost** is based on the amount of shares left unexecuted in the order and reflects the cost of not being able to execute all shares at the decision price. Opportunity cost can be calculated as follows:

$$\text{Opportunity cost} = \left(S - \sum s_j\right)(p_n - p_d)$$

$$= (100{,}000 - 80{,}000)(\$30.65 - \$30.00)$$
$$= \$13{,}000$$

c **Fixed fees** are equal to total explicit fees paid and can be calculated as follows:

$$\text{Fees} = 80{,}000 \times \$0.02 = \$1{,}600$$

d Implementation shortfall can be calculated as follows:

$$\text{Implementation shortfall (\$)} = \underbrace{\$25,000}_{\text{Execution cost}} + \underbrace{\$13,000}_{\text{Opportunity cost}} + \underbrace{\$1,600}_{\text{Fees}}$$

$$= \$39,600$$

The implementation shortfall is expressed in basis points as follows:

$$\text{Implementation shortfall (bps)} = \frac{\text{Implementation shortfall (\$)}}{(\text{Total shares})(p_d)} \times 10,000 \text{ bps}$$

$$= \frac{\$39,600}{(100,000 \times \$30.00)} \times 10,000 \text{ bps}$$

$$= 132 \text{ bps}$$

e Minimizing opportunity cost: Based on the decomposition of IS, the portfolio manager incurred an opportunity cost of $13,000 on 20,000 shares. The opportunity cost could be lowered by reducing order quantity to a size that can be absorbed into the market at the portfolio manager's price target or better. In this example, opportunity cost represented 32.8% ($13,000/$39,600) of the total IS cost. If the portfolio manager had known this in advance, he could have reduced the size of the order to 80,000 shares and invested the extra $600,000 (20,000 shares × $30.00/share = $600,000) in his second most attractive investment opportunity.

f Delay cost can be calculated as follows:

$$\text{Delay cost} = \left(\sum s_j\right) p_0 - \left(\sum s_j\right) p_d$$

$$= 80,000 \times \$30.10 - 80,000 \times \$30.00 = \$8,000$$

g Trading cost can be calculated as follows:

$$\text{Trading cost} = \sum s_j p_j - \left(\sum s_j\right) p_0$$

$$= (30,000 \text{ shares} \times \$30.20 + 20,000 \text{ shares} \times \$30.30 + 20,000 \text{ shares} \times \$30.40 + 10,000 \text{ shares} \times \$30.50) - 80,000 \times \$30.10$$

$$= \$2,425,000 - \$2,408,000$$

$$= \$17,000$$

h Expanded implementation shortfall can be calculated as follows:

$$\text{Expanded IS} = \underbrace{\$8,000}_{\text{Delay cost}} + \underbrace{\$17,000}_{\text{Trading cost}} + \underbrace{\$13,000}_{\text{Opportunity cost}} + \underbrace{\$1,600}_{\text{Fees}} = \$39,600$$

The delay cost is $8,000, which accounts for 20.2% ($8,000/$39,600) of the total IS cost, whereas the opportunity cost of $13,000 accounts for 32.8% ($13,000/$39,600) of the total IS cost.

i Minimizing delay cost: The delay cost of $8,000 accounts for a sizable portion (20.2%) of the total IS cost and could be minimized by having a process in place that provides the buy-side trader with broker performance metrics. This would allow the trader to quickly identify the best broker and/or algorithm to execute the order given its characteristics and current market conditions, thereby minimizing the time between order receipt and market execution.

EVALUATING TRADE EXECUTION

h evaluate the execution of a trade

The evaluation of trade execution is also referred to as trade cost evaluation, trade cost analysis (TCA), and post-trade analysis. Its goal is to evaluate and measure the execution quality of the trade and the overall performance of the trader, broker, and/or algorithm. Here, we discuss different methodologies to evaluate the execution of a trade.

Proper trade cost evaluation enables portfolio managers to better manage costs throughout the investment cycle and helps facilitate communication between the portfolio manager, traders, and brokers to better understand how and why costs occur during the implementation of investment decisions. Trade cost analysis also provides the basis for peer group comparisons, allowing a firm's portfolio managers to compare trading performance and costs with a universe of similar funds trading similar securities.

Trade evaluation helps buy-side traders quantify a broker's performance and rank brokers and/or algorithms most appropriate for implementation of different investment decisions. This helps minimize delay costs associated with trading.

Trade cost evaluation calculates trading costs and performance relative to a specified trading cost or trading performance benchmark. Costs are determined by the transaction amount paid above the reference price benchmark for a buy order and the discount below the reference price benchmark for a sell order. It is important that portfolio managers select the reference price for use on the basis of their selected trading price benchmark. For example, if the portfolio manager selected an arrival price benchmark, it is important to perform trade execution evaluation using the arrival price. If the fund manager selected the VWAP price as the price benchmark, then the reference price used in the post-trade analysis should include the VWAP price. If the fund selected a post-trade benchmark, such as the market on close, it is essential that the fund evaluate trading performance using the closing price benchmark.

Although one benchmark is used in execution, to represent the tradable strategy, multiple reference price benchmarks may be used to measure trading cost and to evaluate performance, typically on an intraday basis. For example, to measure trading costs, a pre-trade benchmark, such as the arrival price benchmark, may be used to provide the portfolio manager or trader with the estimated money required to complete the transaction. The trader may also compare the execution price of the order with an intraday benchmark such as the VWAP of the asset over the trading horizon to determine whether she achieved prices consistent with those of other market participants. Additionally, the trader may compare the last trade price of the order with a post-trade benchmark to understand whether there was price reversion after order completion. The use of multiple price benchmarks may provide valuable insights into different aspects of trading execution.

Trade cost calculations are expressed such that a positive value indicates underperformance and represents underperformance compared with the benchmark. A negative value indicates a savings and is a better performance compared with the benchmark. These calculations are as follows:

Cost in total dollars ($):

$$\text{Cost (\$)} = \text{Side} \times \left(\bar{P} - P^*\right) \times \text{Shares}$$

Cost in dollars per share ($/share):

$$\text{Cost (\$/share)} = \text{Side} \times \left(\bar{P} - P^*\right)$$

Cost in basis points (bps):

$$\text{Cost (bps)} = \text{Side} \times \frac{(\overline{P} - P^*)}{P^*} \times 10{,}000 \text{ bps}$$

$$\text{Side} = \begin{cases} +1 & \text{Buy order} \\ -1 & \text{Sell order} \end{cases}$$

$\overline{P}$ = Average execution price of order

P^* = Reference price

Shares = Shares executed

In most situations, investment professionals express costs in basis points because they represent a standardized measure across order sizes, market prices, and currencies. Portfolio managers will multiply the formulas listed by −1 to represent cost as a negative value and savings as a positive value.

9.1 Arrival Price

The arrival price benchmark measures the difference between the market price at the time the order was released to the market and the actual transaction price for the fund. This benchmark is used to measure the trade cost of the order incurred while the order was being executed in the market. This calculation follows the trading cost component from the expanded implementation shortfall formula.

Consider the following facts. A portfolio manager executes a buy order at an average price of $\overline{P}$ = $30.05. The arrival price at the time the order was submitted to the market was P_0 = $30.00. The arrival cost expressed in basis points is as follows:

$$\text{Arrival cost (bps)} = \text{Side} \times \frac{(\overline{P} - P_0)}{P_0} \times 10^4 \text{ bps}$$

$$= +1 \times \frac{(\$30.05 - \$30.00)}{\$30.00} \times 10^4 \text{ bps}$$

$$= 16.7 \text{ bps}$$

Therefore, the fund incurred an arrival cost of 16.7 bps, underperforming the arrival price benchmark by this amount.

9.2 VWAP

Portfolio managers use the VWAP benchmark as a measure of whether they received fair and reasonable prices over the trading period. Since the VWAP comprises all market activity over the day, all buying and selling pressure of all other market participants, and market noise, it provides managers with a reasonable indication of the fair cost for market participants over the day. In this situation, the VWAP reference price serves as a performance metric.

Consider the following facts. A portfolio manager executes a buy order at an average price of $\bar{P}$ = $30.05. The VWAP over the trading horizon is $30.04. The VWAP cost benchmark is computed as follows:

$$\text{VWAP cost (bps)} = \text{Side} \times \frac{(\bar{P} - \text{VWAP})}{\text{VWAP}} \times 10^4 \text{ bps}$$

$$= +1 \times \frac{(\$30.05 - \$30.04)}{\$30.04} \times 10^4 \text{ bps}$$

$$= 3.3 \text{ bps}$$

Therefore, the fund underperformed the VWAP by 3.3 bps. In most cases, the order will underperform the VWAP generally because of the bid–ask spread and the buying or selling pressure associated with the order.

9.3 TWAP

The TWAP benchmark is an alternative measure to determine whether the fund achieved fair and reasonable prices over the trading period and is used when managers wish to exclude potential trade price outliers.

Consider the following facts. A portfolio manager executes a buy order at an average price of $\bar{P}$ = $30.05. The TWAP over the trading horizon is $30.06. The VWAP cost benchmark is computed as follows:

$$\text{TWAP cost (bps)} = \text{Side} \times \frac{(\bar{P} - \text{TWAP})}{\text{TWAP}} \times 10^4 \text{ bps}$$

$$= +1 \times \frac{(\$30.05 - \$30.06)}{\$30.06} \times 10^4 \text{ bps}$$

$$= -3.3 \text{ bps}$$

Therefore, the fund outperformed the TWAP benchmark by 3.3 bps.

9.4 Market on Close

The closing benchmark, also referred to as an MOC benchmark, is used primarily by index managers and mutual funds that wish to achieve the closing price on the day and compare their actual transaction prices with the closing price. These funds will typically be valued using the closing price, and it is important that the portfolio manager perform benchmark analysis using the execution price of the order and the closing price on the day. Doing so ensures that the benchmark cost measure will be consistent with the valuation of the fund. The closing price benchmark is also the benchmark that is consistent with the tracking error calculation. MOC benchmarks are often used in fixed-income trading.

Consider the following facts. A portfolio manager executing a buy order using an MOC strategy transacts the order at an average price of $30.40. The stock's official closing price is $30.50. The closing benchmark cost is calculated as follows:

$$\text{Close (bps)} = \text{Side} \times \frac{(\bar{P} - \text{Close})}{\text{Close}} \times 10^4 \text{ bps}$$

$$= +1 \times \frac{(\$30.40 - \$30.50)}{\$30.50} \times 10^4 \text{ bps}$$

$$= -32.8 \text{ bps}$$

Thus, a closing benchmark cost of −32.8 bps indicates that the order was executed 32.8 bps more favorably than the closing price of the order. In the case of an index fund, the outperformance would contribute positive tracking error for the fund.

9.5 Market-Adjusted Cost

The market-adjusted cost is a performance metric used by managers and traders to help separate the trading cost due to trading the order from the general market movement in the security price (i.e., the price movement that would have occurred in the security even if the order was not executed in the market). For example, buying stock in a rising market and selling stock in a falling market will cause the fund to incur higher costs than expected, and selling stock in a rising market and buying stock in a falling market will cause the fund to incur lower costs than expected. A market-adjusted cost benchmark will help isolate the price movement due to the general market from the cost due to the impact of the order.

The market-adjusted cost is calculated by subtracting the market cost due to market movement adjusted for order side from the total arrival cost of the trade. The market cost is computed on the basis of the movement in an index and the stock's beta to that index, as follows:

$$\text{Index cost (bps)} = \text{Side} \times \frac{(\text{Index VWAP} - \text{Index arrival price})}{\text{Index arrival price}} \times 10^4$$

The index VWAP is the volume-weighted price of the index computed over the trading horizon. The index VWAP is often computed using an overall market index or a related ETF to compute a volume-weighted price. Alternatively, portfolio managers and traders may use a sector or industry index instead of the overall market index.

The market-adjusted cost is calculated as follows:

$$\text{Market-adjusted cost (bps)} = \text{Arrival cost (bps)} - \beta \times \text{Index cost (bps)}$$

In this case, β represents the stock's beta to the underlying index. The expectation in this formulation is that the stock would have exhibited price movement based on the market movement and the stock's sensitivity to the index measured via its beta to the index. This formulation thus helps remove the movement in the stock that would have occurred even if the order was not entered into the market.

Buying in a Rising Market

Consider a portfolio manager who executes a buy order at an average price of $30.50. The arrival price at the time the order was entered into the market was $30.00. The selected index price at the time of order entry was $500, and market index VWAP over the trade horizon was $505. If the stock has a beta to the index of $\beta = 1.25$, the market-adjusted cost can be calculated as follows:

Step 1 Calculate arrival cost.

$$\text{Arrival cost (bps)} = \text{Side} \times \frac{(\overline{P} - P_0)}{P_0} \times 10^4 \text{ bps}$$

$$= +1 \times \frac{(\$30.50 - \$30.00)}{\$30.00} \times 10^4 \text{ bps}$$

$$= 166.7 \text{ bps}$$

Step 2 Calculate index cost.

$$\text{Index cost (bps)} = \text{Side} \times \frac{(\text{Index VWAP} - \text{Index arrival price})}{\text{Index arrival price}} \times 10^4$$

$$= +1 \times \frac{\$505 - \$500}{\$500} \times 10^4$$

$$= 100 \text{ bps}$$

Step 3   Calculate market-adjusted cost.

$$\text{Market-adjusted cost (bps)} = \text{Arrival cost (bps)} - \beta \times \text{Index cost (bps)}$$
$$= 166.7 \text{ bps} - 1.25 \times 100 \text{ bps}$$
$$= 166.7 \text{ bps} - 125 \text{ bps}$$
$$= 41.7 \text{ bps}$$

The portfolio manager bought stock in a rising market, and prices were generally increasing over the trading horizon because of market movement and the buying pressure of the order. The manager's arrival cost was 166.7 bps, and the market index cost over the period was 100 bps. The stock price would be expected to increase 125 bps over the period on the basis of the movement in the market index and the stock's beta to the index. In this situation, we subtract 125 bps in cost from the arrival cost of 166.7 bps because this amount represents expected market movement not due to the order. The market-adjusted cost due to the order is 41.7 bps, much lower than the total arrival cost.

IN-TEXT QUESTION

Selling in a Falling Market

A portfolio manager executes a sell order at an average price of $29.50. The arrival price at the time the order was entered into the market was $30.00. The selected index price at the time of order entry was $500, and market index VWAP over the trade horizon was $495. The stock has a beta to the index of 1.25.

1   Calculate arrival cost.
2   Calculate index cost.
3   Calculate market-adjusted cost.

Solution:

1   Calculate arrival cost.

$$\text{Arrival cost (bps)} = \text{Side} \times \frac{(\overline{P} - P_0)}{P_0} \times 10^4 \text{ bps}$$
$$= -1 \times \frac{(\$29.50 - \$30.00)}{\$30.00} \times 10^4 \text{ bps}$$
$$= 166.7 \text{ bps}$$

A positive arrival cost in this case indicates that the fund underperformed the arrival price benchmark.

2 Calculate index cost.

$$\text{Index cost (bps)} = \text{Side} \times \frac{(\text{Index VWAP} - \text{Index arrival price})}{\text{Index arrival price}} \times 10^4$$

$$= -1 \times \frac{\$495 - \$500}{\$500} \times 10^4$$

$$= 100 \text{ bps}$$

3 Calculate market-adjusted cost.

$$\text{Market-adjusted cost (bps)} = \text{Arrival cost (bps)} - \beta \times \text{Index cost (bps)}$$

$$= 166.7 \text{ bps} - 1.25 \times 100 \text{ bps}$$

$$= 166.7 \text{ bps} - 125 \text{ bps}$$

$$= 41.7 \text{ bps}$$

In this example, the arrival cost is calculated to be +166.7 bps, indicating that the order underperformed the arrival price. Although this is true, much of the adverse prices were likely due to market movement rather than inferior performance from the broker or algorithm. This sell order was executed in a falling market, which resulted in an arrival cost of 166.7 bps for the investor. However, an estimated 125 bps of this cost was due to market movement, which would have occurred even if the order had not traded in the market. Thus, the market-adjusted cost for this order is 41.7 bps.

9.6 Added Value

Another methodology used by investors to evaluate trading performance is to compare the arrival cost of the order with the estimated pre-trade cost. The expected trading cost is calculated using a pre-trade model and incorporates such factors as order size, volatility, market liquidity, investor risk aversion, level of urgency (i.e., how fast or slow the trade is to be executed in the market), and the underlying market conditions at the time of the trade. If a fund executes at a cost lower than the pre-trade estimate, it is typically considered superior trade performance. If the order is executed at a cost higher than the pre-trade cost benchmark, then the trade is considered to have underperformed expectations. This metric helps fund managers understand the value added by their broker and/or execution algorithms during the execution of the order. The added value metric is computed as follows:

Added value (bps) = Arrival cost (bps) − Est. pre-trade cost (bps)

Consider the following facts. A portfolio manager executes a buy order at an average price of $\overline{P} = \$50.35$. The arrival price at the time the order was entered into the market was $P_0 = \$50.00$. Prior to trading, the buy-side trader performs pre-trade analysis of the order and finds that the expected cost of the trade is 60 bps, based on information available prior to trading. The pre-trade adjustment is calculated as follows:

Pre-trade adjustment = Arrival cost − Est. pre-trade cost

We have,

$$\text{Arrival cost (bps)} = \text{Side} \times \frac{(\bar{P} - P_0)}{P_0} \times 10^4 \text{ bps}$$

$$= +1 \times \frac{(\$50.35 - \$50.00)}{\$50.00} \times 10^4 \text{ bps}$$

$$= 70 \text{ bps}$$

Added value = Arrival cost − Est. pre-trade cost = 70 bps − 60 bps = 10 bps

The pre-trade adjusted cost in this example is 10 bps, indicating that the fund underperformed pre-trade expectations by 10 bps.

Proper trade cost measurement and evaluation are critical to understanding the costs and risks arising from trading. These help inform where a firm's trading activities may be improved through better internal trade management practices, such as the use of appropriate trading partners and venues. Trade governance involves the policies and processes used by firms to manage their trading-related activities.

TRADE GOVERNANCE

10

i. evaluate a firm's trading procedures, including processes, disclosures, and record keeping with respect to good governance

All asset managers should have a trade policy document that clearly and comprehensively articulates the firm's trading policies and escalation procedures (i.e., calling on higher levels of leadership or management in an organization to resolve issues when they cannot be resolved by standard procedures). Such a document is mandated by major market regulators and regulations, including the SEC in the United States, the updated Markets in Financial Instruments Directive (MiFID II) in the European Union, the Financial Services Agency in Japan, and the Securities and Futures Commission in Hong Kong SAR.

The objective of a trade policy is to ensure the asset manager's execution and order-handling procedures are in line with the duty of best execution that is owed to clients. Any trade policy needs to include several key aspects. These include the following:

- **Meaning of best execution:** A trade policy document should outline the meaning of best execution as defined by the relevant regulatory framework. This meaning may be supplemented by additional details. For example, generally best execution does not just mean achieving the best execution price at the lowest possible cost but also involves achieving the right trade-off between different objectives.

- **Factors determining the optimal order execution approach:** A trade policy document should describe the factors used in determining how an order can be executed in an optimal manner for a given scenario. For example, the optimal execution approach may differ by asset class, level of security liquidity, and security trading mechanism (order-driven markets, quote-driven markets, and brokered markets). The optimal execution approach can also depend on the nature of a manager's investment process.

- **Listing of eligible brokers and execution venues:** A trade policy should allow the investment manager flexibility to use different brokers and trading venues to achieve best execution in a particular scenario. To reduce operational risk, checks should be in place to ensure only reputable brokers and execution venues that meet requirements for reliable and efficient order execution are used.
- **Process to monitor execution arrangements:** Optimal order execution arrangements may change over time as markets and securities evolve. Therefore, continual monitoring of current arrangements is needed. The details of the monitoring process should be outlined in a trade policy document.

Asset managers that aggregate trades for client accounts and funds should have a "trade aggregation and allocation" policy in place. These policies seek to ensure executed orders are allocated fairly to individual clients on a pre-trade and post-trade basis, there are remedies for misallocations, and an escalation policy is in place. For example, if several accounts (e.g., pooled funds or separate accounts) follow the same or a similar investment strategy and have similar trading needs, then pooling the trades for trade execution may make sense in some situations. If a pooled trade is not fully executed, the order amount that is executed generally needs to be allocated to accounts on a pro-rata basis so that no account is disadvantaged relative to the others. In all cases, the aggregation and allocation process should be transparent and provide an audit trail in case questions are raised after the fact.

Firms should have a policy in place for the treatment of trade errors. Errors from trading and any resulting gains/losses need to be disclosed to a firm's compliance department and documented in a trade error log. The trade error log should include any related documentation and evidence that trade errors are resolved in a way that prevents adverse impact for the client.

10.1 Meaning of Best Order Execution within the Relevant Regulatory Framework

A trade policy document should outline the meaning of best execution within the relevant regulatory framework. Although there may be slight differences in how best execution is defined by different regulators and in different financial market regulations, the underlying concept requires orders to be executed on terms most favorable to the client, where firms consider the following:

- execution price,
- trading costs,
- speed of execution,
- likelihood of execution and settlement,
- order size, and
- nature of the trade.

Rather than simply trying to obtain the best price at the lowest possible trading cost, best execution involves identifying the most appropriate trade-off between these aspects. For example, although market impact costs can generally be lowered by trading more patiently, patient trading may be suboptimal for an asset manager that uses extremely short-horizon expected return forecasts, which decay quickly.

10.2 Factors Used to Determine the Optimal Order Execution Approach

Firms need to have a list of criteria or factors used in determining the optimal order execution approach to achieve the best possible results for clients on a consistent basis.

Best execution requires investment managers to seek the most advantageous order execution for their customers given market conditions. Best execution includes several key factors that brokers examine, track, and document when choosing how to execute an order. An asset manager needs to ensure that after examining these factors, the broker achieved the best possible execution for the client.

At a firm level, execution policy and procedures need to specify the factors or criteria considered in determining the optimal order execution approach in each scenario. These criteria include the following:

- **Urgency of an order:** Does the order need to be executed aggressively at an accelerated pace, or can it be traded over a longer period of time? What is the size of the order relative to the security's normal liquidity?
- **Characteristics of the securities traded:** How liquid are the securities to be traded (e.g., the average daily volume)? Are the securities standardized or highly customized?
- **Characteristics of the execution venues used:** Which type of trading mechanism or venue is used? Are both lit (on-exchange) markets and dark markets available to trade a security?
- **Investment strategy objectives:** Is the investment strategy short term or long term in nature?
- **Rationale for a trade:** Is a trade intended to capture an investment manager's expected return views? Or is it a risk trade or a liquidity trade? Underlying trade objectives may have important implications for the optimal trade approach.

MiFID II, which came into effect in January 2018 and covers the European Economic Area, provides additional regulations on best execution. MiFID II requires firms to take all sufficient steps to obtain the best possible result in executing client orders. The best possible result is not limited to execution price but also includes consideration of cost, speed, likelihood of execution, likelihood of settlement, and any other factors deemed relevant. MiFID II's "all sufficient steps" test sets a higher standard than the previous "all reasonable steps" standard of MiFID I.

MiFID II prohibits the bundling, or combining, of trading commissions with research provided by brokers, known as a soft dollar arrangement. Under MiFID II, investment managers need the firm to pay for broker research costs or establish a research payment account funded by a special charge to clients. Other jurisdictions place limitations on soft dollar arrangements and are expected to follow MiFID II requirements in making execution and research payments explicit and transparent for clients.

Ensuring best execution often requires different criteria for each asset class that should be incorporated into trade policy and procedures. In terms of execution factors, the relative importance of individual factors often differs by asset class. Exhibit 2 shows key considerations by asset class.

Exhibit 2	Key Considerations for Best Execution
Asset Class	**Considerations**
Equities and Exchange-Traded Options and Futures	An investment manager needs to choose the type of market or venue used for execution. In many cases, there are lit (on-exchange) markets and dark markets available for more liquid securities. Lit markets provide pre-trade and post-trade transparency, whereas dark markets provide post-trade transparency. The liquidity of a security and the percentage of average daily volume traded are critical in the choice of optimal execution algorithm. Historical transaction data—including liquidity characteristics and price volatility—are widely available and can be readily assessed.
Fixed Income	There are two main issues: market transparency and price discovery. Only some of the trading, particularly in corporate bonds, takes place on venues that provide market transparency as well as simultaneous, competitive quotes enabling price discovery, which is a necessary condition to ensure best execution. Generally, trade policy should dictate that, if at all possible, bids/offers should be requested from multiple independent third parties before a trade is executed. This process fosters competition and provides a more precise estimate of the likely market price at a particular time in an effort to achieve the best price possible. If there is no market transparency and if multiple competing quotes cannot or should not be obtained, then a trade policy should outline alternative means to achieve price discovery. These may include data sources (such as TRACE data)* for historical transaction prices or quotes for a given security or comparable securities. In the absence of any relevant transaction prices or quotes, an internal or external pricing model could be used to establish a market price estimate.
OTC Derivatives	Broker selection may depend on the exact terms of the proposed OTC derivative instruments, counterparty risk, and a broker's settlement capabilities.
Spot Currencies	Quotes should be requested from multiple independent dealers before a trade is executed. This process fosters competition in an effort to achieve the best price possible.

* In 2002, the National Association of Securities Dealers introduced TRACE (Trade Reporting and Compliance Engine) in an effort to increase price transparency in the US corporate debt market.

10.3 List of Eligible Brokers and Execution Venues

Asset managers should have a list of approved brokers and execution venues for trading and the criteria used to create this list. In determining the list, there should not be discrimination against brokers or execution venues. Any decisions should be made according to the policy and procedures put in place. Creating and maintaining the list should be a collaborative effort shared by portfolio execution, compliance, and risk management. A best practices approach is to create a Best Execution Monitoring Committee within an investment management firm that is responsible for maintaining and updating the list regularly, or as circumstances require, and distributing the list to all parties involved in trade execution.

Although the criteria used to approve an execution venue or broker differ by asset class, the principles behind the decision and the process followed should be consistent across asset classes, broker firms, regions, and jurisdictions. A number of qualitative and quantitative factors are relevant to this decision, such as the following:

- **Quality of service:** Does a broker provide competitive execution compared with an execution benchmark, such as submission price or VWAP?
- **Financial stability:** Will the broker or execution venue be able to fulfill obligations in all market environments? When such brokers as Lehman Brothers and MF Global went bankrupt, it caused substantial disruption to their clients' activities.

- **Reputation:** Does the broker or execution venue uphold high ethical standards and treat clients fairly?
- **Settlement capabilities:** Are the operations supporting the broker/execution venue robust? Can trades be settled in a reliable and efficient manner?
- **Speed of execution:** Can urgent trades be implemented with minimal delay and at the best price possible? What is the maximum volume that can be traded with minimal delay?
- **Cost competitiveness:** Are the explicit costs (such as commissions or exchange fees) competitive?
- **Willingness to commit capital:** Is the broker willing to act as a dealer to facilitate trading for a client? This can be particularly important for less liquid securities that need to be traded in a timely manner.[9]

A sensible trade policy is particularly important in trade venue selection for transactions that are executed off exchange in so-called over-the-counter markets. Best execution is generally harder to measure for these trades, and there are unique risks associated with OTC trading. For example, OTC trades are not subject to any trading venue rules designed to ensure fair and orderly treatment of orders or minimum levels of price transparency. In addition, there may be counterparty and settlement risk for OTC trades.

10.4 Process Used to Monitor Execution Arrangements

All brokers and execution venues used by the asset manager should be subject to ongoing monitoring for reputational risk, irregularities (such as trading errors), criminal actions, and financial stability. Brokers and execution venues that no longer meet minimum requirements should be promptly removed from the approved list.

Execution quality on realized transactions through different brokers or execution venues should also be monitored continuously. Systems that allow ongoing monitoring of order execution quality should be in place. Although the specific process may vary by asset class and security type, the underlying principles remain the same. Summary reports of execution quality should be produced, examined, and evaluated on a regular basis.

Checkpoints for trade execution monitoring include the following:

- Trade submission: Has the trading/execution strategy been implemented consistent with the investment process (alpha and risk forecasting horizon, rebalancing frequency, etc.), and is it optimal for the asset type traded?
- What was the execution quality of a trade relative to its benchmark (e.g., arrival price, VWAP, TWAP, market close)?
- Is there an appropriate balance between trading costs and opportunity costs (for non-executed trades)?
- Could better execution have been achieved using a different trading strategy, different intermediaries, or different trading venues?

---

9 In this case, the broker, acting as principal rather than agent, is the counterparty to client transactions. Although this can be useful for clients, potential conflicts of interest may arise, and principal trades should be monitored closely by managers for potential conflicts of interest the broker may have.

Asset managers are well advised to have in place the equivalent of a Best Execution Monitoring Committee (BEMC) that has firm-wide responsibility for trade execution monitoring. The BEMC should collaborate with portfolio managers and risk management and legal/compliance departments to ensure potential issues with execution quality are identified, discussed, and acted on in a timely manner.

Trading records and the evaluation of those records should generally be stored and kept accessible by firms for several years (e.g., in the United Kingdom, the requirement is five years). Trading records may be used to do the following:

- **Address client concerns:** For example, trading records can be used as evidence by an investment manager to show clients that their accounts have been treated fairly. This is particularly relevant if an investment manager runs similar strategies that might frequently trade in the same direction. For instance, there may be a need to demonstrate fair trade allocation or that particular strategies are not being favored at the expense of others.

- **Address regulator concerns:** A regulator may be interested in assessing how the investment manager has met best execution standards. In addition, regulators need to monitor market integrity and detect criminal behavior, such as "fake volumes," "quote stuffing," and "spoofing," which are illegal activities in most markets.[10]

- **Assist in improving execution quality:** A database of past transactions may be used to analyze and refine the execution process to control and improve trading costs.

- **Monitor the parties involved in trading/order execution:** Trading records can be used to evaluate how performance by brokers and execution venues may compare in execution quality. This helps inform which services should be retained in the future.

These policies and procedures should be outlined in a comprehensive document and reviewed regularly (for example, quarterly) and when the need arises. Updates should be made when circumstances change. This document could be created by a BEMC and should involve portfolio management, risk management, and legal/compliance departments. If no formal committee is tasked with owning this document, then the legal/compliance department might take responsibility, with collaboration from portfolio management and risk management functions.

IN-TEXT QUESTION

Choice of Broker

ABC Asset Management (ABCAM) is one of the world's largest asset managers. ABCAM has been using AAA Brokerage (AAAB) as its exclusive broker for a number of its funds for many years. Other brokers are used only for market segments in which AAAB does not have business operations. The leadership of ABCAM explains its choice of broker by stating, "Because of its long-standing business relationship with AAAB, ABCAM has a uniquely informed insight into the operations of AAAB, which provides greater comfort and assurance that AAAB will fulfill its duties when compared with other brokers."

---

10 *Fake volumes* refer to the practice whereby a trading venue or exchange executes transactions with itself (i.e., it is on both sides of a trade) to artificially inflate reported trading volume to attract client business. *Quote stuffing* is a practice that has been used by high-frequency traders that involves entering and withdrawing a large number of orders within an extremely short period of time in an attempt to confuse the market and create trading opportunities for the high-frequency trader. *Spoofing* is a manipulative practice defined as bidding or offering with the intent to cancel before execution. All these practices are attempts to gain an unfair advantage over other market participants by engaging in manipulative behavior.

Discuss whether this practice is permissible and can be justified.

Solution:

ABCAM needs to show that it takes all sufficient steps to ensure best execution for its clients' trades. This includes choosing brokers that provide the best service for potential best execution. In order to justify that AAAB is the right broker to use, ABCAM must demonstrate that it has done comparisons of different brokers, that this analysis is regularly conducted with updates, and that each time AAAB is found to be the best choice for order implementation. A thorough and unbiased analysis is required for this. Stating a subjective opinion, such as the explanation provided by ABCAM leadership, is not sufficient justification.

IN-TEXT QUESTION

Trade Policy Document

For several decades, XYZ Capital has been running enhanced index funds. These funds have low levels of target tracking error compared with their market-weighted benchmarks. The firm's trade policy document has a focus on minimizing trading costs and defines best execution as follows:

> "The firm takes all sufficient steps to obtain the best possible result in executing orders; that is, the firm makes its best attempt to achieve the best execution price and lowest trading cost possible for every transaction. In this way, the firm achieves best execution for its client portfolios."

Discuss whether the trade policy statement is in line with regulatory requirements and client best interests.

Solution:

Achieving the best execution price at the lowest trading cost possible is only part of the best execution effort. To ensure that clients and their portfolios are served in the best manner possible, other factors require consideration. These considerations include the speed of execution, the alignment of execution approach and execution horizon with the investment process, the likelihood of execution to be optimal, and so on. An exclusive focus on best execution price and lowest trading cost is too narrow a definition to achieve best client execution. For example, doing so could leave many trades unexecuted, which would result in increased opportunity costs from lost opportunities that could not be implemented.

SUMMARY

- Portfolio manager motivations to trade include profit seeking, risk management (hedging), liquidity driven (fund flows), and corporate actions and index reconstitutions.

- Managers following a short-term alpha-driven strategy will trade with greater urgency to realize alpha before it dissipates (decays). Managers following a longer-term strategy will trade with less urgency if alpha decay is expected to be slower.

- Trading is required to keep portfolios at targeted risk levels or risk exposures, to hedge risks that may be outside a portfolio manager's investment objectives or that the portfolio manager does not have an investment view on.
- Trading may be liquidity driven resulting from client activity or index reconstitutions. In these cases, managers typically trade using end-of-day closing prices because these prices are used for fund and benchmark valuation.
- Inputs affecting trade strategy selection include the following types: order related, security related, market related, and user based.
- Order characteristics include the side (or trade direction) and size of an order. Percentage of average daily volume is a standardized measure used in trading that indicates what order size can realistically be traded. Large trades are generally traded over longer time horizons to minimize market impact.
- Security characteristics include security type, short-term (trade) alpha, security price volatility, and a security's liquidity profile.
- Market conditions at the time of trading (intraday trading volumes, bid–ask spreads, and security and market volatility) should be incorporated into trade strategy since they can differ from anticipated conditions.
- Market volatility and liquidity vary over time, and liquidity considerations may differ substantially during periods of crisis.
- Individuals with higher levels of risk aversion are more concerned with market risk and tend to trade with greater urgency.
- Market impact is the adverse price impact in a security caused from trading an order and can represent one of the largest costs in trading.
- Execution risk is the adverse price impact resulting from a change in the fundamental value of the security and is often proxied by price volatility.
- Reference price benchmarks inform order trading prices and include pre-trade, intraday, post-trade, and price target benchmarks.
- Managers seeking short-term alpha will use pre-trade benchmarks, such as the arrival price, when they wish to transact close to current market prices (greater trade urgency).
- Managers without views on short-term price movements who wish to participate in volumes over the execution horizon typically use an intraday benchmark, such as VWAP or TWAP.
- Managers of index funds or funds whose valuation is calculated using closing prices typically select the closing price post-trade benchmark to minimize fund risk and tracking error.
- The primary goal of a trading strategy is to balance the expected costs, risks, and alpha associated with trading the order in a manner consistent with the portfolio manager's trading objectives, risk aversion, and other known constraints.
- Execution algorithms can be classified into the following types: scheduled, liquidity seeking, arrival price, dark aggregators, and smart order routers.
- Equities are traded on exchanges and other multilateral trading venues. Algorithmic trading is common, and most trades are electronic, except for very large trades and trades in illiquid securities.
- Fixed-income securities are generally traded not on exchanges but in a bilateral, dealer-centric market structure where dealers make markets in the securities. The majority of fixed-income securities are relatively illiquid, especially if they have been issued in prior periods, so-called off-the-run bonds.

Summary

- Most of the trading volume in exchange-traded derivatives is concentrated in futures. Electronic trading is pervasive, and algorithmic trading is growing.
- OTC derivative markets have historically been opaque, with little public data about prices, trade sizes, and structure details. In recent years, regulators have been placing pressure on OTC markets to introduce central clearing facilities and to display trades publicly in an attempt to increase contract standardization and price discovery and reduce counterparty risk.
- There is no exchange or centralized clearing place for the majority of spot currency trades. Spot currency markets consist of a number of electronic venues and broker markets. The currency market is entirely an OTC market.
- The implementation shortfall measure is the standard for measuring the total cost of the trade. IS compares a portfolio's actual return with its paper return (where transactions are based on decision price).
- The IS attribution decomposes total trade cost into its delay, execution, and opportunity cost components.
- Delay cost is the cost associated with not submitting the order to the market at the time of the portfolio manager's investment decision.
- Execution cost is the cost due to the buying and/or selling pressure of the portfolio manager and corresponding market risk.
- Opportunity cost is the cost due to not being able to execute all shares of the order because of adverse price movement or insufficient liquidity.
- Trade evaluation measures the execution quality of the trade and the performance of the trader, broker, and/or algorithm used.
- Various techniques measure trade cost execution using different benchmarks (pre-trade, intraday, and post-trade).
- Trade cost analysis enables investors to better manage trading costs and understand where trading activities can be improved through the use of appropriate trading partners and venues.
- Major regulators mandate that asset managers have in place a trade policy document that clearly and comprehensively articulates a firm's trading policies and escalation procedures.
- The objective of a trade policy is to ensure the asset manager's execution and order-handling procedures are in line with their fiduciary duty owed to clients for best execution.
- A trade policy document needs to incorporate the following key aspects: meaning of best execution, factors determining the optimal order execution approach, handling trading errors, listing of eligible brokers and execution venues, and a process to monitor execution arrangements.

PRACTICE PROBLEMS

The following information relates to Questions 1–9

Robert Harding is a portfolio manager at ValleyRise, a hedge fund based in the United States. Harding monitors the portfolio alongside Andrea Yellow, a junior analyst. ValleyRise only invests in equities, but Harding is considering other asset classes to add to the portfolio, namely derivatives, fixed income, and currencies. Harding and Yellow meet to discuss their trading strategies and price benchmarks.

Harding begins the meeting by asking Yellow about factors that affect the selection of an appropriate trading strategy. Yellow tells Harding:

Statement 1   Trading with greater urgency results in lower execution risk.

Statement 2   Trading larger size orders with higher trade urgency reduces market impact.

Statement 3   Securities with high rates of alpha decay require less aggressive trading to realize alpha.

After further discussion about Yellow's statements, Harding provides Yellow a list of trades that he wants to execute. He asks Yellow to recommend a price benchmark. Harding wants to use a benchmark where the reference price for the benchmark is computed based on market prices that occur during the trading period, excluding trade outliers.

Earlier that day before the meeting, Yellow believed that the market had underreacted during the pre-market trading session to a strong earnings announcement from ABC Corp., a company that Yellow and Harding have been thoroughly researching for several months. Their research suggested the stock's fair value was $90 per share, and the strong earnings announcement reinforced their belief in their fair value estimate.

Right after the earnings announcement, the pre-market price of ABC was $75. Concerned that the underreaction would be short-lived, Harding directed Yellow to buy 30,000 shares of ABC stock. Yellow and Harding discussed a trading strategy, knowing that ABC shares are very liquid and the order would represent only about 1% of the expected daily volume. They agreed on trading a portion of the order at the opening auction and then filling the remainder of the order after the opening auction. The strategy for filling the remaining portion of the order was to execute trades at prices close to the market price at the time the order was received.

Harding and Yellow then shift their conversation to XYZ Corp. Harding tells Yellow that, after extensive research, he would like to utilize an algorithm to purchase some shares that are relatively liquid. When building the portfolio's position in XYZ, Harding's priority is to minimize the trade's market impact to avoid conveying information to market participants. Additionally, Harding does not expect adverse price movements during the trade horizon.

Harding and Yellow conclude their meeting by comparing trade implementation for equities with the trade implementation for the new fixed-income, exchange-traded derivatives, and currency investments under consideration. Yellow tells Harding:

Practice Problems

Statement 4 Small currency trades and small exchange-traded derivatives trades are typically implemented using the direct market access (DMA) approach.

Statement 5 The high-touch agency approach is typically used to execute large, non-urgent trades in fixed-income and exchange-traded derivatives markets.

The next day, Harding instructs Yellow to revisit their research on BYYP, Inc. Yellow's research leads her to believe that its shares are undervalued. She shares her research with Harding, and at 10 a.m. he instructs her to buy 120,000 shares when the price is $40.00 using a limit order of $42.00.

The buy-side trader releases the order for market execution when the price is $40.50. The only fee is a commission of $0.02 per share. By the end of the trading day, 90,000 shares of the order had been purchased, and BYYP closes at $42.50. The trade was executed at an average price of $41.42. Details about the executed trades are presented in Exhibit 1.

Exhibit 1 BYYP Trade Execution Details

Trades	Execution Price	Shares Executed
Trade 1	$40.75	10,000
Trade 2	$41.25	30,000
Trade 3	$41.50	20,000
Trade 4	$41.75	30,000
Total		90,000

While the buy-side trader executes the BYYP trade, Harding and Yellow review ValleyRise's trade policy document. After reviewing the document, Yellow recommends several changes: 1) add a policy for the treatment of trade errors; 2) add a policy that ensures over-the-counter derivatives are traded on venues with rules that ensure minimum price transparency; and 3) alter the list of eligible brokers to include only those that provide execution at the lowest possible trading cost.

1 Which of Yellow's statements regarding the factors affecting the selection of a trading strategy is correct?
   A Statement 1
   B Statement 2
   C Statement 3

2 Given the parameters for the benchmark given by Harding, Yellow should recommend a benchmark that is based on the:
   A arrival price.
   B time-weighted average price.
   C volume-weighted average price.

3 To fill the remaining portion of the ABC order, Yellow is using:
   A an arrival price trading strategy.
   B a TWAP participation strategy.
   C a VWAP participation strategy.

4 What type of algorithm should be used to purchase the XYZ shares given Harding's priority in building the XYZ position and his belief about potential price movements?
  A Scheduled algorithm
  B Arrival price algorithm
  C Opportunistic algorithm

5 Which of Yellow's statements regarding the trade implementation of non-equity investments is correct?
  A Only Statement 4
  B Only Statement 5
  C Both Statement 4 and Statement 5

6 Based on Exhibit 1, the execution cost for purchasing the 90,000 shares of BYYP is:
  A $60,000.
  B $82,500.
  C $127,500.

7 Based on Exhibit 1, the opportunity cost for purchasing the 90,000 shares of BYYP is:
  A $22,500.
  B $60,000.
  C $75,000.

8 The arrival cost for purchasing the 90,000 shares of BYYP is:
  A 164.4 bp.
  B 227.2 bp.
  C 355.0 bp.

9 As it relates to the trade policy document, ValleyRise should implement Yellow's recommendation related to:
  A the list of eligible brokers.
  B a policy for the treatment of trade errors.
  C a policy for over-the-counter derivatives trades.

The following information relates to Questions 10–16

Michelle Wong is a portfolio manager at Star Wealth Management (SWM), an investment management company whose clients are high-net-worth individuals. Her expertise is in identifying temporarily mispriced equity securities. Wong's typical day includes meeting with clients, conducting industry and company investment analysis, and preparing trade recommendations.

Music Plus

Wong follows the music industry and, specifically, Music Plus. After highly anticipated data about the music industry is released shortly after the market opens for trading, the share price of Music Plus quickly increases to $15.25. Wong evaluates the new data

Practice Problems

as it relates to Music Plus and concludes that the share price increase is an overreaction. She expects the price to quickly revert back to her revised fair value estimate of $14.20 within the same day. When the price is $15.22, she decides to prepare a large sell order equal to approximately 20% of the expected daily volume. She is concerned about information leakage from a public limit order. Wong's supervisor suggests using algorithmic trading for the sell order of the Music Plus shares.

West Commerce

Later the same day, West Commerce announces exciting new initiatives resulting in a substantial increase in its share price to $27.10. Based on this price, Wong concludes that the stock is overvalued and sets a limit price of $26.20 for a sell order of 10,000 shares. By the time the order is released to the market, the share price is $26.90. The share price closes the day at $26.00. SWM is charged a commission of $0.03 per share and no other fees. Selected data about the trade execution are presented in Exhibit 1.

Exhibit 1	Selected Trade Data: West Commerce Sell Order	
Trades	Execution price	Shares executed
Trade 1	$26.80	6,000
Trade 2	$26.30	3,000
Total		9,000

The value of the market index appropriate to West Commerce was 600 when the West Commerce sell order was released to the market, and its volume-weighted average price (VWAP) was 590 during the trade horizon. West Commerce has a beta of 0.9 with the index.

Trading Policies

At the end of the day, Wong meets with a long-term client of SWM to discuss SWM's trade policies. The client identifies two of SWM's trade policies and asks Wong whether these are consistent with good trade governance:

Policy 1   SWM works only with pre-approved brokers and execution venues, and the list is reviewed and updated regularly.

Policy 2   SWM is allowed to pool funds when appropriate, and executed orders are allocated to the accounts on a pro-rata basis.

10 The *most appropriate* price benchmark for the sell order of Music Plus shares is the:
   A   closing price.
   B   decision price.
   C   time-weighted average price (TWAP).

11 The *most* appropriate trading strategy for the sell order of Music Plus shares is:
   A   trading in the open market.
   B   selling at the closing auction for the day.
   C   passive trading over the course of the trading day.

12 The trade algorithm that Wong should consider for the sell order of Music Plus shares is:

A a POV algorithm.

B an arrival price algorithm.

C a liquidity-seeking algorithm.

13 The implementation shortfall, in basis points (bps), for the sell order of West Commerce shares is *closest* to:

A 139.

B 198.

C 206.

14 The delay cost in dollars for the sell order of West Commerce shares is:

A $1,800.

B $2,000.

C $2,700.

15 The market-adjusted cost in basis points for the sell order of West Commerce shares is *closest* to a:

A cost of 249 bps.

B savings of 50 bps.

C savings of 68 bps.

16 Which of SWM's trading policies identified by the client are consistent with good trade governance?

A Only Policy 1

B Only Policy 2

C Both Policy 1 and Policy 2

The following information relates to Questions 17–18

Lindsey Morris is a trader at North Circle Advisors, an investment management firm and adviser to a suite of value-oriented equity mutual funds. Will Beamon, portfolio manager for the firm's flagship large-cap value fund, the Ogive Fund, is explaining its investment strategy and objectives to Morris. Morris wishes to know how the Ogive Fund's underlying trading motivations may impact trade urgency and alpha decay. Beamon notes the following relevant characteristics of the Ogive Fund:

- Seeks long-term outperformance vs. S&P 500 by investing in undervalued companies
- Evaluates company fundamentals to identify persistent mispricing opportunities
- Has a three-year average holding period

17 **Determine**, based on Beamon's description of the Ogive Fund's characteristics, his likely inclination to aggressively implement the fund's strategy. **Justify** your response.

Practice Problems

Morris next meets Robin Barker, portfolio manager for North Circle Advisors' small-cap value fund, the Pengwyn Fund, which just received a very large cash inflow. Barker expects equity markets will drift higher in the near-term and asks Morris about the best ways to minimize cash drag for the Pengwyn Fund after the inflow.

18 **Describe** an appropriate cash management strategy for Barker.

The following information relates to Questions 19–20

Last year, Larry Sailors left his trading position at Valley Ranch Partners, a multi-strategy hedge fund, to join North Circle Advisors. Discussing his job experiences with a colleague, Sailors remarks that, prior to starting at North Circle, he didn't fully appreciate the significant differences in trading motivations between the two firms and how such motivations feed into trade strategy. In particular, he notes the following trade characteristics:

Exhibit 1   Features of Trades by Sailors' Employers

Feature	Valley Ranch Partners	North Circle Advisors
Investment Philosophy	Short-term long and short alpha trades across equity and non-equity securities	Long equity value investing
Trade Size	Small	Large
Risk Appetite	Low	Moderate to high
Trading Venue	Listed securities only	Listed and non-listed securities
Bid–Ask Spreads Experienced in Downturn	Moderate-to-wide	Very wide

19 **Identify** one difference between the trading features of Valley Ranch and North Circle, as noted by Sailors, for each trade strategy selection criterion.

Selection Criterion for Trade Strategy	**Identify** one difference between the trading features of Valley Ranch and North Circle, as noted by Sailors, for each trade strategy selection criterion.
Order Characteristics	
Security Characteristics	
Market Conditions	
Individual Risk Aversion	

The next day, Sailors is asked to implement the following buy orders, with target execution price set at Last Trade. He is concerned about minimizing execution risk and market impact.

Exhibit 2 Descriptions of Prospective Buy Orders

Stock	Order Size (#)	Last Trade ($)	Avg. Daily Volume (#)	Price Volatility	Bid–Ask Spread ($)
ABC	45,000	$310.10	195,000	Low	$309.75–$310.35
DEF	55,000	$40.45	4,125,260	Low	$40.39–$40.56
XYZ	8,000	$101.94	750,850	High	$100.82–$102.00

20 **Determine** which trades are *most likely* to exhibit the greatest execution risk and market impact. **Justify** each selection.

Determine which trades are *most likely* to exhibit the greatest execution risk and market impact. (Circle one in each column)

Execution Risk	Market Impact
ABC	ABC
DEF	DEF
XYZ	XYZ

Justify each selection.

The following information relates to Questions 21–23

Although focused on long-term value, North Circle Advisors will exploit temporary mispricings to open positions. For example, portfolio manager Bill Bradley pegged LIM Corporation's fair value per share at $28 yesterday; however, LIM's stock price seems to have overreacted to a competitor announcement prior to market open today. The follow events unfold over the course of the morning:

- PRIOR CLOSE: LIM closed at $30.05
- PRE-MARKET: LIM priced at $20.34
- MARKET OPEN: LIM opens at $22.15
- 10:00 AM: LIM trading at $23.01
- 10:00 AM: Bradley confirms the overreaction with target price of $28
- 10:05 AM: Bradley instructs trader to buy 25,000 shares, with a limit price of $28 when LIM is trading at $23.09
- 10:22 AM: Trader finishes the buy with an average purchase price of $23.45

Practice Problems

Bradley and the trader conduct a post-trade evaluation. In picking an appropriate reference price, the trader asks Bradley if that would be a pre-trade, intraday, post-trade, or price target benchmark.

21 **Identify** the likely appropriate price benchmark for the LIM trade. **Justify** your response.

Identify the likely appropriate price benchmark for the LIM trade. (Circle one)			
Pre-Trade	Intraday	Post-Trade	Price Target
Justify your response.			

Bradley also performs a cost analysis on the LIM trade. Noting the time gap between his trade instructions and the order's submission to the market, Bradley quantifies the cost of the delay.

22 **Calculate** the delay cost incurred in trading the LIM order.

Bradley also sees that following a 10 a.m. Federal Reserve press conference, the market rose significantly throughout that day. He wants to separate out the pricing effect of this general market movement from the cost of trading LIM. Bradley and the trader agree to use an arrival price benchmark for this analysis and gather the following data related to a broad market index:

- Index price at time of order entry: $2,150
- Index volume-weighted average price over trade horizon: $2,184
- LIM beta to Index: 0.95

23 **Calculate** the market-adjusted cost of the trade. **Discuss** the finding.

The following information relates to Questions 24–25

Beatrice Minchow designs and implements algorithmic trading strategies for Enlightenment Era Partners LLC (EEP). Minchow is working with Portfolio Manager James Bean on an algorithm to implement a sell order for Bean's small position in the lightly-traded shares of public company Dynopax Inc. In a conversation with Minchow, Bean states the following:

- I have no expectations of adverse price movements during the trade horizon and would like to use a scheduled algorithm.
- I want to minimize market impact, but I'm more concerned about getting the sell order completely executed in one day.

Based on Bean's comments, Minchow considers three algorithms: POV, VWAP, and TWAP.

24 **Determine** which algorithm Minchow is likely to use for the Dynopax sell order. **Justify** your response.

Determine which algorithm Minchow is likely to use for the Dynopax sell order. (Circle one)

POV	VWAP	TWAP

Justify your response.

Minchow is also tasked to help EEP exit from a large position in a widely-traded blue chip stock. While the trade is non-urgent, given the position's size, Bean is worried about telegraphing intentions to the market. Minchow discusses alternative trading systems with Bean, highlighting dark pools, and makes the following comments:

- Comment 1: A feature of a dark pool is that transactions and quantities won't be reported.
- Comment 2: While a dark pool does provide anonymity, there is less certainty of execution.

25 **Determine** the veracity of each comment. **Justify** each response.

Determine the veracity of each comment. **Justify** each response.

Comment	Veracity (Circle one for each row)	Justification
1	Correct	
	Incorrect	
2	Correct	
	Incorrect	

The following information relates to Question 26

Karen Swanson and Gabriel Russell recently co-founded Green Savanah Securities, an asset management firm conducting various equity and fixed-income strategies. Swanson and Russell are formulating Green Savannah's trade policy. During a meeting, they agree on an initial set of themes regarding trade policy formation:

- Theme 1: We should determine an optimal execution approach and apply that approach to each asset class managed.
- Theme 2: In aggregating trades for pooled accounts, any partially executed orders need to be allocated on a pro-rata basis.
- Theme 3: The principles behind our process to find a broker should be consistent across each asset class managed.
- Theme 4: To act in our clients' best interests, we need to disclose all trade errors to them.

26 **Identify** two inappropriate themes in the partners' set. **Justify** your response.

SOLUTIONS

1. A is correct. Greater trade urgency results in lower execution risk because the order is executed over a shorter period of time, which decreases the time the trade is exposed to price volatility and changing market conditions. In contrast, lower trade urgency results in higher execution risk because the order is executed over a longer period of time, which increases the time the trade is exposed to price volatility and changing market conditions.

2. B is correct. Harding asked Yellow to execute a list of trades, and he wants to use a price benchmark where the reference price for the benchmark is computed based on market prices that occur during the trading period, excluding trade outliers. Portfolio managers often specify an intraday benchmark for funds that are trading passively over the day, seeking liquidity, and for funds that may be rebalancing, executing a buy/sell trade list, and minimizing risk. An intraday price benchmark is based on a price that occurs during the trading period. The most common intraday benchmarks used in trading are volume-weighted average price (VWAP) and time-weighted average price (TWAP). Portfolio managers choose TWAP when they wish to exclude potential trade outliers.

3. A is correct. Given the trade urgency of the order, the very liquid market for ABC shares, and the small order size relative to ABC's expected volume, Yellow is using an arrival price trading strategy that would attempt to execute the remaining shares close to market prices at the time the order is received.

4. A is correct. XYZ shares are relatively liquid, and Harding has prioritized minimizing the trade's market impact to avoid conveying information to market participants. Harding also does not expect adverse price movements during the trade horizon. Scheduled algorithms are appropriate for orders in which portfolio managers or traders do not have expectations for adverse price movement during the trade horizon. These algorithms are also used by portfolio managers and traders who have greater risk tolerance for longer execution time periods and are more concerned with minimizing market impact. Scheduled algorithms are often appropriate when the order size is relatively small (e.g., no more than 5%–10% of expected volume), the security is relatively liquid, or the orders are part of a risk-balanced basket and trading all orders at a similar pace will maintain the risk balance.

5. A is correct. Small currency trades are usually implemented using direct market access (DMA). Buy-side traders generally use DMA for exchange-traded derivatives, particularly for smaller trades.

6. C is correct. Execution cost is calculated as the difference between the cost of the real portfolio and the paper portfolio. It reflects the execution price(s) paid for the number of shares in the order that were actually filled or executed. The execution cost is calculated as:

    Execution cost = $\sum s_j p_j - \sum s_j p_d$

    = [(10,000 shares × $40.75) + (30,000 shares × $41.25) + (20,000 shares × $41.50) + (30,000 shares × $41.75)] − (90,000 × $40.00)
    = $3,727,500 − $3,600,000
    = $127,500

7 C is correct. Opportunity cost is based on the number of shares left unexecuted in the order and reflects the cost of not being able to execute all shares at the decision price. The opportunity cost is calculated as:

$$\text{Opportunity cost} = \left(S - \sum s_j\right)(P_n - P_d)$$
$$= (120{,}000 - 90{,}000) \times (\$42.50 - \$40.00)$$
$$= \$75{,}000$$

8 B is correct. The arrival cost is calculated as:

$$\text{Arrival cost (bp)} = \text{Side} \times \frac{(\overline{P} - P_0)}{P_0} \times 10^4 \text{ bp}$$

$$= +1 \times \frac{(\$41.42 - \$40.50)}{\$40.50} \times 10^4 \text{ bp}$$

$$= 227.2 \text{ bp}$$

9 B is correct. Firms should have a policy in place for the treatment of trade errors. Errors from trading and any resulting gains/losses need to be disclosed to a firm's compliance department and documented in a trade error log. The trade error log should include any related documentation and evidence that trade errors are resolved in a way that avoids adverse impact to the client.

10 B is correct. A pre-trade benchmark is often specified by portfolio managers who are buying or selling securities seeking short-term alpha by buying undervalued or selling overvalued securities in the market. Wong believes the stock of Music Plus is overvalued and is seeking short-term alpha with the sell order. Since Wong has an exact record of the price of Music Plus when the decision for the sell order was made (\$15.22), the decision price is the most appropriate pre-trade benchmark for the sell order.

A is incorrect because a closing price is a post-trade benchmark and is typically used by index managers and mutual funds that wish to execute transactions at the closing price for the day. A portfolio manager who is managing tracking error to a benchmark will generally select a closing price benchmark since the closing price is the price used to compute the fund's valuation and resulting tracking error to the benchmark. This is not the objective of the sell order of Music Plus. Wong's objective is to execute the sell trade as quickly as possible to capture the short-term alpha she identified. She expects the price of Music Plus to revert back to \$14.20 within the day. Therefore, she will need to execute her trading prior to the price when the market closes; thus, the closing price is not the appropriate price benchmark.

C is incorrect because a TWAP benchmark price is used when portfolio managers wish to exclude potential trade outliers. Trade outliers may be caused by trading a large buy order at the day's low or a large sell order at the day's high. Therefore, a TWAP benchmark is not appropriate for the sell order of Music Plus because Wong would like to execute a large sell order near the day's high price, which would likely be an outlier.

11 A is correct. The sell order for the Music Plus shares has associated high trade urgency because Wong determined that the stock is temporarily overvalued and expects others to realize this quickly. Therefore, the trader does not have the benefit of trading the order passively (such as by using a VWAP or TWAP participation strategy) during the day, since the share price could decrease to fair

Solutions

value at any time. Because the trade order for Music Plus shares is submitted after the market opened that day, the opening auction is not an option and the whole order is traded in the open market.

B is incorrect because selling at the closing auction for the day is an appropriate trading strategy for trades when the portfolio manager would like to receive proceeds at NAV. An example of such a trade is a trade to meet a redemption request from a client. The trade for Music Plus shares has associated high trade urgency and must be executed as quickly as possible to capture the short-term alpha. Waiting until the closing auction is not an appropriate trading strategy.

C is incorrect because passive trading is appropriate for trades associated with low trade urgency. The sell order of Music Plus shares has associated high trade urgency because Wong determined that the stock is temporarily overvalued and expects the new data to be reflected in the price by the end of the day. Therefore, the trader does not have the benefit of trading the order passively (such as by using a VWAP or TWAP participation strategy) during the day, since the share price could decrease to fair value at any time.

12 C is correct. Liquidity-seeking algorithms are appropriate for large orders that the portfolio manager or trader would like to execute quickly without having a substantial impact on the security price. The sell order for Music Plus shares is for 20% of the expected volume and therefore is a large order. Liquidity-seeking algorithms are also used when displaying sizable liquidity via limit orders could lead to unwanted information leakage and adverse security price movement. In these cases, the priority is to minimize information leakage associated with order execution and avoid signaling to the market the trading intentions of the portfolio manager or trader. Wong is concerned that a large limit order will reveal to the market her opinion the shares are overvalued.

A is incorrect because POV algorithms (also known as participation algorithms) send orders following a volume participation schedule. As trading volume increases in the market, these algorithms will trade more shares, and as volume decreases, these algorithms will trade fewer shares. Wong needs to execute the sell order for Music Plus shares as quickly as possible because she expects the new information to be reflected in the share price quickly. Therefore, a POV algorithm is not appropriate.

B is incorrect because even though arrival price algorithms are used for orders in which the portfolio manager or trader believes prices are likely to move unfavorably and wishes to trade more aggressively to capture alpha, they are used when the security is relatively liquid or the order is not outsized (size less than 15% of the expected volume). The order size for Music Plus shares is large, at 20% of the expected volume.

13 C is correct. The implementation shortfall in basis points is calculated as follows:

$$\text{Implementation shortfall (bps)} = \frac{\text{Implementation shortfall (\$)}}{(\text{Total order shares})(p_d)} \times 10{,}000 \text{ bps}$$

$$\text{Implementation shortfall(\$)} = \underbrace{\sum s_j p_j - \sum s_j p_d}_{\text{Execution Cost}} + \underbrace{(S - \sum s_j)(P_n - P_d)}_{\text{Opportunity Cost}} + \text{Fees.}$$

$$\text{Fees} = \text{Absolute value of } \sum s_j \times \text{Fee per share}$$

where

> $S > 0$ indicates a buy order and $S < 0$ indicates a sell order
> P_d represents the price at the time of the investment decision
> P_n represents the current price

s_j and p_j represent the number of shares executed and the transaction price of the jth trade

> Execution cost = $[(-6{,}000 \times 26.80) + (-3{,}000 \times 26.30)] - (-9{,}000 \times 27.10) =$ 4,200.
>
> Opportunity cost = $[-10{,}000 - (-9{,}000)] \times (26.00 - 27.10) = 1{,}100$.
>
> Fees = $9{,}000 \; 0.03 = 270$.

So, the implementation shortfall ($) is calculated as

> Implementation shortfall ($) = $4{,}200 + 1{,}100 + 270 = 5{,}570$.

Finally, the implementation shortfall (bps) is calculated as

$$\text{Implementation shortfall (bps)} = \frac{5{,}570}{10{,}000 \times 27.10} \times 10{,}000 \text{ bps} \approx 206 \text{ bps}$$

14 A is correct. The delay cost in dollars is calculated as

$$\text{Delay cost} = \left(\sum s_j\right) p_0 - \left(\sum s_j\right) p_d$$

where

> $S > 0$ indicates a buy order and $S < 0$ indicates a sell order
> p_0 represents the arrival price, defined as the asset price at the time the order was released to the market for execution
> p_d represents the price at the time of the investment decision
> s_j represents the number of shares executed

Therefore, the delay cost in dollars for the sell order is calculated as

> Delay cost = $(-9{,}000 \times 26.90) - (-9{,}000 \times 27.10) = \$1{,}800$

15 B is correct. The market-adjusted cost in basis points is calculated as

> Market-adjusted cost (bps) = Arrival cost (bps) − β × Index cost (bps)

$$\text{Arrival cost (bps)} = \text{Side} \times \frac{(\overline{P} - P_0)}{P_0} \times 10^4 \text{ bps}$$

$$\text{Index cost (bps)} = \text{Side} \times \frac{(\text{Index VWAP} - \text{Index arrival price})}{\text{Index arrival price}} \times 10^4$$

Where

$$\text{Side} = \begin{cases} +1 \text{ Buy Order} \\ -1 \text{ Sell Order} \end{cases}$$

$\overline{P}$ = Average execution price of order

P_0 = arrival price

Therefore,

$$\text{Average execution price} = \frac{(6{,}000 \times 26.80 + 3{,}000 \times 26.30)}{9{,}000} \approx 26.63$$

$$\text{Arrival cost (bps)} = -1 \times \frac{(26.63 - 26.90)}{26.90} \times 10^4 \text{ bps} = 100.37 \text{ bps}$$

$$\text{Index cost (bps)} = -1 \times \frac{590 - 600}{600} \times 10^4 = 166.67 \text{ bps}$$

$$\text{Market-adjusted cost (bps)} = 100.37 \text{ bps} - 0.9 \times 166.67 \text{ bps} \approx -50 \text{ bps}$$

Since the result is negative, the market-adjusted cost for the sell order of West Commerce is a savings of approximately 50 bps.

16. C is correct. Both of SWM's trading policies are consistent with good governance. Asset managers should have a list of approved brokers and execution venues for trading and the criteria used to create this list. Creating and maintaining the list should be a collaborative effort shared by portfolio execution, compliance, and risk management. A best practices approach is to create a Best Execution Monitoring Committee within an investment management firm that is responsible for maintaining and updating the list regularly, or as circumstances require, and for distributing the list to all parties involved in trade execution. Furthermore, if several accounts follow the same or a similar investment strategy and have similar trading needs, then pooling the trades for trade execution may make sense in some situations. If a pooled trade is not fully executed, the order amount that is executed generally needs to be allocated to accounts on a pro-rata basis so that no account is disadvantaged relative to the others.

17. Beamon is likely to take a measured approach in implementing the Ogive Fund's strategy. In particular, trade urgency, which refers to how quickly or slowly an order is executed over the trading time horizon, is likely to be low for the Ogive Fund. Greater trade urgency is associated with executing over shorter horizons, whereas lower trade urgency is associated with executing over longer horizons. To capitalize on views related to mispricing, the Ogive Fund's individual positions may be held for several years. Minimal trading is required, and any necessary trading can often be carried out in a more patient manner. Additionally, the return payoffs associated with the Ogive Fund's long-term investment views and value orientation are not likely to be rapidly acted on by other market participants. Thus, the rate or level of expected alpha decay, which refers to the erosion or deterioration in short-term alpha once an investment decision is made, is low.

18. To minimize cash drag on a portfolio, or fund underperformance from holding uninvested cash in a rising market, Barker may use a strategy known as equitization. In this case, equitization refers to temporarily investing cash using futures or ETFs to gain the desired equity exposure before investing in the underlying securities longer term. Equitization may be required if large inflows into a portfolio are hindered by lack of liquidity in the underlying securities. So, if the Pengwyn Fund's large inflow cannot be invested immediately, Barker can equitize the cash using equity futures or ETFs and then gradually trade into the underlying positions and trade out of the futures/ETF position.

19

Selection Criterion for Trade Strategy	**Identify** one difference between the trading features of Valley Ranch and North Circle, as noted by Sailors, for each trade strategy selection criterion.
Order Characteristics	Key differences include: (i) the sizes of the orders, with larger orders at North Circle; and (ii) the side of the orders, with North Circle skewing more toward buy orders.
Security Characteristics	Key differences include: (i) security type, with North Circle trading only equities; (ii) short-term alpha focus, with more focus on short-term price movements at Valley Ranch; and (iii) security liquidity, with North Circle buying non-listed securities.
Market Conditions	While both North Circle and Valley Ranch are impacted by market conditions overall, North Circle's investments in non-listed securities are more likely to have a greater potential exposure to adverse market liquidity conditions.
Individual Risk Aversion	The portfolio managers at North Circle and Valley Ranch have different aversions to risk, with North Circle's managers having higher risk aversion than the Valley Ranch managers.

20

Determine which trades are *most likely* to exhibit the greatest execution risk and market impact. (Circle one in each column)

Execution Risk	Market Impact
ABC	**ABC**
DEF	DEF
XYZ	XYZ

Justify each selection.

The XYZ trade exhibits the greatest execution risk because XYZ has the highest price volatility of the three stocks. Execution risk is the risk of an adverse price movement occurring over the trading horizon owing to a change in the fundamental value of the security or because of trading-induced volatility. Execution risk is often proxied by price volatility. Securities with higher levels of price volatility have greater exposure to execution risk than securities with lower price volatility.

The ABC trade exhibits the greatest market impact risk as it represents the highest percentage of ADV (45,000 / 195,000 = 23.07%). The permanent component of price change associated with trading an order is the market price impact caused by the information content of the trade. The larger the size of the trade expressed as a percentage of ADV, the larger the expected market impact cost.

21

Identify the likely appropriate price benchmark for the LIM trade. (Circle one)

Pre-Trade	Intraday	Post-Trade	Price Target

Solutions

> **Justify** your response.
>
> A pre-trade benchmark is a reference price that is known before the start of the period over which trading will take place. For example, pre-trade benchmarks include decision price, previous close, opening price, and arrival price. A pre-trade benchmark is often specified by portfolio managers who are buying or selling securities on the basis of decision prices. In this case, Bradley's target price had been set based on his valuation principles before the opening, whereas waiting for the other benchmarks as inputs would result in the perceived opportunity expiring before it could be exploited.
>
> For Bradley and his trader, two of these pre-trade benchmarks are potentially appropriate. Those are either the decision price, which was the price when Bradley made the decision to buy or sell the security, or the arrival price, which is the price of the security at the time the order is entered into the market for execution. Portfolio managers who are buying or selling on the basis of alpha expectations or a current market mispricing will often specify an arrival price benchmark.

22 The delay cost reflects the adverse price movement associated with the untimely submission of Bradley's order and is calculated as follows:

$$\text{Delay cost} = \left(\sum s_j\right) P_0 - \left(\sum s_j\right) P_d = (25{,}000 \times 23.09) - (25{,}000 \times 23.01) = \$2{,}000.$$

23 Bradley and the trader's analysis will show that the market-adjusted cost calculates as follows:

$$\text{Arrival cost (bps)} = \text{Side} \times \frac{(\bar{P} - P_0)}{P_0} \times 10^4 \text{ bps}$$

$$= +1 \times \frac{(\$23.45 - \$23.09)}{\$23.09} \times 10^4 \text{ bps}$$

$$= 155.91 \text{ bps}.$$

$$\text{Index cost (bps)} = \text{Side} \times \frac{(\text{Index VWAP} - \text{Index arrival price})}{\text{Index arrival price}} \times 10^4 \text{ bps}$$

$$= +1 \times \frac{(\$2{,}184 - \$2{,}150)}{\$2{,}150} \times 10^4 \text{ bps}$$

$$\approx 158.14 \text{ bps}.$$

$$\text{Market-adjusted cost (bps)} = \text{Arrival cost (bps)} - \beta \times \text{Index cost (bps)}$$

$$= 155.91 - 0.95 \times 158.14$$

$$= 155.91 - 150.23$$

$$\approx 5.68 \text{ bps}.$$

LIM's market-adjusted cost is thus significantly lower than the total arrival cost. This indicates that most of the expense associated with buying LIM is due to the effect of buying it in a rising market as opposed to the buying pressure induced by the order itself.

24

> **Determine** which algorithm Minchow is likely to use for the Dynopax sell order. (Circle one)

POV	VWAP	**TWAP**

(continued)

Justify your response.

Regarding Bean's alternatives, VWAP and TWAP algorithms release orders to the market following a time-specified schedule, trading a predetermined number of shares within the specified time interval (e.g., one day). Following a fixed schedule as VWAP algorithms do, however, may not be optimal for certain stocks because such algorithms may not complete the order in cases where volumes are low. Furthermore, while POV algorithms incorporate real-time volume by following (or chasing) volumes, they may not complete the order within the time period specified.

TWAP algorithms, which send the same number of shares and the same percentage of the order to be traded in each time period, will help ensure the specified number of shares are executed within the specified time period. Given Bean's stated priority of complete execution in one day, he is likely to use a TWAP algorithm for the Dynopax sell order.

25

Determine the veracity of each comment. Justify each response.

Comment	Veracity (Circle one for each row)	Justification
1	**Correct** / Incorrect	Regardless of the trading venue, transactions and quantities are always reported.
2	Correct / **Incorrect**	Dark pools provide anonymity because no pre-trade transparency exists. Exchanges are known as lit markets (as opposed to dark markets) because they provide pre-trade transparency—namely, limit orders that reflect trader intentions for trade side (buy or sell), price, and size. However, with a dark pool, there is less certainty of execution as compared to an exchange.

26 Theme 1 is inappropriate because the optimal execution approach may differ by asset class, level of security liquidity, and security trading mechanism (order-driven markets, quote-driven markets, and brokered markets). Green Savannah's trade policy document should describe the factors used in determining how an order can be executed in an optimal manner for a given scenario.

Theme 4 is inappropriate because as part of a suitable policy for the treatment of trade errors, those errors and any resulting gains/losses need to be disclosed to Green Savannah's compliance department and documented in a trade error log. The priority is to ensure errors are resolved in a way that prevents adverse impact for the client, not to ensure complete disclosure.

READING 26

Portfolio Performance Evaluation

edited by Marc A. Wright, CFA

Marc A. Wright, CFA, is at Russell Investments (USA).

LEARNING OUTCOMES

Mastery	The candidate should be able to:
☐	a. explain the following components of portfolio evaluation and their interrelationships: performance measurement, performance attribution, and performance appraisal;
☐	b. describe attributes of an effective attribution process;
☐	c. contrast return attribution and risk attribution; contrast macro and micro return attribution;
☐	d. describe returns-based, holdings-based, and transactions-based performance attribution, including advantages and disadvantages of each;
☐	e. interpret the sources of portfolio returns using a specified attribution approach;
☐	f. interpret the output from fixed-income attribution analyses;
☐	g. discuss considerations in selecting a risk attribution approach;
☐	h. identify and interpret investment results attributable to the asset owner versus those attributable to the investment manager;
☐	i. discuss uses of liability-based benchmarks;
☐	j. describe types of asset-based benchmarks;
☐	k. discuss tests of benchmark quality;
☐	l. describe problems that arise in benchmarking alternative investments;
☐	m. describe the impact of benchmark misspecification on attribution and appraisal analysis;

(continued)

© 2019 CFA Institute. All rights reserved.

LEARNING OUTCOMES

Mastery	The candidate should be able to:
☐	n. calculate and interpret the Sortino ratio, the appraisal ratio, upside/downside capture ratios, maximum drawdown, and drawdown duration;
☐	o. describe limitations of appraisal measures and related metrics;
☐	p. evaluate the skill of an investment manager.

1 INTRODUCTION

Performance evaluation is one of the most critical areas of investment analysis. Performance results can be used to assess the quality of the investment approach and suggest changes that might improve it. They are also used to communicate the results of the investment process to other stakeholders and may even be used to compensate the investment managers. Therefore, it is of vital importance that practitioners who use these analyses understand how the results are generated. By gaining an understanding of the details of how these analyses work, practitioners will develop a greater understanding of the insights that might be gathered from the analysis and will also be cognizant of the limitations of those approaches, careful not to infer more than what is explicit or logically implicit in the results.

We will first consider the broad categories of performance measurement, attribution, and appraisal, differentiating between the three and explaining their interrelationships. Next, we will provide practitioners with tools to evaluate the effectiveness of those analyses as we summarize various approaches to performance evaluation. We will cover returns-based, holdings-based, and transactions-based attribution, addressing the merits and shortcomings of each approach and providing guidance on how to properly interpret attribution results. Again, by reviewing how each approach generates its results, we reveal strengths and weaknesses of the individual attribution approaches.

Next, we will turn to the subject of benchmarks and performance appraisal ratios. We will review the long-standing tests of benchmark quality and differentiate market indexes from benchmarks. We will also review different ratios used in performance appraisal, considering the benefits and limitations of each approach.

Lastly, we will provide advice on using these tools to collectively evaluate the skill of investment managers. This advice relies heavily on understanding the analysis tools, the limitations of the approaches, the importance of data to the quality of the analysis, and the pitfalls to avoid when making recommendations.

2 INTRODUCTION TO PERFORMANCE EVALUATION AND ATTRIBUTION

a explain the following components of portfolio evaluation and their interrelationships: performance measurement, performance attribution, and performance appraisal

b describe attributes of an effective attribution process

Introduction to Performance Evaluation and Attribution

   c contrast return attribution and risk attribution; contrast macro and micro return attribution

   d describe returns-based, holdings-based, and transactions-based performance attribution, including advantages and disadvantages of each

Performance evaluation includes three primary components, each corresponding to a specific question we need to answer to evaluate a portfolio's performance:

- Performance measurement—what was the portfolio's performance?
- Performance attribution—how was the performance achieved?
- Performance appraisal—was the performance achieved through manager skill or luck?

We will consider each of these components on their own and the interrelationships between them.

Performance measurement provides an overall indication of the portfolio's performance, typically relative to a benchmark. In its simplest form, performance measurement is the calculation of investment returns for both the portfolio and its benchmark. This return calculation is a critical first step in the performance evaluation process, building the foundation on which performance evaluation is based. The investment return tells us what the portfolio achieved over a specific period, irrespective of peer or benchmark performance. For purposes of this reading, we will call this the *absolute return*. But it also provides the basis to understand the difference between the portfolio return and its benchmark return, the **excess return**.

In addition to return, performance measurement must consider the risk incurred to achieve that return. We measure risk using a variety of *ex post* (looking back in time) and *ex ante* (looking forward in time) techniques. For *ex post*, we might consider the volatility or standard deviation of the past returns, along with many other performance appraisal ratios considered later in this reading. The calculation of a portfolio's value at risk (VaR) at a point in time is an example of an *ex ante* measure. These measures of risk allow us to quantify the risk in a portfolio and better assess the performance.

Performance attribution then builds on the foundation of the investment returns and risk, helping us explain *how* that performance was achieved or that risk was incurred. Performance attribution can be used to explain either absolute returns or relative returns. It can be used to understand what portion of returns was driven by active manager decisions and what portion was a result of exposures not specifically targeted by the portfolio manager. Performance attribution can also be used to decompose the excess return into its component sources, where it is used to help explain why a manager over- or underperformed the target benchmark. Similarly, risk attribution can be used to decompose the risk incurred in the portfolio.

The third component of performance evaluation, performance appraisal, makes use of risk, return, and attribution analyses to draw conclusions regarding the *quality* of a portfolio's performance. Performance appraisal attempts to distinguish manager skill from luck. Did the portfolio manager's decisions help achieve a better outcome, or was the outcome due to market changes outside of the manager's control? If superior results can be attributed to skill, there is a higher likelihood that the manager will generate superior performance in the future. The analysis may affirm the management process or may contain insights for improving the process. This is a key feedback loop in the investment management process.

> **EXAMPLE 1**
>
> **Performance Evaluation**
>
> 1 Performance attribution:
>   **A** measures the excess performance of a portfolio.
>   **B** explains the proportion of returns due to manager skill.
>   **C** explains how the excess performance or risk was achieved.
> 2 Performance appraisal:
>   **A** identifies the sources of under- or outperformance.
>   **B** decomposes a portfolio's risk and return into their constituent parts.
>   **C** uses the results of risk, return, and attribution analyses to assess the quality of a portfolio's performance.
>
> **Solution to 1:**
>
> C is correct. Performance attribution identifies the drivers of investment returns. A is not correct because measuring the excess performance of a portfolio is the subject of performance measurement. B is not correct because it is performance appraisal that distinguishes skill from luck.
>
> **Solution to 2:**
>
> C is correct. Performance appraisal combines all the techniques of performance measurement and attribution to assess the quality of performance. Both A and B describe performance attribution.

2.1 Performance Attribution

As previously described, performance attribution is a critical component of the portfolio evaluation process. Used by senior management, client relationship specialists, risk controllers, operations staff, portfolio managers, and sales and marketing professionals, attribution analysis provides important insights to the investment decision-making process. Clients and prospects also use attribution analysis as part of their evaluation of that process. Effective performance attribution analysis requires a thorough understanding of the investment decision-making process and should reflect the active decisions of the portfolio manager.

An effective performance attribution process must

- account for *all* of the portfolio's return or risk exposure,
- reflect the investment decision-making process,
- quantify the active decisions of the portfolio manager, and
- provide a complete understanding of the excess return/risk of the portfolio.

If the return or risk quantified by the attribution analysis does not account for all the return or risk presented to the client, then at best the attribution is incomplete and at worst the quality of the attribution analysis is brought into doubt. If the attribution does not reflect the investment decision-making process, then the analysis will be of little value to either the portfolio manager or the client. For example, if the portfolio manager is a genuine bottom-up stock picker who ignores sector benchmark weights, then measuring the impact of sector allocation against these weights is not measuring decisions made as part of the investment process; sector effects are merely a byproduct of the manager's investment decisions.

Introduction to Performance Evaluation and Attribution

Performance attribution includes return attribution and risk attribution (although in practice, "performance attribution" is often used to mean "return attribution"). **Return attribution** analyzes the impact of active investment decisions on *returns*; **risk attribution** analyzes the *risk* consequences of those decisions. Depending on the purpose of the analysis, risk may be viewed in absolute or benchmark-relative terms. For example, when risk relative to a benchmark is the focus, a risk attribution analysis might identify and evaluate a portfolio's deviations from a benchmark's exposures to risk factors.

Performance attribution provides a good starting point for a conversation with clients, explaining both positive and negative aspects of recent performance. Return attribution analysis is particularly important when performance is weak; portfolio managers must demonstrate an understanding of their performance, provide a rationale for their decisions, and generate confidence in their ability to add value in the future. When it accurately reflects the investment decision-making process, return attribution provides quality control for the investment process and provides senior management with a tool to manage a complex business with multiple investment strategies.

The attribution process described earlier—understanding the drivers of a manager's returns and whether those drivers are consistent with the stated investment process—is a common application of attribution analysis. But attribution can also be conducted to evaluate the asset owner's tactical asset allocation and manager selection decisions (called **macro attribution**) or to evaluate the impact of the portfolio manager's decisions on the performance of the asset owner's total fund (called **micro attribution**). A defined-benefit pension plan makes the decision to allocate a given percentage of the fund to each asset class and decides which manager(s) to hire for each asset class. Macro attribution measures the effect of the sponsor's choice to deviate from the strategic asset allocation, including the effect of "gaps" between the strategic asset allocation and its implementation (e.g., where the sum of the managers' benchmarks is equal to something other than the benchmark index).

Micro attribution measures the impact of portfolio managers' allocation and selection decisions on total fund performance.

Performance attribution may be either returns based, holdings based, or transactions based. The decision to use one set of inputs rather than another depends on the availability of data as well as the investment process being measured.

Returns-based attribution uses only the total portfolio returns over a period to identify the components of the investment process that have generated the returns. Returns-based attribution is most appropriate when the underlying portfolio holding information is not available with sufficient frequency at the required level of detail. For example, one might use returns-based attribution to evaluate hedge funds, because it can be difficult to obtain the underlying holdings of hedge funds. Returns-based attribution is the easiest method to implement, but because it does not use the underlying holdings, it is the least accurate of the three approaches and the most vulnerable to data manipulation.

Unlike returns-based attribution, **holdings-based attribution** references the beginning-of-period holdings of the portfolio. Calculated with monthly, weekly, or daily data, the accuracy of holdings-based attribution improves when using data with shorter time intervals. For longer evaluation periods, we link together the attribution results for the shorter measurement periods. Because holdings-based attribution fails to capture the impact of any transactions made during the measurement period, it may not reconcile to the actual portfolio return. For example, in a daily holdings-based attribution, securities are included at the end of the day they are purchased and excluded at the end of the day they are sold. If the transaction price is significantly different from the closing price, the attribution analysis can differ significantly from the actual performance.

The residual caused by ignoring transactions might be described as a timing or trading effect. Holdings-based analysis is most appropriate for investment strategies with little turnover (e.g., passive strategies). Holdings-based analysis may be improved by valuing the portfolio with the same prices used to calculate the underlying benchmark index, removing one potential difference between the portfolio and benchmark returns that is not a management effect.

The third approach, **transactions-based attribution**, uses both the holdings of the portfolio and the transactions (purchases and sales) that occurred during the evaluation period. For transaction-based attribution, both the weights and returns reflect *all transactions* during the period, including transaction costs. Transaction-based attribution is the most accurate type of attribution analysis but also the most difficult and time-consuming to implement. To obtain meaningful results, the underlying data must be complete, accurate, and reconciled from period to period. Because all the data are available, the entire excess return can be quantified and explained. The return used in the attribution analysis will reconcile with the return presented to the client, and attribution analysis can be used as a diagnostic tool to identify errors.

The choice of attribution approach depends on the availability and quality of the underlying data, the reporting requirements for the client, and the complexity of the investment decision-making process.

EXAMPLE 2

Performance Attribution

1. Effective attribution analysis must:
   - **A** use intraday transaction data.
   - **B** reconcile to the total portfolio return or risk exposure.
   - **C** measure the contribution of security and sector selection decisions.
2. Which of the following most accurately describes macro attribution?
   - **A** Attribution analysis at the portfolio level
   - **B** Attribution analysis of the fund sponsor decisions
   - **C** Attribution analysis of asset allocation decisions
3. Risk attribution differs from return attribution in that it:
   - **A** is not conducted relative to a benchmark.
   - **B** quantifies the risk consequences of the investment decisions.
   - **C** quantifies the investment decisions of the investment manager.
4. An analyst is *most likely* to use returns-based attribution when:
   - **A** the portfolio has a low turnover.
   - **B** the holdings for the portfolio are not available.
   - **C** she wants the analysis to be as accurate as possible.

Solution to 1:

B is correct. An effective attribution process accounts for all of the portfolio's return or risk exposure. A is not correct; an attribution analysis is improved with intraday transaction data, but an effective attribution analysis can be produced with a returns- or holdings-based approach. C is not correct because an attribution process that measures the sector selection effects of a bottom-up stock-picker does not measure the effectiveness of the investment decision-making process.

Solution to 2:

B is correct. Macro attribution measures the effect of the sponsor's choice to deviate from the strategic asset allocation and the sponsor's manager selection decisions. A is not correct because attribution analysis at the portfolio level may be either macro attribution or micro attribution. C is not correct because macro attribution measures both asset allocation and manager selection decisions of the asset owner.

Solution to 3:

B is correct. Risk attribution, unlike return attribution, attempts to quantify the risk consequences of the investment decisions. A is not correct because risk attribution may be conducted on either an absolute or a relative basis. C is not correct because risk attribution does not capture the return impact of a manager's investment decisions.

Solution to 4:

B is correct. Returns-based attribution is typically used when the holdings data are not available. Neither A nor C is correct because returns-based attribution is the least accurate of the three approaches.

EQUITY RETURN ATTRIBUTION

e   interpret the sources of portfolio returns using a specified attribution approach

Return attribution allows us to look across a specific time horizon and identify which investment decisions have either added value to or detracted value from the portfolio, relative to its benchmark. As feedback to the portfolio management process, return attribution quantifies the active decisions of portfolio managers and informs management and clients. In this way, return attribution can be thought of as "backward looking" or *ex post*, meaning that it is used to evaluate the investment decisions for some historical time horizon.

Return attribution is a set of techniques used to identify the sources of excess return of a portfolio against its benchmark, quantifying the consequences of active investment decisions.

Specific return attribution approaches have been designed to evaluate particular types of assets. In this section, we will consider two common approaches for equity attribution: Brinson–Fachler and factor-based attribution. We will also review the output and findings from a typical fixed-income attribution approach.

Practitioners may also encounter the concept of geometric attribution and arithmetic attribution, two approaches to measuring attribution effects over longer periods. **Arithmetic attribution** approaches are designed to explain the **excess return**, the arithmetic difference between the portfolio return, R, and its benchmark return, B.

When using an arithmetic attribution approach, the attribution effects will sum to the excess return. Arithmetic approaches are straightforward for a single period, for which there is no difference between the sum of the attribution effects and the excess return. However, when combining multiple periods, the sub-period attribution effects will *not* sum to the excess return. Because the excess return is calculated by *geometrically* linking the sub-period returns, adjustments must be made to "smooth" the *arithmetic* sub-period attribution effects over time. Multiple smoothing approaches exist in the industry, including algorithms suggested by David Cariño (1999) and Jose Menchero (2000).

Geometric attribution approaches extend the arithmetic approaches by attributing the geometric excess return (*G*), as defined below:

$$G = \frac{1+R}{1+B} - 1 = \frac{R-B}{1+B}$$

Note that the geometric excess return is simply the arithmetic excess return divided by the wealth ratio of the benchmark (1 plus the return on the benchmark during the period).

In a geometric attribution approach, the attribution effects will compound (multiply) together to total the geometric excess return. Because the attribution effects compound together to exactly equal the geometric excess return, the compounding works across multiple periods. Therefore, no smoothing is required to adjust the geometric attribution effects across multiple periods.

Practitioners typically choose arithmetic attribution approaches when they want to use the attribution analysis with non-practitioner clients or in marketing reports. With results that add up to the total excess return for all periods, arithmetic approaches are more intuitively understood. Geometric approaches tend to be limited to practitioners who understand the approach and who appreciate that they do not have to adjust the attribution effects over time.

3.1 A Simple Return Attribution Example

Suppose a portfolio's return for the past year was 5.24% and the portfolio's benchmark return for that same period was 3.24%. In this case, the portfolio achieved a positive arithmetic excess return of 2.00% (5.24% − 3.24% = 2.00%) over the past year.

To understand how the 2.00% was achieved, we apply return attribution. In this example, return attribution will quantify two typical sources of excess return: *security selection* and *asset allocation*. Security selection answers the question, Was the return achieved by selecting securities that performed well relative to the benchmark or by avoiding benchmark securities that performed relatively poorly? Asset allocation answers the question, Was the return achieved by choosing to overweight an asset category (e.g., economic sector or currency) that outperformed the total benchmark or to underweight an asset category that underperformed the total benchmark? (The term "allocation" is used somewhat differently here. It is not measuring the plan sponsor's asset allocation decision but, rather, the *manager's* decision to allocate among countries, sectors, or, in cases where the manager has a broad mandate, asset classes.)

Models of equity return attribution often attempt to separate the investment process into those two key decisions—selection and allocation—assigning each a magnitude and direction (plus or minus) for both decisions. For instance, for the portfolio referenced previously, we might calculate the return attribution results shown in Exhibit 1:

Exhibit 1	Total Portfolio Return Attribution Analysis (Time Period: Past 12 Months)				
Portfolio Return	Benchmark Return	Excess Return	Allocation Effect	Selection Effect
5.24%	3.24%	2.00%	−0.50%	2.50%

As we noted, the investment decisions generated a positive excess return of 200 basis points (bps) relative to the benchmark. We use the "return attribution analysis" to see how this 200 bps was generated. First, note that the *negative* allocation effect indicates that the allocation decisions over the past 12 months, whatever they were, had a negative impact on the total portfolio performance. They *subtracted* 50 bps from the excess return. In contrast, the *positive* selection effect indicates that the security selection decisions—decisions to overweight or underweight securities relative to their benchmark weights—*added* 250 bps to the excess return. Our return attribution analysis implies that the portfolio manager's security selection decision was far superior to his or her asset allocation decision for the past 12 months.

3.2 Equity Return Attribution—The Brinson–Hood–Beebower Model

The foundations of return attribution were established in two articles, one written by Brinson and Fachler (1985) and the other by Brinson, Hood, and Beebower (1986). The Brinson–Fachler model is more widely used in performance attribution today, but we introduce the Brinson–Hood–Beebower (BHB) model first to lay an important foundation.

BHB is built on the assumption that the total portfolio and benchmark returns are calculated by summing the weights and returns of the sectors within the portfolio (Equation 1) and the benchmark (Equation 2):

$$\text{Portfolio return } R = \sum_{i=1}^{i=n} w_i R_i \quad (1)$$

$$\text{Benchmark return } B = \sum_{i=1}^{i=n} W_i B_i \quad (2)$$

where

w_i = weight of the *i*th sector in the portfolio
R_i = return of the portfolio assets in the *i*th sector
W_i = weight of the *i*th sector in the benchmark
B_i = return of the benchmark in the *i*th sector
n = number of sectors or securities

The sum of the weights in both the portfolio and the benchmark must equal 100%. The presence of leverage would require a position with a negative weight (borrowings or short positions) to balance to 100%.

Attribution analysis quantifies each of the portfolio manager's active decisions that explain the difference between the portfolio return, R, and the benchmark return, B. Note that for this example, we are concerned with only single-period, single-currency return attribution models.

Exhibit 2 provides data for a three-sector domestic equity portfolio, used to illustrate the BHB model.

Sector	Portfolio Weight	Benchmark Weight	Portfolio Return	Benchmark Return
Energy	50%	50%	18%	10%
Health care	30%	20%	–3%	–2%

Exhibit 2 BHB Model Illustration—Portfolio and Benchmark Data

(continued)

Exhibit 2 (Continued)

Sector	Portfolio Weight	Benchmark Weight	Portfolio Return	Benchmark Return
Financials	20%	30%	10%	12%
Total	**100%**	**100%**	**10.1%**	**8.2%**

Total portfolio return $R = (50\% \times 18\%) + (30\% \times -3\%) + (20\% \times 10\%) = 10.1\%$

Total benchmark return $B = (50\% \times 10\%) + (20\% \times -2\%) + (30\% \times 12\%) = 8.2\%$

Thus, the excess return is 1.9% (10.1% − 8.2% = 1.9%), or 190 bps.

We will use the weights and returns data shown in Exhibit 2 to calculate the basic attribution effects using the BHB model, including the allocation effect, the security selection effect, and the interaction effect. The allocation effect refers to the value the portfolio manager adds (or subtracts) by having portfolio sector weights that are different from the benchmark sector weights. A sector weight in the portfolio greater than the benchmark sector weight would be described as *overweight*, and a sector weight less than the benchmark sector weight would be described as *underweight*.

To calculate allocation, we first calculate the contribution to allocation (A_i) for each sector. The contribution to allocation in the *i*th sector is equal to the portfolio's sector weight minus the benchmark's sector weight, times the benchmark sector return:

$$A_i = (w_i - W_i)B_i \quad (3)$$

Using the data from Exhibit 2, we calculate individual sector allocation effects as follows:

- Energy: (50% − 50%) × 10% = 0.0%
- Health care: (30% − 20%) × −2.0% = −0.2%
- Financials: (20% − 30%) × 12% = −1.2%

To find the total portfolio allocation effect, A, we sum the individual sector contributions to allocation:

$$A = \sum_{i=1}^{i=n} A_i \quad (4)$$

Total allocation effect = 0.0% − 0.2% − 1.2% = −1.4%

We can then use the results to state the following conclusions:

- The portfolio weight in the energy sector is equal to the benchmark weight; therefore, there is no contribution to allocation in energy.
- In health care, the portfolio manager held a higher weight than the benchmark (30% versus 20%), but the sector underperformed the aggregate benchmark (−2.0% versus 8.2%). Therefore, the decision to overweight health care lowered the overall excess return; the contribution to allocation is −0.2%.

- In financials, the portfolio manager chose to underweight versus the benchmark (20% versus 30%). But because financials outperformed the aggregate benchmark (12% versus 8.2%), the decision to underweight financials also lowered the overall excess return; the contribution to allocation is −1.2%.
- Overall, the combined allocation effect for this portfolio was −1.4%, demonstrating that the weighting decisions negatively contributed to the performance of the portfolio.

The other attribution effect in the BHB model is security selection—the value the portfolio manager adds by holding individual securities or instruments within the sector in different-from-benchmark weights.

To calculate selection, we first calculate the contribution to selection (S_i) for each sector. The contribution to selection in the ith sector is equal to the benchmark sector weight times the portfolio's sector return minus the benchmark's sector return.

$$S_i = W_i(R_i - B_i) \qquad (5)$$

Using the data from Exhibit 2, we calculate individual sector selection effects as follows:

- Energy: 50% × (18% − 10%) = 4.0%
- Health care: 20% × (−3% − −2.0%) = −0.2%
- Financials: 30% × (10% − 12%) = −0.6%

To find the total portfolio selection effect, S, we sum the individual sector contributions to selection:

$$S = \sum_{i=1}^{i=n} S_i \qquad (6)$$

Total selection effect = 4.0% + −0.2% + −0.6% = 3.2%

We can use the results to state the following conclusions:

- The portfolio's energy sector outperformed the benchmark's energy sector by 800 bps (18% − 10%); 800 bps times the benchmark weight of 50% for this sector results in a 4.0% contribution to selection.
- The portfolio's health care sector underperformed the benchmark's health care sector by 100 bps [(−3%) − (−2%)]; 100 bps times the benchmark weight of 20% for this sector results in a contribution of −0.2%.
- The portfolio's financials sector underperformed the benchmark's financials sector by 200 bps (10% − 12%); 200 bps times the benchmark weight of 30% to this sector results in a contribution of −0.6%.
- Overall, the combined selection effect for this portfolio was 3.2%.

In the BHB model, selection and allocation do not completely explain the arithmetic difference. For example, in the attribution analysis based on Exhibit 2, allocation (−1.4%) and selection (3.2%) together represent just 1.8% of the arithmetic difference between the portfolio return of 10.1% and the benchmark return of 8.2%; 0.1% is missing. To explain this remaining difference in the excess return, the BHB model uses a third attribution effect, called "interaction." The **interaction effect** is the effect resulting from the interaction of the allocation and selection decisions combined.

To calculate interaction, we first calculate the contribution to interaction for each sector. The contribution to interaction in the ith sector is equal to the portfolio sector weight minus the benchmark sector weight, times the portfolio sector return minus the benchmark sector return:

$$I_i = (w_i - W_i)(R_i - B_i) \qquad (7)$$

Using the data from Exhibit 2, we calculate individual sector selection effects as follows:

- Energy: (50% − 50%) × (18% − 10%) = 0.0%
- Health care: (30% − 20%) × (−3% − −2.0%) = −0.1%
- Financials: (20% − 30%) × (10% − 12%) = 0.2%

To find the total portfolio interaction effect, we sum the individual sector contributions to interaction:

$$I = \sum_{i=1}^{i=n} I_i \qquad (8)$$

Total interaction effect = 0.0% + −0.1% + 0.2% = 0.1%

We can use the results to state the following conclusions:

- For the energy sector, the portfolio weight equals the benchmark weight and thus there is no contribution to interaction.
- Because the manager had an overweight to a sector in which selection was negative, the contribution from interaction in health care was also negative, −0.1%.
- In the financials sector, the manager was underweight by 10% and selection was negative. The effect of being underweight in a sector in which the manager underperforms leads to a contribution from interaction of +0.2%.
- Total contribution from interaction is +0.1%, representing the combined effect of the interaction of the selection and allocation effects.

EXAMPLE 3

Interpreting the Results of a BHB Attribution

BHB Attribution Analysis Results Table

Region	Portfolio Return	Benchmark Return	Portfolio Weight	Benchmark Weight	Allocation	Selection	Interaction	Total
Americas	2.80%	1.20%	30%	30%	0.00%	0.48%	0.00%	0.48%
APAC	−1.50%	−0.50%	20%	30%	0.05%	−0.30%	0.10%	−0.15%
EMEA	0.70%	1.50%	50%	40%	0.15%	−0.32%	−0.08%	−0.25%
Total	0.89%	0.81%	100%	100%	0.20%	−0.14%	0.02%	0.08%

Use the table above to answer the following questions.

1. Why is the contribution to selection for Europe, the Middle East, and Africa (EMEA) negative?

   A The total benchmark return is less than the total portfolio return.

   B The manager selected securities in EMEA that underperformed the benchmark.

   C The manager underweighted an outperforming sector.

2. Why is the contribution to allocation for Asia Pacific (APAC) equal to +5 bps?

   A The benchmark weight and the portfolio weight are equal.

- **B** The manager has an overweight position in an overperforming region.
- **C** The manager has an underweight position in an underperforming region.

3 Which of the following conclusions from the above attribution analysis is *most* correct?
- **A** The manager's security selection decisions were better in the Americas than in APAC.
- **B** The manager's security selection decisions were better in EMEA than in APAC.
- **C** The manager's allocation decisions were better in APAC than in EMEA.

4 Which of the following conclusions from the above attribution analysis is *most* correct?
- **A** Overall, the manager made better allocation decisions than selection decisions.
- **B** Overall, the manager made better selection decisions than allocation decisions.
- **C** Contribution from interaction was most noticeable in the Americas.

Solution to 1:

B is correct. The manager selected securities that underperformed the benchmark, with a portfolio return for EMEA of 0.7% versus a benchmark return for EMEA of 1.5%.

Solution to 2:

C is correct. The manager is underweight in APAC, 20% versus a benchmark weight of 30%. The APAC portion of the portfolio underperformed, with a −0.50% benchmark return versus the total benchmark return of 0.81%.

Solution to 3:

A is correct. As reflected in the contribution to selection, the manager's security selection decisions were better in the Americas (0.48%) than in APAC (−0.30%).

Solution to 4:

A is correct. Overall, the manager made better allocation decisions (0.20%) than selection decisions (−0.14%).

3.3 Brinson–Fachler Model

The Brinson–Fachler (BF) model differs from the BHB model only in how individual sector allocation effects are calculated.

In the BHB model, all overweight positions in sectors with positive returns will generate positive allocation effects irrespective of the overall benchmark return, whereas all overweight positions in negative markets will generate negative allocation effects. Thus, overweighting a sector i that earns a positive return, $B_i > 0$, results in a positive allocation effect, $A_i = (w_i - W_i)B_i > 0$, even when the sector return is less than the overall benchmark return (i.e., $B_i < B$). When the sector return is negative, $0 > B_i$, overweighting produces a negative allocation effect, $A_i = (w_i - W_i)B_i < 0$.

Clearly, if the portfolio manager is overweight in a negative market that has outperformed the overall benchmark, the effect should be positive.

The BF model solves this problem by modifying the asset allocation factor to compare returns with the overall benchmark as follows:

$$B_S - B = \sum_{i=1}^{i=n}(w_i - W_i)B_i = \sum_{i=1}^{i=n}(w_i - W_i)(B_i - B) \qquad (9)$$

Because $\sum_{i=1}^{i=n} w_i = \sum_{i=1}^{i=n} W_i = 1$, the constant B can be introduced. The contribution to asset allocation in the ith sector is now:

$$A_i = (w_i - W_i)(B_i - B) \qquad (10)$$

Note that in Equation 10, the allocation effect at the portfolio level, $B_S - B$, is unchanged from the BHB model.

The contribution to arithmetic excess return from sector allocation for the portfolio data shown in Exhibit 2 is $B_S - B = 6.8\% - 8.2\% = -1.4\%$. Revised BF sector allocation effects are calculated for the portfolio data in Exhibit 2 as follows, using $A_i = (w_i - W_i)(B_i - B)$:

Energy	(50% − 50%) × (10% − 8.2%) = 0.0%
Health care	(30% − 20%) × (−2.0% − 8.2%) = −1.02%
Financials	(20% − 30%) × (12% − 8.2%) = −0.38%
Total	0.0% − 1.02% − 0.38% = −1.4%

The impact in health care is much greater. In addition to being overweight in a negative market, which costs −0.2%, the portfolio manager is correctly penalized the opportunity cost of not being invested in the overall market return of 8.2%, generating a further cost of 10% × −8.2% = −0.82% and resulting in a total impact of −1.02%. To describe it another way, the portfolio is 10% overweight in a market that is underperforming the overall market by −10.2% (i.e., −2.0% − 8.2%) and generating a loss of −1.02%

The impact in financials is much smaller. Although being underweight in a positive market cost −1.2%, we must add back the opportunity cost of being invested in the overall market return of 8.2%, generating a contribution of −10% × −8.2% = 0.82% and resulting in a total impact of −0.38%. To describe it another way, the portfolio is 10% underweight in an industry that is outperforming the overall market by 3.8% (i.e., 12.0% − 8.2%), generating a loss of −0.38%. As expected, at the portfolio level, the allocation effect of −1.4% remains the same as that calculated with the BHB model.

The revised attribution effects are summarized in Exhibit 3.

Exhibit 3 BF Return Attribution Results

	Portfolio Weight	Benchmark Weight	Portfolio Return	Benchmark Return	Allocation	Selection	Interaction
Energy	50%	50%	18%	10%	0.0%	4.0%	0.0%
Health care	30%	20%	−3%	−2%	−1.02%	−0.2%	−0.1%
Financials	20%	30%	10%	12%	−0.38%	−0.6%	0.2%
Total	100%	100%	10.1%	8.2%	−1.4%	3.2%	0.1%

Fixed-Income Return Attribution

> **EXAMPLE 4**
>
> ## Allocation Using the BF Model
>
> **Exhibit 4   Sample Portfolio Data**
>
> | | Portfolio Weight | Benchmark Weight | Portfolio Return | Benchmark Return |
> |---|---|---|---|---|
> | Technology | 20% | 30% | −11.0% | −10.0% |
> | Telecommunications | 30% | 40% | −5.0% | −8.0% |
> | Utilities | 50% | 30% | −8.0% | −5.0% |
> | Total | 100% | 100% | −7.7% | −7.7% |
>
> Using the BF method, the allocation effect of utilities based on the portfolio data in Exhibit 4 is:
>
> **A** −1.50%.
>
> **B** 0.54%.
>
> **C** 1.35%.
>
> ### Solution:
>
> B is correct: $(w_i - W_i)(B_i - B) = (50\% - 30\%)(-5.0\% + 7.7\%) = 0.54\%$. The portfolio is 20% overweight in a sector outperforming the overall benchmark by 2.7%, therefore contributing 0.54% to the overall allocation effect.
>
> A is incorrect: $W_i B_i = 30\% \times -5.0\% = -1.5\%$ is the contribution to the benchmark return from utilities.
>
> C is incorrect: $w_i(B_i - B) = 50\% \times (-5.0\% + 7.7\%) = +1.35\%$. Only the portfolio weight of 50% has been used, not the overweight position of 20%.

FIXED-INCOME RETURN ATTRIBUTION

f   interpret the output from fixed-income attribution analyses

As we have seen, return attribution allows us to analyze a portfolio's excess return by comparing the accounting information (weights and returns) in the portfolio with the information in the benchmark. The Brinson–Fachler model focuses on security selection, asset allocation, and the interaction of selection and allocation. But what if we want to assess other decisions within the investment process?

Another type of return attribution uses fundamental factor models to decompose the contributions to excess return from *factors*. Fundamental factor analysis allows us to quantify the impact of specific active investment decisions within the portfolio, showing how they add or remove value relative to the benchmark. We want to remove the effects of the market to identify the excess return generated by the active investment decisions. To do that, we return to our definition of excess return: Excess return = $R - B$.

Many different factor models can be used to decompose excess returns. The choice of factor model is driven by which aspects of the investment process you want to measure. One of the factor models commonly used in equity attribution analyses is the Carhart four-factor model, or simply the **Carhart model**, given in Equation 11 (Carhart 1997). The Carhart model explains the excess return on the portfolio in terms of the portfolio's sensitivity to a market index (RMRF), a market-capitalization factor (SMB), a book-value-to-price factor (HML), and a momentum factor (WML).

$$R_p - R_f = a_p + b_{p1}\text{RMRF} + b_{p2}\text{SMB} + b_{p3}\text{HML} + b_{p4}\text{WML} + E_p \qquad (11)$$

where

R_p and R_f = the return on the portfolio and the risk-free rate of return, respectively

a_p = "alpha" or return in excess of that expected given the portfolio's level of systematic risk (assuming the four factors capture all systematic risk)

b_p = the sensitivity of the portfolio to the given factor

RMRF = the return on a value-weighted equity index in excess of the one-month T-bill rate

SMB = small minus big, a size (market-capitalization) factor (SMB is the average return on three small-cap portfolios minus the average return on three large-cap portfolios)

HML = high minus low, a value factor (HML is the average return on two high-book-to-market portfolios minus the average return on two low-book-to-market portfolios)

WML = winners minus losers, a momentum factor (WML is the return on a portfolio of the past year's winners minus the return on a portfolio of the past year's losers)

E_p = an error term that represents the portion of the return to the portfolio, p, not explained by the model

By analyzing the results of a factor return attribution analysis, we can identify the investment approach and infer the relative strengths and/or weaknesses of the investment decisions. For example, using the Carhart factor model, we calculate the following results for a hypothetical manager.

Exhibit 5 Sample Carhart Factor Model Attribution

	Factor Sensitivity				Contribution to Active Return	
	Portfolio	Benchmark	Difference	Factor Return	Absolute	Proportion of Total
Factor	(1)	(2)	(3)	(4)	(3) × (4)	Active
RMRF	0.95	1.00	−0.05	5.52%	−0.28%	−13.30%
SMB	−1.05	−1.00	−0.05	−3.35%	0.17%	8.10%
HML	0.40	0.00	0.40	5.10%	2.04%	98.40%
WML	0.05	0.03	0.02	9.63%	0.19%	9.30%
				A. Factor tilts return =	2.12%	102.40%
				B. Security selection =	−0.05%	−2.40%
				C. Active return (A + B) =	2.07%	100.00%

Fixed-Income Return Attribution

This attribution analysis yields information about this portfolio's investment approach, how the manager generated excess return, and his or her ability to consistently add value relative to the benchmark.

Let's first look at the analysis of the benchmark (column 2). The sensitivity to RMRF of 1 indicates that the assigned benchmark has average market risk, consistent with it being a broad-based index. The benchmark's negative sensitivity to SMB indicates a large-cap orientation. Assuming, of course, that the benchmark is a good fit for the manager's stated strategy, we can describe the approach as large cap without a value/growth bias (HML is zero) or a momentum bias (WML is close to zero).

Let's now look at where the portfolio manager's approach differed from that of the benchmark. Based on the factor sensitivities shown in column 1 (positive sensitivity to HML of 0.40) and the differences relative to the benchmark shown in column 3, we can see that the manager likely had a value tilt but was otherwise relatively neutral to the benchmark. We would expect the portfolio to hold more value-oriented stocks than the benchmark, and we would want to evaluate the contribution of this tilt.

We can examine the effects of this decision by looking at the balance of the table. Positive active exposure to the HML factor—the bet on value stocks—contributed 204 bps to the realized active return, about 98% of the 207 bps of total realized active return. The manager's minor active exposures to small stocks and momentum also contributed positively to return, whereas the active exposure to RMRF was a drag on performance. However, because the magnitudes of the exposures to RMRF, SMB, and WML were relatively small, the effects of those bets were minor compared with the value tilt (HML).

What about the manager's ability to contribute return through stock selection? Again, assuming that the benchmark is a good fit for the manager's investment process, the overall active return from security selection is the portion of return not explained by factor sensitivities. In this period, the contribution from selection was slightly negative (–0.05%).

In the aggregate, the manager's positive active return was largely the result of the large active bet on HML (+0.40) and a high return to that factor during the period (+5.10%). Is this type of tilt consistent with the manager's stated investment process? If yes, the manager can be credited with an active decision that contributed positively to return. If no, then the excess return in the period is unlikely to result from manager skill but, rather, is a byproduct of luck. What does the manager's investment process say about the role of security selection? If the manager does not profess skill in security selection but instead focuses on sector or factor allocation, then the minimal contribution of security selection should not be perceived as a negative reflection on manager skill.

EXAMPLE 5

Factor-Based Attribution

Use the data from Exhibit 5 to answer the following questions.

1. Which of the following statements is *not* correct?
    A The manager's slight small-cap tilt contributed positively to return.
    B The manager's slight momentum tilt contributed positively to return.
    C The manager's below-benchmark beta contributed negatively to return.

2. What investment approach, not taken by the portfolio manager, could have delivered more value to the portfolio during the investment period?
    A A momentum-based approach

B A growth-oriented approach

C A small-cap-based approach

Solution to 1:

A is the correct answer. The negative coefficient on SMB indicates that the manager had a slight large-cap bias relative to the benchmark. The slight tilt on WML (+0.02) combined with a positive return to the factor resulted in a positive contribution to return. The below-benchmark beta of RMRF (−0.05) combined with a positive return to the factor resulted in a negative contribution to return.

Solution to 2:

A is correct. Had the manager overweighted momentum stocks during the period, the momentum factor (WML) return of 9.63% would have contributed significant positive performance to the portfolio.

4.1 Fixed-Income Return Attribution

Fixed-income portfolios are driven by very different sources of risk, requiring attribution approaches that attribute returns to decisions made with respect to credit risk and positioning along the yield curve. Building on work by Groupe de Reflexion en Attribution de Performance, or GRAP, outlined in Giguère (2005) and Murira and Sierra (2006), we will discuss three typical approaches to fixed-income attribution:

- Exposure decomposition—duration based
- Yield curve decomposition—duration based
- Yield curve decomposition—full repricing based

Candidates are not responsible for *calculating* fixed-income attribution but should be able to interpret the results of a fixed-income attribution analysis.

4.1.1 Exposure Decomposition—Duration Based

Exposure decomposition is a top-down attribution approach that seeks to explain the active management of a portfolio relative to its benchmark, typically working through a hierarchy of decisions from the top to the bottom. These decisions might include portfolio duration bets, yield curve positioning or sector bets, each relative to the benchmark. The term "exposure decomposition" relates to the decomposition of portfolio risk exposures by means of grouping a portfolio's component bonds by specified characteristics (e.g., duration, bond sector). The term "duration based" relates to the typical use of duration to represent interest rate exposure decisions.

Models that take an exposure decomposition approach are similar to Brinson-type equity attribution models, where we might group the portfolio by its market value weights in different economic sectors. In this case, however, we group the portfolio by its market value weights in duration buckets (i.e., exposure to different ranges of duration). This approach simplifies the data requirements and allows straightforward presentation of results relative to other fixed-income approaches. For these reasons, the exposure decomposition approach is used primarily for marketing and client reports, where an important benefit is that users can easily understand and articulate the results of active portfolio management.

4.1.2 Yield Curve Decomposition—Duration Based

The duration-based yield curve decomposition approach to fixed-income attribution can be either executed as a top-down approach or built bottom-up from the security level. This approach estimates the return of securities, sector buckets, or years-to-maturity buckets using the known relationship between duration and changes in yield to maturity (YTM), as follows:

% Total return = % Income return + % Price return,

where % Price return ≈ –Duration × Change in YTM.

Duration measures the sensitivity of bond price to a change in the bond's yield to maturity. So, the percentage price return of a bond will be approximately equal to the negative of its duration for each 100 bp change in yields. The change in yield to maturity of the portfolio or instrument can be broken down into yield curve factors and spread factors to provide additional insights. These factors represent the changes in the risk-free government curve (e.g., changes in level, slope, and curvature) and in the premium required to hold riskier sectors and bonds. When they are combined and applied to the duration, we can determine a percentage price change for each factor.

For example, a manager may have a view as to how the yield curve factors will change over time. We can use the attribution analysis to determine the value of the yield curve views as they unfold over time.

This approach is applied to both the portfolio and the benchmark to identify contributions to total return from changes in the yield to maturity. Comparing the differences between the benchmark's return drivers and the portfolio's return drivers gives us the *effect of active portfolio management decisions.*

In this regard, this group of models is quite different from the exposure decomposition. One consequence of this difference is that we require more data points to calculate the separate absolute attribution analyses for the portfolio and the benchmark. Thus, the yield decomposition approach exchanges better transparency for more operational complexity. These models are typically used when preparing reports for analysts and portfolio managers, rather than in marketing or client reports.

4.1.3 Yield Curve Decomposition—Full Repricing

Instead of estimating price changes from changes in duration and yields to maturity, bonds can be repriced from zero-coupon curves (spot rates). Recall that a bond's price is the sum of its cash flows discounted at the appropriate spot rate for each cash flow's maturity. The discount rate to compute the present value depends on the yields offered on the market for comparable securities and represents the required yield an investor expects for holding that investment. Typically, we discount each cash flow at a rate from the spot curve that corresponds to the time the cash flow will be received.

As with the duration-based approaches, instruments can be repriced following incremental changes in spot rates, whether resulting from changes in overall interest rates, spreads, or bond-specific factors. This bottom-up security-level repricing can then be translated into a contribution to a security's return and aggregated for portfolios, benchmarks, and active management.

This full repricing attribution approach provides more precise pricing and allows for a broader range of instrument types and yield changes. It also supports a greater variety of quantitative modeling beyond fixed-income attribution (e.g., *ex ante* risk). This approach is better aligned with how portfolio managers typically view the instruments. However, it requires the full capability to reprice all financial instruments in the portfolio and the benchmark, including the rates and the characteristics of the instrument. Its complex nature can make it more difficult and costly to administer operationally and can make the results more difficult to understand, particularly for non-fixed-income professionals.

All three approaches can be applied to single-currency and multi-currency portfolios. We can most clearly demonstrate the principles of fixed-income attribution by using a single-currency domestic portfolio, without digressing into the relative merits of the various multi-currency approaches. Therefore, this example is a single-currency example.

4.1.4 Fixed-Income Attribution—Worked Example

Let's begin with an example of exposure decomposition analysis.

Exhibit 6 shows a breakdown of the portfolio and the benchmark by weights, duration, and each bucket's contribution to duration, aggregated by sector and duration buckets. For this example, the short-, mid-, and long-duration buckets are defined as follows:[1]

Bucket	Duration
Short	Less than or equal to 5
Mid	Greater than 5 and less than or equal to 10
Long	Greater than 10

Exhibit 6 Sample Exposure Decomposition: Relative Positions of Portfolio and Benchmark

	Portfolio Weights				Portfolio Duration				Portfolio Contribution to Duration			
	Short	Mid	Long	Total	Short	Mid	Long	Total	Short	Mid	Long	Total
Government	10.00%	10.00%	20.00%	40.00%	4.42	7.47	10.21	8.08	0.44	0.75	2.04	3.23
Corporate	10.00%	20.00%	30.00%	60.00%	4.40	7.40	10.06	8.23	0.44	1.48	3.02	4.94
Total	20.00%	30.00%	50.00%	100.00%	4.41	7.42	10.12	8.17	0.88	2.23	5.06	8.17

	Benchmark Weights				Benchmark Duration				Benchmark Contribution to Duration			
	Short	Mid	Long	Total	Short	Mid	Long	Total	Short	Mid	Long	Total
Government	20.00%	20.00%	15.00%	55.00%	4.42	7.47	10.21	7.11	0.88	1.49	1.53	3.91
Corporate	15.00%	15.00%	15.00%	45.00%	4.40	7.40	10.06	7.29	0.66	1.11	1.51	3.28
Total	35.00%	35.00%	30.00%	100.00%	4.41	7.44	10.14	7.19	1.54	2.60	3.04	7.19

	Portfolio Weights				Portfolio Returns				Portfolio Contribution to Return			
	Short	Mid	Long	Total	Short	Mid	Long	Total	Short	Mid	Long	Total
Government	10.00%	10.00%	20.00%	40.00%	−3.48%	−5.16%	−4.38%	−4.35%	−0.35%	−0.52%	−0.88%	−1.74%
Corporate	10.00%	20.00%	30.00%	60.00%	−4.33%	−6.14%	−5.42%	−5.48%	−0.43%	−1.23%	−1.63%	−3.29%
Total	20.00%	30.00%	50.00%	100.00%	−3.91%	−5.81%	−5.00%	−5.03%	−0.78%	−1.74%	−2.50%	−5.03%

---

[1] Note that the practitioner should take care when selecting the upper and lower bands of each duration bucket. By grouping bonds of different durations in the same bucket, one is measuring the combined impact of those bonds relative to the combined impact of similar bonds in the benchmark. In this example (Exhibit 6 and the related discussion), for instance, a bond with a duration of 5.5 is treated the same as a bond with a duration of 9.5 in terms of its relative impact on the portfolio versus its benchmark.

Exhibit 6 (Continued)

	Benchmark Weights				Benchmark Returns				Benchmark Contribution to Return			
	Short	Mid	Long	Total	Short	Mid	Long	Total	Short	Mid	Long	Total
Government	20.00%	20.00%	15.00%	55.00%	−3.48%	−5.16%	−4.38%	−4.34%	−0.70%	−1.03%	−0.66%	−2.39%
Corporate	15.00%	15.00%	15.00%	45.00%	−4.33%	−6.14%	−5.86%	−5.44%	−0.65%	−0.92%	−0.88%	−2.45%
Total	35.00%	35.00%	30.00%	100.00%	−3.84%	−5.58%	−5.12%	−4.83%	−1.35%	−1.95%	−1.54%	−4.83%

From Exhibit 6, we can make the following inferences regarding the manager's investment decisions:

- With a higher duration than the benchmark (8.17 compared with 7.19 for the benchmark), the manager likely expected the rates to fall and took a bullish position on long-term bonds (interest rates) by increasing exposure to the long end of the interest rate curve (e.g., investing 50% of the portfolio in the longest-duration bucket versus 30% for the benchmark).

- Based on the overweight in the corporate sector (60% versus the 45% benchmark weight), the manager likely expected credit spreads to narrow.[2] Notice that this bet increases the 4.94 contribution to duration of the corporate sector in the portfolio compared with the 3.28 contribution to duration for the benchmark. This allocation makes the portfolio more exposed to market yield fluctuations in the corporate sector.

- The total portfolio return is −5.03%, relative to a total benchmark return of −4.83%, showing an underperformance of −0.20% over the period.

We can then use the portfolio and benchmark information from Exhibit 6 to calculate the portfolio's attribution results. These results are summarized in Exhibit 7. (Note that candidates are expected to be able to interpret, but not calculate, these results.)

Total interest rate allocation is the contribution from active management resulting from the manager's active exposures to changes in the level and shape of the yield curve. This can be decomposed into the duration effect (the contribution to active management from taking a different-from-benchmark aggregate duration position) and the curve effect (the specific points along the yield curve at which the manager made his benchmark-relative duration bets).

Sector allocation measures the effect of the manager's decision to overweight corporate bonds, whereas the selection effect measures the impact of the manager's decision to hold non-benchmark bonds in the portfolio. The hypothetical portfolio underlying this example contains only one bond that is not in the benchmark—a long-duration corporate bond, Corp. (P). Accordingly, there is no selection effect in the other duration buckets.

---

[2] If corporate yields were at a historically large spread with respect to governments, the overweight to corporates might also have been a yield bet. Even if spreads do not narrow, the higher-yielding corporates are likely to outperform the government bonds in the portfolio.

Exhibit 7 Sample Exposure Decomposition: Attribution Results

Duration Bucket	Sector	Duration Effect	Curve Effect	Total Interest Rate Allocation	Sector Allocation	Bond Selection	Total
Short	Government					0.00%	0.00%
	Corporate				0.04%	0.00%	0.04%
	Total	0.40%	0.12%	0.52%	0.04%	0.00%	**0.56%**
Mid	Government					0.00%	0.00%
	Corporate				−0.05%	0.00%	−0.05%
	Total	0.23%	0.03%	0.26%	−0.05%	0.00%	**0.21%**
Long	Government					0.00%	0.00%
	Corporate				−0.22%	0.07%	−0.15%
	Total	−1.25%	0.37%	−0.88%	−0.22%	0.07%	**−1.03%**
Total		**−0.62%**	**0.52%**	**−0.10%**	**−0.23%**	**0.07%**	**−0.26%**

Using the results from Exhibit 7, we can draw the following conclusions about the investment decisions made by this manager:

- The portfolio underperformed its benchmark by 20 bps.
- 62 bps were lost by taking a long-duration position during a period when yields increased (benchmark returns were negative in each duration bucket).
- 52 bps were gained as a result of changes in the shape of the yield curve. Given the manager's overweighting in the long-duration bucket, we can infer that the yield curve flattened.
- 23 bps were lost because the manager overweighted the corporate sector during a period when credit spreads widened (the benchmark corporate returns in each duration bucket were less than the government returns in those same duration buckets).
- 13 bps were added through bond selection.

Exhibit 8 provides an example of a sample duration-based yield curve decomposition attribution analysis. Again, we do not include the calculations for this analysis but instead present the results and suggested interpretations.

Exhibit 8 Yield Curve Decomposition—Duration Based: Active Return Contribution

Bond	Yield	Roll	Shift	Slope	Curvature	Spread	Specific	Residual	Total
Gov't. 5% 30 June 21	−0.19%	−0.04%	0.43%	0.01%	0.15%	0.00%	0.00%	−0.01%	0.35%
Gov't. 7% 30 June 26	−0.22%	−0.03%	0.71%	0.04%	0.04%	0.00%	0.00%	−0.03%	0.52%
Gov't. 6% 30 June 31	0.12%	0.01%	−0.48%	0.05%	0.09%	0.00%	0.00%	−0.01%	−0.22%
Corp. 5% 30 June 21	−0.11%	−0.02%	0.21%	0.05%	0.05%	0.04%	0.02%	−0.02%	0.22%
Corp. 7% 30 June 26	0.12%	0.01%	−0.35%	−0.02%	−0.02%	−0.07%	0.00%	0.02%	−0.31%
Corp. (B) 6% 30 June 31	−0.39%	−0.03%	1.41%	−0.26%	−0.11%	0.30%	0.00%	−0.04%	0.88%
Corp. (P) 6% 30 June 31	0.78%	0.06%	−2.82%	0.52%	0.33%	−0.60%	0.15%	−0.05%	−1.63%

Fixed-Income Return Attribution

Exhibit 8 (Continued)

Bond	Yield	Roll	Shift	Slope	Curvature	Spread	Specific	Residual	Total
Total	0.11%	−0.04%	−0.89%	0.39%	0.53%	−0.33%	0.17%	−0.14%	−0.20%
	Time:	0.08%	*Curve Movement:*		0.03%				

Note: There may be minor differences due to rounding in this table.

Using the data from Exhibits 6 and 8, we can infer the following about the portfolio investment process over this period:

- *Yield*: The portfolio overweighted corporate bonds and longer-term maturities relative to the benchmark (from Exhibit 6), which generally offer higher yield than government bonds and short-term maturities. This decision contributed 11 bps to the excess return (from Exhibit 8).
- *Roll*: The portfolio overweighted longer maturities (from Exhibit 6). Because of the shape of the yield curve, bonds with longer maturities generally sit on a flatter part of the yield curve, where the roll return is limited. The overweighting of the longer maturities reduced the portfolio roll return by 4 bps.
- *Shift*: The portfolio overall duration of 8.17 is greater than the benchmark duration of 7.19 (from Exhibit 6), which reduced the portfolio return by 89 bps.
- *Slope*: The slope flattening caused the long-term yields to increase less than yields on shorter terms to maturity. The overweight at the long end of the curve contributed 39 bps to the excess return.
- *Curvature*: The reshaping of the yield curve resulted in a larger yield increase at the five-year maturity point. The manager underweighted that part of the yield curve. This decision contributed 53 bps to the excess return.
- *Spread*: The manager overweighted the corporate sector, which resulted in a 33 bp reduction in return because corporate spreads widened.
- *Specific spread*: Looking at the bond-specific spreads in Exhibit 8, the corporate 5% 30 June 2021 bond added 2 bps of selection return and the corporate (P) 6% 30 June 2031 bond added 15 bps of selection return. These decisions added a total of 17 bps to active return.
- *Residual*: A residual of −0.14% is unaccounted for because duration and convexity can only *estimate* the percentage price variation. It is not an accurate measure of the true price variation. The residual becomes more important during large yield moves, which is the case here, with a +1% yield shift.

EXAMPLE 6

Fixed-Income Return Attribution

Use the data in Exhibits 7 and 8 to answer the following questions.

1. Which decision had the most positive effect on the overall performance of the portfolio?
   - **A** Taking a long-duration position
   - **B** Security selection of bond issues
   - **C** Overweighting the long end of the yield curve
2. Explain the contribution of the long-duration bucket to overall portfolio performance.

> **Solution to 1:**
>
> C is correct: 52 bps were gained by overweighting the long end of the yield curve during a period when the slope of the yield curve flattened.
>
> **Solution to 2:**
>
> The long-duration bucket cost the portfolio 97 bps of relative return. From Exhibit 7, the curve and selection effects were positive (37 bps and 13 bps, respectively) whereas the duration and sector allocation effects were negative (–125 bps and –22 bps, respectively). The negative duration effect indicates that the manager took a longer-than-benchmark-duration position in the long-duration bucket, a decision that hurt performance because interest rates rose. The positive curve effect implies that the manager's specific positioning along the long end of the yield curve benefited from changes in the shape of the yield curve. This implication is further supported by the positive slope effect shown in Exhibit 8. Taken together, the duration and curve effects accounted for the majority of the manager's underperformance relative to the benchmark. In the long-duration bucket, the manager overweighted corporate bonds relative to the benchmark. This decision penalized returns because credit spreads widened, which can be inferred from the weaker performance of the long-duration corporate segment of the benchmark (–5.42%) relative to the long-duration government segment (–4.38%). The positive selection effect of 13 bps implies that the manager's specific bond selections added to return. This implication is supported by the specific spread contribution reflected in Exhibit 8.

5. RISK ATTRIBUTION

g discuss considerations in selecting a risk attribution approach

Performance attribution, on its own, is typically insufficient to evaluate the investment process. In addition to performance, we need to understand the impact of exposure to risk by including risk attribution.

Risk attribution identifies the sources of risk in the investment process. For absolute mandates, it identifies the sources of portfolio volatility. For benchmark-relative mandates, it identifies the sources of tracking risk. Managers seek opportunities for profit by taking specific exposures to risk (e.g., portfolio volatility or tracking risk). Risk attribution identifies these risks taken and, together with return attribution, quantifies the contributions to both the return and risk of the investment manager's active decisions.

Risk attribution should reflect the investment decision-making process. Exhibit 9 classifies investment decision-making processes and suggests appropriate risk attribution approaches. The columns indicate whether the focus is absolute risk or benchmark-relative risk. The rows categorize investment decision-making processes as bottom up, top down, or factor based. A bottom-up approach focuses on individual security selection. Top-down approaches focus first on macro decisions, such as allocations to economic sectors, and then on security selection within sectors. A factor-based approach looks for profits by taking different-from-benchmark exposures to the risk factors believed to drive asset returns.

Exhibit 9: Selecting the Appropriate Risk Attribution Approach

Investment Decision-Making Process	Type of Attribution Analysis	
	Relative (vs. Benchmark)	Absolute
Bottom up	Position's marginal contribution to tracking risk	Position's marginal contribution to total risk
Top down	Attribute tracking risk to relative allocation and selection decisions	Factor's marginal contribution to total risk and specific risk
Factor based	Factor's marginal contribution to tracking risk and active specific risk	

For portfolios that are managed against benchmarks, a common measure of risk is tracking risk (TR), also often called tracking error. The objective of an attribution model for a benchmark-relative portfolio is to quantify the contribution of active decisions to TR. For bottom-up benchmark-relative investment processes, each position's marginal contribution to TR multiplied by its active weight gives the position's contribution to TR. For benchmark-relative top-down investment processes, the active return is explained first by the allocation decisions. Risk attribution, accordingly, will identify the total contribution of allocation and selection to TR.

For absolute mandates, the risk of the portfolio is explained by exposures to the market, size and style factors, and the specific risk due to stock selections. The attribution model quantifies the contribution of each exposure and of specific risk. Suppose that the manager follows an absolute bottom-up process where the measure of risk is the volatility (standard deviation) of returns. In this case, we want to measure the contribution of selection decisions to overall portfolio risk. To do this, we need to know the marginal contribution of each asset to the portfolio risk—the increase or decrease in the portfolio standard deviation due to a slight increase in the holding of that asset. If we know the marginal contribution of a security to absolute portfolio risk, we can then calculate the overall risk contribution of the portfolio manager's selection decisions.

In all cases, risk attribution explains only where risk was introduced into the portfolio. It needs to be combined with return attribution to understand the full impact of those decisions. For example, if a manager has added to excess return through asset allocation (e.g., positive return attribution allocation effect), we use risk attribution to understand whether those allocation decisions introduced additional risk. As such, risk attribution complements the return attribution by evaluating the risk consequences of the investment decisions.

EXAMPLE 7

Risk Attribution

Manager A is a market-neutral manager following a systematic investment approach, scoring each security on a proprietary set of risk factors. He seeks to maximize the portfolio score on the basis of the factor characteristics of individual securities. He has a hurdle rate of T-bills plus 5%.

Manager B has a strong fundamental process based on a comprehensive understanding of the business model and competitive advantages of each firm. He also uses sophisticated models to make explicit three-year forecasts of the growth of free cash flow to determine the attractiveness of each security's current valuation. His objective is to outperform the MSCI World ex-US Index by 200 bps.

Manager C specializes in timing sector exposure and generally avoids idiosyncratic risks within sectors. Using technical analyses and econometric methodologies, she produces several types of forecasts. The manager uses this information to determine appropriate sector weights. The risk contribution from any single sector is limited to 30% of total portfolio risk. She hedges aggregate market risk and seeks to earn T-bills plus 300 bps.

1 Which risk attribution approach is most appropriate to evaluate Manager A?
   A Marginal contribution to total risk
   B Marginal contribution to tracking risk
   C Factor's marginal contributions to total risk and specific risk

2 Which risk attribution approach is most appropriate to evaluate Manager B?
   A Marginal contribution to total risk
   B Marginal contribution to tracking risk
   C Factor's marginal contributions to total risk and specific risk

3 Which risk attribution approach is most appropriate to evaluate Manager C?
   A Marginal contribution to total risk
   B Marginal contribution to tracking risk
   C Factor's marginal contributions to total risk and specific risk

Solution to 1:

A is correct. Manager A is a bottom-up manager with an absolute return target. B is incorrect because tracking risk is not relevant to an absolute return mandate. C is incorrect because, as a market-neutral manager, Manager A is not seeking to take different-from-market exposures.

Solution to 2:

B is correct. Manager B is a bottom-up manager with a relative return target. A and C are incorrect because they are best suited to absolute return mandates.

Solution to 3:

C is correct. Manager C is a top-down manager with an absolute return target. A factor-based attribution is best suited to evaluate the effectiveness of the manager's sector decisions and hedging of market risk.

6 RETURN ATTRIBUTION ANALYSIS AT MULTIPLE LEVELS

h identify and interpret investment results attributable to the asset owner versus those attributable to the investment manager

Return Attribution Analysis at Multiple Levels

To this point, the return attribution presented in the Brinson examples focused on the bottom-up approach, where we calculated attribution effects at security and sector levels and summed those effects to determine their impact at the total portfolio and fund levels. We can use a similar return attribution approach at multiple levels of the decision process to evaluate the impact of different decisions.

6.1 Macro Attribution—An Example

Consider an example in which the top level is the fund sponsor (e.g., a university endowment or a defined-benefit pension plan sponsor). At the fund sponsor level, the first decision might be to allocate a certain weight to asset classes—the strategic asset allocation. If the fund sponsor does not manage funds internally, it would delegate a second investment decision to the investment managers to decide on any tactical deviations from the strategic asset allocation. The sponsor might also select multiple portfolio managers to manage against specific mandates within a given asset class.

The attribution analysis that we use to determine the impact of these fund sponsor decisions is sometimes called macro attribution. The attribution of the individual portfolio manager decisions is sometimes called micro attribution.

Assume our hypothetical fund sponsor has the following total equity benchmark:

- 50% large-cap value equities
- 25% small-cap value equities
- 25% large-cap growth equities

The fund sponsor hires two investment managers to manage the equity portion of the fund. Value Portfolio Manager manages the large-cap and small-cap value allocations, and Growth Portfolio Manager manages the growth equity allocation. The investment returns are shown in Exhibit 10.

Exhibit 10 Performance of Value and Growth Equity Managers

	Fund Weight	Fund Return	Benchmark Weight	Benchmark Return
Total	100%	0.95	100%	−0.03
Value Portfolio Manager	78%	0.99	75%	0.32
Small-cap value equities	20%	2.39	25%	1.52
Large-cap value equities	58%	0.51	50%	−0.28
Growth Portfolio Manager	22%	0.82	25%	−1.08
Large-cap growth equities	22%	0.82	25%	−1.08

To evaluate the decisions of the fund sponsor, we perform a return Brinson–Fachler attribution analysis using the set of weight and return data in Exhibit 10. "Allocation" measures the tactical asset allocation decision of the sponsor against its own strategic benchmark. In this example, the fund sponsor overweighted value equities and underweighted growth equities. "Selection" measures the fund sponsor's manager selection decision: Did the selected managers add value relative to their assigned benchmarks?

For the decision to hire the Value Portfolio Manager, we would calculate the effects as follows:

Allocation = (78% − 75%)[0.32 − (−0.03)] = 0.01

- The fund sponsor overweighted value equities (78% − 75%).
- Value equities outperformed the fund's aggregate benchmark [0.32 − (−0.03)].
- The decision to overweight value equities added to portfolio return.

Selection + Interaction = [(75%)(0.99 − 0.32)] + [(78% − 75%)(0.99 − 0.32)] = 0.52

- The value manager outperformed the value benchmark (0.99 − 0.32). Thus, the fund sponsor's manager selection decision, independent of the decision to overweight value equities, added value.
- The fund sponsor overweighted a manager who outperformed his benchmark [(78% − 75%)(0.99 − 0.32)]. This is the interaction effect. (For simplicity, we combine interaction with selection, rather than showing interaction separately. By combining with selection, we assume that the selection decisions include the interaction and leave the allocation decision separate.) The interaction effect was positive.

For the decision to hire the Growth Portfolio Manager, we would calculate the effects as follows:

Allocation = (22% − 25%)[−1.08 − (−0.03)] = 0.03

- The fund sponsor underweighted growth equities (22% − 25%)
- Growth equities underperformed the fund's aggregate benchmark (−1.08 versus −0.03)
- The decision to underweight growth equities added to portfolio return

Selection + Interaction = [(25%)(0.82 − (−1.08)] + [(22% − 25%)(0.82 − (−1.08)] = 0.42

- The growth manager outperformed the growth benchmark (+0.82 versus −1.08). Thus, the fund sponsor's manager selection decision, independent of the decision to underweight growth equities, added value.
- The fund sponsor underweighted a manager who outperformed his benchmark [(− 3%)(0.82 − (− 1.08)]. The interaction effect was negative.

The results are summarized in Exhibit 11.

Exhibit 11 Macro Attribution

Return Attribution (Plan Sponsor Level)	Selection + Interaction	Allocation	Total
Total	0.94	0.04	0.98
Value Portfolio Manager	0.52	0.01	0.53
Growth Portfolio Manager	0.42	0.03	0.45

Return attribution analysis is most often calculated with reference to the portfolio's agreed-upon benchmark. But it is entirely possible to attribute one portfolio against another when both are using the same or a similar investment strategy. The purpose of such analysis might be to explain an unexpected difference in return between two portfolios managed by the same portfolio manager using the same investment decision-making process.

6.2 Micro Attribution—An Example

Using the same return data, we now move to the next level of the investment decision-making process and will evaluate the impact of the portfolio managers' decisions on total fund performance. We calculate the return attribution effects using the Brinson–Fachler approach at the segment level (i.e., small-cap value, large-cap value, and large-cap growth):

Allocation = $(w_i - W_i)(B_i - B)$

Selection + Interaction = $W_i(R_i - B_i) + (w_i - W_i)(R_i - B_i)$

We calculate the attribution effects for the small-cap value equities:

Allocation = $(20\% - 25\%)[1.52 - (-0.03)] = -0.08$

Selection + Interaction = $[(25\%)(2.39 - 1.52)] + [(20\% - 25\%)(2.39 - 1.52)] = 0.17$

Using the same approach for large-cap value equities and large-cap growth equities yields the results shown in Exhibit 12. (Note that the numbers are rounded to two decimal places and may not sum because of this rounding.)

Exhibit 12   Segment-Level Return Attribution

Return Attribution (Segment Level)	Fund Weight	Selection + Interaction	Allocation	Total
Total	100%	1.05	−0.07	0.98
Value Portfolio Manager	78%	0.63	−0.10	0.53
Small-cap value equities	*20%*	*0.17*	*−0.08*	*0.10*
Large-cap value equities	*58%*	*0.46*	*−0.02*	*0.44*
Growth Portfolio Manager	22%	0.42	0.03	0.45
Large-cap growth equities	*22%*	*0.42*	*0.03*	*0.45*

In Exhibit 12, the attribution results in italics are calculated at the segment level. The attribution results at the next level above, the Value Portfolio Manager and Growth Portfolio Manager, are sums of the segment-level results. For example, the allocation effect for the Value Portfolio Manager is equal to the sum of the small-cap and large-cap segments: −0.08 + −0.02 = −0.10.

Summing up the segment-level results for each manager, we reach the following conclusions:

- The total outperformance at the overall fund level of 98 bps is almost entirely the result of positive security selection decisions (105 bps in total).

- The decision of the Value Portfolio Manager to underweight small cap in favor of large cap detracted from total fund performance because the small-cap value benchmark outperformed the total benchmark (1.52% versus −0.03%), leading to an allocation effect of −0.10.

- The large-cap value benchmark underperformed the total benchmark (−0.28% versus −0.03%). Because the portfolio was underweight large-cap value, this led to a positive allocation effect of 0.03.
- In total, allocation decisions contributed −7 bps.

Note that in using the total fund benchmark in this analysis, we are evaluating the *impact* of the Value Portfolio Manager's decision on the performance of the total fund.

We can extend the attribution analysis down another level and examine the investment manager's results relative to the investment process. The manager may have an investment process that specifically targets country allocations.[3] At this level of analysis, the same allocation formula will calculate the impact of country allocation decisions within the manager's portfolio and the selection formula will calculate the impact of selection decisions within each country.

If the portfolio manager has an investment process that specifically targets sector allocations within each country, the allocation formula can be used to calculate the impact of sector selection decisions within countries and the selection decisions within sectors.

Whatever the level of analysis, the return attribution must reflect the decision-making process of the portfolio manager. For example, a eurozone investment strategy might use a country allocation process with security selection within each country or a sector allocation process with security selection within each industrial sector. Exhibits 13 and 14 illustrate the different results that might be reached from an analysis based on the investment process. In each case, an arithmetic Brinson approach has been used.

Exhibit 13   Country Allocation

	Portfolio Weight	Benchmark Weight	Portfolio Return	Benchmark Return	Allocation	Selection + Interaction
France	20%	30%	8.0%	6.0%	0.15%	0.40%
Germany	20%	35%	8.0%	7.0%	0.07%	0.20%
Holland	20%	10%	9.0%	15.0%	0.76%	−1.20%
Italy	30%	15%	10.0%	9.0%	0.23%	0.30%
Spain	10%	10%	3.0%	3.5%	0.00%	−0.05%
Total	**100%**	**100%**	**8.3%**	**7.45%**	**1.20%**	**−0.35%**

Exhibit 14   Industry Sector Allocation

	Portfolio Weight	Benchmark Weight	Portfolio Return	Benchmark Return	Allocation	Selection + Interaction
Energy	25%	30%	18.0%	12.0%	−0.23%	1.50%
Health care	30%	20%	−3.0%	−6.0%	−1.35%	0.90%
Financial	20%	30%	10.0%	12.0%	−0.46%	−0.40%
Transportation	10%	15%	12.0%	8.0%	−0.03%	0.40%

---

[3] For some portfolios, the next level may be asset classes (as an example).

Return Attribution Analysis at Multiple Levels

Exhibit 14   (Continued)

	Portfolio Weight	Benchmark Weight	Portfolio Return	Benchmark Return	Allocation	Selection + Interaction
Metals and mining	15%	5%	10.0%	5.0%	−0.25%	0.75%
Total	100%	100%	8.3%	7.45%	−2.30%	3.15%

Exhibit 13 suggests that the manager demonstrated good country allocation but negative security selection within countries, whereas Exhibit 14 suggests that the manager demonstrated poor sector allocation but strongly positive security selection within industrial sectors. This apparent "contradiction" illustrates the importance of designing an attribution approach around the investment decision-making process used by the manager.

Drilling down to the lowest level, the same allocation and selection formulas can be used to calculate the contribution of individual security decisions within sectors. For example, the allocation formula can be used to determine the impact of over- or underweighting individual securities, whereas the selection formula can be used to determine the contribution arising from a difference in the return of a security in the portfolio and the return of the same security in the benchmark. If the pricing sources used in the portfolio and the benchmark are identical, then any difference in return will be caused by transaction activity. Transaction activity because of trading expenses and bid–offer spreads will negatively affect returns, but occasionally because of timing, the portfolio manager may be able to trade at advantageous prices during the day and recover all the transaction costs by the end of the day, resulting in a positive effect.

Exhibit 15 shows the security-level return attribution effects for a small portfolio of oil stocks against a customized benchmark consisting of the same oil stocks. This approach would be used by a pure stock picker, the only decisions in the portfolio being individual stock weighting and timing decisions.

Exhibit 15   Security-Level Return Attribution Effects of Pure Stock Picker

	Portfolio Weight	Benchmark Weight	Portfolio Return	Benchmark Return	Allocation	Transaction Costs and Timing Effects
Chevron	24%	30%	10%	10%	−0.18%	0.00%
ConocoPhillips	21%	25%	8%	8%	−0.04%	0.00%
ExxonMobil	41%	35%	5%	6%	−0.06%	−0.41%
Marathon Oil	6%	5%	4%	4%	−0.03%	0.00%
Newfield Expl.	8%	5%	−5%	−5%	−0.36%	0.00%
Total	100%	100%	5.97%	7.05%	−0.67%	−0.41%

The arithmetic allocation effects of each security using the Brinson approach are as follows:

Chevron	(24% − 30%) × (10% − 7.05%) = −0.18%
ConocoPhillips	(21% − 25%) × (8.0% − 7.05%) = −0.04%
ExxonMobil	(41% − 35%) × (6.0% − 7.05%) = −0.06%
Marathon Oil	(6% − 5%) × (4.0% − 7.05%) = −0.03%
Newfield Exploration	(8% − 5%) × (−5.0% − 7.05%) = −0.36%

Allocation in this context measures the value added from individual security selection. Transactions occur for only one security during the period—ExxonMobil. Therefore, the only selection effects (transaction costs and timing) occur for this security. The calculation is as follows:

ExxonMobil	41% × (5.0% − 6.0%) = −0.41%

EXAMPLE 8

Macro Attribution

AAA Asset Management runs a fixed-income fund of funds. The fund's benchmark is a blended benchmark comprising 80% Bloomberg Barclays Global Aggregate Index and 20% Bloomberg Barclays Global Treasury Index (both in US dollars, unhedged). Two internal investment teams have been selected to manage the fund's assets. The allocations to the two products are determined by the firm's chief fixed-income strategist. The fund has underperformed its benchmark in each of the last three years. You are a member of the board of directors, which is meeting to determine what action should be taken. Based solely on the data in the table below, which of the following courses of action would you recommend? Justify your response.

A Terminate the manager of Product A.

B Terminate the manager of Product B.

C Remove the chief fixed-income strategist as manager of the fund of funds.

	Fund-of-Funds Return			
	Year 1	Year 2	Year 3	Cumulative Return
Total Fund	3.72%	−3.00%	−0.13%	0.47%
Benchmark:	3.84%	−2.94%	0.07%	0.86%

	Product Returns						
	Year 1		Year 2		Year 3		
	Weight	Return	Weight	Return	Weight	Return	
Product A	0.7	4.45%	0.75	−2.50%	0.8	−0.10%	1.74%
Benchmark: Bloomberg Barclays Global Aggregate		4.32%		−2.60%		0.29%	1.90%
Product B	0.3	2.00%	0.25	−4.50%	0.2	−0.25%	−2.83%
Benchmark: Bloomberg Barclays Global Treasury		1.93%		−4.30%		−0.79%	−3.22%

Solution:

C is correct. Based solely on the information provided, the chief fixed-income strategist's allocation decision was the main driver of the fund's underperformance. Product A modestly underperformed its benchmark over the three-year period (−16 bps). Product B outperformed its benchmark (+39 bps). The strategist's allocation decisions were strongly negative in Years 1 and 2, when he overweighted the Treasury allocation and the Treasury index underperformed the aggregate fund benchmark. The results of the attribution analysis are shown below:

AAA Asset Management Fixed-Income Fund-of-Funds Attribution Analysis

	Year 1		Year 2		Year 3	
	Allocation	Selection	Allocation	Selection	Allocation	Selection
Product A	−0.05%	0.10%	−0.02%	0.08%	0.00%	−0.31%
Product B	−0.19%	0.01%	−0.07%	−0.04%	0.00%	0.11%
Total	−0.24%	0.12%	−0.09%	0.04%	0.00%	−0.20%

ASSET-BASED AND LIABILITY-BASED BENCHMARKS | 7

i. discuss uses of liability-based benchmarks

j. describe types of asset-based benchmarks

An investment benchmark is typically a collection of securities that represents the pool of assets available to the portfolio manager. For example, an investor in Japanese small-cap stocks might have a benchmark consisting of a broad portfolio of small-cap Japanese equities. A benchmark should reflect the investment process and the constraints that govern the construction of the portfolio. If the benchmark does not reflect the investment process, then the evaluation and analysis that flow from the comparison with the benchmark are flawed.

Benchmarks communicate information about the set of assets that may be considered for investment and the investment discipline. They provide investment managers with a guidepost for acceptable levels of risk and return and can be a powerful influence on investment decision making.

In investment practice, we use benchmarks as

- reference points for segments of the sponsor's portfolio,
- communication of instructions to the manager,
- communication with consultants and oversight groups (e.g., a board of directors),
- identification and evaluation of the current portfolio's risk exposures,
- interpretations of past performance and performance attribution,
- manager selection and appraisal,

- marketing of investment products, and
- demonstrations of compliance with regulations, laws, or standards.

Benchmarks help analysts measure the effectiveness of a manager's decisions to depart from benchmark weights.

When considering benchmarks, we need to understand the differences between a "benchmark" and a "market index." A market index represents the performance of a specific security market, market segment, or asset class. For example, the FTSE 100 Index is constructed to represent the broad performance of large-cap UK equities. The S&P US Aggregate Bond Index is designed to measure the performance of publicly issued US dollar-denominated investment-grade debt. The constituents of these indexes are selected for their appropriateness in representing the target market, market segment, or asset class.

A market index may be considered for use as a benchmark or a comparison point for an investment manager. Consider the case of passive managers, who typically invest in portfolios designed to closely track the performance of market indexes. For example, the iShares Core S&P 500 ETF seeks investment results, before fees and expenses, that correspond to the price and yield performance of US large-cap stocks as represented by the S&P 500 Index. Because the investment objective of the iShares Core S&P 500 ETF is to track the performance of the S&P 500, the S&P 500 is the appropriate benchmark for the iShares Core S&P 500 ETF.

However, the most appropriate benchmark for an investment manager is not necessarily a market index. Many active managers follow specific investment disciplines that cannot be adequately described by a security market index. For example, market-neutral long–short managers typically have absolute return benchmarks—a specific minimum rate of return or a specified spread over a risk-free rate. Benchmarks must be suitable to the specific needs of the asset owner and any investment manager hired to manage money; market indexes are typically meant to serve the general public's purposes and to have broad appeal. Nonetheless, indexes can sometimes serve as valid benchmarks.

Another category of benchmarks is liability-based benchmarks, which focus on the cash flows that the asset must generate. Liability-based benchmarks are most often used when the assets are required to pay a specific future liability (e.g., as in a defined benefit pension plan). They allow the asset owner to track the fund's progress toward fully funded status (assets greater than or equal to liabilities) or, if fully funded, to track the performance of assets relative to the changes in liabilities. The performance relative to liabilities is important because it would be possible for the portfolio to outperform a market index but still not meet its liabilities. Furthermore, a market-value-weighted index would likely be an inappropriate benchmark because the liability often has a targeted asset allocation and risk exposures that are different from those of the index.

As an example, consider the fixed-income portion of a pension fund. A cap-weighted index is typically not a suitable benchmark because the duration of the index is usually shorter than the duration of most pension plans' liabilities. Furthermore, many fixed-income indexes are heavily weighted toward corporate bonds in the short maturities, which may represent a greater degree of credit risk than the plan desires. As an alternative, a well-diversified portfolio of individual bonds that minimizes idiosyncratic risk could be used as the benchmark. A more recent innovation is liability-driven investment (LDI) indexes. The Bloomberg Barclays LDI Index Series is a series of six investible indexes designed specifically for portfolios intended to hedge pension liabilities. However, they may not describe a plan's liability structure as accurately as a benchmark constructed specifically for the plan.

Asset-Based and Liability-Based Benchmarks

To best determine how a liability-based benchmark should be constructed, the manager first needs to understand the nature of the plan's liabilities and the plan's projected future cash flows. Although each plan will have its own unique characteristics, the following plan features will influence the structure of the liability:

- the average number of years to retirement in the workforce,
- the percentage of the workforce that is retired,
- the average participant life expectancy,
- whether the benefits are indexed to inflation,
- whether the plan offers an early retirement option,
- whether the sponsor could increase its plan contributions (e.g., whether the sponsor is profitable and diversified),
- the correlation between plan assets and the sponsoring company's operating assets (a lower correlation is desired so that the sponsor can make contributions when the plan requires funds), and
- whether the plan is a going concern (e.g., plans will eventually terminate if the sponsor has exited its business).

These characteristics influence the composition of the pension plan portfolio and hence its liability-based benchmark. Nominal bonds, real return bonds, and common shares are the assets most commonly found in liability-driven portfolios. The allocation to each asset class is driven by the proportion of accrued versus future obligations, whether the benefits are inflation indexed, and whether the plan is growing. A younger workforce means that more is allocated to equities. Greater inflation indexing of the benefits would imply more inflation-indexed bonds. If the fund's managers outperform the benchmark constructed according to these principles, the pension obligations should be met. Risk and noise that cannot be modeled in the benchmark may require additional future contributions.

EXAMPLE 9

Liability-Based Benchmarks

1. Which of the following portfolios is most likely to use a liability-based benchmark?
    - **A** A portfolio managed for a private client with a goal of capital appreciation
    - **B** An intermediate-duration fixed-income portfolio managed for a defined benefit pension fund
    - **C** The total portfolio for a defined benefit pension fund with an asset allocation of 80% fixed income/20% equity

2. Which of the following most accurately describes a liability-based benchmark?
    - **A** It focuses on the cash flows that the benchmarked asset must generate.
    - **B** It represents the performance of a specific security market, market segment, or asset class.
    - **C** It is a collection of securities that represents the pool of assets available to the portfolio manager.

> **Solution to 1:**
>
> C is correct. A liability-based benchmark is most likely to be used for the total pension fund portfolio as the plan sponsor tracks its funded status.
>
> **Solution to 2:**
>
> A is correct. A liability-based benchmark is constructed according to the cash flows that the benchmarked asset must generate.

7.1 Asset-Based Benchmarks

Benchmarks are an important part of the investment process for both institutional and private wealth clients. In the following discussion, we introduce the types of benchmarks based on the discussion in Bailey, Richards, and Tierney (2007). The seven types of benchmarks introduced in this section are

- absolute (including target) return benchmarks,
- broad market indexes,
- style indexes,
- factor-model-based benchmarks,
- returns-based (Sharpe style analysis) benchmarks,
- manager universes (peer groups), and
- custom security-based (strategy) benchmarks.

An **absolute return benchmark** is a minimum target return that the manager is expected to beat. The return may be a stated minimum (e.g., 9%), stated as a spread above a market index (e.g., the Euro Interbank Offered Rate + 4%), or determined from actuarial assumptions. An example of an absolute return benchmark is 20% per annum return for a private equity investment. Market-neutral long–short equity funds often have absolute return benchmarks. Such funds consist of long and short positions in perceived undervalued and overvalued equities. Overall, the portfolio is expected to be insensitive to broad equity market movements (i.e., market neutral with a market beta of zero). Therefore, market-neutral fund benchmarks may be specified as a three-month Treasury bill return; the investment objective is often to outperform the benchmark consistently by a given number of basis points.

Broad market indexes are measures of broad asset class performance, such as the JP Morgan Emerging Market Bond Index (EMBI) for emerging market bonds or the MSCI World Index for global developed market equities. Broad market indexes are well known, readily available, and easily understood. The performance of broad market indexes is widely reported in the popular media.

Market indexes have also been more narrowly defined to represent investment styles within asset classes, resulting in style indexes. An **investment style** is a natural grouping of investment disciplines that has some predictive power in explaining the future dispersion of returns across portfolios.[4] In the late 1970s, researchers found that stock valuation (e.g., the price-to-earnings ratio) and market capitalization explained much of stock return variation. In response, many index providers created various style versions of their broad market indexes (e.g., the Russell 2000 Value and Russell 1000 Growth Indexes).

Factor-model-based benchmarks can be constructed to more closely capture the investment decision-making process. Building a factor model identifies the relative explanatory powers of each factor in the portfolio return. Examples of factors include

---
[4] Brown and Goetzmann (1997).

broad market index returns, industry exposure, and financial leverage. To determine the factor sensitivities, the portfolio's return is regressed against the factors believed to influence returns. The general form of a factor model is:

$$R_p = a_p + b_1 F_1 + b_2 F_2 \ldots b_k F_k + \varepsilon_p \qquad (12)$$

where

R_p = the portfolio's periodic return

a_p = the "zero-factor" term, which is the expected portfolio return if all factor sensitivities are zero

b_k = the sensitivity of portfolio returns to the factor return

F_k = systematic factors responsible for asset returns

ε_p = residual return due to nonsystematic factors

The sensitivities (b_k) are then used to predict the return the portfolio should provide for given values of the systematic-risk factors. Earlier, we discussed the four-factor Carhart model, but any key element of the investment process can be considered for inclusion in a factor model. As an example, if the investment manager believes that interest rates are inversely related to security prices, then the model can incorporate an interest rate factor. If interest rates unexpectedly rise, then security returns can be expected to fall by an amount determined by the security's sensitivity (b_k) to interest rate changes.

Returns-based benchmarks (Sharpe style analysis) are like factor-model-based benchmarks in that portfolio returns are related to a set of factors that explain portfolio returns. With returns-based benchmarks, however, the factors are the returns for various style indexes (e.g., small-cap value, small-cap growth, large-cap value, and large-cap growth). The style analysis produces a benchmark of the weighted average of these asset class indexes that best explains or tracks the portfolio's returns. Unlike the investment-style indexes previously discussed, returns-based benchmarks *view style on a continuum*. For example, a portfolio may be characterized as 60% small-cap value and 40% small-cap growth. To create a returns-based benchmark using Sharpe style analysis, we use an optimization procedure to force the portfolio's sensitivities (analogous to the b_k's in factor-model-based benchmarks) to be non-negative and sum to 1.

A **manager universe**, or **manager peer group**, is a broad group of managers with similar investment disciplines. Although not a benchmark, per se, a manager universe allows investors to make comparisons with the performance of other managers following similar investment disciplines. Managers are typically expected to beat the universe's median return. Manager universes are typically formed by asset class and the investment approach within that class.

Peer groups as benchmarks suffer from some significant weaknesses. Although managers within a peer group may all nominally be classified as "large-cap value" or "small-cap growth," for example, they may not truly be substitutable for one another. Some may have tilts or constraints that create an investment product very different from that of the median manager. A manager's ranking within the peer group might change considerably with very small changes in performance, often in response to factors outside of the manager's control: A change in the ranking may be driven not by something he did but by the actions of others in the peer group (e.g., other managers in the peer group may have chosen to overweight a "hot" sector, whereas the target manager's investment discipline constrains him from making a similar bet).

Lastly, **custom security-based benchmarks** are built to more precisely reflect the investment discipline of an investment manager. Such benchmarks are developed through discussions with the manager and an analysis of past portfolio exposures. After identifying the manager's investment process, the benchmark is constructed by selecting securities and weightings consistent with that process and client restrictions.

If an allocation to cash is a key component of the investment process, an appropriate cash weight will be incorporated into the benchmark. The benchmark is rebalanced on a periodic basis to ensure that it stays consistent with the manager's investment practice. Custom security-based benchmarks are also referred to as *strategy benchmarks* because they should reflect the manager's strategy. Custom security-based benchmarks are particularly appropriate when the manager's strategy cannot be closely matched to a broad market index or style index. These benchmarks are costly to calculate and maintain.

8. BENCHMARK PROPERTIES, EVALUATING BENCHMARK QUALITY, AND CHOOSING THE CORRECT BENCHMARK

k discuss tests of benchmark quality
m describe the impact of benchmark misspecification on attribution and appraisal analysis

The choice of benchmark often has a significant effect on the assessment of manager performance. Investment managers should be compared only with benchmarks that reflect the universe of securities available to them. A valid benchmark must satisfy certain criteria. We examine the characteristics of a valid benchmark by using the definitive list from Bailey and Tierney (1998).

- *Unambiguous*—The individual securities and their weights in a benchmark should be clearly identifiable. For example, we should be able to identify whether Nestlé is included in a global equity benchmark and its weight.

- *Investable*—It must be possible to replicate and hold the benchmark to earn its return (at least gross of expenses). The sponsor should have the option of moving assets from active management to a passive benchmark. If the benchmark is not investable, it is not a viable investment alternative.

- *Measurable*—It must be possible to measure the benchmark's return on a reasonably frequent and timely basis.

- *Appropriate*—The benchmark must be consistent with the manager's investment style or area of expertise.

- *Reflective of current investment opinions*—The manager should be familiar with the securities that constitute the benchmark and their factor exposures. Managers should be able to develop an opinion regarding their attractiveness as investments; they should not be given a mandate of obscure securities.

- *Specified in advance*—The benchmark must be constructed prior to the evaluation period so that the manager is not judged against benchmarks created after the fact.

- *Accountable*—The manager should accept ownership of the benchmark and its securities and be willing to be held accountable to the benchmark. The benchmark should be fully consistent with the manager's investment process, and the manager should be able to demonstrate the validity of his or her benchmark. Through acceptance of the benchmark, the sponsor assumes responsibility for any discrepancies between the targeted portfolio for the fund and the benchmark. The manager becomes responsible for differences between the benchmark and her performance.

Benchmark Properties, Evaluating Benchmark Quality, and Choosing the Correct Benchmark

The properties outlined by Bailey and Tierney help ensure that a benchmark will serve as a valid instrument for the purposes of evaluating the manager's performance. Although these qualities for a desirable benchmark may seem straightforward, we will show later that many commonly used benchmarks do not incorporate them.

> **EXAMPLE 10**
>
> ## Benchmarks
>
> 1. You have hired a bond manager to run an intermediate-duration government fixed-income portfolio. Which type of benchmark is most suitable for this portfolio?
>   - **A** A broad market index
>   - **B** A liability-based benchmark
>   - **C** A factor-model-based benchmark
>
> 2. You have hired a top-down quantitative equity manager who has built a proprietary process based on timing the fund's exposures to systematic risks. Which type of benchmark is most suitable for this portfolio?
>   - **A** A broad market index
>   - **B** A liability-based benchmark
>   - **C** A factor-model-based benchmark
>
> 3. You are on the board of a pension fund that is seeking to close the gap between its assets and its liabilities. What is the most appropriate benchmark against which to measure the performance of the plan's outsourced chief investment officer?
>   - **A** A broad market index
>   - **B** A liability-based benchmark
>   - **C** A factor-model-based benchmark
>
> 4. You are a portfolio manager at JEMstone Capital. Your firm has been hired to run a global small-cap developed market equity portfolio. The agreement with the client sets a minimum market cap of US$500 million and a liquidity constraint that states that a portfolio holding is capped at 5 times its average daily liquidity over the past 12 months. Most portfolios managed by the firm are managed without constraint against the MSCI ACWI Small Cap Index, which has an average market cap of approximately $1.2 billion and a median market cap of approximately $650 million. A stock is eligible for inclusion in the index if the shares traded over the prior three months are equal to at least 20% of the security's free-float-adjusted market capitalization.[5] Your team is discussing the suitability of the MSCI ACWI Small Cap Index for this portfolio. Discuss the validity of this benchmark using the Richards and Tierney framework.

---

[5] This is a very abbreviated representation of the liquidity constraint used in the construction of the MSCI indexes. For a more complete description of the liquidity requirements, refer to "MSCI Global Investable Market Indexes Methodology": www.msci.com/eqb/methodology/meth_docs/MSCI_GIMIMethodology_Nov2018.pdf (accessed 5 December 2019).

> **Solution to 1:**
>
> A is correct. A broad market index is a suitable benchmark for a government bond portfolio provided the maturity and duration characteristics of the benchmark align with those of the investment mandate.
>
> **Solution to 2:**
>
> C is correct. Factors represent systematic risks. The manager's approach attempts to create alpha by timing the portfolio's exposure to factors. A factor-model-based benchmark can be constructed to represent the manager's investment approach.
>
> **Solution to 3:**
>
> B is correct. The primary investment objective of the pension portfolio is to close the gap between assets and liabilities. The performance of the pension fund's manager should be evaluated relative to this objective.
>
> **Solution to 4:**
>
> - The benchmark meets the criteria of *unambiguous*. The individual securities and their weights are clearly identifiable.
> - The benchmark most likely meets the criteria of *investable*. The shares in the index are freely tradeable.
> - The benchmark meets the criteria of *measurable*. Index returns are published daily.
> - The benchmark *does not* meet the criteria of *appropriate*. The liquidity and capitalization constraints imposed by the client are not consistent with the manner in which the manager runs other portfolios managed by the firm.
> - The benchmark meets the criteria of *reflective of current investment opinions*. The benchmark was selected by the manager and is presumed to be representative of the manager's investment process.
> - The benchmark meets the criteria of *specified in advance*. The benchmark is not created after the fact.
> - The manager may choose to be *accountable* to this index if the liquidity and capitalization constraints are not expected to interfere with the ability to execute the investment strategy. The client should be made aware of the discrepancies between the portfolio constraints and the benchmark.

8.1 Evaluating Benchmark Quality: Analysis Based on a Decomposition of Portfolio Holdings and Returns

Once a benchmark is constructed, we can evaluate its quality using tests. To understand these tests, it helps to first decompose the benchmark's returns. Using the decomposition from Bailey et al. (2007), we can first state the identity where a portfolio's return (P) is equal to itself:

$$P = P \qquad (13)$$

Then, add an appropriate benchmark (B) to, and subtract this benchmark from, the right-hand side of the equation:

$$P = B + (P - B) \qquad (14)$$

Benchmark Properties, Evaluating Benchmark Quality, and Choosing the Correct Benchmark

The term P − B is the result of the manager's active management decisions, which we denote as A. Thus, we have

$$P = B + A \qquad (15)$$

From Equations 13–15, we see that the portfolio return is a function of the benchmark and the manager's active decisions.

Next, add the market index return (M) to and subtract it from the right-hand side of the equation:

$$P = M + (B − M) + A \qquad (16)$$

The difference between the benchmark return and the market index (B − M) is the manager's style return, which we denote as S:

$$P = M + S + A \qquad (17)$$

Equation 17 states that the portfolio return (P) is a result of the market index return (M), a style return (S), and the active management return (A).

If the manager's portfolio is a broad market index where S = 0 and A = 0, then the portfolio earns the broad market return: P = M.

If the benchmark is a broad market index, then S is assumed to be zero and the prediction is that the manager earns the market return and a return to active management: P = M + A. However, if the benchmark is a broad market index and the manager *does* have style differences from the benchmark, the analysis using the broad market benchmark is incorrect. In this case, any style return (S) will be lumped together with the measured active management component (A), such that an analysis of a manager's true added value will be obscured.

We can use these benchmark building blocks to further search for systematic biases between the active management return and the style return, identified through correlation. For instance, if we measure the correlation between active management return, A = (P − B), and style return, S = (B − M), we can identify whether the manager's active selection decisions align with the style currently favored by the market. A good benchmark should not reflect these systematic biases, where the correlation between A and S should not be statistically different from zero. Likewise, we define the difference between the portfolio and the broad market index as E = (P − M). When a manager's style (S) is in (out of) favor relative to the market, we expect both the benchmark and the account to outperform (underperform) the market. Therefore, a good benchmark will have a statistically significant positive correlation coefficient between S and E.

EXAMPLE 11

Decomposition of Portfolio Return

1. Assume that the Courtland account has a return of −5.3% in a given month, during which the portfolio benchmark has a return of −5.5% and the market index has a return of −2.8%.

   A Calculate the Courtland account's return due to the manager's style.

   B Calculate the Courtland account's return due to active management.

2. Assume that Mr. Kuti's account has a return of 5.6% in a given month, during which the portfolio benchmark has a return of 5.1% and a market index has a return of 3.2%.

   A Calculate the return due to the manager's style for Mr. Kuti's account.

   B Calculate the return due to active management for Mr. Kuti's account.

3. An actively managed mid-cap value equity portfolio has a return of 9.24%. The portfolio is benchmarked to a mid-cap value index that has a return of 7.85%. A broad equity market index has a return of 8.92%. Calculate the return due to the portfolio manager's style.

4. A US large-cap value portfolio run by Anderson Investment Management returned 18.9% during the first three quarters of 2019. During the same time period, a US large-cap value index had a return of 21.7% and a broad US equity index returned 25.2%.

   A Calculate the return due to style.

   B Calculate the return due to active management.

   C Using your answers to A and B, discuss Anderson's performance relative to the benchmark and relative to the market.

Solution to 1:

A The return due to style is $S = B - M = -5.5\% - (-2.8\%) = -2.7\%$.

B The return due to active management is $A = P - B = -5.3\% - (-5.5\%) = 0.2\%$.

Solution to 2:

A The return due to style is $S = B - M = 5.1\% - 3.2\% = 1.9\%$.

B The return due to active management is $A = P - B = 5.6\% - 5.1\% = 0.5\%$.

Solution to 3:

The return due to style is the style-specific benchmark return of 7.85% minus the broad market return of 8.92%: −1.07%.

Solution to 4:

A The return due to style is the difference between the benchmark and the market index, or $S = (B - M) = (21.7\% - 25.2\%) = -3.5\%$.

B The return due to active management is the difference between the portfolio and the benchmark, or $A = (P - B) = (18.9\% - 21.7\%) = -2.8\%$.

C Anderson's underperformance relative to the broad US equity index is partly a function of style and partly a function of the manager's weak performance within the style. Given that the US large-cap value index underperformed the US market index by 3.5%, we can infer that large-cap value was out of favor during the period measured. Provided the US large-cap value index is an appropriate benchmark for Anderson, the manager's underperformance bears further investigation. The client would want to understand the specific drivers of the underperformance and relate those decisions to the manager's stated investment process.

8.2 Importance of Choosing the Correct Benchmark

As we have described, performance evaluation and attribution require appropriate benchmarks. When benchmarks are misspecified, subsequent performance measurement will be incorrect; both the attribution and the appraisal analyses will be useless.

For example, consider a manager who invests in Japanese stocks. The sponsor uses the MSCI Pacific Index to evaluate the manager. Japanese stocks constitute most of the MSCI Pacific, but the index also includes four other developed markets (Australia, New Zealand, Hong Kong SAR, and Singapore). Thus, the MSCI Japan Index more closely represents the manager's normal portfolio. The 2018 returns are as follows:

- Manager return: 24.7%
- MSCI Pacific (investor's benchmark) return: 25.0%
- MSCI Japan (normal portfolio) return: 24.0%

Although the manager *underperformed* the investor's benchmark (24.5% for the manager versus 25.0% for the MSCI Pacific), the manager *outperformed* when correctly benchmarked against the normal portfolio (24.5% for the manager versus 24% for the normal portfolio). In summary,

- True Active Return = Mgr Return − Normal Portfolio Return = 24.7 − 24.0 = 0.7%
- Investor (Mismeasured) Active Return = Mgr Return − Investor Benchmark return = (Mgr Return - Normal portfolio Return) + (Normal Portfolio Return - Investor Benchmark return) = True Active Return + Misfit Active Return = 24.7 − 25.0 = 0.7 + (−1.0) = −0.3%

Measuring the manager's results against the normal portfolio instead of the investor's benchmark more accurately evaluates the manager's performance. The manager's negative "true" active return indicates that the manager outperformed the normal portfolio. Fundamentally, any further performance attribution against the investor's benchmark will also be useless. By using the incorrect benchmark, the attribution would attempt to explain an underperformance, rather than the true active return, which contributed positively to the investor's return.

Peer group benchmarking is particularly susceptible to selection problems. For example, practitioners must select the appropriate peers without suggesting to the portfolio managers that median peer group performance is the target. Peer group benchmarks provide an incentive not to underperform the peer group median, often leading to herding around the median return. As a result, the investment decisions of the fund manager can be biased by the structure of the benchmarks chosen.

Sometimes, benchmarks are chosen for the wrong reasons. Underperforming managers have been known to change benchmarks to improve their measured excess return, which is both inappropriate and unethical.

Benchmark misspecification can lead to mismeasurement of the value added by the portfolio managers. A "normal portfolio" or "normal benchmark" is the portfolio that most closely represents the manager's typical positions in his investment universe. The manager's "true" active return is equal to his return minus his normal portfolio return.

Most investors, however, tend to use a broad market benchmark for manager evaluation. The manager's active return is thus measured as the manager's return minus the investor's benchmark return. There is a mismatch between the broad market benchmark and the manager's "normal" portfolio or benchmark; this is not the manager's "true" active return but is more appropriately termed the "misfit active return" (see, e.g., Gastineau, Olma, and Zielinski 2007). Using a broad market index typically misses the manager's style (i.e., creates style bias). This decomposition is useful for understanding the impact of a misspecified benchmark on performance appraisal.

For example, consider a manager who invests in US value stocks. The sponsor uses the broad Russell 3000 equity index (the "investor's benchmark") to evaluate the manager. However, the manager's normal portfolio is better represented by his or her universe of value stocks. In this example, the manager returns 15%, the Russell 3000 (the investor's benchmark) return is 10%, and the manager's normal portfolio return is 18%. Although the manager has outperformed the investor's benchmark (15% versus 10%), the manager has underperformed when correctly benchmarked against the normal portfolio (15% versus 18%).

9. BENCHMARKING ALTERNATIVE INVESTMENTS

l. describe problems that arise in benchmarking alternative investments

Performance evaluation for alternative asset classes presents many challenges. The selection of an appropriate benchmark is stymied by the lack of high-quality, investible market indexes, the frequent use of leverage in many strategies, the limited liquidity and lack of readily available market values for many underlying assets, and the use of internal rates of return rather than time-weighted rates of return.

In the following sections addressing each of the major alternative asset classes, we will consider how these challenges affect performance evaluation.

9.1 Benchmarking Hedge Fund Investments

Hedge funds do not represent an asset class, such as equities or fixed income. Rather, hedge funds encompass a broad range of possible strategies designed to exploit market inefficiencies. Hedge funds may have an unlimited investment universe, vary substantially from one to another, and can vary their asset allocations over time. Hedge funds also use leverage, sell assets short, take positions in derivatives, and may be opportunistic in their choice of strategy. These characteristics make it difficult to create a single standard against which hedge funds should be judged.

Some hedge funds lever many times their capital base, which increases their expected return and risk. Short positions and derivatives used in long–short strategies can increase return or reduce risk. A manager's use of style, leverage, short positions, and derivatives may change over time. Hedge funds also typically lack transparency, are difficult to monitor, and are often illiquid.

These characteristics of hedge funds make it clear that broad market indexes are unsuitable as hedge fund benchmarks.

The risk-free rate (e.g., Libor) plus a spread (e.g., 3%–6%) is sometimes advocated as a hedge fund benchmark for arbitrage-based hedge fund strategies. The argument for using the risk-free rate is that investors desire a positive return and that arbitrage strategies are risk free, with the spread reflecting the active management return and management costs.

However, most funds, even those that target market-neutral strategies, are not completely free of systematic risk, and the use of leverage could magnify that systematic risk. In this case, the spread relative to the risk-free rate should be adjusted upward.

Both broad market indexes and the risk-free rate will be weakly correlated or uncorrelated with hedge fund returns, thus failing the benchmark quality test of Bailey et al. (2007) that states that portfolio and benchmark factor sensitivities should be similar.

Because of the shortcomings of broad market indexes and the risk-free rate, hedge fund manager universes from such providers as CSFB/Tremont are often used as hedge fund benchmarks. Hedge fund peer universes are subject to a number of limitations:

1 The risk and return characteristics of a strategy peer group is unlikely to be representative of the approach taken by a single fund.

2. Hedge fund peer groups suffer from survivorship and backfill bias. Backfill bias occurs when the index provider adds a manager to the index and imports the manager's entire return history.

3. Hedge fund performance data are often self-reported and typically not confirmed by the index provider. A fund's reported net asset value may be a managed value. Even if the manager has no intention to misreport the data, hedge funds hold illiquid assets that require some subjectivity in pricing. If the previous period's price is used as the current price or an appraisal is used, then the data will be smoothed. The presence of stale pricing will result in downward-biased standard deviations and temporal instability in correlations, with hedge funds potentially given larger portfolio allocations as a result.

9.2 Benchmarking Real Estate Investments

There are numerous private real estate indexes offered by industry associations, large and small index providers, investment consultants, and others who collect real estate data. There are indexes and sub-indexes for nearly all the major developed countries, major sectors, investment styles, and structures (open-end and closed-end funds). Choosing the appropriate real estate benchmark requires careful consideration and an understanding of the limitations of such benchmarks—and their relevance to the investment strategy under evaluation. The following are some limitations of the available real estate benchmarks:

1. The benchmarks are based on a subset of the real estate opportunity set and, therefore, are not fully representative of the asset class.

2. Index performance is likely to be highly correlated with the returns of the largest fund data contributors.

3. Benchmark returns are based on manager-reported performance and may be inherently biased.

4. Benchmarks weighted by fund or asset value may place a disproportionate emphasis on the most expensive cities and asset types.

5. Valuations of the underlying properties are typically based on appraisals because there are few transactions to measure. Appraisals are infrequent, they smooth changes in property values, and they can lag underlying property performance. Transaction-based indexes are becoming more readily available.

6. Some benchmark returns are unlevered, whereas others contain varying degrees of leverage based on the structure used by the investor that contributed the data.

7. Real estate indexes do not reflect the high transaction costs, limited transparency, and lack of liquidity that drive performance for actual real estate investments.

Further complicating the performance evaluation of real estate funds is the selection of the appropriate return measure. Open-end funds, for which the contributions and withdrawals are at the discretion of the investor, generally use time-weighted rates of return. Closed-end funds, however, for which the timing of the contributions and withdrawals is at the discretion of the fund manager, generally report using internal rates of return.

9.3 Benchmarking Private Equity

When measuring the performance of a private equity investment, investors typically calculate an internal rate of return (IRR) based on cash flows since inception of the investment and the ending valuation of the investment (the net asset value or residual value). Similarly, major venture capital benchmarks, such as those of Cambridge Associates, provide IRR estimates for private equity funds that are based on fund cash flows and valuations. Major indexes serving as benchmarks for US and European private equity include those provided by Cambridge Associates, Preqin, and LPX.

These benchmarks can be used to compare the managers' individual funds with an appropriate peer group, normally defined by subclass, geography, and vintage year of the underlying fund. Benchmarks commonly used for this purpose include ones prepared by Burgiss, Cambridge Associates, and the Institutional Limited Partners Association.

Although relative performance measures help an investor understand how a fund performs relative to peers or a relevant public index, there are several limitations to be aware of when comparing returns among managers:

1. The valuation methodology used by the managers may differ.
2. A fund's IRR can be meaningfully influenced by an early loss or an early win in the portfolio.
3. The data are from a specific point in time, and the companies in a fund can be at different stages of development.

The public market equivalent (PME) methodology has been developed to allow comparisons of private equity IRRs with returns of publicly traded equity indexes. The methodology uses cash flow data to replicate the general partner's capital calls and distributions, assuming these same cash flows were invested in the chosen equity index. Comparing the performance of the PME index with the net IRR of the fund reveals the extent of over- or underperformance of the PME index relative to the public index. Several PME methodologies exist, the most common being Long–Nickels PME, PME+, Kaplan and Schoar PME, and Direct Alpha PME. It is important to choose the appropriate PME for each private equity fund; a poorly chosen PME raises the risk of leading the investor to an incorrect conclusion.

9.4 Benchmarking Commodity Investments

Commodity benchmarks tend to use indexes based on the performance of futures-based commodity investments. These include the Reuters/Jefferies Commodity Research Bureau (RJ/CRB) Index, the S&P Goldman Sachs Commodity Index (GSCI), and the Bloomberg Commodity Index (BCOM). However, because the indexes use futures, rather than actual assets, they attempt to replicate the returns available to holding long positions in commodities. The S&P GSCI, the BCOM, and the RJ/CRB Index provide returns comparable to those of passive long positions in listed futures contracts. Because the cost-of-carry model ensures that the return on a fully margined position in a futures contract mimics the return on an underlying spot deliverable, futures contract returns are often used as a surrogate for cash market performance.

These indexes are considered investable. The major indexes contain some common groups of underlying assets. For example, the RJ/CRB Index, the BCOM, and the S&P GSCI all include energy (oil and gas), metals (industrial and precious), grains (corn, soybeans, and wheat), and soft commodities (cocoa, coffee, cotton, and sugar). However, beyond these basic groupings, they and other commodity indexes vary greatly in their composition and weighting schemes. A market-cap-weighting scheme, so common for equity and bond market indexes, cannot be carried over to indexes of commodity futures. Because every long futures position has a corresponding short futures position, the market capitalization of a futures contract is always zero.

Benchmarking of commodity investments presents similar challenges to other alternatives, including

1. the use of derivatives to represent actual commodity assets,
2. varying degrees of leverage among funds, and
3. the discretionary weighting of exposures within the index.

9.5 Benchmarking Managed Derivatives

Because market indexes do not exist for managed derivatives, the benchmarks are typically specific to a single investment strategy. For example, the Mount Lucas Management Index takes both long and short positions in many futures markets based on a technical (moving-average) trading rule that is, in effect, specific to an active momentum strategy.

Other derivative benchmarks are based on peer groups. For example, the BarclayHedge and CISDM CTA trading strategy benchmarks are based on peer groups of commodity trading advisers (CTAs). The CISDM CTA Equal Weighted Index reflects manager returns for all reporting managers in the CISDM CTA database. These indexes suffer from the known limitations of peer group–based benchmarks, including survivorship bias.

9.6 Benchmarking Distressed Securities

Distressed securities are illiquid and almost non-marketable at the time of purchase, making it very difficult to find suitable benchmarks. If the companies' prospects improve, the values of the distressed securities may go up gradually and liquidity may improve. Typically, it takes a relatively long time for this strategy to play out; thus, valuing the holdings may be a challenge. It is difficult to estimate the true market values of distressed securities, and stale pricing is almost inevitable.

One possible strategy is to use market indexes, such as the Barclay Distressed Securities Index. This index is constructed from fund managers who invest in distressed securities. Because this index is constructed from multiple strategies, however, it is difficult to discern whether the index is suitable for a given investment approach. In addition, because the valuations for the member funds are calculated at random intervals, it doesn't necessarily correct for the valuation issues noted previously.

PERFORMANCE APPRAISAL: RISK-BASED MEASURES — 10

- n calculate and interpret the Sortino ratio, the appraisal ratio, upside/downside capture ratios, maximum drawdown, and drawdown duration
- o describe limitations of appraisal measures and related metrics

Investment performance appraisal identifies and measures investment skill, providing the information to assess how effectively money has been invested given the risks that were taken. (Risk-adjusted past performance is just one of many considerations when choosing investment managers. Qualitative considerations, although not within the scope of this reading, are also very important.)

Performance appraisal is most often concerned with ranking investment managers who follow similar investment disciplines. Return attribution provides information that can complement a performance appraisal analysis by providing more details about the consequences of managerial decisions. Performance attribution identifies and quantifies the sources of added value, whereas performance appraisal seeks to ascertain whether added value was a result of managerial skill.

Skill in any profession can be thought of as the ability to influence outcomes in desired directions. We define active investment management skill as the ability of a portfolio manager to add value on a risk-adjusted basis through investment analysis and insights. In everyday language, active investment skill is typically viewed as the ability to "beat the market" or an assigned benchmark with some consistency. The evaluation of active management skill is the focus of performance appraisal and this reading.

10.1 Distinguishing Investment Skill from Luck

An investment manager's record for any specific period will reflect good luck (unanticipated good developments) and bad luck (unanticipated bad developments). One reason that luck should be considered important when appraising investment performance is the paradox of skill. As people become more knowledgeable about an activity, the difference between the worst and the best performers becomes narrower. Thus, the ever-increasing aggregate skill level of investment managers, supplemented by massive computing power and access to "big data," may lead to narrower investment performance differentials and a greater likelihood that these differentials can be explained by luck.

Deciding whether a portfolio manager has or lacks active investment skill on the basis of past returns is difficult and always subject to error. Financial market returns have a large element of randomness. Some of this randomness reflects the impact of news and information that relate directly or indirectly to asset values. Trading motivated by liquidity needs and by the emotions of investors adds to return volatility.

When we observe the historical performance of an investment portfolio, we see only one out of a potentially unlimited number of outcomes for a manager applying the same investment discipline but with different luck. Perhaps we gain additional insight into skill by examining the consistency of performance over time. But the hypothesis that the manager's underlying mean return exceeds the benchmark's mean return may require many years of observations to confirm with a reasonably high degree of confidence.[6]

10.2 Appraisal Measures

The academic and the professional investment literatures have developed several returns-based measures to assess the value of active management. Important measures include the following:

- Sharpe ratio
- Treynor ratio
- Information ratio

---

[6] Can you be lucky once and correctly pick the flip of a fair coin? Of course! How about four times in a row? Yes, although this outcome is much less likely. Can a portfolio manager be lucky enough to generate 15 continuous years of superior investment performance? This outcome is very unlikely, but with hundreds or even thousands of portfolio managers, a few might succeed solely because of luck. One problem faced in investment performance appraisal is that many investment management performance records are only a few years long, making it difficult to distinguish between luck and skill.

Performance Appraisal: Risk-Based Measures

- Appraisal ratio
- Sortino ratio
- Capture ratios

The selection of an appropriate appraisal measure requires an understanding of which aspect of risk is most important given the role of the investment in the client's total portfolio. It is also important to understand the assumptions a measure makes about the probability distribution of possible returns and any assumptions regarding the underlying theoretical pricing model. The Sharpe, information, and Treynor ratios are covered elsewhere in the curriculum and are not covered in depth here. This section will focus primarily on the remaining measures.

10.2.1 The Sharpe Ratio

The **Sharpe ratio** measures the additional return for bearing risk above the risk-free rate, stated per unit of return volatility. In performance appraisal, this additional return is often referred to as **excess return**. This use contrasts with how "excess return" is used in return performance attribution—that is, as a return in excess of a benchmark's return.

The Sharpe ratio is commonly used on an *ex post* basis to evaluate historical risk-adjusted returns, as in

$$S_A = \frac{\overline{R}_A - \overline{r}_f}{\hat{\sigma}_A} \qquad (18)$$

One weakness of the Sharpe ratio is that the use of standard deviation as a measure of risk assumes investors are indifferent between upside and downside volatility. For example, for an investor looking for a potentially high-rewarding investment, volatility on the upside is not necessarily a negative. Similarly, risk-averse investors concerned about the preservation of capital are clearly most concerned with downside risk.

10.2.2 The Treynor Ratio

The Treynor ratio (Treynor 1965) measures the excess return per unit of systematic risk. With the Treynor ratio, as well as the systematic-risk-based appraisal measures that follow, we must carefully choose an efficient market benchmark against which to measure the systematic risk of the manager's fund. In contrast, the Sharpe ratio can be compared among different funds without the explicit choice of a market benchmark.

$$T_A = \frac{\overline{R}_A - \overline{r}_f}{\hat{\beta}_A} \qquad (19)$$

The usefulness of the Treynor ratio depends on whether systematic risk or total risk is most appropriate in evaluating performance. Because of its reliance on beta, the Treynor ratio shows how a fund has performed in relation not to its own volatility but to the volatility it would bring to a well-diversified portfolio. Thus, a ranking of portfolios based on the Treynor ratio is most useful if the portfolios whose performance is being evaluated are being combined in a broader, fully diversified portfolio. The ratio is most informative when the portfolios being evaluated are compared with the same benchmark index.

10.2.3 The Information Ratio

The information ratio (IR) is a simple measure that allows the evaluator to assess performance relative to the benchmark, scaled by risk. The implicit assumption is that the chosen benchmark is well matched to the risk of the investment strategy. The IR is calculated by dividing the portfolio's mean excess return relative to its benchmark by the variability of that excess return, as shown in Equation 18. The denominator of the information ratio, $\sigma(r_p - r_B)$, is the portfolio's tracking risk, a measure of how closely a portfolio follows the index to which it is benchmarked. (Many writers use "tracking error" in the sense of "tracking risk," although, confusingly, tracking error is also used to refer to simply the return difference between a passive portfolio and its benchmark.)

$$\text{IR} = \frac{E(r_p) - E(r_B)}{\sigma(r_p - r_B)} \qquad (20)$$

10.2.4 The Appraisal Ratio

The appraisal ratio (AR) is a returns-based measure, like the IR. It is the annualized alpha divided by the annualized residual risk. In the appraisal ratio, both the alpha and the residual risk are computed from a factor regression. Although the AR can be computed using any factor model appropriate for the portfolio, the measure was first introduced by Treynor and Black (1973) using Jensen's alpha and the standard deviation of the portfolio's residual or non-systematic risk. Treynor and Black argued that security selection ability implies that deviations from benchmark portfolio weights can be profitable and showed that the optimal deviations from the benchmark holdings for securities depend on what they called an "appraisal ratio." The appraisal ratio is also referred to as the *Treynor–Black ratio* or the *Treynor–Black appraisal ratio*.

The appraisal ratio measures the reward of active management relative to the risk of active management (alpha from a factor model):

$$\text{AR} = \frac{\alpha}{\sigma_\varepsilon} \qquad (21)$$

where σ_ε equals the standard deviation of ε_t, commonly denoted as the "standard error of regression," which is readily available from the output of commonly used statistical software.

10.2.5 The Sortino Ratio

The Sortino ratio is a modification of the Sharpe ratio that penalizes only those returns that are lower than a user-specified return. The Sharpe ratio penalizes both upside and downside volatility equally.

Equation 22 presents the *ex ante* Sortino ratio, where r_T is the minimum acceptable return (MAR), which is sometimes referred to as a *target rate of return*.[7] Instead of using standard deviation in the denominator, the Sortino ratio uses a measure of downside risk known as target semi-standard deviation or target semideviation, σ_D, as shown in Equation 23. By using this value, the Sortino ratio penalizes managers only for "harmful" volatility and is a measure of return per unit of downside risk.

$$\text{SR}_D = \frac{E(r_p) - r_T}{\sigma_D} \qquad (22)$$

$$\widehat{\text{SR}}_D = \frac{\bar{r}_p - \bar{r}_T}{\hat{\sigma}_D} \qquad (23)$$

---

[7] The MAR is the lowest rate of return at which an investor will consider investing. For example, an MAR set equal to the expected rate of inflation would be associated with capital preservation in real terms. It is possible to use the benchmark return as the MAR. The MAR does not determine intrinsic value. Rather, it is a constraint or decision criterion that applies to all investment considerations.

Performance Appraisal: Risk-Based Measures

$$\sigma_D = \left[\frac{\sum_{t=1}^{N} \min(r_t - r_T, 0)^2}{N}\right]^{1/2} \tag{24}$$

Assume a portfolio has an MAR of 4.0%. The portfolio's returns over a 10-year period are given in Exhibit 16. The numerator of the Sortino ratio is the average portfolio return minus the target return: $\bar{r}_p - \bar{r}_T = 6.0\% - 4.0\% = 2.0\%$. The calculation of target semi-standard deviation is reported in Exhibit 16. Based on the information in the table, the Sortino ratio is approximately 0.65.

Exhibit 16 Sortino Ratio Using Target Semi-Standard Deviation

Year	Rate of Return: r_t	Target Return: $r_T = 4\%$ $\min(r_t - r_T, 0)^2$
1	6.0%	0
2	8.0%	0
3	−1.0%	0.0025
4	18.0%	0
5	12.0%	0
6	3.0%	0.0001
7	−4.0%	0.0064
8	5.0%	0
9	2.0%	0.0004
10	11.0%	0

$$\sum_{t=1}^{N} \min(r_t - r_T, 0)^2 = 0.0094$$

$$\sigma_D = \left[\frac{\sum_{t=1}^{N} \min(r_t - r_T, 0)^2}{N}\right]^{1/2} = \left(\frac{0.0094}{10}\right)^{1/2} = 3.07\%$$

More so than traditional performance measures, the Sortino ratio offers the ability to accurately assess performance when return distributions are not symmetrical. For example, because of its underlying assumption of normally distributed returns, the Sharpe ratio would not effectively distinguish between strategies with greater-than-normal upside volatility (positively skewed strategies, such as trend following) and strategies with greater-than-normal downside volatility (negatively skewed strategies, such as option writing). Both types of volatility are penalized equally in the Sharpe ratio. The Sortino ratio is arguably a better performance metric for such assets as hedge funds or commodity trading funds, whose return distributions are purposefully skewed away from the normal.

The Sortino ratio formula is not a risk premium. It is the return a portfolio manager generates that is greater than what is minimally acceptable to the investor. Essentially, the Sortino ratio penalizes a manager when portfolio return is lower than the MAR; it is most relevant when one of the investor's primary objectives is capital preservation.

Although there are arguments in favor of both the Sharpe ratio and the Sortino ratio, the Sharpe ratio has been much more widely used. In some cases, this preference may reflect a certain comfort level associated with the use of standard deviation, which is a more traditional measure of volatility. Also, cross-sectional comparisons of Sortino ratios are difficult to make applicable to every investor, because the MAR is investor-specific.

EXAMPLE 12

Performance Appraisal Measures

1. Portfolio B delivered 10.0% annual returns on average over the past 60 months. Its average annual volatility as measured by standard deviation was 14.0%, and its downside volatility as measured by target semi-standard deviation was 8.0%. Assuming the target rate of return is 3.0% per year, the Sortino ratio of portfolio B is closest to:
   A   0.66.
   B   0.77.
   C   0.88.

2. Why might a practitioner use the Sortino ratio, rather than the Sharpe ratio, to indicate performance?
   A   He is measuring option writing.
   B   The return distributions are not symmetrical.
   C   The investor's primary objective is capital preservation.
   D   All of the above

3. Portfolio Y delivered an average annualized return of 9.0% over the past 60 months. The annualized standard deviation over this same time period was 20.0%. The market index returned 8.0% per year on average over the same time period, with an annualized standard deviation of 12.0%. Portfolio Y has an estimated beta of 1.40 versus the market index. Assuming the risk-free rate is 3.0% per year, the appraisal ratio is closest to:
   A   −0.8492.
   B   −0.0922.
   C   −0.0481.

4. The appraisal ratio is the ratio of the portfolio's alpha to the standard deviation of its:
   A   total risk.
   B   systematic risk.
   C   non-systematic risk.

5. Assume a target return of 3.0%. Annual returns over the past four years have been 6.0%, −3.0%, 7.0%, and 1.0%. The target semi-standard deviation is closest to:
   A   1.33%.

B   3.16%.

C   4.65%.

Solution to 1:

C is correct.

$$\widehat{SR}_D = \frac{\bar{r}_p - \bar{r}_T}{\hat{\sigma}_D} = \frac{0.10 - 0.03}{0.08} = 0.88$$

Solution to 2:

D is correct, because the Sortino ratio is more relevant when return distributions are not symmetrical, as with option writing. The Sortino ratio is also preferable when one of the primary objectives is capital preservation.

Solution to 3:

B is correct. Jensen's alpha is –1.0%: $\alpha_p = 9.0\% - [3.0\% + 1.40(8.0\% - 3.0\%)] = -1.0\% = -0.01$. Non-systematic risk is 0.011776: $\sigma^2_{\varepsilon_p} = 0.20^2 - 1.40^2(0.12^2) = 0.011776$. The appraisal ratio is approximately –0.0922: $\widehat{AR} = \frac{-0.01}{\sqrt{0.011776}} = -0.0922$.

Solution to 4:

C is correct. The appraisal ratio is the ratio of the portfolio's alpha to the standard deviation of the portfolio's non-systematic risk. Essentially, this ratio allows an investor to evaluate whether excess returns warrant the additional non-systematic risk in actively managed portfolios.

Solution to 5:

B is correct.

Year	Rate of Return: r_t	Target Return: $r_T = 3\%$ $\min(r_t - r_T, 0)^2$
1	6.0%	0
2	–3.0%	0.0036
3	7.0%	0
4	1.0%	0.0004
	$\sum_{t=1}^{N} \min(r_t - r_T, 0)^2 =$	0.004

$$\hat{\sigma}_D = \left[\frac{\sum_{t=1}^{N} \min(r_t - r_T, 0)^2}{N}\right]^{1/2} = \left(\frac{0.004}{4}\right)^{1/2} \approx 0.0316 = 3.16\%$$

11 PERFORMANCE APPRAISAL: CAPTURE RATIOS AND DRAWDOWNS

n calculate and interpret the Sortino ratio, the appraisal ratio, upside/downside capture ratios, maximum drawdown, and drawdown duration

o describe limitations of appraisal measures and related metrics

In investing, we understand that large losses require proportionally greater gains to reverse or offset. Performance measures used to monitor this aspect of manager performance include capture ratios and drawdowns. Capture ratios have several variations that reflect various aspects of the manager's gain or loss relative to the gain or loss of the benchmark. Capture ratios also help assess manager suitability relative to the investor, especially in relation to the investor's time horizon and risk tolerance. **Drawdown** is the loss in value incurred in any continuous period of negative returns. A manager who experiences larger drawdowns may be less suitable for an investor with a shorter time horizon. This section reviews capture ratios and drawdowns, their implications for performance, and their use in evaluating manager performance and suitability.

11.1 Capture Ratios

Capture ratios measure the manager's participation in up and down markets—that is, the manager's percentage return relative to that of the benchmark. The upside capture ratio, or upside capture (UC), measures capture when the benchmark return is positive. The downside capture ratio, or downside capture (DC), measures capture when the benchmark return is negative. Upside capture greater (less) than 100% generally suggests outperformance (underperformance) relative to the benchmark, and downside capture less (greater) than 100% generally suggests outperformance (underperformance) relative to the benchmark. Practitioners should note that when the manager and benchmark returns are of the opposite sign, the ratio will be negative—for example, a manager with a 1% return when the market is down 1% will have a downside capture ratio of −100%.

The expressions for upside capture and downside capture are

$UC(m,B,t) = R(m,t)/R(B,t)$ if $R(B,t) \geq 0$

$DC(m,B,t) = R(m,t)/R(B,t)$ if $R(B,t) < 0$

where

$UC(m,B,t)$ = upside capture for manager m relative to benchmark B for time t
$DC(m,B,t)$ = downside capture for manager m relative to benchmark B for time t
$R(m,t)$ = return of manager m for time t
$R(B,t)$ = return of benchmark B for time t

The upside/downside capture, or simply the capture ratio (CR), is the upside capture divided by the downside capture. It measures the asymmetry of return and, as such, is like bond convexity and option gamma. A capture ratio greater than 1 indicates positive asymmetry, or a convex return profile, whereas a capture ratio less than 1 indicates negative asymmetry, or a concave return profile. Exhibit 17 illustrates what is meant by concave and convex return profiles. The dotted-line curve for a concave return profile resembles a downward-facing bowl, and the solid-line curve for a convex return profile resembles an upward-facing bowl. The horizontal and vertical axes are, respectively, benchmark returns [$R(B)$] and portfolio returns [$R(m)$]. As benchmark returns increase (i.e., moving to the right on the horizontal axis), portfolio returns increase—but at a *decreasing* rate for a concave return profile and at an *increasing* rate for a convex return profile. The expression for the capture ratio is

$$CR(m,B,t) = UC(m,B,t)/DC(m,B,t)$$

where

$CR(m,B,t)$ = capture ratio for manager m relative to benchmark B for time t

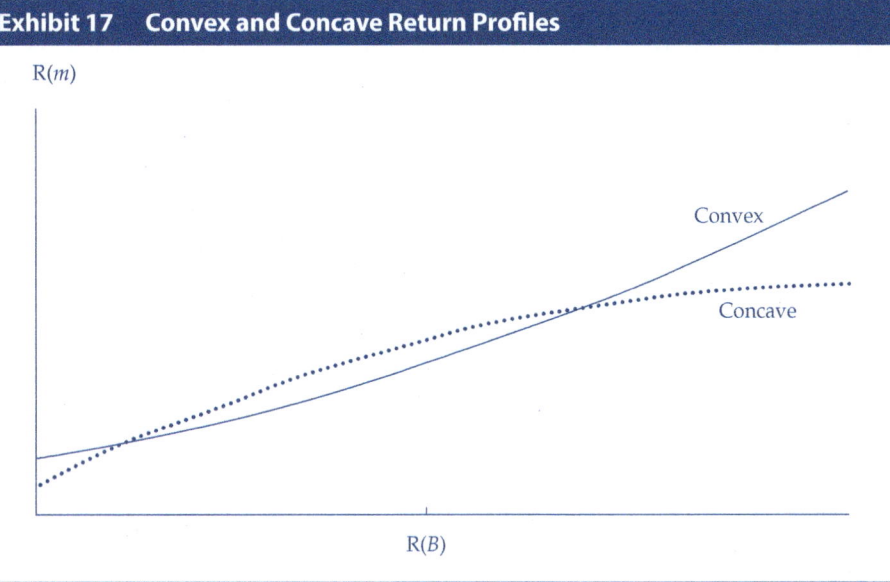

Exhibit 17 Convex and Concave Return Profiles

Consider the following return series for the manager, $R(m)$, and the benchmark, $R(B)$, shown in Exhibit 18. The upside columns calculate the cumulative return for the manager, Cum $R(m)$, and the benchmark, Cum $R(B)$, for those periods when the benchmark return is positive. The downside columns calculate the cumulative returns when the benchmark return is negative.

Exhibit 18 Capture Ratio

			Upside Return				Downside Return			
t	R(m)	R(B)	R(m)	R(B)	Cum R(m)	Cum R(B)	R(m)	R(B)	Cum R(m)	Cum R(B)
1	0.6%	1.0%	0.6%	1.0%	0.60%	1.00%			0.00%	0.00%
2	−0.3%	−0.5%			0.60%	1.00%	−0.3%	−0.5%	−0.30%	−0.50%
3	1.0%	1.5%	1.0%	1.5%	1.61%	2.52%			−0.30%	−0.50%
4	0.1%	0.2%	0.1%	0.2%	1.71%	2.72%			−0.30%	−0.50%
5	−1.0%	−2.0%			1.71%	2.72%	−1.0%	−2.0%	−1.30%	−2.49%
6	0.5%	0.6%	0.5%	0.6%	2.22%	3.34%			−1.30%	−2.49%
7	0.2%	0.1%	0.2%	0.1%	2.42%	3.44%			−1.30%	−2.49%
8	−0.8%	−1.0%			2.42%	3.44%	−0.8%	−1.0%	−2.09%	−3.47%
9	0.8%	1.0%	0.8%	1.0%	3.24%	4.47%			−2.09%	−3.47%
10	0.4%	0.5%	0.4%	0.5%	3.65%	5.00%			−2.09%	−3.47%
Geometric average			0.51%	0.70%			−0.70%	−1.17%		

(continued)

Exhibit 18 (Continued)

			Upside Return				Downside Return			
t	R(m)	R(B)	R(m)	R(B)	Cum R(m)	Cum R(B)	R(m)	R(B)	Cum R(m)	Cum R(B)
Upside capture			0.51%/0.70% = 72.8%				Downside capture		−0.70%/−1.17% = 59.8%	
Capture ratio			72.8%/59.8% = 121.7%							

During up markets, the geometric average return is 0.51% for the manager and 0.70% for the benchmark, giving an upside capture of 72.8%. During down markets, the geometric average return is −0.70% for the manager and −1.17% for the benchmark, giving a downside capture of 59.8%. The manager's capture ratio is 1.217, or 121.7%. Exhibit 19 shows a graph of the cumulative upside and downside returns.

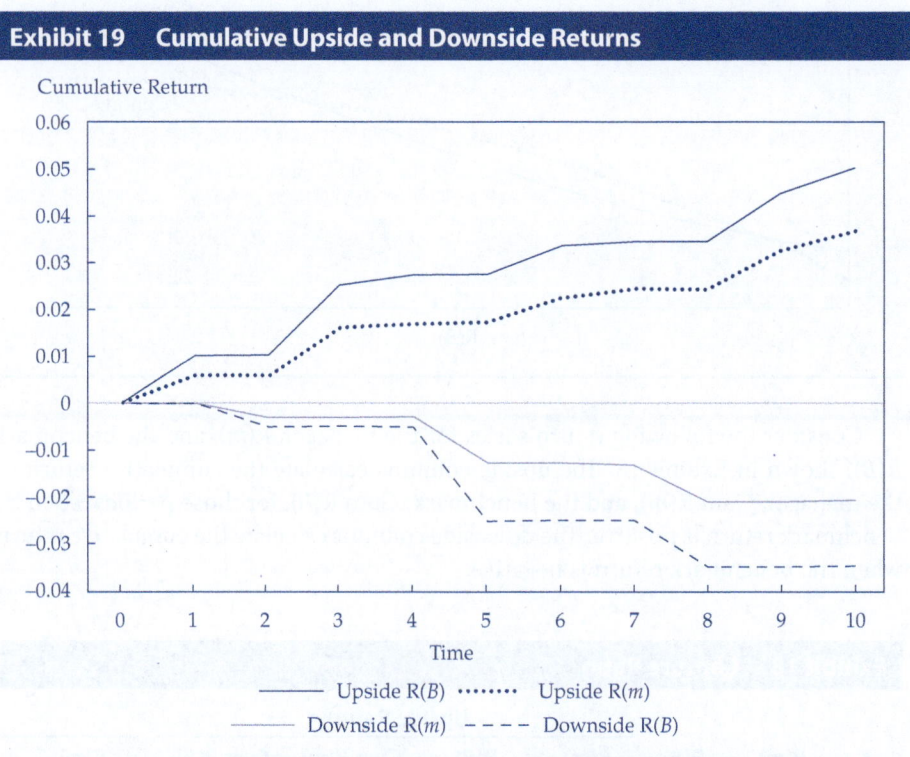

Exhibit 19 Cumulative Upside and Downside Returns

11.2 Drawdown

Drawdown is measured as the cumulative peak-to-trough loss during a continuous period. Drawdown duration is the total time from the start of the drawdown until the cumulative drawdown recovers to zero, which can be segmented into the drawdown phase (start to trough) and the recovery phase (trough-to-zero cumulative return).

$$\text{Maximum DD}(m,t) = \min([V(m,t) - V(m,t^*)]/V(m,t^*), 0)$$

where

$V(m,t)$ = portfolio value of manager m at time t
$V(m,t^*)$ = peak portfolio value of manager m
$t > t^*$

Consider the return on the S&P 500 Index from January 2011 to February 2012, shown in Exhibits 20 and 21. The drawdown is 0% until May 2011, when the return is –1.13% and the drawdown continues to grow, reaching a maximum of –16.26% in September 2011. The strong returns from October 2011 to February 2012 reverse the drawdown. The total duration of the drawdown was 10 months, with a 5-month recovery period.

Exhibit 20	Drawdown				
Month	R(m)	Cumulative R(m)	Drawdown	Cumulative Drawdown	
January 2011	2.37%	2.37%		0.00%	
February 2011	3.43%	5.88%		0.00%	
March 2011	0.04%	5.92%		0.00%	
April 2011	2.96%	9.06%		0.00%	
May 2011	–1.13%	7.83%	–1.13%	–1.13%	Drawdown begins
June 2011	–1.67%	6.03%	–1.67%	–2.78%	
July 2011	–2.03%	3.87%	–2.03%	–4.75%	
August 2011	–5.43%	–1.77%	–5.43%	–9.93%	
September 2011	–7.03%	–8.67%	–7.03%	–16.26%	Maximum drawdown
October 2011	10.93%	1.31%		–7.11%	Recovery begins
November 2011	–0.22%	1.09%	–0.22%	–7.31%	
December 2011	1.02%	2.12%		–6.36%	
January 2012	4.48%	6.69%		–2.17%	
February 2012	4.32%	11.30%		0.00%	Drawdown recovered

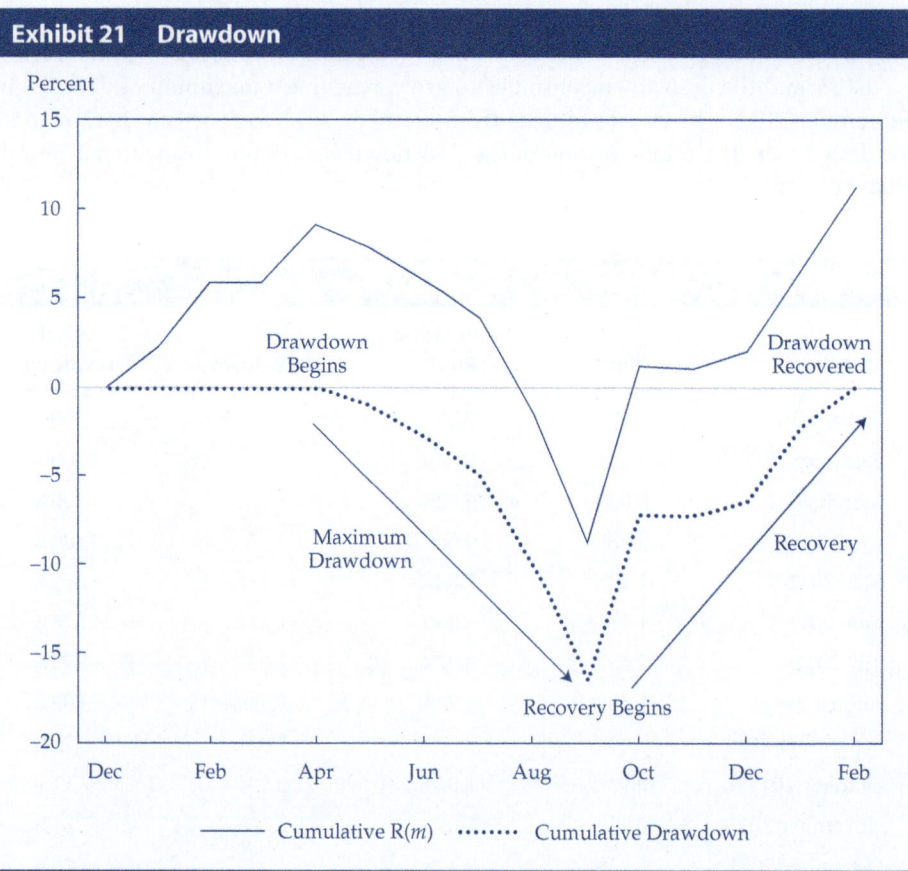

Exhibit 21 Drawdown

An asymmetrical return profile or avoiding large drawdowns, particularly during periods when the market is not trending strongly upward, can result in higher risk-adjusted returns. The reason is the all-too-familiar reality for investors that it takes proportionally larger gains to recover from increasingly large losses. This asymmetry arises from basis drift, from the change in the denominator when calculating returns, or from the practical problem of recovering from a smaller asset base after a large loss. For example, a portfolio decline of 50% must be followed by a gain of 100% to return to its previous value. Exhibit 22 illustrates this relationship.

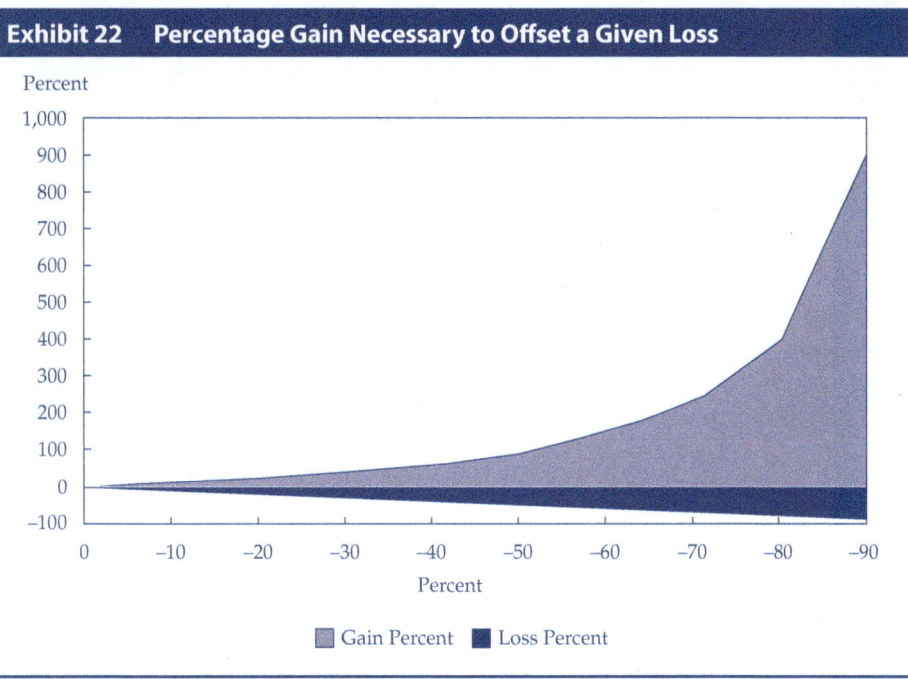

Exhibit 22 Percentage Gain Necessary to Offset a Given Loss

To further illustrate, consider the four return profiles with different upside and downside capture ratios shown in Exhibit 23.

Exhibit 23 Return Profile Summary

Profile	Upside Capture	Downside Capture	Ratio
Long only	100%	100%	1.0
Positive asymmetry	75%	25%	3.0
Low beta	50%	50%	1.0
Negative asymmetry	25%	75%	0.3

We designed these four trading strategies to illustrate the potential effects of the capture ratio and drawdown on return performance and to highlight why understanding the capture ratio and drawdown is important for manager selection.[8] Each strategy's allocation to the S&P 500 Total Return (TR) Index and to 90-day T-bills (assuming monthly rebalancing to simplify the calculations) is based on the realized monthly return from January 2000 to December 2013. (We chose this time period to illustrate the need to examine the asymmetry in a strategy's returns specifically because it encompasses the extreme drawdown of 2008–2009.)

- The long-only profile is 100% allocated to the S&P 500 throughout the period.
- The low-beta profile is allocated 50% to the S&P 500 throughout the period.

---

8 If the market return is known beforehand, the correct strategy is to allocate 100% to the S&P 500 Total Return (TR) Index in up months and 100% to 90-day T-bills in down months (or –100% S&P 500 TR Index if shorting is allowed).

- The positive asymmetry profile is allocated 75% to the S&P 500 for months when the S&P 500 return is positive and 25% when the S&P 500 return is negative.
- The negative asymmetry profile is allocated 25% to the S&P 500 for months when the S&P 500 return is positive and 75% when the S&P 500 return is negative.

The remainder for all profiles is allocated to 90-day T-bills. Exhibit 24 shows each profile's cumulative monthly return for the period.

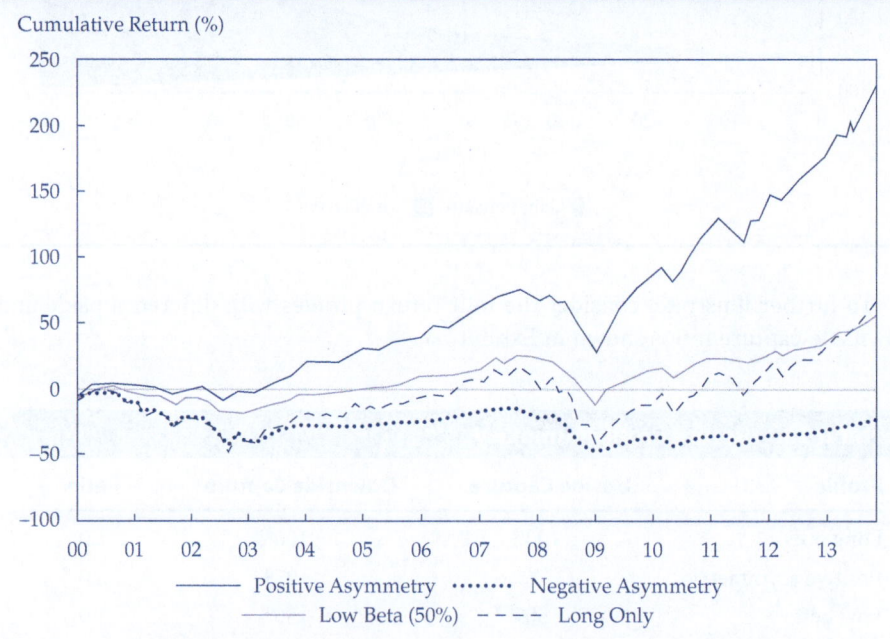

Exhibit 24 Each Profile's Cumulative Monthly Return, January 2000–December 2013

Exhibit 25 provides summary statistics for each profile based on monthly returns from January 2000 to December 2013. Although the long-only profile outperformed the low-beta profile, this outperformance resulted from the strong up market of 2013. The low-beta profile outperformed the long-only profile for most of the period, with lower realized volatility and higher risk-adjusted returns during the entire period. The low-beta profile declined only 18.8%, compared with the long-only decline of 42.5%, from January 2000 to September 2002. As a result, the low-beta profile had higher cumulative performance from January 2000 to October 2007 despite markedly lagging the long-only profile (56.0% to 108.4%) from October 2002 to October 2007.

Although a low-beta approach may sacrifice performance, it shows that limiting drawdowns can result in better absolute and risk-adjusted returns in certain markets. Not surprisingly, positive asymmetry results in better performance relative to long only, low beta, and negative asymmetry. Although the positive asymmetry profile lags in up markets, this lag is more than offset by the lower participation in down markets. Not surprisingly, the negative asymmetry profile lags, with lower participation in up markets insufficient to offset the greater participation in down markets.

Exhibit 25 Summary Statistics for Each Profile, January 2000–December 2013

Strategy	Long Only	Low Beta	Positive Asymmetry	Negative Asymmetry
Cumulative return	64.0%	54.2%	228.1%	−24.4%
Annualized return	3.60%	3.14%	8.86%	−1.98%
Annualized standard deviation	15.64%	7.79%	9.61%	10.01%
Sharpe ratio	0.10	0.14	0.71	−0.40
Beta	1.00	0.50	0.61	0.64
Drawdown (maximum)	−50.9%	−28.3%	−26.9%	−48.9%

Although positive asymmetry is a desirable trait, only some strategies are convex. We need to understand the strategy and how the return profile is created, particularly whether the strategy is inherently convex or whether convexity relies on manager skill. For example, a hedging strategy implemented by rolling forward out-of-the-money put options will typically return many small losses because more options expire worthless than are compensated for by the occasional large gain during a large market downturn. This strategy will likely exhibit consistent positive asymmetry because it depends more on the nature of the strategy than on investment skill.

We should also evaluate the consistency between the stated investment process and reported investment performance. An inconsistency could indicate issues with the strategy's repeatability and implementation or more serious reporting and compliance concerns. Capture ratios can be useful in evaluating consistency issues. We also need to understand the strategy's robustness and potential risks. For example, the expected benefits of diversification—in particular, mitigating downside capture—might not be realized in a crisis if correlations converge toward 1.

Manager responses to a large drawdown provide evidence of the robustness and repeatability of the investment, portfolio construction, and risk management processes, as well as insight into the people implementing the processes. This information requires an understanding of the source of the drawdown and the potential principal–agent risk, operational risk, and business risk that it entails. Drawdowns are stress tests of the investment process and provide a natural point to evaluate and improve processes, which is particularly true of firm-specific drawdowns.

As noted, practitioners should also consider investment horizon and its relationship with risk capacity. An investor closer to retirement, with less time to recover from losses, places more emphasis on absolute measures of risk. In addition, even if the manager maintains her discipline during a large drawdown, the investor may not. This dynamic arises if the investor's perception of risk is path dependent or the drawdown changes risk tolerance. If there has been no change to investment policy and no change in the view that the manager remains suitable, the temptation to exit should be resisted to avoid exiting at an inauspicious time. Investors with shorter horizons, with lower risk capacity, or who are prone to overreact to losses may bias selection toward managers with shallower and shorter expected drawdowns.

EXAMPLE 13

Capture Ratios and Drawdown

1. Do losses require proportionally greater gains to reverse or offset? Choose the best response.

   A Yes, because in investing, it is easier to lose than to gain.

   B No, gains should reflect losses.

   C Yes, because we calculate percentage gains/losses on the basis of the starting amount of portfolio holdings.

2.

t	R(m) (%)	R(B) (%)
1	−3.06	−3.60
2	6.32	3.10
3	6.00	6.03
4	3.21	1.58
5	−9.05	−7.99
6	−4.09	−5.23
7	4.34	7.01
8	−5.72	−4.51
9	12.76	8.92
10	5.38	3.81
11	0.33	0.01
12	5.68	6.68

Using the return information in the table above, what is the manager's downside capture ratio?

   A 103%

   B 108%

   C 115%

Solution to 1:

C is the correct response. If the denominator of the gain calculation is lower, a higher percentage gain is required to offset the loss. For example, if you lose 10% of $100, your new holding is $90. To earn back the $10 loss, you must earn 10/90, or 11%. A is not correct because the "ease" of gaining or losing is not relevant. B is not correct because proportionally higher gains are required.

Solution to 2:

A is the correct answer. See the table below.

| t | R(m) | R(B) | Upside Return | | | | Downside Return | | | |
			R(m)	R(B)	Cum R(m)	Cum R(B)	R(m)	R(B)	Cum R(m)	Cum R(B)
1	−3.06%	−3.60%			0.00%	0.00%	−3.06%	−3.60%	−3.06%	−3.60%
2	6.32%	3.10%	6.32%	3.10%	6.32%	3.10%			−3.06%	−3.60%
3	6.00%	6.03%	6.00%	6.03%	12.70%	9.32%			−3.06%	−3.60%
4	3.21%	1.58%	3.21%	1.58%	16.32%	11.04%			−3.06%	−3.60%
5	−9.05%	−7.99%			16.32%	11.04%	−9.05%	−7.99%	−11.83%	−11.30%

			Upside Return				Downside Return			
t	R(m)	R(B)	R(m)	R(B)	Cum R(m)	Cum R(B)	R(m)	R(B)	Cum R(m)	Cum R(B)
6	-4.09%	-5.23%			16.32%	11.04%	-4.09%	-5.23%	-15.44%	-15.94%
7	4.34%	7.01%	4.34%	7.01%	21.36%	18.83%			-15.44%	-15.94%
8	-5.72%	-4.51%			21.36%	18.83%	-5.72%	-4.51%	-20.28%	-19.73%
9	12.76%	8.92%	12.76%	8.92%	36.85%	29.43%			-20.28%	-19.73%
10	5.38%	3.81%	5.38%	3.81%	44.21%	34.36%			-20.28%	-19.73%
11	0.33%	0.01%	0.33%	0.01%	44.69%	34.37%			-20.28%	-19.73%
12	5.68%	6.68%	5.68%	6.68%	52.91%	43.35%			-20.28%	-19.73%
Geometric average			5.45%	4.60%			-5.51%	-5.35%		
Upside capture			5.45%/4.60% = 118%				Downside capture		-5.51%/-5.35% = 103%	
Capture ratio			118%/103% = 115%							

EVALUATION OF INVESTMENT MANAGER SKILL

12

p   evaluate the skill of an investment manager

Using the tools and principles of performance evaluation presented in this reading, this section presents a specific case to use those tools in an evaluation of manager skill.

For this section, we will consider the case of Manager A, benchmarked against the MSCI Pacific Index. Drawing from the previous sections in this reading, we compiled sample data to evaluate the skill of Manager A. For simplicity of analysis and presentation, we exclude the impact from currency.

Over a five-year period, Manager A's performance is 9.42%, versus the benchmark performance of 9.25%. So, we know that the manager added 17 bps (9.42 – 9.25) of outperformance. But did the manager earn the 17 bps through skill, or was she the beneficiary of luck?

To further evaluate the outperformance, we turn to the tools presented throughout this reading. We include a sample attribution analysis to tell us how the outperformance was achieved. We then use appraisal ratio analysis to compare Manager A's performance to other managers during the same period. Combining the analyses helps present a more balanced assessment of the manager's skill.

12.1 Performance Attribution Analysis

Attribution analysis, as we have shown, is one of the most important tools for evaluating manager skill. Attribution will tell us how the outperformance was achieved, distinguishing the stock selection from country allocation. In the Exhibit 26, we present the sample attribution analysis (for simplicity, we have combined the interaction effect with stock selection).

Exhibit 26 Sample Attribution Analysis

	Manager A		MSCI Pacific		Attribution Effects		
Market	Weight	5-Year Return	Weight	5-Year Return	Allocation	Selection + Interaction	Total
Japan	51.0%	12.40%	60.5%	11.48%	−0.21%	0.47%	0.26%
Australia	30.0%	5.12%	25.4%	4.10%	−0.24%	0.31%	0.07%
Hong Kong SAR	15.0%	8.90%	10.0%	10.08%	0.04%	−0.18%	−0.14%
Singapore	3.5%	5.10%	3.0%	5.38%	−0.02%	−0.01%	−0.03%
New Zealand	0.5%	8.75%	1.0%	9.08%	0.00%	0.00%	0.00%
Total	100%	9.42%	100%	9.25%	−0.43%	0.59%	0.17%

Using this analysis, let us consider the impacts of country allocation weights versus the benchmark weights. Overall, the portfolio manager lost 43 bps of performance as a result of allocation decisions. Specifically, the manager's decision to overweight Australia (30% to 25%) lost 24 bps, because Australia underperformed the total MSCI Pacific benchmark (4.10% versus 9.25%). In addition, the decision to underweight Japan (51% to 60%) lost 21 bps, because Japan outperformed the total benchmark (12.4% versus 9.25%). With this attribution analysis, we can say the manager did not make good weighting decisions over the five-year period.

Now, let us consider the impact from the manager's stock selection decisions. Overall, the portfolio manager gained 59 bps of performance from stock selection decisions. Specifically, the manager added 47 bps through selecting Japanese stocks and 31 bps from selecting Australian stocks. Stock selection in Hong Kong SAR was not as successful, where the manager lost 18 bps.

Overall, we can conclude from the attribution analysis that the manager is a good stock picker, especially for Japanese and Australian stocks. But the manager has not been as successful in choosing the markets to allocate assets. We infer these conclusions on the basis of an analysis of the manager's performance attribution over a five-year period. To better evaluate the manager's performance, we need to understand the risk incurred to achieve that performance. For that risk assessment, we will consider Manager A relative to other managers, using a sample appraisal ratio analysis over the same five-year period.

12.2 Appraisal Measures

As described previously, appraisal analysis uses techniques to review past periods of performance and risk. Consider the sample results presented in Exhibit 27. For the same five-year period, we have calculated a set of performance appraisal measures for Manager A, presented previously, as well as two other managers with the same benchmark over the same period, Managers B and C.

Exhibit 27 Sample Analysis Using Various Appraisal Measures

	Appraisal Measures			
	Manager A	Manager B	Manager C	Benchmark
Annualized return	9.42	8.23	10.21	9.25
Annualized std. dev.	10.83	8.10	12.34	9.76
Sharpe ratio	0.68	0.76	0.66	0.73

Exhibit 27 (Continued)

	Appraisal Measures			
	Manager A	**Manager B**	**Manager C**	**Benchmark**
Treynor ratio	0.35	0.32	0.19	0.57
Information ratio	0.43	0.41	0.30	0.00
Sortino ratio (MAR = 3%)	0.82	0.51	1.03	0.97

In considering this historical analysis, note that Manager A has a higher volatility of returns than the benchmark (manager standard deviation of 10.83 versus benchmark standard deviation of 9.76). This volatility is greater than that for Manager B (8.10) but is less than that for Manager C (12.34). In general, Manager A's return is slightly more volatile—riskier—than the benchmark's and slightly more and less volatile than that of Managers B and C, respectively.

This consistency is demonstrated in the Sharpe ratio measurement as well. Recall that the Sharpe ratio indicates the amount of performance earned over a risk-free proxy per unit of risk. In this assessment, Manager A's Sharpe ratio is less than the benchmark's Sharpe ratio (0.68 versus 0.73) and less than Manager B's Sharpe ratio (0.76). Thus, for this period, we know Manager A certainly incurred more risk than the benchmark and Manager B did for the same amount of return generated. Is the manager incurring too much risk for the return generated? To answer this question, we should consider some of the other appraisal measures as well.

Unlike the Sharpe ratio, the Treynor ratio measures the return earned per unit of *systematic* risk. The information ratio indicates how well the manager has performed relative to the benchmark, *after accounting for the differences in the volatility of the portfolio and the benchmark*. Given that Manager A has the highest Treynor and information ratios for this period, she has been able to produce a higher return relative to systematic risk. In addition, consider her Sortino ratio of 0.82, not significantly higher than the Sharpe ratio, but again indicative of an ability to generate higher returns relative to downside risk (where the target is 3%).

12.3 Sample Evaluation of Skill

In summary, the analysis based on these appraisal measures supports the conclusion generated by the performance attribution analysis that Manager A has been able to generate excess return over the benchmark through stock selection. She has done so without incurring significant excess risk relative to the benchmark and two similar managers. Therefore, within the limits of these analyses, Manager A has exhibited some level of skill worthy of further analysis.

The analysis does not, however, help us evaluate the country allocation conclusions of our attribution analysis. We know that the manager made incorrect bets in Japan and Australia. What beliefs about country selection are embedded in her investment philosophy? Are country allocations an integral part of her investment approach, or are they a by-product of her stock selection? Answers to these questions will help us determine whether our assessment of skill should be penalized by the poor outcomes of the country selection decisions in this period.

It is important to recognize that our analysis encompasses only a small sample of the possible outcomes that are not necessarily indicative of future outcomes. A long track record is necessary to have any statistical certainty in a conclusion of skill or no skill. Practitioners will want to conduct additional analyses to increase their confidence in their conclusions. These additional studies could include some of the other tools presented in this reading, such as risk attribution or *ex ante* analyses. In addition, practitioners will want to include qualitative analyses of the manager (e.g., direct interviews with management to assess abilities), assessment of investment goals and management fees, and so on. In the end, we must understand and acknowledge the limits of all tools, being careful to qualify any conclusions regarding investment skill with the appropriate level of prudence.

> **EXAMPLE 14**
>
> ### Investment Manager Skill
>
> Use the examples in Exhibits 26 and 27 to help answer the following questions.
>
> 1 Which statement *best* describes Manager A's performance during this five-year period?
>   - **A** On an absolute basis, Manager A performed better than either Manager B or Manager C.
>   - **B** Relative to systematic risk, Manager A performed better than either Manager B or Manager C.
>   - **C** Manager C incurred the least risk.
> 2 Which of the following *best* provides evidence of manager skill?
>   - **A** Security selection attribution effect of 47 bps
>   - **B** Annualized performance equal to 9.42%
>   - **C** Annualized standard deviation equal to 12.34%
> 3 How can a practitioner *best* distinguish manager skill from luck?
>   - **A** Run thousands of analyses of the same manager over an extended period.
>   - **B** Avoid making broad-based judgments without statistical evidence.
>   - **C** Use multiple analysis tools to jointly infer conclusions, sensitive to the limits of those tools.
>
> ### Solution to 1:
>
> B is correct. The Treynor ratio measures performance relative to systematic risk. Manager A's Treynor ratio was better than that of both Manager B and Manager C for the period. A is not correct because Manager A's return for the period was less than Manager C's return. C is not correct because Manager C's annualized standard deviation (volatility) was highest.
>
> ### Solution to 2:
>
> A is correct. Performance attribution can be indicative of manager skill, especially over longer historical time periods. Neither B nor C is correct because neither performance nor standard deviation, on their own, is necessarily indicative of manager skill.
>
> ### Solution to 3:
>
> C is correct. Practitioners should use multiple analyses with different tools to find multiple sources that agree on evidence of skill. A is not correct, because thousands of analyses, especially the same types of analyses, may not necessarily lead to more conclusive results. B is not correct because it states best practice but not necessarily techniques to distinguish skill from luck.

SUMMARY

Performance evaluation is an essential tool for understanding the quality of the investment process. Practitioners must take care, however, to understand how performance results are generated. They need a good understanding of the performance methods used, the data inputs, and the limitations of those methods. They particularly need to be careful not to infer results beyond the capabilities of the methods or the accuracy of the data. In this reading, we have discussed the following:

- Performance measurement provides an overall indication of the portfolio's performance.
- Performance attribution builds on performance measurement to explain how the performance was achieved.
- Performance appraisal leverages both returns and attribution to infer the quality of the investment process.
- An effective attribution process must reconcile to the total portfolio return/risk, reflect the investment decision-making process, quantify the active portfolio management decisions, and provide a complete understanding of the excess return/risk of the portfolio.
- Return attribution analyzes the impact of investment decisions on the returns, whereas risk attribution analyzes the risk consequences of the investment decisions.
- Macro attribution considers the decisions of the fund sponsor, whereas micro attribution considers the decisions of the individual portfolio manager.
- Returns-based attribution uses returns to identify the factors that have generated those returns.
- Holdings-based attribution uses the holdings over time to evaluate the decisions that contributed to the returns.
- Transactions-based attribution uses both holdings and transactions to fully explain the performance over the evaluation period.
- There are various techniques for interpreting the sources of portfolio returns using a specified attribution approach.
- Fixed-income attribution considers the unique factors that drive bond returns, including interest rate risk and default risk.
- When selecting a risk attribution approach, practitioners should consider the investment decision-making process and the type of attribution analysis.
- Attribution is used to calculate and interpret the contribution to portfolio return and volatility from the asset allocation and within-asset-class active/passive decisions.
- Liability-based benchmarks focus on the cash flows that the assets are required to generate.
- Asset-based benchmarks contain a collection of assets to compare against the portfolio's assets.
- Valid benchmarks should be unambiguous, investable, measurable, appropriate, reflective of current investment opinions, specified in advance, and accountable.
- Benchmark misspecification creates subsequent incorrect performance measurement and invalidates the attribution and appraisal analyses.

- Alternative investments are difficult to benchmark because they are typically less liquid, have fewer available market benchmarks, and often lack transparency.
- Investment performance appraisal ratios—including the Sortino ratio, upside/downside capture ratios, maximum drawdown, and drawdown duration—measure investment skill.
- Appraisal ratios must be used with care, noting the assumptions of each ratio and affording the appropriateness to the measured investment process, risk tolerance, and investor time horizon.
- Although appraisal ratios help identify manager skill (as opposed to luck), they often are based on investment return data, which are often limited and subject to error.
- Evaluation of investment manager skill requires the use of a broad range of analysis tools, with fundamental understanding of how the tools work, how they complement each other, and their specific limitations.

REFERENCES

Bailey, Jeffery V., and David E. Tierney. 1998. *Controlling Misfit Risk in Multiple-Manager Investment Programs.* Charlottesville, VA: Research Foundation of CFA Institute.

Bailey, Jeffery V., Thomas M. Richards, and David Tierney. 2007. "Evaluating Portfolio Performance." In *Managing Investment Portfolios: A Dynamic Process.* 3rd ed., ed. Maginn, John, Donald Tuttle, Dennis McLeavey, and Jerald Pinto. Hoboken, NJ: John Wiley & Sons.

Brinson, Gary, and Nimrod Fachler. 1985. "Measuring Non-US Equity Portfolio Performance." *Journal of Portfolio Management* 11 (5): 73–76.

Brinson, Gary, Randolph Hood, and Gilbert Beebower. 1986. "Determinants of Portfolio Performance." *Financial Analysts Journal* 42 (4): 39–44.

Brown, Stephen, and William Goetzmann. 1997. "Mutual Fund Styles." *Journal of Financial Economics* 43 (3): 373–99.

Carhart, M. M. 1997. "On Persistence in Mutual Fund Performance." *Journal of Finance* 52 (1): 57–82.

Cariño, David. 1999. "Combining Attribution Effects over Time." Summer *Journal of Performance Measurement.*

Gastineau, Gary L., Andrew L. Olma, and Robert G. Zielienski. 2007. "Equity Portfolio Management." In *Managing Investment Portfolios: A Dynamic Process.* 3rd ed., ed. Maginn, John, Donald Tuttle, Dennis McLeavey, and Jerald Pinto. Hoboken, NJ: John Wiley & Sons.

Giguère, C. 2005. "Thinking through Fixed Income Attribution—Reflections from a Group of French Practitioners." *Journal of Performance Measurement* (Summer): 46–65.

Khandani, Amir E., and Andrew W. Lo. 2011. "What Happened to the Quants in August 2007? Evidence from Factors and Transactions Data." *Journal of Financial Markets*, 14 (1): 1–46.

Menchero, Jose. 2000. "An Optimized Approach to Linking Attribution Effects over Time." Fall *Journal of Performance Measurement.*

Murira, Bernard, and Hector Sierra. 2006. "Fixed Income Attribution: A United Framework—Part 1." *Journal of Performance Measurement* 11 (1): 23–35.

Treynor, J. 1965. "How to Rate Management of Investment Funds." *Harvard Business Review* 43 (1): 63–75.

Treynor, J., and F. Black. 1973. "How to Use Security Analysis to Improve Portfolio Selection." *Journal of Business* 46 (1): 66–86.

PRACTICE PROBLEMS

The following information relates to Questions 1–5

Alexandra Jones, a senior adviser at Federalist Investors (FI), meets with Erin Bragg, a junior analyst. Bragg just completed a monthly performance evaluation for an FI fixed-income manager. Bragg's report addresses the three primary components of performance evaluation: measurement, attribution, and appraisal. Jones asks Bragg to describe an effective attribution process. Bragg responds as follows:

Response 1: Performance attribution draws conclusions regarding the quality of a portfolio manager's investment decisions.

Response 2: Performance attribution should help explain how performance was achieved by breaking apart the return or risk into different explanatory components.

Bragg notes that the fixed-income portfolio manager has strong views about the effects of macroeconomic factors on credit markets and follows a top-down investment process.

Jones reviews the monthly performance attribution and asks Bragg whether any risk-adjusted historical performance indicators are available. Bragg produces the following data:

Exhibit 1	10-Year Trailing Risk-Adjusted Performance
Average annual return	8.20%
Minimum acceptable return (MAR)	5.00%
Sharpe ratio	0.95
Sortino ratio	0.87
Upside capture	0.66
Downside capture	0.50
Maximum drawdown	−24.00%
Drawdown duration	4 months

1. Which of Bragg's responses regarding effective performance attribution is correct?
   - A Only Response 1
   - B Only Response 2
   - C Both Response 1 and Response 2

2. The *most appropriate* risk attribution approach for the fixed-income manager is to:
   - A decompose historical returns into a top-down factor framework.
   - B evaluate the marginal contribution to total risk for each position.

© 2019 CFA Institute. All rights reserved.

C   attribute tracking risk to relative allocation and selection decisions.

3 Based on Exhibit 1, the target semideviation for the portfolio is *closest to:*
   A   2.78%.
   B   3.68%.
   C   4.35%.

4 Based on Exhibit 1, the capture ratios of the portfolio indicate:
   A   a concave return profile.
   B   positive asymmetry of returns.
   C   that the portfolio generates higher returns than the benchmark during all market conditions.

5 The maximum drawdown and drawdown duration in Exhibit 1 indicate that:
   A   the portfolio recovered quickly from its maximum loss.
   B   over the 10-year period, the average maximum loss was −24.00%.
   C   a significant loss once persisted for four months before the portfolio began to recover.

The following information relates to Questions 6–14

Stephanie Tolmach is a consultant hired to create a performance attribution report on three funds held by a defined benefit pension plan (the Plan). Fund 1 is a domestic equity strategy, Fund 2 is a global equity strategy, and Fund 3 is a domestic fixed-income strategy.

Tolmach uses three approaches to attribution analysis: the return-based, holdings-based, and transaction-based approaches. The Plan's investment committee asks Tolmach to (1) apply the attribution method that uses only each fund's total portfolio returns over the last 12 months to identify return-generating components of the investment process and (2) include the impact of specific active investment decisions and the attribution effects of allocation and security selection in the report.

Tolmach first evaluates the performance of Fund 1 by constructing a Carhart factor model; the results are presented in Exhibit 1.

Exhibit 1   Fund 1 Factor Model Attribution

	Factor Sensitivity				Contribution to Active Return	
Factor*	Portfolio (1)	Benchmark (2)	Difference (3)	Factor Return (4)	Absolute (3) × (4)	Proportion of Active Return
RMRF	1.22	0.91	0.31	16.32%	5.06%	−126.80%
SMB	0.59	0.68	−0.09	−3.25%	0.29%	−7.33%
HML	−0.17	0.04	−0.21	−9.60%	2.02%	−50.53%
WML	−0.05	0.07	−0.12	3.38%	−0.41%	10.17%
			A. Factor Tilt Return:		6.96%	−174.49%

Practice Problems

Exhibit 1 (Continued)

Factor*	Factor Sensitivity			Factor Return (4)	Contribution to Active Return	
	Portfolio (1)	Benchmark (2)	Difference (3)		Absolute (3) × (4)	Proportion of Active Return
			B. Security Selection:		−10.95%	274.49%
			C. Active Return (A + B):		−3.99%	100.00%

* RMRF is the return on a value-weighted equity index in excess of the one-month T-bill rate, SMB is the small minus big market capitalization factor, HML is the high minus low factor, and WML is the winners minus losers factor.

Tolmach turns her attention to Fund 2, constructing a region-based, Brinson–Fachler micro attribution analysis to evaluate the active decisions of the portfolio manager. The results are presented in Exhibit 2.

Exhibit 2 Fund 2 Performance—Allocation by Region

Return Attribution (Region Level)	Portfolio Weight	Benchmark Weight	Portfolio Return	Benchmark Return
North America	10.84%	7.67%	16.50%	16.47%
Greater Europe	38.92%	42.35%	23.16%	25.43%
Developed Asia and Australasia	29.86%	31.16%	11.33%	12.85%
South America	20.38%	18.82%	20.00%	35.26%
Total	100.00%	100.00%	18.26%	22.67%

Next, Tolmach evaluates Fund 3 and the appropriateness of its benchmark. The benchmark is a cap-weighted bond index with daily reported performance; the index is rebalanced frequently, making it difficult to replicate. The benchmark has a meaningful investment in foreign bonds, whereas Fund 3 invests only in domestic bonds.

In the final section of the report, Tolmach reviews the entire Plan's characteristics, asset allocation, and benchmark. Tolmach observes that the Plan's benefits are no longer indexed to inflation and that the workforce is, on average, younger than it was when the current fund allocations were approved. Tolmach recommends a change in the Plan's asset allocation policy.

6 Of the three attribution approaches referenced by Tolmach, the method requested by the committee:
  A is the least accurate.
  B uses the underlying holdings of the actual portfolio.
  C is the most difficult and time consuming to implement.

7 Based on Exhibit 1 and relative to the benchmark, the manager of Fund 1 *most likely* used a:
  A growth tilt.
  B greater tilt toward small cap.
  C momentum-based investing approach.

8 Based on Exhibit 1, which of the following factors contributed the *least* to active return?
   A HML
   B SMB
   C RMRF

9 Based on Exhibit 1, the manager could have delivered more value to the portfolio during the investment period by weighting more toward:
   A value stocks.
   B small-cap stocks.
   C momentum stocks.

10 Based on Exhibit 2, the allocation effect for South America is *closest* to:
   A −0.04%.
   B 0.03%.
   C 0.20%.

11 Based on Exhibit 2, the decision to overweight or underweight which of the following regions contributed positively to performance at the overall fund level?
   A North America
   B Greater Europe
   C Developed Asia and Australasia

12 Based on Exhibit 2, the underperformance at the overall fund level is predominantly the result of poor security selection decisions in:
   A South America.
   B greater Europe.
   C developed Asia and Australasia.

13 The benchmark for Fund 3 has which of the following characteristics of a valid benchmark?
   A Investable
   B Measurable
   C Appropriate

14 Based on the final section of Tolmach's report, the Plan should use:
   A a liability-based benchmark.
   B an absolute return benchmark.
   C a manager universe benchmark.

SOLUTIONS

1. B is correct. Performance attribution helps explain how performance was achieved; it breaks apart the return or risk into different explanatory components. Effective performance attribution must account for all of the portfolio's return or risk exposure, reflect the investment decision-making process, quantify the active decisions of the portfolio manager, and provide a complete understanding of the excess return/risk of the portfolio.

2. C is correct. The portfolio is managed against a benchmark, which indicates a relative-risk type of risk attribution analysis. For a top-down investment approach, the analysis should attribute tracking risk to allocation and selection decisions relative to the benchmark.

3. B is correct. The target semi-standard deviation or target semideviation is the denominator of the Sortino ratio. The numerator of the Sortino ratio is the average portfolio return minus the target rate of return (minimum acceptable return, or MAR).

$$\text{Sortino ratio} = \frac{(\text{Average portfolio return} - \text{MAR})}{\text{Target semideviation}}$$

Substituting the values provided in Exhibit 3, the target semideviation is as follows:

$$\text{Target semideviation} = \frac{8.20\% - 5.00\%}{0.87}$$
$$= 3.678\% = 3.68\%$$

4. B is correct. The upside/downside capture, or simply the capture ratio (CR), is the upside capture ratio divided by the downside capture ratio.

(Upside capture)/(Downside capture) = 0.66/0.50 = 1.32.

A capture ratio greater than 1 indicates positive asymmetry of returns, or a convex return profile.

5. A is correct. Maximum drawdown is the cumulative peak-to-trough loss during a continuous period. Drawdown duration is the total time from the start of the drawdown until the cumulative drawdown recovers to zero, which can be segmented into the drawdown phase (start to trough) and the recovery phase (trough to zero cumulative return). The maximum drawdown was −24.00%, with a drawdown period of four months. Given the 10-year time frame, the portfolio recovered quickly from its maximum loss.

6. A is correct. The committee described a return-based attribution, which is the least accurate of the three approaches (the return-based, holdings-based, transaction-based approaches). Return-based attribution uses only the total portfolio returns over a period to identify the components of the investment process that have generated the returns.

7. A is correct. Based on the factor sensitivities in column 1 (negative sensitivity of −0.17 to HML) and the differences relative to the benchmark shown in column 3, the manager likely had a growth tilt.

8. B is correct. With an absolute return of 0.29% and with 7.33% of the contribution to return, SMB contributed far less than HML (2.02% and 50.53%, respectively) and RMRF (5.06% and 126.80%, respectively).

9 C is correct. Had the manager weighted more toward momentum stocks during the period, the momentum factor (WML) return of 3.38% would have contributed positively to the portfolio.

A is incorrect because the HML factor return was −9.60%; thus, weighting more toward value stocks would have detracted from portfolio returns.

B is incorrect because the SMB factor return was −3.25%; thus, weighting more toward small-cap stocks would have detracted from portfolio returns.

10 C is correct. The allocation effect for South America is 0.20%.

$$\text{Allocation} = (w_i - W_i)(B_i - B)$$
$$= (20.38\% - 18.82\%)(35.26 - 22.67\%)$$
$$= 0.1964\% = 0.20\%$$

11 C is correct. The decision to underweight developed Asia and Australasia was a good one because the benchmark for this region underperformed the total benchmark (12.85% versus 22.67%). Alternatively, the question can be answered by calculating the allocation effects for the three regions, as follows:

$$\text{Allocation} = (w_i - W_i)(B_i - B)$$
$$\text{North America} = (10.84\% - 7.67\%)(16.47\% - 22.67\%)$$
$$= -0.20\%$$
$$\text{Greater Europe} = (38.92\% - 42.35\%)(25.43\% - 22.67\%)$$
$$= -0.09\%$$
$$\text{Developed Asia and Australasia} = (29.86\% - 31.16\%)(12.85\% - 22.67\%)$$
$$= 0.13\%$$

Developed Asia and Australasia is the only region of the three that had a positive allocation effect.

12 A is correct. The total −441 bps of underperformance from security selection and interaction at the overall fund level is predominantly the result of poor South American security selection decisions (−311 bps = 3.11%).

Return Attribution (Segment Level)	Allocation	Selection + Interaction	Total
North America	−0.1966%	0.0033%	−0.1934%
Greater Europe	−0.0946%	−0.8835%	−0.9781%
Developed Asia and Australasia	0.1277%	−0.4539%	−0.3262%
South America	0.1964%	−3.1100%	−2.9136%
Total	0.0329%	−4.4441%	−4.4112%

$$\text{Allocation} = (w_i - W_i)(B_i - B)$$
$$\text{North America} = (10.84\% - 7.67\%)(16.47\% - 22.67\%)$$
$$= -0.20\%$$
$$\text{Greater Europe} = (38.92\% - 42.35\%)(25.43\% - 22.67\%)$$
$$= -0.09\%$$
$$\text{Developed Asia and Australasia} = (29.86\% - 31.16\%)(12.85\% - 22.67\%)$$
$$= 0.13\%$$
$$\text{South America} = (20.38\% - 18.82\%)(35.26\% - 22.67\%)$$
$$= 0.20\%$$

$$\text{Selection + Interaction} = W_i(R_i - B_i) + (w_i - W_i)(R_i - B_i)$$
$$\text{North America} = 7.67\%(16.50\% - 16.47\%) + (10.84\% - 7.67\%)(16.50\% - 16.47\%)$$
$$= 0.00\%$$

$$\text{Greater Europe} = 42.35\%(23.16\% - 25.43\%) + (38.92\% - 42.35\%)(23.16\% - 25.43\%)$$
$$= -0.88\%$$
$$\text{Developed Asia and Australasia} = 31.16\%(11.33\% - 12.85\%) + (29.86\% - 31.16\%)(11.33\% - 12.85\%)$$
$$= -0.45\%$$
$$\text{South America} = 18.82\%(20.00\% - 35.26\%) + (20.38\% - 18.82\%)(20.00\% - 35.26\%)$$
$$= -3.11\%$$

13. B is correct. Daily reported performance is available for the benchmark; thus, it is possible to measure the benchmark's return on a reasonably frequent and timely basis.

A is incorrect because the benchmark is a cap-weighted bond index that is rebalanced frequently, making it difficult to replicate. For a benchmark to be investable, it must be possible to replicate and hold the benchmark to earn its return (at least gross of expenses). The sponsor should have the option of moving assets from active management to a passive benchmark. If the benchmark is not investable, it is not a viable investment alternative. Bond indexes are often not investable and are rebalanced frequently over time.

C is incorrect because the index has a meaningful investment in foreign bonds, whereas Fund 3 invests only in domestic bonds, making the benchmark inappropriate. The benchmark must be consistent with the manager's investment style or area of expertise.

14. A is correct. Based on the Plan's type (defined benefit) and its characteristics as detailed in the final section of Tolmach's report, a liability-based benchmark is most appropriate. Liability-based benchmarks are used most frequently when assets are required to pay a specific future liability, as in a defined benefit pension plan.

READING
27

Investment Manager Selection

by Jeffrey C. Heisler, PhD, CFA, and Donald W. Lindsey, CFA

Jeffrey C. Heisler, PhD, CFA, is at TwinFocus Capital Partners (USA). Donald W. Lindsey, CFA (USA).

LEARNING OUTCOMES	
Mastery	The candidate should be able to:
☐	a. describe the components of a manager selection process, including due diligence;
☐	b. contrast Type I and Type II errors in manager hiring and continuation decisions;
☐	c. describe uses of returns-based and holdings-based style analysis in investment manager selection;
☐	d. describe uses of the upside capture ratio, downside capture ratio, maximum drawdown, drawdown duration, and up/down capture in evaluating managers;
☐	e. evaluate a manager's investment philosophy and investment decision-making process;
☐	f. evaluate the costs and benefits of pooled investment vehicles and separate accounts;
☐	g. compare types of investment manager contracts, including their major provisions and advantages and disadvantages;
☐	h. describe the three basic forms of performance-based fees;
☐	i. analyze and interpret a sample performance-based fee schedule.

INTRODUCTION 1

Most investors do not hold securities directly but rather invest using intermediaries. Whether the intermediary is a separately managed account or a pooled investment vehicle, such as mutual funds in the United States, unit trusts in the United Kingdom, Undertakings for the Collective Investment of Transferable Securities (UCITS) in the European Union, hedge funds, private equity funds, or exchange-traded funds

© 2020 CFA Institute. All rights reserved.

(ETFs), a professional investment manager is being entrusted with helping investors achieve their investment objectives. In all of these cases, the selection of appropriate investment managers is a challenge with important financial consequences.

Evaluating an investment manager is a complex and detailed process that encompasses a great deal more than analyzing investment returns. The investigation and analysis in support of an investment action, decision, or recommendation is called **due diligence**. In conducting investment manager due diligence, the focus is on understanding how the investment results were achieved and on assessing the likelihood that the investment process that generated these returns will produce superior or at least satisfactory investment results going forward. Due diligence also entails an evaluation of a firm's integrity, operations, and personnel. As such, due diligence involves both quantitative and qualitative analysis.

This reading provides a framework that introduces and describes the important elements of the manager selection process. Although it is important to have a well-defined methodology, this reading is not intended to be a rigid checklist, a step-by-step guide, or an in-depth analysis but rather to present a structure from which the reader can develop their own approach.

We assume that the investment policy statement (IPS) has been drafted, the asset allocation determined, and the decision to use an outside adviser has been made. As a result, the focus is on determining which manager offers the "best" means to implement or express those decisions. The discussion has three broad topics:

- Outlining a framework for identifying, evaluating, and ultimately selecting investment managers (Sections 2 and 3).
- Quantitative considerations in manager selection (Sections 4 and 5).
- Qualitative considerations in manager selection (Sections 6–9).

The reading concludes with a summary of selected important points.

2. A FRAMEWORK FOR INVESTMENT MANAGER SEARCH AND SELECTION

a describe the components of a manager selection process, including due diligence;

An underlying assumption of investment manager due diligence is that a consistent, robust investment process will generate a similar return distribution relative to risk factors through time, assuming the underlying dynamics of the market have not dramatically changed. One important goal of manager due diligence is to understand whether the manager's investment process, people, and portfolio construction satisfy this assumption—that is, will the investment process generate the expected return from the expected sources? The manager search and selection process has three broad components: the universe, a quantitative analysis of the manager's performance track record, and a qualitative analysis of the manager's investment process. The qualitative analysis consists of investment due diligence, which evaluates the manager's investment process, and operational due diligence, which evaluates the manager's infrastructure and firm. Exhibit 1 details these components.

Exhibit 1 Manager Selection Process Overview

Key aspects	Key Question
Universe	
Defining the universe	What is the feasible set of managers that fit the portfolio need?
◻ Suitability	Which managers are suitable for the IPS?
◻ Style	Which have the appropriate style?
◻ Active vs. passive	Which fit the active versus passive decision?
Quantitative Analysis	
Investment due diligence	Which manager "best" fits the portfolio need?
Quantitative	What has been the manager's return distribution?
◻ Attribution and Appraisal	Has the manager displayed skill?
◻ Capture ratio	How does the manager perform in "up" markets versus "down" markets?
◻ Drawdown	Does the return distribution exhibit large drawdowns?
Qualitative Analysis	
Investment due diligence	Which manager "best" fits the portfolio need?
Qualitative	Is the manager expected to continue to generate this return distribution?
◻ Philosophy	What market inefficiency does the manager seek to exploit?
◻ Process	Is the investment process capable of exploiting this inefficiency?
◻ People	Do the investment personnel possess the expertise and experience necessary to effectively implement the investment process?
◻ Portfolio	Is portfolio construction consistent with the stated investment philosophy and process?
Operational due diligence	Is the manager's track record accurate, and does it fully reflect risks?
◻ Process and procedure	Is the back office strong, safeguarding assets and able to issue accurate reports in a timely manner?
◻ Firm	Is the firm profitable, with a healthy culture, and likely to remain in business? Is the firm committed to delivering performance over gathering assets?
◻ Investment vehicle	Is the vehicle suitable for the portfolio need?
◻ Terms	Are the terms acceptable and appropriate for the strategy and vehicle?
◻ Monitoring	Does the manager continue to be the "best" fit for the portfolio need?

> **EXAMPLE 1**
>
> **Components of the Manager Selection Process**
>
> 1 Qualitative analysis of the manager selection process includes:
>   A attribution.
>   B defining the universe.
>   C investment and operational due diligence.
> 2 Which of the following is considered a key aspect of operational due diligence?
>   A People
>   B Philosophy
>   C Procedures
>
> **Solution to 1:**
>
> C is correct. Qualitative analysis consists of investment due diligence, which evaluates the manager's investment process, and operational due diligence, which evaluates the manager's infrastructure and firm.
>
> **Solution to 2:**
>
> C is correct. Process and procedures are key aspects of operational due diligence, whereas people and philosophy are key aspects of investment due diligence.

2.1 Defining the Manager Universe

The manager selection process begins by defining the universe of feasible managers, those managers that potentially satisfy the identified portfolio need. The objective is to reduce the manager universe to a manageable size relative to the resources and time available to evaluate it. This process also involves balancing the risks of too narrow a search, which potentially excludes interesting managers, and too broad a search, which leads to little gain in reducing the list of potential managers. Like many interesting problems, this step is a combination of art and science. In the initial screening process, the search parameters can be narrowed and widened to determine which managers enter and exit and to evaluate whether these additions or deletions improve the universe.

The IPS and the reason for the manager search largely determine the universe of managers considered and the benchmark against which they are compared. A new search based on a strategic or tactical view, such as adding a new strategy or risk exposure, will examine a broad universe of comparable managers and look to select the best within the universe. Adding a manager to increase capacity or diversification within a strategy already held will look for a complement to current holdings. Replacing a single manager in a particular strategy will look for the best manager within the strategy universe. The IPS in part determines what the relative terms "best," "complement," and "cost/benefit" mean.

Typically, a search starts with a benchmark that represents the manager's role within the portfolio. The benchmark also provides a reference for performance attribution and appraisal. There are several approaches to assigning a manager to a benchmark:

- **Third-party categorization:** Database or software providers and consultants typically assign managers to a strategy sector. This categorization provides an easy and efficient way to define the universe. The risk is that the provider's definition may differ from the desired portfolio role. As such, it is important to understand the criteria used by the provider.
- **Returns-based style analysis:** The risk exposures derived from the manager's actual return series has the advantage of being objective. The disadvantage is additional computational effort and the limitations of returns-based analysis.
- **Holdings-based style analysis:** This approach allows for the estimation of current factor exposures but adds to computational effort and depends on timing and amount of transparency.
- **Manager experience:** The assignment can be based on an evaluation of the manager and observations of portfolios and returns over time.

Not surprisingly, a hybrid strategy that combines elements of each approach is recommended. Using third-party categorizations is an efficient way to build an initial universe that can then be complemented and refined with quantitative methods and experience. The screening should avoid using performance at this point. The focus should be on understanding the manager's risk profile and identifying candidates to fill the desired role in the portfolio. Lastly, the universe of potential managers is not static—it will evolve through time not only as manager strategies evolve but also as a result of the entry and exit of managers.

TYPE I AND TYPE II ERRORS IN MANAGER SELECTION

b contrast Type I and Type II errors in manager hiring and continuation decisions;

Certain concepts from the area of inferential statistics known as hypothesis testing can be relevant to the decision to hire an investment manager or to retain or dismiss a manager previously hired.

The determination of whether a manager is skillful typically starts with the null hypothesis (the hypothesis assumed to be true until demonstrated otherwise) that the manager is not skillful. As a result, there are two types of potential error:

- Type I: Hiring or retaining a manager who subsequently underperforms expectations. Rejecting the null hypothesis of no skill when it is correct.
- Type II: Not hiring or firing a manager who subsequently outperforms, or performs in line with, expectations. Not rejecting the null hypothesis when it is incorrect.

Exhibit 2 Type I and Type II Errors

		Realization	
		Below expectations (no skill)	At or above expectations (skill)
Decision	Hire/Retain	Type I	Correct
	Not Hire/Fire	Correct	Type II

Type I and Type II errors can occur anytime a decision is made regarding the hiring or firing of a manager. The decision maker must determine which error is preferred based on the expected benefits and costs of changing managers.

3.1 Qualitative considerations in Type I and Type II errors

Decision makers appear predisposed to worry more about Type I errors than Type II errors. Potential reasons for this focus on Type I errors are as follows:

- Psychologically, people seek to avoid feelings of regret. Type I errors are errors of commission, an active decision that turned out to be incorrect, whereas Type II errors are errors of omission, or inaction. As a result, Type I errors create explicit costs, whereas Type II errors create opportunity costs. Because individuals appear to put less weight on opportunity costs, Type I errors are psychologically more painful than Type II errors.

- Type I errors are relatively straightforward to measure and are often directly linked to the decision maker's compensation. Portfolio holdings are regularly monitored, and managers' out- and underperformance expectations are clearly identified. Type II errors are less likely to be measured—what is the performance impact of not having selected a particular manager? As such, the link between compensation and Type II errors is less clear.

- Similarly, Type I errors are more transparent to investors, so they entail not only the regret of an incorrect decision but the pain of having to explain this decision to the investor. Type II errors, firing (or not hiring) a manager with skill, are less transparent to investors, unless the investor tracks fired managers or evaluates the universe themselves.

Although Type I errors are likely more familiar and more of a concern to most decision makers, a consistent pattern of Type II errors can highlight weaknesses in the manager selection process. One approach to examine this issue is to monitor not only managers currently held but also managers that were evaluated and not hired as well as managers that were fired. The goal of monitoring is to determine the following:

- Are there identifiable factors that differentiate managers hired and managers not hired?
- Are these factors consistent with the investment philosophy and process of the decision maker?
- Are there identifiable factors driving the decision to retain or fire managers?
- Are these factors consistent with the investment philosophy and process of the decision maker?
- What is the added value of the decision to retain or fire managers?

The objective is to avoid making decisions based on short-term performance (trend following) and to identify any evidence of behavioral biases (regret, loss aversion) in the evaluation of managers during the selection process.

3.2 Performance implications of Type I and Type II errors

The cost of Type I errors is holding a manager without skill, as opposed to the cost of Type II errors, which is not holding managers with skill. The cost is driven by the size, shape, mean, and dispersion of the return distributions of the skilled and unskilled managers within the universe. The smaller the difference in sample size and distribution mean and the wider the dispersion of the distributions, the smaller the expected cost of the Type I or Type II error. More-efficient markets are likely to exhibit smaller differences in the distributions of skilled and unskilled managers, indicating a lower opportunity cost of retaining and the lower the cost of hiring an unskilled manager.

The extent to which a strategy is mean-reverting also has a bearing on the cost of Type I and Type II errors. If a strategy's performance is mean reverting, firing a poor performer (or hiring a strong performer) only to see a reversion in performance results is a Type I error. A Type II error would be trimming or not hiring strong performers and hiring managers with weaker track records. There is evidence that individual investors significantly underperform the average mutual fund because of poor timing and fund selection decisions. A study of institutional plan sponsor allocation decisions found that investment products receiving contributions subsequently underperformed products experiencing withdrawals. The study estimated that more than $170 billion was lost during the period examined (Stewart, Neumann, Knittel, and Heisler 2009).

EXAMPLE 2

Type I and Type II Errors

1. A Type I error is:
   - **A** hiring or retaining a manager that subsequently underperforms expectations.
   - **B** hiring or retaining a manager that subsequently outperforms, or performs in line with, expectations.
   - **C** not hiring or firing a manager who subsequently outperforms, or performs in line with, expectations.

2. A Type II error is:
   - **A** hiring or retaining a manager that subsequently underperforms expectations.
   - **B** hiring or retaining a manager that subsequently outperforms, or performs in line with, expectations.
   - **C** not hiring or firing a manager who subsequently outperforms, or performs in line with, expectations.

3. The difference in expected cost between Type I and Type II errors is *most likely*:
   - **A** higher the smaller the perceived difference between the distribution of skilled and unskilled managers.
   - **B** lower the smaller the perceived difference between the distribution of skilled and unskilled managers.
   - **C** zero.

Solution to 1:

A is correct. The error consists of rejecting the null hypothesis (no skill) when it is correct.

Solution to 2:

C is correct. The error consists of not rejecting the null hypothesis (no skill) when it is incorrect.

Solution to 3:

B is correct. The less distinct the distribution of skilled managers from unskilled managers, the lower the opportunity cost of retaining and cost of hiring an unskilled manager. That is, the smaller the perceived difference between the distribution of skilled and unskilled managers, the lower the cost and incentive to fire a manager.

4. QUANTITATIVE ELEMENTS OF MANAGER SEARCH AND SELECTION

c describe uses of returns-based and holdings-based style analysis in investment manager selection;

Performance appraisal captures most aspects of quantitative analysis, evaluating a manager's strengths and weaknesses as measured by that manager's ability to add value to a stated benchmark. Although the determination of whether the manager possesses skill is important, it is equally important to understand the manager's risk profile. The manager has likely been selected to fill a particular role in the portfolio. As such, although it is important to select a skillful manager, the "best" manager may be one that delivers the desired exposures and is suitable for the investor's assumptions, expectations, and biases.

4.1 Style Analysis

An important component of performance appraisal and manager selection is understanding the manager's risk exposures relative to the benchmark and how they evolve over time. This understanding helps define the universe of potential managers and the monitoring of selected managers. The process is referred to as style analysis.

A manager's self-reported risk exposures, such as portfolio concentration, industry exposure, capitalization exposure, and other quantitative measures, are the starting point in style analysis. They provide a means to classify managers by style for defining the selection process, a point of reference for evaluating the returns-based and holdings-based style analysis, and an interesting operational check on the manager.

The results of the returns-based style analysis (RBSA) and the holdings-based style analysis (HBSA) should be consistent with the manager's philosophy and the investment process. If not, the process might not be repeatable or might be implemented inconsistently. It is essential to look at all portfolio construction and risk management issues.

The results of the returns-based style analysis and the holdings-based style analysis should be tracked over time in order to ascertain if the risk trends or exposures are out of line with expectations or the manager's stated style. Deviations may signal that issues, such as style drift, are developing.

Returns-based and holdings-based style analyses provide a means to determine the risks and sources of return for a particular strategy. To be useful, style analysis must be:

- *Meaningful:* The risks reported must represent the important sources of performance return and risk.
- *Accurate:* The reported values must reflect the manager's actual risk exposures.
- *Consistent:* The methodology must allow for comparison over time and across multiple managers.
- *Timely:* The report must be available in a timely manner so that it is useful for making informed investment decisions.

Style analysis is most useful with strategies that hold publicly-traded securities where pricing is frequent. It can be applied to other strategies (hedge funds and private equity, for example), but the insights drawn from a style analysis of such strategies are more likely to be used for designing additional lines of inquiry in the course of due diligence rather than for confirmation of the investment process.

Returns-based style analysis (RBSA) is a top-down approach that involves estimating a portfolio's sensitivities to security market indexes representing a range of distinct factors. Although RBSA adds the additional analytical step of estimating the risk factors, as opposed to using a third-party or self-reported style categorization, the analysis is straightforward and typically does not require a large amount of additional, or difficult to acquire, data. RBSA should identify the important drivers of return and risk factors for the period analyzed and can be estimated even for complicated strategies. In addition, the process is comparable across managers and through time, and the use of returns data provides an objective style check that is not subject to window dressing. The analysis can be run immediately after the data is available, particularly in the case of publicly traded securities. As such, RBSA has many of the attributes of effective risk reporting.

The disadvantage is that RBSA is an imprecise tool. Although the additional computational effort required is not onerous, accuracy may be compromised, because RBSA effectively attributes performance to an unchanging average portfolio during the period. This attribution limits the ability to identify the impact of dynamic investment decisions and may distort the decomposition across sources of added value. Furthermore, the portfolio being analyzed might not reflect the current or future portfolio exposures. If the portfolio contains illiquid securities, stale prices may understate the risk exposure of the strategy. This is a particular problem for private equity (PE) and venture capital (VC) managers that hold illiquid or non-traded securities. VC and PE firms report performance based on the internal rate of return of cash distributions and appraisals of ongoing projects. As a result, reported performance can understate the volatility of return for shorter horizons or time periods with limited liquidity events. Longer periods generally provide more-accurate estimates of the manager's underlying standard deviation of return. The timeliness of any analysis depends on the securities that take the longest to price, which can be challenging for illiquid or non-traded securities.

Holdings-based style analysis (HBSA) is a bottom-up approach that estimates the risk exposures from the actual securities held in the portfolio at a point in time. This approach allows for estimation of current risk factors and offers several advantages. Similar to RBSA, HBSA should identify all important drivers of return and risk factors; be comparable across managers and through time; provide an accurate view of the manager's risk exposures, although potentially subject to window dressing; and be estimated immediately after the data become available.

Exhibit 3 presents a typical holdings-based style map. The manager being evaluated, along with the other managers in the universe, is placed along the size (y-axis) and style (x-axis) dimensions. The portfolio holdings of the manager being evaluated exhibit a large-cap value bias in what is otherwise a rather diverse universe.

Exhibit 3   Example of Holdings-Based Style Analysis

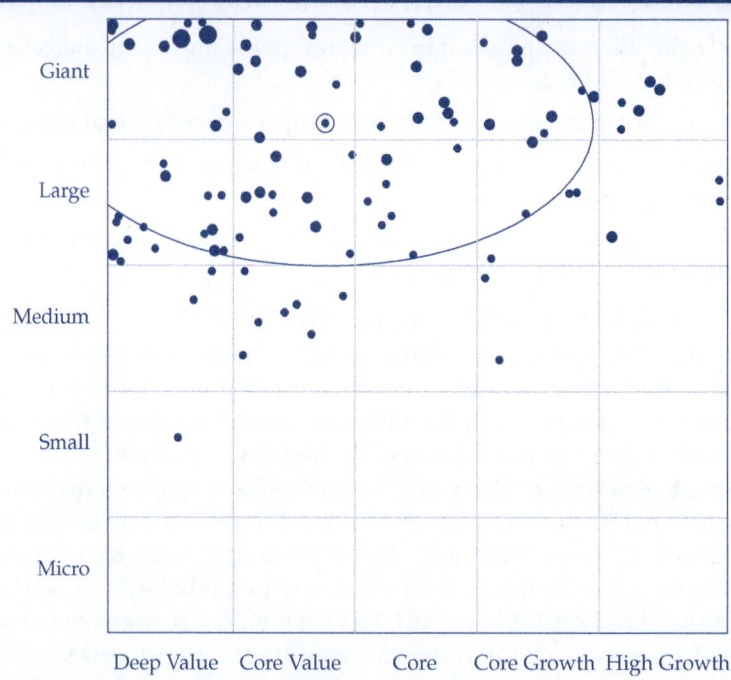

Source: Morningstar Direct, The Mutual Fund Research Center.

As with RBSA, HBSA has some disadvantages. The computational effort increases with the complexity of the strategy and depends on the timing and degree of the transparency provided by the manager. This extra effort can be challenging for hedge fund, private equity, and venture capital managers that may be averse to or unable to provide position-level pricing. Even with mutual funds, the necessary transparency may come with a time lag. The usefulness of the analysis may be compromised, because the portfolio reflects a snapshot in time and might not reflect the portfolio going forward, particularly for high-turnover strategies. Some factors may be difficult to estimate if the strategy is complex because HBSA requires an understanding of the underlying strategy. In general, HBSA is typically easier with equity strategies. If the portfolio has illiquid securities, stale pricing may underestimate the risk exposure of the strategy. The report's timeliness depends on the securities that take the longest to price, which can be challenging for illiquid or non-traded securities.

EXAMPLE 3

Style Analysis

1 Which of the following is an advantage of RBSA?
   A It is a more precise tool than HBSA.
   B It does not require potentially difficult to acquire data.
   C It is more accurate than HBSA when the portfolio contains illiquid securities.
2 Which of the following is an advantage of HBSA?
   A It works well for high-turnover strategies.

B It can identify important drivers of return and risk factors and is comparable across managers and through time.

C It effectively attributes performance to a snapshot of the portfolio at a particular time and thus is not subject to window dressing.

Solution to 1:

B is correct. The data needed for RBSA are usually easier to obtain than the data required for HBSA. RBSA is not a precise tool, and it is not more accurate than HBSA when the portfolio holds illiquid securities.

Solution to 2:

B is correct. Although HBSA allows for estimation of current risk factors and is comparable across managers and through time, the necessary computational effort increases with the strategy's complexity and depends on the timing and degree of the transparency provided by the manager. Some factors may be difficult to estimate if the strategy is complex because this approach requires an understanding of the underlying strategy. In general, HBSA is typically easier for equity strategies. If the portfolio has illiquid securities, stale pricing may underestimate the risk exposure of the strategy. Window dressing and high turnover can compromise the results because the results are attributed to a snapshot of the portfolio.

CAPTURE RATIOS AND DRAWDOWNS IN MANAGER EVALUATION

d describe uses of the upside capture ratio, downside capture ratio, maximum drawdown, drawdown duration, and up/down capture in evaluating managers;

Because large losses require proportionally greater gains to reverse or offset, drawdowns and capture ratios can be important factors in investment manager evaluation. A manager that experiences larger drawdowns may be less suitable for an investor closer to the end of their investment horizon. Capture ratios help assess manager suitability relative to the investor's IPS, especially in relation to the investor's time horizon and risk tolerance.

Recall that: 1) Upside capture (UC) measures capture when the benchmark return is positive. UC greater than 100% suggests out-performance relative to the benchmark. 2) Downside capture (DC) measures capture when the benchmark return is negative. DC less than 100% generally suggests out-performance relative to the benchmark. 3) The **capture ratio** (CR)—upside capture divided by downside capture—measures the asymmetry of return. 4) **Drawdown** is the cumulative peak-to-trough loss during a particular continuous period and **drawdown duration** is the total time from the start of the drawdown until the cumulative drawdown recovers to zero.

Let's illustrate the use of capture ratios in the analysis of manager returns. Consider the four stylized return profiles in Exhibit 4.

Exhibit 4 Return Profile Summary

Profile	Upside Capture	Downside Capture	Ratio
Long only	100%	100%	1.0
Positive asymmetry	75%	25%	3.0
Low beta	50%	50%	1.0
Negative asymmetry	25%	75%	0.3

Each strategy's allocation to the S&P 500 Total Return (TR) Index and to 90-day T-bills (assuming monthly rebalancing to simplify the calculations) is based on the realized monthly return from January 2000 to December 2013. (This time period encompasses two significant drawdowns: the "tech bubble burst" of the early 2000s and the extreme drawdown of the Global Financial Crisis in 2008–2009.)

- The long-only profile is 100% allocated to the S&P 500 throughout the period.
- The low-beta profile is allocated 50% to the S&P 500 throughout the period.
- The positive asymmetry profile is allocated 75% to the S&P 500 for months when the S&P 500 return is positive and 25% when the S&P 500 return is negative.
- The negative asymmetry profile is allocated 25% to the S&P 500 for months when the S&P 500 return is positive and 75% when the S&P 500 return is negative.

The remainder for all profiles is allocated to 90-day T-bills. Exhibit 5 shows each profile's cumulative monthly return for the period.

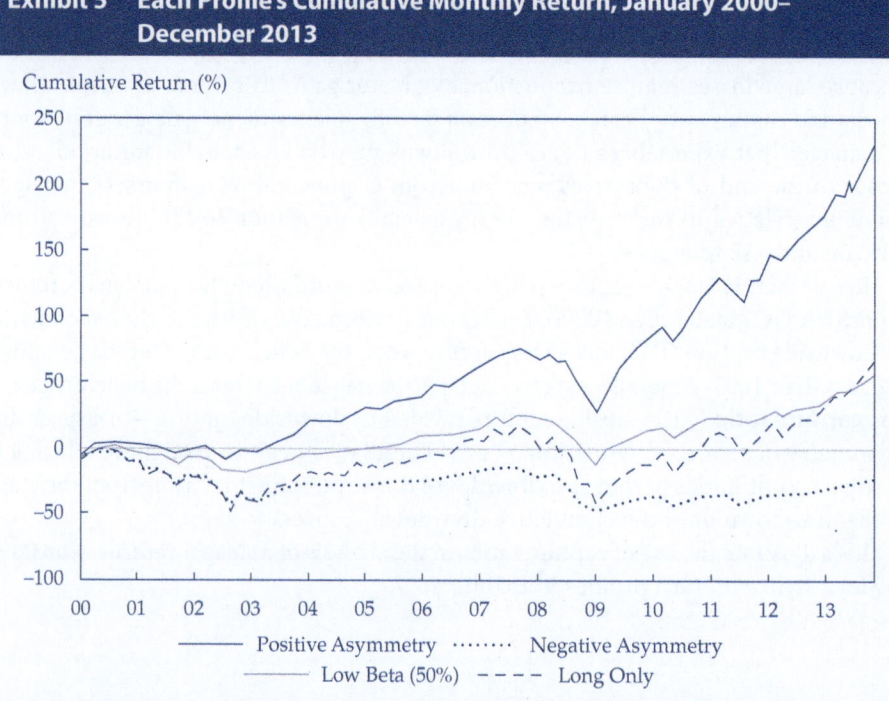

Exhibit 5 Each Profile's Cumulative Monthly Return, January 2000–December 2013

Exhibit 6 provides summary statistics for each profile based on monthly returns from January 2000 to December 2013. Although the long-only profile outperformed the low-beta profile over the full period, this outperformance resulted from the strong up market of 2013—the long-only profile lagged the low-beta profile for most of the period. The low beta profile achieved higher risk-adjusted returns and only half the volatility for the full period. The low-beta profile declined only 18.8% from January 2000 to September 2002, compared with the long-only decline of 42.5%. As a result, the low-beta profile had higher cumulative performance from January 2000 to October 2007 despite markedly lagging the long-only profile (56.0% to 108.4%) from October 2002 to October 2007.

Although a low-beta approach may sacrifice performance, it shows that limiting drawdowns can result in better absolute and risk-adjusted returns in certain markets.

Not surprisingly, positive asymmetry results in better performance relative to long only, low beta, and negative asymmetry. Although the positive asymmetry profile lags in up markets, this lag is more than offset by the lower participation in down markets. Not surprisingly, the negative asymmetry profile lags.

Exhibit 6 Summary Statistics for Each Profile, January 2000–December 2013

Strategy	Long Only	Low Beta	Positive Asymmetry	Negative Asymmetry
Cumulative return	64.0%	54.2%	228.1%	−24.4%
Annualized return	3.60%	3.14%	8.86%	−1.98%
Annualized standard deviation	15.64%	7.79%	9.61%	10.01%
Sharpe ratio	0.10	0.14	0.71	−0.40
Beta	1.00	0.50	0.61	0.64
Drawdown (maximum)	−50.9%	−28.3%	−26.9%	−48.9%

We've shown that positive asymmetry is a desirable trait. When evaluating a manager that exhibits positive asymmetry in its returns, we need to understand whether the strategy is inherently convex or whether the profile is a result of manager skill. For example, a hedging strategy implemented by rolling forward out-of-the-money put options will typically return many small losses because more options expire worthless than are compensated for by the occasional large gain during a large market downturn. A manager employing this strategy will likely exhibit consistent positive asymmetry in his returns, but the positive asymmetry is likely a due to the nature of the strategy rather than on investment skill.

Let's consider now the use of drawdowns in the analysis of manager returns. Drawdowns are stress-tests of the investment process and can expose potentially flawed or inconsistently implemented investment processes, inadequate risk controls, or operational issues. Did the manager implement the stated investment process consistently? If yes, what lessons were learned and how might the investment process have been adapted as a result? If the drawdown resulted from a deviation from the stated investment process, why? During a large or long drawdown, a manager could start to worry more about business risk than investment risk and act in their own best interest rather than that of their investors. How a manager responds to a large drawdown as it occurs, and what lessons are learned, provide evidence of the robustness and repeatability of the investment, portfolio construction, and risk management processes, as well as insight into the people implementing the processes.

> ### Events of August 2007
>
> Starting on 7 August 2007, many quantitative equity long–short strategies began to experience large drawdowns. Many managers had never experienced such losses or market conditions and started to sell positions as stop-loss and risk management policies were triggered (Khandani and Lo 2011). This activity added to additional selling pressure, and the S&P 500 declined 13.4% by 8 August. Those managers that sold ended up locking in large losses because the underperforming stocks and market subsequently recovered, with the S&P 500 down only 5.7% for the month. In many cases, those funds that sold experienced redemptions or ended up closing.

As August 2007 demonstrated, distinguishing prudent risk management from a misalignment of interests is not always straightforward. Should a manager continue to actively trade a portfolio if the market environment no longer reflects their investment philosophy? In addition, traders will claim that it is better to cut losses because losses can signal that something has changed or that the timing of the trade is not right. Conversely, selling into a down market raises the risk of crystallizing losses and missing any subsequent reversal. The decision maker must assess whether the manager's behavior was a disciplined application of the investment process, reflected a misalignment of interests, or simply resulted from panic or overreaction by the manager.

One aspect of suitability for the IPS is the investment horizon and its relationship to risk capacity. An investor closer to retirement, with less time to recover from losses, places more emphasis on absolute measures of risk. If there has been no change to investment policy and no change in the view that the manager remains suitable, the temptation to exit should be resisted to avoid exiting at an inauspicious time. Investors with shorter horizons, with lower risk capacity, or prone to overreact to losses may be better served by allocating to managers with shallower and shorter expected drawdowns.

> ### The Concept of Active Share
>
> **Active share** measures the difference in portfolio holdings relative to the benchmark. A manager that precisely replicates the benchmark will have an active share of zero; a manager with no holdings in common with the benchmark will have an active share of one.
>
> Given a strategy with N securities ($i = 1, 2, ..., N$), active share is calculated as
>
> $$\text{Active Share} = \frac{1}{2}\sum_{i=1}^{N}\left|\text{Strategy Weight}_i - \text{BenchmarkWeight}_i\right|$$
>
> Typically, managers are somewhere along the spectrum. The categorization of active share and tracking risk in Exhibit 7 has been suggested for active managers. It is clear that full replication will appear as a closet indexer. A manager that uses sampling techniques to build the portfolio may, however, appear as a diversified stock picker depending on the universe under consideration and the dispersion of active share of the constituents. Tracking risk will be low, but active share might not be because only a subset of constituents is held. One reason is that high and low are relative to the universe being examined and the category definitions used. As such, it is important to examine risk factors and portfolio construction techniques of both active and passive managers.

Exhibit 7: Active Share vs. Tracking Risk

		Active Share	
		Low	High
Tracking risk	High	Sector rotation	Concentrated stock pickers
	Low	Closet indexer	Diversified stock pickers

THE MANAGER'S INVESTMENT PHILOSOPHY 6

e evaluate a manager's investment philosophy and investment decision-making process;

The goal of manager due diligence is to weigh the potential risks that may arise from entering into an investment management relationship and entrusting assets to a firm. Although it is impossible to eliminate all potential risks, the allocator must assess how the firm will manage the broad range of risks it is likely to face in the future. This section outlines the general aspects of manager due diligence and the particular questions the investor needs to answer.

Investment due diligence examines and evaluates the qualitative considerations that illustrate that the manager's investment process is repeatable and consistently implemented. The objective is to understand whether the investment philosophy, process, people, and portfolio construction satisfy the assumption that past performance provides some guidance for expected future performance. In other words, are the conclusions drawn from performance measurement, attribution, and appraisal reliable selection criteria? In addition, it is important to remember that investment managers are businesses. Regardless of the strength of the investment process or historical performance, investment management firms must be operated as successful businesses to ensure sustainability. Operational due diligence examines and evaluates the firm's policies and procedures, to identify potential risks that might not be captured in historical performance and to assess the firm's sustainability.

6.1 Investment Philosophy

The investment philosophy is the foundation of the investment process. Every investment strategy is based on a set of assumptions about the factors that drive performance and the manager's beliefs about their ability to successfully exploit these sources of return. The investment manager should have a clear and concise investment philosophy.

First, every manager makes assumptions about market efficiency, including the degree and the time frame. Passive strategies assume markets are sufficiently efficient and that active management cannot add value after transaction costs and fees. As a result, passive strategies seek to earn risk premiums. A **risk premium** is the expected return in excess of a minimal-risk ("risk-free") rate of return that accrues to bearing a risk that is not easily diversified away—so-called systematic risk.

Passive strategies seek to capture return through exposure to systematic risk premiums, such as equity risk, duration risk, or credit risk. These strategies can also look to capture alternative risk premiums. such as liquidity risk, natural disaster risk (e.g., insurance-linked securities, such as catastrophe bonds and quota shares), volatility risk, or some combination of these premiums (e.g., distressed strategies seek to capture credit and liquidity risk premiums).

In contrast, active strategies assume markets are sufficiently inefficient that security mispricings can be identified and exploited. These opportunities typically arise when market behavior deviates from the manager's fundamental assumptions. Generally speaking, inefficiencies can be categorized as behavioral or structural.

- *Behavioral inefficiencies* are perceived mispricings created by the actions of other market participants, usually associated with biases, such as trend following or loss aversion. These inefficiencies are temporary, lasting long enough for the manager to identify and exploit them before the market price and perceived intrinsic value converge.

- *Structural inefficiencies* are perceived mispricings created by external or internal rules and regulations. These inefficiencies can be long lived and assume a continuation of the rules and regulations rather than a convergence.

Active strategies also typically make assumptions about the dynamics and structures of the market, such as the following: The correlation structure of the market is sufficiently stable over the investment horizon to make diversification useful for risk management; prices eventually converge to intrinsic value, which can be estimated by using a discounted cash flow model; or market prices are driven by predictable macroeconomic trends.

It is important to evaluate these assumptions and the role they play in the investment process to understand how the strategy will behave through time and across market environments.

- Can the manager clearly and consistently articulate their investment philosophy? It is hard to have confidence in the repeatability and efficacy of an investment process if the manager, and investment personnel, cannot explain the assumptions that underpin the process. This clarity also provides a consistency check that the investment process and personnel are appropriate for the stated philosophy.

- Are the assumptions credible and consistent? That is, does the decision maker agree with the assumptions underlying the strategy, and are these assumptions consistent with the investment process? A decision maker who believes a market is efficient would likely not find the assumptions of an active manager in that market credible. In the decision maker's judgment, the assumptions must support a repeatable and robust investment process.

- How has the philosophy developed over time? Ideally, the philosophy is unchanged through time, suggesting a repeatable process. If philosophy has evolved, it is preferred that changes are judged to be reasonable responses to changing market conditions rather than a series of ad hoc reactions to performance or investor flows. Such changes suggest a lack of repeatability and robustness.

- Are the return sources linked to credible and consistent inefficiencies? The decision maker must judge whether the investment philosophy is based on an inefficiency that is based on an informational advantage, likely a behavioral inefficiency by interpreting information better than other market participants, or a structural inefficiency that suggests the investment process is repeatable.

If the source of return is linked to a credible inefficiency, there is the additional issue of capacity. Capacity has several related aspects, such as the level of assets the strategy or opportunity can absorb without a dilution of returns, the number of opportunities or securities available, and the ability to transact in a timely manner at or near the market price—that is, liquidity. Overall, capacity is the level, repeatability, and sustainability of returns that the inefficiency is expected to support in the future.

- Does the inefficiency provide a sufficient frequency of opportunity and level of return to cover transaction costs and fees? If so, does this require leverage?
- Does the inefficiency provide a repeatable source of return? That is, can the opportunity be captured by a repeatable process, or is each opportunity unique, requiring a different process of skill set to exploit?
- Is the inefficiency sustainable? That is, at what asset level would the realized return from the inefficiency be unacceptably low? Sustainability will be a function of the market's depth and liquidity, as well as how much capital is allocated, either by the manager or competitors, to the inefficiency.

Uncommon Ways of Passing the Investment Philosophy Test

1 Managers that measure the success of the steps of the process and not just the ultimate outcome.

For example, consider a bond manager that makes the claim that his or her credit research not only predicts upgrades and downgrades, but makes those predictions before the expectation of a rating change is reflected in the market price. This manager tracks every prediction to see if the market consensus (as reflected by price) and rating agencies come around to his or her view. I get comfort from the facts that (1) such managers know their views only have value if they are not only correct but different than consensus, and (2) they track how prices eventually come to reflect, or not reflect, their views. Similarly, managers that evaluate their own performance with strategy benchmarks designed to replicate their selection universe demonstrate they understand the importance of attempting to differentiate alpha from noise (see Kuenzi [2003]).

2 Managers that recognize that every strategy they come up with is potentially subject to being arbitraged away.

For example, consider a quantitative equity manager that that plays many themes at once. Each theme is viewed as having a finite life, and the performance of each theme is isolated and monitored so as to observe the decay in the value of the theme. The manager considers his or her competitive advantage to be in the identification of new themes, and in the technology for measuring the contribution of each theme to performance. A similar idea is presented in the adaptive market hypothesis of Lo [2004], where the market is always tending toward efficiency, but the types of trades needed to move it towards efficiency rotate and evolve over time.

3 Managers that claim they exploit inefficiencies, and identify the specific inefficiency they are exploiting with every position they take.

Most managers that say they exploit inefficiencies use this claim as a broad justification for their investment process, but are unable to identify the specific inefficiency they are exploiting in any given decision they make. Those that routinely specify how their information or point of point differs from that reflected in price are much more credible.

4 Managers that know their companies so well that they are quicker to interpret change, even though they have no explicit alpha thesis.

There is always an exception to the rule. Sometimes a manager is simply talented and cannot articulate an alpha thesis.

Despite examples such as these, it remains frustratingly difficult to distinguish between true alpha-generators and alpha-pretenders. I believe there is more that alpha-generators can do to distinguish themselves, and that consultants should be more insistent that they do it.

Excerpted from: John R. Minahan, CFA, "The Role of Investment Philosophy in Evaluating Investment Managers: A Consultant's Perspective on Distinguishing Alpha from Noise," *Journal of Investing*, Vol. 15 (2006). Copyright © 2006 by Institutional Investor Journals. Reprinted with permission.

EXAMPLE 4

Investment Philosophy

1 Which of the following is **not** an important consideration when evaluating a manager's investment philosophy?
   A What are the compensation arrangements of key employees?
   B Are the investment philosophy assumptions credible and consistent?
   C Can the manager clearly and consistently articulate their investment philosophy?

2 Generally speaking, inefficiencies can be categorized as:
   A large and small.
   B internal and external.
   C structural and behavioral.

3 Which of the following is **not** an important consideration when evaluating the capacity of an inefficiency?
   A Does the strategy rely on unique information?
   B Does the inefficiency provide a repeatable source of return?
   C Does the inefficiency provide a sufficient frequency of opportunity and level of return to cover transaction costs and fees?

Solution to 1:

A is correct. Employee compensation is a legal and compliance issue considered as part of operational due diligence.

Solution to 2:

C is correct. Behavioral inefficiencies are created by the actions of other participants in the market. These inefficiencies are temporary, lasting long enough for the manager to identify and exploit them before the market price and perceived intrinsic value converge. Structural inefficiencies are created by external or internal rules and regulations. These inefficiencies can be long lived and assume a continuation of the rules and regulations rather than a convergence.

Solution to 3:

A is correct. The uniqueness of information used by the manager is a consideration when evaluating the assumptions of the investment process.

6.2 Investment Personnel

An investment process can only be as good as the people who create and implement it, and even the best process can be compromised by poor execution by the people involved. This view is not a question of liking the manager or team but of trusting that they possess the expertise and experience to effectively implement the strategy.

- Does the investment team have sufficient expertise and experience to effectively execute the investment process? The need for expertise is self-evident. The greater the experience, particularly managing the current strategy across market environments, the greater the confidence in the manager's ability to effectively execute the investment process. As noted with drawdowns, it is especially instructive to see how the manager responded to stressed markets and poor performance.

- Does the investment team have sufficient depth to effectively execute the investment process? A strategy that focuses on a small universe of publicly traded stocks might not require a large investment team. A global macro or multi-strategy fund, which holds positions across numerous global markets, likely requires a large team with expertise and experience supporting the manager.

- What is the level of key person risk? A strategy that is overly dependent on the judgment or particular skills of an individual or small team of people faces **key person risk**, an overreliance on an individual or individuals whose departure would negatively affect the strategy's performance.

- What kinds of agreements (e.g., non-compete) and incentives (ownership, bonus, pay) exist to retain and attract key employees to join and stay at the firm?

- What has been the turnover of firm personnel? High personnel turnover risks the loss of institutional knowledge and experience within the team.

THE MANAGER'S INVESTMENT DECISION-MAKING PROCESS

e evaluate a manager's investment philosophy and investment decision-making process;

The investment decision-making process has four elements: signal creation, signal capture, portfolio construction, and portfolio monitoring.

7.1 Signal Creation (Idea Generation)

An investment signal is a data point or fact that can be observed early enough to implement as an investment position. The basic question is, how are investment ideas generated? The efficient market hypothesis posits that the key to exploiting inefficiencies is to have information that is all of the following:

- **Unique:** Does the strategy rely on unique information? If so, how is this information collected, and how is the manager able to retain an informational edge, particularly in a regulatory environment that seeks to reduce informational asymmetries?

- **Timely:** Does the strategy possess an information timing advantage? If so, how is this information collected, and how is the manager able to retain a timing edge, particularly in a regulatory environment that seeks to reduce informational asymmetries?
- **Interpreted differently:** Interpretation is typically how managers seek to differentiate themselves. Does the manager possess a unique way of interpreting information? Or does the manager claim their strategy possesses a "secret sauce" component or that its team is simply smarter than other managers?

7.2 Signal Capture (Idea Implementation)

The second step is signal capture, translating the generated investment idea into an investment position.

- What is the process for translating investment ideas into investment positions?
- Is this process repeatable and consistent with the strategy assumptions?
- What is the process, and who is ultimately responsible for approving an investment position?

7.3 Portfolio Construction

The third element is portfolio construction; how investment positions are implemented within the portfolio. This element begins to capture the manager's risk management methodology. Good investment ideas need to be implemented properly to exploit opportunities and capture desired risk premiums. It is also important that portfolio construction is consistent with the investment philosophy and process as well as the expertise of the investment personnel.

- How are portfolio allocations set and adjusted? The allocation process should be consistent with investment philosophy and process. For example, if the portfolio is actively managed, its turnover should agree with the frequency of signals generated and the securities' liquidity. The allocation process should be well-defined and consistently applied, supporting the repeatability of the investment process. For example, are allocations made quantitatively or qualitatively?
- Are portfolio allocations based on the manager's conviction? In other words, do the positions the manager believes will most likely outperform or exhibit the greatest outperformance receive the largest active overweighting, and the securities the manager believes will underperform receive the largest active underweighting?
- How have the portfolio characteristics changed with asset growth? Has the number and/or characteristics of the positions held changed to accommodate a larger amount of AUM?
- Does the portfolio use **stop-losses** to manage risk? If so, are they hard (positions are automatically sold when the loss threshold is reached) or soft (positions are evaluated when the loss threshold is reached)? Although stop-losses represent a clear risk management approach, the goal of protecting against large losses must be balanced with the risk of closing positions too frequently.
- What types of securities are used? Does the manager use derivatives to express investment ideas? What experience does the manager have investing in these securities? The manager should be sufficiently well-versed and experienced with the securities used to understand how they will behave in different market environments.

- How are hedges implemented? What security types are used? How are hedge ratios set? Consider a manager that focuses on stock selection to generate alpha and hedges to reduce or remove market risk. The hedges must be sized correctly, or they can be ineffective (underhedged) or they can overwhelm stock selection (overhedged), with performance driven more by beta than by alpha.

- How are long and short ideas expressed? Are they paired—that is, each long position has a corresponding short position—or are long and short positions established independently? How long and short positions are allocated is important for understanding the portfolio's overall exposure. If long and short positions are paired, with the idea of capturing alpha as prices converge while offsetting market risk, the positions must be well-matched and sized correctly.

An important risk is liquidity. Strategies that are not intending to capture a liquidity risk premium must be aware of portfolio liquidity in terms of adapting to changing information, changing market conditions, and changing investor liquidity demands. An existing portfolio consisting of illiquid securities will be more costly to change, not only to take advantage of new opportunities but also to trade because of higher transaction costs. There is the additional cost of having to sell positions at inopportune times as a result of market events or investor liquidity demands. When assessing security liquidity, it is important to consider all of the assets under management for that particular manager and investment process.

- What percentage of the portfolio can be liquidated in five business days or less? What percentage requires more than 10 business days to liquidate? The less liquid the portfolio, the higher the transaction costs if the manager is forced to sell one or more positions. A more liquid portfolio offers flexibility if the manager faces unexpected investor liquidity demands or rapidly changing market conditions.

- What is the average daily volume weighted by portfolio position size?

- Have any of the portfolio holdings been suspended from trading? If so, what is the name of the company, and what are the circumstances pertaining to the suspension?

- Are there any holdings in which ownership by the firm across all portfolios collectively accounts for more than 5% of the market capitalization or float of the security?

- What is the firm's trading strategy? Does the investment manager tend to provide liquidity or demand it? Has the trading strategy changed in response to asset growth?

7.4 Monitoring the Portfolio

The investment decision-making process is a feedback loop that consists of ongoing monitoring of the portfolio in light of new information and analysis. This monitoring includes an assessment of both external and internal considerations. External considerations include the economic and financial market environments. Has anything meaningful occurred that might affect the manager's ability to exploit the market inefficiency that is the strategy's focus? Internal considerations include the portfolio's performance, risk profile, and construction. Has anything changed that might signal potential style drift or other deviations from the investment process? Ongoing monitoring and performance attribution help to ensure that the manager remains appropriate for the clients' mandates.

8. OPERATIONAL DUE DILIGENCE

f evaluate the costs and benefits of pooled investment vehicles and separate accounts;

g compare types of investment manager contracts, including their major provisions and advantages and disadvantages;

Performance appraisal assumes that reported returns are accurate and fully reflect the manager's risk profile. Unfortunately, as we have seen, this assumption is not always true. Although investment due diligence is one step toward understanding these risks, one must remember that investment management firms are *businesses*, and in many cases they are small businesses with a high degree of business risk. Regardless of the strength of the investment process or the historical investment results, investment management firms must be operated as a successful business in order to ensure their sustainability. This requirement creates the potential for a misalignment of interests between the manager and the investor. Operational due diligence analyzes the integrity of the business and seeks to understand and evaluate these risks by examining and evaluating the firm's policies and procedures.

Weaknesses in the firm's infrastructure represent latent risks to the investor. A strong back office (support staff) is critical for safeguarding assets and ensuring that accurate reports are issued in a timely manner. The manager should have a robust trading process that seeks to avoid human error. A repeatable process requires consistent implementation. The allocator needs to understand the following:

- What is the firm's trading policy?
- Does the firm use soft dollar commissions? If so, is there a rigorous process for ensuring compliance?
- What is the process for protecting against unauthorized trading?
- How are fees calculated and collected?
- How are securities allocated across investor accounts, including both pooled and separately managed accounts? The allocation method should be objective (e.g., based on invested capital) to avoid the potential to benefit some investors at the expense of others.
- How many different strategies does the firm manage, and are any new strategies being contemplated? Is the firm's infrastructure capable of efficiently and accurately implementing the different strategies?
- What information technology offsite backup facilities are in place?
- Does the firm have processes, software, and hardware in place to handle cybersecurity issues?

An important constituent of the infrastructure is third-party service providers, including the firm's prime broker, administrator, auditor, and legal counsel. They provide an important independent verification of the firm's performance and reporting.

- Are the firm's third-party service providers known and respected?
- Has there been any change in third-party providers? If so, when and why? This information is particularly important with regard to the firm's auditor. Frequent changes of the auditor is a red flag and may mean the manager is trying to hide something.

Operational Due Diligence

The risk management function should be viewed as an integral part of the investment firm and not considered a peripheral function. The extent to which integration exists provides insight into the firm's culture and the alignment of interests between the manager and the investor. The manager should have a risk manual that is readily available for review:

- Does the portfolio have any hard/soft investment guidelines?
- How are these guidelines monitored?
- What is the procedure for curing breaches?
- Who is responsible for risk management?
- Is there an independent risk officer?

8.1 Firm

An investment management firm must operate as a successful business to ensure sustainability. A manager that goes out of business does not have a repeatable investment process. An important aspect of manager selection is assessing the level of business risk.

- What is the ownership structure of the firm?
- What are the total firm AUM and AUM by investment strategy?
- What is the firm's breakeven AUM (the asset base needed to generate enough fee revenue to cover total firm expenses)?
- Are any of the firm's strategies closed to new capital?
- How much capital would the firm like to raise?

A firm that is independently owned may have greater autonomy and flexibility than a firm owned by a larger organization, but it may have a higher cost structure and lack financial support during market events, raising potential business risks. Outside ownership could create a situation in which the outside owner has objectives that conflict with the investment strategy. For instance, the outside owner might want to increase the asset base to generate higher fee revenue, but this action could prevent the portfolio from holding lower-capitalization stocks. Ideally, ownership should be spread across as many employees as is feasible and practical. A firm managing a smaller asset base may be more nimble and less prone to dilution of returns but will likely have lower revenues to support infrastructure and compensate employees. At a minimum, the asset base needs to be sufficient to support the firm's current expenditures.

Last, and by no means least important, are legal and compliance issues. It is critical that the firm's interests are aligned with those of the investor.

- What are the compensation arrangements for key employees? For example, are any people compensated with stock in the firm, and if so, what happens to this stock when they leave the firm?
- Do employees invest personal assets in the firm's strategies? Investing their own money in the same products in which the firm's clients invest creates an alignment of interests, but too large a proportion of their own assets invested in this one product may create personal/business risk for the manager that overrides the alignment of interests.
- Does the firm foster a culture of compliance?
- What is covered in the compliance manual?
- Has the firm or any of its employees been involved with an investigation by any financial market regulator or self-regulatory organization?

- Has the firm been involved in any lawsuits?
- Are any of the firm's employees involved in legal actions or personal litigation that might affect their ability to continue to fulfill their fiduciary responsibilities?

Hiring a manager requires trust. A firm's culture as expressed by its compliance policies and procedures should provide a level of confidence that the manager's and investor's interests are aligned.

The Investment Process

Bernard "Bernie" L. Madoff ran one of the biggest frauds in Wall Street history. One of the first indications that something was amiss at Bernard L. Madoff Investment Securities arose when Harry Markopolos was unable to reconcile the return track record with the investment process. In addition to observing the unrealistically consistent nature of the claimed returns, Markopolos concluded that there was no way to generate the returns using the claimed investment process. Further analysis convinced him that Madoff's returns resulted not from front running—that is, taking positions to exploit knowledge of investor trade flows—but rather from fraud.

In hindsight, there were many red flags over the years that indicated there was something wrong with Madoff's investment management process. The firm claimed to generate steady returns in every market environment. Mr. Madoff was known to dismiss questions about his strategy, arguing that his business was too complicated for outsiders to understand. He also operated as a broker/dealer with an asset management division, profiting from trading commissions rather than the investment management fees that hedge funds charged. The structure seemed odd to other investment professionals, raising concerns about the firm's legitimacy. Another red flag was raised when it became known that the firm used a small, unknown auditor with only three employees. If, as Mr. Madoff claimed, the strategy was so complex that no one could understand it, a small, three-person audit firm would be unlikely to be able to effectively audit the financial statements (Zuckerman 2008).

Self-Reported Risk Factors

Requesting and obtaining self-reported risk factors not only is important for understanding the manager's investment process but also provides an interesting operational check. A manager should readily comply with all requests for risk reporting. If not, it suggests a lack of transparency that may become challenging for monitoring the manager and strategy in the future. Additionally, it might indicate an inability to generate essential reports, which raises questions about the firm's policies and procedures.

All risk reporting should be meaningful, consistent, accurate, and timely. A lack of meaningful reporting indicates that the reports are not useful in monitoring the manager and that there is a lack of transparency. In the worst case, the manager does not understand the risk exposures or does not want to disclose them.

A lack of consistent reporting also reduces the usefulness of the reporting. Inconsistent reports preclude the ability to track levels and trends of important risk factors. The manager may be choosing to selectively report particular risks that they deem important or interesting. In the worst case, it may mean that the manager is selectively reporting in order to hide risks created by deviations from the stated investment process.

> A lack of accuracy suggests that the manager cannot properly measure portfolio risks or is intentionally misreporting results. A lack of timeliness reduces the reports' usefulness and suggests either inefficient procedures or attempts to manipulate the flow of information. In all of these cases, poor risk reporting, at a minimum, suggests a reevaluation of the manager and, if issues are identified, potential termination.

8.2 Investment Vehicle

There are two broad options for implementing investment strategies: individual separate accounts and pooled (or commingled) vehicles. An additional operational consideration is the evaluation of the investment vehicle—its appropriateness to the investment strategy and its suitability for the investor. Separate accounts offer additional control, customization, tax efficiency, reporting, and transparency advantages, but these come at a higher cost.

In a pooled or commingled vehicle, the money from multiple investors is held as a single portfolio and managed without potential customization for any investor. Such vehicles include open-end funds, closed-end funds, exchange-traded funds, exchange-traded notes, and hedge funds. As the name infers, a separately managed account (SMA) vehicle holds the money in a segregated account in the investor's name. The funds are managed to a particular mandate with the potential to customize the strategy for each investor. The advantages of SMA vehicles include the following:

- **Ownership:** In an SMA, the investor owns the individual securities directly. This approach provides additional safety should a liquidity event occur. Although the manager continues to make investment decisions, these decisions will not be influenced by the redemption or liquidity demand of other investors in the strategy. An SMA also provides clear legal ownership for the recovery of assets resulting from unforeseen events, such as bankruptcy or mismanagement.
- **Customization:** SMAs allow the investor to potentially express individual constraints or preferences within the portfolio. SMAs can thus more closely address the investor's particular investment objectives.
- **Tax efficiency:** SMAs offer potentially improved tax efficiency because the investor pays taxes only on the capital gains realized and allows the implementation of tax-efficient investing and trading strategies.
- **Transparency:** SMAs offer real-time, position-level detail to the investor, providing complete transparency and accurate attribution to the investor. Even if a pooled vehicle provides position-level detail, such information will likely be presented with a delay.

If the SMA is customized, additional investment due diligence may be required to account for differences in security selection or portfolio construction. In addition, there are operational due diligence considerations.

- **Cost:** Separate accounts represent an additional operational burden on the manager, which translates into potentially higher costs for the investor. SMAs do not scale as easily as pooled vehicles. Once a pooled investment is established and the fixed costs paid, the cost of each new investor is largely the incremental costs of custody, trading larger positions, and generating an additional report. With an SMA, a new account must be established for each investor. In addition, SMAs are likely to face higher transaction costs to the degree that trades cannot be aggregated to reduce trade volumes. These costs are a function of the extent to which the strategy is customized or traded differently to accommodate different investor needs.

- **Tracking risk:** Customization of the strategy creates tracking risk relative to the benchmark, which can confuse attribution because performance will reflect investor constraints rather than manager decisions.
- **Investor behavior:** Transparency, combined with control and customization, allows for potential micromanagement by the investor—that is, the investor attempting to manage the portfolio. Such an effort not only negates the benefit of hiring a manager but is particularly problematic if these changes decrease the portfolio's value. Potential investor behaviors include performance chasing, familiarity bias (being overly averse to unfamiliar holdings), and loss aversion (a tendency to disaggregate the portfolio and not appreciate the value of hedging).

The allocator's goal is to evaluate the costs and benefits of the vehicle used and judge its suitability for the IPS:

- Is the vehicle structure consistent with the investment process?
- Does the manager have the operational infrastructure necessary to manage the SMA?
- Is there a benefit to holding the securities in a separate account? If so, are these benefits sufficient to compensate for additional costs?
- Is tax efficiency an important objective of the IPS?
- Are there concerns that the available transparency and ability to customize will result in decisions by the investor that do not add value?

EXAMPLE 5

Pooled Investments and Separate Accounts

Which of the following are advantages of separately managed accounts compared with pooled investments?

A Typically lower cost

B Potential management of the portfolio by the investor

C Ability to take close account of individual client constraints or preferences

Solution:

C is correct. With SMAs, the investor owns the individual securities directly and can potentially express individual constraints or preferences within the portfolio. In particular, SMAs offer potentially improved tax efficiency because the investor pays taxes only on the capital gains realized and allows the implementation of tax-efficient investing and trading strategies.

8.3 Evaluation of the Investment's Terms

An additional and important aspect of manager selection is understanding the terms of the investment as presented in the prospectus, private placement memorandum, and/or limited partnership agreement. These documents are, in essence, the contract between the investor and the manager, outlining each party's rights and responsibilities. Although these documents cover numerous topics, this section focuses on liquidity and fees. The objective of the decision maker is to determine whether the liquidity and fee structure make the manager suitable for the investor's needs and the "best" manager for expressing a particular portfolio need.

8.3.1 Liquidity

Different vehicles provide different degrees of liquidity. Liquidity is defined as the timeliness with which a security or asset can be sold at or near the current price. The same criteria can be applied to managers.

The most liquid vehicles are closed-end funds and ETFs. As listed securities, they can be bought and sold intra-day, and the price received will depend on the trading volume and depth of the fund. The obvious advantage of these funds is ease of trading, although there can be some price uncertainty for less liquid funds, particularly when trying to buy or sell a large number of shares. Open-end funds are slightly less liquid, providing daily liquidity but also price certainty; shares are bought and sold at the end-of-day NAV.

Unlike open-end funds, ETFs, or closed-end funds, limited partnerships, such as hedge funds, venture capital funds, and private equity funds, typically require investors to invest their money for longer periods. Hedge fund liquidity has four basic features: redemption frequency, notification period, lockup, and gates. Redemption frequency indicates how often an investor can withdraw capital from the fund, and the notification period indicates how far in advance of the redemption investors must tell the fund of their intention to redeem. A lockup is the initial period, after making an investment, during which investors cannot redeem their holding. Lockups have two types: a hard lock, which allows for no redemptions, and a soft lock, which charges a fee, paid into the fund, for redemptions. A mutual fund redemption fee is equivalent to a hedge fund soft lock. Gates limit the amount of fund assets, or investor assets that can be redeemed at one redemption date.

Private equity and venture capital funds provide the least liquidity. Investors are contractually obligated to contribute specific amounts (capital calls) during the investment phase and then receive distributions and capital as investments are harvested during the remaining term of the fund. A typical investment phase is 5 years. The typical life of a fund is 10 years, with the option to extend the term for two 1-year periods.

The obvious disadvantage of partnership liquidity terms is the reduced flexibility to adjust portfolio allocations in light of changing market conditions or investor circumstances, as well as the reduced ability to meet unexpected liquidity needs. The advantage of such terms is that they do lock up capital for longer horizons, allowing funds to take long-term views and hold less liquid securities—such as start-up companies, buyouts, turnarounds, real estate, or natural resources—with reduced risk of having to sell portfolio holdings at inopportune times in response to redemption requests. An additional advantage, which was apparent during the 2008 financial crisis, is that limited liquidity imposes this long horizon view on investors, reducing or removing their ability to overreact.

Because SMA assets are held in the investor's name, the securities in the portfolio can be sold at any time. As a result, an SMA's liquidity will depend on the liquidity of the securities held. An SMA holding listed large-cap stocks will likely be highly liquid, whereas an investor in an SMA that holds unlisted or illiquid securities will have to accept a discount when selling.

9. MANAGEMENT FEES[1]

h describe the three basic forms of performance-based fees;
i analyze and interpret a sample performance-based fee schedule.

Investors seek strong performance net of fees. Managers charge fees to cover operating costs and earn a return on their capital—primarily human capital. A manager's fixed costs are relatively small and primarily cover the costs of technology and the long-term lease of office space. Variable costs, which consist largely of payroll and marketing costs, dominate the income statements of asset management companies. Because a considerable portion of employee compensation comes in the form of bonuses, senior management can reduce bonus payouts as fee revenue declines in order to smooth a company's profitability.

Investors are increasingly sensitive to management fees. Average asset-weighted expense ratios (management fees and fund expenses) incurred by mutual fund investors have fallen substantially. In 2000, equity mutual fund investors incurred expense ratios of 0.99 percent, on average, or 99 cents for every $100 invested. By 2016, that average had fallen to 0.63 percent, a decline of 36 percent. Hybrid and bond mutual fund expense ratios also have declined. The average hybrid mutual fund expense ratio fell from 0.89 percent in 2000 to 0.74 percent in 2016, a reduction of 17 percent. The average bond mutual fund expense ratio fell from 0.76 percent in 2000 to 0.51 percent in 2016, a decline of 33 percent. The decline is a function of several factors: the allocation of the fixed portion of expenses over a larger asset base, increasing investor preference for no-load share classes, and the increasing allocations to lower-cost index funds. Aside from these structural factors lowering average expense ratios, there has been more generalized downward pressure on fees—the average expense ratio of actively managed equity mututal funds has declined from 1.06% in 2000 to 0.82% in 2016. Likewise, the average expense ratio of actively managed bond mutual funds has declined from 0.78% in 2000 to 0.58% in 2016.[2]

Investment firms charge fees in several different ways. In general, mutual funds charge fees based on assets under management in a fund.[3] Some classes of mutual funds, including those with reduced fees, require minimum balances. In contrast, institutional managers frequently offer declining percentage fees on increasing account sizes for separate or commingled pool accounts. Institutional accounts frequently specify minimum account sizes or minimum dollar fees. Fixed-percentage fees facilitate managers' and investors' planning for future cash flows, whereas dollar fees are subject to the variability of asset values.

Fee structures can influence which managers will be willing to accept a particular investment mandate. They can also strongly affect manager behavior. Economic theory suggests that the principal–agent problem is complicated by the fact that an agent's skills and actions are not fully visible to the principal. Although principals control asset availability, agents control both their expenditure of effort and portfolio risk. Moreover, the agent and principal may have different preferences; each might care about different time horizons and agents might not view losses the same way that principals do.[4] Finally, total performance is, to some extent, beyond the control of

---

[1] This section based on Chapter 6 in Essays on Manager Selection, by Scott D. Stewart, PhD, CFA, Research Foundation of CFA Institute. © 2013 CFA Institute. All rights reserved.
[2] ICI Investment Company Fact Book, 2017
[3] Although mutual funds may offer a declining management fee as fund assets increase, the individual investor does not benefit from investing more money unless the extra money qualifies the investor for a lower-fee fund class.
[4] For a summary of theoretical research on investment compensation, see Stracca (2006).

Management Fees

either party. As a result of these factors, the principal's and agent's interests may not be fully aligned. In reality, managers are motivated to work hard even without incentive fees because they want to retain current clients and expand their client base and pricing power. Incentives are useful, however, to help *ensure* that managers routinely act in their clients' best interest.

9.1 Assets under Management Fees

Assets under management fees, also called *ad valorem* fees (from the Latin for "according to value"), result from applying stated percentage rates to assets under management. These fees reward managers who attract and retain assets, generate added value, and experience benefits from rising markets. Managers primarily grow their assets through skillful investing, hard work, and effective marketing. A manager's success, however, also results partly from luck, especially in the short term. Managers benefit from rising portfolio values, which are attributable to the combination of alpha and beta decisions, but are also, at least for long-only managers, greatly affected by market cycles beyond the manager's control. A decline in *ad valorem* percentages as assets grow helps reduce the fee impact on investors from rising markets, but does not eliminate it.

Once a manager's assets are large, he might not want to risk losing them. Assets are typically "sticky"—that is, once investors allocate their assets to a manager, the manager often does not need to generate the same level of returns to retain the assets as he did to attract them. Empirical evidence suggests this stickiness is the case, to some extent, for mutual fund assets. To motivate such managers to work harder or discourage them from closet indexing, an incentive fee determined by future performance may be useful.

9.2 Performance-Based Fees

Performance-based fees are determined by portfolio returns and are designed to reward managers with a share of return for their skill in creating value. Performance can be calculated by using either total or relative return, and the return shared can be a percentage of total performance or performance net of a base or fixed fee. Performance-based fees are structured in one of three basic ways:

1. A symmetrical structure in which the manager is fully exposed to both the downside and upside (Computed fee = Base + Sharing of performance);

2. A bonus structure in which the manager is not fully exposed to the downside but is fully exposed to the upside [Computed fee = Higher of either (1) Base or (2) Base plus sharing of positive performance]; or

3. A bonus structure in which the manager is not fully exposed to either the downside or the upside [Computed fee = Higher of (1) Base or (2) Base plus sharing of performance, to a limit].

Performance fees are paid annually or, in some cases, less frequently. These fees may include maximum and high-water mark (or clawback) features that protect investors from situations such as paying for current positive performance before the negative effects of prior underperformance have been offset. Private equity, hedge fund, and real estate partnerships commonly earn performance fees on total returns and typically do not limit the amount of the performance fee. Hedge funds commonly include high-water mark features.

Consider the example of private equity partnerships, in which base fees are commonly applied to committed (not just invested) capital. Performance fees are earned as profits are realized, and invested capital is returned to investors. A common provision that helps protect private equity limited partners (the investors) is a requirement that the limited partners receive their principal and share of profits before performance fees are distributed to the general partner (the manager).

Specific performance-based fee structures are designed by both clients and managers. A formula is agreed upon based on the anticipated distribution of returns and the perceived attractiveness of the investment strategy. Managers who can command attractive terms, such as real estate managers that are in high demand and have limited capacity, have the power to stipulate the highest base fees and profit sharing in their fee agreements. Fee schedules are typically designed by fund managers, included in marketing materials, and set forth in partnership agreements. Large investors may influence the terms of fee schedules or negotiate side letters for special treatment.

A simple performance-based fee, as illustrated in Exhibit 8, specifies a base fee below which the computed fee can never fall. In this case, the manager is protected against sharing for performance below 25 bps. To make the result symmetrical around the commonplace 50 bps fee, the manager does not share in active performance beyond 2.75%.

Exhibit 8   Sample Performance-Based Fee Schedule

Panel A. Sample Fee Structure

Standard fee	0.50%
Base fee	0.25%
Sharing*	20%
Breakeven active return	1.50%
Maximum annual fee	0.75%

Panel B. Numerical Examples for Annual Periods

	Active Return				
	≤ 0.25%	1.00%	1.50%	2.00%	≥ 2.75%
Billed fee	0.25%	0.40%	0.50%	0.60%	0.75%
Net active return	≤ 0.00%	0.60%	1.00%	1.40%	≥ 2.00%

* On active return, beyond base fee.

If investment outcomes result from a mix of skill and luck (i.e., a probability distribution around a positive mean alpha), then performance fees constitute risk sharing. Fee structures must be designed carefully to avoid favoring one party over the other. Performance-based fees work to align the interests of managers and investors because both parties share in investment results. Investors benefit by paying performance-based fees, rather than standard fees, when active returns are low. Managers may work harder to earn performance-based fees, inspiring the term "incentive based." Empirical evidence suggests a correlation between performance-based fees and higher alphas (also, lower fees) for mutual funds and higher risk-adjusted returns for hedge funds.[5] Asset managers may consider performance-based fees attractive because such fees provide an opportunity to enhance profits on the upside and ensure guaranteed, although perhaps minimal, streams of revenue from base fees when performance is poor.

---

5 See Elton, Gruber, and Blake (2003) and Ackermann, McEnally, and Ravenscraft (1999).

Performance-based fees can also create tensions between investors and managers. Investors must pay base fees even when managers underperform. Management firm revenues decline when cash is needed to invest in operations or retain talent. In fact, the failure rate for poor-performing and even zero-alpha managers may tend to be higher when performance-based rather than standard fees are used.[6]

Performance-based fee structures may also lead to misestimates of portfolio risk. Such fee structures convert symmetrical gross active return distributions into asymmetrical net active return distributions, reducing variability on the upside but not the downside. As a result, a single standard deviation calculated on a return series that incorporates active returns, above and below the base fee, can lead to the underestimation of downside risk.[7]

Investors and managers may have different incentives when performance-based fees are used. For example, according to a utility maximization model, fully symmetric fees, in which the manager is fully exposed to the downside, tend to yield closer alignment in risk and effort than bonus-style fees.[8] Understandably, symmetrical fee structures are unpopular with managers because of their impact on bankruptcy risk.

Bonus-style fees are the close equivalent of a manager's call option on a share of active return, for which the base fee is the strike price. Consider Exhibit 9, which shows a familiar-looking option payoff pattern using the fee parameters defined in Exhibit 8. In this case, the option payoff is modified by a maximum fee feature. The graph illustrates three fee components: a 25 bps base fee, plus a long call option on active return with a strike price equal to the minimum (base) fee, minus another (less valuable) call option with a strike price equal to the maximum fee.

Exhibit 9 Payoff Line of Sample Performance-Based Fee Schedule

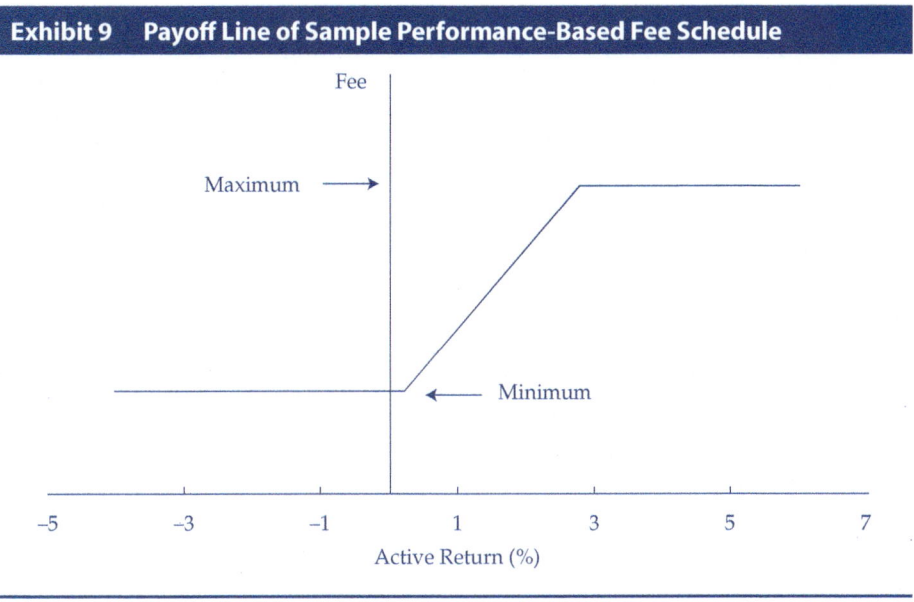

Managers must retain clients year to year, avoid poor performance, and not violate management guidelines. But managers also tend to have an interest in increasing risk, which may conflict with these goals. Based on option pricing theory,[9] higher volatility leads to higher option value, which encourages managers to assume higher portfolio

---

6 See Grinold and Rudd (1987).
7 See Kritzman (2012).
8 See Starks (1987).
9 Margrabe (1978) notes that an incentive fee (without a maximum) consists of a call option on the portfolio and a put on the benchmark. As a result, the value depends on the volatility of the portfolio and the benchmark and the correlation between the two—in other words, the active risk.

risk. This behavior has been observed in the marketplace.[10] As a result, investors, when possible, should carefully select benchmarks and monitor risk in their portfolios.[11] Senior management at investment firms should also ensure that their compensation systems penalize portfolio managers for assuming excessive risk as well as reward them for earning superior returns.[12]

Real Story: The Client's Free Option in a Performance Fee Agreement

Consider the case of an equity manager in the early 1990s offering a performance-based fee that consisted of a 10 bp base fee and a 20% share of active return in excess of the benchmark index (net of the 10 bps). The fee structure also included a maximum annual fee provision that reserved excess fees for subsequent years. Because there was no penalty for cancelling the fee agreement, clients could opt out of the performance-based fee in exchange for a standard flat fee when performance was particularly strong. This arrangement allowed them to avoid paying the manager's accrued, fully earned share, and is precisely what many clients did in the mid-1990s following a period of high active returns.

Other problems exist with performance-based fees. When managers have clients with varying fee structures, it is in their (short-term) interest to favor customers that have performance-based fees. Although doing so may be unethical or potentially illegal, managers can direct trades or deals (including initial public offerings) to performance-fee clients to their benefit and to the detriment of others. It may be difficult for clients to monitor this activity. Fortunately, most managers recognize that such actions, once discovered, could destroy their careers or lead to criminal charges. Here again, due diligence, including the review of internal compliance systems, will help limit an investor's exposure to unscrupulous managers.

When managers can control the timing of profit realization, as is often the case with private equity partnerships, they may have an incentive to hold on to assets until a profit can be realized. Managers may do so even when clients would benefit from selling assets at a loss and investing the proceeds outside of the partnership. In contrast, hedge fund managers have an incentive to return assets in poor-performing partnerships when the high-water mark is substantially above current value (i.e., the performance-fee option is considerably out of the money). This action results in the investor missing the opportunity to recoup previously paid fees based on future strong performance.

Funds of funds (FoFs) commonly charge fees in addition to the fees charged by the underlying funds.[13] These fees pay for the investor's access to the underlying funds and for the FoFs' due diligence, portfolio construction, and monitoring. In addition to these two sets of fees, investors are required to share the profits from well-performing underlying funds but incur the full loss from poorly performing funds.[14] To protect

---

10 See Elton et al. (2003).
11 Starks (1987) notes that an investor can simply set a fee schedule incorporating penalties for observed risk to align interests regarding risk levels.
12 Although it adds a layer of complexity to the evaluation process, an active-risk-adjusted bonus formula can be specified.
13 When funds of funds were popular in the 2000s, it was common for them to charge a performance-based fee.
14 Kritzman (2012) calls this result an "asymmetry penalty."

Management Fees

investors from paying overly high fees, hedge fund consortiums have recently begun to offer fee structures based on the total portfolio value of underlying funds, rather than the sum of fees computed at the individual fund level.

The Impact of Fee Structure on Net Returns

Consider four fee structures applied to the same 12-month return series gross of fees:

- 0.50% management fee, 0% performance fee
- 0.50% management fee, 15% performance fee
- 1.50% management fee, 0% performance fee
- 1.50% management fee, 15% performance fee

The fees are accrued at the end of each month. This example is a simplification but illustrates the important effects of fee level and structure on net performance. As Exhibit 10 shows, the average monthly gross return is 0.72% with a 1.37% monthly standard deviation. Not surprisingly, charging a management fee (MF) lowers the level of realized return without affecting the standard deviation of the series. The management fee is a constant shift in the level and thus does not affect volatility. The addition of a performance fee (PF) also lowers the level of realized returns but has the added effect of lowering the realized standard deviation. This dynamic occurs because in up months, the performance fee is accrued, and in down months, it is subtracted from the accrual balance to reflect the appropriate fee for the cumulative performance. This accounting has the effect of adjusting the monthly returns toward zero and lowering the measured volatility. The larger the performance fee, the more pronounced this effect. Exhibit 11 shows a graph of the cumulative returns for each fee structure.

Exhibit 10 Effects of Expense on Portfolio Performance

	Monthly Gross Return				
	MF = 0%	MF = 0.5%		MF = 1.5%	
Month	PF = 0%	PF = 0%	PF = 15%	PF = 0%	PF = 15%
1	2.00%	1.96%	1.66%	1.88%	1.59%
2	3.00%	2.96%	2.51%	2.88%	2.44%
3	−0.20%	−0.24%	−0.21%	−0.32%	−0.28%
4	−0.50%	−0.54%	−0.46%	−0.62%	−0.53%
5	0.50%	0.46%	0.39%	0.37%	0.32%
6	0.90%	0.86%	0.73%	0.77%	0.66%
7	1.00%	0.96%	0.81%	0.88%	0.74%
8	−2.00%	−2.04%	−1.74%	−2.12%	−1.81%
9	1.50%	1.46%	1.24%	1.37%	1.17%
10	2.00%	1.96%	1.66%	1.88%	1.59%
11	−0.50%	−0.54%	−0.46%	−0.62%	−0.53%
12	1.00%	0.96%	0.81%	0.88%	0.74%
Average Return	0.72%	0.67%	0.57%	0.59%	0.50%
S.D.	1.37%	1.37%	1.16%	1.37%	1.16%

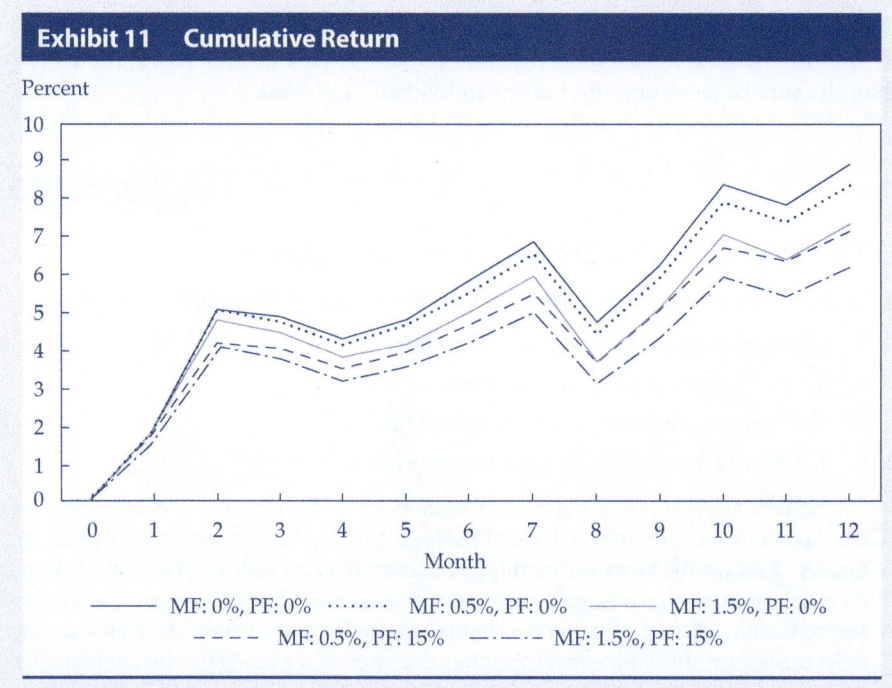

Exhibit 11 Cumulative Return

Given the potentially significant effect of expenses, a clear distinction must be drawn between performance analysis based on gross returns and net of expenses returns.

An additional consideration is the different degree of uncertainty between expenses and the potential added value of the active portfolio manager. Expenses are paid for certain, whereas the added value of the active strategy compared with the passive strategy is uncertain. For example, suppose an active strategy is expected to generate a gross return that is 2% greater than the passive strategy, but the cost of the active strategy is 2% greater than the passive strategy. A risk-averse investor would likely prefer the passive strategy; although the expected net return of the strategies is the same, the uncertainty of the outperformance would be unappealing. The riskier the active strategy, the greater the return volatility and the greater the volatility of the added value relative to the passive strategy. The significance is, the added value of the active strategy has to be sufficiently large and certain to justify the higher cost of the strategy.

In sum, the presence of positive significant average excess return is evidence for manager skill. This excess return, however, must be net of fees and expenses for the benefit of this skill to accrue to the investor.[15] The preference is for more linear compensation to the manager to reduce the incentives to change the portfolio's risk profile at inflection points.

SUMMARY

Evaluating an investment manager is a complex and detailed process. It encompasses a great deal more than analyzing investment returns. In conducting investment manager due diligence, the focus is on understanding how the investment results were

---

[15] Ultimately, the net return to the investor accounts not only for fees and expenses but also for taxes. This more complex issue is beyond the scope of this reading.

Summary

achieved and assessing the likelihood that the manager will continue to follow the same investment process that generated these returns. This process also entails operational due diligence, including an evaluation of the integrity of the firm, its operations, and personnel, as well as evaluating the vehicle structure and terms. As such, due diligence involves both quantitative and qualitative analysis.

This reading provides a framework that introduces and describes the important elements of the manager selection process:

- Investment manager selection involves a broad set of qualitative and quantitative considerations to determine whether a manager displays skill and the likelihood that the manager will continue to display skill in the future.

- The qualitative analysis consists of investment due diligence, which evaluates the manager's investment process, investment personnel, and portfolio construction; and operational due diligence, which evaluates the manager's infrastructure.

- A Type I error is hiring or retaining a manager who subsequently underperforms expectations—that is, rejecting the null hypothesis of no skill when it is correct. A Type II error is not hiring or firing a manager who subsequently outperforms, or performs in line with, expectations—that is, not rejecting the null hypothesis when it is incorrect.

- The manager search and selection process has three broad components: the universe, a quantitative analysis of the manager's performance track record, and a qualitative analysis of the manager's investment process. The qualitative analysis includes both investment due diligence and operational due diligence.

- Capture ratio measures the asymmetry of returns, and a ratio greater than 1 indicates greater participation in rising versus falling markets. Drawdown is the loss incurred in any continuous period of negative returns.

- The investment philosophy is the foundation of the investment process. The philosophy outlines the set of assumptions about the factors that drive performance and the manager's beliefs about their ability to successfully exploit these sources of return. The investment manager should have a clear and concise investment philosophy. It is important to evaluate these assumptions and the role they play in the investment process to understand how the strategy will behave over time and across market environments. The investment process has to be consistent and appropriate for the philosophy, and the investment personnel need to possess sufficient expertise and experience to effectively execute the investment process.

- Style analysis, understanding the manager's risk exposures relative to the benchmark, is an important component of performance appraisal and manager selection, helping to define the universe of suitable managers.

- Returns-based style analysis is a top-down approach that involves estimating the risk exposures from an actual return series for a given period. Although RBSA adds an additional analytical step, the analysis is straightforward and should identify the important drivers of return and risk factors for the period analyzed. It can be estimated even for complicated strategies and is comparable across managers and through time. The disadvantage is that RBSA is an imprecise tool, attributing performance to an unchanging average portfolio during the period that might not reflect the current or future portfolio exposures.

- Holdings-based style analysis is a bottom-up approach that estimates the risk exposures from the actual securities held in the portfolio at a point in time. HBSA allows for the estimation of current risk factors and should identify all important drivers of return and risk factors, be comparable across managers and through time, and provide an accurate view of the manager's risk exposures. The disadvantages are the additional computational effort, dependence on the degree of transparency provided by the manager, and the possibility that accuracy may be compromised by stale pricing and window dressing.

- The prospectus, private placement memorandum, and/or limited partnership agreement are, in essence, the contract between the investor and the manager, outlining each party's rights and responsibilities. The provisions are liquidity terms and fees. Limited liquidity reduce the investor's flexibility to adjust portfolio allocations in light of changing market conditions or investor circumstances. On the other hand, limited liquidity allows the funds to take long-term views and hold less liquid securities with reduced risk of having to divest assets at inopportune times in response to redemption requests. A management fee lowers the level of realized return without affecting the standard deviation, whereas a performance fee has the added effect of lowering the realized standard deviation. The preference is for more-linear compensation to reduce the incentives to change the portfolio's risk profile at inflection points.

- The choice between individual separate accounts and pooled (or commingled) vehicles is dependent upon the consistency with the investment process, the suitability for the investor IPS, and whether the benefits outweigh the additional costs.

- Investment management fees take one of two forms: a fixed percentage fee based on assets under management or a performance-based fee which charges a percentage of the portfolio's total return or excess return over a benchmark or hurdle rate. Performance-based fees work to align the interests of managers and investors because both parties share in investment results. Most managers that charge a performance fee also charge some level of fixed percentage fee to aid business continuity efforts. Fee structures must be designed carefully to avoid favoring one party over the other.

REFERENCES

Ackermann, Carl, Richard McEnally, and David Ravenscraft. 1999. "The Performance of Hedge Funds: Risk, Return and Incentives." *Journal of Finance* 54 (3): 833–74.

Elton, Edwin, Martin Gruber, and Christopher Blake. 2003. "Incentive Fees and Mutual Funds." *Journal of Finance* 58 (2): 779–804.

Grinold, Richard, and Andrew Rudd. 1987. "Incentive Fees: Who Wins? Who Loses?" *Financial Analysts Journal* 43 (1): 27–38.

Khandani, Amir E., and Andrew W. Lo. 2011. "What Happened to the Quants in August 2007? Evidence from Factors and Transactions Data." *Journal of Financial Markets*, vol. 14, no. 1 (February):1–46.

Kritzman, Mark. 2012. "Two Things about Performance Fees." *Journal of Portfolio Management* 38 (2): 4–5.

Kuenzi, David E. 2003. "Strategy Benchmarks." *Journal of Portfolio Management* 29 (2): 46–56.

Lo, Andrew W. 2004. "*The Adaptive Markets Hypothesis: Market Efficiency from an Evolutionary Perspective.*" Journal of Portfolio Management, vol. 30, no. 5 (30th Anniversary):15–20.

Margrabe, William. 1978. "The Value of an Option to Exchange One Asset for Another." *Journal of Finance* 33 (1): 177–86.

Starks, Laura. 1987. "Performance Incentive Fees: An Agency Theoretic Approach." *Journal of Financial and Quantitative Analysis* 22 (1): 17–32.

Stewart, Scott D., John J. Neumann, Christopher R. Knittel, and Jeffrey Heisler. 2009. "Absence of Value: An Analysis of Investment Allocation Decisions by Institutional Plan Sponsors." *Financial Analysts Journal*, vol. 65, no. 6 (November/December):34–51.

Stracca, Livio. 2006. "Delegated Portfolio Management: A Survey of the Theoretical Literature." *Journal of Economic Surveys* 20 (5): 823–48.

Zuckerman, Gregory. 2008. "Fees, Even Returns and Auditor All Raised Red Flags." *Wall Street Journal* (13 December 2008).

PRACTICE PROBLEMS

1. Which of the following qualitative considerations is *most* associated with determining whether investment manager selection will result in superior repeatable performance?
   A Transparency
   B Investment process
   C Operational process

2. Which of the following is *most likely* a key consideration in investment due diligence?
   A Suitability of the investment vehicle
   B Back office processes and procedures
   C Depth of expertise and experience of investment personnel

3. A decision-making investor is *most likely* to worry more about making a Type I error than a Type II error because:
   A Type II errors are errors of commission.
   B Type I errors are more easily measured.
   C Type II errors are more likely to have to be explained as to why a skilled manager was fired.

4. An investor is considering hiring three managers who have the following skill levels:

Manager	Large-cap skill level	Small-cap skill level
1	Skilled	Unskilled
2	Skilled	Skilled
3	Unskilled	Unskilled

   Type I and Type II errors both occur when the investor is:
   A hiring Manager 1 for large-cap stocks and not hiring Manager 3 for small-cap stocks.
   B hiring Manager 3 for large-cap stocks and not hiring Manager 2 for small-cap stocks.
   C hiring Manager 3 for large-cap stocks and not hiring Manager 1 for small-cap stocks.

5. Suppose that the results of a style analysis for an investment manager are not consistent with the stated philosophy of the manager and the manager's stated investment process. These facts suggest the:
   A absence of style drift.
   B investment process may not be repeatable.
   C manager should be included in the universe of potential managers.

6. Compared with holdings-based style analysis (HBSA), a returns-based style analysis (RBSA):
   A is subject to window dressing.
   B requires less effort to acquire data.
   C is more accurate when illiquid securities are present.

7 A manager whose relative performance is worse during market downturns *most likely* has a capture ratio that is:
   A   less than one.
   B   equal to one.
   C   greater than one.

8 Which of the following is consistent with the expectation that exploiting a structural inefficiency is repeatable?
   A   The inefficiency is a unique event that occurs infrequently.
   B   The level of gross return is equal to the amount of transaction costs and expenses.
   C   The aggregate value of all assets affected by the inefficiency is larger than the AUM of the manager and its competitors.

9 Which of the following is **not** a reason that an investor might favor a separately managed account rather than a pooled vehicle? The investor:
   A   is tax exempt.
   B   requires real-time details on investment positions.
   C   has expressed certain constraints and preferences for the portfolio.

10 Which of the following investment vehicles provide investors with the highest degree of liquidity?
   A   Open-end funds
   B   Private equity funds
   C   Limited partnerships

11 Which of the following statements is consistent with the manager adhering to a stated investment philosophy and investment decision-making process?
   A   Senior investment team members have left to form their own firm.
   B   A senior employee has been cited by the SEC for violating insider trading regulations.
   C   A large drawdown occurs because of an unforeseen political event in a foreign country.

12 A manager has a mandate to be fully invested with a benchmark that is a blend of large-cap stocks and investment-grade bonds. Which of the following is **not** an indication that style drift has occurred? The manager:
   A   initiates an allocation to small-cap stocks.
   B   decreases investments in investment-grade corporate bonds.
   C   increases allocation to cash in anticipation of a market decline.

13 The manager selection process begins by defining the universe of feasible managers. When defining this manager universe, the selection process should avoid:
   A   excluding managers based on historical risk-adjusted returns.
   B   identifying the benchmark against which managers will be evaluated.
   C   using third-party categorizations of managers to find those that might fill the desired role in the portfolio.

14 A return distribution of skilled managers that is highly distinct from the return distribution of unskilled managers, *most likely* implies a:
   A   highly efficient market.
   B   low opportunity cost of not hiring a skilled manager.
   C   high opportunity cost of not hiring a skilled manager.

Practice Problems

15 An advantage of a returns-based style analysis is that such analysis:
   A is comparable across managers.
   B is suitable for portfolios that contain illiquid securities.
   C can effectively profile a manager's risk exposures using a short return series.

16 Which of the following types of style analysis use(s) a bottom-up approach to estimate the risk exposures in a portfolio?
   A Returns-based style analysis only
   B Holdings-based style analysis only
   C Both return-based and holdings-based style analysis

17 In a quarter, an investment manager's upside capture is 75% and downside capture is 125%. We can conclude that the manager underperforms the benchmark:
   A only when the benchmark return is positive.
   B only when the benchmark return is negative.
   C when the benchmark return is either positive or negative.

18 Which of the following fee structures *most likely* decreases the volatility of a portfolio's net returns?
   A Incentive fees only
   B Management fees only
   C Neither incentive fees nor management fees

19 An investor should prefer a pooled investment vehicle to a separately managed account when she:
   A is cost sensitive.
   B focuses on tax efficiency.
   C requires clear legal ownership of assets.

20 Which of the following investment types is the most liquid?
   A ETFs
   B Hedge funds
   C Private equity funds

The following information relates to Questions 21–26

The Tree Fallers Endowment plans to allocate part of its portfolio to alternative investment funds. The endowment has hired Kurt Summer, a consultant at Summer Brothers Consultants, to identify suitable alternative investment funds for its portfolio.

Summer has identified three funds for potential investment and will present the performance of these investments to the endowment's board of directors at their next quarterly meeting.

Summer is reviewing each of the fund's fee schedules and is concerned about the manager's incentive to take on excess risk in an attempt to generate a higher fee. Exhibit 1 presents the fee schedules of the three funds.

Exhibit 1 Fee Schedules

Fund	Computed Fee	Base Fee	Sharing	Maximum Annual Fee
Red Grass Fund	Higher of either (1) base or (2) base plus sharing of positive performance; sharing is based on return net of the base fee.	1.00%	20%	na
Blue Water Fund	Higher of either (1) base or (2) base plus sharing of positive performance, up to a maximum annual fee of 2.50%; sharing is based on active return.	0.50%	20%	2.50%
Yellow Wood Fund	Base plus sharing of both positive and negative performance; sharing is based on return net of the base fee.	1.50%	20%	na

Exhibit 2 presents the annual gross returns for each fund and its respective benchmark for the period of 2016–2018. All funds have an inception date of 1 January 2016. Summer intends to include in his report an explanation of the impact of the fee structures of the three funds on returns.

Exhibit 2 Fund and Benchmark Returns

	2016		2017		2018	
Fund	Gross Return (%)	Benchmark Return (%)	Gross Return (%)	Benchmark Return (%)	Gross Return (%)	Benchmark Return (%)
Red Grass Fund	8.00	8.00	−2.00	−10.00	5.00	4.50
Blue Water Fund	10.00	9.00	−4.00	−1.50	14.00	2.00
Yellow Wood Fund	15.00	14.00	−5.00	−6.50	7.00	9.50

The board of directors of the Tree Fallers Endowment asks Summer to recalculate the fees of the Red Grass Fund assuming a high-water mark feature whereby a sharing percentage could only be charged to the extent any losses had been recouped.

21 Based on Exhibit 1, which fund has a symmetrical fee structure?
   A Red Grass
   B Blue Water
   C Yellow Wood

22 Based on the fee schedules in Exhibit 1, the portfolio manager of which fund has the greatest incentive to assume additional risk to earn a higher investment management fee?
   A Red Grass
   B Blue Water
   C Yellow Wood

23 Based on Exhibit 1 and Exhibit 2, the Yellow Wood Fund's 2016 investment management fee is:

A 3.00%.

B 4.20%.

C 4.50%.

24 Based on Exhibit 1 and Exhibit 2, the Red Grass Fund's 2017 investment management fee is:

A 0.40%.

B 1.00%.

C 2.60%.

25 Based on Exhibit 1 and Exhibit 2, the Blue Water Fund's 2018 investment management fee is:

A 2.40%

B 2.50%.

C 2.90%

26 In which year would the Red Grass Fund's investment management fee be affected by Summer's recalculation using the high-water mark?

A 2016

B 2017

C 2018

The following information relates to Questions 27–29

John Connell inherited $700,000 at the beginning of the year and has been developing related investment goals and policies with a financial adviser. The adviser has identified three potential investment funds for consideration. All three have earned similar returns over the last five years and are expected to earn similar returns going forward. Publishing their investment results on a timely and routine basis, they include the following asset classes:

- US equities
- Global equities
- Venture capital
- Corporate bonds
- Government bonds
- Cash reserves

Exhibit 1 presents information about the funds.

Exhibit 1   Fund Characteristics

Characteristic	Zeta	Eta	Theta
Organization	Independent investment fund	Part of a medium-sized investment firm with multiple funds	Part of a large investment firm that rotates investment professionals among funds
Team Size	Small	Small	Small
Staff Turnover	High	Medium	Low
Incentive Compensation	Salary adjustment when returns exceed benchmark	Annual salary adjustment	Annual salary adjustment and performance-based bonus
Key People	Founder directs all trades and investment decisions	Fund manager and assistant fund manager make investment decisions	Fund manager and assistant fund manager lead team in selecting investments
Longevity/Experience	Founder in the investment business for > 25 years	Fund manager in the investment business for > 15 years; assistant fund manager for > 12 years	Fund manager in the investment business for > 20 years; assistant fund manager for > 10 years. Fund family is more than 50 years old.

27 **Select** the fund, based on the Exhibit 1 data, that is *most appropriate* for Connell's needs. **Justify** your selection with *two* reasons.

Select the fund, based on the Exhibit 1 data, that is *most appropriate* for Connell's needs. (Circle one)	**Justify** your selection with *two* reasons.
Zeta	
Eta	
Theta	

Connell elects to defer fund selection and places his inheritance in a short-term money market account. A year later, Connell reviews the one-year performance results of the three funds compared to the benchmark, as shown in Exhibit 2.

Practice Problems

Exhibit 2	Fund Performance Compared to Benchmark*		
Fund	Underperforms	In Line	Outperforms
Zeta		X	
Eta	X		
Theta			X

*Assume performance is mean reverting within this period.

Connell believes he now has two main alternatives for fund investment:

- Alternative 1: Keep his inheritance in the money market account to avoid the Eta fund.
- Alternative 2: Place his inheritance in the Theta fund.

28 **Identify** the type of error Connell is at risk of committing and its associated cost for *each* alternative. **Justify** your selection.

Connell asks the adviser about the conditions under which any form of style analysis would be useful for understanding the funds he is considering.

29 **Identify** the conditions under which the adviser would find style analysis *most* useful.

The following information relates to Questions 30–31

Cassandra Yang, age 59, is a manager at a large US manufacturing firm. Yang is single, owns a home, is debt free, and saves 20% of her pre-tax income in a company retirement plan and 15% of her after-tax income in a short-term money market account. Her accounts are self-directed; Yang makes all related decisions independently.

While Yang hates to suffer investment losses, she now seeks higher returns on 80% of the funds in her money market account. To help achieve her goal of retiring within three years, she is considering the actively managed investment funds listed in Exhibit 1.

(continued)

Exhibit 1 Return Profile Summary

Fund	Upside Capture	Downside Capture	Most Recent Drawdown Loss	Most Recent Drawdown Duration
Alpha	80	20	57%	21 months
Beta	55	45	38%	15 months
Gamma	50	50	28%	12 months

30 **Select** the *best* fund for Yang, using only the information provided. **Justify** your selection.

Select the *best* fund for Yang, using only the information provided. (Circle one)	Justify your selection.
Alpha	
Beta	
Gamma	

Yang is also considering Aspen Investments (Aspen) for a portion of her money market funds. Aspen's investment philosophy states: "We pursue a passive investment strategy, which seeks to identify and exploit structural inefficiencies through identifying mispricings created by loss aversion. Our strategy and philosophy have evolved over time in response to fund and market performance."

31 **Determine** whether Yang is likely to judge that Aspen follows a consistent investment philosophy, using only the information provided. **Justify** your response with *two* reasons.

Determine whether Yang is likely to judge that Aspen follows a consistent investment philosophy, using only the information provided. (Circle one)	Justify your response with *two* reasons.
Yes	
No	

The following information relates to Questions 32–33

Donna Grimmett is working with a financial adviser to establish her investment goals for €850,000, which she recently earned as a bonus. She asks the adviser about how to best select a manager for her funds.

Practice Problems

The adviser responds that both qualitative and quantitative components are involved in outlining a framework for identifying, evaluating, and ultimately selecting a manager.

32 **Describe** *two* considerations for *each* type of component recommended to Grimmett for her manager selection process.

Manager Selection Components	Describe *two* considerations for *each* type of component recommended to Grimmett for her manager selection process.
Qualitative	
Quantitative	

Grimmett asks the adviser if any other preparatory steps should be taken before choosing the best investment manager(s). The adviser produces a checklist related to manager selection in response to Grimmett's question.

33 **Describe** the content of the adviser's checklist related to manager selection.

Describe the content of the adviser's checklist related to manager selection.

The following information relates to Question 34

Boinic Corporation introduced an employee pension plan and set aside $20 million to fund the plan. Assessing five investment management firms, A through E, and expecting all to perform in line with their benchmarks, Boinic selected three firms (A, D, and E) to manage part of the pension plan assets. Exhibit 1 shows the managers' performance compared to their benchmark in the one year after being selected.

Exhibit 1 Year 1 Investment Firm Performance versus Benchmark

	Firm A	Firm B	Firm C	Firm D	Firm E
Year 1 performance versus benchmark	Above	Above	Below	Below	Above

On analyzing these results, Boinic determines that it has made both a Type I and Type II error.

34 **Identify** the firm associated with Boinic's Type I and Type II error. **Justify** your selection for *each* error type, discussing the psychological effects of its Year 1 performance on Boinic.

Identify the firm associated with Boinic's Type I and Type II error. (Circle one for each error type)	**Justify** your selection for *each* error type, discussing the psychological effects of its Year 1 performance on Boinic.

Type I Error	
Firm A	
Firm B	
Firm C	
Firm D	
Firm E	

Type II Error	
Firm A	
Firm B	
Firm C	
Firm D	
Firm E	

The following information relates to Question 35

Susan Patnode, age 66, was recently widowed and received £2,000,000 from a spousal life insurance policy. Patnode would like to invest the proceeds to generate predictable income to cover her ongoing living expenses.

Patnode is considering three investment managers, Laurbær Partners, Alcanfor Limited, and Mylesten Management, to manage the insurance policy proceeds. All three take an active investment approach. Further information regarding each of the investment manager's investment philosophy and approach is provided in Exhibit 1

Exhibit 1 Information on Investment Manager Philosophy/Approach

Investment Manager	Investment Philosophy / Approach
Laurbær Partners	Seeks to produce returns through investing in new investment themes and emphasizes measuring the contribution of each to performance.
Alcanfor Limited	Seeks to produce returns through investing in securities that appear to be mispriced in their industry sectors and tracks their ultimate performance against market benchmarks.
Mylesten Management	Seeks to produce returns through investing with maximum flexibility to the most popular investor sentiments worldwide

35 **Identify** which investment manager is *most* suitable for Patnode. **Justify** your response based solely on *each* manager's investment philosophy and approach

Practice Problems

Identify which investment manager is *most* suitable for Patnode. (Circle one)	**Justify** your response based solely on *each* manager's investment philosophy and approach.
Laurbær Partners	
Alcanfor Limited	
Mylesten Management	

The following information relates to Questions 36–37

Frances Lute is an investment manager for a large institutional investment management firm in London. His client, Parade University (Parade), has an endowment worth approximately GBP1.6 billion. Lute is considering three active investment managers in order to add one new style. Parade's investment policy statement (IPS) highlights the endowment's preference for low turnover and trading costs.

Lute is particularly concerned about portfolio construction and the prospective implementation of investments within the portfolio. All else equal, Lute has identified these distinguishing characteristics for the processes affecting portfolio construction by the three managers.

- Manager A uses hard-stop losses to manage risk.
- Manager B's portfolio can be liquidated within five business days or less.
- Manager C's portfolio turnover is greater than the frequency of signals generated.

36 **Identify** which manager is *most* appropriate for Parade. **Justify** your response.

Identify which manager is *most* appropriate for Parade. (Circle one)		
Manager A	Manager B	Manager C
Justify your response.		

Upon choosing a manager, Lute must allocate the funds either to a separately managed account (SMA) customized for Parade or a pooled vehicle called Diversified. In addition to low turnover and trading costs, Parade's IPS also prioritizes the following characteristics for its investment: transparency, investor behavior, cost, liquidity, and tracking risk. While each type of investment vehicle offers distinct advantages, Parade is unclear as to which advantage is applicable by type.

37 **Identify** which investment vehicle *best* addresses *each* characteristic highlighted in Parade's IPS by placing a check mark where appropriate. **Justify** your response.

Identify which investment vehicle *best* addresses *each* characteristic highlighted in Parade's IPS by placing an x where appropriate.	**Justify** your response.

Characteristic	SMA	Diversified	Justification
Transparency			
Investor Behavior			
Cost			
Liquidity			
Tracking Risk			

The following information relates to Questions 38–40

Jack Porter and Melissa Smith are co-managers for the Circue Library Foundation (Circue) in Canada. Within the next six months, Porter and Smith will be replacing one of Circue's underperforming active managers. This choice will rely on the terms of investment management contracts—specifically, liquidity and management fee structure. Circue's IPS indicates some tolerance for lower liquidity, a moderate sensitivity to management fees, and a heightened sensitivity to closet indexing.

Circue is considering the following three investment vehicles with distinct fee structures:

- Hedge funds with a soft lock
- Open-end funds with an incentive fee
- Closed-end funds with no incentive fee

38 **Determine** which of the three investment vehicles is *most* appropriate for Circue's IPS. **Justify** your response.

Determine which of the three investment vehicles is *most* appropriate for Circue's IPS. (Circle one)		
Hedge funds with a soft lock	Open-end funds with an incentive fee	Closed-end funds with no incentive fee
Justify your response.		

Porter and Smith next consider how the performance-based fee structures of the prospective managers may affect portfolio risk.

Porter states: "I've noticed more managers are applying a bonus structure in which the manager is not fully exposed to the downside but is fully exposed to the upside."

Smith states: "Circue's current market view is that there are increasing risks to the downside."

39 **Discuss** how Smith's stated expectation would be reflected in estimated portfolio risk under the fee structure identified by Porter.

After narrowing their choice to three managers with different fee structures, Porter and Smith analyze the effect of the performance-based fee structure for each manager. Exhibit A provides applicable data for one of the managers.

Practice Problems

Exhibit A Selected Performance-Based Fee Data for a Prospective Manager

Fee Structure	Fee (%)
Standard Fee	0.35
Base Fee	0.20
Sharing*	0.25
Breakeven Active Return	1.25
Maximum Annual Fee	0.90

*On active return, beyond base fee.

To understand the effect each fee structure has on its respective portfolio, Porter and Smith must estimate the net active return for several possible gross active returns, including less than or equal to 0.20%, 0.75%, 1.25%, and 1.75%.

40 Calculate the net active return based on each possible gross active return provided using the selected data in Exhibit A. **Show** your calculations.

Calculate the net active return based on each possible gross active return provided using the selected data in Exhibit A.

Gross Active Return	≤ 0.20%	0.75%	1.25%	1.75%
Net Active Return				

Show your calculations.

The following information relates to Question 41

Brickridge Investment Consultants meets weekly to review the positives and negatives of investment managers being considered for client portfolios. In the latest meeting, analyst Brad Moore discusses investment manager Lyon Management (Lyon). His in-depth analysis of one of Lyon's investment strategies includes the following summary details:

Detail 1: Long and short positions are paired.

Detail 2: Investment strategy relies on unique information.

Detail 3: AUM connected with the strategy have grown substantially, while the number and characteristics of positions have stayed the same.

Asked about Lyon's regulatory context, Moore states, "The regulatory environment is strong and seeks to decrease information symmetries."

41 Identify whether each detail from Moore's summary is *most likely* a benefit or a drawback of the strategy. **Justify** your selection.

Identify whether each detail from Moore's summary is *most likely* a benefit or a drawback of the strategy. (Place an x in the preferred box.)	Justify your selection.

Detail	Benefit	Drawback	Justification
1			
2			
3			

The following information relates to Question 42

Institutional investment consultant Wilsot Consultants (Wilsot) is reviewing multiple investment managers within a prospective client's portfolio. Two of the managers, Vaudreuil Capital Management (Vaudreuil) and Pourtir Investments (Pourtir), have similar strategies that show comparable performance on a net-of-fees basis. Assessing the portfolio effects of management fees, a Wilsot analyst reviews both manager contracts to determine their advantages and disadvantages to the client. Checking client fee structures, the analyst notes Vaudreuil's fees are AUM-based while Pourtir's are performance-based.

42 Discuss *one* advantage and *one* disadvantage to the client of *each* manager's contracted fee structure.

Discuss *one* advantage and *one* disadvantage to the client of *each* manager's contracted fee structure.

Manager	Advantage	Disadvantage
Vaudreuil		
Pourtir		

The following information relates to Question 43

At a meeting for the local municipal pension fund, a group of beneficiaries expressed concern about current investment management fees. The beneficiaries asked the Investment Committee for a fee summary of each manager in the portfolio.

The next day, a pension fund staff member briefed the Committee on the managers' full contracted fee schedules. The Committee was surprised to hear that the managers work under numerous different fee structures and rates. A sample of these fee schedules for two managers is provided in Exhibit 1:

Practice Problems

Exhibit 1 Fee Schedules for Selected Managers: Hidden Lake and Carpenter Management

Fee Type	Hidden Lake	Carpenter Management
Base Fee	0.30%	0.18%*
Sharing**	15%	20%
Maximum Annual Fee	N/A	0.80%

*Minimum fee.
**On active return, beyond base fee.

In explaining the differences, the staff member said that fee structures may lead to misestimates of portfolio risk. She also noted that performance-based fees sometimes are a close equivalent to a manager's call option on active return.

43 **Identify** which manager's fee structure is *most* similar to a call option on a share of active return. **Justify** your selection.

Identify which manager's fee structure is *most* similar to a call option on a share of active return. (Circle one)

Hidden Lake	Carpenter Management

Justify your selection.

SOLUTIONS

1. B is correct. A critical element of manager selection is to assess if the investment process is superior, repeatable, and can be consistently applied.

2. C is correct. Experienced investment personnel is a key aspect of investment due diligence. A strong back office and suitable investment vehicles are key aspects of operational due diligence.

3. B is correct. Type I errors are more easily measured than Type II errors. In addition, Type I errors may be linked to the compensation of the decision maker. Type I errors are errors of commission, whereas Type II are errors in omission. Firing a skilled manager is less transparent to the investor.

4. B is correct. Hiring unskilled Manager 3 for large-cap stocks is an error of commission or Type I error, whereas not hiring skilled Manager 2 for small-cap stocks is an error of omission or Type II error.

5. B is correct. The results of the returns-based style analysis and the holdings-based style analysis should be consistent with the philosophy of the manager and the investment process. If this is not the case, it may suggest that the process is not repeatable or not consistently implemented. For these results the manager should not be included in the universe of potential managers, whereas if the results track over time they may suggest style drift.

6. B is correct. RBSA typically does not require a large amount of additional, or difficult to acquire, data. HBSA requires data on each security in the investment portfolio. HBSA is a snapshot of the portfolio at a single point of time and thus is subject to window dressing. Both HBSA and RBSA are subject to difficulties in interpreting returns when illiquid securities are present.

7. A is correct. A capture ratio less than one indicates the downside capture is greater than upside capture and reflects greater participation in falling markets than in rising markets.

8. C is correct. Given the amount of inefficient assets compared with the AUM of managers likely to exploit them provides some assurance that the inefficiency is repeatable. It would likely take some time for the inefficiency to converge to efficient valuation. The infrequent nature of the inefficiency and the zero marginal return suggest that the inefficiency is probably not worthwhile to pursue.

9. A is correct. The tax advantages to separately managed accounts do not accrue to a tax exempt investor. Choices B and C are considerations that reflect the investor's preferences and could be better satisfied using a separately managed account.

10. A is correct. Open-end funds provide daily liquidity; shares are bought and sold at the end-of-day NAV. Limited partnerships and private equity funds typically require investors to invest their money for longer periods.

11. C is correct. A large drawdown that results from an unforeseen event is explainable as a single isolated event that does not prohibit the manager from adhering to its investment philosophy and process. The events of senior team members leaving to form their own investment firm and an insider trading investigation by the SEC call into question the ability of the firm to adhere to its philosophy and decision-making process.

12. B is correct. In the normal course of business, the manager conforms to its style by reducing exposure to some class of investment grade bonds. Increasing allocation to cash and small-cap stocks is in violation of the mandate to be fully invested with equity exposure to large-cap stocks.

Solutions

13. A is correct. The focus of the initial screening process is on building a universe of managers that could potentially satisfy the identified portfolio need and should not focus on historical performance. Identifying a benchmark is a key component of defining the manager's role in the portfolio, and third-party categorizations are an efficient way to build an initial universe which can then be further refined.

14. C is correct. When the two distributions are highly distinct, the unskilled managers are expected to significantly underperform the skilled managers, implying a high opportunity cost of not hiring the skilled managers. Efficient markets are likely to exhibit smaller differences of returns between skilled and unskilled managers.

15. A is correct. Returns-based style analysis on portfolios of liquid assets is generally able to identify the important drivers of return and the relevant risk factors for the period analyzed, even for complicated strategies. In addition, the process is comparable across managers and through time. If the portfolio contains illiquid securities, the lack of current prices on those positions may lead to an underestimation of the portfolio's volatility in a returns-based style analysis. Longer return series generally provide a more accurate estimate of the manager's underlying standard deviation of return.

16. B is correct. Holdings-based style analysis estimates the portfolio's risk exposures using the securities held in the portfolio (a bottom-up approach), whereas returns-based style analysis uses portfolio returns to estimate a portfolio's sensitivities to security market indexes (a top-down approach).

17. C is correct. Upside capture of 75% suggests that the manager only gained 75% of benchmark increase when the benchmark return was positive. Downside capture of 125% suggests that the manager lost 125% as much as the benchmark when the benchmark return was negative. Therefore, the manager underperformed the benchmark in both scenarios.

18. A is correct. Because incentive fees are fees charged as a percentage of returns (reducing net gains in positive months and reducing net losses in negative months), its use lowers the standard deviation of realized returns. Charging a management fee (a fixed percentage based on assets) lowers the level of realized return without affecting the standard deviation of the return series.

19. A is correct. Pooled investment vehicles are typically operated at a lower cost than separately managed accounts because operational costs can be spread among multiple investors. An investor who is focused on tax efficiency would prefer a separately managed account because a separate account allows the implementation of tax-efficient investing and trading strategies, and the investor pays taxes only on capital gains realized. If the investor requires clear legal ownership, they would prefer a separately managed account in which the investor owns the individual security directly.

20. A is correct. ETFs, as listed securities that can be bought and sold intra-day, are the most liquid vehicles. Hedge fund liquidity features—such as redemption frequency, notification period, lockup, and gates—limit the liquidity of hedge funds. Private equity funds return capital and make profit distributions to investors only as investments are sold during the life of the fund, which is often 10 years and may be extended.

21. C is correct. A symmetrical fee structure is one in which the fees are affected by both positive and negative performance. Of the three funds in Exhibit 1, only Yellow Wood has a symmetrical structure. Yellow Wood's profit sharing component will be negative if its return is negative and positive if it is positive.

22 A is correct. Red Grass's fee arrangement allows for unlimited performance-based fees on the upside and no negative consequences on the downside.

23 B is correct. The fund's fee schedule includes a base fee of 1.50% and a 20% performance-based fee. The performance-based fee is applied after the base fee is deducted. The total fee is calculated as follows:

$$1.5\% + [20\% \times (15\% - 1.5\%)] = 4.20\%$$

24 B is correct. Red Grass Fund's fee schedule states that the fee will be the higher of either (1) the base fee or (2) the base fee plus the sharing of the positive performance. The 2017 return was negative and only the base fee should be applied.

25 B is correct. The fee schedule states that the fee will be the higher of either (1) the base fee or (2) the base fee plus sharing of the positive performance, with a maximum fee of 2.50%. Furthermore, it states that the performance-based fee is assessed on the active return. Without an upper limit, the fee would be 0.5% + [20% × (14% − 2%)] = 2.90%, which is greater than 2.50%; so, the 2.50% fee is assessed.

26 C is correct. The 2016 fee calculation would not be affected by the high-water mark provision because it is the first year of operation of the fund and the return is positive (no prior losses to be offset). The investment management fee in 2016 is calculated as follows:

Investment management fee = 1.00% + [20% × (8.0% − 1.00%)] = 2.4%.

The 2017 fee calculation would also not be affected by the high-water mark provision because the profit sharing component of the fee is zero as a result of a negative return in that year. The investment management fee is calculated as follows:

Investment management fee = 1.00% + 0.00% = 1.00%.

The 2018 fee would be affected by the high-water mark provision because the sharing fee percentage would now be part of the 2018 gain and will need to offset the prior year losses, and only the remaining gains will generate a fee. The performance-based fee would be based on only the gains in excess of the high-water mark. The actual investment management fee charged (percentage and dollar value) will depend on the specific feature of the calculation, which is beyond the scope of this reading. Note that the correct answer can be identified by observing that 2018 is the only year in which a positive return follows a negative return in the prior year.

Solutions

27

Select the fund, based on the Exhibit 1 data, that is *most appropriate* for Connell's needs. (Circle one)	Justify your selection with *two* reasons.
Zeta	The Theta fund, which is managed by an investment team rather than a single manager (as at Zeta) or by two managers (as at Eta), has lower key person risk. If the single manager at Zeta leaves or either manager at Eta leaves, the fund's performance could suffer.
Eta	
Theta	The Theta fund has the lowest level of staff turnover among the three funds. This higher level of personnel continuity limits the risk of the loss of institutional knowledge and experience within the investment team. The Theta fund offers a more attractive compensation package than Eta or Zeta. This incentivizes its investment professionals to stay at Theta, leading to greater longevity and experience over time. Additionally, Theta's package, unlike those of the other funds, will directly increase the rewards to its managers when performance exceeds benchmarks. This better aligns their interests with those of Connell.

28 Alternative 1

If Connell avoids the Eta fund because of its recent underperformance, with performance reverting to the mean, he is at risk of making a Type II error (by not retaining managers with skill). A Type II error is an error of omission or inaction, or in this case, the opportunity cost associated with not hiring Eta and seeing its performance improve.

Alternative 2

If Connell selects the Theta fund because of its recent superior performance, with performance reverting to the mean, he is at risk of making a Type I error. A Type I error occurs when hiring or retaining a manager who subsequently underperforms expectations. The cost of a Type I error is explicit and relatively straightforward to measure.

In deciding which fund to hire, the goal is to avoid making decisions based on short-term performance (trend following) and to identify evidence of behavioral biases in the evaluation of managers during the selection process.

29 The adviser would find style analysis most useful, whether it be returns-based (RBSA) or holdings-based (HBSA), when applied to strategies that hold publicly-traded securities where pricing is frequent. It can be applied to other strategies (hedge funds and private equity, for example), but the insights drawn from a style analysis of such strategies are more likely to be used for designing additional lines of inquiry in the course of due diligence rather than for confirmation of the investment process.

In addition, style analysis, whether returns-based or holdings-based, must be meaningful, accurate, consistent, and timely in order to be useful. Accordingly, style analysis would be most useful to Connell in understanding most of the asset classes in the funds he is considering, including the equities and bonds. However, it would be less meaningful for evaluating the venture capital assets since they are not traded and are thus illiquid.

30.

Select the *best* fund for Yang, using only the information provided. (Circle one)	**Justify** your selection.
Alpha	With Yang hoping to retire in three years and not wanting to suffer investment losses, she has less time to recover from losses than someone with a longer time horizon. Yang should seek a fund with a shallower and shorter expected drawdown. The Gamma fund has the smallest drawdown and the shortest drawdown duration.
Beta	
Gamma	

31.

Determine whether Yang is likely to judge that Aspen follows a consistent investment philosophy, using only the information provided. (Circle one)	**Justify** your response with *two* reasons.
Yes	Passive strategies seek to earn risk premiums, which are defined as the return in excess of a minimal risk ("risk-free") rate of return that accrues to bearing a risk that is not easily diversified away—so-called systematic risk. Active strategies, in contrast, assume markets are sufficiently inefficient that security mispricings can be identified and exploited.

So, in assessing Aspen, Yang first would find its investment philosophy to be inconsistent because it states an active strategy but labels its strategy as a passive one. Aspen is unable to clearly and consistently articulate its investment philosophy.

Yang would also note that Aspen has altered its investment philosophy over time in response to market performance. This suggests Aspen is reacting to markets, not pursuing a consistent philosophy. With this approach, Aspen's performance results may not be repeatable. |
| **No** | |

32

Manager Selection Components	Describe *two* considerations for *each* type of component recommended to Grimmett for her manager selection process.
Qualitative	Process and People: Evaluating the manager's investment process, including the manager's philosophy, process, people, and portfolio. This consideration is broadly described as part of "investment due diligence." Operational due diligence: Evaluating the manager's infrastructure and firm, including the accuracy of the manager's track record and whether the record fully reflects risks; the back office processes and procedures; the terms and if they are acceptable and appropriate for the strategy and vehicle; and the firm's profitability, its culture, and if it's likely to remain in business. This and the following bulleted considerations as a whole are broadly described as part of "operational due diligence": • Investment vehicle: Is the investment vehicle suitable for the portfolio need? • Terms: Are the terms acceptable and appropriate for the strategy and vehicle? • Monitoring: Does the manager continue to be the "best" fit for the portfolio need?
Quantitative	Attribution and appraisal: To assess if the manager has displayed skill in investing. The capture ratio: How has the manager performed in "up" versus "down" markets? Drawdown: Does the return distribution exhibit large drawdowns?

33

Describe the content of the adviser's checklist related to manager selection.

Grimmett, with her adviser, would ensure the following tasks were performed prior to manager selection:
• Decide that outside support is necessary.
• Complete an investment policy statement (IPS).
• Determine the appropriate asset allocation..
Short of these key actions, Grimmett will be unable to identify the managers who fit her needs, confirm that the managers are suitable for her IPS, and be confident that they will act upon the appropriate asset allocation.

34

Identify the firm associated with Boinic's Type I and Type II error. (Circle one for each error type)	**Justify** your selection for *each* error type, discussing the psychological effects of its Year 1 performance on Boinic.

Type I Error	
Firm A	Hiring Firm D, which later underperformed expectations, resulted in a Type I error. A Type I error occurs when a manager is hired or retained who subsequently underperforms expectations. This situation involves rejecting the null hypothesis of no skill when it is correct.
Firm B	
Firm C	
Firm D	
Firm E	It is most likely Boinic will find its hiring of Firm D to be psychologically troubling. Decision makers appear predisposed to worry more about Type I errors than Type II errors. Potential reasons for this focus are as follows: • Psychologically, people seek to avoid feelings of regret. Type I errors are errors of commission, active decisions that turn out to be incorrect, whereas Type II errors are errors of omission, or inaction. Type I errors create explicit costs, whereas Type II errors create opportunity costs. Because individuals appear to put less weight on opportunity costs, Type I errors are psychologically more painful than Type II errors. • Type I errors are more transparent to investors, so they entail not only the regret of an incorrect decision but the pain of having to explain this decision to the investor. Type II errors, such as firing (or not hiring) a manager with skill, are less transparent to investors—unless the investor tracks fired managers or evaluates the universe themselves.
Type II Error	
Firm A	Not hiring Firm B, which later outperformed expectations, resulted in a Type II error. A Type II error occurs when a manager who subsequently outperforms, or performs in line with, expectations is not hired. This situation involves not rejecting an incorrect null hypothesis. As noted previously, a Type II error is typically less psychologically troubling than a Type I error.
Firm B	
Firm C	
Firm D	
Firm E	The other three decisions did not result in either a Type I or Type II error.

Solutions

35

Identify which investment manager is most suitable for Patnode. (Circle one)	Justify your response based solely on each manager's investment philosophy and approach.
Laurbær Partners	Given Patnode's goal of predictably covering expenses and given the choice among these three active managers to invest her insurance policy proceeds, Laurbær is most suitable. Laurbær recognizes its strategy is exposed to potentially being arbitraged away and is more likely to evolve over time to deliver the ongoing returns desired by Patnode.
Alcanfor Limited	
Mylesten Management	Alcanfor and Mylesten, in contrast, are making more generic claims that have a weaker foundation for long-term results. Alcanfor is making its judgments based on performance in industry sectors but is judging effectiveness based on overall market benchmarks. This is not providing evidence related to success within its selection domain but instead gauging itself against a broader market standard. Mylesten is offering a more *ad hoc* reaction to changing market conditions and investment flows, suggesting a lack of repeatability and robustness. So, both of them would have greater uncertainty as to the production of the income Patnode needs.

36

Identify which manager is *most* appropriate for Parade. (Circle one)

Manager A	**Manager B**	Manager C

Justify your response.

All else equal, Manager B is most appropriate for Parade because the portfolio is liquid. That will reduce trading costs in comparison to a portfolio consisting of illiquid securities. Investment strategies not intending to capture a liquidity risk premium must be aware of portfolio liquidity. An existing portfolio consisting of illiquid securities will be more costly to change, not only to take advantage of new opportunities but also to trade because of higher transaction costs. Manager A is not the most appropriate choice because its use of hard-stop losses can risk closing positions too frequently. That, in turn, will increase turnover as well as trading costs. Manager C is problematic because in the case of an actively managed portfolio, the portfolio turnover should agree with (not be greater than) the frequency of signals generated and the securities' liquidity.

37

Identify which investment vehicle *best* addresses *each* characteristic highlighted in Parade's IPS by placing an x where appropriate.

Justify your response.

Characteristic	SMA	Diversified	Justification
Transparency	x		Offering real-time, position-level detail to the investor, SMAs provide complete transparency and accurate attribution. Even if Diversified offers position-level detail, it is likely available with a delay.
Investor Behavior		x	Diversified is not as susceptible to investor micromanagement. Decisions are set by the manager, and portfolio value is determined by the related strategy without investor modification.
Cost		x	Diversified tends to have lower costs from scaling easily and by not imposing upon the manager a higher operational burden of disaggregated trading due to customization.
Liquidity	x		An SMA investor owns individual securities directly, which provides additional safety should a liquidity event occur. Although the manager continues to make investment decisions, those will not be influenced by the redemption or liquidity demands of other investors in the strategy.
Tracking Risk		x	Diversified would have lower tracking risk compared to SMAs, whose customization increases the chances of tracking risk relative to the benchmark. This can confuse attribution because performance will reflect investor constraints rather than manager decisions.

38

Determine which of the three investment vehicles is *most* appropriate for Circue's IPS. (Circle one)

Hedge funds with a soft lock	Open-end funds with an incentive fee	Closed-end funds with no incentive fee

Solutions

Justify your response.

Open-end funds with an incentive fee are the most appropriate among the three investment vehicles being considered by Circue. Although slightly less liquid than closed-end funds, open-end funds still offer daily liquidity—with Circue indicating some tolerance for lower liquidity. An incentive fee is applicable in this case as mutual fund assets are often "sticky"; investors are reluctant to switch allocations once made and may accept lower returns. This outcome decreases manager motivation and leads to closet indexing, to which Circue has a heightened sensitivity among its active managers. Thus, the incentive fee can help motivate managers to work harder to improve performance. Closed-end funds are the most liquid of the three choices. Without an accompanying incentive fee, however, the closed-end fund manager may not have the same motivation to work harder than the open-end fund manager, who does have an incentive fee. Hedge funds are inappropriate here because they are the least liquid of the three options. A soft lock charges a redemption fee, paid into the fund, which is inconsistent with Circue's moderate sensitivity to fees.

39 Under the fee structure identified by Porter, Smith's stated expectation would be reflected in a misestimation of portfolio risk because performance-based fee structures may lead to such misestimates. Performance-based fee structures convert symmetrical gross active return distributions into asymmetrical net active return distributions, reducing variability on the upside but not the downside. As a result, a single standard deviation calculated on a return series that incorporates active returns, above and below the base fee, can lead to the underestimation of downside risk. In contrast, fully symmetric fees (fully exposing the manager to both upside and downside results) tend to yield closer alignment in risk and effort than bonus-style fees.

40

Calculate the net active return based on each possible gross active return provided using the selected data in Exhibit A.

Gross Active Return	≤ 0.20%	0.75%	1.25%	1.75%
Net Active Return	≤ 0.00%	0.41%	0.90%	1.16%

(continued)

	Show your calculations.
	Gross Active Return ≤ 0.20%:
Gross Active Return at or below the Base Fee − Base Fee = Net Active Return
0.20 − 0.20 = 0.00
=> Net Active Return ≤ 0.00%

Base Fee = Billed Fee (No Sharing Fee)
0.20

Gross Active Return = 0.75%:
Active Return − Base Fee = Return Subject to Sharing Fee
0.75 − 0.20 = 0.55

Return Subject to Sharing Fee × Sharing Fee = Additional Fee Due to Sharing Fee
0.55 × 0.25 = 0.1375

Base Fee + Additional Fee Due to Sharing Fee = Billed Fee
0.20 + 0.1375 = 0.3375

Active Return − Billed Fee = Net Active Return
0.75 − 0.3375 = 0.4125, rounded to 0.41%

Gross Active Return = 1.25% is the breakeven active return (No Sharing Fee):
Gross Active Return − Standard Fee = Net Active Return
1.25 − 0.35 = 0.90 or 0.90%

Standard Fee = Billed Fee (No Sharing Fee)
0.35

Gross Active Return = 1.75%:
Gross Active Return − Base Fee = Return Subject to Sharing Fee
1.75 − 0.20 = 1.55

Return Subject to Sharing Fee × Sharing Fee = Additional Fee Due to Sharing Fee
1.55 × 0.25 = 0.3875

Base Fee + Additional Fee Due to Sharing Fee = Billed Fee
0.2 + 0.3875 = 0.5875

Gross Active Return − Billed Fee = Net Active Return
1.75 − 0.5875 = 1.1625, rounded to 1.16% |

41

Identify whether each detail from Moore's summary is *most likely* a benefit or a drawback of the strategy (Place an x in the preferred box.)	**Justify** your selection.

Detail	Benefit	Drawback	Justification
1	x		This is a benefit if Lyon's positions are paired with the idea of capturing alpha as prices converge while offsetting market risk and are well-matched and sized correctly.
2		x	The reliance of Lyon's strategy on unique information is a drawback as it is difficult for Lyon to have an informational edge in a regulatory environment that seeks to reduce informational symmetries.
3		x	This is a drawback because in a context of significant asset growth, Lyon should adjust the number and/or characteristics of the positions held to accommodate the increase in AUM.

42

Discuss *one* advantage and *one* disadvantage to the client of *each* manager's contracted fee structure.

Manager	Advantage	Disadvantage
Vaudreuil	The impact of Vaudreuil's fees on the client is lower as assets grow in a rising market. This is a benefit to the client.	The client might not achieve the same level of returns as would be available under a different fee structure. Vaudreuil might not want to risk losing assets once they are large and may not work to generate the same level of returns to retain assets because they tend to be "sticky."
Pourtir	Performance-based fees work to align the interests of Pourtir and the client because both parties share in the investment results. The client benefits by paying lower fees when active returns are low. Pourtir may work harder.	Tension can be created between the client and Pourtir, as the client must pay base fees even if Pourtir underperforms. Pourtir's fee structure may lead to misestimates of portfolio risk and may incentivize Pourtir to assume higher portfolio risk. The client and Pourtir may have different incentives when performance-based fees are used, specifically in the case of bonus-style fees. Performance-based fees may incentivize Pourtir to hold on to assets until a profit can be realized even if the client would benefit from selling the assets at a loss and investing the proceeds elsewhere.

43

Identify which manager's fee structure is *most* similar to a call option on a share of active return. (Circle one)

Hidden Lake	Carpenter Management

(continued)

Justify your selection.

Carpenter Management has a bonus-style fee with a maximum fee feature. Bonus-style fees are the close equivalent of a manager's call option on a share of active return, for which the base fee is the strike price—for example, the 18 bps base fee, plus a long call option on active return with a strike price equal to the minimum (base) fee, minus another (less valuable call option) with a strike price equal to the maximum fee. Hidden Lake has a symmetrical fee structure in which the manager is fully exposed to both the downside and upside. So, of the two firms, Carpenter Management's fee structure is most similar to a call option.

PORTFOLIO MANAGEMENT
STUDY SESSION

14

Cases in Portfolio Management and Risk Management

This study session provides three cases that integrate material across Level III study sessions. Each case provides a stylized scenario involving several issues that are used to illustrate how to evaluate the needs of a client and synthesize techniques to provide appropriate solutions.

The first case study considers issues associated with the development of a strategic asset allocation (SAA) for a long-horizon institutional investor—a university endowment—with special challenges including supporting spending policies while ensuring the long-term sustainability of the endowment and establishing optimal exposure to illiquid investment strategies in the context of a diversified portfolio. These issues are explored from the perspective of a large university endowment undertaking a review of its asset allocation and then implementing proposed allocation changes and a tactical overlay program.

The second case study explores issues raised in a private wealth management setting of providing advice on risk management to individuals and families. These issues include the extent to which identified and evaluated risks can be reduced, addressed using insurance policies, or self-insurance. Families' financial circumstances and risks evolve over time, and the arrangements addressing the risks should be reviewed and updated. Risk management solutions recommended by advisers should take the overall wealth of the family into consideration. The choice of an adviser may also pose practical and ethical challenges.

The third case study looks at various challenges faced by institutional investors from a risk management perspective including: financial risks, enterprise risk management, environmental risks, and social risks. The focus of the reading is a theoretical case study addressing risk management aspects of a Sovereign Wealth Fund's (SWF) potential long-term direct investments in infrastructure and private equity. The structure of the case itself brings the learner inside two Investment Committee (IC) meetings where various aspects of risk are discussed, and potential investments evaluated. The learner is expected to review IC memos and IC discussions and analyze various risk elements of the investment opportunities as the case unfolds over a 5-year period. Ultimately, the learner is expected to make recommendations for improvement.

READING ASSIGNMENTS

Reading 28	Case Study in Portfolio Management: Institutional by Gabriel Petre, CFA
Reading 29	Case Study in Risk Management: Private Wealth by Giuseppe Ballocchi, PhD, CFA
Reading 30	Case Study in Risk Management: Institutional by Steve Balaban, CFA, Arjan Berkelaar, PhD, CFA, Nasir Hasan, and Hardik Sanjay Shah, CFA

READING 28

Case Study in Portfolio Management: Institutional

by Gabriel Petre, CFA

Gabriel Petre, CFA, is at World Bank (USA).

LEARNING OUTCOMES	
Mastery	The candidate should be able to:
☐	a. discuss tools for managing portfolio liquidity risk;
☐	b. discuss capture of the illiquidity premium as an investment objective;
☐	c. analyze asset allocation and portfolio construction in relation to liquidity needs and risk and return requirements and recommend actions to address identified needs;
☐	d. analyze actions in asset manager selection with respect to the Code of Ethics and Standards of Professional Conduct;
☐	e. analyze the costs and benefits of derivatives versus cash market techniques for establishing or modifying asset class or risk exposures;
☐	f. demonstrate the use of derivatives overlays in tactical asset allocation and rebalancing.

INTRODUCTION 1

The development of a strategic asset allocation (SAA) for long-horizon institutional investors like university endowments raises special challenges. These include supporting spending policies while ensuring the long-term sustainability of the endowment and establishing optimal exposure to illiquid investment strategies in the context of a diversified portfolio.

Large university endowments typically have significant exposure to illiquid asset classes. The exposure to illiquid asset classes impacts the portfolio's overall liquidity profile and requires a comprehensive liquidity management approach to ensure liquidity needs can be met in a timely fashion.[1] In addition, capital market conditions and asset prices change, resulting in a need to change asset allocation exposures and/or rebalance the portfolio to maintain a profile close to the strategic asset allocation.

Derivatives are often used by institutions to manage liquidity needs and implement asset allocation changes. The cash-efficient nature of derivatives and their high levels of liquidity in many markets make them suitable tools for portfolio rebalancing, tactical exposure changes, and satisfying short-term liquidity needs—all while maintaining desired portfolio exposures.

This case study explores these issues from the perspective of a large university endowment undertaking a review of its asset allocation and then implementing proposed allocation changes and a tactical overlay program. Rebalancing needs for the endowment arise as market moves result in the drift of the endowment's asset allocation.

The case is divided into two major sections. The first section addresses issues relating to asset allocation and liquidity management. The case introduces a framework to support management of liquidity and cash needs in an orderly and timely manner while avoiding disruption to underlying managers and potentially capturing an illiquidity premium. Such concepts as time-to-cash tables and liquidity budgets are explored in detail. Aspects relating to rebalancing and maintaining a risk profile similar to the portfolio's strategic asset allocation over time are also covered.

The second section explores the use of derivatives in portfolio construction from a tactical asset allocation (TAA) overlay and rebalancing perspective. The suitability of futures, total return swaps, and exchange-traded funds (ETFs) is discussed based on their characteristics, associated costs, and desired portfolio objectives. The case also presents a cost–benefit analysis of derivatives and cash markets for implementing rebalancing decisions. Environmental, social, and governance (ESG) considerations arising in the normal course of investing are also explored.

2 BACKGROUND: LIQUIDITY MANAGEMENT

a discuss tools for managing portfolio liquidity risk

b discuss capture of the illiquidity premium as an investment objective

For an institutional investor, such as an endowment or a pension fund, liquidity management refers to the set of policies and practices that ensure the portfolio complies with investment policy yet can meet cash outflow needs in a timely and orderly manner without incurring excessive costs. Optimal liquidity management helps ensure that distressed sales of illiquid assets are avoided, especially in weak market conditions, and that the portfolio can benefit from the expected illiquidity premium associated with long-term private market allocations.

The importance of liquidity management was emphasized in the 2008 global financial crisis when many institutional investors with significant allocations to illiquid asset classes and regular cash outflow requirements struggled to meet these outflows.

During this time, public markets experienced significant losses, liquidity conditions deteriorated, and distributions from many private market investments stopped. For many university endowments, another source of liquidity—donations—also dropped significantly, further amplifying liquidity issues. In some cases, endowments were forced

---

[1] In this context, 'liquidity' refers to the ability to exchange assets into cash for an expected value within a known time frame.

to liquidate securities at steep discounts, drastically cut funding for some programs dependent on endowment distributions, and/or borrow funds collateralized by the endowment, increasing leverage and the risk profile of the portfolio.

Institutional investors have several important "tools" at their disposal to manage a portfolio's liquidity risk. These include:

- liquidity profiling and time-to-cash tables,
- rebalancing and commitment strategies,
- stress testing analyses, and
- derivatives.

2.1 Liquidity Profiling and Time-to-Cash

For any investor, the assessment of liquidity needs starts with identifying potential cash inflows and cash outflows for a defined investment horizon. In the case of endowments, cash outflows include distributions to the university and meeting capital call requirements for illiquid investments (e.g., real assets, private equity, hedge funds, and structured products). Once the sources and uses of cash have been identified, the institutional investor establishes the need for liquidity and the desired liquidity maturity profile for the overall portfolio. As part of this process, a **liquidity classification schedule** (**time-to-cash table**) is created and an overall **liquidity budget** is defined.[2] The liquidity classification schedule defines portfolio categories (or "buckets") based on the estimated time it would take in the normal course of business to convert assets in that particular category into cash. The liquidity budget assigns portfolio weights considered acceptable to each liquidity classification in the time-to-cash table and establishes a liquidity benchmark for the portfolio construction process.

An example of a time-to-cash table is provided in Exhibit 1. It defines liquidity classifications based on the time expected to liquidate an investment without liquidation having a significant impact on market conditions and the resulting sale price for the investment. The impact on market conditions is based on the expected market price immediately before and after trading if the sell order was executed. In the case of investments managed by third-party managers, the time-to-cash also depends on the contractual terms governing the type of investment vehicle used. Typically, private investments requiring more than one year to exit are viewed as illiquid. In the case of hedge funds, contractual terms (e.g., lockups, notification periods, withdrawal windows) vary based on the manager and underlying strategy. A manager's ability to deny withdrawal requests during stress periods ("to activate gates") to protect fund investors and prevent forced liquidations will impact time-to-cash.

Exhibit 1	Time-to-Cash Table and Liquidity Budget	
Time to Cash	**Liquidity Classification**	**Liquidity Budget (% of portfolio)**
< 1 Week	Highly Liquid	At Least 10%
< 1 Quarter	Liquid	At Least 35%
< 1 Year	Semi-Liquid	At Least 50%
> 1 Year	Illiquid	Up to 50%

---

[2] See also Russell Investments (2013).

The granularity of a time-to-cash table may vary to include monthly or semi-annual categories depending on the investor's liquidity preferences, liquidity needs, and other circumstances. The core principle is to identify liquidity categories relevant to the types of cash outflows the investor will face and to match overall portfolio characteristics with liquidity needs through the design of the resulting asset allocation. The next step is to define an overall liquidity budget specifying portfolio allocations for the different time-to-cash buckets (as shown in the last column of Exhibit 1).[3] In the case of highly liquid, liquid, and semi-liquid categories, minimum portfolio weights are identified. For the illiquid category, a maximum portfolio weight is identified.

The liquidity budget reflects the acceptable liquidity requirements that the portfolio must meet, even in a liquidity stress scenario. The results of stress test analyses are therefore important inputs in developing the liquidity budget.

To operationalize the concepts represented in the liquidity budget, the institutional investor does an analysis of the underlying liquidity characteristics of the portfolio investments and monitors these characteristics over time. The analysis should look through the broad definition of asset classes to the underlying investments used for exposure. Different investments within the same asset class (such as public equities) may have very different liquidity profiles. Commingled funds (funds that are pooled and managed together in a single account) may be less liquid than exchange-traded funds (ETFs) or mutual funds and may have different liquidity profiles than separate accounts. Furthermore, there could be differences in the liquidity profile of similar investment vehicles in the same asset class depending on the underlying strategy used by the investment manager. For example, a commingled fund following a concentrated, small-cap active strategy in emerging market equities may offer investors only quarterly liquidity as compared to a commingled fund investing in large-cap emerging market equities, which may offer monthly or weekly liquidity. For these reasons, it is appropriate to conduct liquidity analysis on a bottom-up basis for each investment, aggregate at the portfolio level, and monitor changes over time to keep the portfolio within liquidity budget parameters. An example of liquidity profiling for a portfolio's underlying investments is shown in Exhibit 2. The portfolio example uses investments in separate accounts, commingled funds, futures, ETFs, and active managers to achieve its asset class exposure to both public and private markets.

Exhibit 2 Liquidity Profiling for a Portfolio

Asset Class	Asset Class Allocation (% of portfolio)	Investment Allocation (% of overall portfolio)	Investment Vehicle	Liquidity Classification			
				Highly Liquid	Liquid	Semi-Liquid	Illiquid
Cash	1%	1%	Separate Account	100%	0%	0%	0%
Fixed Income	14%	5%	Separate Account	100%	0%	0%	0%
		8%	Commingled Fund	100%	0%	0%	0%
		1%	Futures	100%	0%	0%	0%

---

[3] Mercer (2015).

Exhibit 2   (Continued)

Asset Class	Asset Class Allocation (% of portfolio)	Investment Allocation (% of overall portfolio)	Investment Vehicle	Liquidity Classification			
				Highly Liquid	Liquid	Semi-Liquid	Illiquid
Domestic Equity	17%	8%	Commingled Fund	0%	50%	50%	0%
		8%	Separate Account	0%	100%	0%	0%
		1%	Futures	100%	0%	0%	0%
International Developed Equity	10%	6%	Commingled Fund	0%	50%	30%	20%
		4%	Separate Account	0%	80%	20%	0%
Emerging Market Equity	12%	9%	Commingled Fund	0%	75%	25%	0%
		3%	ETF	100%	0%	0%	0%
Private Equity	18%	18%	Funds 1–85	0%	0%	0%	100%
Real Assets	13%	4%	Funds 1–8	0%	0%	75%	25%
		6%	Funds 9–33	0%	0%	0%	100%
		3%	Funds 34–50	0%	0%	20%	80%
Diversifying Strategies	15%	4%	Funds 1–5	0%	0%	100%	0%
		6%	Funds 6–11	0%	25%	25%	50%
		5%	Funds 12–19	0%	0%	75%	25%
Overall Portfolio	**100%**	**100%**		19%	26%	22%	33%

2.2 Rebalancing, Commitments

The discussion so far has focused on liquidity management and the ability of an institutional portfolio to meet cash outflows in an orderly manner as they come due. Another consideration is the impact of changes in the liquidity profile on the overall risk of the investment portfolio and the ability to keep the portfolio close to desired risk targets. Illiquid assets carry extremely high rebalancing costs. Because asset liquidity tends to decrease in times of market stress, it is important to have sufficient liquid assets and rebalancing mechanisms in place. This will ensure the portfolio's risk profile remains within acceptable risk targets and does not "drift" as the relative valuations of different asset classes fluctuate during stress periods. Rebalancing mechanisms include the following:

> **Systematic rebalancing policies**. Rebalancing disciplines, such as calendar rebalancing and percent-range rebalancing, are intended to control risk relative to the strategic asset allocation. In these cases, pre-specified tolerance bands for asset class weights are used. The size or width of the bands should consider the underlying volatility of each investment category to minimize transaction costs. This means more-volatile investment categories should usually have wider rebalancing bands. Transaction costs, correlations between asset classes, and investor risk tolerance are other factors that may influence the size of the band selected.

Automatic adjustment mechanisms. These are mechanisms designed to maintain a stable risk profile when exposure drifts from targeted exposure. An example is using adjustments to a public market allocation that is correlated to a private market allocation to rebalance private market risk. This approach uses liquid public assets as a proxy for illiquid private assets. For example, assume private equity investments have an equity beta of 1. In a situation where the allocation to private equity increases by 1% versus the target, the allocation to public equities would automatically be adjusted down by 1% to maintain a stable systematic market risk profile. Note, however, that although systematic market risk is unchanged, illiquidity risk of the portfolio is now higher. Alternatively, the adjustment could be further refined to maintain a constant equity beta, assuming private equity has a beta to public equities of greater than 1 (caused by leverage, for example).[4] Similar public market proxies can be used to represent private real estate, infrastructure, or other illiquid instruments based on their underlying risk characteristics.

Multi-year funding strategies for private markets that incorporate a steady pace of commitments to reach a target allocation and/or to keep the allocation close to target over time are other means to ensure the portfolio remains consistent with desired risk objectives. Private market funds pose specific challenges for investors in maintaining a desired exposure over time as investors do not control the pace at which committed capital is drawn or the pace at which capital distributions are returned. Although unpredictable at an individual fund level, these patterns become more predictable within a portfolio of private market investments.

The objective of a multi-year funding strategy is to design a commitment-pacing strategy that will result in the desired portfolio exposure to the asset class over time. The commitment-pacing strategy translates into an annual level of commitments and is typically the result of a cash flow modeling exercise that takes into account expectations about the speed at which committed capital is drawn, the pace of distributions, the evolution in overall asset size, as well as other circumstances specific to the investor. The cash flow modeling exercise would project forward the expected asset class exposure (as a percentage of the overall portfolio) at various commitment levels, thus reducing the risk of overshooting the target allocation. Scenario analysis should also be used to consider the impact of different market stress conditions. The evolution of the asset allocation must be monitored over time, with adjustments to the commitment pace made as necessary.

2.3 Stress Testing

A robust liquidity framework ensures that liquidity needs can be met in a timely fashion during periods of normal market and stress market conditions. Understanding how the portfolio's liquidity profile may change in addition to how the liquidity needs of the institution may change during stress periods is therefore critical. Comprehensive stress testing exercises would seek to "stress" (i.e., presume extremely adverse market conditions for) both assets and liabilities simultaneously to understand how these may be impacted during stress conditions. With respect to assets, the stress test can cover distributional assumptions regarding prices (e.g., volatility, return), correlations across assets, as well as liquidity characteristics. Liability shocks can also be factored in, for example, by increasing expected endowment distributions to support the university during the stress periods. The design of the stress tests can be informed by historical

---

[4] See also Raymond (2009).

events (e.g., the 2008 global financial crisis), statistical models (e.g., extreme value theory), and/or by scenario analysis (e.g., analyzing the potential impact of a hypothetical scenario with respect to a set of variables on the overall portfolio).

2.4 Derivatives

Derivatives can be used to manage cash outflow needs and changing risk exposures. The cash-efficient nature of derivatives makes them desirable tools for rebalancing. A futures overlay program allows an institutional investor to rebalance exposures to public asset classes (for example, on a monthly or quarterly basis) while leaving allocations to external active managers unchanged. Derivatives can also be used to modify a portfolio's liquidity profile through the use of leverage—for example, using futures contracts (long futures position) to gain economic exposure to US equities and then deploying the cash that is not required for posting margin into other investments with different liquidity profiles or to satisfy short-term liquidity needs. Derivatives can also be used to generate additional cash by employing leverage at the overall portfolio level.

2.5 Earning an Illiquidity Premium

An attractive feature for investors in illiquid investments, such as private equity or private real estate, is the expectation of extracting an illiquidity premium in addition to premiums associated with underlying market risk factor exposures in an illiquid strategy. The illiquidity premium (also called the liquidity premium) is the expected compensation for the additional risk of tying up capital for a potentially uncertain time period. Quantitative estimates for the illiquidity premium suggest evidence of a positive illiquidity premium in private equity and private real estate and of illiquidity premium size being positively correlated to the length of the illiquidity horizon.[5]

An alternative approach for estimating the illiquidity risk premium is based on the idea that the size of the discount an investor should receive in return for committing capital for an uncertain period of time can be represented by the value of a put option with an exercise price equal to the marketable price of the illiquid asset at the time of purchase. (The "marketable price" is a hypothetical price at which the illiquid asset could be sold if it were freely traded; it can be estimated by various means.) In this case, the price of the illiquid asset can be derived by subtracting the put price from the marketable price of the asset. If both the marketable price and the illiquid asset price are estimated or known, then the expected return for each can be calculated, with the difference in expected returns representing the illiquidity premium (in %). This approach was initially developed by Chaffe (1993) and later improved upon by Staub and Diermeier (2003). They also find there should be a positive correlation between the length of the illiquidity horizon and the size of the illiquidity premium.

A significant body of literature documents a positive relationship between lack of liquidity and expected returns in the case of public equity. For example, Pastor and Stambaugh (2001) find that expected returns are impacted by systematic liquidity risk and estimate a 3% return over the 1996–2003 period in the United States for a zero-net-investment portfolio that holds low-liquidity stocks long and high-liquidity stocks short.

Overall, though, it is difficult to isolate the illiquidity premium with precision and separate its effects from such other risk factors as the market, value, and size in the case of equity investments. Furthermore, estimates of the illiquidity premium are based on broad market indexes, yet an investor in these asset classes would typically invest in only a small subset of the universe with the result that individual investment

---

[5] See also Green (2015).

experience could be very different and more susceptible to idiosyncratic factors.[6] These challenges further emphasize the importance of liquidity budgeting in facilitating capture of the illiquidity premium while controlling for risk.

3. QUINCO CASE: BACKGROUND

c analyze asset allocation and portfolio construction in relation to liquidity needs and risk and return requirements and recommend actions to address identified needs

Quadrivium University (QU) is an independent liberal arts college located in a vibrant mid-sized city with a growing and diverse population. The university was founded in 1916 by James Greaves and Colin Healey, two entrepreneurs with a passion for astronomy and mathematics who settled in the area in the early 1900s. Over time, the university has built an outstanding reputation as one of the top schools in the country. Consistent with the founders' interests, the programs in astronomy and mathematics are highly regarded, attracting applicants from all over the world.

The Quadrivium University endowment was established in 1936 through a $15 million donation from Healey, whose goal was to provide financial aid to new undergraduate students. A quarter of new students receive Healey grants, and this percentage has increased steadily over time.

As of the current fiscal year, QU has an endowment of $8 billion, of which $6 billion represents funds used for general unrestricted support and unrestricted funds functioning as endowment. The remaining funds have various donor-specified use restrictions. Although a significant portion of the endowment's growth has been from investment returns, the endowment also benefits from a strong and deep alumni network that provides regular donations and access to highly regarded industry contacts and money managers. Exhibit 3 shows the market value of the endowment over recent years, and Exhibit 4 shows the realized investment returns over the same period.

Exhibit 3 Market Value of QU Endowment

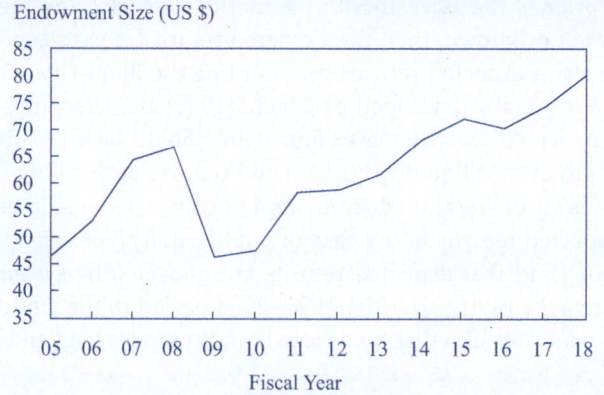

---

[6] Ang, Papanikolaou, and Westerfield (2014).

QUINCO Case: Background

Exhibit 4 Investment Returns for QU Endowment

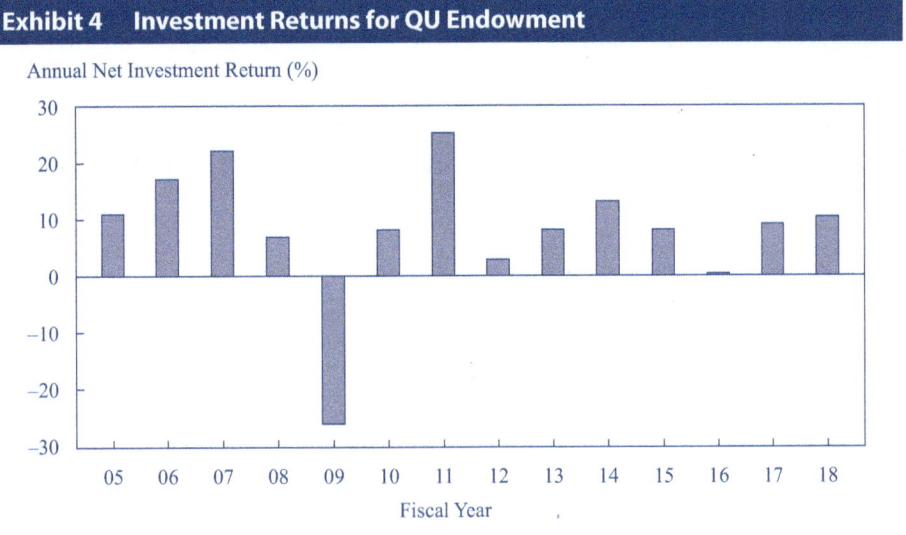

QU has an annual operating budget of $583 million, and 70% of the operating budget is used to fund salaries and benefits for faculty and administrative staff. In addition, the budget is used to pay down debt associated with a major upgrade of the main campus facilities, pay expenses associated with the maintenance of physical infrastructure, and fund various research and financial aid programs.

Annual distributions from the endowment provide funding for approximately 60% of the university's operating budget, including its financial aid programs. In absolute dollar terms, the size of annual distributions has increased steadily in the last five years as the size of the endowment fund has grown. Similarly, the percentage of the operating budget covered by distributions from the endowment has increased. The board of the university has recently expressed a preference for a predictable pattern of distributions to allow for better planning of resource deployment through its programs. Consistent with that preference, the spending policy of the endowment was changed following the 2008 global financial crisis. Pre-crisis, the university used a simple spending rule: Spending equaled the long-term desired spending rate of 5% multiplied by the market value of the endowment at the beginning of the fiscal year. Post-crisis, the university changed its spending rule to a geometric smoothing rule, sometimes called the Yale formula.

The current spending rule is designed to produce a 5% long-term spending rate in a way that shields annual distributions from fluctuations in the endowment's market value. The endowment uses a weighted-average formula of the previous year's spending amount and the endowment's market value at the end of the previous fiscal year multiplied by the long-term desired spending rate:

Spending for current fiscal year = (66% × Spending for previous fiscal year) + 34% × (5% × Endowment market value at the end of previous fiscal year).

For QU, the previous fiscal year's spending was $358.1 million, while the endowment's market value at the end of the previous fiscal year was $7,002.3 million. In this case, QU's spending for the current fiscal year would be:

Spending for current fiscal year = (66% × $358.1 million) + 34% × (5% × $7,002.3 million) = $355.4 million.

Consistent with the spending policy, the endowment's investment objective is to achieve long-term returns that support the spending rate while preserving the value of the endowment in real terms over time (thus safeguarding the long-term sustainability of the program). For QU, a 5% spending rate per year combined with long-term expected inflation for colleges and universities of 2–3% per year translates into a 7–8% nominal return per year objective over the long term. QU's associated risk objective is 12–14% annualized return volatility (standard deviation of portfolio returns must be between 12–14%).

3.1 Quadrivium University Investment Company (QUINCO)

Quadrivium University is overseen by a board of trustees ("the Trustees"), generally consisting of prominent, wealthy alumni who are elected to the position. QUINCO is the university investment office, which manages QU's endowment. The office was established in 1993 at a time when endowment assets were $1 billion. From a governance perspective, the office is organizationally distinct from the university, although it is not a separate legal entity. The president of the investment office, Aaron Winter, reports to the university president and to the QUINCO board of directors ("the Board"). The Board is comprised of 11 members appointed by the Trustees. The president of QUINCO, the university president, and the treasurer of the university serve as ex-officio members. The QUINCO Board is responsible for approving investment policy and guidelines and providing guidance on key policy matters. Implementation of the investment policy has been fully delegated to QUINCO staff, who are empowered to make changes to the portfolio within the parameters of the investment guidelines.

QUINCO has 13 investment professionals, who are university employees. The investment model is one where the investment strategy is implemented through external investment managers. The Board has consistently re-affirmed its view that such a model provides greater flexibility for changing investment portfolio exposures when circumstances warrant while reducing internal staffing needs compared to an in-house investment management model. Internal investment staff are focused on asset allocation, risk management, and selecting, monitoring, and terminating external investment managers.

The following five investment categories are part of the current asset allocation: fixed income, public equities, private equity, real assets (composed of primarily private real estate and natural resources), and diversifying strategies (primarily hedge fund strategies targeting high absolute returns with low correlations to traditional asset classes, like public equity and fixed income). Alternative investments are considered to be private equity, real assets, and diversifying strategies. Private equity and real assets are recognized as illiquid (alternative) investments. The investment team is organized by investment category, with a senior portfolio manager leading each area and supported by an analyst. In addition, the team includes a portfolio strategist in charge of asset allocation and risk management, also supported by an analyst, and the president of the office, who acts as the chief investment officer (CIO). Senior portfolio managers have primary responsibility for investment decisions within their investment category, while the portfolio strategist has responsibility for ongoing endowment rebalancing decisions, overlays, and tactical asset allocation tilts. All external investment manager decisions and tactical asset allocation deviations are discussed and approved by the internal investment committee. Winter chairs the committee, which includes all senior portfolio managers and the portfolio strategist. The QUINCO Board is responsible for granting final approval of external investment managers.

3.2 Investment Strategy: Background and Evolution

QUINCO has distinguished itself as a steady and progressive institutional investor with a focus on long-term objectives; it is unlikely to make abrupt wholesale changes to its investment strategy. This strategy is, in part, driven by leadership stability, with the investment office having had the same president (Winter's predecessor) for the

QUINCO Case: Background

first 25 years of existence. Another important factor has been an established culture focused on maintaining best-in-class investment practices and institutionalizing that knowledge through robust processes and systems.

For the first years of existence, the endowment invested only in public markets, mostly equities and bonds. In its early days, the belief was that the limited size and investment resources of the endowment would present challenges in accessing, monitoring, and properly managing complex, nontraditional investment strategies. Since the mid-1990s, as the size of the endowment grew, the QUINCO Board has embraced the belief that exposure to nontraditional, or alternative, asset categories is beneficial for the long-term prospects of the endowment—enhancing investment risk diversification and providing potentially higher risk-adjusted returns in a greater variety of market environments. To express this belief, the Board has supported an increase in internal investment expertise by hiring seasoned investment professionals and expanding QUINCO's investment staff. Over the next two decades, the endowment portfolio increased its exposure to such alternative investments as private equity, real assets, and hedge funds.

These investments have performed well for the endowment; in particular, private equity and real assets were very strong contributors to the portfolio return over that period, in line with expectations. In aggregate, however, exposure to alternatives in the portfolio is still below the average exposure of other large university endowments that are considered by the Board to be the endowment's relevant peer universe.

The evolution of the endowment's asset allocation is shown in Exhibit 5.

Exhibit 5   Evolution of the Strategic Asset Allocation

	Evolution of Investment Policy Targets							
	1996	1999	2002	2005	2008	2011	2014	2017
Cash	1%	1%	1%	1%	1%	1%	1%	1%
Fixed Income	29%	24%	24%	19%	16%	16%	14%	14%
Domestic Equity	40%	35%	26%	24%	23%	21%	20%	17%
International Developed Equity	24%	24%	20%	17%	15%	15%	12%	10%
Emerging Market Equity	0%	3%	10%	15%	15%	12%	12%	12%
Private Equity	3%	5%	8%	10%	12%	14%	16%	18%
Real Assets	3%	5%	6%	7%	9%	11%	12%	13%
Diversifying Strategies	0%	3%	5%	7%	9%	10%	13%	15%

The QUINCO Board oversees a comprehensive strategic asset allocation review every three years. The last review of the asset allocation occurred two years ago. At that time, the Board approved a continued increase to alternative investments at the expense of developed market equities (both domestic and international).

3.2.1 Current Scenario

Winter, a QU alumnus who joined QUINCO five years ago, took over the role of investment office president and CIO last year. This is the first time he will be overseeing an asset allocation review. The endowment's current asset allocation is shown in Exhibit 6.

Exhibit 6 Current Strategic Asset Allocation

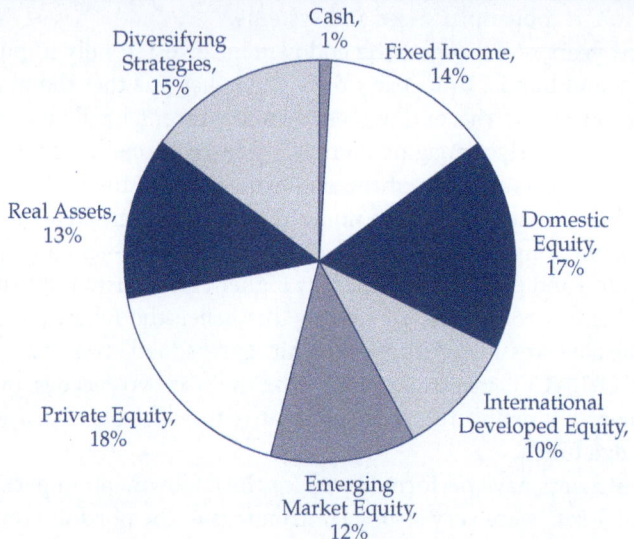

Based on discussions with the Board, Winter asks his portfolio strategy team—consisting of team lead, Julia Thompson, her asset allocation analyst, and the senior portfolio managers for fixed income and public equities—to address the following considerations during the review process:

- The desired liquidity profile for the endowment and corresponding framework for liquidity management.
- The investment outlook and efficiency of the strategic asset allocation. A long period of falling interest rates and rising asset prices in the developed world drove most traditional asset classes to the upper bounds of historical valuation ranges, lowering future expected returns in these markets.
- The role of tactical asset allocation (TAA) in QU endowment's investment strategy. Given the long-term nature of the strategic asset allocation, some Board members are wondering whether a tactical asset allocation program might improve risk-adjusted returns for the portfolio.
- Endowment underperformance relative to a peer universe of large endowments. Although the QU endowment had better returns than most of its peers during the 2008 global financial crisis, the portfolio has largely underperformed its peers since then.

4   QUINCO CASE: STRATEGIC ASSET ALLOCATION

c   analyze asset allocation and portfolio construction in relation to liquidity needs and risk and return requirements and recommend actions to address identified needs

QUINCO Case: Strategic Asset Allocation

Thompson and the strategy team have completed their analysis, including the considerations raised by Winter and the Board, and are now ready to present to the Board. As part of their work, Thompson updated the long-term, forward-looking capital market assumptions used for the mean–variance optimization process and asset allocation recommendations.

In developing their long-term capital market assumptions, Thompson and the strategy team considered and applied unsmoothing (or de-smoothing) techniques. These techniques were applied to illiquid investments to remove the impact of positive serial correlation on risk estimates caused by stale market pricing. From experience, Thompson knows that the uncertainty of risk and return estimates for illiquid assets is amplified by such aspects as infrequent trading, associated leverage, and long investment horizons. In attempting to estimate risk for illiquid assets, the team's challenges include the availability, quality/reliability, and frequency of pricing data. Thompson knows these issues would result in stale pricing or a smoother pattern of reported returns because of fewer data points with lower observed return volatility. If used as an input in their mean–variance optimization models without adjustment, the artificially low volatility would make illiquid asset classes appear more attractive, resulting in higher allocations to illiquids in the "optimal" portfolio. To prevent this, Thompson and her team applied unsmoothing techniques to better reflect the underlying risk of illiquid asset classes. After applying unsmoothing techniques to private equity, resulting volatility ends up being significantly higher than volatility that is observed or experienced for these assets. Exhibits 7 and 8 show these updated assumptions.

Exhibit 7 Long-Term Expected Return (Net of Fees) and Volatility Assumptions

Asset Class	Expected Real Return (annual geometric mean, next 10 years)	Expected Nominal Return (annual geometric mean, next 10 years)	Standard Deviation of Returns (annual)	Sharpe Ratio
Cash	0.9%	3.4%	1.7%	
Fixed Income	1.8%	4.3%	6.3%	0.14
Domestic Equity	5.0%	7.6%	18.1%	0.23
International Developed Equity	4.8%	7.4%	19.7%	0.20
Emerging Market Equity	6.0%	8.7%	26.6%	0.19
Private Equity	8.5%	11.2%	24.0%	0.32
Real Assets	4.5%	7.1%	13.3%	0.27
Diversifying Strategies	4.0%	6.6%	10.0%	0.31

Note: Inflation assumed to be 2.5% per year.

Exhibit 8 Forward-Looking Correlation Matrix

	Cash	Fixed Income	Domestic Equity	International Developed Equity	Emerging Market Equity	Private Equity	Real Assets	Diversifying Strategies
Cash	1.00							
Fixed Income	0.11	1.00						
Domestic Equity	0.03	0.13	1.00					
International Developed Equity	0.02	0.14	0.91	1.00				
Emerging Market Equity	0.04	(0.18)	0.69	0.71	1.00			
Private Equity	0.02	(0.11)	0.68	0.65	0.59	1.00		
Real Assets	0.07	(0.16)	0.35	0.35	0.25	0.42	1.00	
Diversifying Strategies	0.18	0.18	0.40	0.40	0.45	0.35	(0.04)	1.00

Analysis by Thompson and her team uncovered the main reasons for peer underperformance since the 2008 crisis: a lower risk profile of the portfolio and a lower allocation to illiquid investments, in particular, private equity. As such, an important change being proposed by Thompson and the team is an increase in exposure to private markets. The change would increase the private equity allocation from 18% to 23% and the real assets allocation from 13% to 16%. To accommodate both increases, the allocations to public equities and fixed income would decrease. The proposed target allocations are presented in Exhibit 9.

In terms of implementation, Thompson and her team expect that the transition to the higher target allocations in private equity and real assets will occur gradually over the next two to three years.

Exhibit 9 Proposed Strategic Asset Allocation Targets

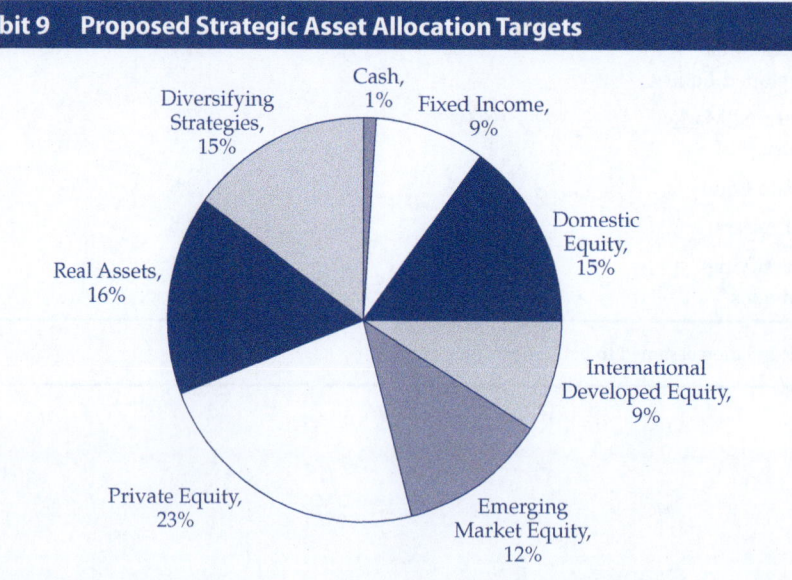

Optimization results in Exhibit 10 are based on the team's assumptions (Exhibits 7 and 8) and show that a higher allocation to private equity and real assets would improve the expected long-term risk–return profile of the endowment. The team also includes the results of Monte Carlo simulations that show the probability of an erosion in longer term purchasing power. Thompson notes that the resulting risk profile measured by the volatility is consistent with quantitative guidelines developed for the endowment's risk tolerance. Based on interaction with the Board, the risk tolerance has been specified as a volatility range of 12% to 14% based on long-term measures of risk.

Exhibit 10 Proposed vs. Current SAA: Expected Risk/Return Properties

Portfolio Characteristic	Proposed SAA	Current SAA
Expected nominal return (annual average, geometric, next 10 years)	7.8%	7.5%
Expected real return (annual average, geometric, next 10 years)	5.3%	5.0%
Standard deviation of returns (annual)	13.2%	12.5%
Sharpe ratio	0.34	0.33
Probability of 25% erosion in purchasing power over 20 years with 5% spending rate	30%	35%

Note: The probability of erosion in purchasing power was derived based on a Monte-Carlo simulation with a 20-year investment horizon, assuming expected return and volatility characteristics will be the same as for the next 10 years.

When asked to justify the proposed strategic asset allocation (SAA), including the higher allocation to private markets, Thompson highlights the optimization results from Exhibit 10 to the Board, noting that the primary driver of the proposed asset allocation changes is the expected improvement in the portfolio's long-term risk/return profile.

Thompson is aware the proposed asset allocation implies a small increase in the overall risk profile of the endowment as measured by the volatility of portfolio returns (13.2% for the proposed SAA versus 12.5% for the current portfolio). She believes that the increase in risk is justified by the following:

- Lower return expectations for all asset classes relative to past expectations due to higher current valuations. This implies that a higher level of risk must be taken to achieve the same level of returns. At the time of the last review, the then-current SAA had an expected return of 5.3% in real terms, although now it is expected to generate a 5.0% real return going forward. Lower return expectations can only be compensated in part by efficiency improvements in the asset allocation. Although the proposed SAA is slightly more efficient (higher Sharpe ratio of 0.01), this efficiency improvement alone is not enough to generate a 5.3% expected real return for the same level of short-term risk/volatility as the current SAA.
- A portfolio risk profile that is currently more conservative when compared to other endowment peers.
- A lower expected Sharpe ratio (expected risk–return profile) for fixed income (compared with recent history), suggesting a lower allocation to these strategies may be warranted.

- Monte-Carlo simulations, suggesting that the proposed asset allocation has a higher probability of achieving the real return target over a 20-year horizon, while better preserving the purchasing power of the endowment with the current spending policy of 5%.

IN-TEXT QUESTIONS: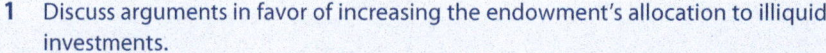

1. Discuss arguments in favor of increasing the endowment's allocation to illiquid investments.
2. Using additional information provided in Exhibit 10 and your knowledge of illiquid investments from prior curriculum content, justify Thompson's proposed asset allocation and explain the trade-offs involved in terms of portfolio volatility.

Guideline Answers:

1. In general, for a long-horizon institutional investor, the ability to tolerate illiquidity creates an opportunity to improve portfolio diversification and expected returns as well as access a broader set of investment strategies. In mean–variance optimization models, the inclusion of illiquid assets in the eligible investment universe may shift the efficient frontier upwards, theoretically resulting in more-efficient investment portfolios (i.e., portfolios with a higher expected return for a given level of risk).

   Thompson and her team believe the above to be true in the case of QU's endowment. In addition, further arguments are in favor of increasing the allocation to illiquidity risk. Thompson believes the specific circumstances of the endowment continue to support an increase in exposure to illiquid investments. To date, the team's historical experience with illiquid investments has been positive with strong realized returns. The endowment has been building exposure to these strategies over the last two decades in a gradual manner. As a result, the illiquid portfolios are now well-established, mature, and well-diversified in terms of fund managers, strategies, and vintages. At the same time, the long presence in the market and the ability to access QU alumni networks have helped the endowment develop a strong network of connections in the industry and gain access to best-in-class managers in these spaces—building a reputation as a well-informed, patient, and reliable long-term investor. As revealed in the case text, the QU endowment has a lower exposure to illiquid investments than most institutional investor peers with similar risk profiles and objectives. Analysis by Thompson and her team has identified this as one of the reasons for the QU endowment's underperformance in recent years relative to peers.

   Thompson and the strategy team should also examine whether the allocation to private equity and real assets is exposed to idiosyncratic risk factors. Avoiding large allocations to a small number of funds helps ensure that idiosyncratic risk factors are largely diversified away.

2. As Thompson highlights to the Board, the primary driver of the proposed asset allocation is the expected improvement in the portfolio's long-term risk/return profile. The proposed SAA has a higher expected real return compared to the current SAA (5.3% vs. 5.0% in real terms) and a slightly higher Sharpe ratio (0.34 vs. 0.33).

   The proposed asset allocation also has a higher probability of achieving the endowment's return target over the long-term. One way to get a better sense of this is through Monte Carlo simulations. For example, using such simulations, the team concludes that there is a 70% chance of maintaining at least 75% of purchasing power over a 20-year horizon for the proposed SAA versus a 65% chance for the current SAA, assuming a 5% spending rate.

There is an implicit trade-off in this case between the short-term risk measure (volatility) and the long-term risk represented by the probability of purchasing power erosion over a 20-year horizon.

Trade-off 1: Portfolio volatility

Thompson has considered the increase in overall risk profile for the endowment (portfolio return volatility increases from 12.5% to 13.2%) and believes the increase to be justified.

Thompson believes future returns will be lower for all asset classes. Lower return expectations imply that a higher level of risk must be taken to achieve the same level of returns. Although the proposed SAA is slightly more efficient, as indicated by its higher Sharpe ratio, this improvement in portfolio efficiency is not sufficient to generate the 5.3% expected real return for the same level of short term risk/volatility as the current SAA.

Optimization results also suggest that the proposed asset allocation has a higher probability of achieving the real return target while preserving the purchasing power of the endowment given the current 5% spending policy. Finally, Thompson also considers that QU's portfolio risk profile is still currently more conservative than its peers.

Trade-off 2: Implementation costs

Thompson and her team analyzed the costs associated with implementing the proposed portfolio allocation changes. Private equity and private real estate strategies typically have higher investment management fees and performance fees than fixed-income and public equity strategies. By using "net of fees" return assumptions, Thompson and her team incorporated the impact of higher expected investment management fees arising from higher allocations to more-illiquid investments.

Before concluding that the QU endowment should adjust its asset allocation to illiquid investments, Thompson should confirm that the resulting risk profile (return volatility of 13.2% and the probability of erosion in purchasing power shown in Exhibit 10) is consistent with the endowment's risk tolerance (willingness and capacity to bear risk). Thompson also should confirm that with the increased allocation to illiquid investments, the resulting asset allocation remains consistent with the liquidity budget.

QUINCO CASE: LIQUIDITY MANAGEMENT

5

c   analyze asset allocation and portfolio construction in relation to liquidity needs and risk and return requirements and recommend actions to address identified needs

Given the increasing complexity in the investment portfolio and the university's reliance on regular distributions from the endowment, QUINCO needs a robust framework for managing liquidity. During her time at QUINCO, Thompson has worked to enhance QUINCO's overall liquidity management framework. This includes improving the tools used in that process and taking a comprehensive, enterprise-wide approach. Using her approach, the expected cash outflows and inflows for the endowment portfolio are modeled over various time horizons both under normal circumstances and in periods of severe market stress.

Thompson is concerned that the portfolio's liquidity characteristics will deteriorate in periods of severe market stress. She believes a deterioration in liquidity could potentially occur for the following reasons:

- **Capital calls in private markets exceeding capital distributions.** This would increase the allocation to private markets in the overall portfolio.

- **Activation of gates.** Some investment vehicles that provide quarterly or annual liquidity, like hedge funds or real estate funds, have provisions in their investment prospectuses allowing the investment manager to refuse investor withdrawal requests (activate gates) during stress periods to protect remaining investors in the fund. The inability to withdraw from funds leads to a more illiquid profile overall.

- **The smoothing effect.** Investments in private markets tend to incorporate market valuations with a lag that leads to a relative increase in their portfolio weighting during periods of market stress and a relative decrease in the portfolio weighting of more liquid assets. This does not reduce the effective liquidity of the portfolio in dollar terms, but it does impact the percentage of assets in the overall portfolio that could be used to satisfy liquidity needs in periods of market stress.

To address her concerns, Thompson asks her team for an analysis of the current and proposed QU portfolios under normal and stress market conditions. The team's analysis of each portfolio's liquidity profile is shown in Exhibits 11 and 12.

Exhibit 11 shows the current QU portfolio under normal and stress conditions.

Exhibit 11 QU Endowment Liquidity Profile: Current Portfolio (Normal and Stress Conditions)

A. Liquidity Profile - Normal Conditions

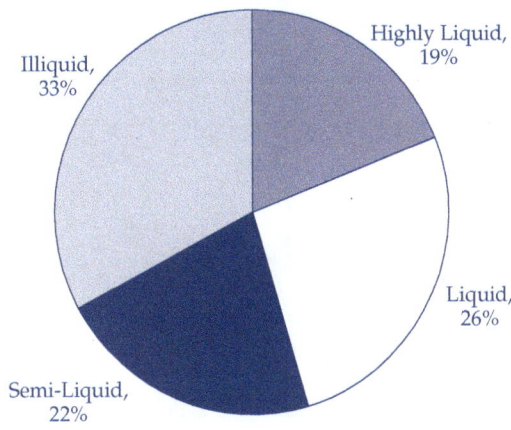

B. Liquidity Profile - Stress Conditions

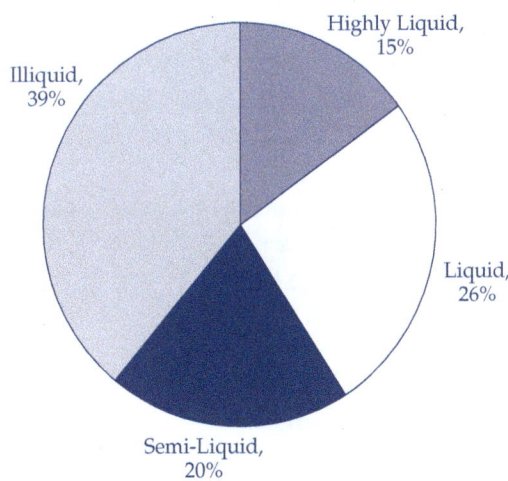

Exhibit 12 shows the proposed QU strategic asset allocation portfolio under normal and stress conditions.

Exhibit 12   QU Endowment Liquidity Profile: Proposed Strategic Asset Allocation (Normal and Stress Conditions)

A. Liquidity Profile - Normal Conditions

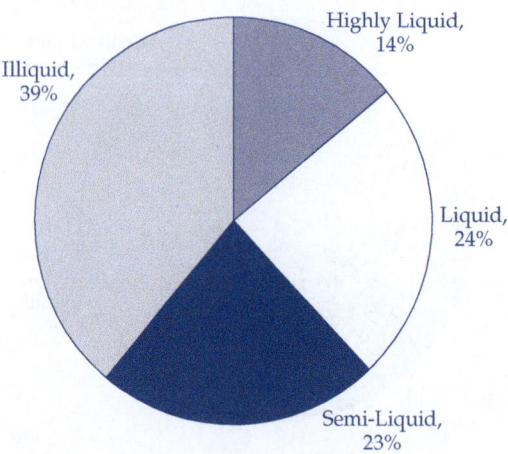

B. Liquidity Profile - Stress Conditions

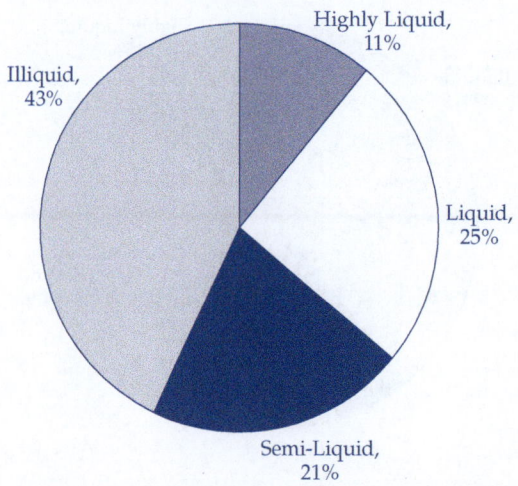

IN-TEXT QUESTIONS:

1. Explain how current spending policy might affect liquidity needs in a market downturn.
2. Describe various tools that QUINCO might use to manage its portfolio liquidity risk.
3. What impact will the proposed asset allocation changes have on the endowment's liquidity profile?

QUINCO Case: Liquidity Management

Guideline Answers:

1. The design of the spending rate policy incorporates a smoothing, countercyclical element leading to spending rates below 5% in a period of sustained strong investment returns but higher than 5% in a protracted weak return environment. This design of the spending rate policy exacerbates the endowment's liquidity needs in severe market downturns.

2. Among the tools QUINCO could use are cash flow-forecasting and commitment-pacing models, liquidity budgets, and stress test analyses. To begin, Thompson estimates expected cash outflows and inflows. For cash outflows, Thompson projects distributions from the endowment to the university. These uses of cash can then be factored into the estimation of expected outflows and inflows through the spending rate policy in which the university seeks to spend, on average, 5% annually of the endowment while preserving the endowment's purchasing power over time.

   For the private equity and real estate portfolios, Thompson and her team can use cash flow-forecasting models and commitment-pacing models to project the expected increase in the allocation to private markets. These help the team project cash outflows needed for future investment commitments (committed but undrawn capital calls) in private markets. These flows could become particularly relevant in stress periods when distributions from prior investments in those markets might cease as general partners find it difficult to exit investments (because of depressed valuations and lack of transaction activity). Future investment commitments are legal obligations of the endowment, so the staff needs to ensure capital calls are met because the general partner may accelerate capital calls as opportunities arise in depressed markets. Thompson and her team should ensure diversification across fund vintage years to avoid overexposure to particular parts of the economic cycle and should also follow a strategy that commits capital on a steady and regular basis to minimize the need to make large allocation changes (or adjustments) with associated transaction costs. Avoiding large allocations to very few funds will help minimize idiosyncratic portfolio risk.

   At the same time, cash inflows into the endowment from donors will likely drop significantly during stress periods, further increasing liquidity needs. Liquidating risk assets or high-beta assets after periods of negative return is often not desirable from a valuation standpoint when future returns may be expected to be more attractive, particularly following periods of sharp drawdowns. Given her experience with these markets, Thompson should recognize the need for the team's approach to be flexible. Access to the top private market managers is often highly competitive, and opportunities to invest with these managers may not be available at times when the portfolio is making allocation increases.

   Incorporating this information, Thompson can develop a liquidity budget for the endowment like that shown in Exhibit 1, which specifies minimum acceptable liquidity targets based on the expected time needed to convert portfolio holdings to cash. The liquidity budget should be monitored by Thompson and her team on a regular basis as part of the liquidity management framework in place at QUINCO. Thompson and her team can also do an analysis of the portfolio's current liquidity characteristics under normal market conditions, like that shown in Exhibit 2.

   Thompson and her team should continue to undertake regular stress tests (such as the liquidity profile analysis done by her team) using historical and hypothetical scenarios to estimate how much the liquidity profile of the portfolio could drift under certain assumptions and to assess whether the minimum liquidity budget is still satisfied. The analysis can also be used to inform the team's asset allocation and implementation decisions for investment vehicles and strategies.

3. Compared to the liquidity profile of the current portfolio, the proposed asset allocation implies a shift toward more-illiquid investments, as shown in the following table:

Liquidity Category	Current Portfolio: Normal (%)	Current Portfolio: Stress (%)	Current Portfolio: Stress vs. Normal (%)	Proposed: Normal (%)	Proposed Portfolio: Stress (%)	Proposed Portfolio: Stress vs. Normal (%)	Proposed vs. Current: Normal (%)	Proposed vs. Current: Stress (%)
Highly Liquid	19	15	−4	14	11	−3	−5	−4
Liquid	26	26	0	24	25	1	−2	−1
Semi-Liquid	22	20	−2	23	21	−2	1	1
Illiquid	33	39	6	39	43	4	6	4

As a result, there will be a reduction in the highly liquid and liquid categories in the endowment's liquidity profile and a commensurate increase in the semi-liquid and illiquid categories under both normal and stress conditions. The proposed allocation results in an increase in the overall illiquidity profile because a higher percentage of the portfolio will be invested in private equity and private real estate, which are the most illiquid asset classes in the portfolio.

Thompson needs to ensure that even under stress conditions the proposed allocation continues to comply with the liquidity budgeting framework in place for the fund, which satisfies the various liquidity needs of the portfolio for both cash outflows and rebalancing. From an ongoing management perspective, and particularly at times when the liquidity profile of the proposed allocation is closer to the minimum thresholds set through the liquidity budget, Thompson and her team should plan to closely monitor the portfolio's liquidity profile and stress test it periodically to make sure portfolio liquidity remains adequate.

Based on this analysis, the QUINCO Board approves the proposed changes to the asset allocation and instructs the team to proceed with implementation. These changes are also presented to the Quadrivium Trustees as part of the university treasurer's financial report at the Trustees' next regular meeting.

6. QUINCO CASE: ASSET MANAGER SELECTION

d analyze actions in asset manager selection with respect to the Code of Ethics and Standards of Professional Conduct

It is now three months later, and Winter, Thompson, and the rest of the QUINCO team have begun implementing changes to the strategic asset allocation by seeking additional external managers. Winter is very pleased with their progress to date but has encountered a somewhat interesting situation.

Among the firms responding to QUINCO's request for proposal (RFP) seeking a new private equity manager is Genex Venture Capital (GVC). GVC is proposing that QUINCO invest in its new "GVC Fund II" offering. GVC is a US-based venture capital fund operating in the biotech space. GVC would be a new relationship for QUINCO. The firm has adopted the CFA Institute Asset Manager Code for its employees. The founder and managing partner at GVC is Virginia Hall, CFA, a prominent alumna of Quadrivium University who was elected to the university's board of trustees three years ago. Hall has made several generous donations to the university over the years, and the building that houses the school's student center and main dining facility is

QUINCO Case: Asset Manager Selection

named in her honor. Both the university president and university treasurer have urged Winter to favorably consider GVC's proposal given Hall's importance to the university. Winter has suspicions that Hall has contacted the university president and treasurer to advocate for her company.

The investment committee narrows the competition for the allocation of QUINCO's private market assets to GVC and Beacher Venture Investments (Beacher). Beacher is another venture capital investment firm operating in the same space and is a direct competitor to GVC.

Both GVC and Beacher are invited to make a presentation to QUINCO's investment committee. GVC's presentation is led by Jason Allen, one of Winter's former colleagues from the endowment they both worked for previously. Allen has joined GVC as a managing director as part of GVC's efforts to build the team in preparation for Fund II. Although Allen's presentation on behalf of GVC is thorough and well-documented, Winter is troubled by two aspects. The presentation is targeted to QUINCO but clearly incorporates information that is based on or could only have come from the university treasurer's non-public reports to the Quadrivium board of trustees or another university source. In addition, the performance presentation of GVC's historical returns shows substantially higher returns than performance reported by third-party performance databases.

Of the two finalists, Beacher has a longer track record and is a more established name in the industry; however, there are some concerns over the historical performance of its previous fund. At the same time, some investment committee members have expressed reservations over GVC's short track record. Given the overlap in sector and strategy between the two firms, the investment committee asks Bud Davis, a CFA charterholder and senior portfolio manager on QUINCO's private equity team, to return with a formal proposal to invest in one of the firms.

Davis presents an update on the fundraising efforts of each firm's fund and notes that GVC is facing challenges in raising the desired fund amount of $300 million for Fund II. Potential investors are apparently concerned with the significant increase in funding size of the fund (Fund I had raised $100 million) and question whether GVC has the infrastructure to scale operations.

Davis makes a strong case for investing with GVC, highlighting confidence in the manager and their differentiated approach to sourcing and growing portfolio companies in the biotech space. Davis tells the investment committee that because of the longer-than-expected fundraising period, GVC is eager to secure QU's commitment for Fund II; as a result, Davis has negotiated a discount on GVC's investment management fee. Following that discussion, the investment committee approves the recommendation from the team to invest with GVC.

After the decision is made to hire GVC, Winter calls Allen to tell him the good news and offer his congratulations. During the conversation, Allen expresses his satisfaction in having QUINCO as one of the fund's investors and praises Davis's strong commitment and drive. Allen goes on to mention that Davis's spouse, Andrea, is Hall's daughter. Winter expresses his surprise at this fact and later asks Davis about his wife's relationship to Hall. Davis responds that he believes this information is common knowledge and that he thought Winter and members of the QUINCO investment committee knew this information.

> **IN-TEXT QUESTION:**
>
> What ethical considerations arise regarding the actions and conduct of individuals involved in manager selection?

Guideline Answer:

Aaron Winter, QUINCO CIO

Winter faces several ethical dilemmas in this case. The main issue is the disclosure of a potential conflict of interest, Standard of Professional Conduct VI(A), regarding the hiring of an external investment manager with close ties to the university. Winter's independence and objectivity, Standard of Professional Conduct I(B), in making the hiring recommendation could be compromised by the implicit and explicit pressure he is receiving to hire GVC. He should disclose this conflict to the QUINCO Board as part of the hiring recommendation. He should also disclose that the managing director for GVC is a former colleague since that relationship could also be perceived as impairing his independence and objectivity, creating a conflict of interest. During the presentation, it appears that GVC has based their proposal on confidential information, Standard of Professional Conduct III(E), about the university, potentially obtained by Hall through her role as a Quadrivium Trustee or others at the university. As an employee of the University and QUINCO, Winter should make them aware of the possible breach of confidentiality. He also apparently has questions about the accuracy of the performance information, Standards of Professional Conduct I(C) and III(D), presented by GVC but fails to exercise appropriate due diligence, Standard of Professional Conduct V(A), by following up with GVC or investigating further to determine the veracity of the information.

Virginia Hall, CFA, Quadrivium University Trustee and Managing Partner at GVC

Virginia Hall has a conflict of interest, Standard of Professional Conduct VI(A), if she is pressuring university staff and QUINCO employees to influence the external manager hiring process in her company's favor. Hall's personal/business interests with GVC pose a potential conflict of interest with her duties as a Trustee of the university board. She has a duty as a Board member to act in the best interest of the university without regard to how it may benefit her, but she has an incentive to pressure the university to hire her company. She would be violating her duty of loyalty, Standard of Professional Conduct IV(A), to the university as a Trustee by putting her firm, and therefore her personal interest, ahead of the interests of the university. She should disclose her potential conflict and recuse herself from any part in the external manager hiring process. In addition, she has potentially gone further by sharing confidential information, Standard of Professional Conduct III(E), she has received as a trustee with GVC in an effort to assist GVC's response and boost the prospects of her company in being hired—another violation of her duty of loyalty as a Trustee. GVC neglected to disclose the relationship of one employee's relative (Hall's daughter, who is Davis's spouse) with QUINCO.

Quadrivium University President/Quadrivium University Treasurer

The university president and treasurer, as members of the QUINCO Board, have a duty to act in the best interest, Standard of Professional Conduct IV(A), of the university by hiring the external investment managers most appropriate for managing the private equity portion of the university's endowment. In pressuring Winter to hire GVC, they are clearly letting the outside consideration of maintaining good relations with a Trustee influence their hiring decision. It is also possible they provided confidential information, Standard of Professional Conduct III(E), to Hall or GVC to assist their bid to become an investment manager for QUINCO. They should disclose their conflict, Standard of Professional Conduct VI(A), and recuse themselves from decisions where their independence and objectivity, Standard of Professional Conduct I(B), are compromised. The university president and treasurer should also have in place a due diligence questionnaire/RFP to raise questions to new managers about potential conflicts of interest.

Jason Allen, Managing Director at GVC

Winter has noticed a discrepancy between the performance history of GVC in the presentation made by Allen and the performance record of the company as reported elsewhere. It is possible that Allen is inadvertently using inaccurate information or, worse, knowingly misrepresenting the performance record, Standards of Professional Conduct I(C) and III(D), of GVC.

> *Bud Davis, CFA, Senior Portfolio Manager at QUINCO*
>
> Through his spouse, Davis has a personal relationship with GVC, a company he is tasked with investigating and providing an opinion on the potential hiring as an outside manager. This could affect his independence and objectivity, Standard of Professional Conduct I(B), and creates, at minimum, the perception of a conflict of interest, Standard of Professional Conduct VI(A), that should be disclosed when making his recommendation. Davis should not rely on his belief that the relationship is "common knowledge" or widely known but should make an explicit disclosure of this potential conflict.

QUINCO CASE: TACTICAL ASSET ALLOCATION

e analyze the costs and benefits of derivatives versus cash market techniques for establishing or modifying asset class or risk exposures

f demonstrate the use of derivatives overlays in tactical asset allocation and rebalancing

As part of the investment strategy review, the Board decided to significantly increase the active risk budget assigned to the QUINCO team for use in a new tactical asset allocation (TAA) program. QUINCO's active risk budget measures the deviation of the endowment's portfolio from its investment policy targets and is expressed as an annual tracking error limit. The Board increased QUINCO's active risk budget from 100 bps to 250 bps to allow the team to pursue greater excess returns versus the strategic asset allocation. By taking active risk relative to investment policy benchmarks through external managers in public asset classes as well as TAA positions, the QUINCO team hopes to add additional portfolio performance.

The implementation of the tactical asset allocation program and associated risk budget was fully delegated to Winter and his staff. At that time, the Board also informed that up to 150 bps (of the 250 bps) active risk budget could be used to implement the TAA program. One consideration the Board discussed was the use of leverage. The TAA program implementation could result in a levered position of the endowment portfolio (because derivatives are likely to be used in implementation and not every overweight exposure would be offset by a corresponding underweight in another asset), so the Board agreed to permit a modest leverage position for the overall portfolio of up to 5% of the portfolio's value.

Winter believes that the tactical asset allocation program will accommodate two types of active decisions:

- Overweight and underweight positions in one or more of the asset classes included in the investment policy portfolio.
- Provide exposure to asset classes and/or investment strategies outside the policy portfolio benchmark universe but compliant with the investment policy (e.g., high yield, emerging market, fixed income).

Winter began implementing the TAA program by building on a framework and research by Thompson and the asset allocation team that was informed by external parties (e.g., investment consultants, external tactical asset allocation managers, investment research houses). Using concepts of fair value and mean reversion in financial markets, fair value models were developed for various financial assets. To do this, the framework incorporated economic and financial data that had exhibited predictive power for future returns and risk over an investment horizon of one to three years.

Current market pricing was then compared with output from the valuation models to determine whether the deviation from 'fair value' was large enough to be exploited in a cost-efficient manner.

In extensive out-of-sample backtests, the methodology had produced encouraging results. One of the strongest signals suggested that large-cap US equities, characterized broadly by the S&P 500 Index, were significantly below fair value with mean reversion expected over the next year. Based on this information, Thompson decides to implement a 1% overweight to US equities through a passive exposure.

Thompson is now considering three options to implement her decision: a total return swap, equity futures, and ETFs. Her goal is to implement the overweight position as effectively as possible from a cost and cash usage perspective. Thompson asks her team to look at the associated costs for each option.

The team's cost comparison analysis is shown in Exhibit 13.

Exhibit 13 Cost Comparison Assuming a Fully-Funded Mandate

Cost Component	ETF	Futures	Total Return Swap
Commission (round trip)	4.00	2.00	5.00
Management fee (annual)	9.50	0.00	0.00
Bid/offer spread (round trip)	2.50	2.00	6.00
Price impact (round trip)	15.00	10.00	0.00
Mispricing (tracking error, annual)	4.00	8.00	0.00
Cost to roll the futures contract	0.00	20.00	0.00
Funding cost	0.00	0.00	40.00
Total cost	**35.00**	**42.00**	**51.00**

Notes: The exhibit shows the team's cost comparison for the three implementation options—ETFs, futures, and total return swaps—for an $80 million notional exposure to the S&P 500 Index (assuming a fully funded mandate) over a one-year investment horizon. All numbers are in basis points (bps) unless otherwise indicated.

The comparison assumes no leverage for the ETF and that the entire mandate amount ($80 million) is deposited to earn the 3-month Libor rate for futures and the total return swap as to offset the 3-month Libor component of the implied financing rate (or the funding cost in the case of the swap).

After closely examining the cost comparison analysis, Thompson debates the pros and cons of each option with her team.

From a cash 'usage' perspective, ETFs would be least efficient as she would need to finance the full notional value of the ETF or use the margin features of the account. Even when using the margin, regulations would limit the margin to 50% of account value, implying a maximum of two times the leverage ratio. For example, for an $80 million ETF exposure, the minimum margin that would have to be held in cash would be $40 million. Thompson knows that using futures and total return swaps could generate a similar economic exposure to ETFs with a much lower capital commitment.

From a liquidity perspective, Thompson likes ETFs and futures, which appear efficient given their liquid trading and narrow bid–ask spreads. She also values the flexibility they offer to terminate exposure before intended maturity should the team's views on the market change. Thompson is concerned about the operational implications of holding futures because they require daily monitoring of margin requirements. In addition, she also worries about interest rate risk and exposure of QU to counterparty credit risk.

> **IN-TEXT QUESTION:**
>
> Assuming a fully-funded position (no use of leverage), which implementation option should Thompson choose for the 1% tactical overweight to US equities?
>
> **Guideline Answer:**
>
> **Expected Costs.** In the case of the ETF, the most significant cost component is price impact—the expected impact on market price from entering into (buying) and exiting out of (selling) the ETF position. This is estimated to be approximately 15 bps. The second largest cost component is the management fee charged by the ETF manager, which is expected to be 9.5 bps.
>
> In the case of futures, the largest cost component is expected to be the cost to roll the futures contract on a quarterly basis (5 bps quarterly or 20 bps annual cost). This is driven by the upward-sloping (contango) shape of the yield curve. In addition to the futures roll cost and the price impact, another significant futures cost is the mispricing or tracking error of expected futures performance relative to the underlying index performance. Expected tracking error on the futures contracts is 8 bps.
>
> Finally, for the total return swap, the cost is dominated by the funding cost, which is expected to be 40 bps.
>
> From a total cost perspective, at 35 bps the ETF offers the most cost-efficient vehicle to implement the tactical overlay, with relatively tight bid–ask spreads that are similar to futures.
>
> **Other Considerations.** ETFs and futures are typically standardized products that trade on exchanges. Total return swaps are over-the-counter contracts that are negotiated and customizable in such features as maturity, leverage, and cost. ETFs are the least cash-efficient option requiring the largest cash outlay, and Thompson would be able to gain similar economic exposure with futures and swaps using significantly less cash.
>
> A position in futures contracts would need to be rolled over each quarter to maintain exposure. Given Thompson's concerns about the operational requirements for futures and the need for daily monitoring for margin requirements, a position in futures is likely less desirable to Thompson. For ETFs, ongoing management of the exposure is done by the ETF manager.
>
> Futures and ETFs have associated tracking error versus the index intended to be replicated. For ETFs, the tracking error may result from premiums and discounts to net asset value, cash drag, or regulatory diversification requirements. For futures, tracking error arises because of liquidity (supply/demand conditions), dividend forecast errors, and interest rate differentials. For total return swaps, the replication is exact; Thompson would receive the total return of the index without incurring any tracking error to the benchmark S&P 500 Index because the swap counterparty is obligated to provide the index return.
>
> However, Thompson is concerned about interest rate risk in the case of futures and swaps. She is also concerned about the counterparty credit risk that QUINCO would be exposed to through a swap, which would additionally create complexities in managing net exposures over the duration of the contract.
>
> To implement the tactical overlay given Thompson's considerations, the ETF provides the most cost-efficient vehicle, with adequate liquidity and relatively tight bid–ask spreads. ETFs also provide Thompson with the flexibility (noted as being important to her) to modify exposure before the end of the one-year horizon should her and her team's investment views change.

After considering with her team, Thompson believes implementing with ETFs appears to be the best option.

Later that day after further discussion, Thompson and the management team decide to implement the overlay using leverage. Thompson asks her team to complete a cost comparison analysis assuming a permissible leverage level of 4 times for all three options (meaning that cash needed to support the position would be 25% of the overlay notional amount).[7] The team's work is shown in Exhibit 14.

Exhibit 14 Additional Information with Respect to Impact of Leverage

Cost Component	ETF	Futures	Total Return Swap
Cost of obtaining leverage	187.50	0.00	0.00
Additional financing/funding cost	0.00	150.00	150.00
Total additional cost	187.50	150.00	150.00

Notes: The additional cost components assume 4 times leverage over a one-year investment horizon. All numbers are in basis points (bps) unless otherwise indicated.

The team's assumptions for the analysis are as follows:

- The borrowing cost of obtaining leverage in the case of the ETF is assumed to be 3-month Libor + 50 bps.
- The 3-month Libor assumption used is 2% (opportunity costs).
- The same Libor rate was used to calculate the additional implied financing cost in the case of futures and the additional funding cost for the total return swap.
- The analysis focuses on the implementation cost of trade and does not consider the additional return earned by investing the cash that is not needed to support the transaction (75% of the overlay notional amount).

IN-TEXT QUESTION:

Assuming a permissible leverage level of 4 times for all three options, and using the information in Exhibit 14, would Thompson change her decision?

Guideline Answer:

As shown in Exhibit 14, the additional information changes the total cost estimates for the different implementation options. In the case of ETFs, to generate 4 times leverage, 75% of the desired nominal exposure would have to be borrowed to provide an overall exposure 4 times higher than the original capital. That is, for a desired nominal exposure of $80 million, borrowing $60 million (75% of $80 million) provides 4 times leverage to an original capital amount of $20 million.

The additional cost of obtaining leverage for each option would be as follows:

1 ETFs. ($80 million × 0.75 × 2.5%) / $80 million = 1.875%.

---

[7] Although in the case of the ETF the leverage at the instrument level may be regulated to not exceed 2 times (50% margin requirement), for the purposes of this exercise assume that the endowment can generate leverage at the plan level for ETF usage.

2 Futures. ($80 million × 0.75 × 2%) / $80 million = 1.50%. The additional financing cost for futures in this case (compared to the unlevered option) would occur because 75% of the amount would not be invested in 3-month Libor to offset the financing cost, thus increasing the overall cost for the futures.

3 Swaps. ($80 million × 0.75 × 2%) / $80 million = 1.50%. The additional financing cost for swaps in this case (compared to the unlevered option) would occur because 75% of the amount would not be invested in 3-month Libor to offset the financing cost, thus increasing the overall cost for the swaps.

Total costs for each option (in bps):

	ETF	Futures	Total Return Swap
Unlevered	35.00	42.00	51.00
Incremental cost	187.50	150.00	150.00
Total	222.50	192.00	201.00

Looking at the data, total costs for futures appear to be the lowest cost alternative (192 bps) followed by the total return swap (201 bps). Given a permissible leverage level of 4 times for all three options, and based on the data in Exhibit 14, ETFs now look to be the most expensive option (222.50 bps).

Given the difference in costs, Thompson would consider implementation through futures. The main consideration between the use of ETFs and futures not captured in the comparative pricing analysis is the additional complexity and operational monitoring associated with a quarterly futures roll. If Thompson and the team can get comfortable with that risk, implementation through futures would be the more efficient option.

Looking at the data, and based on their desire to use leverage, Thompson believes that futures offer the more efficient alternative. She decides to establish a 1% long position to the S&P 500 Index using S&P 500 futures.

QUINCO CASE: ASSET ALLOCATION REBALANCING

e analyze the costs and benefits of derivatives versus cash market techniques for establishing or modifying asset class or risk exposures

f demonstrate the use of derivatives overlays in tactical asset allocation and rebalancing

Three months have passed since Thompson and the team implemented the tactical overweight position to US equities. To date, the position has been performing well and in line with *ex ante* expectations. Global equity markets have rallied, reflecting a favorable global growth environment, and fixed-income markets have sold off as interest rates rose significantly in anticipation of higher inflationary pressures. As a result, the asset allocation of the endowment has drifted from policy targets.

QUINCO follows a calendar quarter rebalancing policy with a rebalancing corridor for each asset class. The allocation drift of the actual portfolio relative to the SAA is monitored monthly; however, to minimize transaction costs, short of extraordinary market circumstances, rebalancing decisions are implemented at the end of each quarter. For public asset classes, systematic rebalancing occurs when the allocation to these assets is outside the rebalancing corridor at quarter end. When the allocation moves outside the corridor, Thompson and her team do have discretion to rebalance back to the target allocation or to the edge of the corridor.

For illiquid asset classes, given high transaction costs and practical challenges in rebalancing the allocation, rebalancing is normally undertaken through the reinvestment/commitment strategy as allocations approach the upper or lower edges of the corridor. In these cases, the pace of commitments could be altered from the expected pace to gradually shift the overall allocation to illiquid assets over time. The SAA, width of the rebalancing corridor, and the current allocation for the various asset classes are shown in Exhibit 15:

Exhibit 15 SAA, Rebalancing Corridors, and Current (Actual) Allocations

	Target Allocation (SAA)	Corridor	Min/Max Target	Current Allocation
Cash	1%	±1%	0%–2%	0.8%
Fixed Income	9%	±3	6%–12%	6.5%
Domestic Equity	15%	±2.5	12.5%–17.5%	17.3%
International Developed Equity	9%	±2	7%–11%	11.5%
Emerging Market Equity	12%	±2%	10%–14%	13.9%
Private Equity	23%	±5	18%–28%	19.2%
Real Assets	16%	±3	13%–19%	13.8%
Diversifying Strategies	15%	±3	12%–18%	17.1%
Total	100.0%			100.0%

Thompson observes that the allocation to international developed equity (11.50%) now exceeds the upper end of its corridor (9.00% + 2.00% = 11.00%) by 0.50%, while the allocation to fixed income (6.50%) is below target (9.00%) but still within its rebalancing corridor (6.00%–12.00%).

Current allocations to private equity (19.20%) and real assets (13.80%) are close to the lower ends of their rebalancing corridors of 18.00%–28.00% and 13.00%–19.00%, respectively, as the team works to move toward the new targets approved by the Board in Exhibit 9 (in the very short term, these allocations cannot be increased).

Based on the information in Exhibit 15, Thompson sees a need to decrease the international developed equity allocation and increase the fixed-income allocation by the same amount. She meets with the team to discuss whether they should execute the rebalancing through the cash or derivatives market.

During the discussion, Thompson and her team consider the following factors: transaction costs, tracking error of the implementation vehicle versus the desired index exposure, tracking error implied by the current and post-rebalancing deviations from the target SAA weights, opportunity cost/impact to active strategies due to manager withdrawals and reallocations, implementation speed, and time horizon of the rebalancing trade.

Thompson knows that executing through the cash markets takes longer to implement than executing in the derivatives markets. Still, allocating to, or reallocating from, external managers may be warranted in certain cases, such as when the adjustments are viewed as more permanent and/or more significant in nature (as compared to smaller, more temporary adjustments that may be reversed within a shorter time frame if investment views change).

After meeting with her team, Thompson decides to rebalance back to the upper edge of the corridor (11.00%) by reallocating 0.50% (50 bps) from international developed equities to fixed income. The team's cost analysis is shown in Exhibit 16.

Exhibit 16 Cost Information: 50 bps Rebalancing Option

Cost Component	Cash Market	Futures (Equity/Fixed Income)
Bid/offer spread	5.00	3.00
Price impact (total trades)	5.00	4.00
Mispricing (tracking error, quarterly)	0.00	17.00
Cash drag (impact of timing delays and disruptions to active manager portfolios)	20.00	0.00
Cost of rolling the futures contract	0.00	0.00
Total cost	30.00	24.00

Notes: This exhibit shows the costs of reallocating 0.5% from international developed equities to fixed income in the cash and futures markets. The analysis assumes a 3-month (one quarter) investment horizon because the expectation is that the change in portfolio allocation is for a relatively short time period. Given the length of the investment horizon, no rolling of futures occurs. All numbers are in basis points (bps) unless otherwise indicated.

IN-TEXT QUESTIONS:

1. Using Exhibit 16, analyze the relative costs of the cash market and derivatives approaches to rebalancing.
2. Explain how considerations of implementation speed and time horizon of the rebalancing trade could affect the implementation choice.

Guideline Answers:

1. Looking at the data in Exhibit 16, Thompson can see that the two options appear similar from a cost perspective. The main cost driver associated with rebalancing through the cash market is cash drag (approximately 20 bps) caused by timing delays and disruptions to active manager portfolios. Rebalancing through cash markets would involve withdrawing funds from international developed equity active managers and increasing funds to current fixed-income managers and/or adding a new fixed-income manager. These activities would generate transaction costs and cash drag because the liquidation process for the equity manager(s) and the investment process for the fixed-income manager(s) would likely not happen simultaneously.

    In the case of derivatives (short equity futures position and long fixed-income futures position), the biggest cost component is mispricing or tracking error. Creating a short exposure position for the MSCI EAFE Index (the benchmark for international ex USA and Canada developed-market equities) and a long fixed-income futures position would involve a higher tracking error (17 bps) compared to the tracking error of using one S&P 500 futures contract discussed previously (8 bps). In this case, using multiple futures instruments increases associated tracking error.

2. An additional factor is speed of implementation. In general, depending on the availability of derivatives for the asset classes involved, rebalancing using derivatives is likely to result in a shorter implementation time frame while leaving the

> active managers in place. Given high levels of liquidity in the equity futures that would be used for MSCI EAFE Index replication, implementing with derivatives could occur quickly.
>
> Another important aspect is rebalancing size and expected time horizon of the trade. The larger the rebalancing, the more likely the rebalance would represent a more permanent re-alignment, as opposed to a temporary adjustment that could be reversed the next quarter.
>
> Based on the expected costs and considerations and the relatively small size of the adjustment, using derivatives to rebalance the portfolio appears to be the best option. Implementing with derivatives gives the team the flexibility to tactically adjust exposure to international developed equities if desired and the ability to quickly reverse decisions in full or in part while leaving the current external managers in place.

After further discussion with her team, Thompson decides to instead rebalance the international developed equity allocation back to the target allocation by reallocating 2.5% from the international developed equity allocation into fixed income. The team's current analysis is shown in Exhibit 17.

Exhibit 17   Cost Information on Rebalancing Options

Cost Component	Cash Market	Futures (Equity/Fixed Income)
Bid/offer spread	5.00	4.00
Price impact (total trades)	5.00	4.00
Mispricing (tracking error, annual)	0.00	68.00
Cash drag (impact of timing delays and disruptions to active manager portfolios)	50.00	0.00
Cost of rolling the futures contract	0.00	6.00
Total cost	**60.00**	**82.00**

Notes: This exhibit shows the costs of reallocating 2.5% from international developed equities to fixed income in the cash and futures markets. The analysis assumes a one-year investment horizon because the expectation is that the change in portfolio allocation is more permanent. Under normal market conditions, it would not be expected for these asset classes to move outside of the corridor again over that investment horizon. All numbers are in basis points (bps) unless otherwise indicated.

IN-TEXT QUESTION:

What implementation option should Thompson use in this case?

Guideline Answer:

Based on relative expected costs, Thompson would likely decide to rebalance the portfolio in the cash markets by reallocating between international developed equity and fixed-income investment managers.

Exhibit 17 shows that the cost of rebalancing back to target allocation using derivatives is higher than implementing through the cash markets. Specifically, the implementation cost with derivatives is 82 bps, while the implementation cost for the cash markets is 60 bps. The higher derivatives cost is primarily caused by expected tracking error of the replication using derivatives, which is 68 bps on an annual basis. In general, the cost of rebalancing through futures is expected to increase with investment time horizon as mispricing or tracking risk increases. In this case, the impact of the cost of rolling the

> futures is not viewed as material given that the roll of the short equity futures position would likely offset most of the cost of holding the long fixed-income futures position. With respect to the cash market implementation, given the size of the rebalancing trade (2.5% of the overall portfolio), potential cash drag is expected to increase to 50 bps as compared to the previous scenario.
>
> Other considerations besides expected cost may be relevant. A faster desired speed of implementation would favor implementation using derivatives, while the size of the planned rebalancing implies a longer time horizon for the trade and favors implementation through the cash market. Based on the facts given, Thompson would likely decide to rebalance the portfolio in the cash markets.

QUINCO CASE: ESG INTEGRATION

Nine months have passed, and the QUINCO team is facing a new challenge. Earlier in the week, the university president had informed Winter of an upcoming student protest planned against the university and the endowment.

Student Activity

The students in the QU Student Association have seen a recent report published by the International Labour Organization (ILO) highlighting social issues in the supply chain of a US-based apparel company named Portro Inc. The report detailed a number of emerging social issues, including terrible labor conditions and allegations of child labor, as well as health and safety issues at two of Portro's largest suppliers. One of the suppliers named is also a supplier for the QU-branded apparel sold at the university stores. The students are further outraged after discovering from various public sources, including QUINCO's annual report, that the endowment is a significant shareholder in Portro Inc.

The students are expected to demand the following actions: The university must drop the supplier, and the endowment must divest its Portro Inc. holdings.

QUINCO ESG Approach

QUINCO has had an ESG responsible investing policy in place for the last seven years. The policy is based on the following considerations and objectives:

a Acknowledgment that ESG factors along with traditional financial factors affect the risk and return of investments;

b Promotion of greater transparency on material ESG issues that impact QUINCO's investment activities;

c Pursuit of long-term sustainability for companies and markets in which the endowment invests.

Rather than a strategy of exclusion that prohibits a priori investments in certain countries, sectors, or companies, QUINCO's approach focuses on ESG integration. ESG integration is defined as "the explicit and systematic inclusion of ESG factors in investment analysis and investment decisions." [8] Using this approach, the investment committee expects all material factors (ESG and traditional financial factors) will be considered in the investment process. Since the endowment's investment strategy is

---

[8] CFA Institute and Principles for Responsible Investment (PRI) (2018, p. 9).

to use external asset managers, the policy relies on external managers to integrate ESG factors into their investment processes through research, materiality analysis, and active ownership assessment.

At its initiation, however, QUINCO's policy did not specify the tools and analyses required for the endowment to assess ESG manager implementation. Because of this, Winter and his team had struggled in recent years to adequately respond to issues similar to the Portro Inc. case.

To address these considerations, Winter had recently hired an ESG integration specialist, Natalya Long, CFA. Since joining QUINCO, Long has been instrumental in updating the responsible investment policy to include the following:

- Enhanced due diligence in manager selection and monitoring with an ESG element. Specifically, to document:
  - whether the manager has a formal ESG integration policy,
  - how the manager incorporates ESG factors into the investment process,
  - what the manager's commitment to timely reporting and disclosure of material ESG issues is, and
  - how consistent the manager's ESG integration approach is with QUINCO's ESG responsible investing policy.

- Specific recognition of responsible ownership, reporting, and communication as key components of the ESG responsible investing policy. In addition to ESG integration, the responsible ownership component is implemented through proxy voting activities and corporate engagement on ESG issues, such as reporting and disclosure, climate change, and human capital.

- Monitoring of available ESG metrics for the QUINCO portfolio. These include aggregating available data on the carbon footprint and carbon intensity of endowment portfolio companies; developing an analytical framework to assess portfolio sensitivities to a wide range of climate-related risks; and sourcing and comparing ESG ratings or scores for portfolio companies from industry providers with peer companies and the policy benchmark. Trends in metrics for a portfolio company or the portfolio are monitored over time for changes.

- Public demonstration and signaling of commitment to responsible investing by being a signatory to the internationally recognized UN Principles for Responsible Investment (PRI).

The enhancements that Long made to the ESG policy provide the framework for QUINCO and thus Winter's response to the Portro Inc. situation.

QUINCO

While Winter had known about the ILO report on Portro Inc., he was not aware of the relationship between the supplier and the university stores. He does know the endowment has two sources of potential exposure. Portro Inc. is a constituent in the benchmark index for the US public equity allocation. As a result, most of QUINCO's equity managers in the US portfolio likely have some exposure to the company. Additionally, one of QUINCO's US equity managers runs a concentrated portfolio strategy and holds Portro Inc. as a core holding, with a significant overweight in the company.

The university president recognizes that in regard to QUINCO investment activity, the students' issues cannot be addressed on a stand-alone basis but must be considered within the context of the endowment's responsible investing strategy. He asks Winter to prepare a formal response to the students' grievances consistent with the endowment's ESG responsible investing policies.

Investment Response

The ESG metrics monitoring system had alerted Winter's team to Portro Inc.'s poor ESG ratings versus its peers, specifically with respect to social factors; the issues with Portro's suppliers had been identified for some time. Consequently, as part of the team's systematic manager engagement strategy, these issues had been raised at the last quarterly review meeting, which had occurred several weeks before the ILO report was published. At that meeting, the QUINCO US public equity portfolio manager raised the Portro supplier issues to the external manager during the discussion on the overweight position in Portro Inc. The QUINCO team sought to understand whether the external manager could identify the risks arising from the supply chain and then report them and how they would be managed to clients in a timely and transparent manner. The discussions at that time had confirmed that while the external manager did not have a formal ESG integration policy in place, she did have a robust framework for considering ESG factors in the investment analysis. While she was concerned about a short-term negative impact to Portro's valuation, she remained confident in the long-term potential of the company, even after accounting for the expected costs of fixing its supply chain problems. She had no plans to reduce position size. She did mention she would be monitoring Portro's management response to the issues in the coming months to determine whether to trim or sell out of the position. After that meeting, the QUINCO team concluded the external manager had followed an adequate due diligence process that considered material ESG factors alongside traditional financial factors as required by QUINCO's ESG integration framework. However, the QUINCO team felt further manager and corporate engagement was still necessary to address the situation.

Consistent with its responsible ownership strategy, the QUINCO team then prepares to engage with Portro on the specific issues highlighted in the ILO report. This engagement includes joining other like-minded institutional investors in a dialogue with Portro's management (through the convening power of PRI) and/or using proxy voting to support shareholder resolutions aimed at increasing the company's corporate disclosure and reporting transparency regarding human capital management in the supply chain.

At the request of the university president, Winter prepares a formal response to share with the QU Student Association. He summarizes QUINCO's responsible investing policy and its application to the endowment's Portro Inc. holdings. Winter highlights the endowment's long-term commitment to promote the sustainability of the companies and markets in which the endowment invests and to integrate relevant ESG factors into the endowment's investment process. Winter's response also articulates that under the endowment's responsible investing strategy, divestment of the investment is considered a suboptimal risk mitigation strategy to be taken as a last resort. Winter highlights the plan to use the responsible ownership tools, such as proxy voting and manager and corporate engagement, to maintain awareness of Portro's company management on the specific issues at hand and to focus discussion on possible mitigating actions. Once he completes his report, Winter turns his attention to the issue of the supplier's apparel being sold in the university stores. He asks the head of the University Administration Office to immediately remove the merchandise in question from the university stores. He plans to revisit this decision once further progress has occurred with corporate engagement efforts, and then he heads home for the day.

SUMMARY

The QU endowment case study covers important aspects of institutional portfolio management involving the illiquidity premium capture, liquidity management, asset allocation, and the use of derivatives versus the cash market for tactical asset allocation and portfolio rebalancing. In addition, the case examines potential ethical violations in manager selection that can arise in the course of business.

From an asset allocation perspective, the case highlights potential risk and rewards associated with increasing exposure to illiquidity risk through investments like private equity and private real estate. Although this exposure is expected to generate higher returns and more-efficient portfolios in the long-run, significant uncertainties are involved both from a modeling and implementation perspective. Finally, the case highlights social considerations that may arise with investing.

REFERENCES

CFA Institute and Principles for Responsible Investment (PRI). 2018. *Guidance and Case Studies for ESG Integration: Equities and Fixed Income.* Charlottesville, VA: CFA Institute.

Green, Katie. 2015. "The Illiquidity Conundrum: Does the Illiquidity Premium Really Exist?" Schroders (August). http://www.schroders.com/hu/sysglobalassets/digital/insights/pdfs/the-illiquidity-conundrum.pdf.

Mercer. 2015. "Setting an Appropriate Liquidity Budget: Making the Most of a Long Investment Horizon" (February). https://www.mercer.com/content/dam/mercer/attachments/global/investments/setting-an-appropriate-liquidity-budget-mercer-february-2015-a4.pdf.

Pastor, Lubos, and Robert F. Stambaugh. 2001. "Liquidity Risk and Expected Stock Returns." NBER Working Paper w8462. https://ssrn.com/abstract=282688. doi:

Investments, Russell. 2013. *"Liquidity Management: A Critical Aspect of a Successful Investment Program for Non-Profit Organizations"* (October). https://russellinvestments.com/-/media/files/nz/insights/1310-liquidity-management.pdf.

Ang, Andrew, Dimitris Papanikolaou, and Mark M. Westerfield. 2014. "Portfolio Choice with Illiquid Assets." *Management Science* 60 (11). doi: https://pubsonline.informs.org/doi/abs/10.1287/mnsc.2014.1986

Chaffe, David B.H. III 1993. "Option Pricing as a Proxy for Discount for Lack of Marketability in Private Company Valuations." *Business Valuation Review* 12 (4): 182–88. doi:

Raymond, Donald M. 2009. "Integrating Goals, Structure, and Decision-Making at Canada Pension Plan Investment Board." *Rotman International Journal of Pension Management* 2 (1).

Staub, Renato, and Jeffrey Diermeier. 2003. "Segmentation, Illiquidity and Returns." *Journal of Investment Management* 1 (1).

PRACTICE PROBLEMS

The following information relates to Questions 1–2

Joe Bookman is a portfolio manager at State Tech University Foundation and is discussing the $900 million university endowment with the investment committee. Exhibit 1 presents selected data on the current university endowment.

Exhibit 1: Selected Data for State Tech University Endowment

Asset Class	Investment Allocation (% of portfolio)	Liquid	Semi-Liquid	Illiquid	Rebalancing Band Policy	Standard Deviation of Returns (annual)
Cash	1%	100%	0%	0%	0% – 15%	1.5%
Fixed Income	24%	100%	0%	0%	20% – 30%	5.9%
Public Equity	39%	50%	50%	0%	30% – 40%	15.4%
Private Equity	21%	0%	0%	100%	20% – 25%	27.2%
Real Assets	15%	0%	50%	50%	10% – 20%	11.7%

The university investment committee is performing its quarterly assessment and requests that Bookman review the rebalancing band policy.

1. **Identify** which asset class(es) Bookman is *most likely* to note as in need of rebalancing band policy adjustment. **Justify** your selection(s).

Identify which asset class(es) Bookman is *most likely* to note as in need of rebalancing band policy adjustment. [Circle choice(s)]	**Justify** your selection(s).
Cash	
Fixed Income	
Public Equity	
Private Equity	
Real Assets	

The investment committee also asks Bookman to investigate whether the endowment should increase its allocation to illiquid investments to take advantage of higher potential returns. The endowment's liquidity profile policy stipulates that at least 30%

of investments must be classified as liquid to support operating expenses; no more than 40% should be classified as illiquid. Bookman decides to perform a bottom-up liquidity analysis to respond to the committee.

2 **Discuss** the elements of Bookman's analysis and the conclusions he will draw from it.

The following information relates to Question 3

Laura Powers is a senior investment analyst at Brotley University Foundation and works for the university endowment. Powers is preparing a recommendation to allocate more funds into illiquid investments for a higher potential return and is discussing the rationale with junior analyst Jasper Heard. Heard makes the following statements to Powers:

Statement 1 The endowment should shift funds into private equity and real estate. Specifically, within these asset classes the endowment should target shorter-term investments. These tend to be the most illiquid and offer the highest liquidity premium.

Statement 2 The endowment should consider low liquidity public equity investments because they are shown to be close substitutes for private equity and real estate investments in terms of liquidity premium.

3 **Determine if** Heard's statements are correct. **Justify** your response.

Determine if Heard's statements are correct.	
Statement 1 (Circle one)	Statement 2 (Circle one)
Correct Incorrect	Correct Incorrect
Justify your response.	**Justify** your response.

The following information relates to Questions 4–5

Rob Smith, as portfolio manager at Pell Tech University Foundation, is responsible for the university's $3.5 billion endowment. The endowment supports the majority of funding for the university's operating budget and financial aid programs. It is invested in fixed income, public equities, private equities, and real assets.

The Pell Tech Board is conducting its quarterly strategic asset allocation review. The board members note that while performance has been satisfactory, they have two concerns:

1 Endowment returns have underperformed in comparison to university endowments of similar size.

2 Return expectations have shifted lower for fixed-income and public equity investments.

Practice Problems

Smith attributes this underperformance to a lower risk profile relative to its peers due to a lower allocation to illiquid private equity investments. In response to the board's concerns, Smith proposes an increase in the allocation to the private equity asset class. His proposal uses option price theory for valuation purposes and is supported by Monte Carlo simulations.

Exhibit 1 presents selected data on the current university endowment.

Exhibit 1: Selected Data for Pell Tech University Endowment

Portfolio Characteristic	Current Allocation	Proposed Allocation
Expected return (next 10 years)	7.8%	8.3%
Standard deviation of returns (annual)	13.2%	13.9%
Sharpe ratio	0.44	0.45
Probability of 30% erosion in purchasing power over 10 years	25%	20%

4. **Discuss** Smith's method for estimating the increase in return expectations derived from increasing the endowment allocation to private equity.

5. **Discuss** *two* reasons why the increased risk profile is appropriate. **Justify** your response.

The following information relates to Questions 6–7

Frank Grides is a portfolio manager for Kemney University Foundation and manages the liquidity profile of the university endowment. This endowment supports some of the funding for the university's operations. It applies the following spending policy designed to produce a 5% long-term spending rate while shielding annual distributions from fluctuations in its market value:

Spending for current fiscal year = (60% × Spending for previous fiscal year) + [40% × (5% × Endowment market value at the end of previous fiscal year)].

Grides is considering allocating more funds to illiquid investments to capture higher potential returns and is discussing this strategy with senior analyst Don Brodka. Brodka has three related concerns given that the higher allocation to illiquid investments may

- reduce the liquidity profile of the endowment,
- induce "drift" in the portfolio's risk profile in times of market stress, or
- alter the endowment's overall risk profile.

Assessing his concerns, Brodka performs a stress test on the portfolio with both current and proposed investments.

Exhibit 1 presents selected data on the university endowment.

Exhibit 1 Selected Data for Kemney University Endowment

Liquidity Category	Current Portfolio: Normal	Current Portfolio: Stress	Proposed Portfolio: Normal	Proposed Portfolio: Stress
Liquid	42%	38%	37%	33%
Semi-liquid	31%	28%	31%	28%
Illiquid	27%	34%	32%	39%

6 **Discuss** the relevance of the endowment's spending policy to Brodka's expressed concerns.

7 **Discuss** actions that Grides should take to alleviate Brodka's concerns.

The following information relates to Question 8

Mason Dixon, CFA, a portfolio manager with Langhorne Advisors (Langhorne), has just completed the request for proposal (RFP) for the Academe Foundation's (the Foundation) $20 million fixed-income mandate. In the performance section of the RFP, Dixon indicated that Langhorne Advisors is a member firm of CFA Institute and has prepared and presented this performance report in compliance with the Global Investment Performance Standards (the GIPS® standards). The performance report presented Langhorne's fixed-income composite returns on the actual net-of fees basis and benchmark returns net of Langhorne's highest scheduled fee (1.00% on the first $5 million; 0.60% thereafter). The report also indicated that as of the most recent quarter, the composite comprised 10 portfolios totaling $600 million of assets under management (AUM).

Upon returning the completed RFP, Dixon thanked the Foundation's chief investment officer, who is also a charterholder, for considering Langhorne. Dixon also indicated that regardless of the outcome of the manager search, he would like to have the CIO and the Foundation's president join him on Langhorne's corporate jet to spend a day at an exclusive California golf club where the firm maintains a corporate membership.

8 **Identify** the ethical concerns posed by Dixon's actions and conduct.

The following information relates to Question 9

In its quarterly policy and performance review, the investment team for the Peralandra University endowment identified a tactical allocation opportunity in international developed equities. The team also decided to implement a passive 1% overweight ($5 million notional value) position in the asset class. Implementation will occur by either using an MISC EAFE Index ETF in the cash market or the equivalent futures contract in the derivatives market.

Practice Problems

The team determined that the unlevered cost of implementation is 27 basis points in the cash market (ETF) and 32 bps in the derivatives market (futures). This modest cost differential prompted a comparison of costs on a levered basis to preserve liquidity for upcoming capital commitments in the fund's alternative investment asset classes. For the related analysis, the team's assumptions are as follows:

- Investment policy compliant at 3 times leverage
- Investment horizon of one year
- 3-month Libor of 1.8%
- ETF borrowing cost of 3-month Libor plus 35 bps

9. **Recommend** the most cost-effective strategy. **Justify** your response with calculations of the total levered cost of each implementation option.

The following information relates to Question 10

Clive Staples is a consultant with the Leedsford Organization (Leedsford), a boutique investment consulting firm serving large endowments and private foundations. Leedsford consults on tactical asset allocation (TAA) program development, implementation, and ongoing TAA idea generation.

Staples has just completed his quarterly client review of the Narnea Foundation. Based on the Foundation's current asset allocation and Leedsford's updated fair value models, Staples believes there is an exploitable TAA opportunity in US large-cap growth stocks. He recommends a 2% overweight position to the US equities policy allocation either through an unlevered ETF or total return swap exposures to the Russell 1000 Growth Index.

10. **Compare** the efficiency of the ETF and total return swap TAA implementation alternatives from the perspectives of capital commitment, liquidity, and tracking error.

Compare the efficiency of the ETF and total return swap TAA implementation alternatives from the perspectives of capital commitment, liquidity, and tracking error.

Capital Commitment:

Liquidity:

Tracking Error:

The following information relates to Question 11

The Lemont Family Foundation follows a systematic quarterly rebalancing policy based on rebalancing corridors for each asset class. In the latest quarter, a significant sell-off in US public equities resulted in an unusually large 1.2% underweight position relative to the applicable lower corridor boundary. This is the only policy exception requiring rebalancing attention.

The Foundation's investment team views the sell-off as temporary and remains pleased with the performance of all external managers, including that of its US public equities manager. However, the sell-off has increased the significance of liquidity and flexibility for the team. As a result, the team now considers whether to rebalance through the cash market or the derivatives market.

11 **Determine** the *most appropriate* rebalancing choice for the Foundation's investment team. **Justify** your response.

Determine the *most appropriate* rebalancing choice for the Foundation's investment team. (Circle one)	
Cash Market	Derivatives Market
Justify your response.	

SOLUTIONS

1

Identify which asset classes Bookman is *most likely* to note as in need of rebalancing band policy adjustment. [Circle choice(s)]	**Justify** your selection(s).
Cash	As part of effective portfolio management, rebalancing disciplines, such as calendar rebalancing and percent-range rebalancing, are intended to control risk relative to the strategic asset allocation. In these cases, pre-specified Tolerance bands for asset class weights are used. The size or width of the bands should consider the underlying volatility of each investment category to minimize transaction costs. This means more-volatile investment categories usually have wider rebalancing bands.
Fixed Income	
Public Equity	
Private Equity	
Real Assets	Cash Rebalancing: In reply to the university investment committee as it performs its quarterly assessment, Bookman notes that the cash asset classes have the lowest standard deviation with one of the widest rebalancing band policies. The cash rebalancing band should be evaluated and suitably reduced. Private Equity Rebalancing: The private equity asset class also has the highest standard deviation with one of the tightest rebalancing band policies. The private equity rebalancing band should be evaluated and suitably expanded.

2 To operationalize the concepts represented in the liquidity budget, it is appropriate to analyze the underlying liquidity characteristics of the portfolio investments and monitor these characteristics over time. The analysis should look beyond the broad definition of asset classes to the underlying investments used for exposure as different investments within the same asset class may have very different liquidity profiles.

In performing a bottom-up liquidity analysis on the State Tech endowment, Bookman multiplies each asset class allocation by its matching liquidity classification and then aggregates across asset classes. Based on this analysis, 44.5% of investments are currently classified as liquid and 28.5% are classified as illiquid, calculated as follows:

Investments classified as liquid = (Cash allocation × %Liquid) + (Fixed-income allocation × %Liquid) + (Public equity allocation × %Liquid)

Investments classified as liquid = (1% × 100%) + (24% × 100%) + (39% × 50%) = 44.5%.

Investments classified as illiquid = (Private equity allocation × %Illiquid) + (Real asset allocation × % Illiquid)

Investments classified as illiquid = (21% × 100%) + (15% × 50%) = 28.5%.

The liquid investment allocation of 44.5% is well above the 30% liquid requirement, and the 28.5% illiquid investment allocation is well below the 40% illiquid limit. As a result, there is enough capacity to re-allocate more funds from liquid investments into illiquid investments to take advantage of the higher potential returns. Thus, Bookman can recommend that shift.

3

Determine if Heard's statements are correct.

Statement 1 (Circle one)		Statement 2 (Circle one)	
Correct	**Incorrect**	Correct	**Incorrect**
Justify your response.		**Justify** your response.	
Statement 1 is incorrect because of a misunderstanding of the characteristics of particular investments. The endowment should shift funds into private equity and real estate as these asset classes generally offer a higher return potential due to higher liquidity premiums. However, within these asset classes the endowment should target longer-term investments, not shorter term. Longer-term investments tend to be the most illiquid and offer the highest liquidity premium. Quantitative estimates for the illiquidity premium suggest evidence of a positive illiquidity premium in private equity and private real estate and of illiquidity premium size being positively correlated to the length of the illiquidity horizon.		Statement 2 is incorrect because of a misinterpretation of the effects of the illiquidity premium. Heard's statement on public equities is partially true, but it does not rely on a fully defensible basis for an investment recommendation. While a significant body of literature documents a positive relationship between lack of liquidity and expected returns in the case of public equity, overall it is difficult to isolate the illiquidity premium with precision and separate its effects from such other risk factors as the market, value, and size in the case of equity investments. Furthermore, estimates of the illiquidity premium are based on broad market indexes, yet an investor in these asset classes would typically invest in only a small subset of the universe with the result that individual investment experience could be very different and more susceptible to idiosyncratic factors. These challenges further emphasize the importance of liquidity budgeting in facilitating capture of the illiquidity premium while controlling for risk.	

4 Private equity is recognized as an illiquid alternative investment and may offer higher returns via a liquidity premium.

The illiquidity premium (also called the liquidity premium) is the expected compensation for the additional risk of tying up capital for a potentially uncertain time period. It can be estimated, as Smith has done, by using the idea that the size of a discount an investor should receive for such capital commitment is represented by the value of a put option with an exercise price equal to the hypothetical "marketable price" of the illiquid asset as estimated at the time of purchase. Smith can derive the price of the illiquid private equity asset by subtracting the put price from the "marketable price." If both the "marketable price" and the illiquid asset price are estimated or known, then the expected return for each can be calculated, with the difference in expected returns representing the illiquidity premium (in %).

5 Reasons to justify the increased risk profile include the following:
   a The board members' lower return expectations for public equity and fixed-income asset classes imply a higher level of risk must be taken to achieve the same level of returns.
   b For a long-horizon institutional investor like Pell Tech, the ability to tolerate illiquidity creates an opportunity to improve portfolio diversification and expected returns as well as access a broader set of investment strategies. In mean–variance optimization models, the inclusion of illiquid assets in the eligible investment universe may shift the efficient frontier for their portfolio upwards, theoretically resulting in greater efficiency (i.e., higher expected returns will be gained across all given levels of risk).
   c The portfolio risk profile for the endowment is currently more conservative in comparison to those of peer universities.
   d Smith's Monte Carlo simulations suggest that the proposed asset allocation has a higher probability of achieving the return target while better preserving the purchasing power of the endowment.

6 In voicing his concerns, Brodka is cautioning that a higher allocation to illiquid investments may have adverse effects on the endowment's spending rate and risk profile. Kemney University's spending policy is an example of a geometric smoothing rule, sometimes called the Yale formula. It is intended to bring about a predictable pattern of distributions for better planning of resource deployment through its programs across varying conditions, even as extreme as the 2008 global financial crisis.

While this spending policy would be consistent with an investment objective of achieving long-term returns that support the spending rate while preserving the value of the endowment in real terms over time, the policy design also incorporates a smoothing, countercyclical element. This leads to lower spending rates in a period of sustained strong investment returns but higher spending rates in a protracted weak return environment.

7 As a result of the allocation changes, there will be a reduction in the liquid and semi-liquid categories and an increase in the illiquid category under both normal and stress conditions. The proposed allocation shifting 5% of the endowment's investments from liquid to illiquid assets would result in an increase in the overall illiquidity profile.

Regarding Brodka's concern about the liquidity profile, Grides needs to ensure that even under stress conditions the proposed allocation continues to comply with the liquidity budgeting framework in place. From an ongoing management perspective—and particularly at times when the liquidity profile of the proposed allocation is closer to the minimum thresholds set through the liquidity budget—Grides should plan to closely monitor the portfolio's liquidity profile and stress test it periodically to make sure portfolio liquidity remains adequate.

Regarding Brodka's concern of risk profile "drift," illiquid assets carry extremely high rebalancing costs. Because asset liquidity tends to decrease in periods of market stress, it is important to have sufficient liquid assets and rebalancing mechanisms in place to ensure the portfolio's risk profile remains within acceptable risk targets and does not "drift" as the relative valuations of different asset classes fluctuate during stress periods. Since liquid assets will decrease due to the proposed allocation, Grides must ensure an effective rebalancing mechanism is adopted prior to the investment and is consistently followed thereafter. That mechanism can either be through a systematic discipline, such as calendar rebalancing or percent-range rebalancing that set pre-specified tolerance bands for asset weights. Or, an automatic rebalancing method can be adopted, such as by using adjustments to a public market allocation that is correlated to a private market allocation (likely a more illiquid exposure) to rebalance private market risk.

Contrary to its desired intent, and providing grounds for Brodka's concerns, this design would exacerbate the endowment's liquidity needs in severe market downturns. Given the possibility of such adverse events within Kemney's long-term planning horizon, the policy is very relevant as potentially introducing undesired risks.

8 Dixon's actions and conduct pose multiple ethical concerns.

Dixon's claim of compliance statement and cover letter, along with Langhorne's performance report, violate both the CFA Institute Code of Ethics and Standards of Professional Conduct (Code and Standards) and the GIPS standards. Regarding the Code and Standards, Dixon's statement improperly asserts that CFA Institute has designated Langhorne as a 'member firm.' Membership is held by practitioners as individuals, with no related rights extended to the firms at which they work. With this assertion, Dixon has misrepresented Langhorne's claim of compliance, Standard I(C): Professionalism, Misrepresentation; engaged in conduct that compromised the reputation or integrity of CFA Institute, Standard VII(A): Responsibilities as a CFA Institute Member or CFA Institute Candidate, Conduct as Participants in CFA Institute Programs; and misrepresented or exaggerated the meaning or implications of membership in CFA Institute, Standard VII(B): Responsibilities as a CFA Institute Member or CFA Institute Candidate, Reference to CFA Institute, the CFA Designation, and the CFA Program.

Regarding the GIPS standards and the performance report, presenting composite returns on a net-of-fees basis is acceptable under the GIPS standards. However, it is not appropriate to adjust benchmark returns with a hypothetical fee for comparative purposes (i.e., composite gross-of-fees returns should be compared to unadjusted benchmark returns). This adjustment of Langhorne's performance report is invalid under the GIPS standards under Section 4.a.1: Disclosure—Requirements. The 1.00% hypothetical fee deducted from benchmark returns is surely greater than the average fee deducted in arriving at composite net-of-fees returns. An average portfolio size of $60 million implies a composite fee percentage of roughly 0.63%, or: {(0.0100 × $5 million) + [0.0060 × ($60 million − $5 million)]}/$60 million = 0.0063 or 0.63%. So, on a relative basis, deducting a larger cost against the benchmark will show Langhorne with a phantom outperformance.

In terms of the Code and Standards, at a minimum, Dixon has presented an inaccurate performance comparison—Standard III(D): Duties to Clients, Performance Presentation—and may have engaged in misrepresentation to the point of misconduct—Standard I(D): Professionalism, Misconduct—since it may be deceitful to cast a more favorable light on the Langhorne composite net-of-fees returns (Section 0.A.7 under Fundamentals of Compliance—Requirements of the GIPS standards).

Dixon's cover letter invitation for an all-expenses paid outing to an exclusive golf destination can be construed as an attempt to influence the independence and objectivity of the Foundation's CIO and president—Standard I(B): Professionalism, Independence and Objectivity. While Dixon's invitation was extended 'regardless of the outcome of the manager search,' the offer could be interpreted as a *quid pro quo*, with future attractive personal benefits available to the Foundation's executives if a continuing relationship was established by their hiring of Langhorne as a manager.

Solutions

9   As the lower cost alternative, the endowment's investment team should implement the 1% overweight position using futures.

The additional cost of obtaining leverage for each option is as follows:

ETF: ($5 million × 0.6667 × 2.15%) / $5 million = 1.43% (or 143 bps) and

Futures: ($5 million × 0.6667 × 1.80%) / $5 million = 1.20% (or 120 bps),

where the inputs are derived as follows:

0.6667 reflects the 3 times leverage factor (66.67% borrowed and 33.33% cash usage),

2.15% reflects the ETF borrowing rate (3-month Libor of 1.80% + 35 bps), and

1.80% reflects the absence of investment income offset (at 3-month Libor) versus the unlevered cost of futures implementation.

The total levered cost of each option is the sum of the unlevered cost plus the additional cost of obtaining leverage:

ETF: 27 bps + 143 bps = 170 bps and

Futures: 32 bps + 120 bps = 152 bps.

This 18 bps cost advantage would make futures the appropriate choice for the endowment's investment team.

10

Compare the efficiency of the ETF and total return swap TAA implementation alternatives from the perspectives of capital commitment, liquidity, and tracking error.

Capital Commitment:
From a cash 'usage' perspective, a Russell 1000 Growth ETF would be less efficient (requiring a larger cash outlay) than a total return swap replicating the Russell 1000 Growth Index. The capital commitment of an unlevered ETF equals the full notional value. In contrast, a total return swap generates a similar economic exposure to ETFs with much lower capital. The cash-efficient nature of derivatives, such as total return swaps, makes them desirable tools for gaining incremental exposure to a particular asset class.

Liquidity:
From a liquidity perspective, a Russell 1000 Growth ETF would be more efficient than the total return swap. As exchange-traded standardized products, ETFs enjoy liquid trading and narrow bid–ask spreads. In contrast, total return swaps are over-the-counter contracts (not exchange traded) that are negotiated and customizable on such features as maturity, leverage, and cost.

Tracking Error:
From a tracking error perspective, ETFs would be less efficient than the total return swap. A Russell 1000 Growth ETF would have associated tracking error, which may result from premiums and discounts to net asset value, cash drag, or regulatory diversification requirements. In contrast, for total return swaps, the replication is exact. The Foundation would receive the total index return without incurring any tracking error to the benchmark index because the swap counterparty is obligated to provide the index return. This would, however, expose the Foundation to counterparty credit risk and introduce additional complexities in managing net exposure over the duration of the contract.

11

Determine the *most appropriate* rebalancing choice for the Foundation's investment team. (Circle one)

Cash Market	Derivatives Market

Justify your response.

The Foundation's investment team should execute the rebalancing in the derivatives market rather than the cash market. The team could, for example, establish a 1.2% long position to the S&P 500 Index using short-term S&P 500 futures to rebalance the US public equities asset class back to its policy allocation corridor.

Execution in the derivatives market offers the following advantages:
- Quick implementation
- Flexibility to tactically adjust exposure and quickly reverse decisions
- Ability to leave external managers in place
- High levels of liquidity

The team views the sell-off as temporary and is pleased with external manager performance. This suggests a short-term rebalancing approach is warranted rather than reallocating amongst managers. Execution in the derivatives market will enable quick rebalancing while leaving current allocations in place.

The sell-off has increased the significance of liquidity and flexibility. The derivatives market offers flexibility to quickly adjust market exposures with high levels of liquidity.

While derivatives can present tracking error and operational risks, the expected short-term nature of the rebalancing serves to contain their effects. The benefits to be gained using derivatives appear to more than outweigh the associated cost and risk.

… READING 29

Case Study in Risk Management: Private Wealth

by Giuseppe Ballocchi, PhD, CFA

Giuseppe Ballocchi, PhD, CFA, is at Alpha Governance Partners (Switzerland).

LEARNING OUTCOMES	
Mastery	The candidate should be able to:
☐	a. identify and analyze a family's risk exposures during the early career stage;
☐	b. recommend and justify methods to manage a family's risk exposures during the early career stage;
☐	c. identify and analyze a family's risk exposures during the career development stage;
☐	d. recommend and justify methods to manage a family's risk exposures during the career development stage;
☐	e. identify and analyze a family's risk exposures during the peak accumulation stage;
☐	f. recommend and justify methods to manage a family's risk exposures during the peak accumulation stage;
☐	g. identify and analyze a family's risk exposures during the early retirement stage;
☐	h. recommend and justify a plan to manage risks to an individual's retirement lifestyle goals.

1. INTRODUCTION AND CASE BACKGROUND

Giving advice on risk management to individuals and families raises a number of challenges. These challenges include the extent to which identified and evaluated risks can be reduced and/or addressed using insurance policies or self-insurance. Families' financial circumstances and risks evolve over time, and financial advisers should review and update the solutions addressing these risks accordingly. Risk management solutions recommended by advisers should consider the family's overall health, wealth, and long-term goals.

© 2019 CFA Institute. All rights reserved.

This case study explores some of the risk management issues for a married couple living in a hypothetical country in the Eurozone. The case spans several decades and follows the couple through different stages of life from their early career phase, when they are in their late twenties, all the way to retirement. We will show how risk management methods need to change as the family's circumstances evolve. Particularly important prior readings related to this case are the Level III readings "Risk Management for Individuals" and "Overview of Private Wealth Management."

The assumptions used are drawn from what is typical for many countries in Europe. The circumstances and risks that this married couple face are influenced by the environment in which they find themselves. Despite the differences between Europe and other parts of the world, however, their goals, the risks they face, and the assessment of their circumstances, as well as the suggested methods, are by no means unique to the region. The risk analysis methodology and its application would therefore be valid in a much broader context.

For simplicity, we assume that economic conditions and tax rates remain unchanged throughout the four decades that this case study spans. The terms "adviser" and "wealth manager" are used interchangeably throughout this case study. The amounts that appear in exhibits throughout the case study are rounded.

The case is divided into six major sections. Section 1.1 provides background information about the hypothetical country in which the Schmitt family resides. Sections 1–4 provide initial case facts relating to the family's early career stage and risk management analysis, as well as solutions relevant to that stage. In Sections 5 and 6, we revisit the couple in their career development stage when they are 45 years old. In Sections 7–10, we examine their lives at age 55, in peak accumulation phase, and age 64, when they are preparing to retire. The final section provides a summary of the case.

1.1 Background of Eurolandia

This section provides background information about the social security system, healthcare, education and tax rates in the hypothetical country of Eurolandia. The case study assumes that the local social security system and regulatory conditions remain unchanged throughout the period under consideration. Economic conditions are assumed to be stable, with low but stable growth, inflation at 1%, and the risk-free rate (the yield-to-maturity of 30-year government bonds) at 3%. Unless stated otherwise, the amounts of the state pension and social security benefits are expected to increase by 1% annually in real terms.

1.1.1 Government Pension Plan

All Eurolandia residents who are employed are enrolled in the mandatory government pension plan. The plan is expected to provide retirement income for participants who have been enrolled for most of their working lives (35 years at a minimum in most cases) to cover at least basic living expenses upon retirement. This pay-as-you-go scheme fulfills that role at present, but its long-term viability is not necessarily guaranteed. Those who have paid the contributions for most of their working lives can expect to receive about a €13,500 annual pension from the government system. Those who have worked for the government (civil servants) enjoy a higher level of benefits and can expect to receive the higher of €20,000 per year, or 55% of their final salary. The foregoing amounts are what is currently paid to retirees. Unlike the arrangements in many other European countries, in Eurolandia the entitlement to civil servants' pension ends when the retiree dies, and surviving family members are not entitled to further payments. The foregoing amounts are expected to increase by 2% per year in nominal terms, more than offsetting the 1% inflation rate. Eurolandia's mean annual salary is €35,000.

1.1.2 Health System

Basic health insurance is compulsory for Eurolandia residents, and contributions to the scheme are normally deducted from salary along with the government pension plan contributions. The health insurance offers comprehensive coverage of the vast majority of health care expenses and is considered adequate. It requires those seeking treatment to make small co-payments for a particular service. Supplemental health insurance is available through private companies. It covers optional treatments and offers shorter waiting times as well as access to a selection of privately run facilities that provide a high degree of comfort and that are not covered by the basic health insurance. The government provides basic long-term care.

1.1.3 Unemployment Insurance

Unemployment insurance is compulsory in Eurolandia, and premiums are paid in the form of social security contributions. Unemployment benefits are capped at a low amount, however, far below what a successful professional would earn. Although the modest benefits (€800 per month) run for a limited amount of time, those in long-term unemployment still receive a form of means-tested income support and a range of means-tested benefits, such as housing benefit. Means testing involves assessment of the person's financial resources to determine the need for state benefit support. Those dependent on the social security system would qualify for up to €12,000 per adult per year.

1.1.4 Disability Insurance

As with unemployment insurance, the compulsory social security contributions provide basic disability insurance. This insurance provides benefits in the form of regular income if one is unable to work because of serious illness or disability. As with unemployment insurance, the level of benefits, however, is capped at what is considered to be a low amount of €1,500 per month (€18,000 per year), far below what a successful professional would earn. Government employees, including those working for state schools, qualify for a higher level of coverage after 10 years of service, providing benefits in the form of income replacement of €1,800 per month (€21,600 per year).

1.1.5 Education

Education for children aged six and older is provided and funded by the government. University education up to the first degree level is also funded by the government and is almost free to residents of the European Economic Area (EEA), a free trade zone that, among others, includes European Union countries. Government funding extends to master's-level degrees that are also made accessible through a public subsidy. Government-funded schools and universities enjoy very good reputations.

1.1.6 Social Security Contributions and Tax Rates

To be entitled to the aforementioned social security benefits, employees pay 9% social security contributions on the portion of gross salaries that exceed €15,000 per year. The contributions are deductible from taxable income at source and are capped to a maximum of €10,000 per family per year. The marginal income tax rates for individuals are listed in Exhibit 1. Unemployment and disability benefits are not subject to income tax.

Exhibit 1	Marginal Tax Rates
Yearly Taxable Income (€)	Marginal Tax Rate
0 to 15,000	0%
15,000 to 50,000	30%
Above 50,000	40%

Note: The €15,000 and €50,000 thresholds and the €10,000 cap are annually adjusted for inflation. Mortgage interest is not tax deductible.

The government encourages residents to save for retirement. There are tax incentives for voluntary contributions to government-regulated defined contribution (DC) occupational (employer-sponsored) and private pension savings plans. The government adds 25% to the amount of a member's contribution, meaning that for every €100 a member contributes to the scheme, the amount added becomes €125 thanks to €25 that comes from the government. Members of such schemes can, within certain limits, decide on the asset allocation. There is no tax on investment returns within regulated pension savings plans. Normal retirement age for both men and women is 65 and is expected to remain unchanged. Tax-free lump sum withdrawals from private pension savings plans, amounting to a maximum 25% of the fund, are allowed from age 55. Realized net capital gains on investments held outside regulated pension schemes (including rental property investments) are subject to capital gains taxes of 30% on amounts of gains exceeding €25,000 per person per year. No distinction is made between short-term and long-term holding periods, and the €25,000 level is expected to remain unchanged in the future.

1.2 The Schmitt Family in Their Early Career Stage

The following section provides initial facts as they apply to the Schmitt family. The subsequent sections then explain the risks the Schmitts face as well as the methods for addressing those risks.

1.2.1 Initial Case Facts

Paul and Jessica Schmitt, both 28 years old, recently got married. They are in their early career phase. Both graduated three years ago with master's degrees in, respectively, mathematics and computer science. Upon graduation, Paul found the teaching job to which he aspired, and he has been teaching mathematics at a local school ever since, earning a gross yearly salary of €45,600. After social security and tax deductions, his take-home pay is €33,670. Jessica, a born entrepreneur, joined an IT startup after graduating. Her gross yearly salary is now €24,000, which translates into €20,490 after taxes and social security contributions. Her salary has potential for a significant increase from the current relatively low level. She is also entitled to receive a discretionary bonus if her company becomes profitable. A bonus would potentially constitute a significant portion of her compensation. She could earn a far better fixed salary elsewhere, but she prefers the upside potential that her current position could offer, and she really believes that her company will succeed.

Paul and Jessica have combined savings of €15,000. They have no other financial assets, except for their participation in the government pension plan, to which they have been contributing since they started working three years ago. Their only other notable asset is their old car. The Schmitts have no debt, because their living expenses while they were students were covered by their parents and by government funding. Tuition costs at the state university they attended were negligible. Their monthly expenses are €2,900, including rent of €1,000. Exhibit 2 summarizes the Schmitts' circumstances.

Exhibit 2 Summary of the Schmitts' Circumstances

	Jessica	Paul	Combined
Annual gross income (€)	24,000	45,600	69,600
Annual net income (€)	20,490	33,670	54,160
Source of income	Information technology start up	Teaching job at state school	
Annual Living expenses (€)			34,800
Financial assets (€)			15,000
Debt (€)			0
Car (€)			7,000

The Schmitts would like to ensure long-term financial security for the family that they are hoping to start soon. They would also like to buy a house in an area that is very popular with young couples and has seen substantial appreciation of property values. The Schmitts would welcome competent and unbiased financial advice, but they are unsure where to get it. They mention their wish to a relative, Mr. Muller, CFA. He is a retired financial advisor and is happy to help them.

IDENTIFICATION AND ANALYSIS OF RISK EXPOSURES: EARLY CAREER STAGE

a identify and analyze a family's risk exposures during the early career stage

Muller follows the four key steps in the risk management process for individuals:

1. Specify the objective.
2. Identify risks.
3. Evaluate risks and select appropriate methods to manage the risks.
4. Monitor outcomes and risk exposures and make appropriate adjustments in methods.

2.1 Specify the Schmitts' financial objectives

Muller discusses the couple's financial objectives with Paul and Jessica. They describe those objectives as a house purchase in the very near future and hopefully starting a family. They wish to ensure long-term financial security and, looking ahead, a comfortable retirement. Muller acknowledges that most couples of their age usually do not pay much attention to the distant future. Although the Schmitts have almost their entire working career ahead of them, he confirms to them that it is essential to start planning for this long-term objective as early as possible. Moreover, there are likely to be tax advantages to be reaped by optimizing retirement savings, although there may be limited financial resources available to devote to that objective in the Schmitts' current stage of life—the early career stage.

Muller questions the couple about their current circumstances, including employment, and inquires further about the proposed house purchase. The Schmitts are keen to purchase a condominium they like very much at a cost of €270,000. If fully funded by a 25-year repayment mortgage at an initial interest rate of 3.6% per year fixed for 5 years, the monthly mortgage cost would come to approximately €1,360, compared with the €1,000 monthly rent that they are currently paying.

2.2 Identification of risk exposures

To better understand the young couple's financial health and to identify and analyze risks the Schmitts face, Muller lists the couple's assets, liabilities, and financial objectives and assesses the characteristics of human capital as components of the Schmitts' total wealth. He observes that they are richly endowed with human capital:

- They are highly trained in fields that are, and are expected to remain, in high demand.
- They are young, in the career development phase, with many working years ahead of them.
- They have been employed for nearly three years, accruing valuable working experience.
- As citizens of an EU country, they are geographically mobile and legally entitled to work in other countries in the region.

Muller describes Paul's human capital, if he continues in his chosen career as a teacher, as very much bond-like. He has the status of a civil servant, a term used to describe someone who works in the state sector. His income is expected to increase with seniority, but has very modest upside potential. Paul benefits from excellent job security, limiting earnings risk from unemployment. Although Paul is entitled to work in many countries, the portability of his human capital as a teacher is limited because the required qualifications to obtain a teaching position vary significantly from country to country. Moreover, the privileges and accrued seniority related to his civil servant status are not easily transferable when moving to another country.

Jessica's human capital, if she remains in the same or a similar role, is very much equity-like. She faces significant uncertainties in her future cash flows from employment, but she can also benefit from substantial rewards if she meets her job objectives and her company does well. Muller and Jessica agree that she faces significant earnings risk, much more so than her husband. This is because she works for a startup that offers no coverage for loss of income resulting from disability or premature death. Only the coverage provided by the country's social insurance system would be available. Unemployment is also much more of a concern for her because, unlike her husband, she does not enjoy the job security of a civil servant. There can also be ambiguity in what triggers her bonus payments and her participation in the company profits. If she becomes a shareholder, following the award of stock options, the resulting asset will have some of the characteristics of a business asset. Jessica's human capital, driven by her globally applicable IT skill set, is portable across countries.

Muller notes that from a financial point of view, the Schmitts' marriage results in human capital diversification, with Paul's human capital being bond-like and Jessica's human capital being equity-like, subject to far more risk and upside than that of her husband.

Identification and Analysis of Risk Exposures: Early Career Stage

Exhibits 3 and 4 show the assumptions and the economic balance sheet as summarized by Muller. He repeatedly stresses that any calculations are subject to substantial uncertainty, especially in the early career stage, but such exercise provides a good starting point for the risk analysis that needs to be performed. The asset side at this stage features the rather limited liquid financial assets, the vested state pension benefits (the mortality-weighted net present value [NPV] of the accrued benefit amount), and human capital. Human capital, reflecting the present value (PV) at a wage-risk adjusted discount rate, of the expected stream of income from employment, is calculated using the formula

$$HC_0 = \sum_{t=1}^{t=N} \frac{p(s_t)w_{t-1}(1+g_t)}{(1+r_f+y)^t} \quad (1)$$

where

HC_0 = human capital
$p(s_t)$ = the probability of surviving to a given year (or age)
w_t = the income from employment in period t
g_t = the annual wage growth rate
r_f = the nominal risk-free rate
y = the risk adjustment based on occupational income volatility
N = the length of working life in years

The human capital values, shown in Exhibit 4, are calculated using the formula in Equation 1 and are based on the assumptions in Exhibit 3.

Exhibit 3   Assumptions for the Calculation of Human Capital at Age 28

	Jessica	Paul
Starting salary (net)	€20,490	€33,666
Assumed nominal salary growth rate	6%	3%
Discount rate (nominal risk-free)	3%	3%
Risk adjustment based on occupational income volatility	3%	0%
Remaining length of working life assuming retirement at age 65	37	37

Note: The probability of surviving to a given age is based on mortality tables (not shown here) used in Eurolandia.

The liability side shows financial objectives that can be modeled as liabilities. The €1.87 million present value of lifetime consumption needs is based on an assumed initial €2,900 monthly expenditure (€34,800 per year). Because the Schmitts do not know when they are likely to have children and when they will be incurring higher expenditures, Muller assumes that their expenses will rise by 6% (5% above inflation and assuming they will have a growing family) in each of the next 10 years and increase in line with 1% inflation from then on. Assuming life expectancy of 90 years, the PV of lifetime consumption calculation would cover 62 years in total.

Exhibit 4 The Schmitts' Economic Balance Sheet at the Age of 28

Assets (€)		Liabilities (€)	
Savings account	15,000	Debt	0
Accrued entitlement to state retirement benefits (Paul)	21,000		
Accrued DB government retirement plan (Jessica)	11,800		
Paul's human capital	1,174,800	PV of lifetime consumption	1,868,000
Jessica's human capital	694,700		
Total assets	**1,917,300**	**Total liabilities**	**1,868,000**
		Net wealth	**49,300**

Note: Figures are rounded. Because we take a holistic view of assets and liabilities, we include the participation in the country's compulsory retirement program as an asset. The Schmitts' ownership of an old car is disregarded for the purposes of the economic balance sheet.

Miller notes at the outset that both Paul and Jessica are in the early career stage, and they are rich in human capital but have very limited financial assets. They face the financial challenges of starting a family, with the possible purchase of a property. Given their very modest level of financial assets and the fact that their liabilities are very limited, the risk analysis at this stage of life focuses on human capital. The estimation of its present value depends on a range of assumptions and is subject to uncertainty. But liabilities need to be met, especially if the couple has children. For this reason, a careful analysis of any gaps in the current insurance coverage must be conducted. Such analysis will lead to recommendations for risk management in order to preserve and optimize human capital, the most valuable asset that the Schmitts own, and also to meet lifestyle goals. Following systematic examination of their circumstances, Muller identifies the following risks that the Schmitts face and that he will need to evaluate:

- earnings risk resulting from loss of employment
- earnings risk resulting from health and disability
- premature death risk leading to costs imposed on the surviving partner
- car accident and repair costs
- liability risk (e.g., the risk of bodily injury or property damage caused when driving)

In addition to these risks, Muller wants to consider the effect of the proposed house purchase on the Schmitts' financial circumstances.

2.3 Analysis of identified risk

Having identified the key risks facing the Schmitts, Mr. Muller, CFA, proceeds to evaluate those risks one by one, considering any existing coverage provided by the employer or the government social security system.

2.3.1 *Earnings risk*

Earnings risk resulting from loss of employment is particularly relevant for Jessica because of the nature of her employer's business. The likelihood of loss of employment is difficult to estimate but is higher than the probability of Paul's loss of employment.

Because of her limited number of years of service, the amount of any statutory redundancy payments (required by law and related to the number of years of service) due from the employer would be limited. Because they have both been paying social security contributions, they would at least initially be entitled to €800 per month of unemployment benefit, representing just under half of Jessica's net salary and just under a third of Paul' monthly net pay.

Earnings risk resulting from health or disability is highly relevant despite the fact that both Paul and Jessica are young and in good health. If Jessica or Paul were unable to work because of illness or disability, both events more likely than premature death, the benefits from the state social security system would amount to approximately €1,500 per month, replacing most of Jessica's initial €1,708 monthly after-tax income but only just over half of Paul's monthly after-tax income of €2,806. In Jessica's case, one needs to consider that her salary is expected to show healthy growth, as reflected in her human capital estimates, and social security benefits are, over time, set to replace decreasing proportion of her income from employment. Jessica's employment package does not include any disability coverage, while Paul's enhanced coverage resulting from his government employee status would apply only after another seven years of employment.

2.3.2 Premature death risk

In the case of an unlikely scenario of premature death, the risk to the remaining spouse is at this stage of life twofold. First, one-off costs such as the funeral would have to be paid and an emergency fund would have to be established, because the surviving spouse would have no partner to help deal with emergencies. Second, his or her lifestyle would be affected by the fact that the monthly household costs that they currently cover jointly, including rent, would become the remaining spouse's sole responsibility.

2.3.3 Car accident and repair costs

The Schmitts use an old car and have a compulsory third-party insurance policy in place, protecting them in case they need to pay other parties' repair costs or compensation. Given the basic nature of the policy, they are not protected from costs that would arise should they need to have their own car repaired or replaced, exposing them to risk. During their discussions with Muller, however, Paul and Jessica explain that they do not use their car very often.

2.3.4 Liability risk

Muller considers the bulk of liability risk arising from car accidents or from injuries sustained by those who visit one's property. The existing compulsory car policy is basic but does provide liability coverage. Because the Schmitts' property liability (as well as buildings and contents) is insured as part of their rental agreement, he does not consider any other liability risks significant given the local culture.

2.3.5 House purchase

In addition to the aforementioned risks that they already face, the proposed house purchase would increase the couple's vulnerability to unexpected short-term expenditures. The Schmitts already have significant mismatch between financial assets and the sum of liabilities and financial objectives. Human capital is illiquid and represents future cash flows from earnings. The Schmitts' objective of purchasing a property requires a substantial amount of cash for the deposit (down payment), legal/notary's fees, additional transaction costs, and moving expenses. Significant sudden cash needs may arise if, for example, they need to replace their old car. To some extent, such cash needs, except for the house down payment, can be met through borrowing. The interest rates for consumer finance, however, are quite high and typically linked to a floating reference rate, thereby exposing the Schmitts to interest rate risk. Their ability to meet even small, short-term bills and cope with any unexpected expenditures would be limited if they decide to buy a property and use their limited savings to cover the transaction costs.

Muller explains that the house purchase decision itself should be weighed against continuing to rent. Paul and Jessica argue that their monthly spend on rent of €1,000 is not that different from the likely monthly mortgage payment of €1,360, so the house purchase should make little difference to their monthly budget that currently stands at €2,900. Muller points out, however, that the difference that does exist should not be disregarded and that property-related service charges and maintenance costs should be taken into consideration. At an annual 1% of property value (annual cost of €2,700 or €225 per month), the additional cost would dent the Schmitts' ability to build up any savings buffer.

3 RISK MANAGEMENT RECOMMENDATIONS: EARLY CAREER STAGE

b recommend and justify methods to manage a family's risk exposures during the early career stage

Having assessed the risks that the Schmitts face, Muller provides the following recommendations to the young couple:

3.1 Recommendations for managing risks

3.1.1 Earnings risk

Earnings risk arising from loss of employment cannot be easily insured. Muller's recommendation is for the Schmitts to build up a savings "buffer" amounting to at least six months' worth of normal expenditures (buffer of €17,400 based on €2,900 monthly spend). That way they could effectively self-insure over time to be able to cope with circumstances during which they would rely on the unemployment benefits provided by the social security system.

Earnings risk resulting from serious illness or disability, exposing the couple to a shortfall in income if they were to rely on state benefits if one was to fall seriously ill or become disabled, can be addressed by taking out disability insurance. Consequently, Muller recommends that each of them take out a disability insurance policy that would replace their current income over and above the disability benefits insurance that the state provides, to maintain their living standards. As their salaries are expected to increase, in Jessica's case substantially from a low starting level, he recommends they go for a policy that guarantees the option to purchase additional coverage without underwriting. The amount of disability income coverage required to replace earnings and supplement the state social security disability benefit is calculated in Exhibit 5. The difference between the amount of recommended coverage for each person reflects the fact that Paul's salary is notably higher than what the disability benefits from the social security system would replace. Muller recommends they buy policies that would provide benefit of €80,000 and €490,000 for Jessica and Paul, respectively. Muller states that the cost of such policy should be in line with fair value and emphasizes the need to carefully compare costs among different providers (*note: the analysis of the cost is beyond the scope of this case study*). He further adds that the policy purchase decision potentially has long term implications, hence the need for in-depth analysis.

Risk Management Recommendations: Early Career Stage

Exhibit 5 Disability Insurance Coverage Calculation

	Jessica	Paul
Annual salary income (net) to be replaced	€20,490	€33,670
Amount of annual disability coverage provided by the social security system	€18,000	€18,000
Shortfall	€2,490	€15,670
Benefit period (until retirement age)	37 years	37 years
Assumed annual benefit adjustment (nominal)	2%	2%
Discount rate	3%	3%
PV of future earnings replacement required (calculated as PV of annuity due)	€77,700	€489,000

Note: Disability insurance benefits can take the form of a lump sum or a stream of payments over time. Using calculator keystrokes for an annuity due with level payment, the growth of payments can be incorporated by adjusting the discount rate to account for the growth rate. The adjusted rate can be calculated as follows, as long as the discount rate is larger than the growth rate: (1 + Discount rate)/(1 + Growth rate) − 1, or (1.03/1.02) − 1 = 0.98%. Set the calculator for beginning-of-period payments; $n = 37$, payment = €2,490, and $i = 0.98\%$. Then calculate PV.

3.1.2 Premature death risk

Although the couple has no children or mortgage to pay at present, the financial difficulties faced by the surviving spouse in the event of one person's death should be covered using a life insurance policy. Exhibit 6 illustrates how one could establish the level of life insurance coverage required.

Exhibit 6 Calculating the Amount of Life Insurance Coverage

Muller explains that the amount of coverage that the life insurance policy should provide can be calculated using two methods. One is based on the value of human capital (the *human life value* method), which estimates the amount of future earnings that must be replaced. The other is the *needs analysis* method, based on estimating the amount needed to cover survivor's living expenses. He adds that both methods rely on a number of assumptions that may turn out to be inaccurate.

Muller suggests focusing on the needs analysis method at this stage of the Schmitts' careers. He explains that in the absence of debts to be repaid and absence of children whose upbringing would need to be funded, the calculation is relatively simple and involves estimating only two main items:

- Cash needs required upon death of the insured person, including funeral and burial costs, any taxes or debt to be repaid, and establishment of an emergency fund. They agree on a figure of €30,000.
- The surviving spouse's ability to cope with ongoing costs. They currently spend €34,800 per year, of which about half is spent jointly on rent and general expenditures that will remain broadly unchanged in the future. They estimate that the surviving spouse would require at least €25,000 annually for ongoing costs and that those costs would, under such circumstances, grow at 2% in nominal terms. The present value of such annual flow for the rest of the person's life is then compared with the present value of the survivor's earnings.

(continued)

Exhibit 6 (Continued)		
	Paul's Life Cover (from Jessica's perspective)	Jessica's Life Cover (from Paul's perspective)
Cash needs		
Funeral and burial costs plus taxes	15,000	15,000
Emergency fund	15,000	15,000
Debts to be repaid	0	0
Total cash needs	30,000	30,000
Capital needs		
PV of surviving spouse's €25,000 annual living expenses (growing at 2% until death at age 90, discounted at 3%, annuity due)	1,169,000	1,169,000
Less PV of survivor's income until retirement at 65 (annuity due, assuming 3% growth and 3% discount rate for Paul and 6% growth and 3% discount rate plus 3% risk adjustment for Jessica)	758,000	1,246,000
Total capital needs	411,000	−77,000
Total financial needs	441,000	−47,000
Capital available:		
Cash, savings, investments	15,000	15,000
PV of vested retirement accounts (attributable to surviving spouse)	11,800	21,000
Existing life insurance coverage	0	0
Total capital available	27,000	36,000
Additional life insurance needs	414,000	−83,000

Note: Rounding used throughout.

Having analyzed the needs from the surviving partner's point of view, Muller recommends that the couple purchase a life insurance policy on Paul's life. He points out that although life and disability insurance is relevant already, if the Schmitts have children, the level of coverage would need to be reviewed and potentially increased significantly. For now, Paul and Jessica decide on a policy covering Paul's life, providing benefit coverage of €400,000.

3.1.3 Car accident and repair costs

The existing car insurance coverage protects other parties but not the Schmitts. Having considered the cost of taking out more comprehensive coverage and taking into account their sparse use of the car, Muller advises the Schmitts not to spend resources on better coverage but self-insure instead with an adequate savings buffer.

3.1.4 Risks to lifestyle arising from the proposed house purchase

Muller advises the couple against the house purchase at this time. Despite recognizing numerous long-term benefits of home ownership, he argues that delaying the house purchase would lower their risk exposures. Muller also points out that a house cannot be considered fully as an investment asset but rather as a "mixed" asset, with elements of a personal asset (consumer item) as well as an investment asset. In addition, he sees risk to mortgage costs from increasing interest rates (once any fixed-rate period comes to an end). Instead of the house purchase, he suggests the Schmitts draw up a savings plan to build their savings and financial assets, because they risk being left virtually without financial assets if they were to purchase their home in the near future. The Schmitts' total yearly after-tax income of slightly more than €54,000 means that they do have the ability to save, as a simple cash budget in Exhibit 7 shows. The costs of paying the recommended insurance premiums (including the existing car insurance) that Muller estimates could roughly be in the region of €2,500 per year would easily be accommodated by the family budget.

Exhibit 7	Summary Annual Budget of the Schmitt Family at Age 28
Combined yearly gross pay	69,600
Less taxes and Social Security contributions	(15,440)
Net pay	54,160
Living costs (including rent)	(34,800)
Net cash available	19,360

Note: Rounded amounts used.

Muller suggests that a comfortable savings buffer, amounting to at least six months of living expenses (i.e., €17,400), should be set aside and be available on demand (e.g., in an easy-access bank account or equivalent). An investment plan should be drawn up once savings in excess of the buffer become available. He recommends that the Schmitts draw up a contingency plan for the critical first year after the home purchase if indeed they go ahead with their intention to buy, in case a sudden liquidity need arises. After the first year, accumulated savings should provide such liquidity buffer. The contingency plan should identify the cheapest way of borrowing, most probably against the house equity.

3.1.5 Other risks

Property insurance will be required if the Schmitts do decide to purchase a home. It is required as a condition for obtaining the mortgage, although Muller suggests that the amount of coverage equals the purchase cost of the property, not just the amount of mortgage debt. This consideration is particularly relevant as the Schmitts would be required to invest almost all of their liquid assets in their new home if the purchase goes ahead.

After a review of the basic health insurance coverage provided by mandatory social security contributions, Muller recommends not to enter into any additional private medical insurance at this time.

3.2 Monitoring outcomes and risk exposures

Muller adds that no risk management strategy is complete without regular monitoring and reviewing of outcomes and risk exposures. He explains that adjustments to the risk management solutions must be made as circumstances change.

4. RISK MANAGEMENT CONSIDERATIONS ASSOCIATED WITH HOME PURCHASE

b recommend and justify methods to manage a family's risk exposures during the early career stage

Contrary to Muller's recommendation, the Schmitts purchase their home in a sought-after area close to Jessica's workplace. The total purchase costs amount to €285,000, including all transaction costs, financed as follows:

1 Personal loan from Jessica's parents amounting to €80,000. The loan is not secured against the property. A secured loan would make obtaining a mortgage from the bank much more challenging, because the bank would not be the sole holder of a lien on the house if Jessica's parents held a secured loan.

2 Personal funds in the amount of €5,000. They reserve the rest of their assets to pay for moving expenses and furniture and to have a minimal liquidity buffer.

3 A 25-year mortgage of €200,000 at 3.6% fixed for five years, resulting in monthly payments of €1,012 consisting of both interest and capital repayment.

A condition of the mortgage is that the property is insured to at least the amount of the mortgage outstanding. The Schmitts take out property insurance with a coverage of €200,000, matching the mortgage amount, but less than what was suggested by Muller.

4.1 Review of risk Management Arrangements Following the House Purchase

Following the decision to purchase the newly built property, the Schmitts ask Muller to review and update the family's risk management arrangements. They discuss how the risks have changed and how risk management solutions should be modified.

Some risks identified earlier have changed, and new ones have appeared. Earnings risk from unemployment, disability or premature death has not changed, but the level of life coverage needs to be reevaluated because the couple now faces a liability in the form of a mortgage that would, in line with local customs, be expected to be repaid in full if Jessica or Paul died. The same would apply to the loan from Jessica's parents.

> **EXAMPLE 1**
>
> **Calculation of Life Insurance Required**
>
> Using the needs analysis method (Exhibit 6), recalculate the amount of life insurance coverage the Schmitts require.
>
> Assume that the surviving spouse continues to live in the newly purchased house, and also assume the following:
>
> - The emergency fund would need to be increased to €30,000 because of the near-zero liquid cash resources available following the house purchase.

Risk Management Considerations associated with Home Purchase

- The mortgage (€200,000) and loan from Jessica's parents (€80,000) are to be fully repaid, in line with local customs in the country.
- The survivor's annual costs fall to only €19,000 because of the fact that mortgage repayment costs drop out and are only partly offset by maintenance and service charges. Assuming such costs are to be paid for the rest the survivor's life (a further 62 years), and assuming a discount rate of 3% and an annual living cost increase of 2%, the PV of such future costs is about €888,000.
- The PV of the survivor's income from after-tax salary is €758,000 for Jessica and €1,246,000 for Paul, as per Exhibit 6.
- Capital available is now only €12,000 and €21,000, represented by the PV of vested retirement savings accounts for Jessica and Paul, respectively.

Solution:

	Paul's Life Cover (from Jessica's perspective)	Jessica's Life Cover (from Paul's perspective)
Cash needs		
Funeral and burial costs plus taxes	15,000	15,000
Mortgage retirement	200,000	200,000
Other debt (Jessica's parents' loan)	80,000	80,000
Emergency fund	30,000	30,000
Total cash needs	325,000	325,000
Capital needs		
PV of surviving spouse's living expenses (until death assumed at 90)	888,000	888,000
Less PV of survivor's income until retirement at 65 (annuity due, assuming 3% growth and 3% discount rate for Paul and 6% growth and 3% discount rate plus 3% risk adjustment for Jessica)	758,000	1,246,000
Total capital needs	130,000	–358,000
Total financial needs	455,000	–33,000
Capital available:		
Cash, savings, investments	0	0
PV of vested retirement accounts (attributable to surviving spouse)	12,000	21,000
Total capital available (excluding existing insurance coverage)	12,000	21,000
Insurance coverage required	443,000	–54,000

Given that the couple already has policy coverage of €400,000 (Paul's life), they should consider raising the amount of coverage of Paul's life.

The Schmitts' advisor explains that they also face property risk and related liability risk. Their existing coverage, arranged to satisfy the mortgage lender, covers the outstanding loan amount of €200,000. Muller recommends that they increase the homeowner's coverage to the full amount of what the property is worth, currently €280,000. The policy, if the cost is reasonable, should also cover the building contents and should provide coverage of legal liability arising from the property.

Muller also points out that the transaction has left the Schmitts with very limited resources. They should aim to build up a cash cushion in the form of instant-access savings. Because they have chosen to borrow at a fixed rate, the Schmitts do not face any near-term risk from rising interest rates.

> **EXAMPLE 2**
>
> ### Review and Reassessment of Methods
>
> Identify possible upcoming events that should require a reassessment of the family's risk management methods.
>
> ### Guideline answer:
>
> Paul and Jessica are buying their first property, and they hope to start a family. The property purchase and the resulting changes to the risk management solutions have been completed. Preparing for the birth of a child would be the point at which a reassessment of risk management methods becomes highly desirable. This is mainly because a loss of earnings of either Paul or Jessica would seriously impair the Schmitts' ability to pay for the child's upbringing.

5. IDENTIFICATION AND ANALYSIS OF RISK EXPOSURES: CAREER DEVELOPMENT STAGE

c identify and analyze a family's risk exposures during the career development stage

The Schmitts decide to approach Ms. Stein, CFA, a private wealth management practitioner and a partner in the same firm as Mr. Muller, CFA, who has since passed away. To identify and analyze the Schmitts' risk exposures Stein makes a full inquiry into their financial circumstances. She subsequently discusses their goals and proceeds to identify risks.

5.1 Case Facts: The Schmitts Are 45

In the last 17 years, the Schmitts have made significant progress in their careers and remain in good health. Their incomes and assets have increased, particularly Jessica's salary, which has risen substantially. They have been able to repay most of their mortgage and build up a portfolio of shares of 10 local IT companies whose business they believe they know. The couple is also considering making a speculative investment into residential property (similar in size to their existing property) located in the area where the IT industry is based and where Jessica works. They have repaid the loan from Jessica's parents. They continue to put money aside into an instant-access savings account, building up almost an €80,000 liquidity "buffer." Jessica's employer now offers a defined contribution (DC) company pension scheme into which Jessica and her employer make combined annual contributions of €3,000 (includes the top-up

Identification and Analysis of Risk Exposures: Career Development Stage

from government). Paul, having spent a number of years working as a teacher in the state education sector, is now entitled to life insurance coverage at three times his salary as part of his employment package. Because he has spent more than 10 years in the teaching role, he is now also entitled to a higher €2,520 monthly benefit in case of disability. This amount is the original €1,800 per month to which tenured state employees were entitled when Paul was 28, subsequently raised annually.

The Schmitts now have two children, Roxane and Peter, who are 12 and 7 years old, respectively. Peter suffers from mental development problems for which there does not appear to be a solution. He needs extra support at school. The Schmitts' living expenses have increased substantially and stand at €65,000 per year. Although Paul and Jessica increased the amount of life insurance coverage after Roxane's birth, they have not updated their insurance arrangements for many years. Exhibit 8 provides a summary of the Schmitts' financial circumstances.

Exhibit 8   Summary of the Schmitts' Financial Circumstances at Age 45

	Jessica	Paul	Combined
Yearly gross income (€)	80,000	66,000	146,000
Yearly after-tax income (€)	53,650	46,510	100,160
Source of income	Department head, IT	Teacher at state school	
Living expenses (€)			65,000
Pension provisions	Government pension scheme membership as mandated by law Plus Employer's DC scheme (annual contribution of €3,000 from Jessica and employer)	Government pension scheme as mandated by law. As a civil servant, enjoys better pension conditions No separate private pension fund	
Employer-provided insurance		Life, insurance lump sum coverage 3 × €66,000 = €198,000.	
Private life insurance	€200,000 life policy she took out after the birth of their first child.	Life policy of €440,000	
Disability insurance	Government insurance coverage of €25,200 per year. Private coverage of a lump sum of €112,200 (the original €80,000 policy taken out at age 28, reflecting 2% annual benefit adjustment)	Government insurance coverage of €30,245 per year (includes extra payment reflecting more than 10 years of service) Private coverage of a lump sum of €686,100 (the original €490,000 policy taken out at age 28, reflecting 2% annual benefit adjustment)	

5.2 Financial Objectives in the Career Development Stage

Stein first discusses financial objectives with the 45-year-old Schmitts. They wish to achieve the following goals:

- maximize household welfare and reduce the impact of any unexpected events, such as illness, disability, or premature death;
- plan for future costs of support for Peter; and
- have a comfortable retirement.

To help understand the family's circumstances and identify risks, Stein conducts a valuation of Jessica's and Paul's human capital. The exercise is easier now than was the case in the early career stage. The input parameters are less uncertain, because their salary levels now are more stable and predictable than in the early career stage, and the calculation of present values of expected future earnings is conducted over a shorter time horizon. Exhibit 9 shows the assumptions used, including the reduction in risk adjustment on Jessica's salary. It also shows the resulting economic balance sheet. Although the valuation of human capital varies considerably under different assumptions, the result is that the value of the couple's human capital is substantial, amounting to a combined €1.9 million. Stein notes the financial objectives and notices their dependency on the couple's growing earnings.

Exhibit 9 Economic Balance Sheet at the Age of 45

Human Capital Assumptions

	Jessica	Paul
Expected salary growth (nominal)	5%	2%
Discount rate (r_f)	3%	3%
Risk adjustment (y)	1%	0%
Length of working life (up to age 65)	20	20
Probability of surviving to age 65	92%	92%

Note: Probability of surviving to a given age is based on mortality tables (not shown here) used in Eurolandia. They are assumed to be the same for men and women.

Economic Balance Sheet

Assets	€	Liabilities	€
Savings account	77,000	Mortgage debt	35,000
Shares of IT companies	130,000		
Accrued DB government retirement plan (Paul)	227,000		
Accrued DB government retirement plan (Jessica)	130,000		
Employer pension value (Jessica)	10,000		
Property (main residence)	320,000		
Paul's human capital	798,000	PV of lifetime consumption needs	2,379,000
Jessica's human capital	1,093,000		
Total assets	**2,785,000**	**Total liabilities**	**2,414,000**
		Net wealth	391,000

Note: The present value of lifetime consumption needs is based on the assumption that the family's current level of expenditure (€65,000) from this point increases by 2% a year in nominal terms (1% above inflation) for the rest of their lives. Assumes remaining time period of 45 years and discount rate of 3%. Numbers in the exhibit are rounded.

Identification and Analysis of Risk Exposures: Career Development Stage

To better understand the family's regular cash flows, Stein also prepares a summary cash flow budget, shown in Exhibit 10.

Exhibit 10   Summary Annual Budget of the Schmitt Family at Age 45

	€
Combined yearly gross pay	146,000
Less taxes and Social Security contributions	45,800
Net pay	**100,200**
Less living costs (including mortgage cost)	65,000
Less (house repair, maintenance, service charges)	3,500
Cash available for insurance and savings	**31,700**
Insurance premiums	3,500
Funds available to save or invest	**28,200**
Currently used primarily to:	
Fund investment portfolio	22,000
Add to savings accounts	3,200
Contribute to Jessica's employer's pension plan	3,000

5.3 Identification and Evaluation of Risks in the Career Development Stage

> **EXAMPLE 3**
>
> ### Identification of Risks
>
> Identify financial risks the Schmitts face. Discuss each risk in turn.
>
> **Guideline answer:**
>
> The Schmitts face the following main risks:
>
> - Earnings risk resulting from potential loss of employment. The risk of involuntary unemployment remains higher for Jessica than for Paul. Jessica is the higher earner, whereas Paul, a civil servant, could be expected to lose employment only under extreme circumstances. The amount at stake is greater than before because of the salary increases Jessica has enjoyed.
>
> - Earnings risk resulting from disability. The Schmitts remain in good health, so the likelihood of them suffering from disability remains low but is higher than the risk of dying. Their salaries, however, provide their main source of income and funding of their current lifestyles. If one of them were to become disabled, the burden on the rest of the family would not only take the form of lost earnings. It would also limit the range of activities in which the surviving partner could engage, with possible implications for income and costs.
>
> - Premature death risk. This risk remains relevant, because early death could have serious consequences for the family now that children need to be cared for. Not only would costs of bringing up children have to

be covered, the surviving spouse would potentially suffer a reduction in income because all family responsibilities would now be performed only by the surviving spouse.
- Risk to the value of their growing but concentrated investment portfolio of shares of IT companies. This is the couple's main investment vehicle but is focused on a volatile sector, whose performance is correlated with Jessica's career prospects.
- Risk to their retirement lifestyle goals. If the couple's contributions to their retirement plans are insufficient or the plans perform poorly, their retirement funding could be insufficient for the standard of living they desire.
- Other risks include property and liability risks.

5.3.1 Assessment of earnings risk

Earnings risk is significant because loss of employment is particularly relevant for Jessica. She is on a relatively high salary and works in a higher-risk sector compared with Paul. If she were to rely on unemployment benefits, at just under €13,500 per year, they would cover a quarter of her net income. In the event Paul were to become unemployed, such benefits would cover less than a third of his net salary.

Earnings risk resulting from disability would seriously affect the couple's ability to maintain their lifestyle and costs associated with providing for the children. In case of disability, Jessica would be entitled to about €25,200 per year, which is less than half of her net salary. Paul is less exposed because his salary is lower and his entitlement to state disability benefit is higher after more than 10 years of service. Relying on state benefits alone would provide €30,245, amounting to almost two-thirds of his net salary. In addition, the Schmitts have existing disability insurance in place, now providing total payout of €112,000 and €686,100 (if treated as a lump sum) in case of Jessica's or Paul's disability, respectively. Stein suggests that the level of coverage is reassessed before recommendation is made.

Premature death risk, now that the couple has children, requires attention. Death of one of the parents would not only have consequences due to one-off costs resulting from the death but would also mean that family expenditures, currently covered jointly, would have to be funded from the survivor's income. Furthermore, the surviving spouse would potentially suffer a reduction in income because family responsibilities would now be performed only by the surviving spouse, most likely preventing him or her from career progression and possibly forcing the person to work part time. Alternatively, such services would have to be provided by others at a cost.

Although the amount of financial assets available to the family has increased substantially in recent years, at an aggregate amount approaching €210,000, they amount to more than the Schmitts' joint yearly gross earnings of €146,000. Stein points out, however, that those amounts are not significant for the couple to be able to cope with unexpected events beyond the short term. The adviser notes the Schmitts would like to avoid the extreme situation where the children would face not only the tragic loss of a parent (or both) but also a deterioration in living standards. Life insurance would provide support for their young children, who are likely to rely on them for financial support for at least the next 10 years and possibly longer in the case of their son Peter.

5.3.2 Analysis of the investment portfolio risks

Risk to the investment portfolio stems from the fact that Jessica and Paul prefer to invest in a relatively small number of companies they believe they know, all of which are IT companies in their home country. Stein points out the correlation between their

IT stock holdings and Jessica's human capital, which is also tied to the prospects for the IT sector. If prospects for IT companies suffer, both the value of Jessica's human capital and that of their investment portfolio would decrease at the same time. Their risk-bearing ability is rather limited, which is important because their financial assets are rather modest compared with their spending needs—particularly in the presence of earnings risk related to Jessica's employment, a risk that is difficult to insure against. Moreover, because there is a relatively high concentration of IT employees where the Schmitts live, the value of the real estate that the Schmitts own there is likely to be positively correlated with Jessica's human capital as well.

5.3.3 Analysis of the retirement savings plans

Stein then takes a closer look at the risk to the Schmitts' retirement lifestyle goals. Through their mandatory social security contributions, the couple will be entitled to a government pension. In addition, Jessica's employer now provides a DC company pension, albeit with a limited amount of employer contributions. At the current rate of recently started contributions of €3,000 per year (combining those from Jessica's employer, her own payments, and the tax incentive), and assuming they grow at 3% annually, the estimated fund value would be near €150,000 at the age of 65, according to the fund administrator. At a typical annuity yield of 5%, such a sum would provide annual retirement income of €7,500. Stein estimates that if they remain employed until their retirement, and if there is no impairment in the benefits that are promised, the Schmitts will have a total gross retirement income, including state pensions, amounting to €76,000. This figure is about half of what they are earning now. Although their spending in retirement is likely to be lower than their current consumption, there is a risk that retirement income will be insufficient. Moreover, it is possible, and even likely, that the benefits offered by the state pension may be reduced before they retire, because the state pay-as-you-go system is under a significant strain.

5.3.4 Other risks

Stein also reviews the property and liability risks. The Schmitts have what is considered to be adequate health insurance through the government-mandated plan, which provides even quite advanced and costly treatment. It is a "no frills" arrangement, however, without any additional comfort or luxury environment. Property risk is covered by their existing buildings insurance, which includes liability coverage. The property value insured is the one they took out when buying their property: €200,000, well below the current estimated value of €320,000.

RISK MANAGEMENT RECOMMENDATIONS: CAREER DEVELOPMENT STAGE

6

d recommend and justify methods to manage a family's risk exposures during the career development stage

6.1 Disability insurance

Exhibit 11 shows Stein's calculation of disability coverage requirement based on the amount of earnings potentially lost in the case of disability.

Exhibit 11 Disability Insurance Coverage Calculation at Age 45

	Jessica	Paul
Salary income (net) to be replaced	53,650	46,510
Amount of annual disability coverage currently provided by the social security system	25,200	30,245
Annual shortfall	28,400	16,265
Benefit period (until retirement age)	20 years	20 years
Assumed annual benefit adjustment	2%	2%
Discount rate	3%	3%
PV of future earnings replacement required (annuity due)	519,000	297,000

Note: The purpose is to provide replacement for current income. This table shows the benefit in the form of a lump sum payout.

The current level of coverage is €112,200 for Jessica and €686,100 for Paul. Stein explains that because Paul would now be entitled to a much higher level of disability income from the state system, his level of additional required coverage is now lower. Given Jessica's pay rises in recent years, resulting in higher amounts of income to be replaced in case of disability, Stein recommends that the Schmitts change the level of coverage. Her suggestion is to increase the amount of coverage to €520,000 for Jessica and to reduce it to €300,000 for Paul.

6.2 Life insurance

Stein explains that the amount of coverage that a life insurance policy should provide can be calculated using either the human capital (the human life value method), which estimates the amount of earnings that must be replaced, or the needs analysis method, based on estimating the amount needed to cover survivors' living expenses. Stein adds that although the methods are distinct in their approach, both rely on a number of assumptions that may turn out to have been inaccurate. For example, it is very difficult to estimate the financial needs of surviving children who are still very young. Exhibit 12 illustrates the two methods.

EXHIBIT 12 LIFE INSURANCE AMOUNT REQUIRED AT AGE 45

Human life value method

Stein first works out the amount of lost income replacement, adjusting after-tax income for the amount of annual expenses and the value of the person's employee benefits. Assuming the survivors would need the lost income replacement immediately, she works out the present value of an annuity due.

Human life value method at age 45

	Paul's Life Cover (from Jessica's perspective)	Jessica's Life Cover (from Paul's perspective)
	€	€
Pretax income	66,000	80,000
After-tax income	46,510	53,650
Less adjustment for the deceased person's annual expenses that would not exist	10,000	10,000
Add value of employee benefits (retirement contribution) that family will no longer receive	10,000	4,000
Subtotal (after taxes)	46,510	47,650
Amount of pretax income required to replace after-tax income (30% rate assumed)	66,440	68,070
Annual growth rate (to reflect career advancement)	2%	5%
Discount rate	3%	3%
Present value of annuity due	1,213,000	1,644,000
Less existing life insurance (including €198,000 provided by Paul's employer)	638,000	200,000
Recommended additional life insurance	575,000	1,444,000

Note: Amounts are rounded.

Needs analysis

Stein estimates the cash needs required upon death of the insured person, including funeral and burial costs as well as mortgage debt. She next estimates capital needed to fund the family's living expenses by discounting future cash flow needs to their present value. Stein then considers the amount of the surviving spouse's future income, which she assumes would remain unchanged in real terms because the surviving spouse, being a single parent, would most likely be unable to achieve career progression. Finally, she deducts capital and savings available.

Needs analysis method at age 45

	Paul	Jessica
	€	€
Cash needs		
Cash needs (funeral and burial costs & taxes)	30,000	30,000
Mortgage retirement	35,000	35,000
Total cash needs	**65,000**	**65,000**
Capital needs		
PV of surviving spouse's living costs (assumed to be currently €35,000 for 45 years)	1,281,000	1,281,000

(continued)

(Continued)		
	Paul	Jessica
	€	€
PV of Roxane's living cost (€9,000 for 10 years until graduation at age 22)	86,000	86,000
PV of Peter's living cost (€13,000 for 83 years until age 90)	743,000	743,000
Less PV of survivor's income until retirement at 65	824,000	777,000
Total capital needs	**1,286,000**	**1,333,000**
Total financial needs	**1,351,000**	**1,398,000**
Capital available:		
Cash, savings, investments	207,000	207,000
PV of vested retirement accounts (attributable to surviving spouse)	140,000	227,000
Existing life insurance coverage (including benefit provided by Paul's employer)	638,000	200,000
Total capital available	**985,000**	**634,000**
Additional life insurance needs	366,000	764,000

Note: The annuity-due PV calculations of living costs assume a 2% annual increase and 3% discount rate. A 1% nominal increase in survivor's income is also assumed.

Stein notes that the human life method suggests a significantly higher increase in the recommended life insurance coverage that stems from different approaches used by the two methods. One may view the differing amounts as a range within which to choose the amount of coverage, taking into account the cost of premiums. The amount of life cover selected may depend on which method is more relevant to the family's circumstances. Taking into account the Schmitts' focus on their ability to meet family expenses, Stein recommends that the Schmitts increase their private insurance coverage from the existing €440,000 to €900,000 in the case of Paul and from €200,000 to €1 million in the case of Jessica.

She adds that it is quite important to obtain such coverage while the Schmitts enjoy good health. If they were to develop any medical conditions later in life, obtaining such insurance would be much more problematic, and available coverage would be subject to exclusions and other limitations. She also suggests that the needed coverage can be met by a temporary life insurance, providing coverage until retirement age in about 20 years, when at least one child is expected to be (or is well on its way to being) independent.

6.3 Investment risk recommendations

EXAMPLE 4

Investment Risk Recommendations

Recommend and justify changes to the Schmitts' investment portfolio.

Guideline answer:

Stein has noted the correlation of the €130,000 of investment holdings in IT companies with Jessica's human capital. They should aim to hold an investment portfolio with as low correlation to one's human capital as possible. They should also move away from the concentrated nature of holdings of which they usually hold 10. In order for the Schmitts to achieve better diversification, Stein recommends that, at a minimum, any new investments are no longer made directly into shares of IT companies. Instead, they should be making regular investments into pooled investment vehicles—such as funds that are diversified across a wide range of regions, sectors, and securities—which can be done at low cost. Cost efficiency is paramount because any amount saved from initial charges or annual costs, compounded over many years, may make significant difference to long-term returns. If an active approach to investing is chosen, the additional costs that stem from such an approach should be justified by sufficient active risk-adjusted return.

EXAMPLE 5

Real Estate in Investment Portfolio

The Schmitts earlier mentioned the possibility of making speculative investment in residential property (similar in size to their existing property) in the area where IT companies, including Jessica's offices, are based. Identify issues that an adviser should consider before making a recommendation.

Guideline answer:

The issue to consider is how the prospects for the local property market depend on the performance for and employment in the local IT industry. Jessica's own employment prospects depend on this industry, and purchasing a property in the area would increase the Schmitts' exposure to the local IT industry.

Funding of the purchase would also need to be considered because the cost could exceed €300,000 given that the Schmitts' property, similar in size and value to the one they are considering, is worth about €320,000. The Schmitts do not have sufficient resources available. Devoting a large proportion of their investment portfolio to a deposit and funding the rest of the purchase price using a loan would expose them to risks such as interest rate risk. A greater share of their wealth would be tied to the prospects of the local IT industry as they would no longer hold exposure to equities, foregoing benefits from diversification. They should be made aware of the fact that holding an investment property would represent a large, concentrated, illiquid position and that there are costs associated with owning and managing rental property.

6.4 Retirement planning recommendation

EXAMPLE 6

Recommendation for Retirement Saving at the Career Development Stage

Recommend methods to manage risk to retirement lifestyle goals.

> **Guideline answer:**
>
> Analysis of retirement plans identified a significant shortfall in the Schmitts' projected retirement income. To address the risk of having insufficient funds to maintain their lifestyle in retirement, the couple should give serious consideration to increasing the amount dedicated to retirement needs. Their monthly after-tax income of €8,350 exceeds their monthly expenditures by about €2,700, which even after the payment of insurance premiums leaves them with €2,350 (€28,200 per year) to invest. This provides them with an opportunity to boost retirement savings and build up their investment portfolio instead of continuing to build up their liquidity buffer, which is now approaching €80,000 (invested in a low-interest, instant-access bank account). The Schmitts should instead increase contributions into Jessica's pension scheme or open separate private pension plans. Doing so would also allow them to take advantage of the tax benefits of retirement saving because income and capital gains within the regulated plans are tax free, and contributions into the plans are supplemented with the 25% top-up payments from the state. Although the funds from pension plans are normally inaccessible before retirement, the tax advantages, compared with investing outside such plans, can be significant.

6.5 Additional suggestions

Stein recommends that they update their property insurance coverage to reflect the current market value.

Supplementary private health insurance could be considered to cover dental care, alternative medicine, hospitalization in a private room, and other health costs. The reason in favor of obtaining such coverage now is that it will be cheaper while they are still relatively young and healthy, whereas it would be much more costly to obtain if and when they suffer from preexisting conditions. An important consideration is the lack of portability of such supplementary medical insurance were the Schmitts to move and/or to retire to another country.

Stein concludes her recommendations by adding that a risk management strategy for individuals should not only consist of establishing objectives, identifying risks, evaluating risks, and selecting methods to manage those risks, but also that outcomes and risk exposures should be monitored and methods for addressing them reviewed and adjusted as necessary.

The Schmitts accept their adviser's recommendations. They drop the idea of purchasing a property near the IT business district; they stop adding to their instant-access savings that form their liquidity buffer and instead increase their contributions to Jessica's employer pension plan. The Schmitts continue their contributions to the investment portfolio but start moving away from individual securities, instead investing in diversified equity funds.

7. IDENTIFICATION AND ANALYSIS OF RISK EXPOSURES: PEAK ACCUMULATION STAGE

e identify and analyze a family's risk exposures during the peak accumulation stage

f recommend and justify methods to manage a family's risk exposures during the peak accumulation stage

Identification and Analysis of Risk Exposures: Peak Accumulation Stage

The Schmitts are now 55 years old and are in their peak accumulation phase. In the last 10 years, they made further progress in their careers. Their incomes continued to increase. Correspondingly, Jessica's employer's contributions into the company pension scheme have increased meaningfully. Jessica herself has also been actively contributing to her employer's occupational pension scheme and into her recently opened private pension, taking advantage of tax incentives. The part of the technology sector in which Jessica's company operates is experiencing volatility arising from a rapidly changing market environment. Paul's employment remains stable. He has been regularly contributing to a private pension plan.

The Schmitts' assets, invested in a number of diversified funds now with a 70% equity (mostly global equity with a small amount in Eurolandia equities) and 30% fixed income mix (split about evenly between domestic government bonds and corporate bonds), have grown substantially thanks to regular investing and investment returns. The value of their property has suffered a decline in real terms as a consequence of the stagnation in Eurolandia's real estate market and of the fact that the area where the property is located has lost its earlier appeal.

Although the Schmitts have already repaid their mortgage, their liabilities have increased. They are still supporting Roxane's living expenses because she just completed her bachelor's degree and is starting post-graduate studies. They are providing the best possible special needs education for Peter, who is now 17 and has made progress but will most likely need assistance for the rest of his life. The Schmitts feel retirement planning has become a crucial issue because they plan to retire in 10 years. They maintain a healthy lifestyle. They meet with Stein to review their risk management arrangements in relation to their lifestyle goals. Together they produce a summary of their financial circumstances, shown in Exhibit 13.

Exhibit 13 Summary of the Schmitts' Financial Circumstances at the Age of 55

	Jessica	Paul	Combined
	€	€	€
Yearly gross income	120,000	80,000	200,000
After-tax income	77,888	53,888	131,776
Source of income	Department head, IT	State teaching job	
Living expenses			75,000
Property			340,000
Bank accounts			80,900
Investment portfolio			611,400
Pension provisions	As mandated by law (state pension), plus a company-sponsored pension scheme €113,000 plus €15,000 in private pension savings	As mandated by law. Paul, as a civil servant, plus €47,500 in private pension savings	

(continued)

Exhibit 13 (Continued)

	Jessica	Paul	Combined
	€	€	€
Disability insurance	Government insurance coverage of €30,720 per year. Private coverage of a lump sum of €633,900 (policy benefit was increased to €520,000 at age 45, adjusted for 2% annual benefit adjustment)	Government insurance cover of €36,870 per year (includes extra payment reflecting more than 10 years of service). Private coverage of a lump sum of €365,700 (policy provided €300,000 at age 45, adjusted for 2% annual benefit adjustment)	
Life insurance coverage (up to age 65)	€1,000,000 private policy. *Note*: This amount reflects the recommendation given at age 45.	€900,000 private policy plus 3× salary insurance coverage of €240,000 provided by the employer	

7.1 Review of Objectives, Risks, and Methods of Addressing Them

Stein sets out to establish the Schmitts' financial objectives and review the financial risks they face. She then proceeds to provide recommendations.

7.1.1 Financial objectives

Stein asks the Schmitts to update her on their financial objectives. Paul and Jessica explain that their objectives remain broadly unchanged. They wish to achieve the following:

- Provide financial security for the family in the next 10 years while they remain in full-time employment.
- Have a comfortable retirement, which they anticipate will happen in 10 years when they both reach the age of 65.
- Be in a position (after their retirement) to provide long-term support and assistance for their son Peter for the rest of his life,
- Leave a meaningful inheritance for Roxane.

Stein explains that she will assess the couple's existing insurance arrangements with regard to their financial security while they still are working and earning salaries. She will then focus on assessing risks relating to their three long-term planned goals: the "comfortable retirement," "Peter's long-term assistance," and "inheritance for Roxane" goals.

Stein proceeds to update the Schmitts' financial and economic balance sheets, shown in Exhibit 14.

Exhibit 14 Financial and Economic Balance Sheet at Age 55

Human Capital Assumptions

	Jessica	Paul
Expected salary growth (nominal)	2%	2%
Discount rate (r_f)	3%	3%
Risk adjustment (y)	1%	0%
Remaining length of working life (up to age 65)	10	10

Note: Probability of surviving to a given age is based on mortality tables (not shown here) used in Eurolandia.

Economic Balance Sheet (€)

Assets		Liabilities	
Savings account	80,900	Mortgage debt	0
Investment portfolio	611,400		
Accrued DB government retirement plan (Paul)	457,000		
Accrued DB government retirement plan (Jessica)	263,000		
Employer pension value (Jessica)	113,500		
Private pension fund (Jessica)	15,000		
Private pension value (Paul)	47,500		
Property (main residence)	340,000		
Paul's human capital	486,600	PV of lifetime consumption needs	2,235,000
Jessica's human capital	668,100		
Total assets	3,083,000	Total liabilities	2,235,000
		Net wealth	848,000

Note: Human capital values are calculated based on an assumption of 2% nominal salary growth rate until retirement in 10 years, discounted at 3%, adjusted for mortality rates and applying a further 1% risk adjustment to Jessica's income.

Lifetime consumption needs are calculated as annuity due based on annual costs of €75,000 over 35 years, with an annual increase of 2%, discounted at 3%.

EXAMPLE 7

Comparison of Economic Balance

Compare the economic balance sheet at age 55, shown in Exhibit 14, with the one produced 10 years ago, shown in Exhibit 9.

Guideline answer:

The Schmitts' human capital has decreased in absolute terms over time as they approach retirement, which is now 10 years away. Their human capital has also decreased relative to their financial resources, which have seen a significant increase. The Schmitts have repaid their debts, and their net wealth is now much more substantial than 10 years earlier.

EXAMPLE 8

Liquidity Needs

Discuss the Schmitts' financial position with regard to their ability to meet any unexpected liquidity needs.

Guideline answer:

The level of their financial assets provides sufficient liquidity if their circumstances were to change. The Schmitts are now significantly richer in financial assets than they were 10 years earlier. They have a balance of almost €81,000 in their instant-access savings account and more than €600,000 in diversified funds that they should be able to easily exit if such need arose.

7.1.2 Review of Risks and Related Risk Management Methods

Having gathered information about the Schmitts' financial circumstances and goals, Stein identifies the risks and prepares summary information (in Exhibits 15, 16, and 17) to help analyze those risks.

Exhibit 15   Earnings Shortfall in Case of Disability at Age 55

	Jessica	Paul
Salary income (net) to be replaced	€77,900	€53,900
Amount of annual disability coverage currently provided by the social security system	€30,720	€36,870
Annual shortfall	€47,180	€17,030

Note: Jessica and Paul's annual earnings shortfalls at the age of 45 were €28,450 and €16,265, respectively. Rounding is used throughout.

Exhibit 16   Disability Insurance Coverage Assumptions

Benefit period (until retirement age)	10 years	10 years
Assumed annual benefit adjustment	2%	2%

Exhibit 16	(Continued)		
Discount rate		3%	3%
PV of future earnings replacement required		€452,000	€163,000

> **EXAMPLE 9**
>
> ### Analysis of Earnings Risk during Peak Accumulation Stage
>
> Using the information provided by the Schmitts to their adviser and the information in Exhibits 13, 15, and 16, analyze the earnings-related risks arising from unemployment and disability that the Schmitts face now that they are in the peak accumulation life stage.
>
> ### Guideline answer:
>
> The Schmitts continue to face earnings risk resulting from unemployment. Jessica continues to work in a sector that shows volatile profitability. A loss of her job at her current age of 55 could make it difficult for her to find alternative employment at significantly above-average salary and level of seniority. Two facts mitigate the seriousness of this concern. First, the Schmitts have a substantial amount of savings and investments to buffer any loss of earnings. Second, Paul's employment appears secure.
>
> The risk to their earnings from disability remains, but the level of coverage should be reassessed because their circumstances have changed and they are closer to retirement.
>
> The amount of annual earnings not protected by the social security system is higher than was the case at age 45 for Jessica because of her salary growth. But the fact that the period over which they would rely on such benefit payments is now only 10 years means that the present value of the disability protection needed is now lower: €452,000 for Jessica and €163,000 for Paul, well below the level of their existing coverage (€633,900 and €365,700).

Stein assesses the level of life insurance coverage needed using the human life and needs analysis methods. Starting with the human life method, the higher level of salaries would be expected to increase the amount of income required to replace the deceased person's earnings. Because the remaining period of earning a salary is now reduced to 10 years until retirement, however, the present value of future earnings would be expected to decline, as Exhibit 17 shows.

Exhibit 17	Human Life Method Insurance Coverage Calculation at Age 55	
	Paul	Jessica
	€	€
Pretax income	80,000	120,000
After-tax income	53,900	77,900
		(continued)

Exhibit 17 (Continued)

	Paul	Jessica
	€	€
Less adjustment for the deceased person's annual expenses that will not exist	10,000	10,000
Add value of employee benefits that the family will no longer receive	10,000	4,000
Subtotal (after taxes)	53,900	71,900
Amount of pretax income required to replace after-tax income (30% tax rate)	77,000	102,700
Annual growth rate	2%	2%
Discount rate	3%	3%
Present value of pretax income to be replaced (annuity due, 10 years)	737,000	983,000
Less existing life insurance (including current benefit €240,000 provided by Paul's employer)	1,140,000	1,000,000
Recommended additional life insurance	−403,000	−17,000

Stein should also carry out needs analysis method to help establish the necessary amount of life insurance coverage. The calculation is made simpler by the fact that there are no further debts to repay. The couple's daughter Roxane has graduated and is expected not to require ongoing support once she completes her post-graduate studies in less than two years (Stein excludes the short-term support for Roxane from her calculation in Exhibit 18).

Exhibit 18 Needs Analysis Method Insurance Coverage Calculation at Age 55

	Paul's Life Cover (from Jessica's perspective)	Jessica's Life Cover (from Paul's perspective)
Cash needs	€	€
Funeral and burial costs plus taxes	35,000	35,000
Total cash needs	**35,000**	**35,000**
Capital needs		
PV of surviving spouse's living expenses (until age 90)	1,191,800	1,191,800
PV of Peter's living cost (€13,000 per year, growing at 2%, until age 90)	682,000	682,000
Less PV of survivor's income until retirement at 65	685,000	494,000
Total capital needs	**1,188,800**	**1,379,800**
Total financial needs	**1,223,800**	**1,414,800**
Capital available:		
Cash, savings, investments	692,300	692,300

Exhibit 18   (Continued)

Cash needs	Paul's Life Cover (from Jessica's perspective) €	Jessica's Life Cover (from Paul's perspective) €
PV of vested retirement accounts (attributable to surviving spouse)	392,000	505,000
Existing life insurance coverage (including current benefit €240,000 provided by Paul's employer)	1,140,000	1,000,000
Total capital available	**2,224,300**	**2,197,300**
Additional life insurance needs	−1,000,500	−782,500

Note: The PV of the surviving spouse's expenses is based on annual spend of €40,000 for 35 years, annual growth rate of 2%, and discount rate of 3%. Annuity due is used. The same growth and discount rates are used to calculate the PV of Peter's living cost, and the benefit period is 73 years. The PV of the survivor's income is based on a period of 10 years, 1% growth resulting from limited career progress opportunities in such circumstances, a 3% discount rate, and a 1% additional discount rate risk adjustment for Jessica.

Both the human life value and needs analysis methods suggest that premature death risks are covered by the Schmitts' existing insurance. The amount of existing coverage now substantially exceeds the coverage suggested by the two methods. Stein recommends they reduce the amount of coverage, lowering their monthly premiums. She does point out, however, that one of their objectives is to provide adequate long-term support for Peter and plan for an increase in the cost of doing so when they are no longer able to support him the way they do now (the €13,000 per year would increase substantially then). If Paul or Jessica died before retiring, it would no longer be possible to set funds aside for Peter's future care. Stein suggests the Schmitts consider this factor before adjusting their policy coverage.

Stein notes that the Schmitts have adequate life insurance and satisfactory, although no-frills, health coverage provided by the state. They also have sufficient liquidity to cover incidental expenses—for example, in relation to health care needs not covered by their health insurance. By maintaining a healthy lifestyle, the Schmitts are helping to reduce the health risk. The combination of their existing coverage, government-mandated programs, and the ability to self-insure through their own assets is sufficient. As such, no additional insurance is recommended.

8. ASSESSMENT OF AND RECOMMENDATIONS CONCERNING RISK TO RETIREMENT LIFESTYLE AND BEQUEST GOALS: PEAK ACCUMULATION STAGE

e identify and analyze a family's risk exposures during the peak accumulation stage

f recommend and justify methods to manage a family's risk exposures during the peak accumulation stage

Next, Stein considers the risk to the Schmitts' retirement lifestyle goal. She provides a summary of the retirement assets and then proceeds to establish how much the couple expects to be spending in retirement. Exhibit 19 provides a summary of the retirement plans assuming that the Schmitts retire in 10 years when they are 65. Further assumptions are as follows:

- The Schmitts continue to make social security contributions to the mandatory government pension scheme.
- They also continue making regular payments into their private pensions and Jessica's occupational pension scheme.
- The investment returns of the DC plans remain at 4% per year, slightly lower than the 5% rate seen over the last 10 years, as the assets in the retirement portfolios are gradually moved to lower-risk asset allocation as the retirement date nears.
- The DC plans' final values at age 65 are used to buy an immediate fixed annuity (we assume a 5% annuity "income yield" and no inflation adjustment thereafter).

Exhibit 19 The Schmitts' Retirement Assets and Main Risks (not including their investment portfolio)

Assets	Type and Current Value	Expected Growth Rate	Expected Value at Age 65	Expected Annual Gross Pension Benefit (€)	Risks
Paul's mandatory government pension plan	DB pension plan	—	—	€48,950 (55% of the estimated final salary)	Government may reduce retirement benefits due to fiscal pressures
Jessica's mandatory government pension plan	DB pension plan	—	—	€28,191	As above
Jessica's company pension	DC plan, Current value €113,500 Balanced fund	Annual contributions of €14,000, growing at 2% 4% annual investment returns	€350,000	€17,515	Investment risk and interest rate risk that could result in lower annuity income yield

Assessment of and Recommendations concerning Risk to Retirement Lifestyle and Bequest Goals

Exhibit 19   (Continued)

Assets	Type and Current Value	Expected Growth Rate	Expected Value at Age 65	Expected Annual Gross Pension Benefit (€)	Risks
Paul's private pension savings plan	DC plan currently valued at €47,500 Balanced fund	€6,000 annual contributions growing at 2% 3% investment returns	€135,900	€6,795	As above
Jessica's private pension savings plan	DC plan opened recently Valued at €15,000 Uses aggressive, actively managed investment strategy with high risk	€10,000 annual contributions growing at 2%. 8% investment returns	€201,600	€10,080	As above

Note: Jessica has no influence over the terms and conditions of her company pension scheme, which is a mandatory DC plan. Like all beneficiaries, she has the right to vote for the employee representatives on the company's pension fund board. Figures and percentage growth rates are assumed to be net of fees.

Stein estimates that their combined annual retirement income from pension schemes could amount to about €111,500. This figure would be subject to income tax, which she estimates will leave them with after-tax income of €84,000, excluding any income from their investment portfolio (treated separately). To be able to judge whether or not the existing retirement provisions are sufficient, Stein needs to better understand what percentage of salary the Schmitts want to replace in retirement. The couple finds it difficult to be precise about the amounts they will need to spend. They conclude that they should require no more than their current level of annual spending of €75,000 (in real terms). Stein explains that they are in a good position to be able to maintain their current lifestyle even in retirement. She points out, however, the risk from loss of employment, the risk to the state pensions system, and the risk of poor investment returns of the DC plans over the next 10 years. Stein explains each risk in turn:

1. If the Schmitts lose their employment and cannot obtain work with comparable compensation, their pension assets growth and the corresponding estimated values would be at risk because they would no longer be able to fund their regular contributions. Their insurance policies do not provide income replacement in the event of unemployment. Statutory redundancy pay and unemployment benefits would cover a small proportion of their current pay.

2. The other main risk is that the government state pension plan gets overhauled in response to the aging population and fiscal pressures. Such an overhaul could take the form of benefit reduction. A less likely scenario is an increase in the retirement age.

3. Investment risk and inflation risk make up a third risk factor. Investment risk affects the non-government, DC plans that the Schmitts hold. Past returns of the Schmitts' retirement funds over the last decade averaged almost 5% per year, but such returns may not continue into the future. Second, inflation may erode the purchasing power of the income from retirement plans.

If the government pension plans continue to provide benefits at the same level enjoyed by current retirees, they will cover the Schmitts' basic living costs. This income would not provide for any other objectives, such as assistance for or bequeathing assets to their children. The arrangements for those other goals are assessed next.

> **EXAMPLE 10**
>
> ### Withdrawal of Tax-Free Lump Sum
>
> Regulations in Eurolandia allow members of private pension schemes to withdraw 25% of their retirement assets as a tax-free lump sum from the age of 55, the Schmitts' current age. Taking into account the analysis of their retirement assets, discuss the merits of withdrawing the tax-free lump sum at this stage.
>
> **Guideline answer:**
>
> The potential logic of withdrawing 25% of the DC funds tax free should be assessed in a broad context. The Schmitts have sufficient cash flows from earnings to be able to fund their ongoing expenses and keep adding to their investment portfolio. They are in their peak accumulation stage of their careers and are accumulating assets rather than spending. There appears to be no need for them to access the funds at this stage.
>
> If they were to withdraw the funds now in order to invest outside their retirement programs, the couple would no longer benefit from the fact that they are accumulating assets without having to pay any capital gains or income taxes within the retirement schemes. Not withdrawing the 25% lump sum now, however, still provides them with the option of withdrawing the tax-free lump sum at a later stage.

8.1 Analysis of Investment Portfolio

Stein turns her attention to the Schmitts' investment portfolio in relation to the couple's two additional goals:

- Provide for their son Peter's care for the rest of his life.
- Leave an inheritance for their daughter Roxane.

She explains to the Schmitts that she needs to understand the time horizon and risk tolerance in relation to the probability of success for each goal. Stein explains that in goals-based investing, their investment portfolio will be treated as a number of sub-portfolios—in this case, only two—each of which is designed to fund an individual goal.

8.1.1 The goal of supporting Peter

Stein first looks into the need to fund support for Peter after the Schmitts' retirement, support that will be required for the rest of Peter's life because he is not expected to ever be in a position to obtain paid employment or to make decisions for himself. Although the state provides a range of benefits to Peter, the Schmitts currently spend €13,000 a year on additional support for their son. They wish to ensure as much as possible that Peter will receive proper assistance, even after they die or otherwise become unable to care directly for him and thus need to hire outside help. This goal is essential for the Schmitts, and they want it to be achieved with the utmost certainty (i.e., with a probability as close to 1 as possible). They are confident that they can fund Peter's long-term care as long as they remain employed for the next 10 years.

Assessment of and Recommendations concerning Risk to Retirement Lifestyle and Bequest Goals

Based on average life expectancy in Eurolandia, Peter is expected to outlive his parents by around 40 years, because he was born when they were 38. The Schmitts struggle to establish the period over which they will be able to care for Peter (incurring the €13,000 cost per year and expected to remain unchanged in real terms) without requiring the use of extensive outside help, which currently costs about €30,000 per year. They are also quite worried about possible future inflation despite Eurolandia's low inflation history.

As a base scenario, the Schmitts and their advisor conclude that they should plan for the higher cost resulting from external care to apply in 20 years' time once they reach the age of 75 and Peter is 37. Stein quantifies the amount required to meet that goal, as illustrated in Exhibit 20.

Exhibit 20 Net Present Value of Peter's Care

The required funding for the goal of providing for Peter's care for the rest of his life can be modelled as the present value of a deferred-start annuity (even though they would not be buying one now) that begins in 20 years' time. Its duration would equal Peter's life expectancy then (an additional 53 years of life up to the age of 90). The following table shows the PV of such an annuity, with different assumptions, considering a yearly cost of €30,000 in real terms. Because the Schmitts emphasized the need to address inflation risks, the calculations are performed in real terms—that is, the amounts are expressed in euros based on their value at present time when the Schmitts are 55. The discount rate represents the real discount rate.

Real Discount Rate	PV
1.0%	€1,018,000
2.0%	€669,000
3.0%	€451,000

Note: The amounts are rounded to the nearest €1000 for the present value of this annuity due lasting 53 years.

Based on the current level of real interest rates of 2%, the net present value of Peter's care exceeds the current value of the Schmitts' €611,000 investment portfolio. When the Schmitts inquire about the calculations' sensitivity to changes in economic conditions and potential solutions to the shortfall, Stein replies that it would be unrealistic to count on a real discount rate much higher than 2% to reduce the net present value, given the very low real rates experienced for quite some time.

Stein notes, however, that the Schmitts are now in the peak accumulation stage of their careers and can continue to add to the investment portfolio on regular basis: approximately €33,000 per year, with the amount slowly increasing. They would be able to do so while also contributing to their pension plans. Failing to continue contributions to the investment portfolio, however, would pose a serious risk of them being unable to completely fund Peter's long-term support. Second, Stein notes that in her retirement planning assessment, their expenditure assumptions reflect the expectation that the €13,000 annual cost (in real terms) of supporting Peter would continue for the rest of their lives and would not stop when they reach the age of 75, which is what the foregoing deferred-start annuity calculation reflected. In other words, the fact that the Schmitts assume they will be paying €13,000 per year (in real terms) even after they reach 75 means that the additional support needed will be closer to €20,000, rather than €33,000, for as long as they live. She therefore suggests that the PV amount they should plan to use for Peter's care should currently be closer to €500,000.

Before advising them on their portfolio's asset allocation, Stein turns to their other goal.

8.1.2 Leaving inheritance to Roxane

The Schmitts would like to leave inheritance for their children, particularly for Roxane, because they are already making arrangements for Peter's long-term care.[1] The required probability of success for this goal, however, is far lower than what was attributed to Peter's care goal, and the time horizon is much longer because they expect to live for more than 30 years. When Stein asks about the amount they would ideally like Roxane to inherit, the Schmitts state that they hope the amount would be as high as possible, so that she inherits more than just their property—their main residence. Exhibit 21 summarizes the three main known goals.

Exhibit 21   The Schmitts' Goals

Goal	NPV	Notes	Time Horizon	Required Probability of Success
Having a comfortable retirement	Not applicable	Goal is already covered by existing pension arrangements, assuming projected earnings growth rates and fund contributions are realized.	10 years	High
Providing for Peter's care	Approximately €500,000	NPV is assumption-dependent	Approximately 20 years	Nearly 100%
Leaving an inheritance for Roxane	As much as possible		>30 years	Around 60%

8.2 Analysis of Asset Allocation

Stein reflects on which asset allocation technique should be used. Using mean–variance optimization is problematic because it is a "single-period" framework," and the Schmitts' stated objectives span multiple periods. She recognizes that asset allocation can be conducted with a goal-based approach, whereby goals are analyzed and modelled and a probability of success specified for each of them. The additional advantage of the goal-based approach is that it enables a far simpler and more intuitive communication with the Schmitts than discussing the risk–return tradeoff in the context of mean–variance optimization.

The idea behind the exercise is to apply goals-based investing techniques by disaggregating the Schmitts' portfolio into two sub-portfolios, each designed to fund a goal with its own time horizon and probability of success.

8.2.1 Peter's care

The Schmitts require that the probability to fulfill this goal be as close as possible to 100%. As such, this sub-portfolio should be worth at least €500,000 in real terms (in today's values) when it becomes necessary to start drawing on it, most probably in

---

[1] In fact, inheritance law in Eurolandia requires the Schmitts to bequeath a minimum proportion of their wealth to each of the surviving children. They could not, therefore, direct that their entire wealth goes to Peter's care. In this case study, we assume that this legal obligation will be satisfied, so we do not discuss it further.

around 20 years. Any volatility in the mark-to-market of this portfolio before then, however, is of secondary importance. Stein believes that such portfolio should be invested in inflation-linked government bonds, with long maturities. Yields (including those on inflation-linked bonds) are currently very low, and Stein expects that they may increase over time because of higher inflation expectations (which the inflation-linked bonds would protect them from) or because real rates could rise. Because the time horizon is relatively long, the allocation to inflation-linked bonds can be implemented gradually. The existing portfolio, from which this "sub-fund" will need to be created, is 70% invested in equities and 30% in bonds. By implementing this switch gradually, the Schmitts should be able to minimize capital gains taxes that would otherwise arise from realizing profits on the existing fund holdings. Eurolandia allows residents to pay no tax on the first €25,000 of realized capital gains per year, a level that has remained and is expected to remain unchanged.

If inflation and, correspondingly, bond coupons on inflation-linked bonds increase in the future, the Schmitts will face a significant tax liability from the income arising from this sub-portfolio. The tax will reduce the inflation protection provided by the portfolio. If this occurs, an adviser can study the possibility of structuring this portfolio as a non-taxable trust but only after considering the costs to create and run the structure, as well as the additional constraints associated with it. Theoretically, the modified duration of this sub-portfolio should match that of the associated goal. Such a match will be challenging, however, because no bonds with such a long modified duration are available.

8.2.2 Leaving an inheritance for Roxane

Given that most of their investment portfolio is allocated to the first sub-portfolio, only €110,000 in investable assets is available to invest in the second sub-portfolio. This sub-portfolio starts off fully allocated to diversified global equity funds to capture the expected returns from equities.

8.3 Recommendations for Risk Management at Peak Accumulation Stage

Having gathered the facts, established the objectives, and analyzed the risks that the Schmitts face, Stein provides a summary of the following recommendations.

8.3.1 Risk to earnings

Stein explains that the risk from unemployment cannot be avoided or insured against using insurance policies but that the Schmitts, thanks to their savings, are self-insuring. Having reviewed their protections against loss of earnings resulting from disability or premature death, she concludes that their existing coverage is more than sufficient. Stein suggests reducing the amount of coverage as well as the premiums they pay where the policies allow for such change.

8.3.2 Recommendations for retirement savings

EXAMPLE 11

Reduction of Risk to Retirement Lifestyle Goals

Recommend and justify methods for reducing risk to retirement lifestyle goals.

> **Guideline answer:**
>
> The Schmitts are in a good position to retire comfortably. They should continue contributing to their private pension savings plans up to the legally specified maximum, thereby obtaining the corresponding tax advantage whereby the government adds 25% to their own contributions. Two of their private pension plans are invested in a portfolio that is diversified across asset classes and regions. Over time, the fund holdings are being gradually moved to a lower-risk asset allocation with an increasing proportion of fixed-income government securities.
>
> Jessica's recently opened private pension plan, however, is managed aggressively at the extreme end of what regulated schemes allow. Stein explains that such a high-risk addition to their substantial retirement savings is not necessarily a cause for concern, but she urges the Schmitts to consider moving the fund choice within the scheme to a less risky, more balanced alternative.

8.3.3 *Recommendations for the investment portfolio*

Stein explains that the first goal, the comfortable retirement, is addressed already through the retirement savings schemes. The other two—funding Peter's support for the rest of his life and leaving an inheritance for Roxane—should be addressed by the following:

- The couple should continue adding to the investment portfolio on regular basis at the existing rate of €33,000 per year or higher. These additional contributions, along with capital gains and reinvested income over time, should result in a healthy growth of the investment portfolio.

- Within the growing portfolio, assets devoted to Peter's care goal, currently amounting to €500,000, should be gradually reallocated from the current 70% equity and 30% fixed income to an increasing proportion of inflation-protected government bonds. Gains on investments should be realized in an orderly fashion to take advantage of the €25,000 of tax-free capital gains per year.

Because the Schmitts continue to save and accumulate assets, it is important to review whether the allocation remains in line with the goals listed in the previous section.

Stein further explains that a detailed Investment Policy Statement will be written for them and further analysis of the actual fund holdings will be carried out. The portfolio allocation will be reviewed periodically, at least once a year. The Investment Policy Statement will be reviewed for any material change in circumstances. She further adds that retirement planning process should also involve an expert, a specialist, on inheritance tax.

9. IDENTIFICATION AND ANALYSIS OF RETIREMENT OBJECTIVES, ASSETS AND DRAWDOWN PLAN: RETIREMENT STAGE

g identify and analyze a family's risk exposures during the early retirement stage

The Schmitts are about to turn 65, and retirement is imminent. They are in good health, although they occasionally make use of the country's health system. They spend less than in earlier stages of life, and their investment portfolio now amounts to more than €1.5 million. Despite the gradual move from equity funds to fixed-income ones, equities still account for a sizable portion of their holdings: 50% of the total, as result of healthy returns from the asset class. The rest is evenly held in inflation-protected government bonds and corporate bonds. Jessica's income has decreased because she decided to step down from her department management job and is currently employed as a senior IT consultant. The family's living expenses have also come down because Roxane is now independent.

The Schmitts' financial situation and pension assets are summarized in Exhibits 22 and 23.

Exhibit 22 Summary of the Schmitts' Financial Circumstances at Age 65

	Jessica	Paul	Combined
Yearly gross income (€)	90,000	89,000	179,000
Source of income	Senior IT consultant	State teaching job	
Living expenses (€)			70,000
Property (€)			420,000
Investment portfolio (€)			1,511,000

Exhibit 23 The Schmitts' Retirement Assets

Asset	Current Value at Age 65
Paul's mandatory government pension plan	Annual pension of €48,950 (55% of final salary of €89,000)
Jessica's mandatory government pension plan	Annual pension of €28,190
Jessica's company pension	DC plan. Fund value of €350,000 corresponding to an annual pension of €17,500
Paul's private pension savings plan	€135,000 corresponding to annual pension of €6,750
Jessica's private pension savings plan	€175,000 corresponding to annual pension of €8,750

Note: The annual pension amounts assume that the fund value at retirement is used to purchase a fixed payment annuity at the current 5% annuity yield.

9.1 Key Issues and Objectives

The Schmitts again meet with Stein. They wish to discuss planning for the retirement decision and the management of the investment portfolio. They repeat their objectives, which are as follows:

- Retire shortly with a comfortable level of secure, predictable retirement income for the rest of their lives, and avoid a situation in which they outlive their assets. The Schmitts consider themselves to be healthy and expect to live longer than the average life expectancy. They also state that they wish to make sure to maintain the purchasing power of their retirement income.

- Continue to provide ongoing financial support for Peter, raising the amount devoted to this purpose in 10 years to what they now estimate will need to be €35,000 per year at today's prices.
- Leave a meaningful but as yet unquantified inheritance for Roxane, over and above their residence.
- Help their daughter Roxane with the purchase of her first property in the very near future, up to €150,000.

The Schmitts would also like to have the option to retire in another country.

9.2 Analysis of Retirement Assets and Drawdown Plan

Stein explains the following:

- Now that the Schmitts are about to retire, there is no further need for life or disability insurance coverage.
- There are no decisions to make with regard to the state pension income that they will soon start drawing, the amounts of which are known with certainty.

Regarding the employer and private pension schemes they have in place, a plan must be established. She explains that the Schmitts have the following options:

- Purchase annuities that would provide a stream of income for the rest of their lives.
- Withdraw lump sums to use as they wish.
- Leave the funds invested in the retirement schemes.

Up to one-third can be withdrawn from the company pension as a lump sum. The private pension assets offer more flexibility. There is the option of using all or part of them to buy a stream of payments (an annuity) while withdrawing the rest as a lump sum. Stein points out that many considerations must be taken into account.

EXAMPLE 12

Addressing longevity risk

Identify an option that would most likely address the Schmitts' concern about outliving their assets.

a   Purchase annuities.

b   Withdraw lump sums.

c   Leave funds invested in the retirement plans.

Solution:

The answer is A. Purchasing annuities would address longevity risk. Annuities involve the purchase of a product that provides a stream of regular income for the rest of the asset owners' lives, regardless of how long they live.

Stein summarizes the key differences between the choice of a lump sum or an annuity:

- With a lump sum withdrawal for the purposes of retirement income, beneficiaries take the longevity risk. The payout is the same regardless of how long they live. This approach normally poses the risk of outliving one's assets. An annuity, instead, is paid for the main beneficiary's entire lifetime, often with residual rights for the spouse (or even children, if below a certain age).
- Ordinary retirement fixed-payment annuities guarantee a nominal amount of regular income. Given the Schmitts' concern about inflation reducing the purchasing power of annuity income, they should consider buying an annuity whose amount is annually adjusted by the inflation index. The drawback is the initial cost, which she estimates would result in them receiving a 4.5% annuity yield instead of 5%.
- The tax treatment of lump sum withdrawals and pension payments varies across jurisdictions. In Eurolandia, lump sums of up to 25% of the total pension plan value can be withdrawn tax free.
- The lump sum payment is final when it occurs. If relevant, any tax arising is also finalized and paid at the same time. With a regular pension, the tax liability cannot be fully estimated in advance because of changes in tax rules and rates. Applicable rules would also change if the Schmitts were to move to another jurisdiction.
- The entitlement to an annuity payment exposes the beneficiary to counterparty risk arising from the provider's inability to honor its obligations.

The relative pretax valuation of a lump sum and the corresponding annuity payment calculation can be performed on the basis of the relevant interest rate curve and life expectancy (including that of any remaining beneficiaries, after the death of the main payee). Stein notes that a number of annuity providers exist on the Eurolandia market and they offer what are considered to be fairly valued annuities. Stein calculates that, on a before-tax basis, the annuity will be more favorable if the Schmitts live past 83 years of age.

With regard to any amounts (of pension fund assets) not used to purchase an annuity, they express preference for a lump sum payment of their pension as opposed to leaving the funds invested in the scheme. This is because of favorable tax treatment of lump sum withdrawals and also because they feel they would have more control of the withdrawn funds, providing them with flexibility. On that note they remind their advisor of their wish to help their daughter Roxane with her planned purchase of a property.

The Schmitts are considering also moving to a sunnier and lower-tax country. In Eurolandia, as in nearly all countries, tax liability depends on tax residence.[2] Some countries offer tax-free status, under certain conditions, to retirees moving there, at least for a certain number of years. One such country is Euromediter, a hypothetical country in the Eurozone.

---

[2] The United States is the most notable exception, because US citizens are liable for US taxes regardless of where they reside.

10 INCOME AND INVESTMENT PORTFOLIO RECOMMENDATIONS: RETIREMENT STAGE

h recommend and justify a plan to manage risks to an individual's retirement lifestyle goals

Stein compares the Schmitts' current, pre-retirement income with what they will be receiving from the government pension, the employer's occupational scheme, and the private pension plans. The objective is to provide the Schmitts with regular, inflation-protected income that is sufficient to fund their current level of expenditure of €70,000. This comparison should help determine how much of the pension plan values need to be converted to annuities, as well as what amount can then be withdrawn as lump sum or simply left in the scheme. Stein presents the Schmitts with the proposals shown in Exhibit 24:

Exhibit 24 Retirement Income Proposal

	€
State pension Jessica	28,200
State pension Paul	48,950
Total pretax income from state pension	**77,150**
Annuity purchased using 75% of Jessica's company pension plan	11,800
Annuity purchased using 75% of Paul's private pension plan	4,600
Total pretax income from pensions/annuities	**93,600**
Less tax	21,600
After-tax income	**72,000**

Note: Assumes 4.5% annuity yield. Purchased annuities would provide inflation protection.

The recommended arrangement would result in the Schmitts relying on the state pension for a large part of their required retirement income. To bring it up to a sufficient level to maintain their current annual expenditures of €70,000 (in real terms), they would need to convert 75% of Jessica's employer's pension plan and 75% of Paul's private pension plan to an annuity that provides annual inflation adjustment. The remaining 25% portions of the two pension plans would be withdrawn as a tax-free lump sum (providing a total one-off sum of €121,250).

The remaining pension plan, Jessica's private pension plan, would not be required to provide retirement income. Stein suggests that 25% of the plan can be withdrawn as a tax-free lump sum of €43,750, with the rest kept invested in the plan.

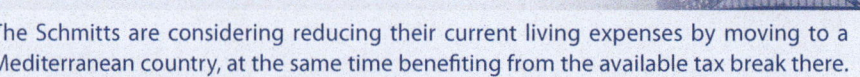

The Schmitts are considering reducing their current living expenses by moving to a Mediterranean country, at the same time benefiting from the available tax break there. Stein provides them with a number of recommendations.

The prospect of retiring to another country has many financial and non-financial implications. It is necessary to consult with experts before making any decisions that are difficult or costly to reverse.

a A tax expert with up-to-date country knowledge must assess whether the claimed tax advantages really hold.

b There are estate planning implications, as it must be understood what the applicable laws are (those of the retirement country, those of Eurolandia, or a combination thereof) and the relevant tax regime for estate taxes.

c The option of moving back to Eurolandia, should the Schmitts wish or need to do so at a later stage, must be examined.

d If the target retirement country is not in Eurozone and hence does not use the euro (€), currency risk must be assessed and managed.

e Efficient and inexpensive arrangements must be made for money transfers and currency conversion (if currency conversion is needed).

f Provision of support for Peter must be assessed.

10.1 Investment Portfolio Analysis and Recommendations

The Schmitts ask Stein for her advice regarding their investment portfolio that stands at €1,511,000. They will also be receiving the tax-free pension lump sum of €165,000 while leaving €131,250 invested in Jessica's private pension plan, bringing the aggregate value of funds available to about €1.8 million.

The Schmitts repeat that, having arranged for regular income stream to cover their retirement expenses, the main objectives for the portfolio are to do the following:

- Provide financial assistance for Peter—a top priority.
- Leave an inheritance for the children, particularly Roxane.
- Provide Roxane with a deposit for her house purchase in the very near future.
- Be able to draw on the investment portfolio to cover unexpected expenses or if a need arises—for example, if their pension income fails to keep up with the rising cost of living, not fully captured by the inflation statistics, or to provide support with their health care if such need arises.

Stein first turns her attention to the Schmitts' top-priority goal: care for Peter, described in Exhibit 25.

Exhibit 25

Peter has just turned 27. The Schmitts explain that their current living expenses of €70,000 include about €13,000 in costs related to the support for Peter. That amount is expected to increase to €35,000 in nominal terms in about 10 years because the Schmitts believe that from that age, they will be unable to provide him with the support they currently provide. That amount is expected to remain broadly unchanged (in real terms) for the rest of Peter's life. It would supplement the support he is and will be receiving from the state. Stein calculates the present value of such contribution to support Peter and arrives at an approximate PV figure of €800,000.

Stein then asks the Schmitts about their investment preferences and willingness to bear risk, beyond what they stated as their top priority: Peter's long-term care.
Paul and Jessica explain that they:

- do not want to see their overall investment portfolio fall in value by more than 20% in any given year;
- wish to invest in instruments that can easily be liquidated, because they like to feel that they are in control;

- worry about inflation despite Eurolandia's stability; and
- do not wish to invest in real estate funds.

Stein points out that because their retirement income covers their current needs, the Schmitts have more room to take risk than other couples who require investment income to supplement their pension and fund ordinary living expenses. Their risk tolerance is limited, however, by their requirement that the portfolio as a whole not suffer a loss of more than 20% in a given year even in the case of a market crash. Stein also points out that real estate funds can provide a degree of protection against inflation.

10.2 The Advisor's Recommendations for Investment Portfolio in Retirement

Having considered the Schmitts' financial circumstances, goals, risk tolerances, and preferences, Stein uses her firm's asset allocation tools that are based on the firm's capital markets expectations, assumptions about asset class volatility, and correlation between asset classes. She suggests the following asset allocation to the Schmitts:

- An allocation to international equities and Eurolandia equities of around 35% and 10%, respectively. This allocation would constitute the "risky" part of the portfolio.
- Allocation of 55% to less risky assets, of which they should aim to have 45% in inflation-linked bond funds and 10% in corporate bond funds.

Exhibit 26 summarizes their goals and Stein's investment recommendations.

Exhibit 26 Goals and Investment Portfolio as the Schmitts Enter Retirement

Existing Assets	Current Allocation	Goals	Time Horizon	Recommended Asset Allocation
Liquid funds (cash proceeds from pension lump sum)	€165,000	Help Roxane with property purchase deposit	<1 year	Keep funds in cash
Investment portfolio for long-term goals				
Inflation-protected government bond funds	€380,000	Care for Peter (PV of €800,000)	10 years	Inflation-protected government bonds 45% (€739,000)
Corporate bond funds	€370,000	Inheritance for Roxane (amount unspecified) and funding for unexpected expenses	Up to 25 years	Corporate bond funds 10% (€164,000)
Passively managed equity funds	€750,000			Global equities 35% (€575,000), including the actively managed equity funds in Jessica's private pension plan
Jessica's private pension plan	€131,250			Eurolandia equities 10% (€164,000)
Total	Approximately €1.8 million			

Note: In addition to these holdings, the Schmitts keep a cash balance of €85,000 in their bank account and do not expect this to change.

Stein notes that her suggested asset mix requires a further switch into inflation-linked government bond funds. She recommends that the necessary reallocation be implemented with capital gains tax implications in mind. Stein also points out that the portfolio's expected return would be higher if the Schmitts dropped their requirement of limiting the maximum drawdown to 20%, thereby allowing a higher allocation to risky assets.

SUMMARY

This case study follows a family from the early career to the retirement stage. It touches on a small and simplified selection of a wide range of issues and considerations that a family may face. A great range of skills and competencies is required to provide financial advice, ranging from the ability to conduct in-depth risk analysis, all the way to making recommendations on risk mitigation strategies, including the choice of insurance products, to perform asset allocation, tax optimization, retirement planning, and estate planning. All of this must be done with a clear understanding of the applicable legal environment and of the level of access and the cost of accessing financial products. In practice, it is very unlikely that a single financial professional can master all the foregoing competencies. The key to success is to understand at what point the generalist needs to bring in, or refer the client to, a subject matter expert.

In this case study:

- We identify and analyze the Schmitts' risk exposures. We observed that the types of risk exposure change substantially from the early career stage to the early retirement stage. We conducted the analysis holistically, starting from the economic balance sheet, including human capital.
- We recommend and justify methods to manage the Schmitt family's risk exposures at different stages of their professional life. We use insurance, self-insurance, and adjustments to their investment portfolio.
- We prepare summaries of the Schmitts' risk exposures and the selected methods of managing those risk exposures.
- We recommend and justify modifications to the Schmitts' life and disability insurance at different stages of the income earners' lives.
- Finally, we recommend a justified a plan to manage risk to the Schmitts' retirement lifestyle goals.

PRACTICE PROBLEMS

The following information relates to Questions 1–2

Recently married, Jennifer and Ron Joseph live in the United States. Jennifer, age 26, and Ron, age 28, both earned master's degrees in the high-demand field of computer science. The young couple are in their early career stage and have combined savings of $50,000 with no other financial assets.

Both Jennifer and Ron are in good health and have been working for a few years. Ron works in the private sector as a programmer for a large information technology company, and Jennifer works in the state sector as a public high school teacher. Jennifer benefits from excellent job security with limited earnings risk from unemployment; however, any salary increases over time are expected to be modest. In contrast, Ron faces significant uncertainties in his future employment income, although he could benefit from significant upside in income if he and his employer achieve performance targets.

The Josephs seek financial advice and ask Jeff Berger, a long-time adviser to Ron's parents, to plan a wealth management strategy. Berger explains the concept of an economic balance sheet and the importance of the value of human capital in meeting their financial objectives.

1. **Discuss** key factors that affect the value of the Josephs' human capital.

Berger is concerned about possible financial difficulties for the surviving spouse in the event of the other's premature death. He advises the Josephs to consider mitigating this risk by purchasing life insurance policies.

Berger suggests using the needs analysis method to determine the required insurance amount. He first estimates cash needs for Jennifer and Ron and then estimates that the surviving spouse would live until age 85 and require $35,000 annually for living expenses, and that those expenses would increase 2% annually in nominal terms. He assumes a 2.5% discount rate. Berger also estimates the present value of the surviving spouse's salary income until retirement at age 65 for both Jennifer and Ron. Exhibit 1 presents an abbreviated life insurance worksheet.

Exhibit 1 Joseph Family Financial Needs: Life Insurance Worksheet

Cash needs	Ron	Jennifer
Funeral and burial costs plus taxes	$20,000	$20,000
Emergency fund	$15,000	$15,000
Debts to be repaid	$0	$0
Total cash needs	**$35,000**	**$35,000**
Total capital needs	?	?
Total financial needs	?	?

© 2021 CFA Institute. All rights reserved.

Exhibit 1 (Continued)

Capital available:		
Cash and investments	$50,000	$50,000
Total capital available	$50,000	$50,000

Supplemental information:		
PV of surviving spouse's income until retirement at age 65	$748,837 (based on $25,000 starting salary for Jennifer)	$1,304,662 (based on $45,000 starting salary for Ron)

2 **Calculate** the amount of life insurance needs for both Jennifer and Ron individually, based on Berger's assumptions and Exhibit 1.

The following information relates to Questions 3–5

Susan and Robert Hunter, both age 47, live in the United States with their two children, ages 10 and 12. The Hunters both plan to retire at age 67. Susan works as a petroleum engineer at a small oil company, and Robert is a nurse at a local state-owned hospital. The Hunters are saving for retirement and for their children's college education expenses. Susan's annual salary is $135,000 ($90,000 after taxes), and Robert's annual salary is $55,000 ($36,000 after taxes). Their annual household living expenses are $90,000.

The Hunters have $50,000 in their bank account. They also have a stock portfolio consisting of five microcap energy stocks worth around $150,000, which they plan to use to partially fund their retirement needs. The Hunters plan to meet their retirement needs through contributions to pension plans offered by their employers, supplemented by government Social Security income payments starting at age 67. Both contribute 5% of their salaries to their respective defined contribution (DC) plans, but only Susan's company offers a matching contribution up to 10% of her base salary. Susan's DC plan has a current value of $80,000, while Robert's plan has a current value of $40,000. Income and capital gain distributions within the plan are tax free.

The Hunters meet with Helen Chapman seeking financial advice. After reviewing the Hunters' financial objectives, which include funding their retirement and the college education for their two children, Chapman discusses several risks facing the Hunters in their efforts to achieve those objectives.

3 **Evaluate** *each* of the following risks facing the Hunters:
   i. Premature death risk
   ii. Investment portfolio risk
   iii. Risk to their retirement lifestyle goals
   iv. Earnings risk resulting from potential loss of employment

Chapman reviews the Hunters' existing life insurance policies. Susan Hunter informs Chapman that she currently has a life insurance policy of $200,000 and his wife has a life insurance policy of $300,000. Only Susan has life insurance coverage at work, with coverage at two times her annual salary.

Chapman believes that the Hunters' current coverage is insufficient to provide support for their family in the event of a death. She suggests using the human life value method to estimate the amount of life insurance required. Chapman estimates the present value of the pretax income needed to replace after-tax income to be $1,700,000 for Susan and $394,000 for Robert.

4   **Recommend** the additional life insurance the Hunters need. **Justify** your recommendation.

Chapman reviews the Hunters' expected spending needs in retirement and is concerned they will not have saved enough by retirement to support their lifestyle thereafter. Chapman recommends that the Hunters raise their DC plan contributions to 10% of their salaries. The Hunters are reluctant to do so, however, telling Chapman that they would rather save the additional funds to continue building up their bank account balance. The bank account savings are readily accessible compared with the contribution to the DC funds, which will be unavailable until they retire.

5   **Discuss** the advantages of the recommendation made by Chapman.

The following information relates to Question 6

James and Wendy Chang, both age 58, plan to retire in nine years. James is a human resource manager for a large US company with a defined contribution (DC) pension plan to which he regularly contributes. Wendy is a freelance computer programmer who works out of a home-based office. She contributes to a private DC plan. Both expect to start receiving Social Security income benefits when they retire at age 67. Their long-term goal is for a comfortable retirement and to provide an inheritance for their two children. The Changs believe they will need to maintain, in real terms, their current level of spending of $100,000 when they retire.

The Changs meet with their financial adviser, Lucie Timan, to discuss the risks to their retirement lifestyle goal. She estimates their Social Security benefit amounts at age 67. In her estimation calculations, Timan assumes a 25% tax rate and a 3% inflation rate. Based on his estimates, the Changs will have total annual pretax retirement income, including Social Security benefits, of $194,500 when they retire at age 67. The Changs tell Timan that they plan to use their DC plans' balances at age 67 to buy an immediate fixed annuity with no inflation adjustment.

6   **Discuss** how *each* of the following risk factors could affect the Changs' projected retirement income:

   i. inflation risk

   ii. loss of employment

   iii. poor investment returns

SOLUTIONS

1. Human capital, which is the present value of the expected stream of income from employment using a wage-risk adjusted discount rate, is an important and large component of the Josephs' total wealth given that they have combined savings of only $50,000 with no other financial assets.

   The Josephs are richly endowed in human capital because they are both highly educated, trained in a high-demand field of computer science, and are in their career development stage. Further, both have been employed for a few years, accruing valuable working experience.

   The value of human capital is a function of several factors:
   - survival probabilities (usually proxied by mortality tables)
   - current employment income
   - expected annual wage growth
   - the risk-free rate
   - a risk adjustment based on occupational income volatility
   - the expected number of working years

   Both Ron and Jennifer are young and in good health, so their survival probabilities are likely to be in line with mortality tables. Their young age also suggests that the expected number of working years for both Ron and Jennifer is probably in the range of 35–40 years. From a financial point of view, the Josephs' marriage results in human capital diversification. As a civil servant, Jennifer's salary income can be described as being bond-like (excellent job security, modest salary increases, limited earnings risk), whereas Ron's salary income can be best described as being equity-like (significant uncertainties in future employment income with significant potential upside). Therefore, the risk adjustment based on occupational income volatility is likely to be low for Jennifer and high for Ron.

2. The needs analysis method determines the amount of life insurance required by estimating the amount needed to cover the surviving spouse's annual living expenses. It is calculated as the difference between the family's total financial needs (total cash needs plus total capital needs) and total capital available.

   The amount of life insurance coverage that the Josephs require is calculated as follows:

Cash needs	Ron	Jennifer
Funeral and burial costs plus taxes	$20,000	$20,000
Emergency fund	$15,000	$15,000
Debts to be repaid	$0	$0
Total cash needs	$35,000	$35,000

Capital needs		
PV of surviving spouse's $35,000 annual living expenses until death at age 85	$1,798,197	$1,745,354
Less PV of surviving spouse's income until retirement at age 65	$748,837	$1,304,662
Total capital needs	$1,049,360	$440,692
Total financial needs	$1,084,360	$475,692

Capital available:		
Cash and investments	$50,000	$50,000
Total capital available	**$50,000**	**$50,000**
Life insurance needs	**$1,034,360**	**$425,692**

The present value of the surviving spouse's annual living expenses of $35,000 until death at age 85 is determined as the present value of an annuity due. Growth in expenses is incorporated into the calculations by adjusting the discount rate to account for the growth in expenses. The adjusted discount rate is calculated as [(1 + Discount Rate)/(1 + Growth Rate in Expenses)] − 1.

The present value of the surviving spouse's annual living expenses of $35,000 until death at age 85 for Jennifer ($n = 59$) in the case of Ron's death is calculated as follows:

First, adjust the discount rate to account for the growth rate:

Adjusted Discount Rate = (1.025/1.02) − 1 = 0.4902% (rounded up)

Now, setting the calculator for beginning-of-period payments, compute the PV:

$n = 59$

I/Y = 0.4902

PMT = $35,000

CPT PV = $1,798,197

Similarly, the present value of the surviving spouse's annual living expenses of $35,000 until death at age 85 for Ron ($n = 57$) in the case of Jennifer's death is calculated as follows:

Again, setting the calculator for beginning-of-period payments, compute the PV:

$n = 57$

I/Y = 0.4902

PMT = $35,000

CPT PV = $1,745,354

The Josephs' additional life insurance needs are summarized in the following table:

	Ron	Jennifer
Total financial needs	$1,084,360	$475,692
Less: total capital available	$50,000	$50,000
Additional life insurance needs	**$1,034,360**	**$425,692**

Based on the needs analysis method, the Josephs should purchase life insurance policies in the amounts of $1,034,360 and $425,692 on Ron and Jennifer, respectively.

3. **Part i:** Premature death risk is high because the Hunters have two young children, ages 10 and 12, who need to be cared for. The death of a parent would mean that the family's household living expenses, now covered jointly, would fall solely to the surviving spouse. The surviving spouse would potentially suffer a reduction in income because all of the family responsibilities would fall to this

Solutions

individual. Alternatively, the surviving spouse could hire outside help, at a cost. Life insurance would provide support for the children and enable the surviving spouse to better cope with unexpected events.

Part ii: Risk in the retirement portfolio is high. Hunter's investment portfolio lacks diversification because it is concentrated in the energy industry and is represented by small, microcap stocks. Further, the investment in the energy stocks is correlated with Susan's human capital. If prospects in the energy industry deteriorate, both Susan's human capital and the stock portfolio value would likely decline at the same time. Finally, their investment portfolio is also rather modest compared with their spending and income.

Part iii: The key risk here is that the Hunters' retirement income is insufficient to meet the standard of living they desire. This risk arises for two reasons. First, the couple's annual contribution to their pension or private saving plans may be insufficient to generate the required fund balance at retirement. Second, the pension plans might perform poorly, generating returns below those expected. This risk can be somewhat offset by the government Social Security benefits the Hunters can elect to receive when they retire at age 67.

Part iv: Earnings risk resulting from potential loss of employment is significant for the Hunters and particularly relevant for Susan given the nature of his employer's business. Susan has a relatively high salary and works for a small oil company in a highly cyclical and risky industry.

Robert's earnings risk is relatively low, because his salary is lower than Susan's. In addition, he works in a highly stable occupation and would lose employment only under extreme circumstances. A job loss for Robert would be less significant for the family because Susan's annual after-tax income of $90,000 would cover all of the family's yearly expenditures of $90,000.

4. The human life value method is based on the value of human capital and estimates the amount of future earnings that must be replaced. The calculations involve adjusting after-tax income for the amount of annual expenses and value of the person's employee benefits. The amount of pretax income needed to replace the lost income is then estimated and assumed to grow until retirement, reflecting career advancement. For both Susan and Robert, the amount of life insurance required is the PV of an annuity due of their respective future pretax incomes, less any existing life insurance policy amounts. The amount of life insurance coverage required by the Hunters is calculated as follows:

	Susan	Robert
Present value of annuity due of pretax income	$1,700,000	$394,000
Less existing life insurance	$200,000	$300,000
Less existing life insurance at Susan's employer (calculated as $135,000 × 2)	$270,000	
Recommended additional life insurance	$1,230,000	$94,000

In conclusion, the Hunters should increase their life insurance coverage by $1,230,000 for Susan and $94,000 for Robert.

5. Chapman suggests that the Hunters increase their contributions to their DC pension plans. The Hunters are able to do so because they have considerable savings with their combined annual after-tax income of $126,000 being well above their current annual household living expenses of $90,000. The additional contributions total only $9,500 (5% of their combined pretax salaries of

$190,000), and the after-tax effect would be only $6,650 (70% of $9,500). Even after increasing their DC contributions, the Hunters would still be able to save about $30,000 each year.

By increasing the contribution to the DC plans, the Hunters would gain the tax advantage of the DC plans because income and capital gain distributions within the plan are tax free. In addition, Susan Hunter could take advantage of the additional 5% contribution match offered as a benefit by her employer. The expected return on the DC plans would likely be significantly higher than in the highly liquid and low-interest bank account preferred by the Hunters. The increased contribution would build up their investment portfolio and boost retirement savings. Thus, the tax and return advantages of making additional contributions to the DC plans reduces the risk of a shortfall in projected retirement income while also leaving a significant amount of current income available for savings.

6. **Part i:** The Changs are in a good position to maintain their current lifestyle in retirement. Their total annual pretax retirement income of $194,500 will leave them with after-tax income of about $145,875 (given the assumption of a 25% tax rate). This expected after-tax income exceeds the expected nominal level of spending in their retirement year of $130,477 (given the assumption of a 3% inflation rate and nine years until retirement). One particular risk that could affect the Changs' projected retirement income, however, is that inflation may reduce the purchasing power of their after-tax income over time. This risk is of particular concern given the expectation that the retirement plan balances are expected to be used to purchase an annuity with no inflation adjustment. Thus, purchasing the fixed annuity with no inflation adjustment should be reconsidered.

   Part ii: Another risk factor that could adversely affect the Changs' projected retirement income is the potential loss of employment. If James were to lose his job or Wendy's freelance work were to decrease unexpectedly, and they were unable to obtain comparable levels of compensation, their projected retirement income would likely be lower.

   Part iii: A third risk factor that could affect the Changs' projected retirement income is poor investment returns. Lower returns resulting from poor market conditions in the equity and bond markets would adversely impact the Changs' pension fund balances at retirement and likely result in lower retirement income.

READING
30

Integrated Cases in Risk Management: Institutional

by Steve Balaban, CFA, Arjan Berkelaar, PhD, CFA, Nasir Hasan, and Hardik Sanjay Shah, CFA

Steve Balaban, CFA, is at Mink Capital Inc. (Canada). Arjan Berkelaar, PhD, CFA, is at KAUST Investment Management Company (USA). Nasir Hasan is at Ernst & Young (UAE). Hardik Sanjay Shah, CFA, is at GMO LLC (Singapore).

LEARNING OUTCOMES	
Mastery	The candidate should be able to:
☐	a. discuss financial risks associated with the portfolio strategy of an institutional investor;
☐	b. discuss environmental and social risks associated with the portfolio strategy of an institutional investor;
☐	c. analyze and evaluate the financial and non-financial risk exposures in the portfolio strategy of an institutional investor;
☐	d. discuss various methods to manage the risks that arise on long-term direct investments of an institutional investor;
☐	e. evaluate strengths and weaknesses of an enterprise risk management system and recommend improvements.

INTRODUCTION   1

The focus of this reading is a fictional "case study." The case itself will focus on the portfolio of a sovereign wealth fund (SWF) specifically looking at risk in terms of the SWF's long-term investments. There are three Learning Outcome Statements (LOS) within the case. Prior to the case, we provide two LOS outside the case. These LOS will provide some background information that will be helpful to the candidate in understanding the case.

© 2021 CFA Institute. All rights reserved.

2 FINANCIAL RISKS FACED BY INSTITUTIONAL INVESTORS

a   discuss financial risks associated with the portfolio strategy of an institutional investor

2.1 Long-Term Perspective

Institutional investors (also referred to as *asset owners*) such as pension funds, sovereign wealth funds, endowments, and foundations are distinct from other institutional investors such as banks and insurance companies in terms of the time horizon over which they invest their assets. This long-term perspective allows these institutions to take on certain investment risks that other institutional investors simply cannot bear and to invest in in a broad range of alternative asset classes, including private equity, private real estate, natural resources, infrastructure, and hedge funds. This section will focus on the financial risks associated with the portfolio strategy of long-term institutional investors and in particular will focus on investments in illiquid asset classes. Banks and insurance companies are excluded from the discussion because they are typically much more asset/liability focused and face much tighter regulatory constraints to ensure capital adequacy.

This section will not cover the quantitative aspects of risk management or the mechanics behind various risk metrics, such as standard deviation and conditional value at risk, or risk management techniques, such as Monte Carlo simulation and factor modelling. Those topics are covered in other parts of the CFA Program curriculum. Instead, this reading will cover key risk considerations faced by long-term institutional investors as they invest in a range of traditional and alternative asset classes, including private equity and infrastructure. An important distinguishing feature of long-term institutional investors is their ability to invest in illiquid asset classes. Since the late 1990s, such asset classes have become an ever more important part of the investment portfolios of pension funds, sovereign wealth funds, endowments, and foundations. In this reading, we put particular emphasis on the financial risks that emanate from illiquid investments because these risks tend to be least well quantified but can pose an existential threat to long-term investors if not addressed and managed carefully. The focus is on how market and liquidity risk interact to create potential challenges at the overall portfolio level and affect the institutional investor's ability to meet its long-term objectives.

Section 2.2 briefly discusses the various lenses through which risk management can be viewed. Risk management is a very broad topic, and the goal is to simply provide the reader with a frame of reference. Section 2.3 focuses on the key financial risks that institutional investors face. The focus is on portfolio-level, top-down, long-term financial risk. Risk management for long-term institutional investors should primarily be concerned with events that may jeopardize the organization's ability to meet its long-term objectives. The interaction between market and liquidity risk plays a critical role. In Section 2.4 we discuss the challenges associated with investing in illiquid asset classes from a risk management perspective. We discuss two important aspects of illiquid asset classes: the uncertainty of cash flows and return-smoothing behavior in the return pattern. Section 2.5 describes how institutional investors address and manage liquidity risk at the overall portfolio level.

2.2 Dimensions of Financial Risk Management

The aim of risk management is to avoid an existential threat to the organization. In other words, risk management should focus on what types of events can jeopardize the organization's ability to meet its long-term objectives. Existential threats can arise from both financial risks (e.g., market losses and liquidity risk in the form of the inability to meet cash flows) and non-financial risks (e.g., reputational risks). In this reading, we solely focus on financial risk. Financial risk needs to be viewed through multiple lenses. There is no simple template to financial risk management. It is not simply a matter of calculating, for example, the value at risk of a portfolio. There are several dimensions to sound financial risk management, and we cover them briefly in the following subsections. Our goal is to simply provide a frame of reference for the reader because risk management is a very broad topic.

2.2.1 Top-down vs. bottom-up risk analysis

Risk management requires both a top-down and a bottom-up perspective. From a top-down perspective, the board and chief investment officer (CIO) set overall risk guidelines for the portfolio that serve as guardrails within which the investment team is expected to operate. Risk management involves measuring, monitoring, and reporting portfolio results versus the guidelines. The investment team is tasked with implementing the overall investment strategy either through hiring external asset managers or by directly purchasing and managing securities and assets. The investment team takes a more bottom-up, sub-portfolio approach to managing the risks of each individual portfolio or asset class, while assessing and monitoring their interaction and impact on the risk level of the overall portfolio.

2.2.2 Portfolio-level risk vs. asset-class-specific risk

Although risk management for an institutional investor is ultimately about controlling overall portfolio-level risk, risks also need to be managed and controlled at the asset-class or strategy level so that no particular asset class or strategy will have an undue adverse effect on the overall portfolio. Different asset classes require different risk management techniques. Some risk metrics and methods make sense for publicly traded asset classes, but they may not be meaningful when assessing the risk of, for example, illiquid asset classes or hedge fund investments. For some asset classes, such as public equities, detailed security-level information might be available, whereas for other asset classes, such as hedge funds, only monthly manager returns may be available. In the case of a public equity portfolio, risk analysis might be very granular and rely on sophisticated factor models, whereas risk analysis for hedge fund investments might simply involve calculating the historical volatility of observed returns. Because of differences in data transparency, data frequency, and risk methods used, it is difficult—if not impossible—to aggregate these results at the overall portfolio level. It is not uncommon for institutional investors to have an overall risk management system for portfolio-wide risk metrics in addition to asset-class-specific systems or approaches that provide a more in-depth risk view tailored to a particular asset class.

2.2.3 Return-based vs. holdings-based risk approaches

Financial risk management systems are typically described as being return based (risk estimation relies on the historical return streams of an external manager or a portfolio of securities) or holdings based (risk estimation relies on individual security holdings and the historical returns of those securities in the portfolio). Both approaches have their pros and cons, and they are not mutually exclusive. Return-based systems are relatively easy to implement but may produce risk estimates that are biased because they rely on past returns from a strategy that may be very different today compared with, for example, five years ago. Holdings-based risk systems, in contrast, tend to be more costly and time-consuming to implement. For many institutional investors that invest in hedge funds and illiquid asset classes, holdings-based risk systems for the entire portfolio are typically not feasible because of a lack of transparency on holdings and their related investment strategy (a multi-strategy fund may maintain a long position in a security within one strategy book and a short position in another strategy book), data being available with a one-month to three-month lag, and significant turnover in certain types of hedge fund investments.

2.2.4 Absolute vs. relative risk

Investors are interested in both absolute risk and relative risk. Absolute risk concerns the potential for overall losses and typically relies on overall portfolio-level metrics, such as standard deviation, conditional value at risk, and maximum drawdown. Relative risk concerns underperformance versus policy benchmarks and relies on such metrics as tracking error (the standard deviation of returns relative to a benchmark).

2.2.5 Long-term vs. short-term risk metrics

Modern risk systems used by institutional investors typically focus on calculating volatility, value at risk, and conditional value at risk using sophisticated risk factor techniques. Given the heavy reliance on the current portfolio composition and the granular modeling of each component in the portfolio, these risk systems are most useful in providing an estimate for the potential for near-term losses. Institutional investors are also interested in calculating longer-term risks, such as the probability of losses, the probability of not being able to meet cash flows, and the probability of maintaining purchasing power or meeting a certain return target over longer time periods, such as 5 years, 10 years, 20 years, and so forth.

These long-term risk metrics are typically calculated using Monte Carlo simulation, where asset-class returns are simulated on the basis of a set of forward-looking capital market assumptions (typically expected returns, volatilities, and correlations) and total assets are calculated including cash flows, such as benefit payments and contributions in the case of pension funds and payouts (spending amounts) in case of endowments and foundations. These methods, although typically much less granular than a risk management system, are better able to incorporate future portfolio changes, different rebalancing methods, and cash flows.

2.2.6 Quantitative vs. qualitative risks

At the end of the day, risk management is not simply a quantitative endeavor. Quantitative risk management techniques are backward looking by nature and typically parametric (i.e., they rely on historical data to estimate parameters). Although history can serve as a guide, it does not provide a prediction of the future. Risk management is about assessing the potential for future losses, and quantitative tools need to be complemented with qualitative assessments. However, with qualitative assessments, it is important for risk managers to be aware of their own biases because they are basing these assessments on their own past experience. Thus, it is important for risk managers to recognize and mitigate the backward-looking bias in both quantitative (explicit) and qualitative (implicit) risk analysis.

2.2.7 Pre- and post-investment risk assessment

Finally, although risk management efforts typically focus on measuring the risks of existing investments, a sound risk management philosophy ensures a proper assessment of financial risks prior to making investments. Institutional investors typically put a lot of effort into operational and investment due diligence prior to making investments. In addition to analyzing past investment performance, it is critical when hiring external managers to evaluate the character of the key decision makers, the business ethics of the firm, the investment experience of the team, the quality of operations (such as accounting and trade settlements), and the risk management practices of the external manager. As part of their investment due diligence, institutional investors also look at the quality of the non-executive directors of the fund, the integrity and independence of external auditors, fee structures, master fund and feeder fund structure, custodians, and safekeeping on assets. These considerations are even more important for illiquid investments because it is very difficult to exit from them (investors cannot easily change their mind). After investing, risk management might take on a more quantitative role, but continued due diligence and monitoring are of equal importance. In the case of external managers, this obligation resides with the team responsible for the hiring and firing of the managers. In the case of internal management, an in-house risk management team may be tasked with the ongoing due-diligence and monitoring responsibilities.

The various risk dimensions we have described should provide a sense of the wide-ranging nature of risk management as a discipline. For this reading, we focus exclusively on the key financial risks that long-term institutional investors face. We take a portfolio-level, top-down perspective and are primarily concerned with how illiquid asset classes and the interaction between market and liquidity risk affect an institutional investor's ability to meet its long-term objectives. This risk is unique to long-term institutional investors. The next section will provide a more in-depth description of this risk.

2.3 Risk Considerations for Long-Term Investors

Long-term institutional investors have the ability to invest a significant part of their portfolio in risky and illiquid assets because of their long-term investment horizon and relatively low liquidity needs. The past two decades have seen a steady increase in the allocation to illiquid asset classes, such private equity, private real estate, and infrastructure, by pension funds, sovereign wealth funds, endowments, and foundations. These asset classes create unique risk management challenges and can pose an existential threat if the risks are not addressed and managed carefully. As stated before, the ultimate objective of risk management is to ensure that the organization survives and can meet its long-term objectives.

We start with briefly describing and reviewing the main objectives of long-term institutional investors and their key risk considerations. Exhibit 1 provides an overview by institutional investor type. The ultimate risk consideration for each of these institutional investors is their ability to meet the payouts that they were set up to provide. This risk is largely affected by how the overall investment portfolio performs over time. On the one hand, a very low-risk portfolio that consists primarily of fixed-income investments is unlikely to cause a problem in providing the required payouts in the short run but will almost certainly jeopardize the organization's ability to provide the required payouts in the long run. On the other hand, a very risky and illiquid portfolio is expected to provide high expected returns in the long run but could cause significant pain in the short run during a significant market downturn or financial crisis. Long-term institutional investors aim to strike the right balance between these two extremes in designing their investment policy or strategic asset allocation.

Exhibit 1 Objectives and Risk Considerations by Institutional Investor Type

Institutional Investor	Main Objective	Key Risk Consideration
Pension funds	Provide retirement income to plan participants	Inability to meet pension payouts to beneficiaries
Sovereign wealth funds	Varies by type of SWF but most have been set up to provide some future financial support to the government	Inability to provide financial support to the government
Endowments and Foundations	Provide financial support in perpetuity while maintaining intergenerational equity	Inability to provide financial support to the institution or to the mission

This process usually involves a Monte Carlo simulation exercise where asset-class returns are simulated on the basis of a set of forward-looking capital market assumptions and total assets are calculated including cash flows, such as benefit payments and contributions in the case of pension funds and payouts (spending amounts) in the case of endowments and foundations. Monte Carlo simulation allows institutional investors to calculate such metrics as the probability of maintaining purchasing power and the probability of a certain loss or drawdown (e.g., 25%) over a specific time period (e.g., 5 or 10 years) and to determine the appropriate trade-off between two such metrics. What is often ignored in this type of analysis, however, is the important interaction between potential market losses and liquidity. Pension funds, SWFs, endowments, and foundations are unique in that they can often tolerate significantly more market and liquidity risk than other investors. Their long-term investment horizon allows them to survive a significant market correction and even operate in a counter-cyclical way during a market crisis. As institutional investors invest more in such illiquid asset classes as private equity, private real estate, and infrastructure, however, their ability to tolerate market losses may diminish.

Institutional investors need liquidity to meet payouts (retirement payments in the case of pension plans, payouts to the university or foundation in the case of endowments and foundations, etc.), meet capital calls on their illiquid investments, and rebalance their portfolios. During a significant market downturn, these needs can become stretched and impact the institution's ability to meet cash flows, particularly if a large part of the portfolio is invested in illiquid asset classes, such as private equity, real estate, and infrastructure. Exhibit 2 shows the main liquidity needs and the main sources of liquidity for long-term institutional investors. Each of these liquidity needs and sources may be adversely affected during a financial crisis.

Exhibit 2 Liquidity Needs and Sources for Institutional Investors

Liquidity Needs	Liquidity Sources
Outflows (e.g., pension payouts to beneficiaries, university payouts, and financial support to the government)	Inflows (e.g., pension contributions, gifts, donations, government savings)
Capital calls for illiquid investments	Distributions from illiquid investments

Exhibit 2 (Continued)	
Liquidity Needs	**Liquidity Sources**
Portfolio rebalancing	Investment income and proceeds from selling liquid asset classes (cash, fixed income, public equities)

We first start with discussing how liquidity needs may increase during a crisis. First, payouts might increase as the beneficiary requires additional financial support. For example, a university may need additional funds from its endowment to support its operations as other sources of income dry up, or a government might require additional financial support from the sovereign wealth fund to mitigate the crisis situation. Second, there might be an acceleration of capital calls as attractive investment opportunities present themselves during a crisis. Finally, rebalancing flows will be more significant during a crisis because of significant market movements. Good governance and best practice suggest that investors rebalance their portfolios at regular intervals. Sticking to rebalancing practices is particularly important during a financial crisis because failure to rebalance may prevent investors from fully participating in the rebound after the crisis.

Having discussed how the needs for liquidity may increase during a significant market downturn, we next turn to how sources of liquidity might dry up under those circumstances. First, inflows might decrease in a crisis. For example, donors might be struggling financially and donate less to their alma mater, or plan sponsors might be faced with budgetary challenges and, therefore, less inclined to contribute to the pension fund. Second, distributions from illiquid investments might be reduced because there are no attractive exit points due to depressed prices or lower profitability. Finally, investments that are otherwise liquid might become less liquid or simply undesirable to exit from. The main sources of liquidity during a financial crisis are typically cash and fixed-income investments. And most long-term institutional investors hold relatively low allocations to cash and fixed income in their portfolios.

Illiquid asset classes (such as private equity, real estate, and infrastructure) are not available to meet liquidity needs during a crisis. These asset classes cannot be rebalanced or redeemed because they are long term in nature and the assets can be locked up for 5–10 years or even longer. Semi-liquid asset classes, such as hedge fund investments, should not be expected to be liquid and available to meet liquidity needs during a financial crisis because many of these managers might impose redemption gates or have lockups in place or their investments might turn out to be less liquid than anticipated. Finally, although public equity investments are technically liquid, investors may be reluctant to sell part of their public equity portfolio to meet liquidity needs because the market value of these investments may have gone down significantly in a crisis. In addition, investors might not want to redeem from certain active external managers, even if the investments are liquid, because it may impact the future relationship with that manager (particularly for high-demand active managers with limited available capacity).

In conclusion, the main risk that long-term institutional investors face is having insufficient liquidity during a significant market downturn to meet their obligations and rebalance their portfolios. Liquidity needs tend to increase in a crisis while sources of liquidity dry up. This risk increases as institutional investors allocate more to illiquid asset classes. The combination of financial losses and not being able to meet cash flows or rebalance the portfolio because of insufficient liquidity can become a matter of survival. Managing this risk is, therefore, very important for long-term institutional investors. In the next section, we will discuss in more detail the risks associated with illiquid asset classes. In Section 2.5, we will discuss the various ways in which institutional managers manage liquidity risk.

2.4 Risks Associated with Illiquid Asset Classes

Illiquid asset classes, such as private equity, real estate, and infrastructure, offer the potential for returns in excess of those on publicly traded asset classes, such as public equity and fixed income. The higher expected return of these asset classes comes at a cost to investors in the form of illiquidity. Illiquid asset classes are typically subject to a drawdown structure where committed capital is called at an unknown schedule and investors receive profits at an unknown schedule. As a result, investors need to hold sufficient liquid assets to meet capital calls from their private fund managers. The uncertain pattern of cash flows poses both a liquidity and a risk management challenge for investors in illiquid asset classes.

In addition to the importance of adequately managing liquidity needs when investing in illiquid assets, these asset classes tend to be subject to stale pricing, appraisal-based valuations, and a lagged response to movements in public markets. As a result, illiquid asset classes exhibit returns that are smooth, understating the true volatility and correlation with publicly traded asset classes. For example, the standard deviation of observed returns for private equity is often smaller than that of public equity. Although this feature may be appealing for institutional investors, it causes traditional asset allocation models, such as mean–variance optimization, to over-allocate to private asset classes because the Sharpe ratios of observed returns are superior to those of publicly traded asset classes.

Finally, illiquid asset classes cannot be rebalanced easily and costlessly. Although investors could potentially, for example, sell their private equity stakes in the secondary market, this cannot be done instantaneously and investors may have to accept a significantly lower price compared with the true market value.

2.4.1 Cash flow modeling

Illiquid asset classes are subject to a drawdown structure. The investor (typically the limited partner, or LP, in the partnership agreement) commits capital, and this capital gets drawn down over time at the discretion of the general partner, or GP. Investors need to figure out both the commitment strategy (i.e., how much to commit each year) to reach a certain target allocation to illiquid assets and the liquidity needs to meet capital calls when required. Committing too much can pose severe liquidity risk because the percentage allocation to illiquid asset classes may soar due to the so-called denominator effect (total assets under management, or AUM, falls by a larger amount than the repricing of illiquid asset classes). Committing too little may prevent the investor from reaching the target allocation and may result in falling short of return expectations.

In managing liquidity needs and determining the appropriate commitment strategy to illiquid asset classes, investors need to be able to predict future cash flows.

2.4.2 Addressing return smoothing behavior of illiquid asset classes

To calculate the true underlying economic risks of illiquid asset classes as part of their risk management efforts, institutional investors typically use one of two approaches: (1) Use public market proxies in place of private asset classes—for example, use small-cap public equities as a proxy for private equity—or (2) unsmooth observed returns of private asset classes. The objective of the latter is to remove the serial correlation structure of the original return series. The implicit assumption is that the serial correlations in reported returns are entirely due to the smoothing behavior funds engage in when reporting results. A common and simple technique to unsmooth the returns of illiquid asset classes and hedge funds is a method developed by Geltner (1993) to address appraisal-based valuations in real estate. The method proposed by Geltner removes only the first-order serial correlation in observed returns. Okunev and White (2003) extended the method of Geltner (1993) to include higher-order serial correlations. An alternative to the Geltner method is the GLM method proposed by Getmansky, Lo, and Makarov (2004). They assumed that observed returns for illiquid asset classes and hedge funds follow a moving-average process.

To show the effect of these different methods on the annualized volatility of various illiquid asset classes, we use quarterly historical returns for global buyouts, global venture capital, global private real estate, and global private natural resources for the period from Q1 1990 until Q4 2019. Exhibit 3 shows the annualized volatility of the observed returns and the volatility of adjusted returns using the three methods briefly discussed earlier. For the Okunev–White and GLM methods, we use up to four lags. Exhibit 4 shows the beta to global equity returns. For global equity returns, we use quarterly returns for the MSCI World Index from 1990 to 2019.

Exhibit 3   Impact of Unsmoothing on Annualized Volatility

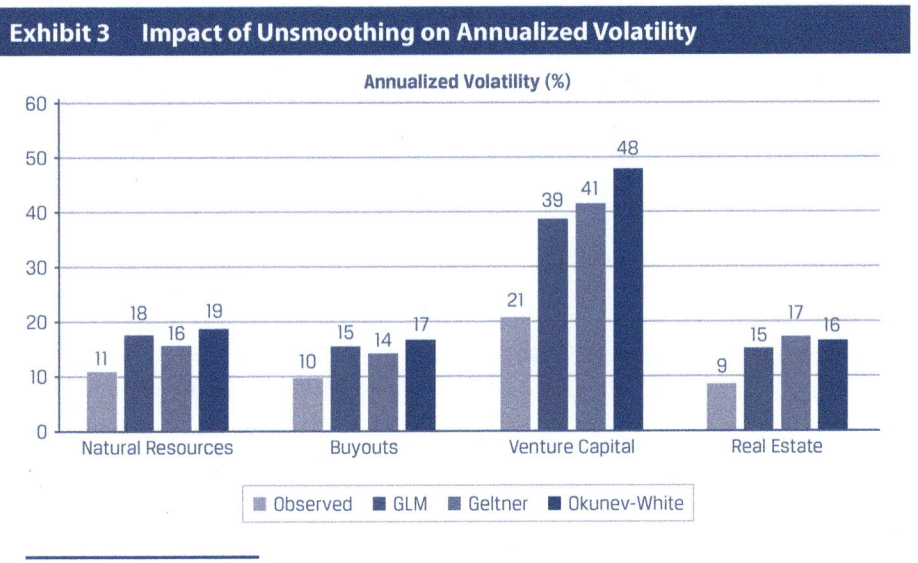

Source: Data is from Cambridge Associates.

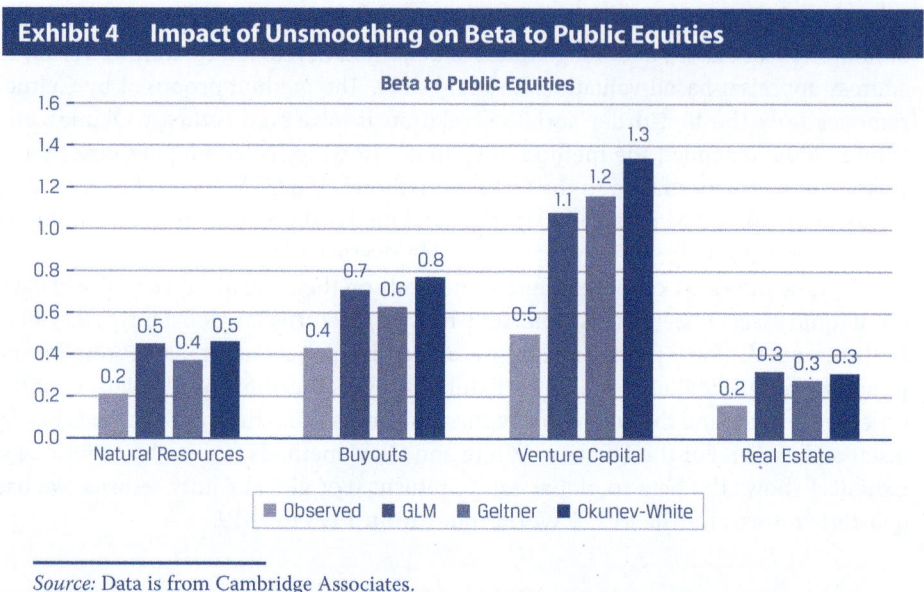

Exhibit 4 Impact of Unsmoothing on Beta to Public Equities

Observed ▪ GLM ▪ Geltner ▪ Okunev-White

Source: Data is from Cambridge Associates.

As illustrated in Exhibits 3 and 4, after applying unsmoothing techniques, the resulting returns exhibit higher volatility and are typically more correlated with public equity markets. These unsmoothed return series can then be used along with returns on publicly traded asset classes to determine the covariance matrix to be used in a mean–variance optimization exercise when determining the appropriate allocation to illiquid asset classes and hedge funds. Mean–variance optimization, however, still falls short as an adequate asset allocation tool for institutional investors because it is not able to take into account the illiquid nature of some asset classes. Illiquid asset classes cannot be rebalanced easily without a potential significant price concession. Single-period optimization methods, such as mean–variance optimization, fail when illiquid asset classes are introduced, because such techniques implicitly assume that investors keep portfolio weights constant over time (i.e., portfolio weights are rebalanced perfectly) and they ignore the drawdown structure of illiquid asset classes and the uncertainty of cash flows. Currently, there are not any widely accepted alternatives. Most investors simply constrain the allocations to illiquid asset classes in the mean–variance optimization to achieve reasonable and practical portfolios.

2.4.3 Direct vs. fund investments in illiquid asset classes

In recent years, large pension funds and sovereign wealth funds have increasingly opted to invest directly in illiquid asset classes rather than through the more typical limited partner (LP)–general partner (GP) setup. Some large pension funds and SWFs have built up a large team of merchant banking professionals who are equally capable as a large private equity fund team. The main motivation behind such a move is to save on the high fees that institutional investors typically pay to GPs (2% base fee on committed capital and 20% fee on profits or over a certain hurdle rate). Being able to save on these fees should make the investments more profitable over the long term. Direct investments provide an institutional investor with control over each individual investment. This situation puts the investor in a better position to manage liquidity. In the case of direct investments, there are no unfunded commitments, making it easier to manage capital. The investor also has full discretion over the decision when to exit investments and will not have to be forced to sell in a down market. As a result, direct investments partially alleviate some of the liquidity challenges typically associated with private asset classes and resolve some of the principal–agent issues associated with fund investing.

There are also disadvantages to direct investments in private asset classes. Direct investments in private equity, real estate, or infrastructure require a dedicated and experienced in-house team. In some instances, rather than building out an in-house team for private investments, large pension funds and sovereign wealth funds acquire a general partner. For example, Ontario Teachers' Pension Plan purchased Cadillac Fairview, a large operating company for real estate. Managing and assembling an in-house team adds several challenges compared with the more nimble setup in the case of fund investing. The sourcing of deals may be constrained by the talent and network of the in-house team. As a result, it may be more difficult to diversify the portfolio across geography and industries. Direct investment portfolios may have higher concentration risk because direct investors opt for larger investments due to staffing issues and scalability. This risk could adversely affect the liquidity of these investments because they might be harder to sell and, therefore, potentially less liquid. If the investor relies on external managers for deal sourcing or a partnership agreement, there is a risk of adverse selection. Finally, the governance structure is not set up as well in the case of direct investing compared with fund investments. In contrast to fund managers, employees of a pension fund or sovereign wealth fund may not be able to sit on the board of a private company. Institutional investors may not be able to afford the liability issues associated with direct investing. For fund investments, the investor is a limited partner and has limited liability, whereas with direct investments, the investor may be considered a general partner, with additional liability risks. Finally, institutional investors may find it difficult to adequately compensate internal staff to ensure that they hire and retain talent. This is usually a problem for public pension funds because there is public pressure to keep compensation down.

2.5 Managing Liquidity Risk

In this section, we discuss some of the tools used by institutional investors to manage overall liquidity risk in their portfolios.

Liquidity management steps:

1 **Establish liquidity risk parameters.**

    Institutional investors typically create liquidity guidelines regarding what percentage of assets needs to be liquid and available on a daily or monthly basis. In addition, given the drawdown structure of illiquid asset classes, institutional investors need to keep track of uncalled commitments, not simply invested capital. It is typical for institutional investors to have internal guidelines or bands around the sum of invested capital and uncalled commitments as a percentage of total assets. In addition to such bands, they may have automatic or semiautomatic escalation triggers, such as reducing commitments to illiquid asset classes or even actively seeking to reduce investments through secondary sales once the sum of invested capital plus uncalled commitments reaches a certain level (expressed as a percentage of total assets). These liquidity risk parameters can either be internal or be included in an investment policy statement approved by the board.

2 **Assess the liquidity of the current portfolio and how it evolves over time.**

    The second step in managing liquidity risk at the overall portfolio level is to have a clear sense of the liquidity of the portfolio and measure liquidity parameters versus guidelines. Most institutional investors have an internal report that shows what percentage of the portfolio can be liquidated within a day, within a week, within a month, within a quarter, and within a year and what percentage of the portfolio takes more than a year to be liquidated. It is important not only to have a snapshot of that report at a given point in time but also to understand how it evolves over time as the portfolio changes. A good starting point for developing these statistics is to simply look at the legal terms that are in place with external managers. This is particularly relevant for active managers and hedge funds that have redemption notices and lockups included in the investment agreement. In the case of internal management, an even more granular assessment can be made depending on the types of securities being held and using market liquidity measures to gauge how much of these securities can be sold over different time frames during a financial crisis. As discussed in Section 2.3, investors may also want to take into account how redeeming from certain external managers during a crisis may impact the future relationship with that manager (in other words, they may not want to redeem even if the investments are liquid and instead include these investments in a less liquid category).

3 Develop a cash flow model and project future expected cash flows.

The third step is to understand and model the various cash flows. As discussed in Section 2.3, institutional investors make payouts (retirement payments, foundation spending, etc.), they receive inflows (gifts and donations for an endowment, pension contributions for a pension plan, etc.), they have to meet capital calls for illiquid asset classes and receive distributions, and they have to rebalance their portfolios. Most institutional investors model each of those cash flows and project future expected cash flows. Section 2.4 briefly discussed how capital calls and distributions are modeled for illiquid asset classes.

4 Stress test liquidity needs and cash flow projections.

The standard cash flow modeling and projections assume business as usual, but it is important to stress test these cash flow projections and liquidity needs. As discussed in Section 2.4, cash flows are affected by market movements. For example, donations might be lower in a crisis and payouts might be higher. Institutional investors stress test their cash flow projections and liquidity needs. It is important to point out that this process is more of an art than a science and there is no universally accepted method for stress testing (as there are universally accepted methods for market risk calculations).

5 Put in place an emergency plan.

Finally, institutional investors should put in place an emergency action plan. Such an action plan should include what to liquidate—and in what order—in a crisis to meet cash flows and how to rebalance the portfolio in a crisis. Having such a plan in place can help avoid the risk of panicking in a crisis. Sharing the emergency action plan with the board to get buy-in can also help when a crisis occurs and mitigate the risk of board members pressuring the investment team to make sub-optimal short-term decisions.

Exhibit 5 summarizes the five steps in developing a liquidity management plan.

Exhibit 5   Liquidity Management Steps

1 Establish liquidity risk parameters.
2 Assess the liquidity of current portfolio, and monitor the evolution over time.
3 Develop a cash flow model and project future cash flows.
4 Stress test liquidity needs and cash flow projections.
5 Develop an emergency action plan.

Financial Risks Faced by Institutional Investors

Long-term institutional investors are able take on certain investment risks that other institutional investors simply cannot bear. Since the late 1990s, they have increasingly invested in a broad range of alternative asset classes, including private equity, private real estate, natural resources, infrastructure, and hedge funds. In this reading, we focus on the financial risks that emanate from illiquid investments because these risks tend to be less well quantified but can pose an existential threat to long-term investors if not addressed and managed carefully. The focus has been on how market and liquidity risk interact to create potential challenges at the overall portfolio level and affect the institutional investor's ability to meet its long-term objectives. We propose several steps institutional investors can take to better manage liquidity at the overall portfolio level.

2.6 Enterprise Risk Management for Institutional Investors

Exhibit 6 provides a high-level view of a risk management framework in an enterprise context:

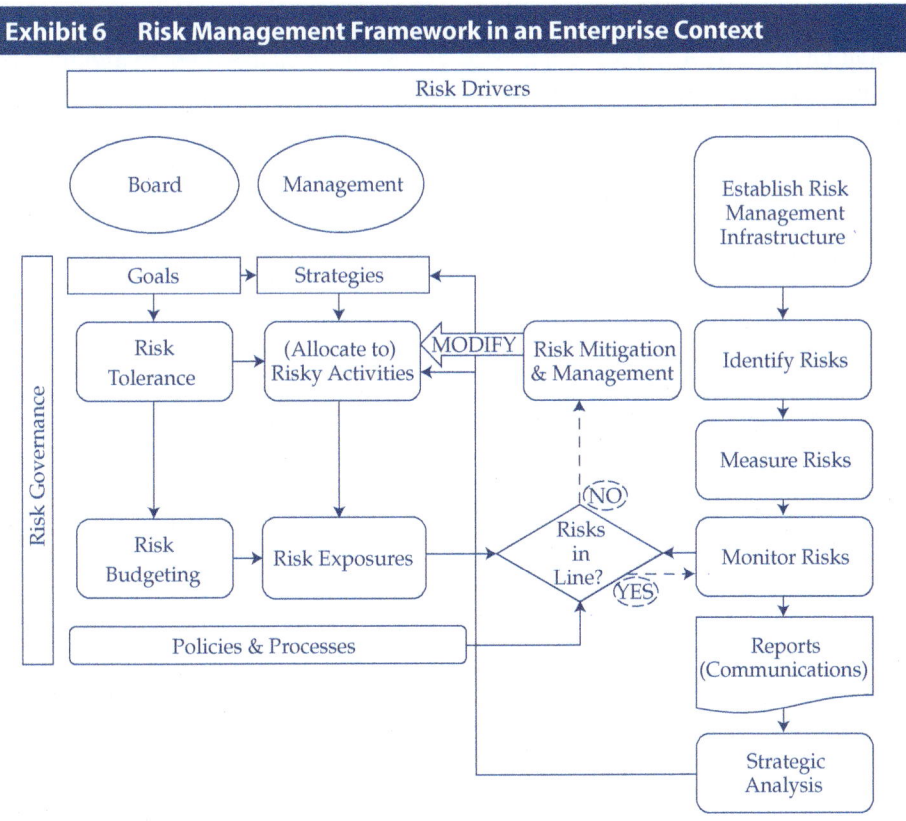

Exhibit 6 Risk Management Framework in an Enterprise Context

Source: "Risk Management: An Introduction," CFA Program Level I curriculum reading (2021).

We can apply this framework to the setting of an institutional investor in the following manner. The risk management process for an institutional investor starts with the board setting the overall risk tolerance for the organization that is consistent with its objectives and constraints. Risk tolerance should capture the amount of market risk that an institutional investor is willing and able to take in order to maximize expected returns, and it informs the most important investment decision that is made by the board—namely, the strategic asset allocation. Risk tolerance can be expressed in asset-only (for sovereign wealth funds, endowments, and foundations) or asset/

liability terms (for pension funds and insurance companies). Typical risk measures used for setting the risk tolerance of institutional investors include volatility, maximum drawdown, and value at risk or conditional value at risk (sometimes referred to as *expected tail loss*, or *ETL*).

In addition to setting the overall risk tolerance (for market losses), the board usually approves additional risk parameters, limits, requirements, and guidelines (some quantitative and others procedural) that are codified in an investment policy statement (IPS). These may include liquidity risk parameters if the institutional investor has a significant allocation to illiquid asset classes, an active risk budget to limit and control the amount of active management pursued by investment staff, restrictions on leverage and the use of derivatives, ethical investment guidelines, and possibly credit risk parameters and constraints in the case of significant fixed-income investments (for example, for an insurance company). These additional guidelines and constraints are put in place to ensure that the investment activities are consistent with the board's risk tolerance and expectations (and with regulatory requirements if applicable).

Management (i.e., the investment team) is tasked with implementing the strategic asset allocation (SAA) and investing the assets either internally or through external managers across the various asset classes included in the SAA. The investment team is also responsible for managing and monitoring the risks associated with the implementation of the SAA and reporting to the board. The objective is not to minimize or eliminate risk but to measure and attribute risk to various risk exposures and factors to ensure that the investments adequately compensate the institution for the risks being taken. Institutional investors typically perform risk factor analysis to better understand the fund's risk exposures, such as exposure to equity risk, interest rate risk, credit risk, inflation risk, currency risk, and liquidity risk. This analysis includes both quantitative modeling and qualitative risk assessments. Quantitative tools may involve sophisticated risk management systems based on returns or holdings, scenario analysis, and stress testing. Other risks are more qualitative in nature, such as potential reputational risk from certain types of investments.

For public equity investments, active risk versus a benchmark needs to be measured and monitored. Institutional investors may have an explicit active risk budget in place. Part of the risk budgeting effort involves ensuring that the active risk budget accurately reflects the areas where most excess return can be expected. In addition, the investment team will want to ensure that most of the active risk in public equities comes from stock picking and not simply from loading on certain equity risk factors, such as growth, momentum, or quality.

For private equity investments, the board may want to understand whether the returns achieved on the investment adequately compensated the fund for giving up liquidity. One way to answer that question is by comparing the returns on the private equity investment with the return of public equities. Currency risk tends to sometimes be overlooked by institutional investors. This risk can have an outsized and unexpected impact on the overall return. Although currency risk can be hedged in some cases, doing so is typically costly or even impossible when investing in emerging and frontier markets. The risk of currency devaluation needs to be acknowledged and assessed prior to making investments. Another risk that gets overlooked is asset allocation drift. The investment portfolio should be rebalanced on a regular basis to bring it back in line with the strategic asset allocation that was approved by the board.

The risk management infrastructure of the institutional investor should be set up to identify and measure the aforementioned risks and monitor how they change over time and whether they are in line with the guidelines set up by the board in the IPS and with additional—more granular—internal guidelines set by the Chief Investment Officer and risk team. The risk team is usually tasked with risk reporting to the various stakeholders, which may include an internal investment committee and the board to ensure adequate risk oversight. The investment team should recognize when risk exposures are not aligned with the overall risk tolerance and guidelines and take action to bring them back into alignment. These actions may involve hedging, rebalancing, and secondary sales or in the case of illiquid investments, reducing commitments.

ENVIRONMENTAL AND SOCIAL RISKS FACED BY INSTITUTIONAL INVESTORS

b   discuss environmental and social risks associated with the portfolio strategy of an institutional investor

3.1 Universal Ownership, Externalities, and Responsible Investing

In this section, we define universal owners as large institutional investors that effectively own a slice of the whole economy and hence are generally managing their total market exposure, instead of focusing on a subset of issuers. Institutional investors such as sovereign wealth funds and public pension funds usually have large portfolios that are highly diversified and built with a long-term focus. Such portfolios are representative of global capital markets, thereby making such investors "universal owners."

Investing long term in widely diversified holdings inevitably exposes such portfolios to increasing costs related to negative environmental and social externalities. An externality is an impact that an individual's or a corporation's activities have on a third party. If everyone acts in their own self-interest, it could lead to an overall negative outcome for society. Examples of negative environmental externalities include plastic pollution in the ocean, poor air quality due to industrial and vehicular emissions, and water toxicity due to improper effluent management.

Universal owners find it challenging to effectively diversify risks arising from negative environmental and social externalities. Costs that are externalized by one portfolio company can negatively affect the profitability of another portfolio company, thereby adversely affecting the overall portfolio return. For example, a sovereign wealth fund invests in a plastic manufacturer that is saving waste treatment and disposal costs by directly releasing waste pellets and other chemical residues into a nearby river. Water toxicity arising as a result of these actions causes reduced productivity in the agriculture operations downstream, which the asset owner is also invested in. In addition, strengthening regulations related to environmental protection, for example, may lead to monetary fines and penalties, thereby leading to financial risks for a company causing such negative externalities.

According to the UN-backed Principles for Responsible Investment (PRI), environmental costs for universal owners are reflected in portfolio impacts via insurance premiums, taxes, inflated input prices, and the physical costs associated with weather-related disasters (PRI Association 2017). Also, the cost of remediating environmental damage is often significantly higher than the cost of preventing it. Given these facts, it is imperative for large institutional investors to internalize the price of such negative externalities by considering the impact of their investments on society and future generations.

Exhibit 7 provides a non-exhaustive list of environmental and social issues that we have introduced in Level I of the CFA Program curriculum.

Exhibit 7   Examples of Environmental and Social Factors

Environmental Issues	Social Issues
Climate change and carbon emissions	Customer satisfaction and product responsibility
Air and water pollution	Data security and privacy
Biodiversity	Gender and diversity
Deforestation	Occupational health and safety
Energy efficiency	Community relations and charitable activities
Waste management	Human rights
Water scarcity	Labor standards

In the next section, we share examples of how some of these environmental and social issues could impact the portfolio strategy for large institutional investors that have a long-term focus toward their investments.

Systemic risks have the potential to destabilize capital markets and lead to serious negative consequences for financial institutions and the broader economy. The unpredictable nature of such megatrends as climate change and their related impacts, both environmental and socioeconomic, pose clear systemic risks to global financial markets. A study carried out by researchers at the Grantham Research Institute on Climate Change and the Environment (2016) at the London School of Economics and Political Science and Vivid Economics projected that climate change could reduce the value of global financial assets by as much as $24 trillion—resulting in permanent damage that would far eclipse that from the 2007–09 financial crisis.

3.2 Material Environmental Issues for an Institutional Investor

For an institutional investor, such as a sovereign wealth fund, such megatrends as climate change and their related risks—both physical and transition risks—have the potential to cause significant harm to a portfolio's value over the medium to long term, particularly for investments in real assets (real estate, infrastructure) and private equity, neither of which are easily divestible. Next, we will discuss the impact of climate-related risks on an institutional investor's portfolio from the perspective of private equity and real asset investments.

3.2.1 *Physical climate risks*

As we have observed since the beginning of the current century, climate change has profoundly affected the physical world we live in. Annual average temperatures across the globe are continuously rising, and 19 of the 20 warmest years have occurred since 2001 (NASA 2019). Erratic weather patterns, such as heavy precipitation, droughts, and hurricanes, are both more frequent and of higher magnitude. Similarly, wildfires are causing more and more devastation every year. In addition, the chronic issue of sea-level rise is causing coastal flooding. As shown in Exhibit 8, an increase in extreme weather events has occurred.

Exhibit 8 Extreme Weather Events on the Rise

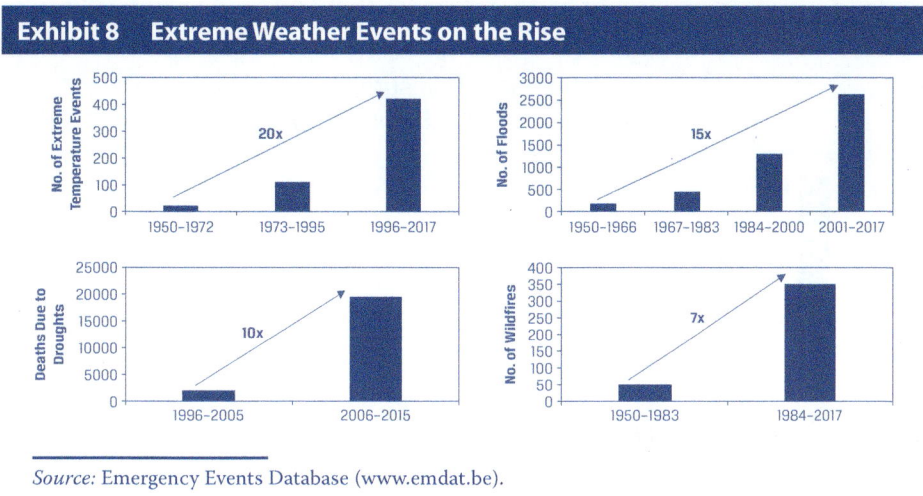

Source: Emergency Events Database (www.emdat.be).

With continued climate change, all these physical climate risks could become more severe in the future and, to a certain extent, become the new normal for the world. Depending on global responses to climate change in the coming decade, the degree of their impact on our economies and investments may be alleviated.

So, what does this mean for the portfolio strategy of large institutional investors with private equity and real asset investments?

3.2.2 Impact on real assets

Should these trends continue, the physical risks that we have discussed could create increased levels of stress on such assets as residential and commercial real estate and infrastructure, such as roads and railways. Rising sea levels that lead to flooding would impact both rents and property valuation for hitherto prime coastal properties. Prolonged exposure to extreme heat would negatively affect the useful life of roads and train tracks, which would lead to accelerated depreciation of such assets and, therefore, more frequent replacement costs for companies and governments (CFA Institute 2020).

Similarly, physical damage caused by frequent, large-scale weather-related events, such as hurricanes or even wildfires—once considered too irregular to insure against— could not only lead to large-scale drawdowns in the portfolio's asset value but also make it difficult or expensive to insure such assets. Most of the flooding-related losses around the world are uninsured, thereby causing additional stress on a country's economy and its people (see Exhibit 9).

Exhibit 9   Global Flood Losses and Insurance Levels

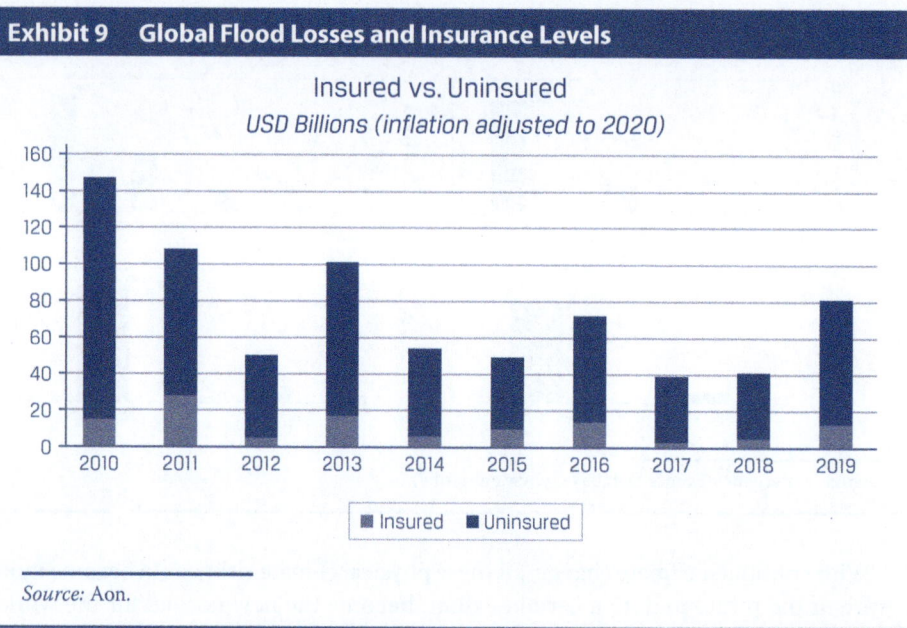

Source: Aon.

Because these physical climate-related risks continue to play out in a much larger and more frequent manner than previously anticipated, they will continue to bring down prices and rental yields of prime real estate, leading to permanent impairments of asset valuations. For a large institutional investor that is looking to preserve capital and provide growth benefits to multiple generations, it is imperative that these risks be factored into the portfolio construction strategies.

3.2.3 *Climate transition risks*

In line with the 2015 Paris Climate Agreement, countries and companies around the world are already making efforts to dramatically reduce or eliminate their CO_2 emissions in order to limit the global temperature increase in this century to 2 degrees Celsius above preindustrial levels. To keep global warming less than 2°C, scientists project that energy-related CO_2 emissions need to fall 25% by 2030 and reach "net zero" by 2070 (Intergovernmental Panel on Climate Change 2018; IEA 2020).

One of the most ambitious efforts to incentivize decarbonization is the European Union's sustainable finance taxonomy, which helps investors understand whether an economic activity is environmentally sustainable. As of October 2020, looking at the scientific evidence about the current and potential impacts of climate change, it has become clear that the world needs to move toward a low-carbon future if we are to cap global warming at less than 2°C and prevent the negative effects that not doing so would bring to our climate, our ecosystems, and human life. What is currently unclear is the pace at which this decarbonization will happen.

Rapid decarbonization will lead to restrictions on carbon emissions, implementation of some form of carbon pricing, introduction of new technologies, and changes in the consumer behavior. All these effects can create massive disruptions in certain sectors, such as electricity generation (with the increasing cost competitiveness of renewable energy sources as compared with coal) and automobiles (with the impending widespread switch from internal combustion engines to electric vehicles. The International Energy Agency has forecast that in order to reach carbon neutrality by 2050, half of all cars in the world should be electric by 2030 (Lo 2020).

The PRI's Inevitable Policy Response (IPR) project aims to prepare financial markets for climate-related policy risks that are likely to emerge in the short to medium term. The IPR forecast a response by 2025 that will be forceful, abrupt, and disorderly because of the delayed action (see Exhibit 10). The PRI argues that markets have inefficiently priced climate transition risks, but its policy forecast is that a forceful policy response to climate change in the near term is a highly likely outcome, leaving portfolios of institutional investors exposed to significant risks that need to be mitigated.

Exhibit 10   IPR Key Policy Forecasts

Coal phase-outs	Sales ban on Internal Combustion Engines (ICE)	Carbon Pricing (Emission Allowances)	Zero carbon power
Early coal phase-out for first mover countries by 2030	Early sales ban for first mover countries by 2035	US$40-80/tCO$_2$ prices by 2030 for first movers	Significant ramp-up of renewable energy globally
Steady retirement of coal-fired power generation after 2030 in lagging countries	Other countries follow suit as automotive industry reaches tipping point	Global convergence accelerated by Border Carbon Adjustment (BCA) to >=$100/tCO$_2$ by 2050	Policy support of nuclear capacity increase in a small set of countries, nuclear phased out elsewhere

Carbon Capture and Storage (CCS) & industry decarbonisation	Energy efficiency	Green House Gas (GHG) removal (Land use-based)	Agriculture
Limited CCS support in power,	Increase in coverage and stringency of performance standards	Improved forestry and nature-based solutions	Technical support to improve agricultural yields
Policy incentives primarily for industrial and bioenergy CCS	Utility obligation programs	Stronger enforcement of zero deforestation	Increasing public investment in irrigation and AgTech
Public support for demonstration, and then deployment of hydrogen clusters	Financial and behavioral incentives	Controlled expansion of bioenergy crops	Incremental behavioural incentives away from beef

Source: PRI IPR (www.unpri.org/the-inevitable-policy-response-policy-forecasts/4849.article).

Given the uncertainty around the precise timing and magnitude of the impact of climate change, organizations are increasingly using climate-related scenario analysis to better understand how their businesses might perform under a variety of global warming scenarios—for example, in a world that is 2°C, 3°C, or 4°C warmer. The Task force on Climate-Related Financial Disclosures (TCFD) recommends organizations, including banks, asset managers, and asset owners, use scenario analysis to estimate the implications of such risks and opportunities for their businesses over time and also to inform their strategic thinking. The International Energy Agency and the Intergovernmental Panel on Climate Change both publicly offer a set of climate-related scenarios that are widely used. To learn more about climate-related scenario analysis, refer to the technical supplement issued by the TCFD.

3.2.4 Climate opportunities

Although most of the investor focus in dealing with climate change has been on managing physical and transition risks, exciting investment opportunities are arising in companies focused on climate change mitigation and adaptation. These opportunities exist in secondary markets and, in some cases, investments in real assets and infrastructure projects, such as wind and solar farms and smart grids.

Because the levelized cost of energy for renewable energy generation technologies has considerably decreased since 2010, these have become cost competitive with some conventional generation technologies, such as coal-based power generation, as shown in Exhibit 11.

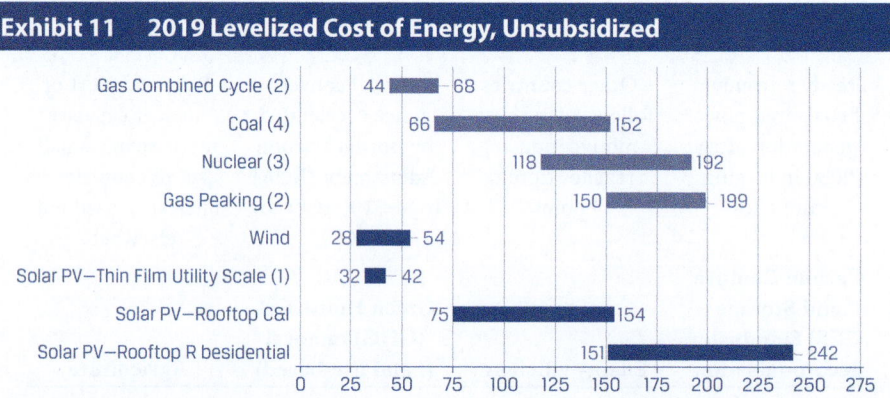

Exhibit 11 2019 Levelized Cost of Energy, Unsubsidized

Note: Levelized cost of energy is a measure of the average net present cost of electricity generation for a power plant over its lifetime.
(1) Unless otherwise indicated herein, the low end represents a single-axis tracking system and the high end represents a fixed-tilt system.
(2) The fuel cost assumption for Lazard's global, unsubsidized analysis for gas-fired generation resources is $3.45/MMBTU.
(3) Unless otherwise indicated, the analysis herein does not reflect decommissioning costs, ongoing maintenance-related capital expenditures or the potential economic impacts of federal loan guarantees or other subsidies.
(4) High end incorporates 90% carbon capture and compression. Does not include cost of transportation and storage.
Sources: Data is from Lazard (www.lazard.com/perspective/lcoe2019).

This cost competitiveness, coupled with the urgency to decarbonize our economies to avoid the potentially catastrophic physical impacts of climate change, has created secular growth opportunity for such businesses and assets, thereby attracting increasingly large investor attention.

A summary of the business segments where such opportunities may lie follows.

Climate mitigation This category includes companies that are positioned to benefit, directly or indirectly, from efforts to curb or mitigate the long-term effects of global climate change, to address the environmental challenges presented by global climate change, or to improve the efficiency of resource consumption.

Exhibit 12 Climate Mitigation Opportunity Examples

Business Segment	Description
Clean energy	Companies in this segment are involved in the generation of clean energy from such sources as wind, solar, and small hydro. This segment also includes manufacturers of such equipment as windmills and solar panels, as well as related service providers.
Energy efficiency	This segment comprises businesses that provide products and services to improve the efficiency of energy consumption in a variety of processes. Examples include energy efficient transportation and building solution providers and recycling technology.
Batteries and storage	This segment includes companies that help improve battery storage capacity and efficiency. These improvements are critical, for instance, to sustainable growth and wider penetration of some of the previously mentioned technologies, such as clean energy generation and distribution and electric vehicles.
Smart grids	Smart grids are digitally enhanced versions of the conventional electricity grid, with a layer of communication network overlaying the traditional grid. They are a key enabler for energy security and reliability and integration of clean energy resources.
Materials	Such materials as copper and battery-grade lithium are key ingredients in the clean energy value chain because they are required in clean energy power generation, storage solutions, and electric vehicles, resulting in a projected demand rise as the world transitions toward a low-carbon future.

Climate adaptation   This category includes companies that would help better adjust to actual or expected future change in climate with an aim to reduce vulnerability to the harmful effects of climate change, such as food insecurity, sea-level rise, and frequent extreme weather events.

Exhibit 13 Climate Adaptation Opportunity Examples

Business Segment	Description
Sustainable agriculture	Companies in this segment are involved in providing products that improve agriculture productivity and reduce the resource consumption in the entire process. Sustainable fish farming and timber production are other activities included here.
Water	This This segment consists of businesses that provide products and services to improve the efficiency of water consumption in a variety of processes, including wastewater treatment and reuse.

Many institutional investors are increasing allocations to such sectors as part of their real-asset allocation or as a potential equity alpha opportunity with the expectation that companies in these sectors will outperform the broad equity market over a long period of time as the world transitions to a low carbon future. Evaluating and sufficiently managing both physical and transition climate risks in the portfolio and capturing some of the aforementioned secular growth opportunities could position large institutional investor portfolios to outperform and grow in value in the long term.

3.3 Material Social Issues for an Institutional Investor

Environmental issues, such as climate change and air pollution, are reasonably mature and quite well understood, making them easier to accommodate in discounted cash flow models. Social issues, such as community relation, occupational health and safety, privacy and data security, modern slavery and other human right violations in the supply chain, and inequality, however, are relatively challenging to quantify and integrate into financial models. Most social issues have largely qualitative data reported by companies, such as health and safety policies and initiatives, lists of product quality certifications, and human capital management policies, rather than metrics on which long-term performance can be judged. Nevertheless, these issues have the potential to cause reputational and financial damage to a company and its investors if not managed sufficiently well.

3.3.1 *Managing community relations and the social license to operate*

For large institutional investors, such as sovereign wealth funds and public pension funds, their investments may have positive social impacts, such as improving essential public infrastructure and services or providing better access to medicine and technology, or negative social impacts, via poor labor standards or forceful relocation and improper rehabilitation of communities by their portfolio companies. Good corporate behavior is usually well received by the community relations, leading to a sustainable and mutually beneficial long-term relationship. In many ways, these aspects are essential to keeping a company's social license to operate.

Let's take a hypothetical example of a sovereign wealth fund (SWF) that has invested in a dam-based hydroelectric power plant in an economically less developed part of its country. Although there will be a positive environmental impact of the project because it will generate electricity from a renewable source, the social impacts of the project could be mixed. On the positive side, rural electrification arising from this project will lead to economic development in the region, thereby improving the standard of living. Dam-based hydroelectric power plants require large-scale land acquisition, often leading to relocation and rehabilitation of indigenous communities. Some locals protest that they have not been sufficiently consulted by the government before issuing consent to establish this project. Moreover, there are allegations of acquisition of land for the project at unfair/poor valuations. In some instances, protesting locals were forcefully removed and relocated by local government authorities, leading to unrest. Eventually, the SWF decides to cease the project implementation owing to this wide variety of instances of pushback from the society.

This example highlights the importance of considering social risks when investing. Despite having the positive intent of supporting development of renewable power generation in a less economically developed part of the country, the SWF faced pushback and reputational damage for not holistically considering the interests of all the stakeholders involved, especially local communities that were the most affected by the project. Some of the best practices in community relation management include extensive stakeholder consultation meetings to better understand their needs and address their concerns, providing alternative employment opportunities to those affected, and ensuring fair land acquisition, rehabilitation, and resettlement practices.

3.3.2 *Labor issues in the supply chain*

Another increasingly important social topic is the one related to poor labor practices, especially in the supply chain. Driven by globalization, a consumption boom across developed and emerging markets, and the availability of cheap labor in certain parts of the world, a large portion of the manufacturing and assembling activities across such key sectors as technology and garments has been outsourced to developing and frontier markets, such as India, Vietnam, and Malaysia. Although access to cheap, semi-skilled labor has led to better bottom lines for multinational companies, it has also come at the cost of exploitation of workers in such supply chains. Labor rights are being compromised in the form of heavy reliance on temporary workers, excessive or forced overtime, and low wages. Moreover, lax regulations in many countries allow legal prevention of unionization or any form of collective bargaining, thereby making such workers more vulnerable.

Large brands in the apparel industry, such as Nike and Gap, and in the technology space, such as Apple and Samsung, have all been accused of various levels of lapses in their supply chain related to the aforementioned labor management issues. Apart from suffering significant damage to their brands and reputations, which could lead to consumer boycotts, such companies may also face additional costs and/or fines related to product recalls and ad hoc shifting of supply chains.

For SWFs with equity exposure to some of the largest apparel brands and branded tech hardware companies, considering such issues while making investments is of paramount importance because lack of transparency in the supply chain and lapses in labor management may weigh heavily on the resilience of such supply chains amid global-scale disruptions, such as that caused by the COVID-19 pandemic. In addition to the financial risks, reputational risks may also arise because of a view that the SWF implicitly supports such improper and unethical business practices.

3.3.3 The "just" transition

Sustainable development involves meeting the needs of the present generation without compromising the ability of future generations to meet their own needs. Sustainable development includes economic, social, and environmental dimensions, all of which are interrelated. In the transition to environmentally sustainable economies and societies, several challenges may arise—for example, displacement of workers and job losses in certain industries, such as coal mining, fossil fuel extraction/production, and fossil fuel-based power generation. Similarly, increased energy costs due to carbon taxes and higher costs of commodities partly resulting from sustainable production practices may have adverse effects on the incomes of poor households. Therefore, a "just" transition is necessary to ensure that there are limited negative social impacts in our pursuit of positive environmental impacts via avoiding fossil fuels and implementing sustainable agriculture and business practices. Although there is no fixed set of guidelines, the just transition encourages a dialogue between workers, industry, and governments influenced by geographical, political, cultural, and social contexts in order to tackle some of the aforementioned challenges.

CASE STUDY

c   analyze and evaluate the financial and non-financial risk exposures in the portfolio strategy of an institutional investor

d   discuss various methods to manage the risks that arise on long-term direct investments of an institutional investor

e   evaluate strengths and weaknesses of an enterprise risk management system and recommend improvements

1 Case Study: Introduction

You are working as a Risk Analyst at a small sovereign wealth fund (SWF) and reporting to the Head of Risk. The SWF is considering making some new investments in direct private equity and direct infrastructure. You have been asked to review risk aspects of these investment opportunities, which will be discussed in an upcoming investment committee meeting. Assuming the investments will be made, you will also have the responsibility to monitor the risk of the investments as well as make recommended improvements to the SWF's risk management system. You are excited about these opportunities and look forward to putting your knowledge and skills learned from the CFA Program to work!

2 Case Study: Background

- Over 20 years ago, the "Republic of Ruritania" discovered an extremely large deposit of crucial rare earth metals that are key elements in the manufacturing of high-speed computers used in science and finance. The entire deposit was sold to various entities allowing Ruritania to secure its financial future. At the same time, the government of Ruritania "dollarized" the economy, moving from the domestic RRR currency to the USD.
- The government of Ruritania (R) decided to form a sovereign wealth fund, R-SWF, in order to grow the capital for future generations. This type of SWF is a "savings fund," intended to share wealth across generations by transforming non-renewable assets into diversified financial assets.
- R-SWF has built up a diversified portfolio of equities, fixed income, and alternative investments.
- In equities and fixed income, the SWF invests in developed markets, emerging markets, and frontier markets through both fund investing and direct investing.
- In alternatives, the SWF invests in private equity (PE), infrastructure, and real estate. Investment methods used include direct investing, making co-investments, and fund investing.
- The case study begins in Section 3 at an investment committee meeting to discuss two potential investments. The next scene, in Section 4, is set three years later, when the performance of the investments are discussed at another investment committee meeting. The final scene, in Section 5, is set five years later and provides additional information on investment performance.

3 R-SWF'S Investments: 1.0

Initial Case Facts (1.0)

Today, the investment committee of R-SWF is considering several new investments, including direct private equity and direct infrastructure investments. The investment committee will be discussing risk aspects of the investments, led by the Head of Risk and supported by *you*, a Risk Analyst.

- The investment committee meeting will open with an overview of asset allocation and a few basic discussions on the two proposed investments. However, the focus of the meeting is on the potential risks of the new investment proposals, not details on the investments themselves. (An in-depth investment committee meeting on the new investments was held last month.)
- The meeting will then move on to a discussion of the potential risks of the two specific direct investments being considered.

Case Study

1. Direct infrastructure investment in an airport
2. Direct PE investment in a beverage manufacturer

- The investment committee meeting will discuss key risks that R-SWF should consider as it decides whether to make new direct investments in PE and infrastructure.
- All investment committee participants (and CFA Program Level III candidates) are provided with a background memo with the following information:

  Memo A: Background on R-SWF's asset allocation and performance

  Memo B: Details on the proposed direct infrastructure investment

  Memo C: Details on the proposed direct private equity investment

INVESTMENT COMMITTEE MEETING MEMO 1.0

To: R-SWF Investment Committee Members

From: R-SWF Chief Investment Officer

Re: Investment Committee Meeting Agenda

Distribution: Head of Risk, Head of PE, Head of Infrastructure, Head of Equities, and Level III Candidates in the CFA Program

An agenda for today's meeting is as follows:

Agenda

- Opening Remarks and Review of Asset Allocation: Chief Investment Officer
- Review of Infrastructure Investment Opportunity: Head of Infrastructure
- Review of Private Equity Investment Opportunity: Head of PE
- Discussion of Risk—Infrastructure Investment: Head of Risk + Everyone
- Discussion of Risk—PE Investment: Head of Risk + Everyone
- Closing Remarks: Chief Investment Officer

The investment committee meeting will discuss key risks that R-SWF should consider as it determines whether to make new direct investments in PE and infrastructure.

Memo 1A: Asset Allocation and Performance

- Since its inception, over a 25+ year period, R-SWF has built a diversified portfolio of investments. As of last month, the fund had AUM of $50 billion USD, with the fund outperforming its overall benchmark by 150 bps net of fees since inception. Of course, there have been short-term periods of underperformance as the fund pursued its long-term strategy.
- Asset allocation as of last month for the overall fund was as follows:

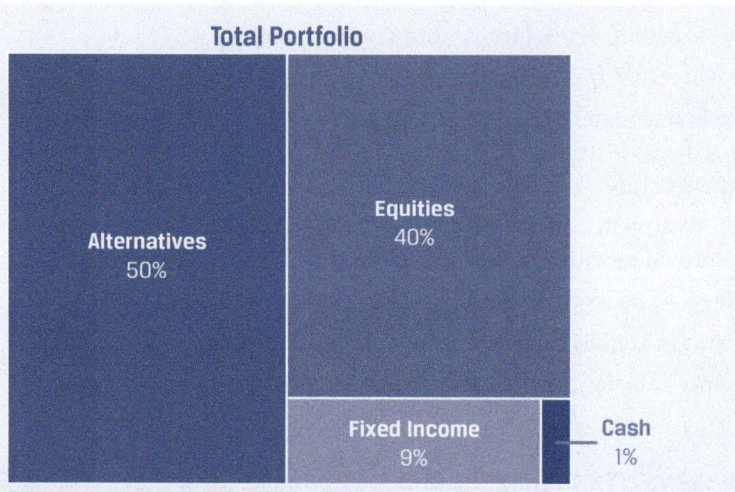

■ As of last month, R-SWF had approximately 50% of assets invested in alternative investments, consistent with its long-term objectives.

■ In today's investment committee meeting, R-SWF is considering two new investments in alternative investments—specifically, in direct private equity and direct infrastructure investments. *(Note: Funding for these two investments will come from a combination of cash, dividends, receivables, and fixed income. The mix will be determined by the Asset/Liability Committee, or ALCO).*

■ Because today's investment committee meeting will focus on alternative investments, we will break the allocation of alternatives down further, as follows:

■ As of last month, R-SWF had approximately 10% of assets invested in private capital and 10% of assets invested in Infrastructure.

■ Next, we provide a breakdown of private capital and infrastructure:

Case Study

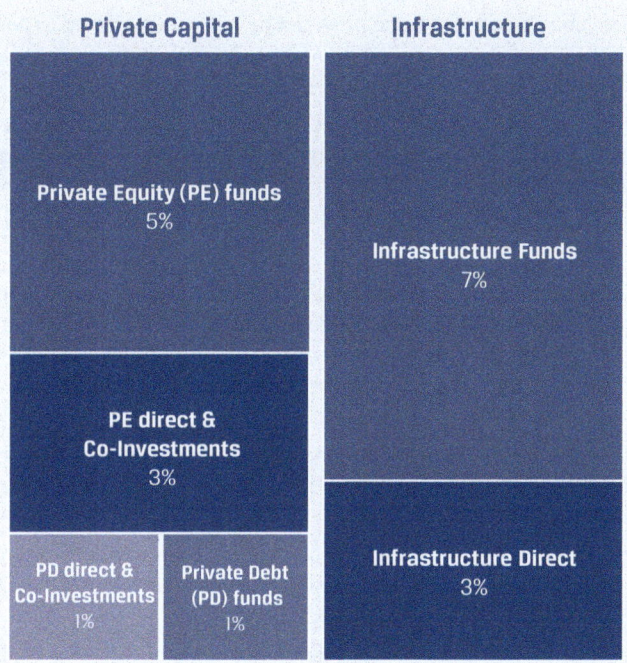

- As of last month, R-SWF had approximately 3% of assets invested in private equity direct and co-investment and 3% of assets invested in direct Infrastructure.
- The investment committee will be discussing risk aspects of the cases, led by the Head of Risk and supported by the Risk Analyst.
- Details on the proposed infrastructure investment are found in Memo 1B.
- Details on the proposed private equity investment are found in Memo 1C.

Memo 1B: Proposed Direct Infrastructure Investment

- The infrastructure direct investment opportunity is an investment in helping modernize an airport in the frontier market island nation of "Sunnyland."
- Sunnyland has beautiful beaches and several hotels, ranging from 3-star to 5-star. However, the Sunnyland Airport has only one small runway that can support airplanes of only up to 10 passengers.
- The Sunnyland government is keen on expanding the airport with a new terminal and new runway. Doing so will allow much larger aircraft to land (up to 150 passengers) and be a major boost to tourism.
- The airport is located about 2 km from the sea, providing scenic views on takeoff and landing. The new runway will be built 1 km from the sea, providing even nicer views.
- R-SWF has been approached by the Sunnyland Airport Authority (SAA) to consider a $100 million investment in a public–private partnership (PPP) on a build–operate–transfer (BOT) basis.
- For R-SWF (with assets of $50 billion), this is a small investment (0.2% of total assets). The investment will be about 2% of total infrastructure assets—$100 million/($100 million + $5,000 million)—which includes investments in funds and direct investments.
- Other facts about this infrastructure investment that are important for the investment committee to understand: *(Note: The focus of the case and investment committee discussion is risks.)*
    - Total project cost of $500 million for new 5 million passenger per annum (pax) terminal

- $33 million investment to be provided by Airport Operating Group (AOG), which will operate the airport under a management agreement (with fixed fee plus/minus performance incentive)
- $300 million funding to be provided through non-recourse project finance debt (i.e., approx. 70/30 debt/equity) with 15–year tenor following 3-year grace period
- 2–year construction period, with fixed price construction contract awarded under tender
- 25–year concession (including 2–year construction period), with investor consortium entitled to collect all regulated airport charges (e.g., passenger departure charge, landing charges) and commercial revenue (duty free, retail, F&B, car parking), subject to payment of quarterly concession fee of 35% of all revenue to SAA
- Airport charges (70% of all revenue) are regulated by concession contract—that is, schedule of charges set and then subject to stated formula for future changes (e.g., CPI)
- Concession agreement includes quality and performance standards to be met for design/construction/development (including timely delivery of new terminal) and operations, respectively
- Expected IRR for full investment term of 25 years of 15%

Risk Discussion: Infrastructure Investment

The Head of Infrastructure believes the potential return on this project far outweighs the potential risk(s). However, she is happy to discuss potential risks with the investment committee.

Memo 1C: Proposed Direct Private Equity Investment

- The private equity direct investment opportunity is an investment in a local beverage company (Atsui Beverage Company Limited (ABC)) that manufactures and sells carbonated beverages. The investment will be used to modernize the plant.
- ABC is an unlisted beverage company located in the tropical, land-locked nation of "Atsui." Atsui has a developing economy and can be considered a frontier market.
- ABC is the only local manufacturer of carbonated beverages in Atsui. All other beverages are imported.
- ABC's factory is located near a river that allows for transport to the port. Also, the river is known for its unique biodiversity.
- R-SWF's Head of Private Equity has been on several vacations to Atsui and saw an investment opportunity.
- ABC is keen on modernizing its plant, but the founder is worried about giving up control. Thus, the founder is willing to sell only a minority stake of 35% in exchange for $25 million.
- For R-SWF (with assets of $50 billion), this is a small investment (0.05% of total assets). The investment will be about 0.4% of total PE assets—$25 million/($25 million + $6,000 million)—which includes investments in funds, co-investments, and direct investments.
- Other facts about this direct PE investment that are important for the investment committee to understand: *(Note: The focus of the case and investment committee discussion is risks.)*
  - R-SWF has been investing in PE for many years in funds. Over the years, R-SWF has developed direct investing capabilities through its co-investments and is now expanding its direct investing program.

Case Study

- Because of the increased direct investing capabilities of R-SWF and recent outperformance in returns, R-SWF is looking to increase its private equity allocation to direct investments over the next five years.
- The government of Atsui has implemented tariffs on all soft drink imports. There is an upcoming election that could change this stance.
- The cost to modernize the ABC plant is estimated to be $20 million.
- Over the last 12 months, ABC had a revenue of $50 million. Revenue is expected to increase significantly over the next 10 years—with a modernized plant.
- Over the last 12 months, ABC had an EBITDA of $7 million. This is an EBITDA margin of 14% and a 10× EBITDA multiple. The Head of PE feels that there is significant room for improvement.
- With the new technology from the plant modernization, ABC will be able to expand into non-carbonated drinks, such as sports drinks and juices.
- Once the plant is modernized, productivity will improve significantly, allowing ABC to reduce factory staff headcount by 40%, from 500 employees to 300 employees, which will drive a higher EBITDA margin in the future.
- With a significant minority, R-SWF will be allowed to have two seats on the board of ABC. So, the board will expand from five members to seven members. R-SWF is planning to have the Head of PE join the board of ABC but hasn't decided on the other board seat.

Risk Discussion: Private Equity Investment

The Head of PE believes the potential return on this project far outweighs the potential risk(s). However, he is happy to discuss potential risks with the Investment Committee.

IN-TEXT QUESTION:

Please respond to the following question based on **Investment Committee Memo 1.0**.

As R-SWF's Risk Analyst, do you anticipate liquidity risk will likely be highlighted as a significant financial risk in the upcoming risk discussions for either investment? Explain your thinking.

Guideline Answer:

No. I do not anticipate the Head of Infrastructure or the Head of PE to highlight liquidity risk as a significant risk for either investment. Although liquidity risk is the main risk that long-term institutional investors face, particularly during a significant market decline, each of these investments represents a small portion of R-SWF's total assets. R-SWF does not have cash flow pressure, unlike many institutional investors that face pressure from the regular payment of liabilities. In addition, R-SWF has been growing over time and is making a concerted effort to expand its direct investment program.

Direct investments typically help mitigate some of the liquidity issues commonly experienced when investing in a fund because direct investment provides a greater amount of control and discretion over when to exit investments. Furthermore, as the direct investment program grows and the proportion of direct investments as part R-SWF's total assets increases, R-SWF's ability to manage capital should improve. I believe there are other financial risks that are more likely to be highlighted as a significant risk for each investment.

Investment Committee Meeting 1.0

Participants

    Chief Investment Officer (CIO)
    Head of Infrastructure
    Head of PE
    Head of Risk
    Head of Equities
    Analysts [no speaking role]

Chief Investment Officer: Good morning, everyone. Welcome to today's investment committee meeting of the sovereign wealth fund of the Republic of Ruritania. After running this money on behalf of our citizens and future generations since its inception, the fund has outperformed our benchmark by 150 basis points, net of fees, and we've grown AUM to $50 billion over 25 years. We are very blessed.

At last month's investment committee meeting, our **Head of Infrastructure** and our **Head of PE** got together to discuss the financials and particulars of two investment opportunities. As they both deserve our attention, today we are joined by our **Head of Risk**, along with our **Head of Equities**, to review them through the lens of risk. Our esteemed junior analysts are in the room with us to observe and provide additional analysis as required.

For now, as we consider our opportunities, I'm mostly here as a facilitator, to pave the way for a robust discussion of investment risk.

Memo A shows us our asset allocation as of mid-June, and we've got 50% in alternatives. We believe in alternatives because our liabilities are negligible and we take a long-term view of things. About 40% of our allocation is in listed equities, with a large portion of that in emerging markets, which we're also big believers in. If we do fund one or both of the two investments on the table, we'll do it with a mix of cash, dividends receivable, and fixed income, but that's not for this committee to decide; the ALCO will go over that at a later date.

In any event, our focus here is private capital, the private equity side. We've got about 3% of our investments in direct private equity and co-investments and about 3% in direct infrastructure.

Again, this meeting is primarily about risk. Let's go to Memo B and ask our **Head of Infrastructure** to talk us through the first investment. It's usually the depth of her infrastructure experience that gives R-SWF the comfort to proceed in the face of risk.

Infrastructure Investment Discussion

Head of Infrastructure: Thank you for the kind words, **CIO**. I'm glad everyone's here so we can apply the full breadth of the investment committee's expertise.

This is an airport BOT project, a PPP in the frontier island nation of Sunnyland, whose primary industry is tourism. The members of our hard-working analyst team who are new to infrastructure have been briefed on the build-operate-transfer models that private developers often adopt under private-public partnerships so they can operate the facilities they have designed and built for a number of years before handing them over to government agencies.

[**Head of Infrastructure** looks around the room to see a few polite nods from the assembled analysts.]

Funds are needed for an airport upgrade: A new terminal and a new, bigger runway will accommodate larger planes. Sunnyland needs to get rid of the passenger bottleneck to allow for an all-important boost in tourism. We're thinking $500 million and two years of construction time should be enough.

Case Study

Ruritania is prepared to contribute $100 million, and we're insisting on bringing in AOG, a properly experienced airport operator, which will also be investing private equity—about $33 million. The rest of the capital will be no-recourse debt, about $300 million, and an equity injection from the government and other infrastructure investors for the remainder. The debt will be 15-year with a 3-year grace period.

With the BOT arrangements, of course, we take over the airport from the beginning under a 25-year concession agreement for all the cash flows from the terminal. So that's airport charges, like aircraft landing and passenger departure fees, as well as the commercial revenue from duty-free concessions, retail, and so forth, and we remit 35% of what we collect to the Sunnyland Airport Authority on a quarterly basis. If we want to charge more, any increases—say, for CPI adjustments—are worked out according to fixed formulas.

CIO has set the stage for this discussion of risk, and in that spirit, everyone should note the standards and conditions of our agreement with the government. You already know we've got a two-year development program—that's two years to see the revamped airport up and running—so if there are delays or shortfalls in quality, the concession agreement sets out the consequences.

Finally, our expected return for the full 25-year term given our fund's $100 million investment is a 15% IRR.

Chief Investment Officer: Thank you, **Head of Infrastructure**. That's a sufficient return, to be sure, but let's also understand that our involvement can help our friends down in Sunnyland. If we execute this project carefully, it means a boost to the wealth of all Sunnylanders.

You've been there recently, right?

Head of Infrastructure: I have. All indications are that it's an attractive tourist destination. Tourism is key to them now; they lack natural and other resources to diversify the economy. That's what they're depending on to build the economy.

Things are constrained because of the airport. The runway allows only for short, smaller aircraft, so just by increasing runway size and the associated facilities, you're paving a path for the whole nation to grow.

Chief Investment Officer: I ask the assembled team to consider for a minute the responsibilities we have to ourselves, to Ruritania; we all feel partly responsible for its success. When we invest in another sovereign country, such as Sunnyland, we may carry over a similar sense of responsibility, and we take that seriously. While our proposed $100 million investment is just 0.2% of our AUM, this single investment in transportation infrastructure will have an outsized impact on our investees.

With that in mind, let's move to the other proposal on the table. Our **Head of PE** has recently returned from Atsui, the site of the proposed private equity investment outlined in Memo C. Over to you, **Head of PE**.

Private Equity Investment Discussion

Head of PE: Yeah, I just got back. The company is called Atsui Beverage Company or ABC for short, and it was kind of "love at first sight"—or sip. I was on the beach, and a waiter brought me a drink and said it was called the "Mango Special." I thanked him but I was barely listening. You know how it is; my mind was elsewhere. But after the third sip, I was paying less attention to my leisure and more attention to just how good this drink was: refreshing, perfectly sweet, and unlike anything I'd tasted before. You know I'm always thinking about investments, ladies and gents, and I began to think I'd stumbled onto a winner.

I've been back to Atsui three times, and I introduced R-SWF to the team at the ABC plant that makes the Mango Special. I explained how sovereign wealth funds usually partner for the long term, and I built some trust while learning about their business. I know how small this is compared to the rest of our portfolio, but I'm still obsessed with this drink, so I figured out that we can invest $25 million for 35% of the business. They've got $50 million in revenue and $7 million in EBITDA. For those on the team who can't do math quickly like I can, that's a 14% EBITDA margin. And we're looking at a company valuation of roughly 10× EBITDA.

So, wait: Is this a good deal or not?

Well, let's think about it. ABC markets the only locally sourced carbonated beverage in Atsui, *and* tariffs are imposed on foreign competitors. That alone seems pretty great. And they'd use $20 million of our $25 million to modernize the plant. That way, they can turn out product way faster while also gearing up to make non-carbonated drinks like sports drinks and juices. We'd drive efficiency enough to cut headcount from 500 to 300, and that's even better for the EBITDA margin: new equipment, big changes.

I've got the most knowledge on the ground, so I could take a board seat along with someone else from our team. We've gotten pretty comfortable with co-investing, making some money, and developing our skills, and since we're expanding our direct investing effort anyway, this seems like a good fit. It's just $25 million out of our $50 billion pool, so it's a good way to learn, even if some of us think it's risky.

And, you know, sun, mango drinks, and the beach—I bet everyone wants to join the board!

Chief Investment Officer: So, the plant modernization allows for both a meaningful expansion of the product line *and* significant cost savings. But you said that a cut of 200 people underpins those savings?

Head of PE: Yeah.

Chief Investment Officer: OK. Any further questions for **Head of PE**?

Head of Risk: A question from me for **Head of PE**. You mentioned that these guys are the sole beverage manufacturer in Atsui and that there are entry barriers on foreign manufacturers coming in. You've been on the ground, so are local competitors raising their voices about giving ABC some competition?

Head of PE: I've done a lot of local research, and I'm not seeing anyone. When ABC thinks about threats, they think of the big international drink players, who are still scared off by the government's import tariffs.

Chief Investment Officer: A lot of senior officials are keen to grow the local industry. It's a small country, and there's a common emotional investment in ABC's success.

Head of Risk: These do seem like heavy tariffs. **CIO** mentioned they're as high as 100% if you try to buy Coke or Pepsi. The memo says there's an election coming up. Surely there's a risk those entry barriers fall away?

Head of PE: A mango drink is much better than cola, I promise!

Chief Investment Officer: I've done a little outreach myself to people in the know. Combining that with **Head of PE**'s research, I'd say a relaxing of tariffs after the election is a fair assumption.

Head of Equities: I have a question. Will this investment allow for ABC to start exports? Is that part of the expansion plan?

Head of PE: The markets nearby are also tropical, frontier nations. Business relations are decent, and the plant is next to a river that connects to a big port.

Case Study

Chief Investment Officer: **Head of PE** has explained that the plant workers fish on the freshwater river during their lunch and during breaks, and the river does indeed connect to Atsui's major port. I see good potential for connecting to neighbouring buyers.

Head of Risk: But let's remember that this is a frontier market with a developing economy.

Chief Investment Officer: Quite right. Beverages are still somewhat of a luxury item. Nevertheless, there's plenty of growth potential for us and for them.

Head of Equities: Sure, that's encouraging on exports, but **Head of PE** said that ABC sees its competition as the big international drink players, who are still scared off by the government's tariffs. If the election brings in a government keen on foreign investment, that could completely overturn the advantage this particular business has.

Let's apply a probability to a tariff reduction and to import markets opening up. Pepsi and Coca-Cola have much deeper pockets for waiting out a price war.

Head of PE: I hear you, but maybe I went too far by saying ABC sees them as competitors. Products like the Mango Special and their other drinks don't actually exist in the Coke and Pepsi product lines, and the Mango Special recipe is so proprietary that if we protect it, it's a real competitive advantage. The other ABC beverages use tropical fruit the multinationals don't have supply chains for, and we believe—I mean, *ABC* believes they have a way of mixing things that no one else can figure out. If that's the case, a path to exports is still there.

With investment, they still have time to get into other juices and diversify. And we're always talking to government officials and to people who could make up the government, and everyone's pretty aligned.

Chief Investment Officer: These risks are tied to the modernization program we're investing in, which means job cuts. In frontier markets, this is very sensitive: Unions may protest, and politicians may make it part of their election agenda, especially given that we're talking about one of the country's more popular companies. We're veering into reputational risk here.

Look, this is a rather small investment, of $25 million, but even a small investment can have an outsized negative impact on us if we don't manage the risk properly.

Thoughts?

Head of PE: We're not just investing and then forgetting things, folks. We're going to be proactive. Before modernization starts, we're going to do some research that shows us what issues are in the minds of all the people of Atsui, not just our workers, and we're going to design new community programs around that. We'll try to make a positive impact first.

We know that cutting employees is sensitive. But by helping many more people than we let go and by giving employees proper training so they have the skills for whatever they're doing next, we're going to be part of a sensible transition.

Head of Equities: That's going to be critical. Community relations is a key component of our social license to operate.

Chief Investment Officer: My dialogue with the **Head of PE** on the ground in Atsui has been ongoing, and he wants us to do right by the community. It's almost an impact investment in and of itself.

Any other questions on the PE investment?

Head of Risk: How comfortable are you with ABC's management? We'll only have a minority stake, and founders are sometimes not the best people to run a business.

So are these people reliable? Do they have the right skill set? The right education? Any worry about potential corruption?

Head of PE: Our due diligence is thorough, and we don't think corruption is an issue. We're new to direct investing, and so we'll be tracking progress extra carefully. And also we're the ones implementing a lot of the modernization, so there'll be more monitoring built in than ever before.

Do we keep management or not? You always have this question in private equity. With all the co-investing we've done, the directors of the funds we partner with find management teams and then keep them and then work *with* them to help them grow.

I see your point that we'd only hold 35% of ABC, but we'll also hold two board seats. I can't predict the future, but we've done a lot of due diligence and we've done a lot of interviews with management, customers, and suppliers. We've interviewed a lot of people who know the management.

We're paying $25 million, and $20 million goes to modernizing the plant. Management will take a little money off the table, and we'll structure it so that they are incentivized in alignment with growth and good oversight. After all, they'll still hold 65%.

We think they'll see that working with us will create success and that willful mismanagement or corruption or taking too much money out of the business works against them in the long run. We're coming to them with our track record through the co-investments we've made, our expertise, and our channels to other markets.

There's always risk, but that's my point of view.

Head of Equities: I support the PE investment. With management having this much skin in the game, their interests are aligned with ours.

Chief Investment Officer: This is a $25 million investment out of our $50 billion fund, and there are impact elements as well that make it more interesting.

Head of PE: Yeah, and to build our direct investment program, we must learn by doing. We've gotten really comfortable with co-investing, and that's great, but to me, it's the people who do this a lot on their own who tend to be really successful.

Yes, there's some risk with management and the government, but a lot of those are risks we're willing to take with one of our first direct investments, where we can get our hands dirty. It's a simple business, right? It's carbonated beverages, and then maybe we go into juices and non-carbonated stuff, right? We can really build the experience of working with management and the other skills that our direct program is going to need.

Hey, maybe our next committee meeting should be in Atsui!

General Discussion on Risk

Chief Investment Officer: I won't argue, but let me ask the committee about a risk that applies to both of these investments. We're an open forum, and so I ask the entire room: What bears more scrutiny?

Head of Risk: The first thing that comes to my mind when we're investing in frontier markets like these is, "How do we deal with the currency risk?" It's hard to hedge these currencies. Meanwhile, they can move wildly against the dollar, turning a really good investment into a really bad investment.

What's your read on this, **Head of PE**?

Head of PE: I'm not stressed about it. When it comes to me and most other visitors to Atsui, we're using US dollars.

Case Study

Head of Infrastructure: I can speak to the currency risk in Sunnyland. When we're talking about the aviation industry and airports, a lot of revenues for infrastructure investors come in the form of regulated charges. Look at our own concession contract: 70% of the revenues are airport charges. It's typical with these arrangements to outsource the collection of these charges to international organizations like IATA. They collect the revenue from the airline, and almost all of that is paid in dollars, so we're comfortable there.

That leaves the 30% of our revenue coming from commercial sources—retail revenue in the terminal and past the gate and all that duty free and parking. In the big international airports, those transactions take place in the local currency, but we're in a locale that's expressly seeking international tourism. Pricing will be geared to international markets, so we'll have the freedom to price everything in dollars and benchmark the pricing against the affluent traveler.

Head of Risk: I'm glad to hear that.

What about the borrowing side, though? To keep people happy and the logistics simple, I assume any borrowings will come from local banks that use their country's currency.

Head of Infrastructure: It's a good thought, but no. The lenders are big international banks. The in-country banks may participate, but given the size of the loans and how long term these arrangements are—at least in Sunnyland—the local banks just don't have the capacity yet.

Whoever the lenders are, they'll be comfortable knowing the investors are getting their returns mostly in US dollars, which is what the $300 million of debt is denominated in.

Head of Risk: Which brings me to defaults.

Head of Infrastructure: Right, well, this is non-recourse financing, and the concession agreement outlines the terms of default and termination. These are matters that impinge on the direct arrangement between the government and the banks, so while it's something to be aware of, I don't see us getting dragged in.

Head of Risk: Thanks.

Head of Equities: I know the **Head of Risk** was coming to this, but the topic is coming up very often recently.

If you look at the World Economic Forum's "Global Risk Report" since 2017, climate risk and extreme weather feature in the top risks every time. Year over year, the weather gets more erratic. Sea-level rise may be gradual, but it doesn't stop. And while I understand the need to support Sunnyland's economy by expanding the airport, the memo says that the new runway is less than a kilometer from the sea.

Sure, you get a fantastic view when you take off and land, but the sea *is* rising, and the risk of flooding could become real even just during high tide. Running an airport in those conditions would not be possible.

It's a 25-year infrastructure investment. That's long enough for climate risks to materialize and impact operations. We've got to factor this in.

Head of Infrastructure These points are well taken, but keep in mind that to even get as far as finding interested lenders for the airport, it means we've gone through the due diligence process. The big banks need environmental-impact statements before they jump on board, and even just in our role as equity investors, we had to satisfy ourselves that these kinds of issues were thought through.

Head of Risk: Sure, and naming risks is necessary and commendable, but—

Head of Infrastructure: —But that doesn't mean the risk goes away. Of course.

I'm obviously not an engineer or a contractor, but what I'd say to the committee is that the experts tells us, in the time frame we're looking at, environmental risks are unlikely to materialize, and even so, they're accounted for during the design process. The drainage systems are modified to handle increases in groundwater levels, and the engineers are building in once-in-50-years and once-in-100-years flood scenarios. Those are risks they're confident they can build for.

Chief Investment Officer: None of us are experts here, but my perspective is that we can take comfort from the fact that these kinds of challenges have been around for decades. Consider Kansai International Airport in Japan: People are always saying that it's sinking—and it *has* gone down a tiny bit—but it's been around for over 25 years and it's been fine.

It's important to be aware of it, and I'm glad you brought it up, but indications are that there's nothing really stopping us on this front.

Head of Infrastructure: That's right. We've come to rely on the reports from the technical adviser, and that's a fairly standard approach for us with these sorts of investments.

Head of PE: Agreed.

Head of Risk: What about previous foreign investment in Sunnyland? Did political risk come into play for other investments? What's the general feeling?

Head of PE: **Head of Infrastructure** called me from Sunnyland when I was on the beach in Atsui planning the ABC upgrades, and he asked me to look into it. Investment in Sunnyland has mostly been on the tourism side. There's a mixture of three- and five-star hotels, so major international hotel operators are around. And they're still arriving, but they feel the transportation bottleneck. Those who are there and the ones who are thinking about coming in are happy about the airport project.

Head of Infrastructure: And I haven't heard any horror stories about investors in Sunnyland getting burned because of unfair rule changes. Plus, relations are good. The Sunnyland authorities approached us as a fellow government institution, so we're comfortable on a sort of government-to-government basis.

Chief Investment Officer: One nice thing about an island nation is that it *is* an island. There's less political interference from the neighbours. From what **Head of Infrastructure** was telling me, we can feel positive that our investment in the airport will help the economy and stabilize the local political situation more than the contrary.

Head of Risk: Good to hear. Let's dig a little deeper on the modeling we've done for the airport investment. We expect a 15% IRR over 25 years. That is our base case. Have we done any stress tests to those baseline expectations? What if there are delays and we have to pay a penalty? What if construction costs overrun the budget? What if revenues fall short? Give us an idea of how bad the IRR could get if we don't achieve the base case.

Head of Infrastructure: Sure. I like how you've framed the question, because it covers some key risks.

From our perspective, the biggest risk is traffic—comparing the actual number of visitors and tourists coming in and out of the airport against our projections. We're not experts here, either, but we hired an established traffic consultant who looks at the global tourism numbers and the particulars of our development to make a determination.

Case Study

The consultant produced a low case and a high case based on different traffic forecasts. The low case is also of interest to the banks, of course, which want confidence that they'll be paid.

Our analysis of the reasonable low case puts IRR down to around 10% or 11%. The high case pushes the return out into the high teens.

There are some sensitivities around CapEx, and we're looking to manage this risk through a fixed-price contract, the language of which says that whatever penalties we'd face for delayed or subpar construction will be passed down to the contractor. We've applied a ±10% sensitivity around that, and it does impinge on the IRR a little bit but not as much as the low-traffic case. If we run into real cost overruns or delays, we're looking at about a 13% IRR.

Head of PE: The airport's key source of revenue is tourist numbers, and we've got an exotic luxury destination on our hands, folks.

Head of Equities: Agreed. And therefore, we need to consider the risk of a prolonged global recession when discretionary vacations and spending take a nosedive. For a small island like Sunnyland, this is a big risk. Some scenario analysis that considers the impact of a downturn that lasts for two or three or even four years seems necessary.

Head of Infrastructure: We've done some work on those scenarios, and it's influenced by a specific responsibility of the government, which they have explicitly accepted, to aggressively promote tourism as soon as, if not before, a recession hits.

Think of the aviation industry, which has been through shocks again and again. With downtimes like the global financial crisis around 2009 and the few instances where travelers were spooked by crashes, the airlines came out with attractive deals and recovery was quick.

Sunnyland's government is used to adjusting and always reduces pricing to attract tourists when they need to. Our sense is that even a prolonged recession isn't a deal killer, because the authorities and the industry will react quickly.

Head of PE: I like your optimism.

Chief Investment Officer Well, beyond optimism, we're starting from a low base; there's enormous room for growth in Sunnyland.

Head of Risk: If I may, **CIO**, just a follow-up question to the **Head of Equities**' point on the recession: We all experienced the coronavirus pandemic in 2020, and plenty of scientists have warned us that pandemics are going to be more likely—

Head of Equities: —Helped along by climate change!

Head of Risk: Yes, thank you, because of how we're damaging the environment, and again, this investment has a 25-year horizon. What if another pandemic causes rampant restrictions and people are simply not allowed to travel? Has that been factored into our scenario analysis?

Head of Infrastructure: To a limited extent, yes. We pass through 35% of whatever revenue we take on, so our payments to the government are handled that way in the concession agreement. That leaves the crucial aspect of defaults to lenders and what would trigger them.

The built-in debt-service reserve covers us for a period of time, and if travel is on hold for too much longer, then we turn to restructuring or rescheduling the financing.

But let's understand that the COVID-19 pandemic in 2020 was a game-changer, and the language and dynamics of certain contractual agreements were adjusted to avoid straight defaults in these cases. And the concern here is about short-term impact, whereas over 25 years, we expect things to gradually recover, so our concerns are more about keeping the project going and avoiding default during the problem period.

Voting on Infrastructure Investment

Chief Investment Officer: OK, I'm grateful for the expertise we have around this table. I think that's probably good for a committee vote. Let's start with our **Head of Infrastructure**: yes or no?

Head of Infrastructure: Yes.

Chief Investment Officer: How about our **Head of Risk**?

Head of Risk: I have my doubts, but because it is a $100 million investment on AUM of $50 billion, we'll give it a shot. I'll say "yes."

Chief Investment Officer: We have to take a little bit of risk, after all. **Head of PE**, how about you?

Head of PE: Before we ultimately pull the trigger, we should take another look at our other investments and similar memos to see if they're related to tourism and it would mean too much correlation. Besides that, I'm a "yes."

Chief Investment Officer: OK. **Head of Equities**?

Head of Equities: Yes from me as well. Given the size of the investment, I think it's worth taking the risk.

Chief Investment Officer: And I vote "yes."
As a sovereign wealth fund, beyond our responsibility to manage risks and returns well, we want to give back, and where our participation helps nations develop, we feel a responsibility there as well.

Voting on Private Equity Investment

Chief Investment Officer: All right, very good. Let's move on to our direct private equity investment in ABC. **Head of PE**, what say you?

Head of PE: I'm in. Yes.

Chief Investment Officer: Very good. How about you, **Head of Equities**?

Head of Equities: I'm supportive of this. For one thing, it presents much less risk than the airport in Sunnyland. Yes.

Chief Investment Officer: OK. And our resident infrastructure expert, what say you?

Head of Infrastructure: Well, you might expect me to disagree with **Head of Equities** in terms of the risk—we have a minority position, for one thing. But the investment is small, so I'm fine. Yes.

Chief Investment Officer: OK. And finally, **Head of Risk**?

Case Study

Head of Risk: **Head of PE** made some very good points. It *is* indeed a simple investment to understand and a chance to gain some experience in direct investment. Even if it doesn't work out financially, there's upside to building our experience and to having a positive impact on the wider community, to name but two areas of non-financial return. Yes from me.

Chief Investment Officer: OK, we have two investments that I'm excited to proceed with. I'd like **Head of Infrastructure** and **Head of PE** to run with those and keep us posted, and now it's time—

Head of PE: —To fight for the open board seat!

Head of Risk: Sounds fun, but actually, let's do this the old-fashioned way by filling the other board seat on the basis of experience?

Head of PE: One free Mango Special to our wise, risk-averse colleague!

Chief Investment Officer: And with that, we'll see everyone for the next investment committee meeting, in a month's time.

—*The End*—

IN-TEXT QUESTIONS

Please respond to the following questions based on **Investment Committee Meeting 1.0**.

1. The Head of Infrastructure identified a key risk to the Sunnyland airport investment. Explain what analysis could be shared with you to increase your confidence that the key risk is properly managed prior to making the investment in the Sunnyland airport.
2. Explain how the upcoming election most likely exposes the R-SWF's investment in ABC to financial risk. Discuss whether or not you believe the Head of PE's approach to managing this particular risk is sufficient.

Guideline Answers:

1. During the investment committee meeting, the Head of Infrastructure identified traffic as the key risk to the Sunnyland airport investment. The island might not draw an increased number of tourists simply because the airport can accommodate larger planes and more passengers. Although the Head of Infrastructure alluded to the fact that he has quantified the financial risk should the level of tourists not meet expectations after the completion of the new airport, I would like to review his scenario analysis to feel comfortable with his assumptions. Scenario analysis would be the best way to manage this financial risk prior to making the investment in Sunnyland.
2. I do not think the Head of PE's approach to managing the financial risk due to the upcoming election is sufficient. My understanding is that the upcoming election will expose ABC to financial risk because the current government has imposed large tariffs on foreign competitors that would like to export their products to Atsui. In the event a different political party, specifically one that opposes such tariffs, wins the upcoming election in Atsui, it could have a significant effect on the profitability of ABC because the company would need to compete for local customers.

   Of course, a change in government is not something that ABC can control. Although I believe the steps the Head of PE has taken to manage this particular risk are good, including building rapport with the current government, it is not clear to me that he has conducted a thorough analysis to illustrate the potential financial impact on ABC should the tariffs be reduced or eliminated after the upcoming election. This analysis should be done using scenario analysis. Despite this being a relatively small investment for R-SWF, the financial risk of a change in the tariff policy should be thoroughly modeled and assessed prior to making the investment.

4 R-SWF'S Investments: 2.0

Extension of Case Facts (2.0)

After Investment Committee Meeting 1.0, the investment committee of the sovereign wealth fund of Ruritania, R-SWF, added two new significant investments to its portfolio. These investments were direct infrastructure and direct private equity investments—the investments in the airport in Sunnyland and the beverage manufacturer in Atsui, respectively.

- Three years have passed, and the investment committee of R-SWF has decided to conduct an investment review of the two projects.
- Note: The focus of the meeting is on the risks (current and potential) of the new investment proposals, not details on the financial performance of the investments. (An in-depth meeting on the financial performance of the investments was held in the previous month).
- All investment committee participants (and Level III candidates in the CFA Program) are provided with a background memo with the following information:
    - Memo A: Update on R-SWF's asset allocation and performance
    - Memo B: Update on the direct infrastructure investment (airport expansion in Sunnyland) and a list of risks for discussion
    - Memo C: Provides details on the proposed direct private equity investment (investment in ABC) and a list of risks for discussion.

INVESTMENT COMMITTEE MEETING MEMO 2.0

To: R-SWF Investment Committee Members
From: R-SWF Chief Investment Officer
Re: Investment Committee Meeting 2.0 Agenda

Distribution: Head of Risk, Head of PE, Head of Infrastructure, Head of Equities, and Junior Staff

Agenda

- Opening Remarks and Asset Allocation CIO—5 minutes
- Infrastructure Update CIO + Head of Infrastructure—5 minutes
- PE Update CIO + Head of PE—5 minutes
- Discussion of Risk—Infrastructure: Head of Infrastructure, Head of Risk, All—10 minutes
- Discussion of Risk—PE: Head of PE, Head of Risk, All—10 minutes
- Other Risks: Head of Equities + All—5–10 minutes
- Closing Remarks: CIO—5 minutes

Memo 2A: Asset Allocation and Performance

- Since its inception, R-SWF has built a diversified portfolio of investments. As of last month, the fund had AUM of $56 billion USD, with the fund outperforming its overall benchmark by 130 bps net of fees since inception. Of course, there have been short-term periods of underperformance as the fund pursued its long-term strategy.
- The asset allocation as of last month for the overall fund was as follows:

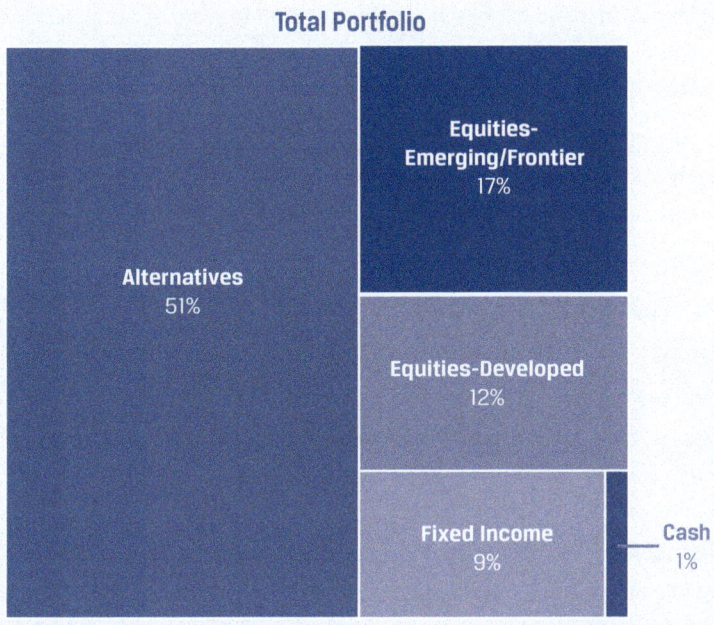

- R-SWF had approximately 51% of assets invested in alternative investments, consistent with its long-term objectives.
- Asset allocation was covered extensively in the prior month's investment committee meeting, so today's meeting will not provide any further breakdown.
- The investment committee will be discussing various points of view on risk aspects of the investments—including risk mitigation.
- The discussion will include "other risks" that were perhaps not covered well in the initial discussion. Discussion of environmental and social risks are challenging for long-term direct investing.
- Updates on the airport expansion in Sunnyland infrastructure investment are found in Memo 2B.
- Updates on the PE investment in ABC in Atsui are found in Memo 2C.

Memo 2B: Update on Infrastructure Investment in Sunnyland Airport

Investment Update

- Based on investment committee approval, the $100 million investment in Sunnyland has moved forward in accordance with agreed plans. This amount represents approximately 0.2% of total R-SWF assets.
- The Sunnyland government is happy with the progress of construction, which was completed recently. There was a delay in getting started, but that is Island life. Thankfully, there were no material cost overruns on the project.
- The new terminal is beautifully built and will be a great addition to the island nation as it further develops its tourism capabilities.

- We expect a grand opening of the new terminal in September, in time for the busy fall season. Tourist season is primarily from October through May, with the summer months being very hot (around 40°C) and humid.
- There are rumors that Airport Operating Group (AOG) is looking to renegotiate its contract for a higher fixed fee.
- One of the advantages of Sunnyland as a tourist attraction is its beautiful beaches with easy access to the airport, with the new runway, only 1 km from the sea, providing spectacular views.
- However, climate change has led to rising seas and more frequent storms. Storms are common in island nations; however, the rising seas are of concern.
- In addition, hotter temperatures are of additional concern. A few years ago, the tourist season was September through June, with only July and August being "too hot." However, in May this year, daytime highs were frequently 42°C or higher. There is a risk that the hotter temperatures lasting longer in the year will reduce tourism (and revenues for the airport project).
- Although this is a small investment in total, there are some risks we should focus on in today's discussion.

Risk Discussion: Infrastructure Investment

The following key risks are highlighted for discussion:

- Currency risk
- Expropriation risk by the Sunnyland government
- Risk that revenue from airport is less than expected
- Risk of project delays
- Risk of operating and maintenance costs being higher than projected
- Risk of default of AOG
- Risk that actual future (borrowing) interest rates will be higher than forecast
- Risk of underperformance regarding service quality–not meeting defined standards
- Other risks

Possible Mitigation of the Key Risks

- What should we do to mitigate the key risks?
- What should be our priorities? Action plan?

Memo 2C: Update on PE Investment in Atsui Beverage Company

Investment Update

- Based on investment committee approval, the $25 million investment in ABC has moved forward in accordance with agreed plans. This amount represents approximately 0.05% of total R-SWF assets.
- The modernization of the ABC plant went well, and the product expansion is starting to take shape. However, there several key updates that are unfortunately negative:
  - Atsui and surrounding nations went into a recession last year. Furthermore, a currency devaluation is anticipated. Beverages are considered a luxury item in Atsui.

- A new government was elected in Atsui last year and took office in January. One of the first orders of business was to reduce tariffs on imported beverages from a 100% tariff to a 20% tariff. This change hurts our cost advantage over foreign brands. It is rumored that tariffs were reduced because Atsui wants to gain favor with foreign governments for potential loans.
- Because the modern equipment will improve productivity, the original plan was to reduce headcount by 40%. In addition, due to slowing sales, management wanted to reduce staff by a total of 50%. However, labor laws are strict in Atsui. In order to terminate the employment of an Atsui citizen, significant notice (two years) is required. Plus, there is reputational risk for R-SWF for firing factory employees in a frontier market during a recession.
- In order to make up for lower profits (due to the above reasons), plant management has started to cut corners to save on costs. Unfortunately, one way to do this was to dump waste into the nearby river rather than transport the waste for proper treatment. Although the waste is not toxic, it is starting to spoil the lovely fishing spot near the factory.
- Another way ABC has tried to cut costs is by reducing employee breaks from one hour to 30 minutes and removing soap from the restrooms, requesting that employees bring their own.
- Although this is a small investment in total, there are some risks we should focus on in today's discussion.

Risk Discussion: Private Equity Investment

The following key risks are highlighted for discussion:

- Currency risk
- Expropriation risk by the Atsui government
- Quality control issues
- Challenges with local management (don't have a majority stake)
- Competitor pressure
- Growing trend of health foods that would result in avoidance of many carbonated beverages
- Elimination of tariffs protecting ABC from foreign-owned manufacturers
- Other risks

Possible Mitigation of the Key Risks

- What should we do to mitigate these risks?
- What should be our priorities? Action plan?

IN-TEXT QUESTIONS

Please respond to the following questions based on **Investment Committee Memo 2.0**.

4 The investment committee has identified several new risks that were not previously discussed (before Memos 2B and 2C). The CIO asks you to recommend how R-SWF can manage each of the following risks:

   a Risk of actual future (borrowing) interest rates will be higher than forecast (Memo 2B)

   b Growing trend of health foods that would result in avoidance of many carbonated beverages (Memo 2C)

> **Guideline Answers:**
>
> 4a: R-SWF can manage the risk that actual future (borrowing) interest rates will be higher than forecast by hedging its interest rate exposure for the Sunnyland airport project.
>
> 4b: R-SWF can manage the risk of carbonated beverages falling out of favor due to an increasing preference for health foods by working to develop new healthy alternatives to carbonated, presumably sugar-filled drinks. As the production facility expands its ability to produce product, ABC could focus its new product development on healthy alternatives. The company can leverage its experience producing such beverages given the success of its natural mango drink in order to differentiate itself and increase market share.

Investment Committee Meeting 2.0

Participants

- Chief Investment Officer (CIO)
- Head of Infrastructure
- Head of PE
- Head of Risk
- Head of Equities
- Analysts [no speaking role]

Chief Investment Officer: Good morning, everyone, and welcome to today's investment committee meeting of the sovereign wealth fund of the Republic of Ruritania. We're grateful for the opportunity to serve our constituents.

During last month's committee meeting, we reviewed the financial statements of the two projects in question—the airport in Sunnyland and the beverage manufacturer in Atsui. Our **Head of PE** provided the Mango Specials, so thank you for that!

It's been three years—wow, time really flies—since we unanimously approved proceeding with both investments. We'll go through some updates, but today's focus is risks and sensible mitigation measures.

First, though, the bigger picture: In those three years, AUM have grown by $6 billion. We're still outperforming our overall benchmark, but our outperformance has been dulled by difficulties with some assets, primarily real estate, because commercial real estate has underperformed. So that's hurt us a little bit, but as ever, we are long-term investors, and we may reap the benefits of those investments yet.

As we discuss risk mitigation, let's consider environmental and social risks. The greater pressure we've put on ourselves to invest responsibly and sustainably is matched by increased scrutiny from outside observers.

Whether we've decided to make an exit on our own or because of outside pressure, our rather long-term horizon doesn't make it any easier for us to step away from an investment when the time comes. As a contrast, our **Head of Equities** was telling me before the meeting started that he wasn't too happy about how much one of his portfolio companies was polluting, and so he just went ahead and sold the position. It was a liquid investment in a public market, and he was done within the hour. That's a contrast we have to keep in mind.

Allow me to read this comment about ABC from the minutes of the last meeting, as a sort of touchstone for us today: "This is a rather small investment, of $25 million, but even a small investment can have an outsized negative impact on us if we don't manage the risk properly."

But let's begin with Sunnyland airport. **Head of Infrastructure**, why don't you start us off?

Head of Infrastructure: Thanks, **CIO**.

The good news is that the new terminal is pretty much complete and in line with specifications. We received some good reviews, both from locals and the international trade press. The downside is delays: At the outset, we expected a two-year construction program, but we're now well into the third year, unfortunately. There were noticeable cost overruns, and those were borne by the contractor, according to the contract, but there are some delay penalties that have yet to be settled.

The government, the contractor, and ourselves and AOG as investors—we're in discussions about these penalties, and the contractors are pointing to variations they say arose from our side. What they're calling "variations" we see as necessary design thinking for optimizing the commerciality of the retail outlets. The "variations" were pretty minimal, so let's see where our discussions end up. And some further disagreements center around the offices of customs and immigration within the terminal, which the contractor is laying at the foot of the government.

We should also highlight that as we're nearing the startup of terminal operations, the operator, AOG, has started complaining that the costs of training local staff are higher than expected. They haven't said anything formally yet, but I imagine they'll want to renegotiate their fixed-fee contract—nothing too serious.

Meanwhile, the grand opening of the terminal is a month away, in late August. It should be a good, high-profile event, and we should make a good showing. At least four Ruritania representatives, I think.

And then always swirling around our work is the focus of the press on the environmental movement and climate change, so we need to think about the impact on tourism. The main tourist season is September through June, historically, but it's just getting too hot, and so really the prime window for visitors will narrow to October through May.

The debate in the local press is frequently about the impact of so many tourists flying to Sunnyland, and AOG is in dialogue with the airlines about it. We have yet to see how that plays out in terms of impact on the airport operations down the road, but at the grand opening, we'll be able to celebrate the start of the upcoming season in September; bookings are in line with optimistic projections for the first year with the new terminal and runway.

Chief Investment Officer: OK, thank you for that update.

And what can we say about ABC in Atsui?

Head of PE: So, there are positives and negatives. A big positive is that this has been a fantastic learning experience for our direct investment program. But there's been a currency devaluation, and you could argue it's going to get worse because of the recession—the recession that started last year and that you all know so well because we're in the middle of it.

Still, is that good or bad? We do sell to tourists who bring their own currency, and we've got a lot of flexibility to shift our pricing so we can keep prices where they should be relative to our costs, which is positive.

But following the recent election, the new administration is talking about dropping all sorts of import tariffs, including the ones on food and drink. They've basically said, "For sure, we're going to cut them from 100% to 20%."

Obviously, this hurts our cost advantage over foreign brands, and the challenge here is that the new government wants to win favor with foreign governments before asking them for big loans, so the issue is about more than just carbonated drinks.

Chief Investment Officer: There's a rumor that the new president likes Pepsi, so it's almost as if she doesn't want to pay double for a can, but 20% more is OK.

Head of PE: ABC's new modernized equipment is ready to go, but here's the problem: Management is now saying they want to reduce headcount by 50%, instead of just 40%, because of the slowing sales. But labor laws in Atsui are strict, and to let someone go, you usually have to give as much as two years' notice.

Head of Risk: Two years?

Head of PE: Yeah, and the other issue is that for us as a sovereign wealth fund, there's reputational risk. Flying in from world cities and firing factory employees in frontier markets mean bad publicity, especially in Atsui and especially during the recession.

And here's another thing: In order to make up for lower profits, management has started cutting corners. They're dumping waste in the nearby river rather than paying to transport it to the treatment site. Do you remember how the plant is right next to the river and the employees fish in it during lunch? It's spoiling the fishing spot. This is a problem. And it gets worse: Scientists are saying that the plant site and the river overlap with the range of a rare reptile that is found here and only one other place on earth. So our site has attracted the attention of people with no interest in soda or mangoes.

Head of Risk: This is a problem.

Head of PE: Now here's another thing: ABC has tried to cut costs by reducing employee breaks from an hour to 30 minutes and—this is probably a little granular for our meeting, but risks are risks, they have removed soap from the restrooms! Everyone has to bring their own soap now.

Now, I know we're a $50 billion sovereign wealth fund—

Chief Investment Officer: —$56 billion.

Head of PE: I know we're a $56 billion sovereign wealth fund, and here we are talking about removing soap from a few bathrooms in the tropics where we have a $25 million direct investment, but stuff like this can have a reputational impact.

Head of Risk: Agreed.

Chief Investment Officer: Our focus right now is risk, and we should be talking about this. We haven't really faced any of these health and safety or social issues before at the individual investment level, and it's a learning opportunity as we expand our direct investing program. **Head of PE**, when you went to the restroom and found out there was no soap, you had to borrow some from the plant manager. Is that right? Did he give it to you for free, or did he charge you?

Head of PE: He wanted to charge me, but I didn't need any soap because I had hand sanitizer with me. I got used to carrying hand sanitizer around with me everywhere back in the coronavirus days, so now I just do that when I'm in Atsui.

Chief Investment Officer: OK, then let's discuss infrastructure.

Three years ago when we approved this investment, we talked potential risks, including climate, and we were comfortable with the position that the threat of rising seas was well into the future. We may have to re-evaluate that position.

Head of Risk: Despite our comfort then, the fact is that storms have become more frequent and the sea level *has* risen measurably—in three short years.

Head of Infrastructure: The lenders have also raised this point, as has our in-country political adviser. I still don't see any impact in the immediate term. If you remember three years ago, much of our comfort came from the environmental-impact assessments, which were required and were factored into the design. What has been constructed can deal with it sufficiently.

The bigger worry is the force of an unanticipated and rare storm that compounds the impact of some already bad flooding. Originally, the engineers planned for a once-in-50-years or once-in-100-years scenario, and it may be that the risk of those events has increased.

There's a discussion to be had with the government about architectural solutions—maybe some proper flood barriers. As for the cost of them, if they'll even work, and whose responsibility that is—those issues are unclear. It's not in anybody's interest for the airport to shut down.

Head of Equities: My experience engaging with large public companies on climate risk tells me that a tiny island like Sunnyland can't have any meaningful impact on a global scale and hence they must focus on adaptation rather than worry too much about mitigation. **Head of Infrastructure** points to one of the more logical solutions: some sort of storm-surge barrier like the Netherlands has relied on for years.

As for who's going to pay for it, let's think beyond our own project for a minute. Rising seas aren't just going to have an impact on the airport; every five-star, beach-facing property will feel it too. The prime hotels feel it, and eventually the whole tourist ecosystem feels it, and with the country so dependent on tourism, my view is that this has to be a government-driven initiative. And a storm-surge barrier that successfully avoids damaging floods will be important enough to private interests, such as real estate and other infrastructure investors, that they'll form part of the funding circle.

Head of Infrastructure: I think that's right. It's a question for the whole economy and for the government. Serious talks are taking place in Sunnyland about a new tax to cover the costs, a sort of climate tax that would go to a host of worsening climate issues.

How the authorities end up structuring that tax will inform whether we can avoid it.

Chief Investment Officer: Understood, but as a sovereign institution, even if we could avoid such a tax to protect our investment value, from a reputational perspective, we should think twice.

Head of PE: **Head of Infrastructure** said that AOG might be asking for a higher fixed fee to operate the new terminal. I'm not sure if this is a question for this point in the meeting, but is there anything we can do to proactively protect ourselves against a higher contract fee in the event AOG gets its renegotiation?

Head of Infrastructure: We all signed a well-structured agreement, and that affords us some decent protection against any meddling in the fee structure, though there are break clauses if anything gets too out of line. Still, there are incentives built into the concession agreement to make sure everyone wins to a greater or lesser extent when traffic goes up.

Equally, we don't want a disgruntled operator. Happy employees, happy travelers, better experience, more traffic.

We haven't been formally approached about this, but let's not dismiss it out of hand just because we have a contract we can hide behind. AOG is a strong global operator. If they did activate a break clause in two or three years' time, that lands us with a responsibility we really don't want, which is finding a new operator. We're still satisfied with their cooperation. I recommend seeing how talks over the delays play out, and if we find that the government is liable for the delay, we'll request an extension to the concession and then sit down with AOG to positively collaborate on retooling the whole picture.

Chief Investment Officer: OK, we've covered the environmental and reputational risks, the climate risk, and the AOG item as well. Are there any other risks we should examine at this point?

Head of Risk: That covers the important ones. Currency risk and the risk of further delays are less of a concern. With climate change, we can't *solve* it; as **Head of Equities** insists, we have to adapt. It affects the entire nation, so hopefully the government will step in.

And I reinforce the idea of positive negotiations with AOG. We want a happy operator.

Chief Investment Officer: Right. OK, very good.

Head of Risk, it looks like something is still on your mind.

Head of Risk: Thanks for noticing. A little more scrutiny of ABC is warranted. I acknowledge its importance for boosting our direct investment know-how. It's been a great learning experience for **Head of PE** and his team, and it's a very small investment. Even if we lose money, it's not going to move the needle for our fund, but—and this is a substantial "but"—the reputational risk is a big concern.

We don't want to end up in the newspaper firing people during a recession, polluting the river, threatening endangered species, and being rather petty about soap.

Head of Infrastructure: True on all counts.

Head of Risk: Ladies and gentlemen, the writing is on the wall. I propose we exit this investment as soon as possible, if we can. Maybe we can't, and if that's the case, I would remain very concerned.

Head of PE: No, I'm happy you mentioned it, and it's good that it's all coming out in this room. Let me tell you how we see things.

Before we jumped into this as one of our first direct investments, we co-invested and participated in many private equity funds that invest in all kinds of things, including special situations and distressed investments, and we've always gone in with third-party experts or used our own experts. Just because things get a little dicey, it doesn't mean we exit.

When we started, ABC was a conventional, if small, investment. If that's changed and it now is a problem business, we've got a team whose job it is to make lemonade out of lemons, so let's think about passing ABC over to the distressed-asset team before it becomes properly distressed. I'm not saying we keep it or some other team takes it. I'm saying let's at least see if it's a better fit for someone else.

What if we keep going? We've got risks around firing employees, dumping waste in the river, and pettiness around soap. And we're shifting our mindset, and the challenge is less about the return and more about the reputational risk.

So we really need to figure out: Can we change how this business functions to manage that risk? We have a 35% interest, we know that management has skin in the game. But in what game? With management incentivized to improve the bottom line, we're motivating them to cut employees instead of keeping employees happy and avoiding resentment.

So we're asking ourselves a new question: How do we motivate management to keep people inside and outside the plant happy? We have two board seats, and investing more money in modernization seems to make less sense now.

Case Study

And we've got employees now who don't have much to do, but they're collecting a salary, so why would they leave? And if we can't fire them, it's an issue. Maybe we pay them a percentage—say, half their regular salary—while offering them good training and assistance for eight months to find another job. At the same time, we'd convince management to shift to a less profit-driven focus.

I don't know if any of that will work. Maybe we should have divested earlier, but that's our thinking if we keep holding on.

Head of Equities: And what about the toxic stuff being released into the river?

Head of PE: It's actually not toxic, technically, but we don't even want to be talking about whether it's toxic or not toxic. Ending that practice is an important piece of our talks with management, and so is removing incentives to cut corners.

Can we fundamentally change the way things are going? If we can't, then maybe this is an investment for someone else. Or perhaps we sell our 35% stake back to management?

Chief Investment Officer: Thanks, **Head of PE**. We talked about this being a learning experience. We also talked about it displaying aspects of impact investment. Maybe part of the value is in education. In some less developed areas, they think it's maybe not a big deal to throw things into the river. Can we inform their thinking with the idea that wanting a beautiful river for fishing and enjoyment is a virtue and that it's not really that hard to dispose of waste properly? What can we intelligently say about impact?

Head of Equities: This line of thinking makes sense to me. Our experience in other developing nations as well as developed nations tells us that you'll save some costs in the short term with actions like dumping waste directly into water bodies, but in the long run, regulations catch up to you and the cost of pre-treatment or appropriate handling of waste is much lower than the penalties you get for taking such shortcuts.

If we decide to stay, we have to paint the picture for management that there's a fatal flaw in our approach at the moment. Public perception is one issue, but eventually regulations will be introduced with penalties and obligations to clean up the river.

If we do try to salvage the situation and continue with our investment, there's a path that involves the government. Our pitch should be that if there are legal roadblocks for cutting 50% of the jobs, you might be putting 100% of the jobs at risk because the company won't survive if tariffs are reduced to 20%. The government doesn't want the factory to shut down because of *its* rigid labor laws, so there may well be room for a more, let's say, negotiated conclusion.

It's worth exploring, again, in consultation with the local management.

Chief Investment Officer: Lobbying the government, reframing management's incentives—these are interesting ways to pivot. We should also consider as a committee the extent to which we want to maintain our direct investing/private equity approach or whether there is wisdom in recasting our work as more of an impact program. The committee's analysis has highlighted the difficulties faced by a sovereign wealth fund in cutting staff. It ends up being a headline risk.

The conventional private equity houses can more easily cut jobs for purely financial reasons. However, as a sovereign wealth fund, it is more complicated for us. Imagine the headline: "Government of Ruritania Cuts Jobs in XYZ during a Recession."

Head of Infrastructure: It's not a good look.

Chief Investment Officer: It's not a good look. Right.

Head of Risk: From my point of view, we've covered the main risks for ABC. I like the sequence: We engage with management to change the mindset, and we lobby government on how a two-year notice period and similar restrictions could jeopardize the whole business. We give it another year, and if we're not making progress, we look for an exit option, maybe handing things over to a team that is comfortable with these thorny issues.

Chief Investment Officer: Well summarized. I'm grateful for the focus we are putting on the risks here.
And as for Sunnyland?

Head of Equities: I'd submit to the team that while the world's major governments have *started* taking action on climate change, we're not going to "fix" these problems easily so the planet can just go back to the way it was 30 years ago. The impact will intensify, and we have to adapt.
In my mind, the focus should be on liaising with the government. They will have to drive things because of the scale of the investment required—

Chief Investment Officer: —And because of how long term the investment horizon is.
Team, this is the sort of experienced scrutiny of risk we needed, so thank you very much. This was a highly worthwhile meeting, and let's keep a keen focus on the risks.

—The End—

IN-TEXT QUESTIONS

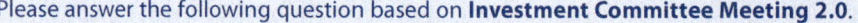

Please answer the following question based on **Investment Committee Meeting 2.0**.

1. In the template provided, state the primary environmental risk that has been identified by R-SWF's investment committee for each investment. Recommend how each risk can be managed in the future.

Investment	Primary Environmental Risk	Risk Management Recommendation
Sunnyland Airport		
Atsui Beverage Company		

2. Identify one significant social risk that both investments have in common and that was not originally identified by the investment committee. Discuss whether or not this risk is easily managed once recognized.

Guideline Answers

1. In the template provided, state the primary environmental risk that has been identified by R-SWF's investment committee for each investment. Recommend how each risk can be managed in the future.

Case Study

Investment	Primary Environmental Risk	Risk Management Recommendation
Sunnyland Airport	Climate change due to rising sea levels	Given the uncertainty around the precise timing and magnitude of the impact of climate change and rising sea levels specifically, R-SWF should use climate-related scenario analysis to better understand how climate change will affect its investment in Sunnyland. In addition, since R-SWF cannot mitigate climate change, it must focus on adaptation strategies. In this case, a strategy to provide protection for the airport against a storm surge or higher sea levels is the most realistic option. An adaptation strategy is consistent with the development mandate of R-SWF's investment in Sunnyland.
Atsui Beverage Company	Waste management due to dumping waste into river	R-SWF must find a way to persuade the board and local management to stop dumping waste in the river in an effort to pursue sustainable development and a "just" transition. Although it might be a cost savings in the short run, in the long run, regulations will catch up. Cleanup of improperly disposed waste is far more costly than appropriately disposing of waste up front. One of the ways to encourage prioritization of protecting the river is to educate the local community about the importance of a healthy river. Community education, the pursuit of sustainable development, and a "just" transition are consistent with the impact investing element of this investment for R-SWF.

2   Reputational risk is very significant in the case of each investment and can have an outsized effect on the performance of the investments. Social issues, such as reputational risk, are generally quite difficult to manage even once identified and understood because they are relatively challenging to quantify and integrate into financial models. Furthermore, best practices include considering the interests of all the stakeholders involved, which is not easy.

In Sunnyland, R-SWF must contribute to any effort to raise funds to implement protection against rising seas. This project will likely be expensive. However, it is not in R-SWF's best interest to appear to be avoiding contributing to the project to accommodate climate change. Doing so could significantly damage R-SWF's reputation in Sunnyland and beyond given the international attention paid to the construction of the new airport. In theory, reputational risk in this case is relatively simple to manage in that R-SWF simply needs to be a contributor to the project and overall community by supporting efforts to adapt to climate change so as to not destroy Sunnyland's tourism industry. However, execution of such a strategy to mitigate R-SWF's reputational risk in Sunnyland will need to be closely monitored in order to effectively execute it. Managing this type of risk is not easy.

Reputational risk is also very significant in the case of ABC because of two major social issues: (1) occupational health and safety and (2) labor standards. Each of these issues could significantly damage R-SWF's reputation. Removing hand soap from the restrooms is an occupational health and safety issue that could cause reputational damage. Shortening employee breaks and firing people during a recession are social issues related to labor standards.

These types of choices indicate that local management is more concerned about profitability than reputational risk. In order to manage its reputational risk, R-SWF needs to persuade the board to adjust its incentive structure in order to encourage local management to reverse course on these short-sighted, destructive social issues, even if it is expensive. R-SWF does not want to be perceived as an investor that exploits its labor force. Soap should be provided for employees, breaks should be reasonable in length, and rather than firing employees, which can't be effectively executed because of the strict labor laws, ABC should focus on retraining employees for the future of the business. This is a complicated, multifaceted course especially as a minority owner. It isn't easily implemented but can be done. Any changes will need to be monitored to ensure they continue and have the desired outcome—a sustainable and mutually beneficial long-term relationship with the local community.

5 R-SWF'S INVESTMENTS: 3.0

Second Extension of Case Facts (3.0)

You left R-SWF at the end of Year 3 and took a position as a Senior Risk Consultant at Kiken Consulting, a risk consulting firm.

In the summer of Year 5, you are reading the newspaper and notice some commentary on two of the R-SWF investments you had been involved with. You read the following excerpts with nostalgic interest.

Update on Infrastructure Investment

- The infrastructure investment continues to perform poorly because of a combination of the following:
  - lower revenue (fewer tourists) vs. forecast (50% lower than base case)
  - higher costs (mitigating flood damage) vs. forecast (50% higher than base case)
- The medium- and long-term forecast on this investment does not look promising.

Update on PE Investment

- The PE team was able to avoid a diplomatic crisis and reputational risk damage by finding a buyer for the 35% stake. They sold the full position at $27 million.
- The stake was sold to an international beverage company that had been exporting to Atsui. The company's sales had been adversely affected by a weaker Atsui currency. Thus, producing locally is advantageous because it provides a natural foreign exchange hedge.

You set the newspaper down and start thinking about Sunnyland and Atsui when your boss suddenly interrupts you with the following news:

> Kiken Consulting has a new client! R-SWF has hired the firm for a risk analysis project. Because you have prior knowledge on R-SWF's approach, your boss has assigned you to the project with a lead role. You are expected to evaluate the strengths and weaknesses of R-SWF's enterprise risk management system and to make recommendations for improvements.

IN-TEXT QUESTION

Please respond to the following question.

1. Provide key facts/inputs from the R-SWF case, use them to evaluate the strengths and weaknesses of R-SWF's enterprise risk management processes, and make recommendations for improvements.

Guideline Answer

1. One of the main strengths of R-SWF's risk management process is that R-SWF dedicated an entire internal investment committee meeting to identifying and discussing the potential risks of two relatively small investment opportunities. Ample time was taken to allow senior management of R-SWF to express their concerns

and discuss mitigation strategies to reduce potential risks. The investment committee was able to identify various potential risk factors, and senior management voted on both investment opportunities.

One of the weaknesses of R-SWF's risk management process is that too little effort was made in trying to quantify the various risks and agreeing on specific actions that could be taken if some of those risk materialized. The team, with the help of the Head of Risk, could have done a better job at performing scenario analysis for both investments and presented a base case, an optimistic case, and a pessimistic case. Although the team identified and discussed several risk factors, they should have put together an action plan for risk mitigation and potential hedging tools prior to making the investments. This action plan would be conditional on certain bad outcomes materializing. Finally, since both investments were quite small in the overall scheme and had limited financial and liquidity risk implications for the fund, more consideration could have been given to identifying potential reputational risks and ESG.

REFERENCES

CFA Institute. 2020. "*Climate Change Analysis in the Investment Process.*" CFA Institute (September). www.cfainstitute.org/en/research/industry-research/climate-change-analysis.

Geltner, D. 1993. "Estimating Market Values from Appraised Values without Assuming an Efficient Market." *Journal of Real Estate Research* 8:325–45.

Getmansky, M., A. W. Lo, and I. Makarov. 2004. "An Econometric Model of Serial Correlation and Illiquidity in Hedge Fund Returns." *Journal of Financial Economics* 74:529–609.

Grantham Research Institute on Climate Change and the Environment."*New Study Estimates Global Warming of 2.5 Centigrade Degrees by 2100 Would Put at Risk Trillions of Dollars of World's Financial Assets.*" Press release (4 April 2016). www.lse.ac.uk/GranthamInstitute/news/us2-5-trillion-of-the-worlds-financial-assets-would-be-at-risk-from-the-impacts-of-climate-change-if-global-mean-surface-temperature-rises-by-2-5c.

IEA. 2020. "*World Energy Outlook 2020*" (October). www.iea.org/reports/world-energy-outlook-2020.

Intergovernmental Panel on Climate Change. 2018. "*Special Report: Global Warming of 1.5 ºC*" (6 October). www.ipcc.ch/sr15/chapter/spm.

Lo, Joe. 2020. "*IEA Outlines How World Can Reach Net Zero Emissions by 2050.*" Climate Home News (13 October). www.climatechangenews.com/2020/10/13/iea-outlines-world-can-reach-net-zero-emissions-2050.

NASA. 2019. "*NASA Global Climate Change: Vital Signs of the Planet.*" https://climate.nasa.gov/vital-signs/global-temperature.

Okunev, J., and D. White. 2003. "*Hedge Fund Risk Factors and Value at Risk of Credit Trading Strategies.*" Working paper, University of New South Wales.

PRI Association."*Macro Risks: Universal Ownership*" (12 October 2017). www.unpri.org/sustainable-development-goals/the-sdgs-are-an-unavoidable-consideration-for-universal-owners/306.article.

Glossary

Absolute return benchmark A minimum target return that an investment manager is expected to beat.

Accounting defeasance Also called in-substance defeasance, accounting defeasance is a way of extinguishing a debt obligation by setting aside sufficient high-quality securities to repay the liability.

Accumulation phase Phase where the government predominantly contributes to a sovereign wealth pension reserve fund.

Active management A portfolio management approach that allows risk factor mismatches relative to a benchmark index causing potentially significant return differences between the active portfolio and the underlying benchmark.

Active return Portfolio return minus benchmark return.

Active risk The annualized standard deviation of active returns, also referred to as *tracking error* (also sometimes called *tracking risk*).

Active risk budgeting Risk budgeting that concerns active risk (risk relative to a portfolio's benchmark).

Active share A measure of how similar a portfolio is to its benchmark. A manager who precisely replicates the benchmark will have an Active Share of zero; a manager with no holdings in common with the benchmark will have an Active Share of one.

Activist short selling A hedge fund strategy in which the manager takes a short position in a given security and then publicly presents his/her research backing the short thesis.

After-tax excess return Calculated as the after-tax return of the portfolio minus the after-tax return of the associated benchmark portfolio.

Agency trade A trade in which the broker is engaged to find the other side of the trade, acting as an agent. In doing so, the broker does not assume any risk for the trade.

Alpha decay In a trading context, alpha decay is the erosion or deterioration in short term alpha after the investment decision has been made.

Alternative trading systems (ATS) Non-exchange trading venues that bring together buyers and sellers to find transaction counterparties. Also called *multilateral trading facilities (MTF)*.

Anchoring and adjustment An information-processing bias in which the use of a psychological heuristic influences the way people estimate probabilities.

Anchoring and adjustment bias An information-processing bias in which the use of a psychological heuristic influences the way people estimate probabilities.

Anomalies Apparent deviations from market efficiency.

Arithmetic attribution An attribution approach which explains the arithmetic difference between the portfolio return and its benchmark return. The single-period attribution effects sum to the excess return, however, when combining multiple periods, the sub-period attribution effects will not sum to the excess return.

Arrival price In a trading context, the arrival price is the security price at the time the order was released to the market for execution.

Asset location The type of account an asset is held within, e.g., taxable or tax deferred.

Asset-only With respect to asset allocation, an approach that focuses directly on the characteristics of the assets without explicitly modeling the liabilities.

Asset swap spread (ASW) The spread over MRR on an interest rate swap for the remaining life of the bond that is equivalent to the bond's fixed coupon.

Asset swaps Convert a bond's fixed coupon to MRR plus (or minus) a spread.

Authorized participants Institutional investors who create and redeem ETF shares using an OTC primary market with an ETF sponsor.

Availability bias An information-processing bias in which people take a heuristic approach to estimating the probability of an outcome based on how easily the outcome comes to mind.

Back-fill bias The distortion in index or peer group data which results when returns are reported to a database only after they are known to be good returns.

Barbell A fixed-income investment strategy combining short- and long-term bond positions.

Base With respect to a foreign exchange quotation of the price of one unit of a currency, the currency referred to in "one unit of a currency."

Base-rate neglect A type of representativeness bias in which the base rate or probability of the categorization is not adequately considered.

Basis risk The risk resulting from using a hedging instrument that is imperfectly matched to the investment being hedged; in general, the risk that the basis will change in an unpredictable way.

Bear flattening A decrease in the yield spread between long- and short-term maturities across the yield curve, which is largely driven by a rise in short-term bond yields-to-maturity.

Bear spread An option strategy that becomes more valuable when the price of the underlying asset declines, so requires buying one option and writing another with a *lower* exercise price. A put bear spread involves buying a put with a higher exercise price and selling a put with a lower exercise price. A bear spread can also be executed with calls.

Bear steepening An increase in the yield spread between long- and short-term maturities across the yield curve, which is largely driven by a rise in long-term bond yields-to-maturity.

Behavioral finance macro A focus on market level behavior that considers market anomalies that distinguish markets from the efficient markets of traditional finance.

Behavioral finance micro A focus on individual level behavior that examines the behavioral biases that distinguish individual investors from the rational decision makers of traditional finance.

Bequest The transferring, or bequeathing, of assets in some other way upon a person's death. Also referred to as a testamentary bequest or testamentary gratuitous transfer.

Best-in-class An ESG implementation approach that seeks to identify the most favorable companies and sectors based on ESG considerations. Also called *positive screening*.

Bid price In a price quotation, the price at which the party making the quotation is willing to buy a specified quantity of an asset or security.

Breadth The number of truly independent decisions made each year.

Buffering Establishing ranges around breakpoints that define whether a stock belongs in one index or another.

Bull flattening A decrease in the yield spread between long- and short-term maturities across the yield curve, which is largely driven by a decline in long-term bond yields-to-maturity.

Bull spread An option strategy that becomes more valuable when the price of the underlying asset rises, so requires buying one option and writing another with a *higher* exercise price. A call bull spread involves buying a call with a lower exercise price and selling a call with a higher exercise price. A bull spread can also be executed with puts.

Bull steepening An increase in the yield spread between long- and short-term maturities across the yield curve, which is largely driven by a decline in short-term bond yields-to-maturity.

Bullet A fixed-income investment strategy that focuses on the intermediate term (or "belly") of the yield curve.

Business cycle Fluctuations in GDP in relation to long-term trend growth, usually lasting 9–11 years.

Butterfly spread A measure of yield curve shape or curvature equal to double the intermediate yield-to-maturity less the sum of short- and long-term yields-to-maturity.

Butterfly strategy A common yield curve shape strategy that combines a long or short bullet position with a barbell portfolio in the opposite direction to capitalize on expected yield curve shape changes.

Calendar rebalancing Rebalancing a portfolio to target weights on a periodic basis; for example, monthly, quarterly, semiannually, or annually.

Calendar spread A strategy in which one sells an option and buys the same type of option but with different expiration dates, on the same underlying asset and with the same strike. When the investor buys the more distant (near-term) call and sells the near-term (more distant) call, it is a long (short) calendar spread.

Canada model Characterized by a high allocation to alternatives. Unlike the endowment model, however, the Canada model relies more on internally managed assets. The innovative features of the Canada model are the: a) reference portfolio, b) total portfolio approach, and c) active management.

Capital gain or loss For tax purposes equals the selling price (net of commissions and other trading costs) of the asset less its tax basis.

Capital market expectations (CME) Expectations concerning the risk and return prospects of asset classes.

Capital needs analysis See *capital sufficiency analysis*.

Capital sufficiency analysis The process by which a wealth manager determines whether a client has, or is likely to accumulate, sufficient financial resources to meet his or her objectives; also known as *capital needs analysis*.

Capture ratio A measure of the manager's gain or loss relative to the gain or loss of the benchmark.

Carhart model A four factor model used in performance attribution. The four factors are: market (RMRF), size (SMB), value (HML), and momentum (WML).

Carry trade A trading strategy that involves buying a security and financing it at a rate that is lower than the yield on that security.

Carry trade across currencies A strategy seeking to benefit from a positive interest rate differential across currencies by combining a short position (or borrowing) in a low-yielding currency and a long position (or lending) in a high-yielding currency.

Cash drag Tracking error caused by temporarily uninvested cash.

Cash flow matching Immunization approach that attempts to ensure that all future liability payouts are matched precisely by cash flows from bonds or fixed-income derivatives.

Cash-secured put An option strategy involving the writing of a put option and simultaneously depositing an amount of money equal to the exercise price into a designated account (this strategy is also called a fiduciary put).

CDS curve Plot of CDS spreads across maturities for a single reference entity or group of reference entities in an index.

Cell approach See *stratified sampling*.

Charitable gratuitous transfers Asset transfers to not-for-profit or charitable organizations. In most jurisdictions charitable donations are not subject to a gift tax and most jurisdictions permit income tax deductions for charitable donations.

Charitable remainder trust A trust setup to provide income for the life of named-beneficiaries. When the last named-beneficiary dies any remaining assets in this trust are distributed to the charity named in the trust, hence the term *charitable remainder* trust.

Closet indexer A fund that advertises itself as being actively managed but is substantially similar to an index fund in its exposures.

Cognitive cost The effort involved in processing new information and updating beliefs.

Cognitive dissonance The mental discomfort that occurs when new information conflicts with previously held beliefs or cognitions.

Cognitive errors Behavioral biases resulting from faulty reasoning; cognitive errors stem from basic statistical, information processing, or memory errors.

Collar An option position in which the investor is long shares of stock and then buys a put with an exercise price below the current stock price and writes a call with an exercise price above the current stock price. Collars allow a shareholder to acquire downside protection through a protective put but reduce the cash outlay by writing a covered call.

Completion overlay A type of overlay that addresses an indexed portfolio that has diverged from its proper exposure.

Completion portfolio Is an index-based portfolio that when added to a given concentrated asset position creates an overall portfolio with exposures similar to the investor's benchmark.

Conditional value at risk (CVaR) Also known as expected loss The average portfolio loss over a specific time period conditional on that loss exceeding the value at risk (VaR) threshold.

Glossary

Confirmation bias A belief perseverance bias in which people tend to look for and notice what confirms their beliefs, to ignore or undervalue what contradicts their beliefs, and to misinterpret information as support for their beliefs.

Conjunction fallacy An inappropriate combining of probabilities of independent events to support a belief. In fact, the probability of two independent events occurring in conjunction is never greater than the probability of either event occurring alone; the probability of two independent events occurring together is equal to the multiplication of the probabilities of the independent events.

Conservatism bias A belief perseverance bias in which people maintain their prior views or forecasts by inadequately incorporating new information.

Contingent immunization Hybrid approach that combines immunization with an active management approach when the asset portfolio's value exceeds the present value of the liability portfolio.

Controlled foreign corporation (CFC) A company located outside a taxpayer's home country in which the taxpayer has a controlling interest as defined under the home country law.

Covered call An option strategy in which a long position in an asset is combined with a short position in a call on that asset.

Covered interest rate parity The relationship among the spot exchange rate, the forward exchange rate, and the interest rate in two currencies that ensures that the return on a hedged (i.e., covered) foreign risk-free investment is the same as the return on a domestic risk-free investment. Also called *interest rate parity*.

Credit cycle The expansion and contraction of credit over the business cycle, which translates into asset price changes based on default and recovery expectations across maturities and rating categories.

Credit default swap (CDS) basis Yield spread on a bond, as compared to CDS spread of same tenor.

Credit loss rate The realized percentage of par value lost to default for a group of bonds equal to the bonds' default rate multiplied by the loss severity.

Credit migration The change in a bond's credit rating over a certain period.

Credit valuation adjustment (CVA) The present value of credit risk for a loan, bond, or derivative obligation.

Cross-currency basis swap An interest rate swap involving the periodic exchange of floating payments in one currency for another based upon respective market reference rates with an initial and final exchange of notional principal.

Cross hedge A hedge involving a hedging instrument that is imperfectly correlated with the asset being hedged; an example is hedging a bond investment with futures on a non-identical bond.

Cross-sectional consistency A feature of expectations setting which means that estimates for all classes reflect the same underlying assumptions and are generated with methodologies that reflect or preserve important relationships among the asset classes, such as strong correlations. It is the internal consistency across asset classes.

Cross-sectional momentum A managed futures trend following strategy implemented with a cross-section of assets (within an asset class) by going long those that are rising in price the most and by shorting those that are falling the most. This approach generally results in holding a net zero (market-neutral) position and works well when a market's out- or underperformance is a reliable predictor of its future performance.

Currency overlay A type of overlay that helps hedge the returns of securities held in foreign currency back to the home country's currency.

Currency overlay programs A currency overlay program is a program to manage a portfolio's currency exposures for the case in which those exposures are managed separately from the management of the portfolio itself.

Custom security-based benchmark Benchmark that is custom built to accurately reflect the investment discipline of a particular investment manager. Also called a *strategy benchmark* because it reflects a manager's particular strategy.

Decision price In a trading context, the decision price is the security price at the time the investment decision was made.

Decision-reversal risk The risk of reversing a chosen course of action at the point of maximum loss.

Decumulation phase Phase where the government predominantly withdraws from a sovereign wealth pension reserve fund.

Dedicated short-selling A hedge fund strategy in which the manager takes short-only positions in equities deemed to be expensively priced versus their deteriorating fundamental situations. Short exposures may vary only in terms of portfolio sizing by, at times, holding higher levels of cash.

Default intensity POD over a specified time period in a reduced form credit model.

Default risk Likelihood that a borrower will default or fail to meet its obligation to make full and timely payments of principal and interest according to the terms of a debt obligation.

Deferred annuity An annuity that enables an individual to purchase an income stream that will begin at a later date.

Defined benefit A retirement plan in which a plan sponsor commits to paying a specified retirement benefit.

Defined contribution A retirement plan in which contributions are defined but the ultimate retirement benefit is not specified or guaranteed by the plan sponsor.

Delay cost The (trading related) cost associated with not submitting the order to the market in a timely manner.

Delta The change in an option's price in response to a change in price of the underlying, all else equal.

Delta hedging Hedging that involves matching the price response of the position being hedged over a narrow range of prices.

Demand deposits Accounts that can be drawn upon regularly and without notice. This category includes checking accounts and certain savings accounts that are often accessible through online banks or automated teller machines (ATMs).

Diffusion index An index that measures how many indicators are pointing up and how many are pointing down.

Direct market access (DMA) Access in which market participants can transact orders directly with the order book of an exchange using a broker's exchange connectivity.

Disability income insurance A type of insurance designed to mitigate earnings risk as a result of a disability in which an individual becomes less than fully employed.

Discount margin The discount (or required) margin is the yield spread versus the MRR such that the FRN is priced at par on a rate reset date.

Discretionary portfolio management An arrangement in which a wealth manager has a client's pre-approval to execute investment decisions.

Discretionary trust A trust that enables the trustee to determine whether and how much to distribute based on a beneficiary's general welfare.

Disposition effect As a result of loss aversion, an emotional bias whereby investors are reluctant to dispose of losers. This results in an inefficient and gradual adjustment to deterioration in fundamental value.

Dividend capture A trading strategy whereby an equity portfolio manager purchases stocks just before their ex-dividend dates, holds these stocks through the ex-dividend date to earn the right to receive the dividend, and subsequently sells the shares.

Domestic asset An asset that trades in the investor's domestic currency (or home currency).

Domestic currency The currency of the investor, i.e., the currency in which he or she typically makes consumption purchases, e.g., the Swiss franc for an investor domiciled in Switzerland.

Domestic-currency return A rate of return stated in domestic currency terms from the perspective of the investor; reflects both the foreign-currency return on an asset as well as percentage movement in the spot exchange rate between the domestic and foreign currencies.

Double taxation A term used to describe situations in which income is taxed twice. For example, when corporate earnings are taxed at the company level and then that portion of earnings paid as dividends is taxed again at the investor level.

Drawdown A decline in value (represented by a series of negative returns only) following a peak fund valuation.

Drawdown duration The total time from the start of the drawdown until the cumulative drawdown recovers to zero.

Due diligence Investigation and analysis in support of an investment action, decision, or recommendation.

Duration matching Immunization approach based on the duration of assets and liabilities. Ideally, the liabilities being matched (the liability portfolio) and the portfolio of assets (the bond portfolio) should be affected similarly by a change in interest rates.

Duration times spread Weighting of spread duration by credit spread in order to incorporate the empirical observation that spread changes for lower-rated bonds tend to be consistent on a percentage, rather than absolute, basis.

Duration Times Spread (DTS) Weighting of spread duration by credit spread to incorporate the empirical observation that spread changes for lower-rated bonds tend to be consistent on a percentage rather than absolute basis.

Dynamic asset allocation A strategy incorporating deviations from the strategic asset allocation that are motivated by longer-term valuation signals or economic views than usually associated with tactical asset allocation.

Dynamic hedge A hedge requiring adjustment as the price of the hedged asset changes.

Earnings risk The risk associated with the earning potential of an individual.

Econometrics The application of quantitative modeling and analysis grounded in economic theory to the analysis of economic data.

Economic balance sheet A balance sheet that provides an individual's total wealth portfolio, supplementing traditional balance sheet assets with human capital and pension wealth, and expanding liabilities to include consumption and bequest goals. Also known as *holistic balance sheet*.

Economic indicators Economic statistics provided by government and established private organizations that contain information on an economy's recent past activity or its current or future position in the business cycle.

Economic net worth The difference between an individual's assets and liabilities; extends traditional financial assets and liabilities to include human capital and future consumption needs.

Effective federal funds (FFE) rate The fed funds rate actually transacted between depository institutions, not the Fed's target federal funds rate.

Emotional biases Behavioral biases resulting from reasoning influenced by feelings; emotional biases stem from impulse or intuition.

Empirical duration Estimation of the price-yield relationship using historical bond market data in statistical models.

Endowment bias An emotional bias in which people value an asset more when they hold rights to it than when they do not.

Endowment model Characterized by a high allocation to alternative investments (private investments and hedge funds), significant active management, and externally managed assets.

Enhanced indexing approach Maintains a close link to the benchmark but attempts to generate a modest amount of outperformance relative to the benchmark.

Enhanced indexing strategy Method investors use to match an underlying market index in which the investor purchases fewer securities than the full set of index constituents but matches primary risk factors reflected in the index.

Equity monetization A group of strategies that allow investors to receive cash for their concentrated stock positions without an outright sale. These transactions are structured to avoid triggering the capital gains tax.

Estate Consists of all of the property a person owns or controls, which may consist of financial assets (e.g., bank accounts, stocks, bonds, business interests), tangible personal assets (e.g., artwork, collectibles, vehicles), immovable property (e.g., residential real estate, timber rights), and intellectual property (e.g., royalties).

Estate planning The process of preparing for the disposition of one's estate upon death and during one's lifetime.

Estate tax Levied on the total value of a deceased person's assets and paid out of the estate before any distributions to beneficiaries.

Evaluated pricing See *matrix pricing*.

Excess return Used in various senses appropriate to context: 1) The difference between the portfolio return and the benchmark return; 2) The return in excess of the risk-free rate.

Excess spread Credit spread return measure that incorporates both changes in spread and expected credit losses for a given period.

Exchange fund A partnership in which each of the partners have each contributed low cost-basis stock to the fund. Used in the United Sates as a mechanism to achieve a tax-free exchange of a concentrated asset position.

Execution cost The difference between the (trading related) cost of the real portfolio and the paper portfolio, based on shares and prices transacted.

Exhaustive An index construction strategy that selects every constituent of a universe.

Expected shortfall The average loss conditional on exceeding the VaR cutoff; sometimes referred to as *conditional VaR* or *expected tail loss*.

Expected tail loss See *expected shortfall*.

Extended portfolio assets and liabilities Assets and liabilities beyond those shown on a conventional balance sheet that are relevant in making asset allocation decisions; an example of an extended asset is human capital.

Factor-model-based benchmarks Benchmarks constructed by examining a portfolio's sensitivity to a set of factors, such as the return for a broad market index, company earnings growth, industry, or financial leverage.

Family constitution Typically a non-binding document that sets forth an agreed-upon set of rights, values, and responsibilities of the family members and other stakeholders. Used by many wealth- and business-owning families as the starting point of conflict resolution procedures.

Family governance The process for a family's collective communication and decision making designed to serve current and future generations based on the common values of the family.

Financial capital The tangible and intangible assets (excluding human capital) owned by an individual or household.

Fixed trust Distributions to beneficiaries of a fixed trust are specified in the trust document to occur at certain times or in certain amounts.

Forced heirship Is the requirement that a certain proportion of assets must pass to specified family members, such as a spouse and children.

Foreign assets Assets denominated in currencies other than the investor's home currency.

Foreign currency Currency that is not the currency in which an investor makes consumption purchases, e.g., the US dollar from the perspective of a Swiss investor.

Foreign-currency return The return of the foreign asset measured in foreign-currency terms.

Forward rate bias An empirically observed divergence from interest rate parity conditions that active investors seek to benefit from by borrowing in a lower-yield currency and investing in a higher-yield currency.

Foundation A legal entity available in certain jurisdictions. Foundations are typically set up to hold assets for a specific charitable purpose, such as to promote education or for philanthropy. When set up and funded by an individual or family and managed by its own directors, it is called a *private foundation*. The term *family foundation* usually refers to a private foundation where donors or members of the donors' family are actively involved.

Framing An information-processing bias in which a person answers a question differently based on the way in which it is asked (framed).

Framing bias An information-processing bias in which a person answers a question differently based on the way in which it is asked (framed).

Fulcrum securities Partially-in-the-money claims (not expected to be repaid in full) whose holders end up owning the reorganized company in a corporate reorganization situation.

Full replication approach When every issue in an index is represented in the portfolio, and each portfolio position has approximately the same weight in the fund as in the index.

Fund-of-funds A fund of hedge funds in which the fund-of-funds manager allocates capital to separate, underlying hedge funds (e.g., single manager and/or multi-manager funds) that themselves run a range of different strategies.

Funding currencies The low-yield currencies in which borrowing occurs in a carry trade.

G-spread Yield spread for a fixed-rate bond over a government benchmark.

Gamblers' fallacy A misunderstanding of probabilities in which people wrongly project reversal to a long-term mean.

Gamma The change in an option's delta for a change in price of the underlying, all else equal.

General account Account holding assets to fund future liabilities from traditional life insurance and fixed annuities, the products in which the insurer bears all the risks—particularly mortality risk and longevity risk.

Generation-skipping tax Taxes levied in some jurisdictions on asset transfers (gifts) that skip one generation such as when a grandparent transfers asset s to their grandchildren. (see related Gift Tax).

Gift tax Depending on the tax laws of the country, assets gifted by one person to another during the giftor's lifetime may be subject to a gift tax.

Goals-based With respect to asset allocation or investing, an approach that focuses on achieving an investor's goals (for example, related to supporting lifestyle needs or aspirations) based typically on constructing sub-portfolios aligned with those goals.

Goals-based investing An investment industry term for approaches to investing for individuals and families focused on aligning investments with goals (parallel to liability-driven investing for institutional investors).

Green bonds Fixed-income instruments issued by private or public sector borrowers that directly fund ESG initiatives.

Grinold–Kroner model An expression for the expected return on a share as the sum of an expected income return, an expected nominal earnings growth return, and an expected repricing return.

Halo effect An emotional bias that extends a favorable evaluation of some characteristics to other characteristics.

Hard-catalyst event-driven approach An event-driven approach in which investments are made in reaction to an already announced corporate event (mergers and acquisitions, bankruptcies, share issuances, buybacks, capital restructurings, re-organizations, accounting changes) in which security prices related to the event have yet to fully converge.

Hazard rate The conditional POD, or the likelihood that default will occur given that it has not already occurred in a prior period.

Health insurance A type of insurance used to cover health care and medical costs.

Health risk The risk associated with illness or injury.

Hedge ratio The relationship of the quantity of an asset being hedged to the quantity of the derivative used for hedging.

Herding When a group of investors trade on the same side of the market in the same securities, or when investors ignore their own private information and act as other investors do.

High-water mark A specified net asset value level that a fund must exceed before performance fees are paid to the hedge fund manager.

Hindsight bias A bias with selective perception and retention aspects in which people may see past events as having been predictable and reasonable to expect.

Holdings-based attribution A "buy and hold" attribution approach which calculates the return of portfolio and benchmark components based upon the price and foreign exchange rate changes applied to daily snapshots of portfolio holdings.

Holdings-based style analysis A bottom-up style analysis that estimates the risk exposures from the actual securities held in the portfolio at a point in time.

Holistic balance sheet See *economic balance sheet*.

Home bias A preference for securities listed on the exchanges of one's home country.

Home-country bias The favoring of domestic over non-domestic investments relative to global market value weights.

Home currency See *domestic currency*.

Human capital An implied asset; the net present value of an investor's future expected labor income weighted by the probability of surviving to each future age. Also called *net employment capital*.

I-spread (interpolated spread) Yield spread measure using swaps or constant maturity Treasury YTMs as a benchmark.

Illusion of control A bias in which people tend to believe that they can control or influence outcomes when, in fact, they cannot. Illusion of knowledge and self-attribution biases contribute to the overconfidence bias.

Illusion of control bias A bias in which people tend to believe that they can control or influence outcomes when, in fact, they cannot. Illusion of knowledge and self-attribution biases contribute to the overconfidence bias.

Immediate annuity An annuity that provides a guarantee of specified future monthly payments over a specified period of time.

Immunization An asset/liability management approach that structures investments in bonds to match (offset) liabilities' weighted-average duration; a type of dedication strategy.

Impact investing Investment approach that seeks to achieve targeted social or environmental objectives along with measurable financial returns through engagement with a company or by direct investment in projects or companies.

Implementation shortfall (IS) The difference between the return for a notional or paper portfolio, where all transactions are assumed to take place at the manager's decision price, and the portfolio's actual return, which reflects realized transactions, including all fees and costs.

Implied volatility The outlook for the future volatility of the underlying asset's price. It is the value (i.e., standard deviation of underlying's returns) that equates the model (e.g., Black–Scholes–Merton model) price of an option to its market price.

Implied volatility surface A three-dimensional plot, for put and call options on the same underlying asset, of days to expiration (x-axis), option strike prices (y-axis), and implied volatilities (z-axis). It simultaneously shows the volatility skew (or smile) and the term structure of implied volatility.

Incremental VaR (or partial VaR) The change in the minimum portfolio loss expected to occur over a given time period at a specific confidence level resulting from increasing or decreasing a portfolio position.

Information coefficient Formally defined as the correlation between forecast return and actual return. In essence, it measures the effectiveness of investment insight.

Inheritance tax Paid by each individual beneficiary of a deceased person's estate on the value of the benefit the individual received from the estate.

Input uncertainty Uncertainty concerning whether the inputs are correct.

Interaction effect The attribution effect resulting from the interaction of the allocation and selection decisions.

Intertemporal consistency A feature of expectations setting which means that estimates for an asset class over different horizons reflect the same assumptions with respect to the potential paths of returns over time. It is the internal consistency over various time horizons.

Intestate A person who dies without a valid will or with a will that does not dispose of their property are considered to have died intestate.

Intrinsic value The difference between the spot exchange rate and the strike price of a currency option.

Investment currencies The high-yielding currencies in a carry trade.

Investment policy statement A written planning document that describes a client's investment objectives and risk tolerance over a relevant time horizon, along with the constraints that apply to the client's portfolio.

Investment style A natural grouping of investment disciplines that has some predictive power in explaining the future dispersion of returns across portfolios.

Irrevocable trust The person whose assets are used to create the trust gives up the right to rescind the trust relationship and regain title to the trust assets.

Key person risk The risk that results from over-reliance on an individual or individuals whose departure would negatively affect an investment manager.

Key rate duration A method of measuring interest rate sensitivities of a fixed-income instrument or portfolio to shifts in key points along the yield curve.

Knock-in/knock-out Features of a vanilla option that is created (or ceases to exist) when the spot exchange rate touches a pre-specified level.

Leading economic indicators A set of economic variables whose values vary with the business cycle but at a fairly consistent time interval before a turn in the business cycle.

Liability-based mandates Mandates managed to match or cover expected liability payments (future cash outflows) with future projected cash inflows.

Liability-driven investing An investment industry term that generally encompasses asset allocation that is focused on funding an investor's liabilities in institutional contexts.

Liability driven investing (LDI) model In the LDI model, the primary investment objective is to generate returns sufficient to cover liabilities, with a focus on maximizing expected surplus return (excess return of assets over liabilities) and managing surplus volatility.

Liability glide path A specification of desired proportions of liability-hedging assets and return-seeking assets and the duration of the liability hedge as funded status changes and contributions are made.

Liability insurance A type of insurance used to manage liability risk.

Liability-relative With respect to asset allocation, an approach that focuses directly only on funding liabilities as an investment objective.

Liability risk The possibility that an individual or household may be held legally liable for the financial costs associated with property damage or physical injury.

Life-cycle finance A concept in finance that recognizes as an investor ages, the fundamental nature of wealth and risk evolves.

Life insurance A type of insurance that protects against the loss of human capital for those who depend on an individual's future earnings.

Life settlement The sale of a life insurance contract to a third party. The valuation of a life settlement typically requires detailed biometric analysis of the individual policyholder and an understanding of actuarial analysis.

Limited-life foundations A type of foundation where founders seek to maintain control of spending while they (or their immediate heirs) are still alive.

Liquidity budget The portfolio allocations (or weightings) considered acceptable for the liquidity categories in the liquidity classification schedule (or time-to-cash table).

Liquidity classification schedule A liquidity management classification (or table) that defines portfolio liquidity "buckets" or categories based on the estimated time it would take to convert assets in that particular category into cash.

Longevity risk The risk of outliving one's financial resources.

Loss-aversion bias A bias in which people tend to strongly prefer avoiding losses as opposed to achieving gains.

Loss severity Also known as loss given default (LGD). The amount of loss if a default occurs, usually expressed as a percentage in annual terms.

Macro attribution Attribution at the sponsor level.

Manager peer group See *manager universe*.

Manager universe A broad group of managers with similar investment disciplines. Also called *manager peer group*.

Matrix pricing An approach for estimating the prices of thinly traded securities based on the prices of securities with similar attributions, such as similar credit rating, maturity, or economic sector. Also called *evaluated pricing*.

Matrix pricing (or evaluated pricing) Methodology for pricing infrequently traded bonds using bonds from similar issuers and actively traded government benchmarks to establish a bond's fair value.

Mental accounting bias An information-processing bias in which people treat one sum of money differently from another equal-sized sum based on which mental account the money is assigned to.

Micro attribution Attribution at the portfolio manager level.

Minimum-variance hedge ratio A mathematical approach to determining the optimal cross hedging ratio.

Mission-related investing Aims to direct a significant portion of assets in excess of annual grants into projects promoting a foundation's mission.

Model uncertainty Uncertainty as to whether a selected model is correct.

Mortality table A table that indicates individual life expectancies at specified ages.

Multi-class trading An equity market-neutral strategy that capitalizes on misalignment in prices and involves buying and selling different classes of shares of the same company, such as voting and non-voting shares.

Multi-manager fund Can be of two types—one is a multi-strategy fund in which teams of portfolio managers trade and invest in multiple different strategies within the same fund; the second type is a fund of hedge funds (or fund-of-funds) in which the manager allocates capital to separate, underlying hedge funds that themselves run a range of different strategies.

Multi-strategy fund A fund in which teams of portfolio managers trade and invest in multiple different strategies within the same fund.

Multilateral trading facilities (MTF) See *Alternative trading systems (ATS)*.

Negative butterfly An increase in the butterfly spread due to lower short- and long-term yields-to-maturity and a higher intermediate yield-to-maturity.

Negative screening An ESG implementation approach that excludes certain sectors or companies that deviate from an investor's accepted standards.

Non-deliverable forwards Forward contracts that are cash settled (in the non-controlled currency of the currency pair) rather than physically settled (the controlled currency is neither delivered nor received).

Nonstationarity A characteristic of series of data whose properties, such as mean and variance, are not constant through time. When analyzing historical data it means that different parts of a data series reflect different underlying statistical properties.

Norway model Characterized by an almost exclusive reliance on public equities and fixed income (the traditional 60/40 equity/bond model falls under the Norway model), with largely passively managed assets and with very little to no allocation to alternative investments.

OAS duration The change in bond price for a given change in OAS.

Offer price The price at which a counterparty is willing to sell one unit of the base currency.

Opportunity cost The (trading related) cost associated with not being able to transact the entire order at the decision price.

Option-adjusted spread (OAS) A generalization of the Z-spread yield spread calculation that incorporates bond option pricing based on assumed interest rate volatility.

Optional stock dividends A type of dividend in which shareholders may elect to receive either cash or new shares.

Options on bond futures contracts Instruments that involve the right, but not the obligation, to enter into a bond futures contract at a pre-determined strike (bond price) on a future date in exchange for an up-front premium.

Overbought When a market has trended too far in one direction and is vulnerable to a trend reversal, or correction.

Overconfidence bias A bias in which people demonstrate unwarranted faith in their own intuitive reasoning, judgments, and/or cognitive abilities.

Overlay A derivative position (or positions) used to adjust a pre-existing portfolio closer to its objectives.

Oversold The opposite of overbought; see *overbought*.

Packeting Splitting stock positions into multiple parts.

Pairs trading An equity market-neutral strategy that capitalizes on the misalignment in prices of pairs of similar under- and overvalued equities. The expectation is the differential valuations or trading relationships will revert to their long-term mean values or their fundamentally-correct trading relationships, with the long position rising and the short position declining in value.

Parameter uncertainty Uncertainty arising because a quantitative model's parameters are estimated with error.

Participant/cohort option Pools the DC plan member with a cohort that has a similar target retirement date.

Participant-switching life-cycle options Automatically switch DC plan members into a more conservative asset mix as their age increases. There may be several automatic de-risking switches at different age targets.

Passive investment In the fixed-income context, it is investment that seeks to mimic the prevailing characteristics of the overall investments available in terms of credit quality, type of borrower, maturity, and duration rather than express a specific market view.

Passive management A buy-and-hold approach to investing in which an investor does not make portfolio changes based upon short-term expectations of changing market or security performance.

Percent-range rebalancing An approach to rebalancing that involves setting rebalancing thresholds or trigger points, stated as a percentage of the portfolio's value, around target values.

Performance attribution Attribution, including return attribution and risk attribution; often used as a synonym for return attribution.

Permanent life insurance A type of life insurance that provides lifetime coverage.

Portfolio overlay An array of derivative positions managed separately from the securities portfolio to achieve overall intended portfolio characteristics.

Position delta The overall or portfolio delta. For example, the position delta of a covered call, consisting of long 100 shares and short one at-the-money call, is +50 (= +100 for the shares and -50 for the short ATM call).

Positive butterfly A decrease in the butterfly spread due to higher short- and long-term yields-to-maturity and a lower intermediate yield-to-maturity.

Positive screening An ESG implementation approach that seeks to identify the most favorable companies and sectors based on ESG considerations. Also called *best-in-class*.

Post-liquidation return Calculates the return assuming that all portfolio holdings are sold as of the end date of the analysis and that the resulting capital gains tax that would be due is deducted from the ending portfolio value.

Potential capital gain exposure (PCGE) Is an estimate of the percentage of a fund's assets that represents gains and measures how much the fund's assets have appreciated. It can be an indicator of possible future capital gain distributions.

Premature death risk The risk of an individual dying earlier than anticipated; sometimes referred to as *mortality risk*.

Present value of distribution of cash flows methodology Method used to address a portfolio's sensitivity to rate changes along the yield curve. This approach seeks to approximate and match the yield curve risk of an index over discrete time periods.

Principal trade A trade in which the market maker or dealer becomes a disclosed counterparty and assumes risk for the trade by transacting the security for their own account. Also called *broker risk trades*.

Probability of default The likelihood that a borrower defaults or fails to meet its obligation to make full and timely payments of principal and interest.

Probate The legal process to confirm the validity of the will so that executors, heirs, and other interested parties can rely on its authenticity.

Program trading A strategy of buying or selling many stocks simultaneously.

Progressive tax rate schedule A tax regime in which the tax rate increases as the amount of income or wealth being taxed increases.

Property insurance A type of insurance used by individuals to manage property risk.

Property risk The possibility that a person's property may be damaged, destroyed, stolen, or lost.

Protective put An option strategy in which a long position in an asset is combined with a long position in a put on that asset.

Pure indexing Attempts to replicate a bond index as closely as possible, targeting zero active return and zero active risk.

Put spread A strategy used to reduce the upfront cost of buying a protective put, it involves buying a put option and writing another put option.

Qualified dividends Generally dividends from shares in domestic corporations and certain qualified foreign corporations which have been held for at least a specified minimum period of time.

Quantitative market-neutral An approach to building market-neutral portfolios in which large numbers of securities are traded and positions are adjusted on a daily or even an hourly basis using algorithm-based models.

Quoted margin The yield spread over the MRR established upon issuance of an FRN to compensate investors for assuming an issuer's credit risk.

Re-base With reference to index construction, to change the time period used as the base of the index.

Realized volatility Historical volatility, the square root of the realized variance of returns, which is a measure of the range of past price outcomes for the underlying asset.

Rebalancing In the context of asset allocation, a discipline for adjusting the portfolio to align with the strategic asset allocation.

Rebalancing overlay A type of overlay that addresses a portfolio's need to sell certain constituent securities and buy others.

Rebalancing range A range of values for asset class weights defined by trigger points above and below target weights, such that if the portfolio value passes through a trigger point, rebalancing occurs. Also known as a corridor.

Rebate rate The portion of the collateral earnings rate that is repaid to the security borrower by the security lender.

Reduced form credit models Credit models that solve for default probability over a specific time period using observable company-specific variables such as financial ratios and macroeconomic variables.

Reduced-form models Models that use economic theory and other factors such as prior research output to describe hypothesized relationships. Can be described as more compact representations of underlying structural models. Evaluate endogenous variables in terms of observable exogenous variables.

Regime The governing set of relationships (between variables) that stem from technological, political, legal, and regulatory environments. Changes in such environments or policy stances can be described as changes in regime.

Regret The feeling that an opportunity has been missed; typically an expression of *hindsight bias*.

Regret-aversion bias An emotional bias in which people tend to avoid making decisions that will result in action out of fear that the decision will turn out poorly.

Relative value A concept that describes the selection of the most attractive individual securities to populate the portfolio with, using ranking and comparing.

Relative value volatility arbitrage A volatility trading strategy that aims to source and buy cheap volatility and sell more expensive volatility while netting out the time decay aspects normally associated with options portfolios.

Glossary

Relative VaR The minimum portfolio loss expected to occur over a given time period at a specific confidence level based on a portfolio containing active positions minus benchmark holdings.

Repo rate The interest rate on a repurchase agreement.

Representativeness bias A belief perseverance bias in which people tend to classify new information based on past experiences and classifications.

Repurchase agreements In repurchase agreements, or *repos*, a security owner agrees to sell a security for a specific cash amount while simultaneously agreeing to repurchase the security at a specified future date (typically one day later) and price.

Request for quote (RFQ) A non-binding quote provided by a market maker or dealer to a potential buyer or seller upon request. Commonly used in fixed income markets these quotes are only valid at the time they are provided.

Reserve portfolio The component of an insurer's general account that is subject to specific regulatory requirements and is intended to ensure the company's ability to meet its policy liabilities. The assets in the reserve portfolio are managed conservatively and must be highly liquid and low risk.

Resistance levels Price points on dealers' order boards where one would expect to see a clustering of offers.

Return attribution A set of techniques used to identify the sources of the excess return of a portfolio against its benchmark.

Returns-based attribution An attribution approach that uses only the total portfolio returns over a period to identify the components of the investment process that have generated the returns. The Brinson–Hood–Beebower approach is a returns-based attribution approach.

Returns-based benchmarks Benchmarks constructed by examining a portfolio's sensitivity to a set of factors, such as the returns for various style indexes (e.g., small-cap value, small-cap growth, large-cap value, and large-cap growth).

Returns-based style analysis A top-down style analysis that involves estimating the sensitivities of a portfolio to security market indexes.

Reverse repos Repurchase agreements from the standpoint of the lender.

Revocable trust The person whose assets are used to create the trust retains the right to rescind the trust relationship and regain title to the trust assets.

Risk attribution The analysis of the sources of risk.

Risk aversion The degree of an investor's unwillingness to take risk; the inverse of risk tolerance.

Risk budgeting The establishment of objectives for individuals, groups, or divisions of an organization that takes into account the allocation of an acceptable level of risk.

Risk capacity The ability to accept financial risk.

Risk perception The subjective assessment of the risk involved in the outcome of an investment decision.

Risk premium An extra return expected by investors for bearing some specified risk.

Risk reversal A strategy used to profit from the existence of an implied volatility skew and from changes in its shape over time. A combination of long (short) calls and short (long) puts on the same underlying with the same expiration is a long (short) risk reversal.

Risk tolerance The capacity to accept risk; the level of risk an investor (or organization) is willing and able to bear.

Sample-size neglect A type of representativeness bias in which financial market participants incorrectly assume that small sample sizes are representative of populations (or "real" data).

Scenario analysis What-if analysis that involves changing multiple assumptions at the same time in order to evaluate the change in an investment's value.

Seagull spread An extension of the risk reversal foreign exchange option strategy that limits downside risk.

Securities lending A form of collateralized lending that may be used to generate income for portfolios.

Selective An index construction methodology that targets only those securities with certain characteristics.

Self-attribution bias A bias in which people take personal credit for successes and attribute failures to external factors outside the individual's control.

Self-control bias A bias in which people fail to act in pursuit of their long-term, overarching goals because of a lack of self-discipline.

Separate accounts Accounts holding assets to fund future liabilities from variable life insurance and variable annuities, the products in which customers make investment decisions from a menu of options and themselves bear investment risk.

Sharpe ratio The average return in excess of the risk-free rate divided by the standard deviation of return; a measure of the average excess return earned per unit of standard deviation of return. Also known as the *reward-to-variability ratio*.

Short-biased A hedge fund strategy in which the manager uses a less extreme version of dedicated short-selling. It involves searching for opportunities to sell expensively priced equities, but short exposure may be balanced with some modest value-oriented, or index-oriented, long exposure.

Shortfall probability The probability of failing to meet a specific liability or goal.

Shrinkage estimation Estimation that involves taking a weighted average of a historical estimate of a parameter and some other parameter estimate, where the weights reflect the analyst's relative belief in the estimates.

Single-manager fund A fund in which one portfolio manager or team of portfolio managers invests in one strategy or style.

Smart beta Involves the use of transparent, rules-based strategies as a basis for investment decisions.

Smart order routers (SOR) Smart systems used to electronically route small orders to the best markets for execution based on order type and prevailing market conditions.

Social proof A bias in which individuals tend to follow the beliefs of a group.

Soft-catalyst event-driven approach An event-driven approach in which investments are made proactively in anticipation of a corporate event (mergers and acquisitions, bankruptcies, share issuances, buybacks, capital restructurings, re-organizations, accounting changes) that has yet to occur.

Special dividends A dividend paid by a company that does not pay dividends on a regular schedule, or a dividend that supplements regular cash dividends with an extra payment.

Spread duration The change in bond price for a given change in yield spread. Also referred to as *OAS duration* when the option-adjusted spread (OAS) is the yield measure used.

Staged diversification strategy The simplest approach to managing the risk of a concentrated position involves selling the concentrated position over some period of time, paying associated tax, and reinvesting the proceeds in a diversified portfolio.

Static hedge A hedge that is not sensitive to changes in the price of the asset hedged.

Status quo bias An emotional bias in which people do nothing (i.e., maintain the "status quo") instead of making a change.

Stock lending Securities lending involving the transfer of equities.

Stop-losses A trading order that sets a selling price below the current market price with a goal of protecting profits or preventing further losses.

Stops Stop-loss orders involve leaving bids or offers away from the current market price to be filled if the market reaches those levels.

Straddle An option combination in which one buys *both* puts and calls, with the same exercise price and same expiration date, on the same underlying asset. In contrast to this long straddle, if someone *writes* both options, it is a short straddle.

Strangle A variation on a straddle in which the put and call have different exercise prices; if the put and call are held long, it is a long strangle; if they are held short, it is a short strangle.

Stratified sampling A sampling method that guarantees that subpopulations of interest are represented in the sample. Also called *representative sampling* or *cell approach*.

Structural credit models Credit models that apply market-based variables to estimate the value of an issuer's assets and the volatility of asset value.

Structural models Models that specify functional relationships among variables based on economic theory. The functional form and parameters of these models are derived from the underlying theory. They may include unobservable parameters.

Structural risk Risk that arises from portfolio design, particularly the choice of the portfolio allocations.

Stub trading An equity market-neutral strategy that capitalizes on misalignment in prices and entails buying and selling stock of a parent company and its subsidiaries, typically weighted by the percentage ownership of the parent company in the subsidiaries.

Support levels Price points on dealers' order boards where one would expect to see a clustering of bids.

Surplus The difference between the value of assets and the present value of liabilities. With respect to an insurance company, the net difference between the total assets and total liabilities (equivalent to policyholders' surplus for a mutual insurance company and stockholders' equity for a stock company).

Surplus portfolio The component of an insurer's general account that is intended to realize higher expected returns than the reserve portfolio and so can assume some liquidity risk. Surplus portfolio assets are often managed aggressively with exposure to alternative assets.

Survivorship bias Bias that arises in a data series when managers with poor track records exit the business and are dropped from the database whereas managers with good records remain; when a data series of a given date reflects only entitites that have survived to that date.

Swaption This instrument grants a party the right, but not the obligation, to enter into an interest rate swap at a pre-determined strike (fixed swap rate) on a future date in exchange for an up-front premium.

Synthetic long forward position The combination of a long call and a short put with identical strike price and expiration, traded at the same time on the same underlying.

Synthetic short forward position The combination of a short call and a long put at the same strike price and maturity (traded at the same time on the same underlying).

Tactical asset allocation Asset allocation that involves making short-term adjustments to asset class weights based on short-term predictions of relative performance among asset classes.

Tax alpha Calculated by subtracting the pre-tax excess return from the after-tax excess return, the tax alpha isolates the benefit of tax management of the portfolio.

Tax avoidance The legal activity of understanding the tax laws and finding approaches that avoid or minimize taxation.

Tax basis In many cases, the tax basis is the amount that was paid to acquire an asset, or its 'cost' basis, and serves as the foundation for calculating a capital gain or loss.

Tax-deferred account An account where investments and contributions may be made on a pre-tax basis and investment returns accumulate on a tax-deferred basis until funds are withdrawn, at which time they are taxed at ordinary income tax rates.

Tax-efficiency ratio (TER) Is calculated as the after-tax return divided by the pre-tax return. It is used to understand if a fund is appropriate for the taxable account of a client.

Tax-efficient decumulation strategy Is the process of taking into account the tax considerations involved in deploying retirement assets to support spending needs over a client's remaining lifetime during retirement.

Tax-efficient strategy An investment strategy that is designed to give up very little of its return to taxes.

Tax evasion The illegal concealment and non-payment of taxes that are otherwise due.

Tax-exempt account An account on which no taxes are assessed during the investment, contribution, or withdrawal phase, nor are they assessed on investment returns.

Tax haven A country or independent area with no or very low tax rates for foreign investors.

Tax loss harvesting Selling securities at a loss to offset a realized capital gain or other income. The rules for what can be done vary by jurisdiction.

Tax lot accounting Important in tax loss harvesting strategies to identify the cost of securities sold from a portfolio that has been built up over time with purchases and sales over time. Tax lot accounting keeps track of how much was paid for an investment and when it was purchased for the portfolio. Not allowed in all jurisdictions.

Taxable account An account on which the normal tax rules of the jurisdiction apply to investments and contributions.

Taylor rule A rule linking a central bank's target short-term interest rate to the rate of growth of the economy and inflation.

Temporary life insurance A type of life insurance that covers a certain period of time, specified at purchase. Commonly referred to as "term" life insurance.

Term deposits Interest-bearing accounts that have a specified maturity date. This category includes savings accounts and certificates of deposit (CDs).

Term structure of volatility The plot of implied volatility (y-axis) against option maturity (x-axis) for options with the same strike price on the same underlying. Typically, implied volatility is not constant across different maturities – rather, it is often in contango, meaning that the implied volatilities for longer-term options are higher than for near-term ones.

Territorial tax systems Jurisdictions operate where only locally-sourced income is taxed.

Testamentary bequest See *Bequest*.

Testamentary gratuitous transfer See *Bequest*.

Testator The person who authored the will and whose property is disposed of according to the will.

Thematic investing An investment approach that focuses on companies within a specific sector or following a specific theme, such as energy efficiency or climate change.

Theta The daily change in an option's price, all else equal. Theta measures the sensitivity of the option's price to the passage of time, known as time decay.

Time deposits Interest-bearing accounts that have a specified maturity date. This category includes savings accounts and certificates of deposit (CDs).

Time-series estimation Estimators that are based on lagged values of the variable being forecast; often consist of lagged values of other selected variables.

Time-series momentum A managed futures trend following strategy in which managers go long assets that are rising in price and go short assets that are falling in price. The manager trades on an absolute basis, so be net long or net short depending on the current price trend of an asset. This approach works best when an asset's own past returns are a good predictor of its future returns.

Time-to-cash table See *liquidity classification schedule*.

Time value The difference between the market price of an option and its intrinsic value, determined by the uncertainty of the underlying over the remaining life of the option.

Total factor productivity A variable which accounts for that part of Y not directly accounted for by the levels of the production factors (K and L).

Total return payer Party responsible for paying the reference obligation cash flows and return to the receiver but that is also compensated by the receiver for any depreciation in the index or default losses incurred by the portfolio.

Total return receiver Receives both the cash flows from the underlying index and any appreciation in the index over the period in exchange for paying the MRR plus a predetermined spread.

Total return swap A swap in which one party agrees to pay the total return on a security. Often used as a credit derivative, in which the underlying is a bond.

Tracking error The standard deviation of the differences between a portfolio's returns and its benchmark's returns; a synonym of active risk. Also called *tracking risk*.

Tracking risk The standard deviation of the differences between a portfolio's returns and its benchmark's returns; a synonym of active risk. Also called *tracking error*.

Trade urgency A reference to how quickly or slowly an order is executed over the trading time horizon.

Transactions-based attribution An attribution approach that captures the impact of intra-day trades and exogenous events such as a significant class action settlement.

Transfer coefficient The ability to translate portfolio insights into investment decisions without constraint.

Trigger points In the context of portfolio rebalancing, the endpoints of a rebalancing range (corridor).

Trust A legal is a vehicle through which an individual (called a settlor) entrusts certain assets to a trustee (or trustees) who manages the assets for the benefit of assigned beneficiaries. A trust may be either a testamentary trust—a trust created through the testator's will—or a living or inter-vivos trust—a trust created during the settlor's lifetime.

Uncovered interest rate parity The proposition that the expected return on an uncovered (i.e., unhedged) foreign currency (risk-free) investment should equal the return on a comparable domestic currency investment.

Unsmoothing An adjustment to the reported return series if serial correlation is detected. Various approaches are available to unsmooth a return series.

Value at risk (VaR) A measure of the minimum portfolio loss expected to occur over a given time period at a specific confidence level.

Variance notional The notional amount of a variance swap; it equals vega notional divided by two times the volatility strike price [i.e., (vega notional)/(2 × volatility strike)].

Vega The change in an option's price for a change in volatility of the underlying, all else equal.

Vega notional The trade size for a variance swap, which represents the average profit and loss of the variance swap for a 1% change in volatility from the strike.

Vesting A term indicating that employees only become eligible to receive a pension after meeting certain criteria, typically a minimum number of years of service.

Volatility clustering The tendency for large (small) swings in prices to be followed by large (small) swings of random direction.

Volatility skew The skewed plot (of implied volatility (y-axis) against strike price (x-axis) for options on the same underlying with the same expiration) that occurs when the implied volatility increases for OTM puts and decreases for OTM calls, as the strike price moves away from the current price.

Volatility smile The U-shaped plot (of implied volatility (y-axis) against strike price (x-axis) for options on the same underlying with the same expiration) that occurs when the implied volatilities priced into both OTM puts and calls trade at a premium to implied volatilities of ATM options.

Will (or Testament) A document that outlines the rights others will have over one's property after death.

Withholding taxes Taxes imposed on income in the country in which an investment is made without regard for offsetting investment expenses or losses that may be available from the taxpayer's other investment activities.

Worldwide tax system Jurisdictions that tax all income regardless of its source.

Yield spread The simple difference between a bond's YTM and the YTM of an on-the-run government bond of similar maturity.

Z-score Credit risk model that uses financial ratios and market-based information weighted by coefficients to create a composite score used to classify firms based on the likelihood of financial distress.

Zero-discount margin (Z-DM) A yield spread calculation for FRNs that incorporates forward MRR.

Zero-volatility spread (Z-spread) Constant yield spread over a government (or interest rate swap) spot curve.